Bankruptcy in Practice

Written by
John D. Ayer and
Michael L. Bernstein

A Publication of the
American Bankruptcy Institute

Additional copies may be purchased from the American Bankruptcy Institute. Discounts are available to ABI members. Copies may also be purchased from ABI's web site, ABI World, at http://www.abiworld.org.

Founded on Capitol Hill in 1982, the American Bankruptcy Institute (ABI) is the only multi-disciplinary, non-partisan organization devoted to the advancement of jurisprudence related to problems of insolvency. The ABI membership includes approximately 8,400 attorneys, bankers, judges, accountants, professors, turnaround specialists and other bankruptcy professionals, providing a forum for the exchange of ideas and information. ABI was founded to provide Congress unbiased testimony and research on insolvency issues. For further information, contact ABI.

1982–2002
AMERICAN BANKRUPTCY INSTITUTE
20th Anniversary

44 Canal Center Plaza • Suite 404 • Alexandria, VA 22314
(703) 739-0800 • FAX (703) 739-1060
http://www.abiworld.org • E-mail: info@abiworld.org

Bankruptcy in Practice

Table of Contents

This Book is
Dedicated to our Wives,
Maryanne Bertram
and Jamie G. Bernstein.

JDA
MLB

John Ayer is a Professor of Law at the University of California at Davis, and a former bankruptcy judge.

Michael Bernstein is a partner in the bankruptcy practice group at Arnold & Porter in Washington, D.C.

Introduction

Bankruptcy in Practice

Introduction: Bankruptcy in Practice

Why This Book Is Different

They say that rugby is a game for ruffians played by gentlemen. We kept this view in mind when we wrote this book. What we try to do here is to marry the classroom with the courtroom: to offer a framework for understanding bankruptcy law, along with equipment with which to face the practical necessities of the day. Our primary target audience is the new or non-specialist lawyer who needs a jump-start in understanding the practice of bankruptcy law. We hope it may be useful to others as well: to accountants, bankers, managers and others on the fringe of bankruptcy law, and perhaps also to law and business students.

We say we offer a mix of doctrine and practical counsel. We try to brief the reader on the governing law and doctrine, but also to provide practical guidance on the problems facing the practicing bankruptcy lawyer day in and day out. And we try to offer some insight into the framework of the bankruptcy system, so that the reader may see the forest as well as the trees.

It is our purpose to provide a general overview, but within the limits of a single paperback we have had to exclude a lot of potential material. In this light, we have tried to focus on problems that are most likely to employ lawyer time and energy—problems of business reorganization in particular, but also issues in bankruptcy litigation such as discharge and dischargeability. We have specifically resisted the temptation to dive deeply into the arcane of complex conceptual problems which, however beguiling, are not necessarily the stuff of everyday life.

On the other hand, in a few cases, we have felt it important to reach outside bankruptcy law narrowly defined—for example, to sketch the outlines of non-bankruptcy lien law (including tax lien law), describe successor liability doctrines, or to say a word about offshore asset protection. Also where appropriate, we have tried to reach beyond ordinary research sources: we offer, for example, a general introduction to bankruptcy-related resources on the Internet.

With respect to presentation, we have tried to keep the tone relaxed and conversational so the book can be read, not merely consulted.

We think this book shows the virtues of collaboration. One of us is a partner in a big firm, one a professor, with experience as a boutique lawyer and as a bankruptcy judge. We believe we have different strengths (and perhaps weaknesses). Each of us drafted individual sections of this manuscript, but after more than two years' cooperative effort, we have each gone over just about every line of it. We know we have learned from each other in the process, and we hope the reader profits.

We share one negative prerequisite, which we hope is itself a virtue. Specifically: neither one of us took a course on bankruptcy in law school. The consequence is that we both underwent the unsettling and sometimes painful process of learning this stuff on the fly. We hope our experience has sharpened our awareness to the needs of our readers, and made us better able to serve those needs.

Acknowledgments: One of the pleasures of doing an introduction is that it gives us a chance to acknowledge the help we have enjoyed from others. Sara Buck, Sue Williams, Diana Johannes and Jane Vogt provided secretarial support. Ann Graham untangled computer problems. Tom Johnston and Matt Seeger provided research assistance. Jack Williams, Eric Gustafson and Nancy Rapoport read and commented on the entire manuscript. Dean Rex Perschbacher of the UC-Davis Law School provided research funding to Ayer. The law firm of Arnold & Porter allowed Bernstein to give time and attention to the project, and also provided valuable support services. George Gold got us started and we are sorry he was not able to work with us through to the end.

We owe a special debt to Richard Meth, who saw virtues in the project and helped to place it with the American Bankruptcy Institute. At the ABI, we had invaluable assistance from Sam Gerdano, Melissa Lanning, and others (some perhaps unknown to us) on the ABI staff.

JDA

MLB

1 What, Who

1 What, Who

§1.1 ~ Introduction: A Good Story

A good story needs characters and plot. Bankruptcy has both. In this chapter, we begin by sketching the plot. We provide an overview of what bankruptcy law is for, and then a brief sketch of a bankruptcy case.

§1.2 ~ What Bankruptcy is About: A Short Description

Bankruptcy is about debtors who cannot, or will not, pay their debts. It offers some solace to debtors seeking relief from the burden of their obligations. It offers some protection to creditors who want an efficient and convenient means to liquidate claims. It seeks to preserve the value of the debtor and its assets. These goals often conflict with one another. In some cases it will be possible to reconcile the conflicts; oftentimes, it will not.

§1.3 ~ Too Many Purposes

"Bankruptcy" is not a single concept. It is a set of loosely connected, more or less overlapping concepts that have to do with the relationship between a debtor and his creditors. Some of these serve the interests of creditors, some of debtors, and some may serve both at once.

For most participants and observers, bankruptcy is first of all a means of getting a discharge, whereby a debtor wipes out some or all of his unpaid debt. In order to get the discharge, the debtor must submit most of his property to a bankruptcy trustee who will liquidate it and distribute the proceeds to his creditors as their interests may appear. But in fact, the vast majority of debtors have no assets to submit, and the case is about the discharge only.

The United States is nearly unique in the scope and extent of its bankruptcy discharge. Most other countries, including the countries with political and legal systems most similar to ours, give nothing like the same protection. But that is perhaps changing, as other countries become more compassionate, and the United States, less so.

A more venerable purpose of bankruptcy law is to orchestrate claims and to marshal the pool of assets when there isn't enough to go around. In the classic model, bankruptcy supplants the race-to-the-court-house grab law of the non-bankruptcy regime with a distribution that is pro rata: if there are enough assets to pay 40 percent of claims, then each creditor gets 40 percent of his claim. This, at any rate, is how the story is told.

But the practical fact is that the Bankruptcy Code articulates its own system of priority claims (for administrative expenses, taxes, wages and so forth). Also, bankruptcy respects otherwise valid and perfected non-bankruptcy security interests. Thus, the practical consequence is that even in the (minority of) cases where there are assets to distribute, most of the assets go to secured or administrative claims, and there is little or nothing for the residual class.

Pro rata bankruptcy distribution is justified as an economy insofar as it substitutes one race to the courthouse for many. A more elegant justification argues that it represents the kind of bargain creditors would make on their own if they could.

But there is a still more subtle justification for pro rata distribution. IndusCo, a mythical heavy-industry manufacturer, runs a factory, where it owns and maintains a boiler. As a going business, IndusCo could be sold for $5 million. Broken up for scrap, the assets would yield $1.5 million—some $1 million from the boiler alone. The factory cannot run without the boiler. IndusCo owes $1 million to Carlos, and $3.5 million to an array of other creditors. Carlos levies on the boiler. He puts it up for sale and liquidates his entire claim. The going concern value of the business dissipates and the remainder is just $500,000, which the other creditors share pro rata.

A bankruptcy proceeding may prevent this "death by a thousand cuts." So another purpose of bankruptcy law is to prevent piecemeal liquidation and to protect asset values. But this term can have at least two different meanings. First and most obvious, we want to make sure that the assets get identified and collected, and that we get top dollar at sale. But second, we want to make sure values do not get dissipated by the very process of collection itself.

What we mean is this. A business might have two different values—the liquidation value of the component assets piecemeal, and the (potentially very different) value of the business kept together as a going concern. Sometimes, but not always, the business is worth more as a going concern than in liquidation. And, a piecemeal liquidation can destroy the value of the going concern.

Now, an individual creditor may have no incentive to care whether he destroys the value of the going concern; as far as he is concerned, if he gets paid, that is the end of it. But the creditors as a whole may have a powerful interest in preserving the going concern. So when we say "protect asset values," then at least part of what we mean is "protect the going concern."

Part and parcel of protecting asset values, bankruptcy (chiefly through chapter 11) offers an opportunity to make and implement deals about the liabilities of the debtor and their satisfaction. Sometimes, it may be in the interest creditors to scale back their claims, particularly if they can rely on others to give the same kind of relief. Nothing bars debtors and creditors from making a deal, even independent of bankruptcy. But a non-bankruptcy deal may be considerably harder to achieve and harder to enforce.

Why does bankruptcy make the deal easier? The most important reason is that the court may impose the deal on a dissenting minority of creditors. This power to impose may spell the difference between the possible and the impossible among deals. It is so important that some plan proponents will make their deal outside bankruptcy and then, if they cannot get unanimous consent, shepherd it through bankruptcy to impose it on dissenters. For more on imposing the deal, *see* Chapter 18, "Confirmation," below.

All these purposes suggest a further purpose whose nature and extent is more contentious. That is: it may be that a purpose of bankruptcy is to give business debtors relief from some or all of their debts, even where creditors do not agree, and even at creditors' expense. There may be a societal interest in preserving going concerns, by adjusting debts to make them serviceable, although some will argue that this runs contrary to the basic concert of the marketplace (competition, businesses that can not service their debts should go out of existence, etc.), constitutes an inappropriate transfer of value from creditors to shareholders, and serves the unfortunate purpose of raising the costs of financing for all businesses. So it is contentious. But the scrutiny of a thousand bankruptcy opinions gives rise to a conviction that bankruptcy judges believe it is their mandate to give some kind of debtor relief, even if its bounds and limits are uncertain.

To repeat, then, here are the five predominant purposes that we see in bankruptcy law:

- To grant a discharge;
- To orchestrate claims;
- To protect asset (and going concern) values;
- To present an opportunity to make and implement deals; and
- To give business debtors "relief."

§1.4 ~ A Bankruptcy Case

Next, the narrative. Most cases begin when the debtor files a voluntary petition for bankruptcy relief.[1] The Code also allows creditors to initiate the process by filing a petition to create an involuntary bankruptcy case (*see* Code Section 303), but it doesn't happen very often. The commencement of the case creates an estate,[2] and operates as a stay of just about anything a creditor would want to do to liquidate or enforce its claim.[3] The debtor must also file schedules of assets and liabilities and a statement of financial affairs giving information on the state of its finances.

After it receives the petition, the court generates a notice of a meeting of creditors.[4] The debtor must appear at this meeting of creditors, but the meeting isn't quite what it sounds like. Generally speaking, particularly in individual debtor cases, creditors' meetings are set wholesale, so a battalion or more of

---

1. Section 301.

2. Section 541.

3. Section 362.

4. Section 341. The meeting is sometimes referred to as the "341 meeting," after the Code section that provides for it.

debtors show up at the same time at a trustee's office, where the trustee asks each of them in turn a few more or less searching questions to see if the debtor (under oath) really appears to be telling the truth on his schedules.

Creditors, if they show up at all, will sometimes find they are discouraged from asking many questions —the trustee has too many cases to process, and he can't hold up the room for detailed individual inquiry. The meeting is not normally recorded by a court reporter, but it is taped, so if you need a record of the meeting, you can get a copy of the tape.[5] In any event, if the creditor really wants to investigate, he has plenty of opportunities elsewhere. *See* Section 2.22 ff.

If the individual debtor plays by the rules, then (with certain exceptions) he gets a discharge, wiping out his unpaid pre-petition debts. If there is any property to distribute (but remember, usually there is not), a trustee takes it in charge. In the ordinary liquidating case, the trustee's job is to turn it into cash and to distribute it among creditors as their interests may appear.[6] After the trustee finishes, the court closes the case and the file goes to storage.[7]

Note that in practice, most bankruptcy is far more an administrative than a judicial proceeding. Most debtors never go to the courthouse except for the creditors' meeting (and even then this is not held in court). Every case is assigned to a judge, but most judges never see most of their cases. Instead, most of the action goes forward in the clerk's office, and between the debtor and the trustee.

§1.5 ~ The Judge and the Courthouse Staff

The central role belongs to the bankruptcy judge who presides over the bankruptcy court. Most bankruptcy matters are litigated before her although, as explained in more detail elsewhere, she operates in the shadow of the federal district judge and derives her jurisdiction from the district court. *See generally* Chapters 3, 4 below.

The bankruptcy judge is appointed by the Court of Appeals. She holds office for a 14-year term. Typically, she has a secretary and a law clerk. She very likely also has the regular services of a deputy clerk assigned to her courtroom, and a court reporter. Communication between counsel and the court may go through the secretary, or the law clerk, or the courtroom deputy, depending on the preference of the particular judge.

Bankruptcy is largely a paper process—huge quantities of documents (or, in the new age, electronic transmissions). It follows that an important role is played by the clerk of the bankruptcy court and his staff. Bankruptcy clerks have been fierce (and, so far, largely successful) in maintaining their independence from the district court. Virtually all bankruptcy filings take place with the bankruptcy clerk and, except for active appeals and matters with respect to which the reference has been withdrawn, remain there.

---

5. *See* Bankruptcy Rule 2003(c).

6. Section 704.

7. Such, at least, is a simple chapter 7 case. For more on reorganization cases, *see* Chapters 6, 10 and 18.

§1.6 ~ Trustees

One trouble with clarifying the role of the trustee is that there are different kinds of trustees. We enumerate:

- There is the case trustee who supervises the individual chapter 7 (or, sometimes, chapter 11).
- There are standing trustees who supervise cases in chapters 13 and 12.
- There is the debtor in possession (DIP) who functions as if he is the trustee in most chapter 11s.
- And there is the U.S. Trustee, an employee of the U.S. Department of Justice, who supervises trustees.

Comment: Responding to local concerns, Congress carved out an exception to the ordinary plan of administration for judicial districts in Alabama and North Carolina. In those, there is no U.S. Trustee and chapter 11 cases are supervised by a "case administrator."

We say a word about each separately.

§1.7 ~ "Case" Trustee

There is a trustee in every chapter 7 liquidating bankruptcy case. He is appointed by the U.S. Trustee, although the statute is somewhat deceptive on the point. What the statute provides is that the U.S. Trustee names an interim case trustee,[8] and that creditors may thereafter elect a trustee.[9] The statute says that if creditors fail to elect a trustee, then the interim trustee continues as case trustee.[10] But the practical fact is that creditors rarely exercise their right to elect a trustee, so the U.S. Trustee's appointee "interim" trustee continues as case trustee.[11]

The duties of the case trustee are set forth in Section 704. In summary, he collects the property of the estate, reduces it to cash, and distributes among creditors. He is charged also to "investigate the financial affairs of the debtor," and "if advisable, oppose the discharge of the debtor."[12]

The Code provides that the U.S. Trustee appoints the interim trustee, but where does the U.S. Trustee find candidates? The answer is that the U.S. Trustee maintains a panel of individuals whom it deems qualified to serve as case trustee and selects from that panel (hence, sometimes, "panel trustee").[13]

---

8. Section 701(a).

9. Section 701(a), 702(b).

10. Section 702(d).

11. Even though it doesn't happen often, still you may want to consider demanding an election when the stakes are high enough, and/or when specialized knowledge will be necessary in order to realize on the value of the debtor's assets. The election (if any) takes place at the meeting of creditors under §341. The request has to have the support of at least 20 percent of all eligible claims. The candidate is elected if he gets a majority in amount of claims voting, and if at least 20 percent vote. *See generally* §702.

12. Section 704.

13. Section 701, 28 U.S.C. §586(a)(1).

Many are lawyers, but there is no requirement that one be a lawyer in order to gain membership on the panel. Many are accountants. Some are people who have simply developed good skills at managing or investigating.

§1.8 ~ How Much Does the Trustee Earn?

How much does the trustee earn? The answer is in Section 326(a), which prescribes that the court may allow compensation that is "reasonable," but not to exceed a prescribed schedule, which is a function of the size of the estate. But every trustee gets a minimum of $60 a case. So, if a trustee gets 150 new cases a month, he books a minimum gross income of $9,000. At least outside of high-priced metropolitan areas, many trustees find this sufficient to pay their office overhead, leaving them free to make an income from their other professional practice activities.

The Code authorizes the trustee to serve as his own attorney or account if he is so authorized "in the best interest of the estate."[14] Read liberally, this would open a large loophole in the limit on trustee compensation, because fees of attorneys and accountants (although subject to court control) are not capped at a percentage of the estate. In part for this reason, many courts are loath to authorize the trustee to represent herself, and some do not allow it at all. And a trustee who does get to represent himself is likely to find himself embroiled with creditors' counsel over which of his services are "attorney" services (entitled to attorney compensation) and which are merely trustee work that comes in under the cap.

On the other hand, trustees may achieve a similar result by simply employing each other: On Monday Ralph as trustee employs Margaret as his lawyer in the case of DebtorCo. On Tuesday Margaret as trustee hires Ralph to represent her in the case of LittleCo. The cynic will detect a hint of reciprocity here, as if (horrors!) Ralph and Margaret might have had some sort of a deal. A response is that all of these appointments (and all relevant compensation) take place under judicial scrutiny, and if the judge doesn't want this sort of thing to go on, she can make it stop.

One practical consequence of the trustee compensation system is that you can't expect the trustee to work hard looking for assets unless someone (that is—an aggrieved creditor) is willing to fund the inquiry. Indeed, the system offers an incentive. Because of the statutory percentages and the minimum, the trustee really doesn't want to find assets unless he is going to find a lot. So estates that are small but not empty tend to go unadministered and debtors who hide $5,000 or $10,000 have a better chance of getting away with a felony than those who hide $1 million.

§1.9 ~ DIP

So far we have been talking mostly about chapter 7. Chapter 11 does not provide for the automatic appointment of a trustee. Rather, Section 1104(a)(1) provides that the Court shall appoint a trustee on motion if there is cause.[15] The statute defines cause to include "fraud, dishonesty, incompetence, or

---

14. Section 327(d).

15. *See also* §1104(a)(2).

gross mismanagement." The practical fact is that creditors rarely ask for a trustee and courts even more rarely order the appointment. In most cases, the debtor remains in possession of the assets as a DIP.[16]

The DIP is not just the old debtor with a new name. The law clothes him with powers and responsibilities much like those of a trustee (but he is not, for example, required to investigate himself, nor is he empowered to pay himself).[17] There is often an obvious tension between the objectives of management (usually, protecting the interests of management and equity) and the new fiduciary duty that the DIP assumes when the bankruptcy petition is filed. *See generally* Section 6.18.

In the ordinary case, the DIP will be just what the statute seems to suggest—the old debtor with new responsibilities and duties. Some larger cases take on a special character. In these cases, creditors (or shareholders) have already forced out old management before the commencement of the case, sometimes replacing them with "turnaround specialists," who thus may function as de facto independent trustees, even though operating under the DIP hat.

§1.10 ~ Chapter 11 Trustee

If the court does order the appointment of a trustee, then the U.S. Trustee appoints "one disinterested person" to serve as trustee.[18] Or, on request of a party in interest, creditors may elect a trustee.[19]

Note that the chapter 11 trustee does not need to come from the trustee panel. Moreover the U.S. Trustee is authorized to make his appointment only after consultation with the parties. Ideally, the trustee and the creditors work together to try to identify a person with skills suitable to the case at hand. There is a growing cadre of "turnaround specialists" who hold themselves out as expert in the matter of managing and reorganizing chapter 11 debtors. Some of these sometimes work as chapter 11 trustees.

Because chapter 11 provides for reorganization, the duties of a chapter 11 trustee are not identical to the duties of a chapter 7 trustee. The chapter 11 trustee is enjoined to be accountable for all property received, to operate the business (if authorized) and (as necessary) to oppose claims.[20] But he is not authorized simply to "collect and reduce to money the property of the estate . . . and close such estate as expeditiously as is compatible with the best interests of the parties in interest"—a duty imposed on the chapter 7 trustee.[21] Unlike the chapter 7 trustee, he is directed to file a plan (or a statement as to why he is not doing so).[22]

---

16. Section 1101(1).

17. Section 1107(a).

18. Section 1104(d).

19. Section 1104(b).

20. Section 1106(a)(1).

21. But excluding the duties imposed by Section 704(1).

22. Section 1106(a)(5).

Since the DIP has most of the rights and powers of a trustee, when one reads "trustee" in the context of a chapter 11 case, we can usually understand the word as meaning "DIP." For example, Section 363 provides terms under which "the trustee" may use, sell or lease property of the estate. But in reality, these "use, sell or lease" powers are asserted by the DIP far more often than by an appointed trustee.

§1.11 ~ Examiners

As an alternative to appointing a trustee, the court may appoint an examiner. The Code provides that if the debts exceed $5 million, then the court, in lieu of appointing a trustee, shall appoint an "examiner" to "investigate" the debtor.[23] In terms of sheer numbers, there aren't very many examiners, but in contested cases, asking for an examiner may be a good litigation strategy. It gives the judge an independent voice to hear from, without imposing as much disruption as a trustee. And it can result in delay, which is sometimes in the tactical interest of a party, such as a creditor trying to slow down a prepackaged plan. Some courts, perhaps pressing the limits of the statute, are experimenting with the use of examiners for services beyond mere investigation—*e.g.*, to try to promote settlement of complex cases. On occasion, one hears a reference to an "examiner with expanded powers," which apparently refers to this practice of enlarging the role of an examiner.

§1.12 ~ Standing Trustees

For cases under chapter 13 (and chapter 12) the statute authorizes the appointment of a standing trustee, if the number of cases so warrants.[24] The standing trustee collects and distributes the debtors' earnings under chapter 13 plans. He is also takes a prominent role in setting standards for plans, and in supporting (or opposing, as the case may justify) motions to dismiss or convert, or motions for relief from the stay. Standing trustee compensation is a function of the amount of money he handles, subject to a statutory cap.

§1.13 ~ U.S. Trustee

At least in an earlier generation, trustees had a bad reputation. To some observers, a trusteeship was seen as an attractive plum, awarded to a crony of the judge as a license to pillage the estate.

In the runup to the 1978 law creating the Code, some critics wanted to do away with the system of appointed trustees altogether. They wanted to bring trusteeship into some sort of government agency. The notion met with resistance, and Congress struck on a compromise. It created the office of the U.S. Trustee as a unit of the Justice Department, and gave it the job of supervising the case trustees.[25] The office's own mission statement says:

---

23. Section 1104(c). If a party moves for examiner, and if the fixed liquidated unsecured debts (other than certain insider debts) total more than $5 million, the court shall appoint examiner. The court may also appoint an examiner if it is the interests of creditors, any equity security holders and other interests of the estate, etc. to have an examiner. In either case, the court has discretion regarding the scope of the engagement.

24. 28 U.S.C. §586(b).

25. The program came into being as a pilot project. The permanent authorization is United States Trustees & Family Farmer Bankruptcy Act of 1986 (Pub. L. 99-554, 100 Stat. 3088, reprinted in part at 28 U.S.C. §581, note). Districts in Alabama and North Carolina remain outside the system. Cases there are supervised by case administrators through the clerk's office.

> The United States Trustee Program acts in the public interest to promote the efficiency and to protect and preserve the integrity of the bankruptcy system. It works to secure the just, speedy, and economical resolution of bankruptcy cases; monitors the conduct of parties and takes action to ensure compliance with applicable laws and procedures; identifies and investigates bankruptcy fraud and abuse; and oversees administrative functions in bankruptcy cases.[26]

The most important part of the job is that the U.S. Trustee maintains and supervises the panel of private trustees—and has the power to remove them.[27] The U.S. Trustee also appoints creditors' committees and comments on professional fee applications. At least some in some districts, the U.S. Trustee has proven aggressive in helping to police bankruptcy fraud.

Bankruptcy lawyers in general tend to feel that the participation of the U.S. Trustee, at least in large chapter 11 cases, is unnecessary or counterproductive. The hostility may rest in part on self-interest: the U.S. Trustee monitors professional fees. But in the major chapter 11 cases, the conflicting interests are typically represented by experienced and sophisticated counsel. The bureaucrat's voice in these cases is unlikely to add anything of value.

Judges, by contrast, often speak well of the U.S. Trustee program. They seem to feel that the U.S. Trustee can help them with some of the most onerous parts of their job—cleaning up the docket, identifying systematic abuses—and, again, policing fees.

§1.14 ~ The Debtor

In some sense, the debtor may be the star of the show, but in a different sense, he isn't there at all. Most cases begin with the individual debtor who files to get a discharge—and end when he gets it. In most of these, either there are no assets, or they are exempt, or they are so heavily encumbered by secured claims that there is nothing to administer.

Contrast this with the class of cases where there are some assets worth saving. These are fewer in number, but they probably absorb a lot more lawyer time and energy. The debtor may be an active participant these asset cases, although in other cases it is just the creditors fighting among themselves.

The Debtor's role is sufficiently qualified that some courts have said he doesn't have standing in an individual chapter 7 case. This is obviously too loose: as to his discharge or in issues of dischargeability, he may be a necessary party. As to issues involving property of the estate, it is closer to the truth. But more alert courts have qualified this proposition to recognize that the Debtor may have a pecuniary interest even in a chapter 7 case. For example, there may be a surplus after the payment of creditors. In cases like this, he certainly ought to be heard if he wants to be.

---

26. From the web site of the United States Trustee program, http://www.usdoj.gov/ust/mission.htm, current as of June 27, 2001.

27. 28 U.S.C. §586(a)(1).

Cult Awareness Network, Inc., v. Martino[28] draws an interesting line. The debtor was a nonprofit corporation dedicated to fighting cults. Because of an adverse judgment, it filed for relief under chapter 11, but subsequently converted to chapter 7. The trustee undertook to sell the trade name. The debtor objected to a prospective sale, fearing that the intended buyer would use the name to promote cults. The court concluded that the debtor lacked standing because he had no financial stake. But it said that if he had shown a "reasonable possibility" of a surplus in the estate, then the result might be different.

§1.15 ~ Professionals—Counsel for the DIP

Section 327 provides that "the trustee, with the court's approval, may employ one or more attorneys [and other professionals] to represent or assist the trustee in carrying out the trustee's duties." This means, *inter alia*, that the DIP is authorized to retain counsel. Indeed, probably the most important single role in the ordinary chapter 11 is that of the lawyer for the DIP. Usually he is the one who has been counseling the debtor outside bankruptcy and usually it is he who recommended the filing in the first place. Typically it is he who speaks for the DIP in court, far more often than the debtor himself. He is typically the center of plan negotiations. Also, for good or ill, the judge is likely to depend on him as if he were a kind of trustee.

This is problematic: it can put counsel to some difficult choices about how to reconcile his obligations as an advocate for his client and his obligations as an officer of the court. *See* Sections 6.18, 16.15. For the moment, the point to remember is that the DIP is an entity separate from the debtor, with differing duties. By corollary, insofar as counsel represents the DIP, he does not represent the debtor. It will not surprise you that this distinction is often lost in practice, where the individual debtor (or the business debtor's management) gives instructions to the DIP's counsel, and is the one who hired that counsel in the first place.

Counsel for the DIP (and indeed, any professional appointed under Section 327(a)) may take his compensation from the estate as an administrative expense—but only with court approval.[29] There is a more extensive discussion of employment compensation in Chapter 16; see especially Section 16.21. For the moment, the point is: he gets no compensation as DIP counsel unless his employment was authorized. If you want to get compensation as counsel for the DIP, make sure that you apply for employment authorization at the beginning of your employment—and make sure the order of authorization is forthcoming.

U.S. Trustee Approval: Many judges look to the U.S. Trustee for help on employment applications. Some require that the U.S. Trustee sign off before the application is approved. In many districts, it is a good idea to ask for U.S. Trustee approval on any application for employment before it is filed, and to get the approval into the record.

---

28. *In re* Cult Awareness Network, Inc., 151 F.3d 605 (7th Cir. 1998). The purchaser was an individual believed to be associated with The Church of Scientology "an organization not in complete harmony with the beliefs of the Cult Awareness Network." *Id.* at 607.

29. Section 330.

But what if you forget to get your appointment at the beginning, and go ahead and do all the work? The answer is not completely bleak. You may be able to get some kind of *nunc pro tunc* (retroactive approval of the employment) or *quantum meruit* (payment for the value of services rendered) relief. But it may take some groveling, or at least a lot of explanation as to why you missed the deadline in the first place. And if the judge has any reason at all not to want to see you compensated, this is a great peg to hang his wishes on.

Comment: For convenience, we have talked here about attorneys. But note that the rules of Sections 327 and 330 apply to *any* "professional person." Just who is a professional person may be open to some debate. But the class certainly includes (in addition to lawyers) accountants and investment bankers. When in doubt, seek Court authorization before employing someone who may be considered a "professional person." We've seen too many real estate brokers go away empty-handed because nobody thought to tell them that they needed court approval for their employment.

§1.16 ~ Note on Petition Preparers

Anyone who needs bankruptcy protection is not going to find it cheap: even the basic $175 filing fee is likely beyond the reach of the most exigent debtors, to say nothing of the fee for an attorney. Yet the protections of bankruptcy are surprisingly easy to obtain—the mere filing of a petition will stop a foreclosure fast in its tracks.

The facts help to explain when the Code was young, why the judges found themselves choking in a deluge of petitions, most of them barely legible, many of them with no purpose other than to get the protection of the automatic stay. It didn't take much detective work to grasp that there was a stratum of debtors coming in below the radar with the aid of non-lawyer drafters who took a fee to write (but not to file) the bankruptcy paper.

Judges quickly developed a settled animosity to these petition preparers and it is not hard to see why. A lot of their work seemed to clutter up the system. And there is no doubt that the preparers, barely visible and unpoliced, often took money from debtors and then did them no service or positive harm.

Yet the problem of the preparers was more complicated than that. The existence of the preparers made it clear that there were plenty of debtors for whom standard legal services weren't available. Moreover, incompetent or irresponsible as some of the preparers might be, the fact was they did seem to provide a service—to get some debtors bargain relief at bargain prices.

The consequence of these competing concerns is that Congress in 1994 adopted new Section 110 of the Code which does not outlaw, but does regulate, the preparers. Now they must sign petitions and disclose their fees. They are even at risk of being disbarred, if they violate the rules. The provision may have done something to limit the abuses of the preparers. But it also provides at least backhanded acknowledgment that they are there, and that they may perform a service.

§1.17 ~ Creditors' Committee

Read the Code on committees and you quickly infer that the drafters anticipated a different sort of chapter 11 than the one that came into being. Section 1102 says that "as soon as practicable after the order for relief . . . the United States trustee shall appoint a committee of creditors. . . ." Section 1103(c) sets forth a detailed catalog of committee powers. You would be entirely justified in concluding that the drafters intended the committee to be a linchpin of the chapter 11 process, policing the debtor and formulating a plan.

Sometimes, it works this way. But in many, perhaps most, cases, either there is no committee at all or it is substantially moribund, a paper committee only. There are at least two reasons why it works this way.

One, there is a class of cases for which a committee makes no intrinsic sense at all. Take Limited LP, a hypothetical limited partnership with one asset, Blackacre, a medical office building, worth $3 million. Limited owes $5 million to BigBank, the mortgagee. It owes $35,000 to suppliers of goods and services including the building management company, the janitorial service, and others. There is just about no point to a committee of creditors in a case like this. BigBank will take care of itself. For the unsecureds, the numbers don't begin to justify the time, effort and expense of a committee—especially since, practically speaking, both Limited and BigBank want the unsecureds to get paid so they will continue to provide the services.

Two, there is a somewhat different class of cases where the potential role of the committee is more problematic.

Example: Consider DebtorCo, a small widget maker with annual gross revenues of about $2 million a year. DebtorCo owes FirstBank $800,000 secured by Whiteacre, its factory-office-warehouse. DebtorCo owes $700,000 to FinCo, an asset-based lender who provides working capital under an agreement secured by inventory and receivables. It owes 30 vendors an aggregate of $240,000. The largest vendor claim is for $25,000.

There may be good arguments in favor of assembly a committee of creditors in this case—but the practical hurdles may be insurmountable. Individual creditors are likely to be unsophisticated or at least uneducated in the niceties of chapter 11. They may be demoralized by their past misfortune and unwilling to send good efforts after bad. On numbers of this size, it may be hard to find a lawyer willing to take the time and effort to give them good representation. So even if a committee is appointed, it is likely to remain moribund. Indeed, if the debtor elects to be treated as a "small business debtor," (and DebtorCo would qualify), then on request of a party in interest, the court may order that a committee not be appointed.[30]

On the other hand, in a (rather small) percentage of cases where the numbers justify, the committee may play an important role. The committee may employ counsel (and other professionals).[31] Like DIP counsel, they may be paid as administrative claimants out of assets of the estate. A well-organized committee of sophisticated creditors, speaking through a competent counsel, can play a major part in shaping a case —and sometimes even dominate a case.

---

30. *See* §§1102(a)(3), 101(51C), 1121(e); *see also* §5.5 on the small business debtors, explaining why there aren't many small business cases.

31. Section 1103(a).

Example: Consider LittleCo with secured claims of $10 million and unsecured claims of $8 million (total = $18 million) but where assets will never, under the most optimistic forecast, be worth more than $14 million.

On these numbers, there will be nothing for equity and so the old residual owners may choose to throw the keys on the table and walk away. This leaves unsecured creditors as the de facto equity class, with the same motivations as any other junior class. Properly organized and represented, they may be able to act to preserve going concern values or otherwise do what is necessary to maximize the value of their claim.

Another basic fact about committees is that judges tend to like them. Or more precisely: In an operating case where there is no trustee, the judge may feel uncomfortable depending solely on the representations of the DIP. He may be eager for another voice, either to challenge or (where appropriate) to confirm what the DIP is telling him. Moreover lawyers for the committee often find they have a freer hand than lawyers for the DIP.

This may seem ironic, in that the committee lawyer has many "clients"—the whole committee—rather than just one. But for any individual creditor, this case is likely to be only a secondary item. The practical result is that he will often leave broad discretion to Committee counsel, and rely on counsel for all but the most technical business judgments. This framework gives committee counsel, in some ways, the best of both worlds—an important voice in the case without the enormous administrative responsibilities that come from representing the DIP.

Committee members are authorized to receive reimbursement of expenses from the estate, but they are not compensated like "professionals."[32] On committee counsel conflicts and compensation, *see* Chapter 18 below.

There is also a provision for a committee of creditors in chapter 7.[33] But it isn't much used because the cases tend to be smaller and creditor's don't have anything to gain from adding another layer of bureaucracy. One important distinction is that the chapter 7 committee is not appointed but elected (just like the equally rare "elected" chapter 7 trustee).

§1.18 ~ Limits on Committee Members

There is a downside to committee service. Pan Am World Airways, once the crown jewel of United States aviation, went into chapter 11 in 1991. Delta Air Lines undertook interim financing and bought some Pan Am routes while negotiating for a broader role. Hoping to keep the airline viable, some unions agreed to concessions. But the deal broke down and the employees howled betrayal, perceiving that

---

32. Section 503(b)(3),(4). But the Third Circuit recently held that creditors may be reimbursed for individual legal fees insofar as they were incurred in their service as committee members, i.e., not as individual creditors. First Merchants Acceptance Corp. v. J.C. Bradford & Cop. (*In re* First Merchants Acceptance Corp.), 198 F.3d 394 (3d Cir. 1999). The decision has sparked some criticism. *See, e.g., In re* Firstplus Financial, Inc., 254 B.R. 888 (Bankr. N.D. Tex. 2000). We would not be surprised to see the First Merchants decision rejected by other courts or overturned by Congress.

33. *See* §705.

Delta had kept Pan Am alive only long enough to skim off the good assets. Thereupon, the employees sued Delta for $2.5 billion.

By way of defense, Delta sought to implead members of the Pan Am creditors' committee, alleging that the committee displaced the DIP in plan negotiations. Committee members in response asserted that they had immunity from suit.[34] The judge, conceding that they had limited immunity, nonetheless found that the complaint alleged willful wrongdoing and thereby survived a motion to dismiss.[35]

Committee members may also be restricted in—or barred from—claims trading or trading in securities of the debtor. In some cases, courts have approved "ethical wall" mechanisms so that committee member institutions could continue to trade, by separating those who serve on the committee (and therefore have access to nonpublic information) from those at the member institution who do the trading. *See* Section 13.51.

§1.19 ~ Additional Committees

The court *may* but is not required to appoint additional committees—either of creditors or of equity security holders.[36] The court shall order such additional committees "if necessary to assure adequate representation of creditors or of equity security holders." After a court order, it is left to the U.S. Trustee to appoint such committees.

Additional committees are sufficiently rare that they do not merit extensive commentary here, but idea of an equity committee does raise an interesting conceptual problem. That is: if the bankruptcy is "for" creditors, then why do you need an equity committee at all? Or, if there is a DIP—and if the DIP is permitted to "tilt to equity,"—then again, what would be the role of the DIP where there is an equity committee? We discuss this topic more at length below; *see* Section 6.18

A partial answer is: courts have permitted equity committees in some cases where there are substantial conflicts between shareholders and managers—as, for example, where shareholders have been trying to oust management either before or in the chapter 11 process. Equity committees have also been appointed where it appears the estate may be solvent.

Whatever nominal purpose, there is dramatic evidence of their real function. LoPucki and Whitford in their study of chapter 11 cases,[37] have shown that when there is an equity committee, equity gets more money out of the case. Of course, if this comes about because equity expands the size of the pie, then everyone should be happy. But if equity gets more by leaving others to get less, then the policy is more questionable. Some lawyers, deploying the LoPucki-Whitford study, have argued that the court ought to

---

34. Luedke v. Delta Air Lines, Inc., 159 B.R. 385 (S.D.N.Y. 1993).

35. *Id.* at 395.

36. Section 1102(a)(2).

37. Lynn M. LoPucki & William C. Whitford, Bargaining over Equity's Share in the Bankruptcy Reorganization of Large, Publicly Held Companies, 139 U. Pa. L. Rev. 125 (1990).

appoint an equity committee because this is the way to assure that the equity gets more! Your authors think this rather puts the cart before the horse and indeed, there is no reported case in support of the view.

Aside from equity committees, we have seen committees appointed to speak for such various constituencies as: subordinated debt holders, employees, personal injury plaintiffs, limited partners and retirees. They are perhaps most common where there is a constituency that doesn't really think of itself as a creditor class, even though they have a creditor stake in the case.

§1.20 ~ Membership

The Code provides that a committee of creditors "shall ordinarily consist of the persons, willing to serve, that hold the seven largest claims against the debtor of the kinds represented on such committee. . . . "[38] But the Code also allows the Trustee to carry over a pre-petition committee "if such committee was fairly chosen and is representative of the different kinds of claims to be represented."[39] This provision allows creditors to organize and negotiate with the debtor outside chapter 11, carrying some expectation that they will be able to continue after the petition.

---

38. Section 1102(b)(1). Cf. Section 1102(b)(3) (seven largest equity security holders).

39. Section 1102(b)(1).

2

How to Find Out About It

2 How to Find Out About It

§2.1 ~ Introduction: Three Jobs

In this chapter we do three jobs. First, we outline the sources of bankruptcy law. Then we offer you some techniques for reading that law. Finally, we give you a sketch of devices you can use to find out about your case.

§2.2 ~ Sources of Law

The bankruptcy lawyer's primary statute is the Bankruptcy Code. But for matters of jurisdiction, he is governed by the bankruptcy provisions of the Judicial Code. Both of these are fleshed out by the bankruptcy rules—chiefly the Federal Rules of Bankruptcy Procedure, but also a wide array of "local rules," not to mention "local, local" rules, as we explain more fully below.

But this is only the beginning. Often bankruptcy operates as a procedural framework to implement other law, sometimes (inexactly) referred to as "state law"—but other law can be any non-bankruptcy law, state or federal—or foreign. As a minimum, the bankruptcy lawyer is likely to need to know something about security interests, either under Article 9 of the Uniform Commercial Code or under state mortgage law. *See* §§12.5-.6. And he will surely need to know something about tax law as it affects bankruptcy cases. *See*, *e.g.* §§8.21ff, §12.11, §13.41.

We deal with all these matters in turn. But in the first instance, bankruptcy draws its authority from the Constitution, with which we begin.

§2.3 ~ The U.S. Constitution

United States bankruptcy law begins with the Constitution, specifically Article I, Section 8, which gives Congress the power to make bankruptcy laws. Surprisingly little is known about the purpose of the drafters in adopting the clause. It is not even clear whether the drafters thought they were adopting a debtor protection, or a creditor protection, or some combination of the two.

Perhaps the most important consequence of the adoption of the bankruptcy clause is negative—the sorts of things that have not happened because it is there. Specifically, because the bankruptcy clause is in the Constitution, it has never been necessary to wrestle with the limits of the commerce clause, as has been the history with so many other kinds of commercial legislation.[1] Similarly, it has not been necessary to enact a uniform code, adopted by individual jurisdictions, as has been the path in commercial law.

1. But all this may be changing before our eyes, given the Supreme Court's new attitude towards the Eleventh Amendment and doctrines of state sovereign immunity. *See* §4.12.

One might expect that there would be disputes concerning the scope of Congressional authority under the bankruptcy clause. Perhaps surprisingly, there is not much. There has been a scattering of cases purporting to explore the nature and limits of the bankruptcy power. But ironically, perhaps the most important case imposing a constitutional limit on a bankruptcy statute was decided on the authority not of the bankruptcy clause but of the Fifth Amendment.[2]

Merely authorizing Congress to adopt bankruptcy laws does not compel it to do so. And indeed, through most of the 19th Century, there was no federal bankruptcy law at all. But Congress adopted a comprehensive Bankruptcy Act in 1898 and we have had federal bankruptcy law continuously ever since.

§2.4 ~ Statutes

The present Bankruptcy Code was adopted as part of a comprehensive Bankruptcy Reform Act in 1978. It remains the point of departure for all inquiry into bankruptcy law today, although it has been amended many times since, and although it is still appropriate to cite pre-1978 cases on matters of basic principle.[3]

The current Code, adopted as part of the 1978 Bankruptcy Reform Act, is set forth in Title 11 of the United States Code. Usually you would cite them as, e.g., 11 U.S.C. §___. In this book, when we refer to a section of the Bankruptcy Code, we will say simply "Section (such and such)." So, Section 303(d) is really 11 U.S.C. §303(d).

Important provisions governing jurisdiction are codified in Title 28. Rules governing the taxation of debtors in bankruptcy, or of bankruptcy estates, are mostly in the Internal Revenue Code, Title 26. Congress has also proscribed a number of crimes in connection with bankruptcy law which are codified in Title 18.[4] For more on jurisdiction, *see* Chapters 3, 4 below. On taxes, *see* §8.21 ff., §12.11, §13.41. On bankruptcy crimes, *see* §2.13.

§2.5 ~ Rules

Rules governing procedure in bankruptcy courts come from the structure set forth in the Rules Enabling Act.[5] This is the same section that governs all other federal procedural rules system, including the Federal Rules of Civil Procedure. Rules are proposed by an advisory committee and approved (or not) by the Supreme Court. Congress reserves (but does not often exercise) the right to override the decision of the Court on this matter if it wishes.[6]

---

2. *See* Louisville Joint Stock Bank v. Radford, 295 U.S. 555, 602 (1935) (holding that the Frazier-Lemke Act violated the secured creditor's Fifth Amendment protection against appropriation of property rights without just compensation).

3. For the text, see http://www.abiworld.org/legis/Title11.pdf.

4. *See* 18 U.S.C. §151-157.

5. 28 U.S.C. §2075.

6. Bankruptcy rules can be found at http://www.abiworld.org/legis/FRBP.pdf. Bankruptcy rules incorporate many provisions of the (general) Federal Rules of Civil Procedure, which can be found at http://www.law.cornell.edu/rules/frcp/overview.htm.

§2.6 ~ Ten Rules You Need to Read

Few law students study the bankruptcy rules. Even in practice people tend not to read the rules until they are impacted by them. But here is a basic list of some of the most important rules to get you started.

- Rule 2002 is a catch-all notice rule that sets time limits for a variety of bankruptcy moves. There are plenty of other time rules. See, e.g., Rule 9006 regarding computation of time and Rule 8002 setting the (short) time deadline for filing a notice or appeal.

- Rule 9014 provides the general framework for contested matters—i.e., conflicts that are not governed by the adversary rules, or by other specific rules.

- Rule 4001 sets far more specific standards for some specific contested matters—including relief from stay, using collateral, borrowing money, as well as settlements and compromises involving these matters.

- Rule 7001 tells you what matters require an adversary proceeding.

- Rule 7004 tells you how to accomplish service in an adversary proceeding.

- Rule 2004 is the bankruptcy discovery rule; and compare also Rules 7026 through 7037 (incorporating Federal Rules 26 through 37 in bankruptcy adversary proceedings).[7]

- Rule 9011, the "good faith pleading" rule. Probably more attorneys get in serious trouble for violating this rule than any other.[8]

- Rule 6004 on use, sale or lease of property. And compare Rule 4001, above.

- Rule 4007 governs dischargeability of a debt. Compare rule 4004 on the discharge.

- Rule 3002 tells you how to file a proof of claim in a chapter 7 case. See the surrounding rules (3001 through 3008) for other claims issues.

§2.7 ~ Local Rules

Bankruptcy courts also generate local rules to flesh out the framework. These local rules have been a persistent (and perhaps) increasing source of complaint in the bar. The complaints are of three sorts: one, the local rules are too diverse and particular; two, that they may sometimes trench upon substantive law, and three, they sometimes exist in "oral tradition," where the outsider can't even find out about them.

---

7. Each of these rules, other than Rule 27, is also applicable in contested matters, pursuant to Bankruptcy Rule 9014.

8. Note that there are minor differences between this rule and Rule 11 of the Federal Rules of Civil Procedure.

The first complaint is understandable: the harried lawyer practicing in multiple districts does not enjoy having to juggle half a dozen different systems in his head. On the other hand, there will always be some matters that are not amenable to general resolution—surely the world would not be a better place if all stay relief motions were heard on Thursdays. Moreover it is surely better to have a set of local rules, printed (or perhaps better, posted on the web site) and accessible, than to be blind-sided by local procedures that are not set forth in rules at all.

This point gains force when you reflect on the reputation of bankruptcy court as an "insider's court" where the regulars enjoy a home court advantage. Set aside the question of whether the reputation is deserved or not. The point is that whatever their vices, rules clearly stated (if consistently enforced) have the virtue of making the same process available to all.

The second complaint—rules as substance—is more difficult to evaluate. The line between substance and procedure is at best shadowy in any case. But some things cross it. For example, consider a rule purporting to grant a discharge to corporations in chapter 7. Such a rule could not be considered mere procedure by any measure.[9] Of course, there are closer cases than this.

Driven by persistent complaints of this sort, the drafters of the bankruptcy rules have promulgated (and repeatedly amended) a Federal rule to govern local rules.[10] The rule provides that local rules must be "consistent with—and not duplicative of—Acts of Congress and these rules." Also, they must "not prohibit or limit the use of Official Forms." A most intriguing provision provides:

> A local rule imposing a requirement of form will not be enforced in a manner that causes a party to lose rights because of a nonwillful failure to comply with the requirement.[11] Another provides:
>
> No sanction or other disadvantage may be imposed for noncompliance with any requirement not in federal law, federal rules, Official Forms, or the local rules of the district unless the alleged violator has been furnished in the particular case with actual notice of the requirement.[12] The drafters seem to be trying to respond to the criticisms set forth above.

Beyond local rules, there are often "standing orders" governing various matters. There are also "local, local" rules, emanating from individual judges. These are least likely to be written and thereby most likely to blindside the unwary. They may be the best argument of all for retaining local counsel in any matter of consequence on unfamiliar turf.

---

9. Section 727(a)(1) (no discharge if the debtor is not an individual).

10. Fed. R. Bankr. Proc. 9029.

11. Fed. R. Bankr. Proc. 9029(a)(2).

12. Fed. R. Bankr. Proc. 9029(b).

§2.8 ~ Official Forms

Just about everything that needs to done to begin a bankruptcy case (and many things that need to be done thereafter) is carried out on official forms, promulgated as part of the rules process. You can buy them at local legal stationery stores. You can also buy sets of forms on disk for computer processing. Or you can download forms from the web.[13]

§2.9 ~ U.S. Trustee Guidelines

The Office of the United States Trustee (a branch of the Justice Department) which supervises a number of activities in bankruptcy courts, promulgates its own principles of behavior. Like them or not, counsel might as well treat them as rules unless she is willing to spend a lot of time and effort seeking to make an issue over their validity.[14] For the most part, they deal with employment and compensation of professionals.

§2.10 ~ Evidence (and "Testimony from the Podium")

The Federal Rules of Evidence apply in bankruptcy court.[15] Bankruptcy court has a reputation, earned or not, for a certain flexibility with the rules of evidence.

Nearly any lawyer who has ever spent so much as a day there will be able to tell you a story of a matter that would have taken a week of trial time in district court, but which breezed through bankruptcy court in half an hour. They joke about "testimony from the podium," where counsel gets a judgment on his assertions of what he will prove, without ever troubling to prove anything at all.

It is easy to deride this kind of free-spirited indifference to form. But the casual style has its defenders. Proponents will argue that the bankruptcy court is best understood as an analog to the European commercial courts, or perhaps to panels of commercial arbitrators, closer to the practical exigencies of commercial practice, undistracted by the excesses of legalism.

The best practical counsel may be that the lawyer who anticipates the need of an appeal will have to be alert to preserve his record, and may sometimes find himself coping with the skepticism of the judge in his efforts to do so.

§2.11 ~ Tactic—For The Record

Don't let the casual style prevent you from protecting your record, particularly if you foresee you will need an appeal. Make evidentiary objections on the record or important points even if you know the ruling will be adverse. And if you need them, ask for findings of fact and conclusions of law under Federal

---

13. For example: http://www.uscourts.gov/bankform/index.html.

14. As a sample, the "United States Trustee Guidelines" for the Ninth Circuit can be found here: http://www.caeb.uscourts.gov/data/trustee/guidelines.htm.

15. Fed. R. Bankr. Proc. 9017. By incorporating Fed. R. Civ. P. 43, the rule permits (*inter alia*) evidence on a motion to be presented by affidavit, although the court may direct otherwise. For text of the rules, *see* http://www.law.cornell.edu/rules/fre/overview.html.

Rule 52, which is incorporated into the bankruptcy rules.[16] When the judge says she doesn't do that in her court, be prepared to say something tactful and firm like, "I know that, judge, but I need to have something on the record for others who aren't familiar with the practices of this court."

Finally, show up to court with admissible evidence sufficient to prove your point. Occasionally, we see lawyers who rely upon the "casual" attitude of bankruptcy courts toward formal evidentiary requirements, assuming they will be able to just argue their point, only to find that the judge will require evidence in admissible form before he will enter the requested order.

§2.12 ~ Non-bankruptcy Law

It is often said that bankruptcy is no more than a procedural framework to receive non-bankruptcy substantive law. Taken at face value, this is a distortion to the point of outright falsehood. But as a point of departure, it is a useful oversimplification. What is "property" for purposes of bankruptcy administration is, with minor exceptions, whatever might be property independent of bankruptcy law. And so also for claims.

Perhaps more importantly, bankruptcy seeks to divide up property when there isn't enough to go around. In so doing, it frequently finds itself entangled with state law rules governing priority of competing claims. Perhaps the most important of these is the Uniform Commercial Code, particularly the UCC's Article 9, governing security interests in personal property. State recording acts, governing priority in title to real estate, also plays a big role. So will other kinds of state "priority" or "lien" law—or indeed, any non-bankruptcy law that may serve to govern or allocate property rights.

§2.13 ~ Bankruptcy Crimes

Bankruptcy clients (and their lawyers) may be liable under any number of criminal laws; but Congress has also specifically proscribed a number of bankruptcy crimes. The so-called bankruptcy crimes statutes prohibit a broad range of activities that involve concealing assets, embezzling from the estate and filing false documents.[17] Some of these are perhaps intuitively obvious but others, less so.

For example, Section 152(6) makes it a crime to "knowingly and fraudulently" give or receive compensation "for acting or forbearing to act in any case under Title 11." Read aggressively, this could put a damper on all kinds of deal-making in chapter 11. Section 3284 adds that concealment of assets in a bankruptcy case is a continuing offense, so the statute of limitation does not begin to run until the discharge is granted (or denied).

The bankruptcy crimes may overlap with noncriminal provisions of the bankruptcy law. For example, Section 152(1) of the criminal statute outlaws fraudulent concealment—an activity which could easily overlap with Section 727(a)(2) which bars a discharge for one who made an intentional fraudulent transfer.

---

16. Fed. R. Bankr. Proc. 7052.

17. 8 U.S.C. §§152-157.

Attorneys are distressingly often participants in, or seeming instigators of, bankruptcy crimes. The cardinal statutes can easily pit lawyer and client against each other. For example, in United States v. Webster,[18] the Seventh Circuit upheld the conviction of an attorney for aiding and abetting in a fraudulent concealment scheme. On the advice of the attorney, the debtor transferred his bar to a corporation in exchange for stock. He then filed for chapter 7 bankruptcy.

On his statement of financial affairs, he said he voluntarily surrendered the bar for release of an unpaid contract obligation. The debtor also failed to list his stock ownership. The debtor later testified that the attorney had orchestrated the scheme, and had told him how to answer questions about it from the trustee. The attorney got a 15-month prison sentence.

On the other hand, in *United States v. McIntosh*,[19] the debtor did what debtors sometimes do when they are in trouble—he tried to blame his lawyer. Convicted of concealing his business he said he had told his attorney about it. The attorney admitted in testimony that he had been told, although he said he was left with the impression the business was not of great value. But the court held that the duty to disclose falls on the debtor, not the attorney, and that the debtor signed schedules over a warning that failure to disclose assets might lead to prosecution.

There is an additional level of complication. These bankruptcy crimes (except for Section 157) are also "RICO predicates." That is, violation of the bankruptcy crimes statute will constitute "racketeering activity" under the Racketeering Influenced and Corrupt Organizations Act.[20] Title 18 also directs the judge or trustee to report any suspected bankruptcy crime to the United States Attorney.[21] Somewhat more surprisingly, Section 3057(b) requires the U.S. Attorney thereafter to "report to the judge" on his investigation, as if the judge had some sort of prosecutorial role in the case (which he does not).

The bankruptcy crimes statutes lay more or less moribund for many years, but lately the U.S. Attorney, in cooperation with the U.S. Trustee, has shown more aggressiveness in prosecuting parties—and professionals representing parties—for supposed offenses in the bankruptcy process.[22] On the U.S. Trustee, *see generally* §1.13.

---

18. 125 F.3d 1024 (7th Cir. 1997).

19. 124 F.3d 1330 (10th Cir. 1997).

20. 18 U.S.C. §1961.

21. *Id.* §3057(a).

22. The Office of the U. S. Trustee has posted summaries of some bankruptcy crimes cases on its official web site. *See* http://www.usdoj.gov/ust/. The government's policy towards bankruptcy crimes prosecution is indicated by the material at http://www.usdoj.gov/ust/ustp_manual/vol5toc.htm.

§2.14 ~ Threatening Prosecution

You won't be around bankruptcy court very long before you will be tempted to use the threat of a criminal charge as leverage to settle civil litigation. You may be able to do it, but be careful: it may be a violation of the rules governing lawyer professional responsibility. *See generally* chapter 16 below.

The difficulty is that the law is in transition. The old ABA Model Code barred a lawyer from "threatening criminal prosecution in connection with a civil case solely to gain an advantage in the civil matter."[23]

The new Model Rules of Professional conduct omitted this provision. An ABA ethics opinion declares that the Model Rules do not prohibit a lawyer from using the possibility of presenting criminal charges against the opposing party in a private civil matter to gain relief for a client, provided that the criminal matter is related to the client's civil claim, the lawyer has a well-founded belief that both the civil claim and the criminal charges are warranted by the law and the facts, and the lawyer does not attempt to exert or suggest improper influence over the criminal process.[24]

But many states retain the express prohibition of the Model Code.

§2.15 ~ Bankruptcy Taxes

Bankruptcy tax law comes from a variety of sources. Some of it is in the Bankruptcy Code itself. For example, the Bankruptcy Code sets rules on the priority and dischargeability of tax claims, §13.41. The Bankruptcy Code also sets fairly elaborate rules governing the treatment of tax attributes in bankruptcy. But because of turf conflicts among federal lawmakers, these rules apply only to state and local taxes, not to Federal taxes—and in this new age of 11th Amendment immunity, there are serious questions as to what extent they apply at all.[25] But apart from the Bankruptcy Code, there are important provisions governing bankruptcy tax attributes in the Internal Revenue Code.[26] And debtors often also run aground on the provisions of the Federal Tax Lien Act; *see* §12.11.

§2.16 ~ How to Read and Interpret Bankruptcy Law

There are a number of threshold principles of interpretation, not set forth explicitly in the statute but deeply rooted in bankruptcy folklore, that will help in reading the statute.

§2.17 ~ Notice and a Hearing

One reason the neophyte finds it hard to read the Bankruptcy Code is that it seems so abstract: the statute says a lot about what happens, but little about how it gets done. Rather, the Code repeatedly says

---

23. ABA Model Code of Professional Responsibility Disciplinary Rule 7-105(a).

24. ABA Ethics Opinion 92-363 (1992).

25. *See* §§326, 738 and 1146. On 11th Amendment immunity, see §4.24.

26. U.S.C. §§108, 1017, 1398, 1399. Some of this material derives from the Bankruptcy Tax Act of 1980, which has a legislative history of its own. *See* Bankruptcy Tax Act of 1980, Pub. L. No. 96-589, 94 Stat. 3389 (codified as amended in scattered sections of Title 26); H. Rep. No. 96-833, 2d Sess., at 33 (1980); S. Rep.96-1035 at 11 (1980).

that such and such will happen "after notice and a hearing," as if everyone knew what sort of notice and what sort of hearing is appropriate. As if to aggravate matters, Section 102 defines notice and a hearing to be such as is "appropriate under the circumstances," which seems not to help at all.

What were the drafters up to here? The point is that they understood that the Code would be fleshed out with bankruptcy rules. *See* §2.5. They made a conscious decision to provide a framework for the rule makers, but otherwise not to get in the way.

But take a second look at Section 102. "Such notice as is appropriate in the particular circumstances, and such *opportunity for a hearing* as is appropriate in the circumstances." Note the italics (added). What do they mean? They mean that for many matters, no hearing is required, so long as the matter is properly noticed and no one objects.

In practice, in many courts this means you put things on a kind of "consent calendar," where you tell the world what you intend to do and let any party object who sees fit. Failing objection, you go ahead and carry out your declared intention. But, we emphasize that the practices in this respect vary from court to court. When in doubt, ask the clerk's office or your local counsel.

An important example is the use, sale or lease of property other than in the ordinary course of business under Section 363(b)(1). Rule 6004(a) specifies the rules governing notice. Rule 6004(b) sets the ground rule for objections.

Note that there is no specific requirement—or even authorization—for an order approving the sale. In a case where there is notice but no objection, one could infer that the judge has neither the obligation nor the power to issue such an order. But most judges will grant a sale approval order if asked, and some require them, at least for sales over a certain dollar limit. To protect both the client and himself, counsel for the buyer will want to insist on an order in any case. *See* §10.5. Another reason buyers will often insist on a sale order, and Court will often accommodate the request, is that many title companies will not give "clean" title opinions on real property purchased from a bankruptcy estate if there is no sale order.

With the procedure under Section 363, contrast the procedure for obtaining credit under Sections 364(b) through (d). These sections provide that the court may authorize credit after notice and a hearing. Here, unlike Section 363, the Code appears to require a court order. In any event, no DIP lender would ever advance funds post-petition without a court order. *See generally* §10.12.

§2.18 ~ When the Legislative History is in Doubt, Read the Statute

Another background condition of Bankruptcy Code reading is the matter of legislative history. In fact, the Code has a lot of legislative history: there are House and Senate committee reports and elaborate (if seemingly manufactured) "floor statements" from the time of the adoption of the 1978 law. There are additional reports and such for some of the later amendments. Particularly in the early years of the Code, lawyers tended to rely heavily on the legislative history—heavily enough to give rise to the quip at the beginning of the section.

But the utility of legislative history has been diminished by the attitude of the Supreme Court, and particularly of Justice Scalia, toward legislative history. Put shortly, he has made it clear that he distrusts it, cleaving rather to a conception of "plain meaning" wherever possible. Justice Scalia's attitude appears to be a general proposition of which bankruptcy offers no more than incidental examples. But he has expressed himself clearly in the context of bankruptcy opinions.[27]

§2.19 ~ Case Law

An additional background condition for reading the Bankruptcy Code is the role of judicial decisions.[28] The bankruptcy judge in reaching a decision is bound by the controlling decision of any authoritative court (for example, her own court of appeals). Absent binding authority, she may be guided by decisions of other courts the judge finds persuasive.

But in bankruptcy, there is a veritable blizzard of opinions that are nonauthoritative. Bankruptcy judges got law clerks in the late 1970s. About the same time, West Publishing Company started publishing volumes of bankruptcy decisions. The combined result was to create a kind of "vanity press," in which the bankruptcy judge is able to publish virtually any opinion she thinks fit. Now, there are new sources for "publishing" decisions. For example, many courts have started publishing their decisions on web sites.

The best of these are wonderfully enlightening insights into the law: taken as a whole, the bankruptcy judges, are after all, perhaps the ablest corps of commercial judges in the country. But some bankruptcy opinions can be obtuse or impenetrable. Perhaps even worse, others amount to no more than findings of fact on well-documented principles. One consequence is that you can find a bankruptcy opinion supporting almost any proposition you want to advance. And many of these are not binding authority for anything at all.

§2.20 ~ The Bankruptcy Court Is a Court of Equity

No principle of bankruptcy jurisdiction is more familiar—and none easier to misunderstand—than the notion that the bankruptcy court is a "court of equity."[29] The trouble is that there are just too many and conflicting meanings to the notion of "equity." It can refer to the historical fact that bankruptcy jurisdiction descends from the jurisdiction exercised by the equity courts in earlier times; or to a supposed general principle that the bankruptcy court ought to "do good" in some general sense—or any number of other meanings in between.[30]

---

27. *See, e.g.*, Bank of Am. Nat'l Trust and Sav. Ass'n v. 203 N. LaSalle St. Partnership, 526 U.S. 434 (1999) (Thomas, J., concurring); Dewsnup v. Timm, 502 U.S. 410, 420-36 (1992) (Scalia, J., dissenting).

28. Major recent decisions on bankruptcy issues for the Supreme Court and for circuit courts of appeal can be accessed through: http://www.abiworld.org/chambers/newchambers.html.

Opinions of lower courts are published in various ways. More and more courts post them on their own web sites.

29. A computer search reveals over 350 published decisions stating that the "Bankruptcy Court is a court of equity."

30. "The English language is overblessed with words that mean several unlike things at the same time. English poetry no doubt benefits from the possibility of shorthand multiple reference but legal analysis does not." GRANT GILMORE, SECURITY INTERESTS IN PERSONAL PROPERTY §7.2 at 198 (1965) (undertaking to identify five different meanings of 'equitable' in the sense of 'equitable lien').

In the narrow sense, it often refers to the power of the bankruptcy court (now codified in Section 510(c)) to "equitably subordinate" a claim to a claim or an interest to an interest.[31] In this sense, its principal sponsor was the architect of modern reorganization law, Justice William O. Douglas.[32]

Given the ambiguity, and the frequency with which bankruptcy courts repeat that they are "courts of equity," one can hardly blame the desperate litigant from using the equity card as a last-ditch appeal. But we caution that too much emphasis by a litigant upon the need for the "Court of Equity" to "do the right thing" may focus the court upon the lack of legal authority for the stated proposition, and then backfire.

§2.21 ~ Section 105

Close kin to the idea that the bankruptcy court is a court of equity is the residual power conferred by Section 105, the "bankruptcy all writs" act, to "enter any order, process, or judgment that is necessary or appropriate to carry out the provisions of this title." Like the "court of equity" ploy, it is probably far more often pleaded than implemented, and counsel needs to beware that appeal to Section 105 may be read as a sign that he has run out of respectable arguments.

Still, the courts have used the section to tease out the limits of the Bankruptcy Code, perhaps particularly in the realm of protecting nondebtor third parties as part of the bankruptcy case, either by extensions of the "automatic stay" to nondebtors or by implementing third party releases under a plan, as in some of the professional partnership cases.[33]

The task of teasing out the exact limits of Section105 is generating a jurisprudence all its own. Generalizations are hazardous, but it's probably fair to say that if the court finds itself confronted with an express rule either inside or outside the Bankruptcy Code, it won't permit the use of Section 105 as a trump card.[34] On the other hand, the courts have been able to take some remarkable steps to implement plans and effectuate other relief in the interstices of other law.[35]

---

31. *See, e.g.*, U.S. v. Noland, 517 U.S. 535, 539 (1996).

32. *See* Sampsell v. Imperial Paper Corp., 313 U.S. 215 (1939).

33. *Compare* A.H. Robins Co.v. Picinin, 788 F.2d 994, 1008 (4th Cir. 1986) (Section 105 authorizes injunction against litigation which could threaten a reorganization) with Official Committee of Equity Security Holders v. Mabey, 832 F.2d 299, 302 (4th Cir. 1987) (same case–Section 105 does not authorize creation of an emergency fund for benefit of unsecured claimants prior to a plan of reorganization).

34. *See, e.g.*, California State Board of Equalization v. Sierra Summit, Inc., 490 U.S. 844, 849-50 (1988) (state may impose sales tax on a bankruptcy liquidation sale, notwithstanding Section105(a)).

35. United States v. Energy Resources Co., 495 U.S. 545, 550-51 (1990) (bankruptcy court may direct Internal Revenue Service to direct plan payments first to trust-fund liabilities).

§2.22 ~ Getting Information from the Bankruptcy System

§2.23 ~ Notice

Here is a nightmare. You know the debtor is in bankruptcy. You know he owes your client a lot of money. But you know that there are a lot of assets in the estate. So you trust that in good time, at least, you will hear about it.

Then one day on the street, an acquaintance tells you that the debtor's property has been spirited out of the estate, the debtor has been discharged, and the case has been closed—all without your knowing about it. What prevents this nightmare from turning into reality? The answer is that the system itself makes elaborate provision for notice of many particular events. In getting familiar with bankruptcy, you want to get familiar with the basic notice rules and the traps that may keep them from working.

§2.24 ~ Rule 2002

One consequence of Section 102 (on notice and a hearing) is that you will have to be alert to look for notice rules in lots of places. The judge may declare that a particular form of notice is "appropriate for" a particular case or circumstance. Lots of courts have special notice provisions in their local rules.

Happily, many of the important notice provisions are collected together in one place. That place is bankruptcy rule 2002. The rule includes three major categories, classified by the time limit required for notice:

- Twenty days.[36] This is the one you will have to watch. It includes eight items, many of them items that come up in ordinary cases a lot.
- Twenty-five days.[37] This category includes two items, approval of disclosure statements and confirmation of plans.[38]
- No time specified, but notice required. This is a residual catch-all category with nine items, but most of them are the sort of chores that are carried out routinely by the court.

Rule 2002 also includes subsections specifying when there shall be notice to the U. S. Trustee and the United States government, and when to committees.[39] A particular subsection specifies when there shall be notice to equity security holders.[40] This is interesting, because it gives some hint as to when the old equity owners have standing in a case, and also because it implies that there are many matters on which they do not have a right to notice at all.

---

36. Fed. R. Bankr. Proc. 2002(a).

37. Fed. R. Bankr. Proc. 2002(b).

38. Fed. R. Bankr. Proc. 2002(f).

39. Fed. R. Bankr. Proc. 2002(j) (U.S. trustee); 2002(j) (U.S. government); 2002(i) (committees).

40. Fed. R. Bankr. Proc. 2002(d).

§2.25 ~ Notice Rules: A Few Examples

If you expect to be around bankruptcy court very much, it is probably worth your while to read rule 2002 now, to get a feel for it. But the practical fact is that there are a lot of internal inconsistencies that may rise to haunt you—or that may turn into weapons that you can use in your favor.

For example: while most of the time the Code just specifies "notice and a hearing" (see above), still there are a few cases where it is very specific. One such is the matter of dismissing an involuntary bankruptcy. Suppose a creditor begins an involuntary, then wants to compromise and dismiss the case. The Code (not the rule) specifies that dismissal may occur only after notice to all creditors.[41] The practical fact is that it makes compromise of a pending involuntary difficult.

For a different kind of example, consider the matter of disposing of an estate asset. The rule provides for 20 days notice to all creditors of sale of an asset (if outside the ordinary course of business).[42] But rights under an executory contract may be just as valuable to the debtor to the estate. Yet there is no rule requiring notice to all creditors of a decision to reject an executory contract.

In the same vein, consider the motion for relief from the automatic stay. Nothing in the Code or rules specifically requires that the motion for relief go to all creditors. Yet in a single asset case, relief from stay can empty the coffers just as much as outright dismissal.[43]

§2.26 ~ Other Means of Protecting Yourself

But even if the notice system works reasonably well, you won't want to sit by and wait. In fact there are a number of things you can do to make sure you learn about the case. You can request in writing that you be added to the notice list for all matters in the case. You can request electronic noticing through the courts' new electronic noticing system.[44] You can take the initiative to consult the schedules and other papers that the debtor must file. You can check dockets on court web sites or on a variety of computer systems, such as PACER. And you can protect yourself with a variety of discovery techniques.

§2.27 ~ Form: Demand for Notice

To make sure you get notice of pleadings, consider filing a "notice of appearance." Here's a form:

---

41. Section 303(k). Rule 2002(b) requires 20 days' notice to all creditors of the hearing on dismissal or conversion.

42. Fed. R. Bankr. Proc. 2002(a)(2).

43. Apparently, some courts do require notice to all creditors, by local rule. And a court has the power to order notice to all creditors if it sees fit.

44. http://www.ebnuscourts.com/.

IN THE UNITED STATES BANKRUPTCY COURT
FOR THE EASTERN DISTRICT OF UTOPIA

In Re:
INSOLVENT DISTRIBUTION CORPORATION,
Debtor in Possession

Case No. 99-1416-BBL (Chapter 11)

NOTICE OF APPEARANCE AND DEMAND FOR NOTICES AND PAPERS

PLEASE TAKE NOTICE that Citistreet Construction, Inc. ("Citistreet"), a creditor and party in interest, hereby appears in the above-captioned case by its counsel, Smith & Jones, LLP; such counsel hereby enters its appearance pursuant to §1109(b) of the Bankruptcy Code and Federal Rule of Bankruptcy Procedure 9010(b); and such counsel hereby requests, pursuant, *inter alia*, to Federal Rules of Bankruptcy Procedure 2002, 3017 and 9007 and §§342 and 1109(b) of the Bankruptcy Code, that copies of all notices and pleadings given or filed in this case and in any adversary proceeding or contested matter filed herein be given to and served upon the undersigned at the following address and telephone number:

Lawrence L. Lawyer, Esq.
Abigail A. Attorney, Esq.
SMITH & JONES, LLP
333 Twentieth Street
Sun City, Utopia 99899
(646) 394-5000

Please take further notice that, pursuant to §1109(b) of the Bankruptcy Code, the foregoing demand includes not only the notices and papers referred to in the rules specified above but also includes, without limitation, any notice, application, complaint, demand, motion, petition, plan of reorganization, disclosure statement, pleading or request, whether formal or informal, written or oral, and whether transmitted or conveyed by mail, delivery, telephone, telegraph, electronic mail, facsimile, or otherwise filed or made in or with regard to the referenced case and proceedings herein.

This notice of appearance and demand for notices and papers shall not be deemed or construed to be a waiver of any of Citistreet's rights (1) to have final orders in non-core matters entered only after de novo review by a United States District Judge; (2) to invoke the right to a trial by jury in any proceeding so triable in this case or any case, controversy, or proceeding related to this case; (3) to ask the United States District Court to withdraw the reference in any matter subject to mandatory or discretionary withdrawal; or (4) to contend that jurisdiction or venue in this Court over any matter is improper or inappropriate.

Respectfully submitted,

SMITH & JONES, LLP
/s/______________________________
By: Lawrence L. Lawyer, Esq. #987654321
333 Twentieth Street
Sun City, Utopia 99899
(646) 394-5000
Attorney for Citistreet Construction Inc.

§2.28 ~ Schedules And Statements of Affairs

Every debtor must file (or there must be filed on its behalf) a set of schedules and a statement of affairs.[45] As a source of information, they aren't perfect. They may not be available until 15 days or more into the case; they may be incomplete or inaccurate; and in a rare case they may even be impounded, out of public view. But they are still the first line of approach for the creditor trying to get information about the case.

§2.29 ~ Meeting of Creditors — Section 341

Section 341 mandates provides that "within a reasonable time after the order for relief . . . the United States trustee shall convene and preside at a meeting of creditors"—more generally, the "341 meeting," or sometimes the "first meeting of creditors." Rule 2003 says the meeting will take place between 20 and 40 days after entry of the order for relief. On the face of things, it would appear that this is the right place to go to interrogate the debtor.

But don't be misled. Meetings of creditors are usually "mass market" affairs. In a chapter 7 case, dozens will typically be scheduled at the same time. The debtor must appear and the assistant U. S. Trustee or chapter 7 Trustee will ask a few questions with the intention of exposing gross anomalies in the case. Sometimes creditors will attend and sometimes even ask questions, but their participation will be limited as a result of the tight schedule. In a chapter 11 case, they tend to be a bit less rushed, but even there a creditor is unlikely to have more than about 10-15 minutes to examine the debtor. For your serious discovery, plan on using Rule 2004, discussed below.

§2.30 ~ DIP Filings

A second source of information may be periodic operating reports filed with the United States Trustee. The bankruptcy rules mandate a quarterly report, although the U. S. Trustee offices typically require monthly reports. Three months is a long time, and a lot of money can funnel out of the estate before you learn about it from the quarterly report, but it can still give you some idea of whether the debtor has any hope of reorganization. Note the monthly operating reports are not routinely served on creditors, so if you want a copy, you will have to get one from the clerk's office or from debtor's counsel.

§2.31 ~ Rule 2004 Exams

Rule 2004 examinations are general bankruptcy depositions. This is the rule to use when a creditor wants to depose the debtor (or another party), but does not have a particular adversary proceeding or contested matter in which to take the deposition. The thorniest question with reference to Rule 2004 is how it relates to the discovery framework of the Federal Rules of Civil Procedure, incorporated for adversary proceedings into the Bankruptcy Code. An occasional case will hold that Rule 2004 is no longer available once an adversary proceeding has begun.[46] But other courts disagree.[47] Sometimes, a party will use a Rule 2004 examination for some discovery before filing an adversary complaint, to determine whether to file the complaint, or to allow for a more specific and well-informed complaint.

45. Section 521, Fed. R. Bankr. Proc. 1007. *See* Official Bankr. Form 6, 7.

46. *See, e.g.*, *In re* Bakalis, 199 B.R. 443, 448 (Bankr. E.D.N.Y. 1996).

47. *See, e.g.*, *In re* Sun Medical Mgt., Inc., 104 B.R. 522, 524 (Bankr. M.D. Ga. 1989).

§2.32 ~ Limitation: Protective Orders

On request of a party in interest, the bankruptcy court may issue orders as necessary to protect trade secrets and such, or to protect with respect to scandalous or defamatory matter. Protection is authorized by the Bankruptcy Code; but also, for adversary proceedings, by the rules of civil procedure.[48]

§2.33 ~ A Short List of Web Sites You Need to Know About

We have scattered references to web sites through the footnotes as we thought convenient for the reader. In this section, we collect some of our favorites. In the next section, we add our second-string choices. Remember that this sort of thing changes as fast as we can type, so some of it is bound to be outdated before you read it.

One of the most convenient bankruptcy web sites is the "Maryland Bankruptcy Bar Association" site: http://bankruptcybar.org/links_main.htm

More good general-information bankruptcy sites include:

http://www.abiworld.org/
http://www.djnewswires.com/fin-pro/overview.html
http://www.banko.com/
http://bankrupt.com/
http://bankruptcydata.com/

Links to all Federal courts are consolidated at: http://www.uscourts.gov/allinks.html

For bankruptcy clerks, go to: http://www.bankruptcydata.com/Courts/Courts.htm

This book is not primarily about consumer bankruptcy cases, but for those who do need quick information on consumer cases, we like: http://nolo.com/encyclopedia/dc_ency.html

§2.34 ~ More Web Sites

Here is a list of other web sites, not quite as essential or pervasive as our first list, but perhaps useful to you for particular purposes. Many of these have links in the Maryland bankruptcy bar web site (listed above).

More good "links of links" include:

http://www.washlaw.edu/bankrupt/ntlsites/ntlsites.htm
http://www.agin.com/lawfind/
http://www.wolfenet.com
http://stinson.com/2cents/

---

48. Section 107; *cf.* Fed. R. Civ. Proc. 26(c)(7), Fed. R. Bankr. Proc. 7026.

Sites for court opinions (including the judicial "link of links" cited earlier) include:
U.S. Supreme Court: http://supct.law.cornell.edu/supct/

Selected Bankruptcy Courts

1st Circuit

Maine District: http://www.meb.uscourts.gov/
Massachusetts District: http://www.mab.uscourts.gov/
New Hampshire: http://www.nhb.uscourts.gov
Rhode Island District: http://www.rib.uscourts.gov/

2nd Circuit

Connecticut: http://www.ctb.uscourts.gov
New York, Northern District: http://www.nynb.uscourts.gov/
New York, Southern District: http://www.nysb.uscourts.gov/
Vermont District: http://www.vtb.uscourts.gov/

3rd Circuit

Delaware: http://www.deb.uscourts.gov
New Jersey District: http://www.njb.uscourts.gov/
Pennsylvania, Middle District: http://www.pamb.uscourts.gov/
Pennsylvania, Eastern District: http://www.paeb.uscourts.gov/

4th Circuit

Maryland District: http://www.mdb.uscourts.gov/
North Carolina, Eastern District: http://www.nceb.uscourts.gov/
North Carolina, Middle District: http://www.ncmb.uscourts.gov/
North Carolina, Western District: http://www.ncbankruptcy.org
Virginia, Eastern District: http://www.vaeb.uscourts.gov/
Virginia, Western District: http://www.vawb.uscourts.gov/

5th Circuit

Louisiana, Western District: http://www.lawb.uscourts.gov/
Texas, Northern District: http://www.txnb.uscourts.gov/
Texas, Southern District: http://www.txs.uscourts.gov/

6th Circuit

Michigan, Western District: http://www.miwb.uscourts.gov/
Ohio, Northern District: http://www.ohnb.uscourts.gov/

7th Circuit

Illinois, Northern District: http://www.ilnb.uscourts.gov
Illinois, Southern District: http://www.ilsb.uscourts.gov/
Indiana, Northern District: http://www.innb.uscourts.gov/
Wisconsin, Western District: http://www.wiw.uscourts.gov/bankruptcy/

8th Circuit

Iowa, Northern District: http://ianb.uscourts.gov/index.html
Minnesota District: http://www.mnb.uscourts.gov/
Missouri, Eastern District: http://www.moeb.uscourts.gov/
South Dakota District: http://www.sdb.uscourts.gov/

9th Circuit

Alaska District: http://www.akb.uscourts.gov/
Arizona District: http://www.azb.uscourts.gov/
California, Central District: http://www.cacb.uscourts.gov/
California, Eastern District: http://www.caeb.uscourts.gov/
California, Northern District: http://www.canb.uscourts.gov/
Hawaii District: http://www.hib.uscourts.gov/
Idaho District: http://www.id.uscourts.gov/
Nevada District: http://www.nvb.uscourts.gov/
Washington, Eastern District: http://www.waeb.uscourts.gov
Washington, Western District: http://www.wawb.uscourts.gov

10th Circuit

Colorado District: http://www.cob.uscourts.gov/bindex.htm
Kansas District: http://www.ksb.uscourts.gov/
New Mexico District: http://www.nmcourt.fed.us/bkdocs/
Utah District: http://www.utb.uscourts.gov/
Wyoming District: http://www.wyb.uscourts.gov/

11th Circuit

Alabama, Northern District: http://www.almb.uscourts.gov/
District of Columbia: http://www.dcb.uscourts.gov/
Florida, Middle District: http://www.flmb.uscourts.gov/
Georgia, Middle District: http://www.gamb.uscourts.gov/
Georgia, Northern District: http://www.ganb.uscourts.gov/

D.C. Circuit

District of Columbia: http://www.dcb.uscourts.gov

Organizations

American Bankruptcy Institute: http://www.abiworld.org

National Bankruptcy Conference: http://www.law.uchicago.edu/NBC/NBC.htm

National Conference of Bankruptcy Judges: http://www.ncbj.org/ncbjhomepage/index.htm

National Conference of Bankruptcy Clerks: http://www.ncbcimpact.org/

National Association of Bankruptcy Trustees: http://www.nabt.com

National Association of Chapter 13 Trustees: http://www.nactt.com

National Association of Consumer Bankruptcy Attorneys: http://www.nacba.org/

Commercial Law League of America: http://www.clla.org

American Bar Association: http://www.abanet.org

INSOL International: http://www.insol.org/

Other Bankruptcy/Financial Resources

Professor LoPucki's data set on major cases: http://teddy.law.cornell.edu:8090/lopucki.htm

Bank/Financial Links: http://www.bankinfo.com/quicklinks.html

Bank Rate Monitor: http://www.bankrate.com

Collectors.com (for valuing stamps, coins, baseball card, etc.): http://www.collectors.com

Currency Converter: http://www.oanda.com/converter/classic

EDGAR (free): http://www.freeedgar.com

Experian Credit Reports (fee required): http://www.experian.com

Kelly Blue Book: http://www.kbb.com

Mortgage Calculator: http://www.interest.com/hugh/calc/mort.html

Real Estate ValueService (free): http://www.homeagain.com

Real Estate Comparable Values: http://www.yahoo.iplace.com/value_search.asp

Reference

Bluebook Online: http://www.cheapestrate.com/auto.html

Oran's Law Dictionary: http://www.wld.com/conbus/orans/welcome.asp

West's Legal Directory: http://www.directory.findlaw.com/

Government Agency Sites

U.S. Trustee, Executive Office: http://www.usdoj.gov/ust/

Department of Justice: http://www.usdoj.gov

Department of Labor: http://www.dol.gov

Federal Bureau of Investigation: http://www.fbi.gov

Federal Judiciary: http://www.uscourts.gov/

Federal Trade Commission: http://www.ftc.gov/

Internal Revenue Service: http://www.irs.ustreas.gov/prod/cover.html

HUD: http://www.hud.gov

Patent and Trademark Office: http://www.uspto.gov

Pension Benefit Guaranty Corp.: http://www.pbgc.gov

Small Business Administration: http://www.sba.gov

Social Security: http://www.ssa.gov/

Treasury: http://www.ustreas.gov/

International Sites

A link of links, with international connections:
http://www.catalaw.com/topics/Bankruptcy.shtml

United Kingdom: http://www.insolvency.co.uk/

Canada: http://strategis.ic.gc.ca/sc_mrksv/bankrupt/engdoc/superint.html

Quebec: http://www.avocat.qc.ca/affaires/iifailliteentreprise.htm

Australia: http://www.law.gov.au/aghome/commaff/itsa

Switzerland: http://www.admin.ch/ch/f/rs/28.html

Teaching Web Sites (For help in learning bankruptcy law)

http://www.law.arizona.edu/faculty/boyd/publications/index.htm

http://mail.law.missouri.edu/lawless/bus_bkr/

http://www.law.duke.edu/curriculum/courseHomepages/287_01

Sample plans and disclosure statements:

http://lopucki.lawlib.ucla.edu/BRD_Documents/

And Your Authors' Web Sites

http://idrive.ucdavis.edu/jdayer/web/index.htm

http://www.arnoldporter.com

3

Bankruptcy Litigation: Jurisdiction and Procedure

3 Bankruptcy Litigation: Jurisdiction and Procedure

§3.1 ~ Introduction: In General

Bankruptcy law is replete with problems of jurisdiction and procedure—so much so that we have divided them into two chapters. In this one, we take up the basic framework of the bankruptcy dispute. In the next, we deal with some more specific jurisdiction issues, as well as with appeals and with some problems of federalism.

§3.2 ~ Sorting It Out

For the newcomer, bankruptcy jurisdiction and procedure can seem like a bad dream. Everything looks familiar, but nothing seems to work the way you expect it to. You find yourself straining to open seemingly unlocked doors, and just when you are about ready to give up and go home, you plunge headlong through a solid wall.

You won't be consoled if we tell you that things are easier once you get used to it although, in fact, they are. The trick is to get from here to there. We explain, first, why things are difficult. Second, ignoring all complications, we give a short summary. Then we offer a catalog of some basic distinctions. Finally, we offer some discussion of specific points.

§3.3 ~ Why Things Are

Why is bankruptcy litigation such a tangle for the beginner? There are two reasons. First is the matter of jurisdiction. As we will explain more fully later, most bankruptcy litigation gets handled by the bankruptcy judge in the bankruptcy court. But the bankruptcy judge is not an Article III Federal judge. So she has to exercise her powers as a kind of extension of the district court. This leads to a lot of cumbersome work-around rules with reference to judicial power, finality of judgments, review and such.

The second problem is the structure of the bankruptcy case. Bankruptcy starts with the global bankruptcy case. But it also includes all kinds of cases within the case that get their own names and rules—adversary proceedings, contested matters, and such.

§3.4 ~ A Summary

The principal theater for bankruptcy practice is the bankruptcy court. The bankruptcy court operates as "a unit" of the district court, and sometimes (though rarely) the district judge hears bankruptcy matters in his own court.

Most matters start and end in the bankruptcy court. But also, one or another of the parties may remove certain matters from other courts into bankruptcy court. For his part, the judge may remand a matter to non-bankruptcy court, or may simply abstain, leaving matters to another court.

Appeals from the bankruptcy court go sometimes to the district court, sometimes to the bankruptcy appellate panel ("BAP"). Appeals from the district court go to the circuit courts of appeal, and ultimately, to the Supreme Court.

§3.5 ~ Jurisdiction Concepts

There is nothing especially arcane about bankruptcy procedure, but there is a fair amount of specialized jargon bound to be off-putting to the outsider. You will want to master these basic principles:

- **Case versus Proceeding.** The bankruptcy "case" is the global bankruptcy—*In re* DebtorCo, or whatever. The proceeding is a matter "arising under, arising in, or related to" the global case. The district court always has jurisdiction over the bankruptcy case (the statute says "original and exclusive"). The district court may have jurisdiction over a proceeding ("original but not exclusive").[1] The bankruptcy court may have the power to do some of the things the district court may do—but not all. And the bankruptcy court never has the power to do any more than the district court can do.

- **Adversary Proceeding versus Contested Matter.** Each of these is a "proceeding" in the sense that it is not a case. The line between them is somewhat shadowy, but the adversary proceeding is the more formal—a separate lawsuit within the bankruptcy case. The adversary begins with the filing of a complaint, much like an ordinary civil case. It gets its own file jacket and docket number, and it functions under a specific set of adversary rules (see Part VII of the Bankruptcy Rules). A contested matter is a disputed matter that does not rise to the dignity of an adversary proceeding. Most of the time, you begin a "contested matter" by "motion," but in some courts you will still see an application or an order to show cause.[2]

- **Core versus Non-core.** As we explain more fully below, in 1982 the Supreme Court struck down the extant bankruptcy jurisdiction statute as unconstitutional, on grounds that it reposed too much power in the bankruptcy judge. Judges and administrators scrambling to salvage bankruptcy jurisdiction hit upon the notion that the bankruptcy judge might hear matters if she operated under the aegis of the district court. They reasoned that the bankruptcy judge might actually have the power to decide a matter if it were part of the core of the bankruptcy estate. If not part of the core, she might at least hear the matter, even if not finally decide it.

---

1. 28 U.S.C. §1334.

2. At the risk of complicating what is already complicated enough, note that there are some instances where you will need to go to court and get an order from the judge even if no one objects to what you propose to do (for example, post-petition borrowing under Section 364).

The distinction has since been cobbled into the statute.[3] The Supreme Court has never explicitly ruled on it, but most people operate on the assumption that it probably passes muster.

People sometimes also make this distinction as "core" versus "related matter." For more on "related matter," see below.

- **"Related to" Jurisdiction.** As noted above, bankruptcy judges may hear and decide "core" matters. This includes matters "arising under" the bankruptcy case (proceedings created by or founded upon the Bankruptcy Code), and matters "arising in" the bankruptcy case (those relating to administration of the bankruptcy case, but not founded upon an express provision in the Code). The category of matters that could have some impact upon the estate or its creditors, but are not "core" matters, are referred to as being within the "related to" jurisdiction of the Bankruptcy Court. Proceedings that do not affect the estate or its creditors, are unrelated, and the Bankruptcy Court will have no jurisdiction over such matters.

  People sometimes treat the distinction between "related to" jurisdiction and "arising under" or "arising in" jurisdiction and no bankruptcy jurisdiction at all as if it were the same as the "core/non-core" distinction. Strictly speaking, this isn't quite right. Related/unrelated goes to the question of jurisdiction—whether there is any bankruptcy jurisdiction at all or not. Core/non-core goes to the question of which judge can decide the matter—the bankruptcy judge or the district judge (or, at any rate, it goes to the question of the power of the bankruptcy judge). But some courts have held that "arising in" and "arising under" matters are all within the Bankruptcy Court's "core" jurisdiction and that "related to" matters are within the court's "noncore" jurisdiction.[4] We can imagine exceptions to this rule, but as a starting point it is probably a reasonable assumption.

- **Reference and Withdrawal.** The bankruptcy court is a unit of the district court. The bankruptcy judge has no power except insofar as a matter is referred to her from the district court. In most districts, referral is by standing order, so most bankruptcy matters go first to the bankruptcy court as a matter of course. But the district judge may withdraw the reference at any time—either for a particular matter or for all matters—for any reason or (apparently) for no reason. There are certain matters with respect to which withdrawal of the reference is mandatory. *See* 28 USC §158.

- **Note—Other Ways to End Up in the District Court**. If you start out in the bankruptcy court, there are at least three ways in which you may wind up in the district court. One, you may ask the district judge to "withdraw the reference" and take the matter back to the district court (but don't expect him to do it very often). Two, if the bankruptcy judge enters a final judgment, you may have the right to appeal (but in some cases, the appeal may also go to the Bankruptcy Appellate Panel) And three, in a case where the bankruptcy judge has the power to hear but not decide a matter, as in a noncore matter, you will go to the district court to get a final order.[5]

---

3. *See* 28 U.S.C. §157.

4. *See, e.g., In re* Poplar Run Five L.P., 192 B.R. 848 (Bankr. E.D. Va. 1995).

5. The distinction doesn't necessarily make a lot of difference in terms of substance, because the district judge has the power to make his own findings of fact in any of the three cases. But it does make a difference as to which set of rules you follow.

- **Abstention and Remand**. The judge exercising bankruptcy power may decide to abstain from hearing the bankruptcy case or some part of the case. Or he may remand a proceeding, once properly removed to the bankruptcy court, back to the originating state court. The principles governing abstention and remand are pretty much the same and courts use similar factors in evaluating the two.[6]

Now we move on to a fuller discussion of some of the issues.

§3.6 ~ Where It Begins: The Constitution

In order to exercise the judicial power of the United States, a judge must be appointed who "shall hold their offices during good behavior,"—which is to say, for life. So says Article III of the Constitution.[7] Thus a U. S. district judge (among others) may exercise the judicial power of the United States.

But a bankruptcy judge is appointed for a term (of 14 years).[8] She derives her power from Article I, Section 8, of the Constitution, the bankruptcy power. So by definition she cannot exercise "the judicial power of the United States" and must exercise, if anything at all, something less. This analysis has led to a complicated and not always successful kind of a two-step in which Congress and the courts sort out the relative roles of the district court and the bankruptcy judge.

§3.7 ~ The Statute

The substantive law of bankruptcy is in Title 11 of the United States Code, the Bankruptcy Code. But most of the jurisdictional rules are in Title 28, the Judicial Code.

§3.8 ~ Jurisdiction—the Basics

Section 1334 says that jurisdiction is "original and exclusive" over all cases under the Bankruptcy Code, and "original but not exclusive" with respect to other matters. See further below.[9] The district court also has exclusive jurisdiction of all property of the debtor and of the estate, wherever located.[10]

But the district judge in fact actually exercises very little of the jurisdiction conferred by Congress. Rather, most of the work is delegated to the bankruptcy judge. How is this done? It is carried out under the process set out in Sections 151 and 157 of the Judicial Code.[11]

---

6. *See* Aetna Life Ins. Co. v. Danbury Square Assocs. (*In re* Danbury Square Assocs.), 150 B.R. 544, 547-48 (Bankr. S.D.N.Y. 1993) (stating that "[t]he courts have generally applied some of the same factors in determining motions for remand as . . . with respect to abstention issues"), *In re* Riverside Nursing Home, 144 B.R. 951, 957 (Bankr. S.D.N.Y. 1992) (stating that '[t]he equitable grounds that warrant a decision to remand under 28 U.S.C. §1452(b) are similar to the factors that authorize abstention under 28 U.S.C. §1334(c)").

7. *See* U.S. Const. Art. III.

8. 28 U.S.C. §152(a)(1) (1994).

9. *Id.*, §1334 (a) and (b).

10. *Id.*, §1334(e)(1994).

11. *Id.*, §§151, 157.

First, Section 151 creates the "bankruptcy court." The bankruptcy court is a unit of the district court, comprising "all bankruptcy judges in regular or active service" in the district. The bankruptcy court itself has no jurisdiction. Rather, the statute says that the bankruptcy judge exercises authority "as a judicial officer of the district court."

Section 157 specifies how this exercise takes place. Specifically it provides that the district judge may refer any and all bankruptcy matters to the bankruptcy judge. As to what the bankruptcy judge can do with these matters so referred, we need to ask an additional question. We need to ask whether the particular matter is part of the core of the bankruptcy case (on the one hand) or merely related to the case (on the other). We can shorthand the distinction as core versus related to, or sometimes simply core versus non-core.

§3.9 ~ "RELATED"

To clarify, turn the point around. In order to be within bankruptcy jurisdiction, the matter must be at least "related to" the bankruptcy case. If unrelated, then there is no bankruptcy jurisdiction at all.

A number of courts have had to grapple with the limits of bankruptcy jurisdiction. The short summary is that it is broad, but not infinite.[12] *Pacor, Inc. v. Higgins*[13] provides the boilerplate standard to determine when a matter is "related." It says the question is "whether the outcome of that proceeding could conceivably have any effect on the estate being administered in bankruptcy."[14] Many circuits have endorsed Pacor, and it has been cited, if not expressly adopted, by the Supreme Court.[15]

Deciding *In re Wood*,[16] the Fifth Circuit undertook a thoughtful exploration of the distinction between related and unrelated matters. The court had to consider a lawsuit between a debtor and a fellow shareholder over share allocations in a closely-held corporation. The district court dismissed the complaint for lack of subject-matter jurisdiction. The appellate court reversed, holding that the matter was within bankruptcy jurisdiction as related to a bankruptcy case under 1334(b). The court found that the suit was related to the bankruptcy case because it had a potential effect on the estate.[17]

---

12. Broad, because just about all the problems of the debtor are somehow related to his bankruptcy. A favorite law professor example is the antitrust suit. There may be all kinds of reasons why the antitrust suit should not be tried in the bankruptcy court (consider abstention, remand, withdrawal of reference, etc., below). But suppose the allegation is that it was the defendant's antitrust violation that put the debtor out of business and the proceeds from the suit if successful, would be available to pay creditors and shareholders. Then pretty clearly the suit is within the bankruptcy court's related to jurisdiction.

13. 743 F.2d 984 (3d Cir.1984).

14. *Id.* at 994.

15. Celotex Corp. v. Edwards, 514 U.S. 300, fn.6 (1995).

16. 825 F.2d 90 (5th Cir. 1987).

17. *But see* §3.10 *infra*.

§3.10 ~ Core v. Non-core: The Role of the Bankruptcy Judge

The core/non-core distinction determines the authority of the bankruptcy judge. The bankruptcy judge has the power to hear and determine any core matter.[18] But if the matter is noncore, then the judge may hear but not determine the matter.[19] Rather, in a noncore matter to the judge shall "submit proposed findings of fact and conclusions of law to the district court." It remains for the district judge to consider the bankruptcy judge's proposals, and to enter the final order. The statute adds that the judge will review de novo those matters to which any party has timely and specifically objected.

But Section 157(c) goes on to say that the bankruptcy judge may determine a non-core matter on consent of all parties. The statute also provides that it is for the bankruptcy judge to decide whether a proceeding is core or non-core.

§3.11 ~ Withdrawal

Finally, the Code also provides that the district judge may withdraw the reference from the bankruptcy judge. Section 157(d) provides for withdrawal at the district judge's discretion. It says she may withdraw any time for cause. Since the district judge has ultimate control via his Article III status, it is hard to imagine what kind of reason would not count as "cause" if she wanted it to.[20]

The practical fact is that most district judges don't want to preside over bankruptcy litigation. They have enough to do with their own dockets, and for the most part, they have confidence in the bankruptcy judges and are happy to let the bankruptcy judges go on about their business (although they do like having the ultimate control).

There are only two situations where you are likely to find a district judge using his discretionary power to withdraw the reference over an entire bankruptcy case. One is where a judge is already deeply involved in a civil lawsuit when one of the parties files for bankruptcy. Particularly if she thinks that the filing was a litigation tactic, the district judge can be expected to withdraw the reference and to treat the bankruptcy as part of the litigation. The other is that rare case where as district judge in a particular district has lost confidence in the bankruptcy judge and doesn't think he should be handling matters at all.

Not too long ago, the District Court in Delaware withdrew the reference generally and started assigning bankruptcy cases to district judges as well as to bankruptcy judges. There was a lot of speculation about the reasons for this. Were the district judges being helpful with a busy docket? Or were they showing their disapproval of the way bankruptcy judges were handling their cases? We will not join in this speculation, but it is worth remembering that in Delaware certain bankruptcy cases may be heard by district judges.

---

18. 28 U.S.C. §157(b)(1).

19. *Id.* §157(c).

20. *Id.* §157(d).

§3.12 ~ Be Diplomatic

The Code provides that the bankruptcy judge shall determine whether a proceeding is core.[21] The rules provide that the district judge shall hear a motion to withdraw the reference.[22] But you should assume that the bankruptcy judge will learn about the motion to withdraw the reference sooner or later. You have to be prepared for the fact that you may lose your motion and find yourself back in front of the same bankruptcy judge you tried to get away from. So it is prudent to be diplomatic in what you say about the bankruptcy judge in your motion to withdraw the reference.

§3.13 ~ Mandatory Withdrawal

The final sentence of Section 157(d) reads:

> The district court shall, on timely motion of a party, . . . withdraw a proceeding if the court determines that resolution of the proceeding requires consideration of both title 11 and other laws of the United States regulating organizations or activities affecting interstate commerce.

Read broadly, the sentence would appear to impose a tight limit on the range of cases that could be referred to the bankruptcy court. But courts have been unwilling to take it at face value. In re Vicars Insurance Agency, Inc.,[23] suggests a typical approach. UNG sued Vicars for fraud and conspiracy, and also alleged violations of the Racketeer Influenced and Corrupt Organizations Act (RICO).[24] UNG also asked the district court to withdraw the reference under Section 157(d).

The district court refused and the court of appeals affirmed. The court held that withdrawal was mandatory under Section 157(d) only when "issues require the interpretation, as opposed to mere application . . . or where the court must undertake analysis of significant open and unresolved issues" of non-bankruptcy law. The opinion also offers a helpful review of other approaches.

Withdrawal of the reference is also mandatory, at least for purposes of trial, where a party has a right to a jury trial and does not consent to the trial being conducted by a bankruptcy judge. *See* §3.24.

§3.14 ~ How We Got Here: Marathon

A bit of background may help to explain this elaborate jurisdictional structure. Under the 1898 Act, the reach of the Federal bankruptcy power was far less extensive than it is today. Matters were heard in the bankruptcy court only if the property was in possession of the bankruptcy court, or if the adverse claimant consented. Over time, by an enterprising exercise of judicial fiction, the courts extended their reach, but the limits remained palpable—and litigation over the limits of jurisdiction thrived in the bankruptcy court.

---

21. 28 U.S.C. §157(b)(3).

22. Fed. R. Bankr. Proc. 5011(a).

23. 96 F.3d 949 (7th Cir. 1996).

24. 18 U.S.C. §1961.

As with the court, so with the judge. Originally under the 1898 Act, the individual who handled bankruptcy matters was virtually a part of the district judge's personal staff. He acted in matters "referred" by the district judge—hence bankruptcy referee (as he was known). Time and circumstance entrenched his position and elevated his dignity. But 1978, he had a courtroom of his own, a staff, and the title of judge. But he remained a term appointee under Article I, not a lifetime appointee under Article III.

In the preliminaries to the 1978 Act, a strong lobby of bankruptcy professionals favored expansion on both fronts. They lobbied for a one-stop bankruptcy forum, armed to do all that was necessary to resolve the problems of the debtor in trouble. To this end, they wanted to expand the reach of the bankruptcy power to its constitutional limits, and they wanted correspondingly to extend the powers of the bankruptcy judge, if necessary by giving him Article III status.

The bankruptcy lobby met resistance more on the second point—judgeships—than on the first. Some of the resistance came from existing federal judges seeking to protect against dilution of their own prestige. Still it is useful to remember that there are good substantive arguments against expanding the Article III bench (for example—how many lifetime judges can a democracy bear)?

In any event, the standoff ended with a kind of a stalemate. Congress chose not to give Article III status to the bankruptcy judges. But it mandated the most extensive jurisdiction possible to the district court. Then—and this became the rub—it provided that this extensive jurisdiction, though mandated to the district court, would be exercised by the bankruptcy judge. The practical effect was to give bankruptcy judges powers almost indistinguishable from those of a district judge, but without lifetime tenure.

This was the scheme that came before the Supreme Court in *Northern Pipeline Construction Co. v. Marathon Pipe Line Co.*[25] Northern filed for bankruptcy, and sued Marathon in the bankruptcy court, seeking damages for breach of warranty. Marathon challenged the constitutionality of bankruptcy court jurisdiction. The Supreme Court held that the grant was unconstitutional.

The decision presents some problems of interpretation. For one, Justice Brennan, who delivered the judgment of the Court, spoke only for a plurality of four (two others concurred and three dissented). But he made it clear that his concern rested on the role of the (Article I) judge and not on the broad grant of jurisdiction itself. He also made it clear that he recognized the validity of certain specialized (non-Article III) courts, at least as long as they stuck to their specialized jobs.

Congress responded with the new jurisdictional statute, effective in 1984. The statute left the broad grant of jurisdiction intact, as well it might have, because no one had questioned its validity. But Congress made clear this time that jurisdiction lay in the first instance with the district court, fleshing it out with the elaborate rules discussed above.

---

25. 458 U.S. 50 (1982).

There are surely those who believe that the 1984 statute is just as defective (in terms of the constitution) as its predecessor. This seems unlikely. In several other cases since *Marathon*, the Court has endorsed the role of specialized courts in the judicial system. Indeed, three years after *Marathon*, the Court interpreted its own decision in a way that seems to warn against broad readings. The Court said that *Marathon* establishes only that Congress may not vest in a non-Article III court the power to adjudicate, render a final judgment, and issue binding orders in a traditional contract action arising under state law, without consent of the litigants, and subject only to ordinary appellate review.[26]

Comment: Clearly, the lifetime Article III judges enjoy more general prestige than the term appointees on the bankruptcy bench. And there are recurrent tidbits of gossip about status wars between district and bankruptcy judges—bankruptcy judges who can't use the judicial elevator, or lunchroom, or something of that sort. Moreover there is no doubt that Article III judges (led by then Chief Justice Warren Burger) for the most part weighed in as opposed to Article III status for bankruptcy judges in the run-up to 1978. Meanwhile the sitting bankruptcy judges waged a fierce campaign for the upgrade.

But too much can be made of these status wars. The bankruptcy judgeship has prestige enough that there will be dozens of applicants for any individual vacancy. Moreover, bankruptcy judges report a lot of job satisfaction. One reason is ironic. That is, on a day to day basis, they have a job that is at least as and perhaps more, interesting than the job of the district judge. They are at least as likely to get substantial commercial cases with complex and challenging facts. They are free of the agonies of the drug docket, and from criminal sentencing. "We have," one bankruptcy judge likes to say "no problems that money can't solve."

This background ought to explain the distinctions set forth in the previous section. It was in the wake of *Marathon* that Congress adopted the present jurisdictional statute, which reposes broad jurisdiction in the district court, and gives the court limited power to delegate matters to the bankruptcy court, functioning as a an adjunct to the district court. It explains why Congress felt it necessary to distinguish "core" from "non-core" matters, giving the bankruptcy judge broader control over the former than the latter.

§3.15 ~ Core versus Non-core—Substance

The historical sketch in the previous section makes it easier to understand the distinction between core and non-core proceeding, as set forth in the Judicial Code in response to *Marathon*. Section 157(b)(2) of Title 28 sets forth a nonexclusive list of 15 items that (per Congress) are core proceedings:

- matters concerning the administration of the estate (except personal injury claims);
- allowance or disallowance of claims against the estate;
- counterclaims by the estate against persons filing claims;
- orders in respect to obtaining credit;

---

26. Thomas v. Union Carbide Agric. Prods. Co., 473 U.S. 568, 584 (1985) (citations omitted).

- orders to turn over property of the estate;
- proceedings to determine, avoid, or recover preferences;
- motions to terminate, annul, or modify the automatic stay;
- proceedings to determine, avoid, or recover fraudulent conveyances;
- determinations as to the dischargeability of particular debts;
- objections to discharges;
- determinations of the validity, extent, or priority of liens;
- confirmations of plans;
- orders approving the use or lease of property, including the use of cash collateral;
- orders approving the sale of property other than property resulting from claim brought by the estate against persons who have not filed claims against the estate; and
- other proceedings affecting the liquidation of the assets the estate or the adjustment of the debtor-creditor or the equity security holder relationship, except personal injury tort or wrongful death claims.

The list is impressive, and it surely represents a conscientious effort to respond to the constraints of *Marathon*. But it is not self-justifying. The question still remains, whether any given matter, though designated core by Congress, can qualify as core under the judicial mandate.

The Ninth Circuit grappled with this question in *In re Castlerock Properties*.[27] In Castlerock the court faced the question whether the bankruptcy judge had power to assert jurisdiction over a counterclaim. The Ninth Circuit concluded that a "court should avoid characterizing a proceeding as 'core' if to do so would raise constitutional problems," It said that the "the apparent broad reading that can be given to §157(b)(2) should be tempered by the Marathon decision." It held the matter to be non-core.

The Fifth Circuit's *Woods* decision, discussed above, having concluded that there was jurisdiction in a conflict between shareholders, also had to decide whether the matter was "core." The plaintiff argued that the matter was core because it could have been a claim.[28] The Fifth Circuit rejected the argument saying that the present action was not, in any event, a claim proceeding.

---

27. 781 F.2d 159 (9th Cir. 1986).

28. *In re* Wood, 825 F.2d at 97-98.

§3.16 ~ Personal Injury Claims

There is a special allocation rule for personal injury or wrongful death claims. It provides that these claims will be tried in the district court—either where the bankruptcy is pending or where the claim arose.[29] The choice of which district is made by the district court where the bankruptcy case is pending.

Note that this provision applies only to the trial of the claim. Presumably the bankruptcy judge retains the power to deal with other "core matters" arising from personal injury claims. This would include pre-trial matters in the bankruptcy case, and the determination of dischargeability. On dischargeability generally *see* §17.12ff.

Comment: The plaintiff or movant should state in his pleading whether the matter is core or non-core. The response should admit or deny the assertion. If the assertion is that the matter is non-core, then the party making the assertion should state whether he consents to a final order by the bankruptcy judge.

§3.17 ~ Form: Foundation Pleading in a Core Matter

Core matters may be contested matters (*e.g.*, a motion to extend exclusivity) or adversary proceedings (*e.g.*, complaint to avoid a preference or fraudulent conveyance). Initial allegations in a "core" adversary proceeding complaint might look something like the following:

> Donald L. Kollektbak, chapter 7 Trustee for the estate of Insolvent Supply Corporation, by his counsel, Smith & Jones, alleges:
>
> 1. This is an action for recovery of a fraudulent conveyance.
>
> 2. The jurisdiction of this Court is founded upon 28 U.S.C. §1334.This adversary proceeding is brought pursuant, *inter alia*, to Rule 7001 of the Federal Rules of Bankruptcy Procedure and §§547, 548 and 550 of Title 11 of the United States Code.
>
> 3. This is a core proceeding within the meaning of 28 U.S.C. §157(b)(2)(F).
>
> 4. On or about October 22, 1999, Insolvent Supply Corporation (hereinafter the "Debtor") filed a petition in this Court for relief under chapter 11 of Title 11 of the United States Code.
>
> 5. By an Order entered on or about November 25, 1999, the Debtor's chapter 11 case was converted to a case under chapter 7 of the Bankruptcy Code.
>
> 6. Donald L. Kollektbak (Trustee) is the duly appointed and qualified Trustee for the Debtor's estate.

---

29. 28 U.S.C. §157(b)(5).

7. Victim, LLP (Defendant), a Utopia limited liability partnership, was a pre-petition lender to the Debtor and, on information and belief, had other pre-petition business dealings with the Debtor.

§3.18 ~ Adversary Proceeding v. Contested Matter

§3.19 ~ Not the Same

For starters, keep in mind that the distinction between adversary proceedings and contested matters is not related to the core versus non-core distinction. Adversary proceeding may be core or non-core, and the same is true with respect to contested matters.

§3.20 ~ A Road Map to the Bankruptcy Rules

Earlier we distinguished between the (global) bankruptcy case and an (individual) bankruptcy proceeding that may arise within a bankruptcy case. Here we draw another kind of distinction between different kinds of proceedings. We recognize (on the one hand) proceedings that will receive full-bore litigation treatment, like ordinary civil lawsuits: call them adversary proceedings. We distinguish these from matters that may be in contest, but where the full-bore treatment will not ordinarily apply: call them contested matters.

The distinction is fundamental to the bankruptcy rules. Part VII of the Rules governs "adversary proceedings." Rule 9014 (and attended rules) govern "contested matters."

Rule 7001 defines adversary proceeding by example. It is a proceeding

- to recover money or property, except a proceeding to compel the debtor to deliver property to the trustee, or a proceeding under (b) or Section 725 of the Code, Rule 2017 or Rule 6002;
- to determine the validity, priority, or extent of a lien or other interest in property, other than a proceeding under Rule 4003(d);
- to obtain approval pursuant to §363(h) for the sale of both the interest of the estate and of a co-owner in property;
- to object to or revoke a discharge;
- to revoke an order of confirmation of a chapter 11, chapter 12, or chapter 13 plan, (6) to determine the dischargeability of a debt;
- to obtain an injunction or other equitable relief;
- to subordinate any allowed claim or interest, except when subordination is provided in a chapter 9, 11, 12, or 13 plan;

- to obtain a declaratory judgment relating to any of the foregoing; or
- to determine a claim or cause of action removed pursuant to 28 U.S.C. §1452.

The adversary proceeding is the part of the case that will seem most familiar to the non-bankruptcy litigator. Most of the adversary rules in Part VII of the Code merely adopt by reference individual rules from the Federal Rules of Civil Procedure. Of those rules not included in Part VII, many are included in other parts of the Code.[30]

Perhaps the most noteworthy difference between the adversary rules and the general Federal rules is that Adversary Rule 7004(b) allows nationwide service of process for all pleadings except a subpoena.[31] This is a much broader service rule than applies in many other fora, and may be reason enough in some cases to justify the filing of the bankruptcy. You can effectuate service simply by dropping the summons and complaint in the mailbox.

§3.21 ~ Form Caption—Commencing an Adversary Proceeding

An adversary proceeding is a "case within a case." It bears the caption of the main case, together with the particular adversary caption. Note that it gets its own file number. Sometimes, an adversary will stay open even after the main case file has been sent to storage. Here is a sample caption:

IN THE UNITED STATES BANKRUPTCY COURT
FOR THE EASTERN DISTRICT OF UTOPIA

In Re:	)	Bankruptcy Case No. 99-1415-BBL
INSOLVENT SUPPLY CORPORATION,	)	Chapter 7
	)	
Debtor	)	
	)	
	)	
DONALD L. KOLLEKTBAK,	)	
Chapter 7 Trustee	)	Adversary Proceeding No. _______
Plaintiff,	)	
v.	)	
VICTIM, LLP	)	
Defendant.	)	

30. For a catalog, FED. R. BANKR. PROC. 7001 advisory committee's note.

31. But there remains a question whether and to what extent there is some sort of Constitutional minimum contacts threshold. *Compare* Diamond Mortgage Corp. v. Sugar, 913 F.2d 1233, 1244 (7th Cir. 1990) *with* Busch v. Buchman, Buchman & O'Brien, 11 F.3rd 1255, 1258 (9th Cir. 1994).

§3.22 ~ Contested Matter

The more flexible "contested matter" is governed by Rule 9014. The form of pleading differs between an adversary proceeding and a contested matter. An adversary proceeding begins by summons and complaint. There is provision for an answer and a counterclaim, and for a motion to dismiss, all on the model of the Federal Rules of Civil Procedure.

For contested matters by contrast, Rule 9014 provides that

> relief shall be requested by motion, and reasonable notice and opportunity for hearing shall be afforded the party against whom relief is sought. No response is required under this rule unless the court orders an answer to a motion.

The rule requires that the motion shall be served in the same manner as a summons and complaint under Rule 7004, but the answer and counterclaim rules do not apply. Rule 9014 lists some 23 other adversary rules that also apply in contested matters, including the discovery rules.[32] And the rule adds that "[t]he court may at any stage in a particular matter direct that one or more of the other rules in Part VII shall apply."

Comment: Motion practice for contested matters is generally faster than the adversary proceeding route. Adversary proceedings require a $150 filing fee; contested matters do not. Many of the adversary rules apply in contested matters in any event, and the judge may at any stage order that any of the other adversary rules apply.

Perhaps the most important item that is clearly a contested matter and not an adversary proceeding is the action for relief from the automatic stay.[33]

Caution: Here is a rule that many lawyers seem to miss: service upon a bank in either an adversary proceeding or a contested matter must be by certified mail upon an officer of the bank, unless (a) the bank has appeared in the case by counsel, or (b) the court orders otherwise, after an application for service by regular mail has been filed and served on the bank officer by certified mail, or (c) the bank waives certified mail service.[34]

§3.23 ~ Jury Trials

Jury trials were not much of an issue in bankruptcy law until recently. The conventional wisdom, not always well articulated, was that the Bankruptcy Court was a court of equity, and that jury trials weren't available in an equity court.

---

32. There is a problem in applying the discovery rules in contested matters, however, in that the time limits are geared to the more leisurely adversary proceeding, not to the quicker contested matter. If you are determined to use the discovery rules in the contested matter, you'll have to be alert to get orders shortening time.

33. Fed. R. Bankr. Proc. 7004 advisory committee's note. If your request for stay relief is joined with another matter that does require an adversary proceeding, then the stay relief goes by adversary proceeding also.

34. Fed. R. Bankr. Proc. 7004(h).

The Supreme Court stood that rule on its head with its decision in *Granfinanciera, S.A. v. Nordberg.*[35] Chase & Sanborn filed for relief under chapter 11. Nordberg, a trustee, sued Granfinanciera to avoid some alleged fraudulent transfer. The defendant asked for a jury trial. The court of appeals held that there was no statutory right to jury trial and that the Constitution didn't require it because the fraudulent transfer action was equitable in nature and in any event because the bankruptcy case was itself inherently equitable.

The Supreme Court reversed. The court took its departure from the mandate of the Seventh Amendment that the defendant had a right to jury trial in any case where jury trial would have been allowed in 1791. The Court then found that there would have been a right to a jury trial in a fraudulent transfer action in 1791, so the transferee had a jury trial right protected by the Constitution.

As with *Marathon*, it is important again to note what the court is not holding. Nothing in *Granfinanciera* casts doubt on the power of the Federal court to conduct a fraudulent transfer trial in the exercise of its bankruptcy jurisdiction—so long as the court recognizes the right to jury trial. Moreover the opinion dangled a couple of tantalizing residual questions.

For one - will the non-debtor lose his right to jury trial if he files a proof of claim and thereby surrenders to the court's equity jurisdiction? The court answered that question a year later in *Langenkamp v. Culp.*[36] The non-debtor filed a proof of claim. The trustee responded with an action to avoid a preference. The court held that the non-debtor had indeed waived the right to jury trial.

§3.24 ~ Preserving Right to a Jury Trial

The *Langkenkamp* decision prompted an abrupt shift in strategy for non-debtors with potential claims against the bankruptcy estate. Prior to 1978 under the old Bankruptcy Act, bankruptcy jurisdiction was narrow, but the bankruptcy court could gain jurisdiction by consent, and filing a claim counted as consent. With the expanded jurisdiction of the 1978 law, creditors had figured there was nothing to lose by filing a claim because the court pretty much had them anyway, and there was nothing to lose by consent.

Langenkamp sent creditors dusting off their old pre-1978 research notes, as they found they had to worry about consent all over again—if not for jurisdiction, then at least on the issue of jury trial. If you represent a creditor who may be a defendant, you need to stop and consider whether you want to forego filing a claim so as to preserve your right to jury trial. For example you will have to weigh the probability (and size) of a recovery against the importance of having a jury in a suit against you.

Also left dangling was the question whether the jury trial could go forward before the (Article I) bankruptcy judge instead of the (Article III) district judge. The Supreme Court still hasn't spoken on this one and the lower courts are split. The Second Circuit has held flatly that the bankruptcy judge does have the power.[37]

---

35. 492 U.S. 33 (1989).

36. 498 U.S. 42 (1990).

37. Ben Cooper, Inc. v. Insurance Co. of Pa. (In re Ben Cooper, Inc.), 896 F.2d 1394, 1403-04 (2d Cir.), *vacated on jurisdictional grounds*, 498 U.S. 964 (1990), *reinstated*, 924 F.2d 36 (2d Cir.), *cert. denied*, 500 U.S. 928 (1991).

Against the Second Circuit, six other circuits have held that the bankruptcy judge does not have the power—but always on grounds that the statute does not authorize it, sidestepping the issue of the Constitutional issue.[38] On the other hand many courts, while refusing to find that the bankruptcy court may hold the trial, have found that the bankruptcy judge may do pre-trial preparation in a jury case—everything but the trial itself.

At least partly sidestepping the Constitutional question, Congress in 1994 added a new subsection (e) to Section 157 providing a structure to help define the role of the bankruptcy court. This new subsection says:

> If the right to a jury trial applies in a proceeding that may be heard under this section by a bankruptcy judge, the bankruptcy judge may conduct the jury trial if specially designated to exercise such jurisdiction by the district court and with the express consent of all the parties.

The rule seems to set forth three conditions to be met before the bankruptcy judge can hear any jury trial:

- The right must arise "in a proceeding that may be heard under this section by a bankruptcy judge." One may wonder whether this denotes only a "core matter," or any matter for which there is bankruptcy jurisdiction. We suspect the latter.

- The judge must be "specially designated." This seems to suggest that a general order of reference is not enough, but we understand that some district courts have entered "standing" special designation orders.

- The parties must give their "express consent." Of course, if the issue is "jurisdictional," then not even consent can confer a power which the judge does not otherwise have. Thus, to take a familiar example, the parties cannot by consent confer jurisdiction on the bankruptcy judge to grant a divorce. The Supreme Court might someday hold that the bankruptcy jury trial falls in the same category.[39]

The advisory committee's note provides that "This rule is not intended to expand or create any right to trial by jury where such right does not otherwise exist."

Comment: Jury trials are a practical headache for the bankruptcy court. They take up time and space and resources. And the care and feeding of jurors is no small responsibility. When jury trials were still a novelty in bankruptcy court, it seemed that some judges were eager to try their hand at them. For most judges, the novelty now has probably worn off—which is to say, they are probably just as happy to avoid the extra headache if they can.

---

38. *In re* Stansbury Poplar Place, Inc., 13 F.3d 122 (4th Cir. 1993); *In re* Clay, 35 F.3d 190 (5th Cir.1994); Rafoth v. Nat'l Union Fire Ins. Co. (*In re* Baker & Getty Fin. Servs., Inc.), 954 F.2d 1169 (6th Cir. 1992); *In re* Grabill Corp., 967 F.2d 1152 (7th Cir. 1992); *In re* United Missouri Bank of Kansas City, 901 F.2d 1449 (8th Cir. 1990); Kaiser Steel Corp. v. Frates (*In re* Kaiser Steel Corp.), 911 F.2d 380 (10th Cir. 1990).

39. *See also* FED. R. BANKR. PROC. 9015 (b) (on the form of consent).

Perhaps more importantly, trying a jury case is a skill. It's not necessarily the kind of skill you would expect from a bankruptcy judge, even a pretty good one. To take just one example—bankruptcy judges sometimes take a somewhat elastic view of the rules of evidence. This may work well enough for bench trials. But it's not the sort of thing you want in a jury trial. If the judge is inexperienced at jury trials (however able), you might not want to be the victim of his first try.

Finally, insisting upon your right to a jury trial, but declining to consent to the trial proceeding before the bankruptcy judge, is a sure-fire way to have the reference withdrawn, since consent is required for the trial to proceed before the bankruptcy judge. But note that many district judges will require all pretrial proceedings to stay in the bankruptcy court, with only the trial—if there ever is one—proceeding in the district court.

4
More on Jurisdiction and Procedure

4 More on Jurisdiction and Procedure

§4.1 ~ Introduction

In this chapter we address a range of more specialized jurisdiction problems. We consider removal and remand, as well as appeals. We also consider the thorny issue of state sovereign immunity.

§4.2 ~ Removal

As noted, you can get into a bankruptcy case by filing (or having filed against you) an adversary proceeding or a contested matter. There is at least one more way in. That is, a party may remove a claim or cause of action to the bankruptcy forum.[1] The path is not intuitively obvious, so the statute needs to be read with care. You remove to the district court in the district where the civil action is pending. So, if the bankruptcy is pending in Los Angeles and the civil action is pending in Boston, you remove to the district court in Boston, not Los Angeles. The matter will then presumably be referred to the bankruptcy court by the district court.[2]

Removal is available for a civil action pending in federal court, or in state court. The only requirement is that the district court have jurisdiction under Section 1334. If the district court has jurisdiction, then of course it is free to refer to the bankruptcy court, as outlined above, or to change venue.

Removal is self-executing; you accomplish the removal by filing a notice of removal with the district court (and filing a copy with the state court in which the litigation was pending). A party who opposes removal attacks it by filing a motion to remand or abstain with the same district court. Removal is not available for a proceeding before the U.S. Tax Court, or for a civil action by a governmental unit to enforce the police or regulatory power.

Any party considering removal ought to keep in mind that one of the parties is ordinarily a debtor in bankruptcy. This may raise the question of whether pursuing the lawsuit is worth the bother. The non-debtor may be able to raise the same issues simply by filing a claim. The decision on issues of this sort will vary from case to case, but counsel at least ought to think them through, rather than charging forward to litigate removal.

1. 28 U.S.C. §1452.

2. There are cases allowing removal direct to the bankruptcy court. *See, e.g.*, *In re* Henderson Condominium Homes, 84 B.R. 510 (M.D. Tenn. 1988); *In re* Aztec Industries, 84 B.R. 464 (Bankr. N.D. Ohio 1987) (citing cases). These seem to us to be wrong, and they represent a minority position.

Non-debtors are more likely than not to resist removal, particularly if counsel is unfamiliar with bankruptcy court and fears that the debtor will enjoy an insider advantage. This may not always be the right strategy. For example suppose the parties are litigating a complicated question of priority on a secured claim. By virtue of its experience in commercial cases, the bankruptcy court may be better equipped to than a state court understand that kind of case. A party who wants a serious hearing on difficult commercial issue may decide that bankruptcy court is exactly the place she wants to be.

§4.3 ~ Getting Out Again

We have talked about a few ways in which a party may get his case in to bankruptcy court. Now we should talk about a few ways to get it out.

§4.4 ~ Abstention

Removal brings a proceeding into bankruptcy. Remand sends it back out. But the bankruptcy judge may also decline to hear a matter that originates on his docket. He may do so by choosing to abstain from hearing the matter. The statute provides two routes to abstention. Section 305 of the Bankruptcy Code authorizes the judge to abstain from hearing the bankruptcy case. Meanwhile Section 1334(c)(1) of the Judicial Code permits her to abstain from a proceeding. The Judicial Code permits abstention in "the interest of justice, or . . . the interest of comity with State courts or respect for State law."[3]

§4.5 ~ Remand

Earlier, we saw how a party may remove a matter to the bankruptcy court. We saw that removal was self-executing. But the bankruptcy court does not need to keep the matter. Rather, the court may choose to remand. The statute provides that the court to which the proceeding is removed may remand "on any equitable ground."[4] The decision is not reviewable by appeal or otherwise by a court of appeals (although it is reviewable by the district court). The language of remand closely parallels the language of the abstention statute discussed above.

§4.6 ~ Caution: A Remand Trap

There is a trap lurking in the removal process for the party who seeks remand. Suppose you represent the plaintiff in an action governed by the National Elixir Relief Act. The defendant files for bankruptcy and removes to the bankruptcy court. For remand, you develop an argument about the specialized statute, the specialized knowledge of the court, not really a bankruptcy issue, etc. First thing you know, your adversary will be on his feet saying—"Judge, he's saying you aren't smart enough to decide an elixir case." No, of course that wasn't what you said, but you may spend the rest of your argument trying to dig yourself out of that hole.

---

3. *In re* Continental Holdings, Inc., 158 B.R. 442 (Bankr. N.D. Ohio 1983).

4. 28 U.S.C. §1452(b).

§4.7 ~ Factors That Encourage Abstention or Remand

Factors the courts have considered as grounds for remand include:[5]

- Inconvenient forum;
- The interest of seeing that the entire case is dealt with by a single judge;
- Whether the non-bankruptcy court is better equipped to deal with non-bankruptcy issues;
- Duplication of effort;
- Risk of inconsistent results;
- Comity.

§4.8 ~ Mandatory Abstention

Section 1334 also calls for so-called "mandatory abstention" for certain state law proceedings.[6] Abstention is mandatory under this section if

- an action could not have been commenced in a court of the United States absent bankruptcy jurisdiction; and
- an action is commenced, and can be timely adjudicated, in a state forum of appropriate jurisdiction.

Mandatory abstention is available proceedings related to bankruptcy cases, but not for proceedings "arising under" the Bankruptcy Code or "arising in" bankruptcy cases. This may be the same as saying that it is not available in a core proceeding.[7]

§4.9 ~ Jurisdiction Over Dischargeability

In Chapter 17, we discuss the dischargeability of debts. Here, a word on jurisdiction. Special rules govern jurisdiction over the determination of dischargeability. Suppose the debtor files a no-asset Chapter 7 case and gets a discharge. Later the government sues him in state court for a liability arising from an environmental cleanup. The debtor believes the claim is barred by the Chapter 7 discharge. The government asserts that the claim is excepted from discharge as a fine, penalty, or forfeiture under Section 523(a)(7). Who gets to decide the question of dischargeability? There are two possible courses.

---

5. *See, e.g.*, Browning v. Navarro, 743 F.2d 1069, 1076 n.21 (5th Cir. 1984).

6. 28 U.S.C. §1334(c)(2).

7. *See also id.* §157(b)(3) (providing that "a determination that a proceeding is not a core proceeding shall not be made solely on the basis that its resolution may be affected by State law").

One, the court may decide the issue as part of the pending litigation. With some important exceptions to be noted below, any court has the power to interpret the meaning of the bankruptcy discharge, just as it would any other court order.

The second possible course is that either party may ask the bankruptcy court for a determination of dischargeability.[8] The action is an adversary proceeding.[9] The rule makes clear that the relief may be sought either before or after the closing of the case, and specifies that there be no filing fee for reopening a case to determine dischargeability.[10]

The trouble with this system is that invites a kind of nondischargeability by ambush. The debtor files for bankruptcy and gets a discharge. Later he is served with a new complaint in an action to pay a pre-petition debt. Knowing that he has the discharge, he drops the complaint in the wastebasket. The next thing he knows, the creditor has taken a default judgment against him, and the protection of the discharge (as to that debt) has been lost.

Back in the 1960s, Congress decided that "professional" creditors— notably small loan companies— were winning too many cases on this tactic. So Congress adopted the predecessor of the current Section 523(c). This section mandates that certain dischargeability actions be brought only in the bankruptcy court. Congress imposed this mandate in cases arising under what are now Sections 523(a)(2), (a)(4) and (a)(6)—the so-called debtor wrongdoing provisions. This was where the abuse was thought to take place. More recently, Congress added Section 523(a)(15), the marital property provision.

For all of these, the adjudication of dischargeability must take place in the bankruptcy court, and it must be brought within the time limits set forth in the rules. The burden is on the creditor to bring the action if he wants the debt to be declared nondischargeable.

What is that limit? The simple answer is that it is the date specified in the notice of bankruptcy filing that is sent to the creditor at the beginning of the case. A longer answer is: in a Chapter 7 liquidating case, the deadline shall be set not later than 60 days after the date set for the meeting of creditors under Section 341.[11] The meeting of creditors must be set for between 20 and 40 days after the filing of the petition.[12] Sixty days plus 40 days equals 100 days. So the deadline will be within 100 days after the filing of the petition.[13]

---

8. Fed. R. Bankr. Proc. 4007.

9. Fed. R. Bankr. Proc. 7001(6).

10. Fed. R. Bankr. Proc. 4007.

11. *See* Fed. R. Bankr. Proc. 4007(c).

12. *See* Fed. R. Bankr. Proc. 2001(a).

13. You can get an extension of time in which to file, but only if you requested it before the original time limit expired. Practically speaking, you also want to have your decision before the time limit expires—in case it goes against you, and you have to make a judgment call as to whether you should go ahead and file anyway. Bankr. R. 4007(c).

§4.10 ~ Venue—Related Cases

The judicial code governs venue of cases.[14] In brief, a case may be commenced in the district court for the district where the debtor has his

- Domicile;
- Residence;
- Principal place of business in the United States; and
- Principal assets in the United States.

If he has moved recently, then the appropriate place is the one where he has been located for the greater portion of the last 180 days. There is also a remarkable and highly controversial rule governing "affiliates." It permits a filing where there is pending a case concerning an "affiliate, general partner, or partnership."

Suppose the (partnership) debtor runs an investment office in Illinois whose only significant asset is an apartment house in Texas. Where is its principal place of business? There is a useful discussion in *In re Peachtree Lane Associates, Ltd.*,[15] where the court recognized two approaches. One looks to the locus of "major business decisions" (the nerve center—in this case, Illinois). The other looks to "operations" (Texas). The court saw the apartment house as an investment. "That its existence as an investment portfolio item was more abstract and less publicly obvious does not make that side of Peachtree's business any less deserving of recognition."[16] Therefore, Illinois.

The residence of a corporation is the place of incorporation. Many large public companies are incorporated in Delaware. So Delaware is the residence, and is an appropriate venue, even though their "real" corporate headquarters may be elsewhere. A few years back, public companies seemed to favor New York as the venue of choice. New York seemed to provide debtors the comfort they needed. New York judges seemed to understand New York billing rates. And anyway, the courthouse was just a subway ride away.

Lately, for whatever reason, the center of the action seems to have moved to Delaware. There is room to speculate on just why this has come to pass but in any event, the Delaware bankruptcy court seems to have developed into a sophisticated, well-oiled machine for public company cases. Indeed, the popularity of Delaware has led to a serious debate regarding whether state of incorporation venue should be eliminated. Although this debate may have a veneer of intellectual honesty, it is really more of a dispute between lawyers over who will have the big cases in their own backyard.

---

14. 28 U.S.C. §1408.

15. 206 B.R. 913 (N.D. Ill. 1997), *aff'd*, 150 F.3d 788 (7th Cir. 1998).

16. *Id.* At 924.

§4.11 ~ CHANGING VENUE

The decision to order (or not to order) a change of venue is one on which the trial judge has a lot of discretion and on which he is not likely to be overruled.[17] But in bankruptcy (unlike general civil litigation), there is an overriding principle that offers some certainty. This is a "general policy . . . to have all proceedings related to a bankruptcy case tried in the court where the case is pending."[18] So if you are arguing for transfer of a proceeding back to the court where the case is pending, you have a pretty good shot.

Aside from the general rule, you are reduced to "factors." One court listed the following factors as relevant to the decision:[19]

- The proximity of creditors of every kind to the court;
- The proximity of the debtor to the court;
- The proximity of the witnesses necessary to the administration of the estate;
- The location of the assets;
- The economic administration of the estate; and
- The necessity for ancillary administration.

Experienced litigators will recognize this as similar to the list of factors that would apply to a venue change in ordinary federal litigation.

§4.12 ~ ROADMAP TO BANKRUPTCY APPEALS

§4.13 ~ IN GENERAL

The matter of appealing bankruptcy orders is one of the trickiest for the outsider. Start with the case where the bankruptcy judge expressed an intention to ruling on a motion or in an adversary proceeding that does not conclude the entire bankruptcy case. Counsel anticipates that the ruling will be adverse. Counsel needs to consider at least the following questions:

- Appeal or something else? Recall that in non-core matters, absent consent by the parties, the bankruptcy judge does not issue final orders; she only recommends to the district judge. So the appropriate route is not an appeal to the District Court, but by written objection to the proposed findings.[20]

---

17. 28 U.S.C. §1412, *See also* Continental Airlines, Inc. v. American Airlines, Inc., 805 F. Supp. 1392, 1395 (S.D. Texas 1992). Peteet v. Dow Chem. Co., 868 F.2d 1428, 1436 (5th Cir. 1989).

18. *In re* Thomson McKinnon Securities, Inc., 126 B.R. 833, 836 (Bankr. S.D.N.Y. 1991).

19. *In re* Commonwealth Oil Refining Co., 596 F.2d 1239, 1247 (5th Cir. 1979).

20. FED. R. BANKR. PROC. 9033.

- When? Bankruptcy Rule 8002 provides that appeal shall be filed with 10 days of the order appealed from. It is shorter than the 30-day appeal period that one encounters in ordinary federal appellate practice.[21] Courts of appeals are fierce about enforcing the limit, and horror stories abound.[22]

- Which court? Appeals generally go to the District Court. But if a Circuit has created a Bankruptcy Appellate Panel, they may go to that panel.[23]

- Final or interlocutory? For "final" orders, and for orders governing plan exclusivity, the notice of appeal is enough.[24] For other "interlocutory" orders, appeal lies only with leave of the court.[25] The notice of appeal must be accompanied by a request for leave to appeal.[26]

- Stay pending appeal? Even though the appellant successfully establishes his appeal, he may find the judgment enforced against him while the matter is still pending—unless he gets a stay pending appeal. A motion for a stay "must ordinarily be presented to the bankruptcy judge in the first instance."[27] The judge may require a bond as a condition of issuing the stay. In addition to the general principle, the Code provides specific rules on stays pending appeal with respect to use, sale, or lease of property, and with respect to post-petition borrowing.[28]

§4.14 ~ Downside of Taking an Appeal

The net effect of all these rules is to make it relatively hard to take an appeal in a bankruptcy case, or at least to take one that is not moot by the time it is decided. Why would this be? The answer must be that delay and excess cost could impair the reorganization process. Keep this policy in mind and fashion your arguments accordingly. Where appropriate, an appellate court may be willing to set an expedited briefing schedule and decide an appeal quickly.

---

21. Strictly speaking, counsel should not file before the final order. The appeal should be filed with the bankruptcy clerk, not the clerk of the appellate court. The rule makers have introduced "saving" language that should correct the errors of counsel who slip up on either of these points. *See* Fed. R. Bankr. Proc. 8002(a), but *see* Fed. R. Bankr. Proc. 8002(b) on the effect of post-decision motions. The bankruptcy judge may extend the time for the filing the notice in some cases. Fed. R. Bankr. Proc. 8002(c).

22. In U.S. v. Henry Bros. Partnership (*In re* Henry Bros. Partnership), 214 BR. 192 (B.A.P. 8th Cir. 1997), the court directed the debtor to serve copies of the order. The debtor mailed them on the eighth day, and they arrived on the tenth. The adverse party waited two more days to file. In Lacey Trust v. Askanase, 114 F.3d 556 (5th Cir. 1997), the notice of appeal was mailed to the court four days before the filing deadline, but was file stamped one day after. In both cases, the court held that it lacked jurisdiction.

23. At this writing, there are bankruptcy appellate panels in the first, second, sixth, eighth, ninth and tenth circuits. Bankruptcy Appellate Panels that publish their opinions online include the Eighth and the Tenth: http://www.ca8.uscourts.gov/index.html; http://www.utb.uscourts.gov/.

24. 28 U.S.C. §158(a)(1), (2), Fed. R. Bankr. Proc. 8001(a).

25. 28 U.S.C. §158(a)(3).

26. If the appellant files a notice of appeal when the appeal is in fact only interlocutory, the court will treat it as a motion for leave to appeal. Fed. R. Bankr. Proc. 8003(c).

27. *Id.* 8005.

28. Sections 363(m), 364(e).

§4.15 ~ Mootness

Another barrier for a party seeking an appeal is the doctrine of mootness. Perhaps especially in bankruptcy matters, the appellate courts are quick to decide that there is nothing to decide, if events have overtaken the issue on appeal. A good example is *Nationwide Mut. Ins. Co. v. Berryman Prods, Inc.*[29] The bankruptcy court confirmed the plan and some creditors appealed. The circuit court dismissed the appeal as moot, holding that implementation of the plan had continued so far that fundamental changes would jeopardize its success. On the problem of mootness in credit extensions, see §10.15 below.

§4.16 ~ Beyond Mootness: "Equitable or Prudential Grounds"

On the outer fringes of mootness, the court has erected yet one more barrier against appeal to apply in the case of confirmed plans—the doctrine of "equitable mootness." For example, the Third Circuit held (7-6, en banc) that an appeal should be dismissed on equitable or prudential grounds after a plan was consummated, even if not moot on traditional grounds.[30] In deciding whether to dismiss, the court said these factors should be considered:

- Whether the plan had been "substantially consummated;"
- Whether a stay had been obtained;
- Whether the relief sought would affect parties not before the court;
- Whether the relief sought would affect the success of the plan; and
- The public policy of affording finality to bankruptcy judgments.

§4.17 ~ Technique for Getting Your Appeal Heard

Although case law states that failure to obtain a stay does not by itself moot an appeal, if you want your appeal to get heard on the merits, you had better get a stay pending appeal. Ask the bankruptcy judge first. If this fails, ask the district judge. If the matter is important enough, go to the Court of Appeals to seek a stay. If you fail to exhaust all efforts to get a stay, it will likely be held against you when your opponent seeks to dismiss your appeal as moot. By contrast, if you are the plan proponent, you have an extra incentive to consummate as quickly as possible, so as to moot all possible appeals.

---

29. *In re* Berryman, 159 F.3d 941 (5th Cir. 1998).

30. *In re* Continental Airlines, 91 F.3d 553, 561-62 (3d Cir.1996) (in banc). *See also In re* Manges, 29 F.3d 1034, 1038-39 (5th Cir. 1994), *cert denied*, 115 S.Ct. 1105, 130 L.Ed.2d 1071 (1995); *In re* Speciality Equip. Cos., 3 F.3d 1043, 1048 (7th Cir. 1993); In re Chateaugay Corp., 988 F.2d 322, 325 (2d Cir. 1993); *In re* Public Serv. Co., 963 F.2d 469, 471-72 (1st Cir.)., *cert. denied*, 506 U.S. 908 (1992); Club Assocs., 956 F.2d 1065, 1069 (11th Cir. 1992); Central States, Southeast and Southwest Areas Pension Fund v. Central Transp., Inc., 841 F.2d 92, 95-96 (4th Cir. 1988).

§4.18 ~ Court of Appeals

After an appellate decision to the District Court or the BAP—and after any decision by the District Court as the initial trial court—then the next appeal is to the Court of Appeals for the appropriate Circuit. Here, more familiar rules of appellate practice apply. The time for appeals is 30 days after the entry of the order, although it may be extended by a timely motion for rehearing.[31]

One difference is that the Court of Appeals is not authorized to hear interlocutory appeals. On the other hand, the rules on what counts as a "final order" for purposes of appeal are looser in bankruptcy than they are in ordinary cases. For a seminal discussion, see the opinion of Justice (then Judge) Breyer for the First Circuit deciding *In re Saco Local Development Corp.*[32] Unfortunately, although the rules are more elastic, it is almost impossible to say just what they are. There are countless decisions on the question of finality for purposes of appeal and they seem to spread pretty much all over the lot.

§4.19 ~ Review of Abstention Orders

Both Section 305 and Section 1344 provide that the decision on abstention "is not reviewable by appeal or otherwise."[33] But, as noted above, this should not prevent review by the District Court of a bankruptcy court decision. And a decision denying mandatory abstention is appealable to the court of appeals.

§4.20 ~ Technique: Which Court Hears the Motion

As between district judge and bankruptcy judge, who hears and decides the motion to abstain? The Code is silent. The rules seem to intend (although they do not quite say) that the motion will be heard by the bankruptcy judge in the first instance but that the final decision rests with the district judge. *See* Bankruptcy Rule 5011 and its Advisory Note, together with rule 9033. In any event, this is probably preferable. There seems to be a good argument that decision by the bankruptcy judge alone would be unconstitutional under *Marathon.*

§4.21 ~ Beyond the Bankruptcy Clause: Other Limits on Bankruptcy Jurisdiction

§4.22 ~ Federal-State Relations

Bankruptcy law is federal law, and federal law is "supreme"—but only up to a point. In fact, there are a number of doctrines that limit or impair the reach of bankruptcy law with respect to claims that involve the individual states. These doctrines may restrict the power of the bankruptcy court to take jurisdiction over actions involving states, or to discharge state debts.

---

31. 28 U.S.C. §158(d).

32. 711 F.2d 441(1st Cir. 1983). "Congress has long provided that orders in bankruptcy cases may be immediately appealed if they finally dispose of discrete disputes within the larger case" (*id.* at 444, emphasis added) and that "a 'final judgment, order, or decree'" for purposes of appeal "includes an order that conclusively determines a separable dispute over a creditor's claim or priority." *Id.* at 445-46.

33. Section 305(c); 28 U.S.C. §1334(d).

§4.23 ~ Eleventh Amendment Immunity (Seminole Tribe)

The Eleventh Amendment to the U.S. Constitution provides:

> The Judicial power of the United States shall not be construed to extend to any suit in law or equity, commenced or prosecuted against one of the United States by Citizens of another State, or by Citizens or Subjects of any Foreign State.

This is often referred to as a sovereign immunity rule, although as we shall see, sovereign immunity is in fact a somewhat different creature. Better to call it "Eleventh Amendment immunity," after its source, as we will try to do here. In any event, Section 106 of the Bankruptcy Code purports to waive this immunity with respect to bankruptcy action involving the state.[34]

You might think that waiver is something that one does by choice, and that it cannot be imposed, but no matter: Congress did it and the statute says what it says. On the other hand, the original legislative history does concede that "Congress does not have the power to waive sovereign immunity completely (emphasis added) with respect to claims of a bankrupt estate against a state." But it adds: "it may exercise its bankruptcy power through the supremacy clause to prevent or prohibit State action that is contrary to bankruptcy policy."[35]

It's tantalizing to wonder just what the drafters had in mind with that cautious qualifier. In any event, it is clear that courts applying bankruptcy law have done many things to trump state policy or state law. A famous example is *Perez v. Campbell*,[36] where the Supreme Court used the supremacy clause to invalidate an Arizona statute that denied a driver's license to anyone who had discharged a debt in bankruptcy.

Section 106 from the start had a rough road. A number of lower courts read it narrowly. Then in 1989, the Supreme Court held that Section 106 did not give the trustee power to recover a money judgment from the state.[37] But this was purely a matter of statutory interpretation, which meant that Congress was free to reverse the result by legislation if it wishes (and Congress, in fact, did undertake to reverse it, by an amendment to Section 106).

The decision was an interpretation of the statute, and Congress responded by trying to mend the statute. But then 1996, in the now-famous *Seminole Tribe* decision, the Supreme Court inaugurated a revolution in federal-state relations.[38] In *Seminole Tribe*, the court stated flatly that Article I of the Constitution did not empower Congress to waive state immunity from suit in federal court.

---

34. Section 106 also purports to waive sovereign immunity with respect to the federal government. This topic has received somewhat less attention in the courts and gets less attention here, *but see* §4.12.

35. H.R. Rep No. 95-595 at 317 (1977); S. Rep. No. 95-989 at 29 (1978).

36. 402 U.S. 637 (1971).

37. Hoffman v. Conn. Dep't of Income Maintenance, 492 U.S. 96, 102-03 (1989).

38. Seminole Tribe of Florida v. Florida, 517 U.S. 44 (1996).

The impact of *Seminole Tribe* and its progeny extends far beyond bankruptcy, of course, but it has sent bankruptcy lawyers and judges scrambling back to their constitutional law notes. By now a host of courts have conceded that the basic grant of Section 106(a) is, on the authority of *Seminole Tribe*, unconstitutional. The question is—are there ways around it? Or, failing that, how do you live in a world where jurisdiction is so much more circumscribed than it seemed to be?

One early response was to try to locate some other Constitutional power which trumped the Eleventh Amendment. Some analysts tried to deploy the bankruptcy clause of Article I, Section 8. Some even sought comfort in the due process clause of the 14th Amendment. But this approach appears to be a non-starter.[39] Another approach, which may have slightly greater promise, is to deploy an "exception" set forth in *Ex parte Young*, allowing action against a state official when there is no "detailed remedial scheme for enforcement against the state."[40] But this exception seems restricted on its own terms. A third approach, which has been accepted in some cases, is to argue that your action against the state is not a "suit" against the state, and so (although it may have adverse consequences to the state) is not barred by the Eleventh Amendment. This has been accepted in some circumstances.[41]

Thus, while the Eleventh Amendment may bar commencing an adversary proceeding against a state in bankruptcy court, it should not preclude the application of general bankruptcy law, which does not require a law suit, to a state. For example, a state should not be able to use an Eleventh Amendment defense to avoid the discharge of its claims against a debtor in bankruptcy or to collect taxes that are exempted under Section 1146(c). Finally, it should be noted that the Eleventh Amendment does not apply to local or municipal entities—only to states themselves.

§4.24 ~ CONSENT

While the state seems to have a great deal of immunity, no one seems to doubt that the state may waive the immunity by consent. Which naturally raises the question. What counts as consent? To take the most important example, does the state consent to waive its immunity by filing a claim in the bankruptcy estate? Most (not all) the cases have held that filing a claim does indeed waive the immunity.[42]

---

39. Dep't of Transp. and Dev. v. PNL Asset Mgmt. Co., LLC (*In re* Estate of Fernandez), 123 F.3d 241 (5th Cir. 1997) rejects both arguments.

40. *Ex Parte* Young, 209 U.S. 123 (1908). The quotation is from *Seminole, 517 U.S.* at *74*, where it explained that *Young* was not available to the plaintiff in that case. *See also* Guiding Light Corp. v. Louisiana (*In re* Guiding Light Corp.), 213 B.R. 489 (Bankr. E.D. La. 1997).

41. Maryland v. Antonelli Creditors' Liquidating Trust, 123 F.3d 777 (4th Cir. 1997); *In re* Collins, 173 F.3d 924 (4th Cir. 1999).

42. *See, e.g., In re* Rose, 187 F.2d 926, 928-29 (8th Cir. 1999); Gardner v. New Jersey, 329 U.S. 565, 573-74 (1947). *But see* Schlossberg v. Maryland (*In re* Creative Goldsmiths of Washington D.C. Inc.), 119 F.3d 1140, 1144-45 (4th Cir. 1997), *cert. denied*, 523 U.S. 1075 (1998).

Another recurrent issue is the question whether the waiver may be void because it is unauthorized (it is easy to picture a mid-level bureaucrat making an apparent waiver in ignorance of some limit on his authority). A number of later cases have held that express authorization is not necessary. But a recent Fifth Circuit case holds that a clause in a contract purporting to waive Eleventh Amendment immunity would not be enforced because it was not expressly authorized by statute.[43]

§4.25 ~ Sue in State Court

Another approach that arose on the heels of *Seminole* was to note that the state still might be sued in its own courts—the Eleventh Amendment only prohibits suit in federal court.[44] This is where the distinction between Eleventh Amendment immunity and "true sovereign immunity" becomes critical. If the immunity is something that belongs to the sovereign because he is sovereign, then the it doesn't matter whether you have sidestepped the Eleventh Amendment—you still can't sue. And indeed, in 1999, that was exactly what the Supreme Court said.

Deciding *Alden v. Maine*, the court held that the state was immune from suit in its own courts from a suit alleging violation of a federal statute. No one doubts that the Bankruptcy Code is a "federal statute" within the meaning of Alden. And so Alden effectively cuts off any cause of action by debtors or trustees against the state.

§4.26 ~ State Officers

In its restrictive *Alden* opinion, the Supreme Court offered one suggestion for possible relief against wrongdoing by a state official. It provided that "[e]ven a suit for money damages may be prosecuted against a state officer in his individual capacity for unconstitutional or wrongful conduct fairly attributable to the officer himself"—adding, in the next breath: so long as the relief is sought not from the state treasury but from the officer personally.[45]

§4.27 ~ Younger v. Harris

Many times, the states will use the criminal courts as (for all practical purposes) collection agencies—for example, prosecuting on bad check charges but then dismissing the prosecution if the debtor pays the check. At least before *Seminole Tribe*, the bankruptcy court might have had the power to enjoin these prosecutions on a "substance over form" finding that they were merely collection efforts and ought to be stayed as such. Indeed, some did so.

---

43. Magnolia Venture Capital Corp. v. Prudential Securities, Inc. 151 F.3d 439, 444-45 (5th Cir. 1998), *cert. denied,* 525 U.S. 1178 (1999). *Cf. in re* Barrett Refining Corp., 221 B.R. 795, 810 (Bankr. W.D. Okla. 1998) holding that the proof of claim waived immunity in the teeth of a statute purporting to preserve it.

44. The Supreme Court had so held as recently as 1994, in Hess v. Port Authority Trans-Hudson Corp., 513 U.S. 30, 39 (1994).

45. Alden v. Maine, 119 S.Ct. 2240, 2267-68 (1999).

But others have forborne to interfere with the state proceedings on the principle of *Younger v. Harris.*[46] *Younger* is the leading authority on the scope of federal power to interfere with state criminal proceedings. It lays down the rule that the federal court will enjoin a state criminal proceeding only if there is "great and immediate danger" of irreparable injury. Relying on *Younger* many courts have refused to look behind the form of the state criminal proceeding. For example, in *In re Rosa*,[47] the court refused to interfere in a criminal proceeding even though the prosecutor had offered to drop the criminal charges if the debtor made restitution to the victim.

§4.28 ~ Rooker-Feldman

The so-called Rooker-Feldman doctrine holds that a federal court does not have subject matter jurisdiction to entertain a claim that is "inextricably intertwined" with a previous state court judgment where the federal decision would effectively constitute appellate review of the state court judgment.[48] For example, the Eighth Circuit, deciding *In re Goetzman*,[49] held that the federal court had no power to second-guess a state court as to the balance remaining on a mortgage debt in a confirmed Chapter 12 plan.

A most interesting case exploring the boundaries of the conflict *is Gruntz v. County of Los Angeles.*[50] Gruntz provided for child support in a Chapter 13 plan, but the case was converted to Chapter 11 and the Chapter 13 trustee did not distribute. Gruntz' ex-wife complained to the district attorney who prosecuted Gruntz for criminal non-support. After he was convicted, Gruntz asked the bankruptcy court for a temporary restraining order. The bankruptcy court refused to grant the TRO. The state court sentenced Gruntz to 360 days in jail.[51]

Gruntz appealed, but then he filed an adversary action in bankruptcy court to declare the criminal proceedings void as violative of the automatic stay. The state court of appeals affirmed the conviction, relying on Rooker-Feldman.[52] The bankruptcy court thereupon dismissed on grounds of collateral estoppel.

A Ninth Circuit panel, voting 2-1, reversed, holding that stay modifications are the exclusive province of the bankruptcy court.[53] The panel specifically acknowledged the Rooker-Feldman doctrine, but held that it did not apply.

The panel decision raised a few eyebrows, even among the partisans of the bankruptcy forum. Not surprisingly, the case moved on to en banc review. In its en banc decision, the Circuit gave with one hand, but then took away with another. It held the bankruptcy forum is indeed supreme with respect to the applicability

---

46. 401 U.S. 37 (1971).

47. 196 B.R. 231 (D. P.R. 1996).

48. Rooker v. Fidelity Trust Co., 263 U.S. 413, 415-16 (1923); D.C. Ct. of App.v. Feldman, 460 U.S. 462, 486-87 (1983).

49. 91 F.3d 1173 (8th Cir. 1996).

50. *In re* Gruntz, 202 F.3d 1074 (9th Cir. 2000).

51. The facts are set forth at in 202 F.3d at 1077.

52. The conviction was upheld in People v. Gruntz, 29 Cal. App. 4th 412 (Cal. D.C.A. 55 1994).

53. *In re* Gruntz, 177 F.3d 728 (9th Cir. 1999) (withdrawn).

of the stay, Rooker-Feldman notwithstanding.[54] But then it fell back on Section 362(b)(1), which provides that the stay does not apply to a criminal action.[55]

So Gruntz is tagged out at second, and we are back where we were under *Younger*.[56] The Circuit did suggest there is a remedy if the state is misusing its criminal process; but the remedy must be habeas corpus, and we suspect it will be a cold day in July before any debtor ever persuades a court to let him use habeas as a means of bankruptcy relief.

§4.29 ~ Competition in the Federal System

Almost lost in the uproar over the Eleventh Amendment is another jurisdictional conflict. That is the battle between the bankruptcy system and other parts of the federal government. The conflict emerges at a number of points in the bankruptcy system; for example, it may arise in disputes over the scope of the "police or regulatory" exception to the automatic stay. We note just a couple of important items here.

§4.30 ~ Federal Sovereign Immunity

Like the states, the federal government may enjoy some sort of immunity from suit. Does this "federal sovereign immunity" impair the power of the bankruptcy court? On the face of things, the answer is: apparently not. Section 106 purports to waive federal (as well as state) sovereign immunity. This provision, at least, would appear to be valid. Recall the linchpin of the Supreme Court's argument in the *Seminole* line: Congress has no power to impose a waiver on an unwilling state. But with the feds, the problem of "voluntariness" cannot be an issue.[57] After all, it is the Congress that "speaks for" the federal government, and so it would seem the legislature has the power to waive all the immunity it wants, up to the limits of the Constitution.

But the courts have not been sympathetic to this waiver, either. In *United States v. Nordic Village, Inc.*,[58] the court held that it did not empower the trustee to collect a post-petition tax payment from the Internal Revenue Service.

§4.31 ~ Competing Powers: NextWave

There are many cases exploring the boundary between the bankruptcy estate and the government's police or regulatory power. But perhaps the most dramatic encounter has been the battle between the Federal Communications Commission and NextWave, a company formed to buy and develop FCC wireless communication licenses.

---

54. 202 F.3d at 1083.

55. 202 F.3d at 1085.

56. The court made an oblique reference to *Younger* but didn't directly rely on it. 202 F.2d at 1087.

57. *See, e.g.*, Jove Engineering, Inc. v. I.R.S., 92 F.3d 1539, 1549 (11th Cir. 1996).

58. 503 U.S. 30 (1992).

Back in the 90s, the FCC undertook a program to auction licenses to distribute wireless service. NextWave was formed to capture part of the market. In 1996, NextWave won two auctions to buy a package of licenses for $4.74 billion, with payment in installments. NextWave paid 10 percent down and the FCC kept a security interest for the unpaid price.

After NextWave won its auction—but before it had paid the balance of the purchase price—the bottom fell out of the wireless market: the licenses when at last transferred were apparently worth just $1.02 billion, less than one quarter of the purchase obligation. NextWave and the FCC negotiated over a "restructuring," but to no avail. Thereupon NextWave filed for relief under Chapter 11, and attacked the $4.74 billion obligation as a fraudulent transfer. NextWave argued that the spread between purchase price ($4.74 billion) and market value ($1.02 billion) was a fraudulent transfer. The bankruptcy court agreed.[59] Thereupon NextWave undertook to pay the $1.02 billion in installments. But the Second Circuit, on appeal, upset the scheme, holding the central issues in the case were "regulatory" and thereby beyond the jurisdiction of the bankruptcy court.[60]

Meanwhile the market for spectrum had begun to recover. NextWave thereupon stumped up new money from investors and undertook to pay the original $4.74 billion price in a single installment. The FCC took the position that the licenses had already been cancelled (as a "regulatory" measure) and that there was nothing to buy. Once again, the bankruptcy judge ruled for NextWave and once again, the Circuit reversed.[61]

From the Second Circuit, the scene shifted back to the regulatory agency in Washington. The FCC undertook to reauction the licenses—for which it received, this time, some $15.85 billion. But NextWave, for its part, took its case before the court with jurisdiction over the regulatory agency—specifically the D.C. Circuit —and ask for a ruling to invalidate the "second sale."

In the summer of 2001, the D.C. Circuit ruled for NextWave and invalidated the sale.[62] The D.C. Circuit held that the purported cancellation was a violation of Section 525. It said the FCC had to obey all federal laws (i.e., including the Bankruptcy Code) and not just the communications statutes. NextWave immediately declared that it was teaming up with the tech giant Lucent to develop its newly-restored rights. With the stakes as high as they are, it is unlikely that we have heard the last of the matter.

---

59. NextWave Personal Communications, Inc. v. FCC (*In re* NextWave Personal Communications, Inc.), 235 B.R. 277, 304 (Bankr. S.D.N.Y. 1999).

60. FCC v. NextWave Personal Communications, (*In re* NextWave Personal Communications, Inc.), 200 F.3d 43 (2d Cir. 1999).

61. *In re* Next Wave Personal Communications Inc., 244 B.R. 253, 262 (Bankr. S.D.N.Y. 2000), rev'd 217 F.3d 12 (2d Cir. 2000).

62. NextWave Personal Communications Inc. v. FCC, 2001 U.S. App. LEXIS 13923 (D.C. Cir. 2001).

§4.32 ~ Jurisdiction Over Tax Claims

There is an inevitable conflict in the bankruptcy system and the tax collector over jurisdiction in tax cases. Perhaps surprisingly, Congress has explicitly granted limited power over tax cases to the bankruptcy court. The statute says that the bankruptcy court "may determine the amount or legality of any tax . . . whether or not preciously assessed, whether or not paid, and whether or not contested before and adjudicated by [a court]".[63] But the power to adjudicate the tax claim does not imply the power to reduce any otherwise valid tax claim.[64]

The court also has limited power to declare the tax effects of a chapter 11 plan. Section 1146(d) permits to the court to authorize the debtor to request a taxing authority to declare the tax effect of a plan. If there is an actual controversy over the tax effect the bankruptcy court may declare it. The Fourth Circuit recently held that the bankruptcy court's declaration of tax effect is *res judicata* even if in error.[65] Perhaps more interesting, the court held that the Eleventh Amendment did not bar the determination.[66]

---

63. Section 505(a)(1).

64. Carlson v. U.S. (Matter of Carlson), 126 F.3d 915, 920 (7th Cir. 1997).

65. State of Maryland v. Antonelli Creditors' Liquidation Trust, 123 F.3d 777, 782 (4th Cir. 1997).

66. *Id.* at 786-87.

5

Going Into Bankruptcy (Or Staying Out)

5 Going Into Bankruptcy (Or Staying Out)

§5.1 ~ Introduction: The Ins and Outs of Bankruptcy

If you think the debtor is concealing or wasting significant assets, you want him in bankruptcy where his conduct is regulated and a trustee may be appointed. If you perceive that he is stalling a foreclosure, you want him out so you can have your way with the property. In short, the question whether to push him in or out is a strategic choice that will depend on the facts of the individual case.

At one extreme is the case where the debtor is concealing or wasting assets and you want him to stop—and there is no other route to relief. Then bankruptcy is the prescription and the involuntary filing may be the solution.

At the other extreme, suppose you are trying to foreclose on your collateral when the debtor files for relief under chapter 11. Your main concern is to get relief from the stay so you can finish your foreclosure. You don't want to push him into a chapter 7. You'd do nothing but buy yourself a new enemy, in the form of a trustee who might challenge your secured position (or whatever)—and you might pick up a host of competing creditors as well. Dismissal wouldn't hurt but you don't need it, certainly not at the cost of provoking opposition from other creditors. What you want is just relief from the stay.

There are any number of positions in between these extremes. The merits will vary depending on the facts of the case.

§5.2 ~ The Case: A Restatement

Earlier we provided a sketch of a simple bankruptcy case (*see* §1.4). To frame up the current discussion, here we offer a slightly different sketch. So, recall that the typical bankruptcy case begins when the debtor files a petition.[1] Along with it (or soon thereafter), he files schedules and a statement of affairs.[2]

---

1. Section 301; *cf.* §§302-4.

2. Fed. R. Bankr. Proc. 1007; Official Bankr. Forms 1-9.

Most debtors are individuals. They file under chapter 7 to get their discharge. Most of them get it, although individual claims may be excepted from discharge.[3] A smaller number of debtors file for relief under chapter 13.[4] Unlike debtors in chapter 7, these chapter 13 debtors surrender a portion of their post-petition earnings to the court for distribution among creditors. In exchange they get a "premium" discharge, broader in scope than they would get in chapter 7.

Smaller in number but perhaps more important to lawyers are the cases filed under chapter 11.[5] Typically no trustee is appointed and the debtor remains in possession (as "DIP") with the powers and responsibilities of a trustee. The premise of chapter 11 is that someone (usually the old equity owners) will propose a plan of reorganization. If it is confirmed, then the debtor is discharged, as he would be in chapter 7.

The drafters set forth threshold requirements for relief in bankruptcy in Sections 109 and Sections 301 through 304, and related rules. The statutes and rules make for intricate reading on first encounter, but they present few practical problems in application.

§5.3 ~ Who May Be a Debtor

Section 109 defines who may be a debtor. Section 109(a) specifies that a "person" may be a debtor. Person is a term defined under the Code. Section 101(41) provides that "person includes individual, partnership, and corporation."[6] Section 101(9) defines corporation. The definition specifies that the term includes business trust. Nonetheless, the courts have encountered occasional difficulty in figuring out where to put specialized entities like the "Illinois Land Trust."[7]

"Individual" and "partnership" are undefined. "Person" does not include a government unit, except in limited cases.[8] Two classes of persons are excluded from chapter 7. The first excluded class is the class of financial intermediaries—banks and insurance companies, both domestic and foreign. The second excluded class is railroads.

---

3. In the year ending Sept. 30, 1998, there were 1,436,964 new cases filed. Of these, 1,026,134, or 71 percent, were filed under chapter 7. Statistics can be found on the Federal Judiciary homepage at http://www.uscourts.gov.

4. For the year ending Sept. 30, 1998, 401, 151 cases, or 28 percent of total filings were under chapter 13. *Id.*

5. In the year ending, Sept. 30, 1998, only 8,765 filings, or just one percent of all cases, were under chapter 11. *Id.*

6. The term seems broad enough to include non-profits. *See, e.g.*, *In re* Joliet-Will County Community Action Agency, 847 F.2d 430, 431 (7th Cir., 1988) (private nonprofit corporation is a proper debtor in bankruptcy).

7. *In re* Treasure Island Land Trust, 2 B.R. 332, 335-36 (Bankr. M.D. Fla. 1980), is an instructive early Code case. The bankruptcy judge dismissed the case of an Illinois Land Trust, on the premise that it was only holding property, not engaging in business. On the facts, the case looks a lot like the notorious single asset real estate cases that gave the courts so much perplexity in later years. But the elaborate reasoning that supports dismissing single-asset real estate cases had not been invented yet.

8. A government unit is a "person" if it acquired an asset from a person in a loan guarantee program or as receiver or liquidating agent of pension assets. Section 101(41)(A), (B). These provisions presumably exist so that these government entities are able to serve on creditors' committees. *See* §1103(b)(1).

The exclusion of financial intermediaries is justified on the grounds that there are fully developed regulatory schemes for financial institutions already in place elsewhere. In the case of insurance companies there is also the deep-rooted Congressional policy of deferring insurance regulation to the states.[9]

Both justifications carry a superficial plausibility. But while regulatory schemes may function for both banks and insurance companies, it is not obvious that regulators have any special competence at liquidation or reorganization. Anyone who watched the regulators administer the crisis in the savings and loan industry during the late 1980s and early 1990s may well wonder whether bankruptcy judges could have done any worse. And in any event, the Bankruptcy Code covers some institutions that resemble banks or insurance companies—specifically, stock and commodity brokers, who are covered by their own subchapters of chapter 7.[10]

There are some curious interpretation problems in deciding just who is an insurance company, particularly in the case of health care providers. A provider who offers to furnish all necessary health care for a fixed fee is, after all, accepting a fee in exchange for bearing a risk—which is exactly what an insurance company does. Some courts, confronted with the question whether a particular health care entity is eligible for bankruptcy relief, seem to have resorted to inquiring whether or not there is any other regulatory scheme in place. If there is no other regulator (so the reasoning seems to go), then the entity must not be an insurance company and correspondingly must be eligible for bankruptcy.[11] This is probably good rough-and-ready justice.

§5.4 ~ Who May Be a Debtor—Chapter 11

Anyone who may be a debtor in chapter 7 may be a debtor in chapter 11, except stock and commodity brokers.[12] The exclusion of brokers can be read as embodying a policy that the failing broker must be disposed of swiftly so as to maintain confidence in the financial system. This is consistent with the general notion of the separateness of financial assets and entities, discussed elsewhere.

At any rate, stock and commodities brokers get their own subchapter in chapter 7.[13] What typically happens to the insolvent broker is that the regulators swoop down and effect a wholesale transfer of assets to another (solvent) entity with the effect of protecting the investor-depositors and with the purpose of seeking to maintain confidence in the financial system.

---

9. McCarren-Ferguson Act of 1945, codified as 15 U.S.C. §1011 *et seq.*

10. While "banks" may be exempt, several bank holdings companies have sought relief under chapter 11. And a number of "bank-life institutions" (e.g., second trust deed brokers) have reorganized under the Bankruptcy Code.

11. *In re* Republic Trust & Savings Co., 59 Bankr. 606, 614 (Bankr. N.D. Okla. 1986); *cf. In re* Grouphealth Partnership, Inc., 137 Bankr. 593, 600 (Bankr. E.D. Pa. 1992) (deference to state regulator).

12. Section 109(d).

13. Subchapter III of chapter 7 applies to securities brokers liquidations, 11 U.S.C. §§741-752; Subchapter IV of chapter 7 applies to commodity brokers liquidations. 11 U.S.C. §§761-66.

Comment. The Securities Investor Protection Act of 1970 (SIPA),[14] created the Securities Investor Protection Corporation (SIPC) to which all registered securities brokers are members. SIPA provides procedures by which SIPC can liquidate troubled dealers. These procedures are intended in large part to protect customers. The filling of chapter 11 is sufficient grounds for a SIPC protective decree.[15] A SIPC liquidation is similar in many ways to a chapter 7 case, and is presided over by a bankruptcy judge, but there are some important differences, particularly relating to claim priorities.[16]

One entity excluded from chapter 7 may seek relief in chapter 11: that is the railroad, which gets its own chapter 11 subchapter. Railroads and insolvency have a long history: indeed virtually every American railroad has been through bankruptcy at least once, some several times. Therefore it is hardly surprising that the deep-rooted history persists in provision for special treatment.

But the policy also bespeaks a deep-rooted and persistent conceptual error. The decision implies that the railroad is too important to fail and (and here comes the error) that "saving" the railroad must mean "reorganizing." The first point (too important to fail) may or may not be correct. But the second loses sight of the fact that you could perfectly well "save" the railroad by selling it as a going concern under chapter 7. But the point is theoretical only: chapter 11 is the only route and in any event, there haven't been any new railroad cases in years.[17]

Note that the statutory framework makes clear that an individual may be a debtor under chapter 11—i.e., that chapter 11 relief is not restricted to businesses like partnerships or corporations. Whatever the merits of the policy, it is hard to see how anyone could read the statute any other way. But it took the Supreme Court to settle the point.[18]

There has never been any great rush on the part of individuals to get into chapter 11. For the most part it the individual cases are limited to those with complex personal investments. In the late 1980s and early 1990s, there were a fair number of real estate developer cases. We may see that again during the next real estate cycle. On the overlap between individual and corporate case, *see* §6.23.

The question of eligibility for chapter 13 deserves some attention because it may be an alternative to chapter 11 in some smaller cases—and because there are recurrent proposals to expand eligibility, so as to include more smaller cases.[19] As it stands now, chapter 13 is available only to an individual (not a corporation or a partnership). The individual must have "regular income." This usually means wages, but it is not so limited—commission salesmen qualify, as do self-employed small business people.

---

14. 15 U.S.C. §§78aaa-78lll.

15. Securities Investor Protection Corp. v. Blinder, Robinson & Co., 962 F.2d 960m 966-67 (10th Cir. Colo. 1992).

16. For more information, *see* SIPC's web site at www.SIPC.org.

17. For a long-running railroad case, *see* Matter of Chicago, Milwaukee, St. Paul & Pacific R. Co., 78 F.3d 285, (7th Cir., 1996) (filing from 1977).

18. Toibb v. Radloff, 501 U.S. 157, 160-61 (1991).

19. Section 109(e).

Perhaps the most important limitation is the dollar cap: the debtor's unsecured debts must not exceed $269,250 and the secured, $807,750.[20] These debts must be noncontingent and liquidated—a condition that has led to some seemingly bizarre high-profile cases in which a defendant facing a multimillion dollar lawsuit has escaped into chapter 13 because he succeeded in filing before the dispute went to trial.

Back in the 1980s, there was sentiment that chapter 11 as it stands was too complex for the small business case. There was sentiment to include a new small-business chapter (thus restoring a separation that had subsisted for a generation under prior law, but had been abolished by the Bankruptcy Act of 1978),

One alternative proposal was to lift or eliminate the cap on chapter 13. One argument against limiting the cap was the nature of the protection available in chapter 13—particularly the "super discharge." It is one thing to let a debtor discharge only (!) a million so in, say, fraud debt—quite another to let the super discharge apply without limit. The upshot was that Congress did neither. Rather, they added special rules for small chapter 11s, and for accelerated relief in certain single-asset real estate cases.

Some of the small chapter 11 cases also fold into chapter 12, the family farmer chapter—sort of a hybrid between chapters 13 and 11. A "family farmer" is defined as a debtor whose debts do not exceed $1.5 million, mostly from farming operations. Notably, unlike chapter 13, the debtor may be an individual (or a couple), or it may be a partnership or corporation, if closely held by one family.[21]

§5.5 ~ Note on the Small Business Debtor

The discussion of chapter 13 suggests a more general problem: Congress has never really figured out whether (or how) to deal with the small business debtor.

The old Bankruptcy Code made a clear cut. Old chapter X was designed for major public corporate cases. Old chapter XI was intended for the small business. But it didn't work out that way. Chapter X was cumbersome, which is to say expensive; chapter XI less so. Not surprisingly, under the old Bankruptcy Act, chapter X languished (and chapter XI flourished) because chapter X was just too big, bulky and expensive for the ordinary case; the protections tended to love the debtor to death. In drafting the new Code, the drafters made an effort to trim down the supposed excesses of old chapter X and to make the new chapter 11 accessible to all.

But again, it didn't work. Almost from the beginning, debtors and their lawyers were howling that chapter 11 was loaded with costly rigidity that drove worthy reorganization cases into liquidation.

For a long time there was talk about how to remedy the situation. One proposal was to expand chapter 13. Another was to create an all-new chapter 10—this time for little cases—to do what chapter 11 seemed not to have done.[22]

---

20. The seemingly arbitrary dollar amounts are the result of a cost of living adjustment. *See* §104.

21. Section 109(f); *see* also §§101(18)-(20).

22. *See* §101(51C) (aggregate unsecured debt no more than $2 million). The small debtor follows a pattern developed by Bankruptcy Judge A. Thomas Small in the Western District of North Carolina, who dubbed it "the rocket docket."

So far, neither has come to pass. Instead, what Congress has done is to provide an *elective* fast-track framework for small businesses inside of chapter 11.

You need to be alert even to find it. The central principle is in section 1121(e), where the debtor is authorized to make the election. If he does, there are two "advantages:"

- He may combine the hearings on disclosure and confirmation.

- He may dispense with committees.

But in exchange for these advantages, he has to settle for a *shorter* exclusivity period—only 100 days, as distinct from 120 in an ordinary case. It is hard to imagine why anyone would accept the inducement for the tradeoff, and in fact very few debtors do.

§5.6 ~ A Non-requirement—You Don't Need to Be Insolvent

The Bankruptcy Code defines "insolvency" in terms of the balance sheet—the debtor is insolvent when his liabilities exceed his assets.[23] One remarkable "non-requirement" for bankruptcy filing is that you don't have to show that you are "insolvent" in this bankruptcy sense. This may strike some readers as odd. What is bankruptcy for, if not to deal with cases of insolvency?

One answer is that there may be debtors who face a liquidity crisis that cannot be untangled without judicial intervention. A notable example is the conflict that arose after Texaco seemingly nosed out Pennzoil in a takeover fight for Getty Oil. A jury in Texas awarded Pennzoil $10 billion for the affront. Texaco thereafter filed for bankruptcy in New York and ultimately settled for around $3 billion.

The numbers were huge, of course, but so is Texaco, and the fact is that even the maximum judgment was not beyond Texaco's capacity to pay. On the other hand, apparently Texaco on the eve of filing did face a commercial paper crisis that would have impaired its capacity to function pending resolution of the dispute. Remarkably, no one ever formally challenged Texaco's right to file.[24]

Another example is Columbia Gas Systems, Inc., the natural gas transmitter. In mid-1991, Columbia found itself found itself whipsawed by its long-term purchase contracts in a rising market. Columbia filed for bankruptcy, rejected the contracts, and spent the next several years negotiating a deal with suppliers. Throughout, Columbia insisted (and the market essentially acknowledged) that Columbia was a viable company with one big problem.

A counter-example is Manville Corp., once the dominate supplier of asbestos. By 1982 Manville faced perhaps 52,000 lawsuits, present and potential. In mid-1982, Manville filed for bankruptcy, declaring that it had to do so to preserve the company in the face of the asbestos litigation. A number of critics

---

23. Section 101(32).
24. Our information comes mostly from conversations with counsel. For background, *see* David M. Cutler & Lawrence H. Summers, *The Cost of Conflict Resolution and Financial Distress: Evidence from the Texaco-Pennzoil Litigation*, 19 Rand J. Econ 157 (1988).

greeted the filing with outrage, alleging that Manville was abusing the process. The financial press in particular howled that Manville shouldn't be permitted to use the bankruptcy process because it was "solvent."

In fact, Manville had reported a profit in each of the five years preceding the petition, and its balance sheet showed a net worth of $1.1 billion. But one informed estimate put the potential asbestos liability (not on the balance sheet) at $2 billion. If this number was correct, then Manville was insolvent in the "liabilities versus assets" sense, no matter what its transitory profitability. In fact, bankruptcy was probably the best available forum to sort out Manville's crippling liabilities.

Whatever the formal rules, the fact is that most businesses ordinarily won't file for bankruptcy unless they face a corporate crisis. Bankruptcy is expensive and very public. It can destroy market value and it is usually terrible for public relations. It often puts a company "in play" and there is a high risk of losing control to creditors. Few companies will accept these downsides unless they are insolvent and cannot find another alternative for turning the business around.

Meanwhile, courts have been resistant to permitting the use of bankruptcy where they perceive that it is nothing more than a litigation tactic. *In re SGL Carbon Corp.*[25] is a remarkable example. The officers of the debtor declared that the company was financially healthy. They said they filed for the sole purpose of pressuring the plaintiffs to settle some anti-trust lawsuits. The District Court sustained the filing. However, the Third Circuit, reversing, held that Section 1122 implies a condition of good faith in filing. It held that the mere possibility that the debtor might need to file if he lost the lawsuits was not enough to satisfy the condition.

§5.7 ~ SAREs

One of the most prominent episodes in the history of modern chapter 11 is the story of the single asset real estate case ("SARE"). For reasons we set forth below, we think this episode is becoming less important. But history has its claims and in any event, some of the law made in the SARE cases will be with us for a long time to come. Here is a classic SARE:

It is 1985. Bruce, Dan and Joel (BDJ) get together to create LimCo, a limited partnership. BDJ will be limited partners in exchange for cash contributions. The general partner will be GenCo, a corporation created for this purpose. LimCo will buy PinkAcre, a strip shopping center, for $100,000 down and a $4.9 million secured promissory note in favor of BigBank.

In fact, PinkAcre doesn't look like all that great an investment. It doesn't make a lot of money—indeed, from a pure accounting standpoint it makes no money at all. But what appeals to BDJ is not necessarily the project per se, but the tax angle. The deal is that all the deductions (including some fast depreciation deductions) will pass straight through to them, and they will be able to use them to offset against the hefty revenues from their professional practices. Since this is a limited partnership, the only money they have at risk is their modest capital contribution.

---

25. 200 F.3d 154 (3rd Cir. 1999), *rev'g,* 233 B.R. 285 (D. Del. 1999).

Jump cut to 1991. BDJ have enjoyed some substantial deductions, but the PinkAcre has been anemic from its inception and now BigBank is ready to foreclose. BDJ learn to their horror that if the bank forecloses, then (a) they will lose PinkAcre; but (b)—much worse—the tax collector will go back and recompute their tax returns and "recapture" their depreciation deductions. Now is the time for BDJ to do something—anything—to keep the partnership from unraveling, mostly so they can avoid liability for depreciation recapture.

This is the model of the case that winds up in bankruptcy as a single asset case. On the face of things, you could make a pretty good argument that they shouldn't be there at all. It doesn't really fit within any traditional bankruptcy category. Orchestrate claims? But there is only one real creditor—the trade debt, if any, is negligible. Discharge? But this is a limited liability entity, with nonrecourse debt, so the owners don't face any liability for deficiency in any event.

Of course, BDJ can get discharges as individuals if they qualify—but that would be in their own bankruptcies (and in any event, it probably wouldn't discharge their tax debts). What these investors seem to be doing is to try to use the (federal) bankruptcy court as a court of appeal for a state mortgage foreclosure, to buy more time in the hope that something will turn up to save the deal.

But you can make an equally good argument that the case belongs in bankruptcy just fine. They were a staple of old chapter XII, which was on the books when Congress adopted the 1978 Bankruptcy Act. And nothing in the Code specifies that you have to have either "orchestration" or "discharge" as your purpose. And clearly, these investors need help.

This is a kind of case that became a staple of the bankruptcy docket from the mid 1980s through to the mid 1990s. Some courts never felt comfortable with them, and often agonized over whether they ought to remain in bankruptcy court.[26] On the other hand, they never issued a blanket per se rule that the cases would be excluded.

Comment: Some judges will dismiss "eve of foreclosure" SARE cases as fast as they arrive—and may even sanction counsel for bringing them in particularly egregious situations. Others are more tolerant, and will rarely dismiss a single asset case. Know your judge before you file.

We think the issue may be diminishing in importance, for one very good reason. That is that the tax law on which the deals were based was repealed effective in 1986.[27] So by this time, most of that entrepreneurial pig has probably worked its way through the juridical python. But it leaves it mark. For example, much of the law of bad faith dismissal and the absolute priority rule was made in SARE cases.

---

26. *See, e.g., In re* Greystone III Joint Venture, 995 F.2d 1274 (5th Cir. 1991).

27. Another reason to suspect that they may not have a bright future is that they pretty much depended on the new value exception, which the Supreme Court has either abolished or at least severely undercut. *See* §9-8.

Remarkably, after years of agony over whether the SARE cases belonged in chapter 11, the Code gave a kind of back-handed recognition to them in a set of amendments specifically designed to govern relief from the automatic stay in such cases.[28]

§5.8 ~ Strategy: Keeping Your Case in Court

The dominant reason why courts feel uneasy with SAREs is that they are essentially two-party disputes. So one way to make sure your case stays in court is to persuade the judge that there are "multiple creditor" issues that can't be dealt with well elsewhere. Show her (if you can) how outside of bankruptcy the secured creditor will walk away with all the assets, leaving nothing for unsecureds (or indeed, for a junior secured).

§5.9 ~ Strategy: Dismissing the SAREs

We can think of at least two devices for a secured creditor who wants to hasten the dismissal of the SARE. One device is to focus on where the debtor will get money to pay its legal fees. This will put the debtor in a twist. The courts are often unwilling to allow debtors to use cash collateral to pay legal fees, which is usually all the cash a single asset debtor has. So, the only option may be capital contributions made to the debtor by its equity holders. At a certain point, they may regard this as throwing good money after bad. A second option is to consider purchasing unsecured claims and moving for relief from the stay on grounds that the debtor won't be able to confirm a plan, because it cannot obtain an impaired accepting class of creditors. Courts will usually uphold claims purchasing by a secured creditor in a SARE case, although debtors often challenge it on "bad faith" grounds.

§5.10 ~ Partnerships and LLCs

Non-bankruptcy law seems to create problems for partnership bankruptcy, but in the end, the problems are mostly illusory. For example, the old Uniform Partnership Act declares that a partnership dissolves on a petition in bankruptcy by a partner or the partnership.[29] But courts have rarely if ever let this rule inhibit them in taking jurisdiction over partnership cases.[30]

There may be a problem if the partnership is in pre-petition dissolution. A Second Circuit decision holds that such a partnership is not a "person" eligible to file for relief.[31] But this case is perhaps better read as an "abstention" case, as if holding that there is no role to play when the state court dissolution is already well under way. So the short point is: the partnership is eligible to be a debtor, but you may occasionally have to jump through a couple of hoops to get there.

A related issue is whether limited liability companies (and limited liability partnerships) are eligible for bankruptcy relief. The issue arises because these entities are not referred to in Section 109 or in the definition

---

28. *See* §362(d)(3).

29. Uniform Partnership Act §31(d)(5). Bankruptcy is not an event of dissolution under the Revised Uniform Partnership Act.

30. *See, e.g., In re* Donald Verona & Bernard Green, 126 B.R. 133 (Bankr. M.D. Fla. 1991).

31. C-TC 9th Ave. Partnership v. Norton Co., 113 F.3d 1304, 1307 (2d Cir. 1997).

of "person." But the omissions are easily explained given that LLCs and LLPs are relatively recent creatures of state law. Perhaps not surprisingly, the courts and commentators who have addressed the issue agree that LLCs and LLPs should be eligible for relief under the Code.[32]

§5.11 ~ BANKRUPTCY-PROOFING

If you are a creditor that has been bruised in the past by bankruptcy, or you want to do a deal without the risk of bankruptcy, you naturally try to think up ways to exempt yourself or your transaction from the bankruptcy laws, or, failing that, to minimize the impact of the bankruptcy.[33] For example, you may try to argue that "your" asset is not really an asset of the estate.[34] Or you try to provide for expedited disposition, as is available to real property lessors[35] or single asset real estate creditors.[36] Or you may try to exempt your type of transaction from the bankruptcy laws, as the securities industry has managed to do for a whole range of financing and securities transactions, such as repos and swaps.[37] Or you try to get the debtor to sign (and the court to enforce) a waiver of the automatic stay.[38] Or you may bargain for a springing guaranty or similar device to create a disincentive for the debtor to file for bankruptcy.

But, these days, far and away the most fertile field for special-protection devices is that of "asset securitization." Securitization lawyers and their close cousins have developed a remarkable array of tactics to "bankruptcy proof" their assets.

To understand securitization, start with Jimmy Stewart as George Bailey in "It's a Wonderful Life." When George Bailey made a loan at his Bedford Falls Building and Loan Association, he could pretty nearly see all his collateral from the front door. There were good business reasons for running a bank this way. George knew that anyone who relies on his contract as his primary assurance of repayment is a fool: to succeed as a lender, you had to judge a man's character and George was in a position to do just that.

George's strategy, in short, was to put all his eggs in one basket, and then to watch the basket. But as Will Rogers said—what if you drop the basket? The hidden peril in George's old-fashioned portfolio was that a single disaster—a flood, or a hurricane, or even a factory closing—might wipe it out with a single blow.

---

32. *In re ICLNDS Notes Acquisition, LLC*, 259 B.R. 289 (Bankr. N.D. Ohio 2001); *see generally* Limited Liability Companies in Bankruptcy, 937 PLI/Corp. 747 (PLI 1996) ("Not surprisingly, the Bankruptcy Code does not specifically refer to limited liability companies in the list of entities eligible for relief. However, LLCs should be eligible for relief as debtors because they arguably fall within the Bankruptcy Code's definition of "person," and there appears to be no reason for their exclusion").

33. You will think of simply writing it into the contract that your debtor agrees not to file for bankruptcy. This is surely a non-starter; otherwise everyone would do it. *But see* §7.27.

34. *See, e.g.*, §541(d), discussed at §8.13.

35. Section 365(d)(2).

36. Section 362(d)(3).

37. *See, e.g.*, §§555, 556, 559, 560.

38. *See, e.g.*, Michael St. Patrick Baxter, *Pre-petition Waivers of the Automatic Stay*, 52 Bus. Law. 577 (1997), discussed §7.26.

For good reasons or bad, no one does business like George Bailey anymore. Instead, the note that you sign at the bank this morning is likely to be winging its way to Wall Street before the end of the week. By the end of the month, it will be wrapped up in a package with a thousand other loans. Investors will buy, not your loan or mine or anybody else's, but a participation in a portfolio of loans—a "security" backed by the anticipated payments from the package of pooled loans—hence "securitization."

The advocates of securitization can recite many advantages for borrower and lender and society as a whole. It's cheaper, for one thing: cheaper to do a thousand deals at once than any one deal a thousand times. It's standardized: anyone, anywhere, can understand it. It provides access to capital and liquidity that would not otherwise exist. It allows investors to buy exactly what they want, because the pool of loans can be split in an infinite number of ways.[39] And because the transactions are rated by rating agencies, the universe of potential investors is broader than it otherwise would be.

But the real virtue of securitization is diversification—the "insurance" effect. Bundle together a thousand loans from a thousand places and you have essentially defanged the ogre of disaster. One loan may go bad in time, maybe a hundred. But you can price the risk into the deal at the beginning, and sell the risk only to those who want it. And the chance of a total wipeout, destroying the whole portfolio, is essentially nil.

Securitization grew up in the home mortgage market, where the great secondary lenders like Fannie Mae and Freddie Mac have become powerhouses that dominate the economy.[40] But that was only the beginning. These days, you can find almost any kind of deal "securitized on the back end," as the new jargon prescribes. The most typical securitized assets are accounts receivable, mortgages, credit card debt, and the like, but we've seen some odd ones too: a portfolio of debt owed by chapter 13 debtors; the future royalty revenue of a rock star; and proceeds owed to a state government from a litigation settlement, to name just a few. The reason for this is simple—people want to turn a future stream of anticipated revenue into current dollars, and the discount they are willing to pay to do so creates an attractive investment for others.

In a typical securitization, the party entitled to receive the receivables or other payments to be securitized will transfer or "sell" the receivables to a "special purpose vehicle" ("SPV")—an entity whose sole purpose is to own the transferred receivables and which is forbidden by charter from engaging in any other business activity.

---

39. For example, an investor who wants a safe investment with a modest return could purchase a highly-rated security, which would be repaid from the first dollars generated by the loan pool. An investor with greater tolerance for risk could purchase a lower-rated or non-rated security, backed by the same pool of loans, but in the first loss position—if some of the loans in the pool go into default, the holder of this security loses his money first. That investor takes more risk, but receives a correspondingly greater return. And there are an infinite number of other ways these things are sliced—an investor can buy a security backed only by interest payments on the loans, or only by principal payments, or only by prepaid principal, or almost anything else you can imagine. This allows an investor to buy exactly the anticipated payment stream that meets its investment criteria, and to manage risk and return with some level of precision.

40. Fannie Mae is the Federal National Mortgage Association. Freddie Mac is the Federal Home Loan Mortgage Corporation. Both are publicly traded corporations, not government agencies. *See generally* PETER J. WALLISON AND BERT ELY, NATIONALIZING MORTGAGE RISK: THE GROWTH OF FANNIE MAE AND FREDDIE MAC (2000), available at the web site of the American Enterprise Institute, http://www.aei.org/shop1/shops/1/7146-5.pdf.

In exchange, the transferor receives all of the stock of the SPV. The articles and bylaws of the SPV are drafted in a way to minimize the risk that the SPV will be able to file a bankruptcy petition. In order for the securities issued as a result of the securitization to be rated by the rating agencies (the key to the success of the transaction), the creation of the SPV, the transfer of the receivables from the parent to the SPV, and virtually every other aspect of the transaction must meet specified guidelines.[41]

Among other functions, the securitization market is processing a lot of the claims that used to go to the bank as security for receivables financing under Article 9 of the Uniform Commercial Code. But an Article 9 lender is vulnerable to all the hazards of the bankruptcy case. The securitization deal-makers argue that they can't be expected to put up with *that*. What they need is a set of rules or procedures that make sure that the bankruptcy of the underlying borrower (the transferor) will not affect the securitization.

Securitization lawyers worry about a number of issues as they try to insulate their deals from the bankruptcy process. First, they seek to argue that the SPV will not file a chapter 11 petition. A popular device is to include a requirement in the organizational documents providing that only a supermajority of directors may initiate a bankruptcy case. A related tactic is to provide that at least one director of the SPV will be an outsider, unconstrained by ties with the original management. And by restricting the ability of the SPV to conduct business or incur debt, they minimize the prospect of an involuntary bankruptcy. In addition, they seek to assure that the SPV is operated as a legally separate entity, so it will not be consolidated with the parent in a parent bankruptcy case.

Addressing bankruptcy law itself, the securitization bar has concentrated its attention on assuring that any transfer of assets to the SPV will be regarded as a true sale and not a mere security interest. The purpose of this device should be obvious: if the asset came by way of true sale, then the entity can continue to manage the asset unconstrained by the bankruptcy of the transferor. But if it was a transfer for security purposes only, then the securitization may be entangled in the bankruptcy of the transferor.[42] They also seek to assure that the transfer of the receivables to the SPV is structured so that it will not be vulnerable to attack as a fraudulent conveyance.

An important part of these transactions is the legal opinions that will be required by the rating agencies. These opinions deal with, among other things, the structure of the SPV, the validity of its articles and bylaws, nonconsolidation between the transferor and the SPV, true sale, and fraudulent conveyance issues. A good deal of the bankruptcy lawyers' time on these transactions is preparing the required opinions and structuring the deals in a way that will allow the lawyers to give the opinions that the rating agencies will require.

---

41. There is a lot more information at www.standardandpoors.com. *See also Structured Financing Techniques*, a report prepared by the Committee on Bankruptcy and Corporate Reorganization of the New York City Bar Association, and published by the ABA Section of Business Law; and WEIL GOTHSHAL & MANGES, REORGANIZING FAILING BUSINESSES (STRUCTURED FINANCING TECHNIQUES CHAPTER), Vol 1 Chapter 4 (ABA 1998).

42. We discuss some of the law on true sale versus "security" at §§8.11 ff., §11.9.

It is tempting to get jaded about the special pleading that you hear from the securitization industry —after all, everyone else has to share in the debtor's rehabilitation, why shouldn't they? But in fact, there is a good deal to be said on their side. For one, these securitizations shouldn't be understood as simple secured loans. Rather, they are (or at least they can be) free-standing financial intermediaries in their own right. As such, they are more akin to banks or insurance companies—for which we have long had special insolvency rules outside the bankruptcy system. In addition, they provide an important source of capital at a lower cost than would otherwise be available. This might entitle them to special merit, as Congress has determined with respect to certain financial transactions and entities in the securities industry.

Related to (but distinguishable from) the securitization problems are the issues surrounding "repos." Repos have a different history and purpose from securitizations. But they are both creatures of the financial bar. And as with securitizations so also with repos, the sponsors have deployed an remarkable fund of energy to assuring that they are insulated from the bankruptcy case. The problem of repos involves attention to particular statutory language, particularly the "property" language of section 541(d).[43]

§5.12 ~ Involuntary Bankruptcy

There was a time when virtually the only kind of bankruptcy was involuntary. As long as bankruptcy was quasi-criminal—and before the advent of the bankruptcy discharge—one would no more readily declare oneself bankrupt than one would indict oneself for grand theft.

Today all that has changed. Only a tiny fraction of bankruptcies are involuntaries—and of that small number, one suspects a good many are ill-advised. It is probably going too far to say that the involuntary never makes sense. But when you consider the costs and risks against the advantages, it is at least no surprise that involuntaries are as uncommon as they are.

§5.13 ~ Does It Ever Make Sense?

Does it ever make sense to file an involuntary? To decide, consider the creditor who is having trouble getting paid because (for example) the debtor is deliberately hiding assets.[44] What are the options for the creditor? Certainly she has available whatever ordinary collection remedies are available under non-bankruptcy law. For example, she may be able to effect a levy and execution after judgment. In some cases, she may be able to get a receiver. (The details vary almost infinitely under the laws of the different states and remain beyond our scope).

She may also be able to get an extraordinary remedy like a pre-judgment attachment or a temporary restraining order if she can persuade a court that waiting for judgment will be futile or self-defeating. These pre-judgment remedies were once fairly common. But the Supreme Court sharply restricted their

---

43. *See* §8.14 ff.

44. *See generally* Susan Block-Lieb, *Why Creditors File so Few Involuntary Petitions and Why the Number is Not Too Small*, 57 Brook L. Rev. 803 (1991).

use during the due process revolution of the 60s and 70s, in cases like *Sniadach v. Family Finance Corp.*[45], *Fuentes v. Shevin*[46] and *Mitchell v. W.T. Grant Co.*[47]

The remedies have never fully recovered. As a minimum, achieving a worthwhile pre-judgment remedy will require that the creditor meet a heavy burden of proof—and the chances are that she will have to post a bond to compensate the debtor in the event that her allegations turn out to be wrong.

All this is enough to make the involuntary a tempting alternative. The filing of the petition counts as the commencement of the case.[48] This event is an important trigger for all kinds of bankruptcy provisions. For example, the commencement of the case creates the estate, and triggers the trustee's strong-arm power. The filing of the petition also triggers the automatic stay, and starts the count on the period for avoiding preferences (there are many other possible examples). The court may require a bond from the petitioners, but only after notice and a hearing.[49] So on the surface, the involuntary looks like a wonderful way to stop the debtor dead in his tracks.

§5.14 ~ Too Good to Be True

For the creditor all this sounds too good to be true, and it is. In the first place, in the ordinary case, the single creditor is not entitled to file the petition alone. Rather, the petition must be filed by *three or more* creditors, each of which is the holder of a claim "that is not contingent as to liability or the subject of a bona fide dispute."[50] The claims must aggregate at least $10,775 more than the value of any lien. Only if there are fewer than 12 creditors overall may just one initiate the case.[51] Just finding the other creditors —or satisfying oneself that there are fewer than 12—can itself be a formidable task.

Second, while the filing of the petition may commence the case, it does not put the debtor in bankruptcy. Rather, the debtor may contest the petition. If the debtor contests, then the court may enter the order for relief only if it finds either

- the debtor is generally not paying its debts as they become due (unless the debts are the subject of a bona fide dispute);[52] or

---

45. 395 U.S. 337 (1969).

46. 407 U.S. 67 (1972).

47. 416 U.S. 600 (1974). Due process limitations on collection protect not only consumers. *See* North Georgia Finishing, Inc. v. Di-Chem, Inc., 419 U.S. 601, 608 (1975) (business assets). And it clearly outlived the 70s. *See* Connecticut v Doehr, 501 U.S. 1, 12 (1991) (prejudgment attachment of real estate).

48. Section 303(b).

49. Section 303(e).

50. Section 303(b)(1).

51. Section 303(b)(2).

52. Section 303(f). Gap creditors may have a second priority (just behind administrative expenses). Section 502(f), 507(a)(2).

- within 120 days before the filing, a custodian such as an assignee for the benefit of creditors was appointed for (or took possession of) substantially all of the debtor's property.

Put differently, this means that if the debtor contests, there will be a trial—in which, on most important issues, the creditor(s) will bear the burden of proof.

§5.15 ~ After the Petition

Given the possibility of contest and trial, you need to know about the rules governing the interim period between petition and order for relief. The Code gives several. For one, it specifies that until the order for relief the debtor's business may continue to operate, unless the court orders otherwise. But it also provides that the court may order the appointment of an interim trustee if it finds that a trustee is "necessary to preserve the property of the estate or to prevent loss to the estate."[53]

Faced with the prospect of extended conflict, the practical-minded litigator will be tempted to use the involuntary as a lever to trigger settlement. But for the creditor, here is where the real trouble starts. The difficulty is that involuntary may be dismissed only after notice to all creditors.[54] If the debtor really is in trouble, then the chance that other creditors will allow a settlement that favors only the petitioning creditor is small.

This translates into a more general point. Once the creditor commences an involuntary, he has transforms the case from the two-party to the multi-party realm—more bluntly, he has bought himself a whole new set of enemies. Bankruptcy is, after all, a collective remedy, and the very collective nature means that it is unattractive to the aggressive or enterprising creditor who gets his claim in first at non-bankruptcy law—in short, to the creditor most likely to bring the involuntary in the first place.

Your authors haven't taken a survey, but they have a strong suspicion that a good many non-bankruptcy lawyers, habituated to two-party thinking, have gotten their clients entangled in the nets of an involuntary case without really thinking through the implications of its multi-party nature.

As an added inducement to reconsider the filing decision, the Code provides that if the court dismisses the involuntary after trial, then the debtor may recover from the petitioning creditors his costs and a reasonable attorney's fee.[55] Against any petitioner who filed in bad faith, the debtor may receive judgment for "any damages proximately caused or for punitive damages."

§5.16 ~ Where Involuntaries Might Be a Good Idea

While involuntaries are not favored, there are three situations in which an involuntary might make sense:

- Where the debtor is spiriting away assets *and he cannot be restrained in any other practical way.*

---

53. Section 302(g).

54. Section 303(i).

55. Section 303(i)(1).

- Where there is need for ongoing supervision/management which the debtor (due either to dishonesty or incompetence) simply cannot provide.

- Where there are preferences to be set aside or other bankruptcy powers to be deployed that won't be available without a bankruptcy petition. Thus typically a preference may be avoided only if it occurred within 90 days of filing. The creditor who confronts an "89-day preference" may have to file an involuntary because there may be no non-bankruptcy alternative.

§5.17 ~ But Still ...

We would suggest that you should do it only (a) after all practical non-bankruptcy remedies have been considered and rejected as inadequate; and (b) if the creditor is willing to bear the burden of translating the case from a two-party into a multi-party dispute, together with (c) after considering the risk of liability for costs and damages.

§5.18 ~ Who?

Who may be a debtor in an involuntary? In general, anyone who may be a debtor in a voluntary chapter 7 and 11, however, there are exceptions. There may be no involuntary petitions against farmers—perhaps an odd sort of exception at first blush, but rooted in the pro-farmer populism of the 1898 Bankruptcy Act. And there may be none against a charitable corporation. Formally there may be no involuntary chapter 13s, though as we shall see elsewhere, some provisions of chapter 7 may be used to leverage the debtor into chapter 13.

A footnote on the rule for petitioning creditors. The Code requires that the three petitioning creditors hold claims aggregating at least $10,775 more than the value of any lien.[56] Typically, we think of bankruptcy as a remedy for unsecured, rather than secured, creditors. But suppose this case: Abel holds a claim for $1 million, fully secured by Blackacre. Baker holds a claim for $1 million fully secured by Whiteacre. Charlie holds a claim for $1,010,775, secured by Greenacre which is worth $1 million.

Since Charlie's claim against Greenacre exceeds the value of his lien by $10,775, the claims of the three would seem to qualify them as petitioning creditors. Whether the drafters intended the involuntary rules to be used to protect creditors whose claims are primarily secured is perhaps an open question. A thoughtful opinion holding that a fully secured creditor may be a petitioner is *Paradise Hotel Corp. v. Bank of Nova Scotia*.[57]

Section 303 provides for a different kind of involuntary bankruptcy case that raises some interesting policy questions all its own. Specifically, the section provides that an involuntary may be filed by one or more *general partners* against other partners in a partnership.[58] A general partner that did not join the petition

---

56. Section 303(b)(1).

57. 842 F.2d 47, 49-50 (3d Cir., 1988).

58. Section 303(b)(3).

may contest it.[59] The practical result is that bankruptcy thus offers a mechanism for winding up a partnership and resolving partnership debts, settling conflicts among (as it were) equity owners, rather than merely among creditors. Interestingly, bankruptcy does not specifically offer a device for winding up corporations, leaving that matter to non-bankruptcy law.[60]

§5.19 ~ Conversion or Dismissal

Sections 109 and 303 specify who can go into bankruptcy. Rules on conversion or dismissal govern who stays there, or who can be moved into which chapter.

Start with Section 1112 (a). It provides that the debtor may convert out of chapter 11 and into chapter 7 at any time, with three exceptions.[61] He cannot convert if

- he is not a DIP (i.e., if a trustee has been appointed);
- the case was begun as an involuntary 11; or
- the case was converted to 11 other than at the request of the debtor.

Compare Section 706, which provides that the debtor may convert from chapter 7 to 11[62] at any time, if the case has not previously been converted from another chapter.

Perhaps of greater interest, the court may dismiss the chapter 11, or convert to chapter 7, after notice and a hearing "for cause."[63] The Code says that cause includes:

- continuing loss to or diminution of the estate and absence of a reasonable likelihood of rehabilitation;
- inability to effectuate a plan;
- unreasonable delay by the debtor that is prejudicial to creditors;
- failure to propose a plan under Section 1121 of this title within any time fixed by the court;
- denial of confirmation of every proposed plan and denial of a request made for additional time for filing another plan or a modification of a plan;

---

59. Section 303(d).

60. But *see In re* Stolrow's Inc, 813 F.2d 997, 998-99 (9th Cir., 1987) (over objection, court allows jurisdiction over a case that is essentially a two-shareholder dissolution proceeding).

61. The Debtor can convert from chapter 12 or 13 to chapter 7 at any time, without exception. *See* §§1209, 1307.

62. Or to chapters 12 or 13.

63. Section 1112(b).

- revocation of an order of confirmation under section 1144 of this title, and denial of confirmation of another plan or a modified plan under section 1129 of this title;
- inability to effectuate substantial consummation of a confirmed plan;
- material default by the debtor with respect to a confirmed plan;
- termination of a plan by reason of the occurrence of a condition specified in the plan; or
- nonpayment of any fees or charges required under chapter 123 of title 28.

Some of these rules raise issues of court management. But others raises fundamental questions of substantive policy. Consider especially Section 1112(b)(3) which provides for dismissal or conversion in the case of "unreasonable delay by the debtor that is prejudicial to creditors." As we try to show elsewhere, time is money for the debtor. It seems clear that the drafters intended the Code to give him *some* time. But how much? We don't know a short answer to that question, but to try to moot the issue out under the adjective "unreasonable" seems to us to be brushing the issue under the rug.[64]

Indeed, even as the rules raise issues of judicial management, they also raise questions of policy. Surely any judge has some residual power to manage his own court and his own docket. But a stated purpose of the 1978 Code was to get the judge *out* of active case management and back into the more traditional role of judging. But ironically, it appears that the management rules in this section are not within his control at all. Rather, he may act on the motion of a U. S. Trustee (or administrator) or "on request of a party in interest," but apparently *not* on his own motion.[65]

The court may also convert from chapter 7 to chapter 11 on request of a party in interest at any time, apparently for any reason.[66] But the court may not use the conversion rules to sidestep the rules on involuntary filings. Thus, the court may not convert from chapter 7 to chapter 12 or 13 without the debtor's consent.[67]

---

64. The question was rhetorical, but here is one answer: seven years is too long. *In re* Jackson, 190 B.R. 808, 811 (W.D. Va. 1995) (IRS the only creditor).

65. *In re* Gusam Restaurant Corp., 737 F.2d 274, 277 (2d Cir. 1984) (the judge does not have the power to convert *sua sponte*). A 1994 amendment added subsection 105(d), which gives the court power to control time "on its own motion or on the request of a party in interest." These days, the U.S. Trustee regularly moves to dismiss dormant cases. In the absence of U.S. Trustee action, many cases may languish for lack of creditor interest. This is in the end probably a problem of court management. If the U.S. Trustee is in fact languishing, nothing prevents the judge from stating clearly and on the record that he'd be happy to entertain a few motions to dismiss.

66. Section 706(b).

67. Section 706(c). *Cf.* §706(d) (no conversion unless debtor is a permissible debtor in the target chapter), and *see* also §1112(d) (limiting conversion from chapter 11 to chapters 12 or 13).

The court may dismiss a chapter 7 for cause after notice and a hearing.[68] Cause is said to include:

- Unreasonable delay by the debtor that is prejudicial to creditors;
- Nonpayment of fees; or
- On motion of the U.S. Trustee, failure to file lists and schedules.

The court may also dismiss certain consumer cases for "substantial abuse."[69]

§5.20 ~ What It Costs

Trying to appraise the cost of a bankruptcy proceeding is bound to be a fool's errand. The debtor will have to count the direct cost of professional fees and so forth along with the indirect cost of any additional loss to a business already in trouble—all this to weigh, of course, against any gains that may come from discharging, restructuring or scaling down debt. But it is possible to get certainty on one issue. That is the amount of the direct cost payable to the sovereign for the privilege of using the courts.

The *filing fee*, payable to the clerk, is $830 for a chapter 11, $175 for a chapter 7, $160 for a chapter 13. In chapter 11, the debtor must also pay a quarterly fee to the United States Trustee. The sum due runs from a minimum of $250 a quarter up to a maximum of $10,000 a quarter on disbursements over $5 million. While these fees may seem trifling for a business debtor, even one in deep trouble, the quarterly fees seem to be high enough to keep the purely frivolous small chapter 11s from cluttering up the court's docket. [70]

§5.21 ~ Checklist: Initial Interview Talking Points

Here is a checklist of topics you will want to think through—and talk through—with the client considering an individual bankruptcy case.

A. *Non-bankruptcy Options*

1. Single Creditor Cases
    a) Are defenses to the obligation available?
    b) Are there claims against the creditor?
    c) Can the obligation be restructured?
    d) Is alternative financing available?
    e) What action is creditor likely to take absent bankruptcy?

---

68. Section 707(a).

69. *See* §707(b).69. 28 U.S.C. §1930. The fees are not trifling to the ordinary consumer debtor. While there is no provision for fee waiver, the individual debtor may pay his fee in installments.

70. 28 U.S.C. §1930. The fees are not trifling to the ordinary consumer debtor.While there is no provision for fee waiver, the individual debtor may pay his fee in installments.

2. Multi-creditor cases

   a) Is there a likelihood that all creditor matters could be resolved favorably either through nonbankruptcy litigation or negotiation?
   b) Is alternative financing available?
   c) Are state law remedies available in lieu of bankruptcy?

3. Other considerations

   a) Relative cost of bankruptcy vs. other alternatives
   b) Timeliness of bankruptcy vs. other alternatives
   c) Adequacy of relief in bankruptcy vs. other alternatives
   d) Need for future credit, access to credit, impact of bankruptcy on credit

B. *Assets*

1. Personal property
   a) Tangible assets and household goods–furniture, cars, etc.
   b) Cash, bank accounts, securities, other financial assets
   c) Tax refunds owed
   d) Wages
   e) Accounts or notes receivable
   f) Expectation of inheritance
   g) Assets in trust
   h) Potential divorce or property settlements
   i) Pensions and retirement accounts (IRA, Keogh, 401(K))
   j) Life insurance - cash value
   k) Expensive or unusual items (art, jewelry, etc.)
   l) Child's assets in parent's name
   m) Claims or causes of action

2. Real property
   a) Personal residence
      1. Value
      2. Liens/mortgages
   b) Other real estate
      1. Value
      2. Liens/mortgages

3. How Assets Titled
   a) Who owns each
   b) Tenancy by entireties
   c) Community property (where applicable)

4. Exemptions (state and federal)

C. *Creditors*

1. Notice to creditors

2. Contingent or unliquidated claims

3. Claims not generally thought of as claims
   a) Guarantees
   b) Co-signers and co-makers
   c) Rights of contribution/indemnity

4. Secured Debts
   a) Reaffirmation
   b) Surrender
   c) Redemption
   d) Continuation of payments
   e) Abandonment by trustee

5. Executory contracts

6. Joint or individual debts

D. *Chapter Selection*

1. Options available in chapters 7, 11, 12 and 13
   a) Feasibility of various chapters
      1. Debt limitations with respect to chapter 13—secured and unsecured
      2. Income for chapter 13 purposes
      3. Prior filings and dispositions
   b) Advantages/Disadvantages of various chapters—what result under each chapter
      1. Need for "super discharge"
      2. Need/desire to retain assets
   c) Possible use of "chapter 20" filing

E. *Venue for Filing?*

1. What choices are available?

2. Which exemption rules apply?

F. *Discharge and Dischargeability Matters*

1. Tax debts

2. Spousal and child support; property settlements

3. Student loans

4. Fraud

5. Financial statements
6. Willful injuries
7. Embezzlement/Larceny
8. Fines and penalties
9. Drunk driving
10. Credit card usage
11. Fraudulent transfers
12. Luxury goods
13. Condominium/homeowners association fees

G. *Preferences/Fraudulent Conveyances*

1. Gifts to friends or relatives
2. Charitable contributions
3. Sales for less than fair value
4. Nature of recent payments on unsecured or undersecured debts
5. Recent liens and encumbrances granted

H. *Taxation*

1. Sale or exchange–foreclosures
2. Split tax year (short year election)
3. Late filed returns or years returns not filed
4. Any tax liens

I. *Timing of Filing*

1. Suits and judgments
2. Executions, foreclosures and repossessions
3. Any tax consequences of timing of filing

J. *Explanations to Client re: How it Works*

1. Preparation of petition, schedules and statement of affairs

2. Filing

3. Meeting of creditors

4. Bar date

5. Discharge

6. Complaints

7. Administration of assets

8. Closing of case

9. Timing of Process

K. *Client Relations*

1. Fee agreement

2. Scope of engagement

3. Adversary complaints and discharge objections

4. Timing of payment of fee and form of payment

L. *General Issues of Strategy; Forecasting*

1. Best guess as to what will happen

2. Risks, unknowns and possibilities

3. Source of potential adverse actions
   a) Trustee
   b) U.S. Trustee
   c) Creditors

4. Impact of bankruptcy on access to credit

5. Importance of honesty and full disclosure

§5.22 ~ Bankruptcy Interview Sheet

Particularly, if you have a high volume individual debtor practice, it is helpful to complete an interview sheet when the client first comes in, to make sure you obtain the essential information and to keep an organized record of it. Below is a sample interview sheet.

BANKRUPTCY INTERVIEW SHEET

Date: ____________________ Attorney: ________________________

Client's Name: ____

Address: ____

____

Telephone: (Bus.) _______________(Res.) __________________

Referred by: ____

Fee Arrangement: Flat Fee: $__________Hourly: $___________

Filing Fees: $_________

/__/ includes discharge and other post-bankruptcy litigation

/__/ does not include discharge and other post-bankruptcy litigation

Installments: _______________

Other Terms: _______________

Previous Address (if less than 5 yrs at current address): ____

Age: ____

Marital Status: Married __ Divorced ___ Separated ___ Single ___

Spouse's Name:_____________ How long married?_________________

Dependents:

Name: ____________________ Age:______

Name: ____________________ Age: ______

Name: ____________________ Age: ______

Place of Employment

Husband: ______________________________

Length of Employment: ______________________________

Take-Home Pay: ______________________________

Place of Employment

Wife: ______________________________

Length of Employment: ______________________________

Take-Home Pay: ______________________________

Other Income (include source): (H) ______________________________

(W) ______________________________

Any prior bankruptcies? ______________________________

Reason(s) for Financial Problems:

____

____

____

____

____

Real Estate Owned:

Address	Date Purchased	Mortgage Company	Original Price	Balance of Mortgage(s)	Current Value	Joint or Individual

Was any mortgage guaranteed by VA, FHA, or anyone else? ______________________

Cars Owned:

Year & Make	Lienholder	Amount Owed	Estimated Value

Contracts and Leases:

Nature of Contract | Non-debtor Party | Summary of Terms

____
____
____
____
____

Other Assets:

Significant/expensive household goods: ______________________

Cash on hand or on deposit: ______________________

Other financial assets: ______________________
(stocks, bonds, etc.)

Luxury goods (jewelry,
furs, artwork, etc.): ______________________

Boats, recreational vehicles: ______________________

Patents, copyrights, trademarks: ______________________

Computers/Electrical/Technical: ______________________

Collections: ______________________

Alimony, child support: ______________________

Expectation of
inheritance: ______________________

Tax refunds: Federal: ____________ State: ____________

Accounts or
notes receivables: ______________________

Retirement accounts: ______________________

Cash value life
insurance: ______________________

Any other
property of value: ______________________

Debts (including contingent debts and debts to friends and relatives):

Name of Creditor	Amount Owed	Who is Liable	Monthly Payment	Number of Months Delinquent

Other debt issues:

Any co-signers or guarantors on any debts: ______________________

Any liens on any property (include PMSI): ______________________

Any debt anticipated to be incurred between now and bankruptcy filing: ______________________

What credit cards held: ______________________

Transfers/Payments:

Any transfers or gifts within the last year: ______________________

Any payments on loans from relatives within the last year: ______________________

Any other debt repayments within the last year, other than ordinary course: ______________________

Dischargeability:

Any charges within
60 days of filing? ________________________________

Recent cash advances? ________________________________

Were credit applications
accurate and complete? ________________________________

Tax debts: ________________________________

Any other Section 523 issues: ________________________________

Budget: (if applicable)

Rent or Home Mortgage ____________________

Utilities (electric, heat, gas, water) ____________________

Food ____________________

Telephone ____________________

Clothing ____________________

Laundry & cleaning ____________________

Medical & drug expenses ____________________

Newspapers, periodicals, books ____________________

Insurance ____________________

Transportation ____________________

Car loan(s) ____________________

Club & Union Dues ____________________

Recreation ____________________

Child care ____________________

Alimony, maintenance
or support payments ____________________

Other payments for support ______________________

Tuition or school expenses ______________________

Other periodic payments (specify) ______________________

TOTAL ______________________

Tax Issues: ______________________

Returns not filed: ______________________

Returns late filed: ______________________

Taxes owed: ______________________

Penalties/Interest/
Tax liens: ______________________

Debtor's Objectives: ______________________

Recommendation and Remarks: ______________________

____

____

____

____

§5.23 ~ Checklist: Paperwork

Here's a basic checklist of documents you will need to file a chapter 11 case for a corporation or a partnership. It is the petition that gets the case into court. As a bare minimum, when you are scrambling for jurisdiction, you will need the petition and list of creditors, with names and addresses (you have up to 15 days to finish the rest).[71] You'll also need the check for the filing fee.[72] Check local rules or the clerk to make sure you bring the right number of copies.

A. Petition [73]

B. Exhibit "A"

C. $830.00 Filing Fee

71. FED. R. BANKR. PROC. 1007.

72. An *individual* may apply to pay the fee in installments, but there is no provision for installment payment by a corporation or a partnership. FED. R. BANKR. PROC.1006(b).

73. *See* OFFICIAL BANKR. FORM 1.

D. Creditor Matrix (note local format requirements)

E. List of equity security holders.

F. Schedules

G. Summary of Schedules
1. Schedule A (Real Property)
2. Schedule B (Personal Property)
3. Schedule C (Property Claimed as Exempt)
4. Schedule D (Creditors Holding Secured Claims)
5. Schedule E (Creditors Holding Unsecured Priority Claims)
6. Schedule F (Creditors Holding Unsecured Non-Priority Claims)
7. Schedule G (Executory Contracts and Unexpired Leases)
8. Schedule H (Codebtors)
9. Schedule I (Current Income of Individual Debtor(s))
10. Schedule J (Current Expenditures of Individual Debtor(s))

H. Declaration Concerning Debtor's Schedules

I. Statement of Financial Affairs

J. Attorney Disclosure of Compensation (Bankr. R. 2016(b))

K. Corporate Resolution (or minutes) or Consent of Partners setting forth authority to file for bankruptcy

L. List of Creditors Holding 20 Largest Unsecured Claims

6
What Is Chapter 11?

6 What is Chapter 11?

§6.1 ~ Introduction

In this section, we offer an outline of the area where we think our reader will spend most of his time —chapter 11, the so-called "reorganization" chapter of the Code. We begin with a brief summary. Then we present a sample case, to sketch some of the possibilities. *See* §§6.3 ff.

Then we offer a somewhat broader sketch, called "What is Chapter 11 For?" *See* §§6.13 ff. This material may seem a bit abstract, and you can skip it without loss of continuity. But in our experience, one problem the young lawyer has with chapter 11 work is trying to get at least a glimmer of the big picture. We end with a miscellany of comparative strategic points.

We elaborate on this discussion in other chapters of this book, chiefly Chapter 10 ("Keeping the Ship Afloat") and Chapter 18 ("Confirmation.").

§6.2 ~ The One-minute Chapter 11

Here is a short summary of chapter 11.

Chapter 11 is the reorganization chapter of the Code. The case begins like any other case with a petition and schedules and a statement of affairs. Usually no trustee is appointed, and the debtor remains in possession as "debtor in possession" ("DIP"), with the powers and responsibilities of a trustee. The debtor's business (if there is one) continues to operate (he may even, with court approval, borrow new money). Creditors are stayed from pursuing their claims. Someone (usually the old equity owners) proposes a plan of reorganization. Creditors may get to vote on the plan. If the plan gets the required votes and satisfies the legal requirements of section, then the court may confirm the plan.[1]

§6.3 ~ What Can You Do in Chapter 11?

What can you do in chapter 11? To explore the question, we start with a classic case—LittleCo, a small business debtor in trouble who may get help from chapter 11. We don't mean to suggest that this is a typical case (in fact, we think it is not), but we think it is probably the kind of case the drafters had in mind when they wrote the statute.

---

1. The Administrative Office of U.S. Courts offers a brief summary of chapter 11 here: http://www.nceb.uscourts.gov/chapter.htm.

We proceed as follows. We tell you a little about LittleCo's business, and about how it got into this mess. We suggest how it might go about trying to solve its problems—by appealing not to the generosity of its creditors, but to their self-interest. We suggest reasons why a negotiated deal may be difficult or impossible. Then we show you what chapter 11 has to offer.

§6.4 ~ LittleCo Balance Sheet

LittleCo
Balance Sheet
(In Millions)

Assets		Liabilities & NW	
Cash	$2	BigBank	$4
Inventory	$3	FinCo	$5
Accts Rec	$3.5	Trade Creditors	$6
Plant	$5	Total L	$15
		Net Worth	<$1.5>
Total Assets	$13.5	Total L & NW	$13.5

LittleCo is a small manufacturer and distributor of widgets. It owns some inventory, some accounts receivable, a factory building, and a little cash. It owes $4 million to BigBank. It owes $5 million to FinCo. It owes $6 million to "the trade"—some 150 vendors and other unsecured creditors with claims ranging from a few hundred thousands down to just nickels and dimes. Lester Little is president and a 60 percent shareholder. Other shareholders are his brothers and sisters.

On a day-to-day basis, LittleCo is a functioning, healthy company—meaning that it can pay its ordinary expenses as they come due from ordinary income. But last year, a series of unexpected misfortunes caused LittleCo to fall behind on many of its obligations. During these unhappy times, LittleCo's trade debt more than doubled and has remained at a high level ever since.

LittleCo has adopted a variety of tactics to fend off its creditors. Most important, the company has slowed down its payments to its vendors. It used to pay in 30 days; now the lag time is more like 45. More passive creditors have had to wait even longer, while more aggressive or threatening creditors got paid. Lester and other family members have had to skip some of their own personal paychecks. Recently Lester was even tempted to dip into the sacrosanct "trust fund account," where he keeps money withheld from employee paychecks that the company is supposed to turn over to the tax collector.

Among the creditors, BigBank has proven most malleable. The reason is easy enough to understand: BigBank's $4 million claim is secured by LittleCo's plant which is worth perhaps $5 million. BigBank sent out an appraiser to assure itself that the plant was really worth as much as the books showed, but after they got a favorable appraisal, BigBank quit pushing for monthly payments. (Lester sometimes suspects that BigBank would actually like to foreclose on the plant so it could sell it at a higher price.)

FinCo, with its claim of $5 million, holds a security interest in inventory and receivables. The books show the inventory value at $3 million and receivables at $3.5 million—a total of $6.5 million—so on the face of things, FinCo has no cause for concern. But LittleCo and FinCo both know these numbers are probably soft. The $3 million inventory number is a signal that inventory simply hasn't been selling, and is piling up in the warehouse. The receivables, too, have been creeping up, as customers pick up rumors that LittleCo may be in trouble. After all, the main reason for paying a creditor like LittleCo is the practical fact that you may need new credit. So why pay LittleCo if it won't be around?

Trade creditors have been ambivalent. They have made a lot of phone calls and sometimes they have delayed or suspended deliveries of new supplies. Some of them—those for whom LittleCo is just a minor customer—have referred their claims out for collection and made it clear they will go to court if necessary. Others—regular suppliers who need LittleCo as a customer—have been more compliant. It is clear that many of these would willingly accept less than full payment on their past claims, if necessary to keep LittleCo in business.

Lester has been working himself to a frazzle trying to climb out of the debt chasm, and to keep the business in good shape. He has an obvious motive: he doesn't want to lose his equity, nor that of his brothers and sisters. But he has an additional motive. As a condition of the FinCo loan, Lester gave FinCo his personal guarantee, secured by a mortgage on his personal residence. So if FinCo goes unpaid, Lester may lose not only his business, but his home as well.

§6.5 ~ "Both Ends of the Boat Are Sinking"

Reaching the end of its tether, LittleCo finally decides to try to cut a deal. Lester (and his lawyer) call a meeting of unsecured creditors.[2] Here is what they say:

"Ladies and gentlemen, thank you for coming. We all know why we are here today: LittleCo is in trouble. If matters continue as they are going now, we will be out of business in a matter of months. Naturally we don't want that: if LittleCo goes broke, the owners lose everything.

But both ends of this boat are sinking. If we lose, you lose. Remember this:

- LittleCo has two different 'values.' One is its value in liquidation; the other is its value as a going concern. LittleCo is worth less in liquidation than it is as a going concern. In liquidation, the receivables don't get paid, and inventory sells for distress prices. Moreover in liquidation you lose the 'goodwill value' of an ongoing business—the customer relationships, the market niche, and the other intangibles that LittleCo has worked so hard to maintain.

---

2. That is, the vendors. Interestingly, they do *not* invite FinCo. FinCo is the largest secured creditor in the case. But if things go badly (and if FinCo comes up short), then FinCo may be the largest unsecured creditor as well. Still, everyone agrees that FinCo's stake is different from the stake of the vendors, so Lester will deal with FinCo separately.

- In liquidation, secured creditors get paid first. Practically everything will go to BigBank and FinCo and you will see little or nothing.

- If we can maintain LittleCo as a going concern, we can pay part or all of your claim.

- But there is another reason why you need as a going concern. The reason is that you need us as a customer. For some of you, we are your major customer: if we go, you go. For others, even if we aren't a major customer, we help you to keep our competitors (your other customers) in line: if we go, they will demand better goods and services at lower prices.

- So clearly, it is in your interest to preserve the going concern. But in order to keep this business in operation as a going concern you need the cooperation of us, the old owner/managers. We have the special knowledge and the institutional memory. These are the assets that create the going concern value. Without us, these assets dissipate and you are left empty-handed."

§6.6 ~ The Offer

"This is our appeal to your self-interest. Now here is our offer. It has three parts:

- Give us some time and some cooperation so we can restore the value of the going concern—thus increasing the asset side of the balance sheet, generating more money with which to pay your claim.

- Accept some reduction in the amount of your claim—thus reducing the liability side of the balance sheet, making it easier for us to pay you.

- Leave something on the table for us—that is, leave us with all (or at least part) of our old equity stake."

§6.7 ~ Will They Buy It?

Such, in summary, is LittleCo's pitch to its creditors. Note that compassion or generosity have nothing to do with it: this is an appeal purely to self interest, as LittleCo tries to persuade unsecured creditors that they have, in effect, a joint problem, which they must solve together. Will it work? One answer is that it has worked a thousand times. Over the generations, countless creditors have recognized that it is in their interest to make a deal on these lines, and have made agreements of just this sort.

§6.8 ~ Technique: Be Prepared

Our experience is that the debtor is most likely to accomplish his purpose at the workout meeting if it presents financial information that is complete, accurate and well organized. The creditor is unhappy just to be there: you've already destroyed his confidence, and he may be more than a little bitter. You've got an uphill fight to convince him that you are honest and competent. Of course you have troubles of your own. But this is the day to put on your very best face.

A deal is possible, but it is not inevitable. After LittleCo makes its pitch, and before they decide whether to take it, creditors will retire for a private conference on their own (while Lester is left to chew his fingernails or pray). Here is the kind of questions that creditors will consider:

- Did Lester get the story right? Is this truly a matter of one-off past misfortune, never to be repeated? Or is this really a failing business—and is Lester too incompetent, or too blinded by self-deception, to understand what is going on?

- Worse, could it be that Lester is lying—that he is embezzling, or siphoning off assets in our ignorance, while trying to deceive us?

- Short of blatant theft, we know that Lester guaranteed the FinCo debt, but he did not guarantee our debt. This gives him a powerful motivation to see to it that FinCo gets paid, even if we get nothing. Is he skewing the story so as to protect FinCo?

- Is this business really worth more as a going concern? Some businesses are worth more as a going concern, but some are worth more in liquidation. For example, consider the building. Maybe it is worth no more than $4 million to LittleCo. But maybe another business would pay us twice as much—in which case, maybe the best thing to do with LittleCo's business is to close it down, and sell the building to a condominium developer.

- Even if the business is worth more as a going concern, do we really want it as a going concern? Some of us creditors are also competitors. Maybe we would rather see LittleCo go out of business so we get rid of the competition?

- If Lester is right that we need the going concern value, is he also right that we need him? If Lester can't pay us, the business really belongs to us. Maybe we should just take it and get someone else to manage it—or, if he has such wonderful knowledge, just hire him back as a salaried manager.

- Even if the deal makes sense, does it strike us as fair? Is Lester insisting on too much for himself and his friends? Has he been taking too much out of LittleCo in this time of trouble?

- Has Lester treated us respectfully and provided complete and honest answers to our questions? Has he been cooperative?

Note that none of these questions affect the economics of the deal itself. But if we aren't happy, we may refuse to deal just to save our dignity, even if we would be better off to scrap the dignity and take the deal.

§6.9 ~ The Deal

After—and only after—they have palavered over this kind of questions, the creditors agree upon a proposal:

- Unsecured creditors agree to settle for payment on their old claims as follows: 30 percent cash within six months of the day the deal closes, plus 40 percent of the net revenues of LittleCo for the next five years.

- Creditors get to name an independent accountant to define the meaning of "net revenues."

- Creditors get "refusal rights" on LittleCo's chief financial officer: that is, Lester may choose the CFO, but creditors get to veto the choice.

- Creditors will appoint one member of LittleCo's board of directors.

- Old equity owners retain their equity stakes unchanged.

This is at least a possible deal, and on the right facts, creditors may decide that it is a very good deal. A not inconsiderable virtue is that it avoids bankruptcy. This is important because bankruptcy has a downside for everybody. For the debtor, it is like major surgery—he's never sure when he goes under the anaesthetic whether he will ever achieve consciousness again. And for the creditors, it means a whole new set of costs and inconveniences. So, weighing costs of bankruptcy against the advantages of the deal, creditors may well decide just to take their money and run.

§6.10 ~ It Makes You Wish for Bankruptcy

All this is true enough in the abstract but, on second look, things are not as simple as they seem. The practical fact is that there are all kinds of obstacles that may keep this deal from being consummated outside of bankruptcy—or, even if consummated, from being carried out.

To see that this is so, start with the size of the creditor body. We saw that there are some 150 unsecured creditors. Just getting many of them together in one place may be impossible. But far worse—suppose we do get them together, and suppose that 90 percent agree on a plan, such as the plan set forth above. The hard fact is that even with 90 percent agreement, there is nothing (absent bankruptcy) to restrain the dissenters. This is important for at least three reasons.

- **Door-shut Panic:** Any individual creditor might choose to go ahead and get a judgment, and execute his claim. We don't need to assume any malice here; we merely assume that he wants to look out for himself. The trouble is that any one creditor can set off a race to the courthouse—as everybody races to get through the closing door.

- **What, Me Worry?** Even if creditors don't sprint for the courthouse, any individual creditor may stymie the whole plan. Suppose the dissenter levies on inventory. Without inventory, there may be no way to preserve the going concern value, and the business may die. The levy may leave all the other creditors holding an empty bag, but the levying creditor may have no incentive to care.

- **Stop, Pay Troll:** Suppose the debtor has assets on hand of $100 and 10 creditors with claims aggregating at $1,000. With the purpose of saving the going concern value, all creditors may agree it is in their interest to settle for the assets on hand, accepting just 10 cents on the dollar and forgiving the balance.

But suppose instead that one creditor, with a claim of $1, refuses to go along with the deal: he demands that he be paid in full; else he will go ahead and liquidate his claim. Fine, he is a nuisance, pay him off and get him out of the case—that is, give him his dollar and let $999 worth of claims share the $99 remainder. The percentage change is almost invisible (creditors now get just 9.91 percent of their claims[3]). Since there is no way to impose the plan on the dissenter, this may be the price of doing the deal.

So any single creditor may have the incentive to be a holdout—the troll at the troll-bridge who demands payment as a condition of getting the deal. The trouble is that if any one creditor has an incentive to be a troll, then all creditors have the incentive to be a troll. And if everyone waits for everyone else to make a deal, then no deal gets made.

All of these problems arise from the difficulty of organizing and controlling a multitude of creditors—the more creditors, the harder it will be to do a deal. But there is another, more basic problem that may arise even in a simple case. That is: are you sure state law allows you even to make an enforceable deal?

Before you reject the question as silly, go back in your mind to your first year in law school, and the course in contracts. Remember the pre-existing duty rule ("PED"). PED holds that payment of less than all you owe cannot be consideration for a promise to release the balance of the claim. Why not? Because you already owed the debt in the first place (this is the "pre-existing duty" part). And so the promise to release is not binding, and the creditor can go ahead and sue for the balance, even though he gave the release.

We suspect that PED isn't very good law any more. But we're not at all sure we want to stake our malpractice insurance on the opinion. If we were representing the debtor trying to cut a deal like the one above, we'd be aching for a device that would give us the assurance to say that the debtor really did get the release he bargained for.

Tactic: Reducing Chances of a Holdout. Because of the holdout problem, it is common for debtors, in soliciting acceptance of a workout agreement, to provide that the agreement will be implemented only if a specified percentage (say, 90 percent) agree to it. Of course, this does not prevent a holdout, but it does reduce the chances.

Lots of deals happen, even in the face of these obstacles. Still these impediments leave us searching for a device that will:

- help us to organize creditors;
- stay the buzzards from picking over the carcass before it is dead;

---

3. 99/999 = 0.0991 = 9.91 percent.

- prevent a holdout from becoming a holdout; and
- assure the enforceability of our deal.

Enter chapter 11.

§6.11 ~ Enter Chapter 11

We think you can understand what chapter 11 can do if you first understand what non-bankruptcy law cannot do. In short, we suggest that chapter 11 offers at least a partial solution to each of the four problems outlined above:

- In chapter 11, the debtor files schedules, and statements of affairs, giving full information about his creditors and his claims. There is a meeting of creditors. There may even be a committee of creditors. All of these help to give some structure and framework, and help to solve the problem of organization.
- The filing of the petition imposes the automatic stay. As we explain elsewhere, the stay may protect the debtor; but it also protects the assets of the estate, and solves the problem of the buzzards. *See* chapter 7 below, "The Automatic Stay."
- If a plan gets the assent of a majority in number and two-thirds in amount of impaired classes, then the plan may be imposed on dissenters. This does not eliminate, but it certainly reduces, the problem of the holdout. *See* Chapter18 below, "Confirming a Plan."
- If the plan is confirmed, then the debtor gets a discharge. Court approval affords all parties assurance that the deal is enforceable. *See* Chapter 17 below, "Discharge and Dischargeability."

In fact, there is a lot more to chapter 11 than this. So far, we have said nothing about secured claims—but in fact, in chapter 11 we may be able to rewrite the contract on the secured claim, even against the secured creditor's will. Moreover, bankruptcy offers a schedule of priorities for payment. Sometimes, this schedule of priorities is different from what is available at state law; so a favored creditor may be motivated to trigger a bankruptcy just to get the bankruptcy priorities, *see* §§13.35 ff.

Further, in some places bankruptcy changes the substantive rights of creditors. For example, it may cap the claims of landlords and terminated employees. Stakeholders who benefit from these impositions may trigger the bankruptcy just to take advantage of them, *see* §11.26. And, of course, bankruptcy may permit the recovery of certain pre-petition payments: this fact alone may be a sufficient motivation for filing, *see* Chapter 14, "Avoiding Powers."

§6.12 ~ Don't Believe a Word of It

Such is a general sketch of a classic chapter 11. The best we can guess, it is pretty much what the drafters had in mind when they wrote the Bankruptcy Code. The problem is, we suspect that there are few cases filed today that look anything like the classic model. The reasons are varied. For one thing, people have figured out ways to sidestep the problems that drive them toward chapter 11 in the first place—or, if the cost of chapter 11 looks too high, simply to bear the cost. Second, lawyers for desperate clients have figured out ingenious uses for chapter 11. And third, the market has changed and deals look different today.

To get a feel for the changes, here are a few other things that you can do via chapter 11—*i.e.*, things that bear little or no resemblance to the classic case set forth above.

- **Sell It to the Creditors.** The plan cancels all the old debt and all the old equity interests. It issues new equity to the old creditors. This is certainly a plan. Some scholars like to say that the point of chapter 11 is to sell the business to the creditors. But it's a plan you almost never see in practice. The old owners won't propose it because it wipes them out. Less obviously, the old creditors won't propose it because they don't want the business either: they just want to get paid. Nevertheless, you do see, with some frequency, plans that convert at least some debt to equity. It is a way to improve the debtor's balance sheet, and creditors who will be forced to take an equity-type risk may want the potential for equity-upside.

- **Sell It to a Stranger.** The plan proposes that the business be sold as a going concern to a third party, after which the proceeds be distributed to creditors as their interests may appear. This kind of plan is undoubtedly lawful under the Code and in fact, these days it is perhaps the commonest kind of chapter 11 plan. But there are several oddities. Most obviously, it looks an awful lot like a liquidation. The alert observer will ask why the case is in chapter 11 (instead of chapter 7) at all. There are several answers to that question. For one, the trustee would rather suffer a root canal than operate a going concern, even for the short time necessary to permit a sale. A second answer is that the creditors may prefer to have the case in chapter 11, where the debtor can remain as DIP, than to put up with the expense of a trustee. Third, of course the old managers will make every effort to stay in chapter 11, where they remain in control. A related puzzle is: What do you do with the case after the sale? Now the DIP holds nothing but a pot of money. He could propose a plan—but the plan would say no more than: We propose to distribute the money among creditors as their interests may appear. At this point, it may well be better and cheaper just to convert to chapter 7—or, if you can get creditor approval, simply to dismiss.

- **Dissolution with Dignity.** This example is a little like putting down a beloved old Doberman. The debtor is (for example) a retailer. Everyone agrees that the business has no future. But everyone also agrees that they can squeeze more out of the assets if they operate through the holiday season and liquidate the inventory at retail, rather than going through a distress sale or a bulk transfer. Under close creditor sponsorship and supervision, the DIP supervises the sale.

- **Impose an Unfriendly Plan.** As we will explain at more length later, it is sometimes possible to impose at least part of a plan on creditors against their will, *see* §18.2. But it's easier said than done. To take just one example, even the most adverse plan requires at least one "impaired consenting class." And chapter 11 is supposedly not meant to enable a debtor to bully its creditors into submission. But surely there is some number of cases where the creditors have accepted a deal that is voluntary only in the most abstract sense—where, in fact, they have simply thrown up their hands and taken a deal to get done with it, rather than suffer worse treatment under an unfriendly plan.

As a general catalog, this is probably a pretty good start. But it hardly the end of things. There are any number of other purposes to which chapter 11 has been turned, limited only by the ingenuity of counsel.

There is nothing inherently wrong with this. The difficulty comes up only when you try to explain chapter 11. It brings us to the central question: What is chapter 11 for?

§6.13 ~ What is Chapter 11 For?

A threshold difficulty of anyone trying to make sense out of chapter 11 is that we can't make up our mind what we want chapter 11 to do. There are two possibilities:

- Chapter 11 is designed to preserve asset value, including going concern values (call it the asset view).
- Chapter 11 is designed to give the old equity[4] owners a second bite at the apple (call it the equity view).

These two goals may go together but there is no certainty that they will, and far more often, the debtor's gain will be the creditor's loss (and vice versa). Similarly, there can be no doubt that some provisions of the Bankruptcy Code serve both purposes, while some serve one alone, and some the other. Moreover, the Bankruptcy Code doesn't always make itself clear as to just which purpose it is serving when. Of course this may be the result of poor drafting. But at least as likely, the confusion is intentional, as if we wanted a Code that lets us work at cross purposes without quite owning up to the fact.

You can see this difficulty when you try to make sense of the concept of "reorganization." The Code says that chapter 7 is about "liquidation" and that chapter 11 is about "reorganization."

But reorganization is nowhere defined in the Code. A common view is that reorganization means to continue the business as a going concern *and* "with the equity interests in the hands of the old equity owners" —the equity view, as set forth above. It is easy to find support for this reading in chapter 11. Most important, only the debtor (for which read: the old equity owners) may propose a plan during chapter 11's exclusivity period. Except in the most special of circumstances, the old equity owners will not propose a plan that wipes out old equity owners. So exclusivity keeps them in control.[5]

Beyond the exclusivity rule, there are other provisions of the Code that appear calculated to keep the old equity in control. Perhaps most notable is the rule that in chapter 11, unless the court orders otherwise, the debtor (read: old equity owners) continues in possession (as DIP), with power to continue to operate

---

4. Except where noted, in this discussion we have in mind an incorporated debtor where the former managers, ultimately answerable to shareholders, remain in control. We recognize that there are at least two other classes of chapter 11 case. One is the case of the individual debtor. And the other is the case of the corporate debtor where the old equity-managers have been kicked out prior to the filing. We don't think our argument would look much different in either of these cases, but for simplicity's sake, we ignore them for now.

5. Section 1121.

the business.[6] We shall see later that there is plenty of uncertainty over just how far the DIP can go in tilting toward equity. For the moment, suffice it to say that he can go far enough to support the equity view.

But this isn't the end of it. The fact remains that on close reading, there is also plenty of support for the contrasting "asset view." For example, the DIP isn't permitted to do just anything in chapter 11. He is specifically enjoined to act as if he were a trustee.[7] A chapter 11 plan may also provide for "sale of all or any part of the property of the estate."[8] So a lawful can plan (and many plans do) provide for sale of all of the property of the estate—perhaps as a going concern, if that is the way to maximize asset value. This may or may not leave value in the hands of the old equity, but it certainly doesn't leave the business under their control.[9]

§6.14 ~ Two Problems That Never Go Away: Risk and Time

We have talked about the DIP acting adversely to the interest of creditors. We have been a little vague on what we meant by that, although it is easy enough to guess. It is easy to picture managers who spirit away assets to private offshore bank accounts, or dissipate them in management perks and high living. But we want to talk now about two demons of DIP management that we think are more pervasive, and harder to cope with. These are the problems of risk and time. Our point is that when the balance sheet is leveraged, the creditors and the equity owners have different stakes, and different motivations. We summarize:[10]

- Equity owners overvalue risk; creditors undervalue it.
- Equity owners of insolvent enterprises always gain from more time.

---

6. Sections 1108, 1107.

7. Section 1107.

8. Section 1123(a)(5)(D); cf. (a)(5)(B), (C).

9. As if to complicate matters, compare what you can do in chapter 7. As a general matter, it's fair to say that chapter 7 foresees piecemeal liquidation of the estate. Section 704. But the court *may* permit the business to continue to operate in chapter 7 as well. Section 721. So the trustee *may*, in chapter 7, arrange to sell the business as a going concern—and probably should do so if that is the way to maximize the estate. In fact, the chapter 7 trustee rarely seeks court approval to operate, nor sell the business as a going concern. Just exactly why not is a topic for speculation. Our own best guess is that the matter is cultural—that people are ingrained to thinking that chapter 11 is for going concerns and chapter 7 is for piecemeal liquidations, even though on the face of things, either chapter would allow the other.

10. We note in passing that strictly speaking, these problems are by no means restricted to the DIP. They would apply to anyone managing a highly leveraged asset pool. But the issue seems to come up most often in DIP cases.

§6.15 ~ Risk: Balance Sheet

First, risk. Consider LittleCo, a corporation. The only asset of LittleCo is $100 cash in the bank. It has no liabilities. The balance sheet looks like this:

LittleCo
Balance Sheet

Assets		Liabilities & NW	
Cash	$100	Liabilities	$ 0
		Net Worth	$100
Total	$100	Total	$100

Now, suppose LittleCo managers have a chance to invest the whole $100 in a project. There is a 10 percent chance that the project will succeed, yielding $900. There is a 90 percent chance it will fail, yielding nothing. Any odds-maker knows that the value of the project is:

$$0.1\ (\$900) + 0.9\ (0) =$$
$$\$90 + 0 = \$90$$

So, in effect, LittleCo is being asked to spend $100 to get $90. No manager in his right mind will take the deal. But suppose that LittleCo is not all-equity financed, but has $75 in debt, so its balance sheet looks like this:

LittleCo
Balance Sheet

Assets		Liabilities & NW	
Cash	$100	Liabilities	$ 75
		Net Worth	$ 25
Total	$100	Total	$100

Reconsider the same offer. Recall that LittleCo is a corporation, so the shareholders have no personal liability for the debts of LittleCo. The only money they have at risk is their equity stake, here $25. If the project succeeds, the shareholders get $900 minus the $75 that it will take to pay the debt. Formally,

$$0.1\ (\$900 - \$75) + 0.9\ (0) = 0.1\ (\$825) = \$82.50$$

Recall that the shareholders have only $25 at risk. This means they are being asked to risk $25 to get $82.50, which is probably a very good deal.

We can make the same kind of analysis of the debt. If the project succeeds, debt gets paid. But there is only a ten percent chance of success. And if the project fails, debt gets nothing. So the stakes for debt are:

$$0.1\ (\$75) + 0.9\ (0) = \$7.50$$

So if LittleCo takes the risky project, the value of the debt falls to $7.50, while the face value remains at $75. We can even put together a "weighted" balance sheet that looks like this:

LittleCo
Balance Sheet

Assets		Liabilities & NW	
Project	$ 90	Liabilities	$7.50
		Net Worth	$ 82.50
Total	$ 90		$ 90

In other words if LittleCo takes the project, equity is *better* off even though LittleCo as a whole (and the creditors) are *worse* off. But managers who are beholden to equity and not to debt will be motivated to take the risk even so. This is what we mean when we say that equity overvalues risk, and debt undervalues it.

§6.16 ~ Time

Next, consider time. For analysis, suppose that LittleCo is insolvent with a balance sheet as follows:

LittleCo
Balance Sheet

Assets		Liabilities & NW	
Cash	$ 80	Liabilities	$ 100
		Net Worth	<$20>
Total	$ 80		$80

If the creditors liquidate today, then creditors get everything and equity gets nothing.

Now, suppose there is a project that costs $80 and offers a 50 percent chance of yielding $220, with a 50 percent chance of yielding nothing. Taking the project as a whole, the weighted value is:

$$0.5\ (\$220) + 0.5\ (0) = \$110$$

From the standpoint of equity, the value is

$$0.5\ (\$220 - \$100) + 0.5\ (0) = \$60$$

And from the standpoint of debt:

$$0.5\ (\$100) + 0.5\ (0) = \$50$$

The "weighted" balance sheet looks like this:

LittleCo
Balance Sheet

Assets		Liabilities & NW	
Project	$110	Liabilities	$ 50
		Net Worth	$60
Total	$110		$ 110

So the equity owners are motivated not to liquidate today, but to wait and try the project. We can generalize the point: risk is always as function of time—the more time you have, the greater the chance that something will turn up. The equity owners of the insolvent enterprise have nothing to lose by waiting—they have lost everything already. Any chance of gain is better than no gain at all. And this is what we mean when we say the equity always gains from more time.[11]

The point is particularly sharp here in a case where the decision to take the project would increase the aggregate value of the assets (from $80 to $110) while reducing the value of the creditor's claim (by imposing more risk).

The math here is noncontroversial. And while the example is stylized, the principles are perfectly well understood in life. Anyone understands the point who ever complained about the debtor "gambling with the creditor's money." So also anyone who ever begged the bank for more time. As in life, so also in law. Every state has statutes governing debt collection and mortgage foreclosure. And virtually every one of these statutes includes some sort of a time rule that assures the debtor will not be sold out "too quickly." Most of these rules are non-waivable—that is, the parties cannot contract around them (at least not in advance of default), not even if both debtor and creditor want to do so.

11. The same can be said about any other out-of-the-money class; you will often see subordinated bondholders playing for more time.

But any way you go at it, the fact remains that equity likes risk and time, while debt doesn't like either. Now we need to go back to the case of the DIP. In reconciling this irreconcilable conflict, how far is the DIP bound to serve debt? And how far can he tilt to equity? To understand this problem, it may be helpful to step back a moment from bankruptcy law, and to consider the problem in the context of general principles of fiduciary duty.

§6.17 ~ Why the DIP?—Two Reasons

Another way to see this double purpose is to consider the role of the DIP. Why leave the debtor in a chapter 11 case? One's first thought is that the purpose must be to give the old equity a tactical advantage. For the practical fact is that DIP surely will not behave with the same detachment you would expect from a trustee, no matter how earnest and high principled.

And this is surely at least one reason why Congress mandated a DIP. The wrinkle is that there is another and very different reason to leave the debtor in possession. That is the matter of creditor economy. Suppose the old owner really is (as the saying goes) "honest but unfortunate." And suppose the alternative is a to put in a stranger—a stranger who may or may not himself be honest but who in any event will face a costly learning curve while he comes to understand the debtor's business. In cases like this, it is easy to see why it may be in the interest of creditors to leave the debtor in possession—and so the DIP rule can be understood as serving the "asset" view of the case, just as much as the "equity" view.[12]

§6.18 ~ Learning from Corporate Law

To understand the question of tilt to equity, we start with (non-bankruptcy) corporate law. What is the duty of directors (or managers) of a corporation before bankruptcy?

Here is a sketch of an answer: Shareholders elect directors who appoint managers. Managers owe duties to both creditors and shareholders. But traditional doctrine says that the managers' duty to shareholders is a fiduciary duty, while they may deal with creditors "at arms' length."[13] This would seem to suggest that managers can "tilt to equity" in making corporate decisions.

By comparison, traditional bankruptcy doctrine says that the trustee for an insolvent estate owes a fiduciary duty to creditors, rather than solely to equity owners.[14] This might seem to be a departure from the

12. A possible third reason for the DIP rule cuts between these first two. The third reason is that a manager will not file a chapter 11 when he should if he knows he will be ousted by a trustee. Allowing the debtor to remain in possession gives the manager the courage to make the right decision.

13. CFTC v. Weintraub, 471 U.S. 343, 354 (1985). A dramatic instance of "no fiduciary duty to creditors" is Metropolitan Life Insurance Co. v. RJR Nabisco, Inc., 716 F. Supp 1504 (S.D.N.Y. 1989), where a management buyout took a conservative old corporate balance sheet and piled on $19 billion of new debt, driving down the value of the old publicly traded bonds. The court rejected all attempts to fashion anything like a fiduciary duty in favor of the old bondholders. *Id.* at 1524.

14. Strictly speaking, the conventional view probably is that he owes a duty to unsecured creditors, in preference either to the secured creditors or equity owners. In fact, none of this is written in the Bankruptcy Code, and one could just as well read the Code as providing that he owes a duty to all parties as their interests might appear. *But see In re* Nadler, 8 B.R. 330 (Bankr. E.D. Pa. 1980) (trustee "primarily represents the unsecured creditors, and represents the secured creditors only in his capacity as a custodian of the property upon which they have a lien," *quoting In re* American Fidelity Corp., 28 F. Supp. 462, 471 (S.D. Cal. 1939)).

corporate rule. But on closer scrutiny, it's not a departure at all. Consider: if the debtor in bankruptcy is truly insolvent, then by definition, the old equity owners are wiped out and the old creditors are the equity in fact if not in name. So to say that the trustee is a fiduciary for creditors is no more than a special case of the general principle that a manager owes a fiduciary duty to the residual class—which is equity in a solvent company, but creditors in an insolvent one.

But a moment's reflection will suggest that there is nothing magical about bankruptcy per se. If there is a duty to creditors when the debtor is insolvent, then the duty ought to apply independent of whether bankruptcy has intervened. On this principle a growing body of case law holds that directors owe a duty to creditors (as well as to shareholders) once the corporation is insolvent even if there has not been a bankruptcy filing.[15]

A wholly different view of the manager's duty tries to bypass the creditor-equity distinction by directing its attention to the asset side of the balance sheet, independent of the liability side. On this view, the duty of the manager is to maximize the value of the assets without regard to who owns them. This is most familiar in its guise as the "Revlon auction doctrine," after the case that gave it birth.[16] Brutally oversimplified, *Revlon* holds that when the company is "in play"—when raiders are trying to stage a takeover—then it is the duty of the manager to get the highest price for the assets on sale.

Revlon created a great stir in the financial community and got a lot of attention from professors. But it is surely about as popular as a rattlesnake in the bathtub with corporate managers. That would include big company managers who believe that their perks and position depend on preventing a takeover. It would just as well include small company managers who think of the company as "their" company, no matter how much of it might belong to the bank. In any event, it isn't really "law" much of anywhere, not even in the jurisdiction that gave it birth.[17]

§6.19 ~ The Courts and the DIP

If it is really so clear that the fiduciary duty runs to "owners," and if that can include creditors whenever the debtor is insolvent, whether or not he is in bankruptcy, then you would think the rest would be easy. But for good reasons or bad, there is a raft of doctrine running the other way.

Foremost, as we suggest above, is the statute itself. The practical result of a DIP rule is to help old equity, even if that is not its only purpose. "Exclusivity" may help to preserve asset values; but its most important practical consequence is that it favors old equity. The courts for their part show an irreconcilable ambivalence over just how much time the equity owners take and what sort of risks they may take.[18]

---

15. *See, e.g.*, Geyer v. Ingersoll Publications Co., 621 A.2d 784, 787 (Del. Ch. 1992).

16. Revlon, Inc. v. MacAndrews & Forbes Holdings, Inc., 506 A.2d 173 (Del. 1985).

17. Or at any rate, sharply restricted. *See, e.g.*, Paramount Communications, Inc. v. QVC Network, Inc., 637 A.2d 34, 43 (Del. Supr. 1994); Paramount Communications, Inc. v. Time Inc., 571 A.2d 1140, 1150 (Del. Supr. 1990).

18. About the strongest recent tilt to equity case —by no means a general rule—is Hansen, Jones & Leta, P.C. v. Segal, 220 B.R. 434 (D. Utah 1988). For what it is worth, outside the United States this is a view is widely held and well established. In many countries, a manager who continues to run his business after he is insolvent may be guilty of fraudulent trading.

At one extreme are cases like *In re Kendavis Industries International, Inc.*,[19] which seem to suggest that any tilt towards equity is improper, no matter how trifling. *Kendavis* is indeed uncompromising in its insistence on the manager's duty not to favor equity. But the facts of *Kendavis* are perhaps distinctive. The record suggest a residuary owner who had determined that he was willing to destroy himself if necessary, so long as he did harm to his creditors.

A much different perspective comes from *Committee of Equity Security Holders v. The Lionel Corporation*,[20] where an equity committee sought to delay the sale of a block of stock in a subsidiary. Creditors wanted the sale to go forward to produce a pot of cash from which to formulate a plan. Lower courts approved the sale but the circuit, in a 2-1 vote, reversed. In one perspective, this would seem to be a classic "debtor gets more time" case. Judge Winter, dissenting, acidly dismissed the ploy as a "Hail Mary pass"—a last-minute desperation maneuver by a residual claimant who had everything to lose by quick sale and everything to gain from delay.

Judge Winter's view is beguiling. An embarrassment is that the Hail Mary pass connected: in the end, Lionel sold the stock for substantially more than the original bid, and the lawyer for the equity committee sought (and got) a premium fee from the estate for his obstructionism (or "contribution," depending on your point of view).

For a different view of risk management, compare *Chrysler Credit Corp. v. Perry Chrysler Plymouth, Inc.*,[21] where the debtor took $100,000 of funds held in trust for Chrysler and took them to Las Vegas, where he lost them in about three days.

The Fifth Circuit held the debt nondischargeable under the "fraud or defalcation" rule of Section 523(a)(6). It's not easy to put your finger on what distinguishes the gamble that was endorsed in Lionel and the one that was denounced in *Perry*. In *Perry*, if the debtor's lawyer had advised him to put everything on "no-pass" and had won, would the lawyer have been entitled to a fee enhancement?

Lionel is hardly alone. In a remarkable recent decision, the judge had to consider the case of some defaulting borrowers who had consented to allow a representative of the mortgagee on each of their boards. The governance documents required unanimous consent for all board decisions—so the lender's designated board member had an effective veto over the board behavior.

The debtors defaulted and the lender began foreclosure proceedings. The principal owner of the borrower, knowing that the borrower could not file chapter 11 because the lender's board member would not approve it, invited unsecured creditors to file an involuntary, which they did (he even paid the retainer).

---

19. 91 B.R. 742 (Bankr. N.D. Tex. 1988).

20. 722 F.2d 1063 (2d Cir. 1983).

21. 783 F.2d 480 (5th Cir. 1986).

The lender moved to dismiss the cases as bad faith filings in violation of Section 1112(b). The court denied the motion and instead criticized the "lender's director" for breaching a fiduciary duty to the limited partners.[22]

Another such is the *Marvel Entertainment* case,[23] where the court held that shareholders are not stayed from voting to replace directors in chapter 11, although the vote was presumptively designed to get a larger share for equity. The court said their action was not a "clear abuse." The court defined a "clear abuse" as "a willingness to risk rehabilitation altogether in order to win a larger share for equity."[24]

Perhaps the most tantalizing case of all is *Fulton State Bank v. Schipper*.[25] The debtor was a farmer. In chapter 11, he sold some farm land to his parents. Later it emerged that the parents had resold the land to a neighbor for a higher price. On inquiry, the bankruptcy judge refused to interfere. He found as a matter of fact that the family relationship was known to everyone prior to sale, and that the resale to the neighbor was part of a deal that came along later, not an under-the-table side arrangement at the time of the first sale. He was upheld by the district and the circuit.[26]

Cases like this are fact-specific and it is impossible to find any direct point of comparison. Still, it is hard to believe that courts would tolerate this kind of self-dealing from other fiduciaries, such as a corporate executive or the trustee under a consensual trust—or, for that matter, from a bankruptcy trustee.[27] One is compelled at least to speculate that the court felt there was something special about a DIP.

A rather different spin on the issue comes from In *re Central Ice Cream Co*.[28] This was a trustee liquidating case, not a DIP chapter 11. The debtor had only one important asset—a lawsuit against MacDonald's. There was a jury verdict for $52 million and an appeal. There was a settlement proposal at $15 million. Since the debtor owed only $11 million, the settlement provided money enough to produce that rarest of all bankruptcy creatures, a solvent estate.

But Judge Easterbrook (in dicta) suggested that it might not be proper to accept the proposal. He argued, in effect, that the trustee should do whatever maximizes the value of the assets. This means, for example, if the risk-adjusted value of the appeal is (say) $26 million, then the trustee should reject the $15 million settlement and risk the appeal.

---

22. *In re* Kingston Square Associates, 214 B.R. 713 (Bankr. S.D.N.Y. 1997). The debtor had allowed the lender to put his representative on the board as part of a deal to make the debtor a bankruptcy remote entity, and to induce a loan.

23. Official Bondholders Committee v. Chase Manhattan Bank (*In re* Marvel Entertainment Group, Inc.), 209 B.R. 832 (D. Del. 1997), contra, *see In re* Johns-Manville Corp., 801 F.2d 60 (2d Cir. 1986).

24. *Id.* at 838.

25. 109 B.R. 832 (Bankr. N.D. Ill. 1989).

26. 112 B.R. 917 (N.D. Ill. 1990); 933 F.2d 513 (7th Cir. 1991).

27. Indeed, it is a crime for a bankruptcy trustee knowingly to buy assets from the estate, 18 U.S.C. §154(1). *But see* Landscape Properties, Inc., v. Vogel, 46 F.3d 1416, 1426 (8th Cir. 1995) (blessing what appears to be a pretty blatant bid-rigging system); Landscape Properties v. Whisenhunt, 127; F.3d 678 (8th Cir. 1997) (imposing Rule 11 sanction on the objecting attorney for raising the issue).

28. 836 F.2d 1068 (7th Cir. 1987).

Judge Easterbrook's opinion is a clear echo of the "*Revlon* auction doctrine" discussed above, which holds that, if the corporation is in play, then the managers should see that it goes to the highest bidder. Judge Easterbrook seems to be treating the bankruptcy estate as an entity like any other, except with a (possible) negative net worth.

Most trustees will respond with incomprehension to Judge Easterbrook's *Central Ice Cream* opinion. They will say: if we reject a $15 million settlement and take the appeal and lose, then the creditors will sue us for putting their money at risk—and the creditors will win.

One answer might be: if the creditor's suit comes before Judge Easterbrook, and if you can satisfy him that the appeal risk was a "good" one (*e.g.*, that it was worth $26 million), then you will win the creditor lawsuit, even if you lost the appeal. Judge Easterbrook himself suggests a different answer. The pending appeal is an asset, just like any other.

One way to find out what it is really worth is to "put it up for auction," and to let prospective bidders decide for themselves just what they think its worth might be. But this view also seems to be out of keeping with conventional bankruptcy law, where a principle seems to be that some transactions cannot be entrusted to the market and that debtors must be insulated from its uncertainties.[29]

§6.20 ~ Technique: Cultivating Directors

If creditors think the debtor is breaching its fiduciary duty, nothing bars them from ventilating their concerns with individual directors. In a public company, there ought to be at least a couple of directors sufficiently independent to make their own evaluation of management's strategy, and perhaps concerned about avoiding personal liability. For its part, the debtor may be able to turn the tables by creating a committee of non-insider independent directors to make their own decisions on questions of bankruptcy strategy, and thereby to deflect criticism.

§6.21 ~ Caution: Weintraub

One important caution for the DIP comes from the Supreme Court's decision in *Commodity Futures Trading Comm. v. Weintraub*.[30] This is the case where the court held that after a bankruptcy has begun, the debtor's attorney-client privilege belongs to the trustee, and can be waived by the trustee in her good judgment.

Weintraub is a chapter 7 liquidating corporate case, and there is some question just how far it will extend to operating cases, or individual cases, or, indeed, to other privileges. But there is an important practical mandate for the attorney counseling the debtor in pre-bankruptcy planning. That is: he must warn the debtor that there is at least a possibility that their conversations, though privileged outside bankruptcy, may not remain so after the case comes under the jurisdiction of the court.

---

29. It may not be out of keeping with the approach of the Supreme Court in *203 N. LaSalle*. *See* §9.8.

30. 471 U.S. 343 (1985).

Weintraub seems straightforward enough on its own, but it leaves a lot of questions open. For example, who gets to exercise the privilege in an individual case? *In re Hunt*[31] holds that the privilege remains with the individual debtor and does not pass to the trustee. Hunt is interesting because it bears a ringing endorsement of the utility of the privilege, as if to suggest that perhaps the Supreme Court was wrong in *Weintraub* to begin with.

Other courts have held that the privilege does pass to the trustee, at least sometimes. For example, Bankruptcy Judge Yacos in New Hampshire found that "extraordinary circumstances" existed sufficient to permit the trustee to waive the privilege in a case where the debtor had fled the jurisdiction.[32]

One important restriction is that *Weintraub* speaks only to the privilege of confidentiality. The privilege overlaps with, but differs from, the privilege for the attorney's work product. In *re JAP Newcor International Inc.*[33] involves a debtor who demanded to see handwritten notes prepared by counsel to the unsecured creditors' committee. The committee had been disbanded, so there was no "client" around to assert the privilege of confidentiality. But the court, reconsidering and reversing its own earlier order, held there was a work-product privilege that could be asserted by the attorney even after the client had ceased to exist.

§6.22 ~ How the Individual Can Get in Trouble in the Corporate Case

Here is a kind of problem you will encounter over and over in the chapter 11 of the closely-held family firm where there is a "corporation" and a controlling individual shareholder/manager. Bill Belton is president of the Belton Suspender company. The company has not yet, but may soon have to, file for relief under chapter 11. In the ordinary case, we would expect the debtor to remain as DIP, and for Bill to speak as its voice. Bill has always worked hard to "maintain the corporate form," so there is no doubt that he and the company are two different entities. Nevertheless, there are any number of ways in which his individual and his corporate problems may become so intertwined as to impair his performance as spokesman for the DIP—or even, in an extreme case, to cause his removal. Here are some of the main ones:

- Bill wants to save his own job.
- As majority shareholder, he wants to save his equity stake.
- The chances are that Bill has given a personal guarantee to some creditors (*e.g.*, his working capital secured lender) but not others (*e.g.*, the trade creditors).

---

31. 153 B.R. 445 (Bankr. N.D. Tex. 1992).

32. 135 B.R. 717, 723 (Bankr. D. N.H. 1991).

33. 204 B.R. 963 (Bankr. N.D. Ill. 1997).

- Bill may be personally liable for unpaid "trust fund taxes" of the corporation.[34]
- Under non-bankruptcy law, he may face civil or even criminal liability for nonpayment of corporate wages.

Courts in general show a fair amount of elasticity in leaving people like Bill as the voice of the DIP even in the face of conflicts of this sort. But in an extreme case, protecting himself at the expense of creditors clearly is grounds for removal.[35]

§6.23 ~ Bankruptcy Alternatives to Chapter 11

In this book we concentrate primarily on chapter 11. Nonetheless, a lot of what we say (automatic stay, avoiding powers) applies to bankruptcy cases across the board. Other discussions (discharge for individuals) apply alike in chapters 7 and 11. Still for perspective, it is useful that we say at least a few specific words about chapters 7 and 13.

§6.24 ~ Throw the Keys on the Table—Chapter 7

In the classic chapter 7 bankruptcy case, the trustee takes charge of the property and reduces it to cash and distributes it among creditors as their interests may appear.[36] If the (individual) debtor plays by the rules, he gets his discharge. In fact, the vast majority of bankruptcies are chapter 7s. Most are filed by debtors with no (nonexempt) assets. Most are looking for their discharge, and most of them get it.

In the typical case, the lawyer's most important role is giving advice on the decision whether (and under what chapter) to file. He is the one who ought to know whether the debtor really needs the good offices of the bankruptcy court, or whether he will, in fact, be able to enjoy the discharge that he seeks. This is not a mere truism: long experience around the bankruptcy court suggests that there are some cases —maybe a lot —where the debtor gains nothing discernible by filing and simply throws away a "discharge card" that he might need even more later. And plenty of debtors have lost their houses, or suffered otherwise, because they filed under the wrong chapter.

Beyond that, the job of the lawyer is to file the petition, the schedules and the statement of affairs. The critical job here is to make sure that the debtor gives you all the information, and gives it to you right, so there will be no occasion for finger-pointing later. And make sure you claim the right exemptions, *see* §9.2.

For this work, the lawyer may take his fee, and he must disclose what he has taken. The court gets to review the fee and may even make him disgorge if he thinks it excessive.[37] But in just about every district, there is an "off-the-rack" standard fee that he will be able to take without serious inquiry.

---

34. 26 U.S.C. §6672.

35. For a suggestion of how far you have to go, *see In re* V. Savino Oil & Heating Co., 99 B.R. 518, 526 (Bankr. E.D.N.Y. 1989).

36. Section 704(1).

37. Section 329.

A difficulty arises if the case is to be more complicated—particularly if there is to be litigation over discharge or dischargeability. As a minimum, we think the fee agreement should specify that the lawyer is getting his flat fee for the chapter 7 filing only—and that if an issue of discharge arises, then the debtor will have to make a new fee arrangement and pay separately.[38] To avoid misunderstandings on this point, you'd better spell out the possibility in the original engagement letter.

§6.25 ~ CHAPTER 13

Chapter 13 is for "individuals with a regular income"—sometimes (though not quite accurately) called the "wage earner" chapter. This is the chapter where the debtor voluntarily submits a portion of his post-petition earnings for a period of between three and five years to pay pre-petition debts. Recall that post-petition earnings are not part of the estate in the ordinary case. And note that chapter 13 is (at least formally) wholly voluntary—there can be no involuntary chapter 13.

The question naturally arises—if the whole point is to get the debtor to surrender voluntarily some earnings that he would not have to surrender under chapter 7, then why does anyone ever do it? We can think of several answers to that question.

- Perhaps most important, chapter 13 offers a "super discharge," where the debtor gets to discharge many of the claims that would not be dischargeable (per Section 523) in chapter 7—or even in an individual chapter 11.[39]

- The debtor gets to keep property he might lose in chapter 7. For example, suppose he has (nonexempt) tools that he needs to run his business and to generate income. In chapter 7 he might have to surrender them to the trustee. Under a confirmed chapter 13 plan, he will be able to hang onto them. Many individuals have filed under chapter 13 in order to keep their houses, when the equity in the house exceeds the applicable state law homestead exemption.

- The chapter 13 may help impose some structure on the payment of a debt nondischargeable in chapter 7.

- There may be some debts that the debtor just can't walk away from, no matter what the Code says (family debts, credit union debts where his foreman is on the credit union board).

---

38. We suspect that some courts will say that the lawyer is bound to the client for the duration of the case and will not be free to abandon him even if the fee relationship breaks down. But the lawyer who is specific about additional fees for additional litigation in his engagement letter probably has the best chance with the court.

39. Section 1328(a). A source of mischievous merriment for law professors teaching chapter 13 is to find a particularly odious recital of facts on which a debtor appears headed for a clean chapter 13 discharge. *See, e.g.*, Solomon v. Cosby (*In re* Solomon), 67 F.3d 1128 (4th Cir. 1995).

- Although chapter 13 is formally voluntary, the court may dismiss certain chapter 7 petitions if the court finds that the petition is a "substantial abuse." We think the drafters of the "substantial abuse"[40] rule hoped that the courts would use it to leverage some debtors into "voluntary" chapter 13s.[41] We suspect it hasn't requited all the hopes of the sponsors, but it does work that way sometimes.

- Chapter 13 provides a co-debtor stay, unavailable in chapters 7 or 11. A lot of chapter 13 debt is "cosigned." The debtor may be able to use the co-debtor stay to protect compassionate relatives, etc., who might be vulnerable elsewhere.

The chapter 13 narrative runs like this: the debtor files his petition, together with schedules and statement of affairs. He proposes a "plan"—almost always an off-the-rack, check-the-boxes affair. There are two key requirements for confirmation:

- The creditor must be getting at least what he would get in chapter 7. This is the chapter 13 equivalent of chapter 11's "best interest" test.[42] So the debtor who chooses chapter 13 rather than 7 because it has substantial equity in his home may have to propose a full-payment chapter 13 plan in order for it to be confirmable.

- If a party raises the issue, the court may not be confirmed unless the debtor is proposing to pay his disposable income over the life of the plan.[43] This is the so-called "best efforts" test.

If the plan is confirmed, and if the debtor completes it, then he gets the deluxe discharge (contrast chapter 11, where the rule is discharge first, performance later).[44] The difficulty with this is that most chapter 13 debtors are on the ragged edge of nothing to begin with—to expect them to complete a three (some times a five) year plan without incident is expecting a lot. Indeed, the typical chapter 13 docket is an array of supplicants with confirmed plans, asking for a little more time, a little more leeway, to carry out the plan.

If the debtor does not complete the chapter 13 plan as promised, he has three options. He can ask the court to approve a non-deluxe chapter 13 discharge. Or he can convert to chapter 7. Or he can dismiss.[45]

There are limits on who can file for chapter 13.[46] The debtor must be an individual—no partnerships or corporations. And he must have debts that do not exceed $269,250 (unsecured) and $807,750 (secured).

40. Section 707(b).

41. *See, e.g.*, U. S. Trustee v. Harris, 960 F.2d 74, 77 (8th Cir. 1992) (capacity to fund a chapter 13 plan is the primary factor to be considered in deciding whether to dismiss for substantial abuse).

42. Section 1325 (a)(4); cf. §1129(a)(7).

43. Section 1325(b)(1)(B).

44. Section 1328; cf. §1141.

45. Sections 1328(b), 1307(a), (b), Fed. R. Bankr. Proc. 1017.

46. Section 109(e).

But note that the code speaks about "noncontingent" and "liquidated" debts. So if the debtor is sued for (say) $40 million and files while the matter is still in dispute, he may be able to get in under the bar. This explains why, every few months, some famous entertainer, whom you would think of as having as lot of money, winds up in chapter 13.

We hope we haven't sounded disdainful of the chapter 13 process. The fact is, we find it fascinating—one of the truly remarkable (if controversial)[47] aspects of bankruptcy law. Indeed, if you are new to bankruptcy practice, we suspect you could learn a lot by doing a few chapter 13s, at least for practice. But McDonald's doesn't make money by selling just a single Happy Meal. Chapter 13, as the "fast food" chapter of the Bankruptcy Code, runs on volume. If you care for your own solvency, and if you do just one chapter 13, then you had better think about doing a lot of them.

§6.26 ~ Strategy: Filing "Chapter 20" Cases

To combine the benefits of chapters 7 and 13, some debtors will file what has become known as "chapter 20" cases. They file a chapter 7 petition, discharge all of the debts that are dischargeable under chapter 7, and then file a chapter 13 case, to pay off the rest of the debts over time, and get the super discharge. It is hard to believe that Congress intended to validate this "chapter 20" arrangement in the Bankruptcy Code (far more likely, Congress never gave it any thought at all). Some judges take a dim view of it, but the Supreme Court specifically held that it is not *per se* grounds for dismissal.[48]

§6.27 ~ Alternatives to Bankruptcy

For perspective, it is useful to keep in mind that the bankruptcy (including chapter 11) is rarely any more than a last resort after better alternatives have failed. For the debtor, there is the allure of protection and a discharge, but only at great cost and hazard to its very existence. For the creditor, there is the appeal of judicial supervision, but (again) at great cost, and with the considerable likelihood that he'll suffer pains beyond what he would face outside of bankruptcy. Therefore both sides, if they know what is good for them, have a motivation to seek a less intrusive alternative. Here are some alternatives.

§6.28 ~ Receivership

In some cases, the creditor will be able to get the protection he wants from a non-bankruptcy receiver, who takes charge of the property and manages it for the interests of the parties as their interests may appear. In many states, for example, creditors regularly use receivers to manage real estate pending foreclosure. Local collection law may allow a kind of receiver (California calls him a "keeper") to tap the till of an ongoing business, as a device to collect an ordinary claim. Many states allow a receiver as a matter of course on a showing of "waste" or "mismanagement," and some will even allow it as a default remedy if it is provided for in the contract.

---

47. Its detractors see it as a government-subsidized debt collection service—or worse, a form of peonage.

48. Johnson v. Home State Bank, 501 U.S. 78, 87 (1991) ("Congress did not intend categorically to foreclose the benefit of chapter 13 reorganization to a debtor who previously has filed for chapter 7").

A receiver's powers are almost never as broad as the powers of a bankruptcy trustee. The compensation is that he is often cheaper and less intrusive.

§6.29 ~ Assignment for the Benefit of Creditors

With or without the aid of a statute, just about every common law jurisdiction allows the debtor to transfer all his assets to a third party who takes the obligation to liquidate and distribute them for the benefit of creditor. This assignee is typically understood as bearing certain fiduciary duties to the creditors as a body, so he functions as a kind of trustee. An experienced assignee may be able to complete a liquidation with more efficiency (equals "at lower cost") than a bankruptcy trustee.

But he doesn't have nearly the powers of a bankruptcy trustee to (for example) investigate, or to unravel the pre-bankruptcy transactions of the debtor. The very lack of power makes the assignee attractive to a debtor who intends to liquidate, but who has some skeletons in the closet he'd rather not call attention to.

§6.30 ~ Bulk Transfer

Consider LittleCo, with an inventory of widgets, when widgets aren't in fashion. Lester Little, the president, decides to liquidate the inventory at the best available distress price, at his creditors' expense.

What will restrain him? In the old days, one thing that would restrain him was Article 6 of the Uniform Commercial Code, the Bulk Sales Act. Under the Bulk Sales Act, the buyer had to give notice of the sale to general creditors, in time so they make a claim against the proceeds. So the Bulk Sales Act was a kind of primitive non-bankruptcy bankruptcy.[49]

The drafters of the Commercial Code have recommended repeal of the Bulk Sales Act, and at this writing, most states have already done away with it.[50] But in those places where it survives, you might think of it as a bankruptcy alternative.

Why are the drafters hostile to the bulk transfer statute? One reason is that bulk sale can turn into a nightmare if the debtor goes into bankruptcy. On this topic, *see* §15.22.

§6.31 ~ Bankruptcy v. Alternatives: Tradeoffs

The possibility of a non-bankruptcy remedy may impel both sides into a tag-team conflict. If the creditor seeks a receiver, the debtor may up the ante, by seeking to invoke the jurisdiction of the bankruptcy court (and to remain as DIP). If the debtor files an assignment with a "friendly" assignee, the creditor may want to file the bankruptcy to wrest control away from him. The fact of a preexisting receivership (or assignment) may impel the bankruptcy judge to abstain under Section 305. And Section 543(d)(1) allows the court to leave the receiver in place.

---

49. "Bulk sale" is defined as "a sale not in the ordinary course of the seller's business of more than half the seller's inventory . . . if on [the day of sale] the buyer has notice, or after reasonable inquiry would have had notice, that the seller will not continue to operate the same or a similar kind of business after the sale." UCC §6-102(c)(ii).

50. Some 37 states have taken the repeal option and only five (California the largest) have opted for revision. ULA UCC Prec. §6-101, Refs & Annos (1999).

7

The Automatic Stay

7 The Automatic Stay

§7.1 ~ Introduction: Where the Action Is

Back in the 80s, we knew a young lawyer whose first job out of law school was to assist in the liquidation of a failed savings and loan association (S&L). One thing a failed S&L has is plenty of nonperforming loans. So our friend's job was to carry a crate full of files into the front passenger seat of her car and drive from court to court (there were five of them), entering her appearance, and seeking relief from the stay, in case after case.

Times are better now, of course, but the story helps to remind us of a basic fact: the automatic stay is (next to the discharge) probably the single most important fact about bankruptcy and (way ahead of the discharge) the principal source of bankruptcy litigation.

We begin with a form of motion for relief. Then, we go on to explain why the stay is in the Code, and how it works.

§7.2 ~ Form Motion for Relief from the Stay

IN THE UNITED STATES BANKRUPTCY COURT
FOR THE EASTERN DISTRICT OF UTOPIA

In Re: INSOLVENT SUPPLY CORPORATION, Debtor-in-Possession	))))	Case No. 99-1415-BBL (Chapter 11)
In Re: INSOLVENT DISTRIBUTION CORPORATION Debtor-in-Possession	)))))))	Case No. 99-1416-BBL (Chapter 11)

MOTION FOR RELIEF FROM AUTOMATIC STAY

Secured Bancorporation ("Lender") hereby moves for relief from the automatic stay, pursuant to 11 U.S.C. Section Section 362(d)(1) and (d)(2) and Federal Rule of Bankruptcy Procedure 4001(a), to foreclose on its collateral and to exercise its other rights and remedies as a secured creditor. In support of its motion, Lender represents as follows:

I. FACTUAL BACKGROUND

1. This case was filed as a a voluntary chapter 11 case on February 23, 2000.

2. The Debtor owns certain real property improved by a twelve-story office building located in Rockville, Utopia, which is described in more detail as Lot 12, Square 473, Erewhon Estates (the "Property").

3. In 1989, Lender made a loan to Debtor in the original principal amount of $7.3 million to purchase the Property (the "Loan"). The Loan was evidenced by a Promissory Note and was secured by a duly recorded first priority mortgage on the Property, an assignment of rents and leases, and certain other instruments and documents, all of which are listed on Attachment A hereto and are referred to collectively hereinafter as the "Loan Documents."

4. The outstanding principal balance of the Loan, as of the petition date, was $6.9 million. With accrued and unpaid pre-petition interest, fees, costs, and expenses allowed under the Loan Documents, the amount of the Debtor's obligation to Lender, in connection with the Loan, as of the petition date, was at least $7.9 million.

5. The Property has a value of $6.1 million. This value is confirmed by an appraisal performed by Robin Allen, MAI, dated as of March 29, 2000.

II. JURISDICTION AND VENUE

6. This Court has jurisdiction over this motion pursuant to 28 U.S.C. §§1334. This is a core matter pursuant to 28 U.S.C. §§157(b)(2)(G).

7. Venue is proper in this Court in accordance with 28 U.S.C. §§1409.

III. RELIEF UNDER SECTION 362(d)(2)

8. The Debtor has no equity in the Property.

9. The Property is not necessary to an effective reorganization.

10. No reorganization of the Debtor is in prospect.

IV. RELIEF UNDER SECTION 362(d)(1)

11. Lender's interest in the Property is not adequately protected.

12. Lender's interest in the rents generated by the Property, which are an additional item of Lender's collateral, is not adequately protected.

13. Debtor is not able to provide to Lender adequate protection for its interest in the Property or the rents.

14. Debtor is committing and suffering waste and deterioration in the Property. The value of the Property has diminished since the petition date and continues to diminish.

15. The Debtor has not paid real property taxes due and owing on the Property for the post-petition period and Lender has been forced to pay those real property taxes, in the amount of $75,000, in order to avoid the taxes becoming a lien on the Property.

16. For all of these reasons, "cause" exists to grant Lender relief from the automatic stay, as that term is used in Section 362(d)(1) of the Bankruptcy Code.

V. MEMORANDUM OF LAW

17. A memorandum of law is being filed along with this motion and is incorporated herein by reference.

WHEREFORE, Lender requests that the Court grant it relief from the automatic stay, pursuant to Sections 362(d)(2) and 362(d)(1) of the Bankruptcy Code, to foreclose on the Property and to exercise each and every one of its other rights and remedies under the Loan Documents, and that the Court afford such other and further relief as it deems appropriate.

Respectfully submitted,
TIMBERS, TOIBB & STRUMF
By:______________________________
Allen B. Cecill
72 Fifteenth Street
Paradise City, Utopia 94943

ATTORNEYS FOR SECURED BANCORPORATION

Dated: April 4, 2000

§7.3 ~ A Typical Case

Here is a classic automatic stay case. The debtor files a petition for relief under chapter 11 (or 13). He may owe unsecured claims, but in any event he owes a large secured claim, perhaps a mortgage on Blackacre. The petition stays all creditor action against the debtor, and against his property. The unsecured creditors would be delighted to be rid of the case, but they recognize that any effort to get it dismissed, or to extricate themselves, is unlikely to succeed, and would be throwing good money after bad.

The mortgagee recognizes that he also might seek dismissal or conversion of the case. But this motion also is unlikely to succeed and in any event, it entangles him in a conflict with other creditors. On the other hand, he is a mortgagee, with priority rights in Blackacre, the collateral.

He decides to ask the court to give him relief from the stay of creditor action so he can go ahead with his foreclosure independent of—and unencumbered by—the bankruptcy case. He files a motion for relief. The debtor/DIP answers. The motion provides a forum for debtor and creditor to thrash out issues of valuation, possibly a schedule of interim payments, and some sort of understanding as to how long the case will last. More often than not, they reach an agreement and submit a stipulation (under Bankruptcy Rule 4001(d)) for a court order without ever actually presenting their cases.

There is more to the stay than this. But the example suggests the scope and significance of the stay.

§7.4 ~ Two Reasons for the Stay

To understand the stay, it helps to recognize that the stay protects two different interests. One is the interest of the debtor in getting a fresh start. Many subsections of Section 362(a) bar action against the debtor.[1] But the other is the interest of creditors (and perhaps also the debtor) in preserving the estate.

So the stay has a role to play in a case where there are no assets, but the debtor will get a discharge. It also has a role to play in a case where there will be no discharge but there are assets to collect and distribute (and, of course, a role where there are both).

The dramatic fact about the stay is that it is a kind of "statutory injunction," if there can be such a thing, that operates on the filing of a petition, without court initiative and without bond. Imagine a debtor under threat of foreclosure. He believes that with a bit more time, he could come up with the cash to reinstate the obligation, or at least to liquidate the claim without losing the collateral. Outside bankruptcy, is there anything he can do to delay the sale?

The answer is: possibly. Perhaps he can persuade the court to issue a temporary restraining order against sale, but there are obstacles. The debtor must take the initiative and draft the pleading, find a court, schedule a hearing, put on a case, and make an extraordinary showing. And even if he is successful there is a great likelihood that the judge won't effectuate the injunction unless the debtor posts a bond—which means yet more money which is, after all, just exactly what the debtor does not have enough of. Against this, compare the sequence in bankruptcy: the debtor files the petition and the stay is in place.

---

1. *See, e.g.*, §§362(a)(1), (2), (5)-(8).

It's probable that courts have always entertained pleas for restraining orders to delay mortgage foreclosures. The automatic stay worked its way into bankruptcy law by stages. It made its first important appearance in old chapter X, the procedure for the reorganization of large public corporations. That was surely consistent with the premise of old chapter X: if the debtor was truly a "public" problem, then surely it made sense to mandate a single forum for the disposition of all claims against which it might be liable. The stay made its way by degrees into old chapter XI, and even into the liquidation provisions of old chapter VII. It was extended to all cases by the 1978 Act.

One unintended consequence was an explosion of cases where the debtor finds a lawyer who will file a petition without schedules, without prospects—indeed with no sense of what will happen next, but simply seeking the stay to give it more time. In its extreme form this is surely improper, probably a grounds for dismissal and (some might contend) for lawyer discipline. The trouble is, no one quite knows what the "extreme form" might be, and so many such cases have perhaps gone unsanctioned or even undismissed. For more on this issue, see the discussion of "more time" in §6.17.

§7.5 ~ How to Read Section 362

The statutory framework is fairly easy to grasp. Most of what counts is in section 362. Section 362(a) provides that the filing of the petition "operates as a stay" of a great variety of actions against the debtor, and against property of the estate. Section 362(b) itemizes a number of exceptions to the automatic stay. Section 362(c) measures its extent. Section 362(d) sets forth the substantive grounds for relief. Sections 362(e) through (g) govern procedure for getting (or resisting) relief. Section 362(h) is a penalty for willful violation.

As to the scope of the stay, we have already seen that it protects actions against the debtor and also actions against property of the estate. The exceptions (under Section 362 (b)) are a mixed bag, but in general they represent decisions by Congress that certain activities are so important that they trump the policies favoring the stay.

§7.6 ~ Causes of Action

We know that the stay operates to suspend a creditor's cause of action to collect a claim. But to explore the nature of the stay, consider a case where it is the debtor, not the creditor, who wants to go forward with litigation. An example is *Farley v. Henson*.[2] Farley got judgment against Henson in a securities fraud suit, and Henson appealed. Henson also filed for bankruptcy. He undertook to continue his appeal but Farley objected, asserting that the action was stayed as an action against the debtor under Section 362(a)(1). It was the debtor and not the creditor who had taken the appeal. But he argued that the underlying action had been brought against the debtor, and so the stay applied.

The court agreed. It said the decision was supported by the language and policy of the Code. It said also that any attempt to apply or not to apply the stay depending on who brought the underlying action would be unworkable. Many other courts agree. So if Henson wants to continue his appeal, he will have to do

---

2. 2F.2d 273 (8th Cir. 1993).

what any party does when he wants relief from the stay—he will have to file a motion pursuant to Section 362(d).

The analysis is attractive at first blush, but it is perhaps not inevitable. Consider the debtor operating as DIP in a chapter 11 case. He has a great deal of leeway to buy and sell property, to incur liabilities—even to bring lawsuits—all without court approval. It seems strange in this context to conclude that he must get court approval before he can take an appeal.

§7.7 ~ Exceptions

The exceptions to the automatic stay are set forth in section 362(b). Three exceptions are most notable. First, Section 362(a) does not stay the commencement or continuation of a criminal action or proceeding against the debtor.[3] Second, it does not stay any action to enforce a governmental unit's police or regulatory power.[4] Third, there are several types of securities and similar financial transactions that are insulated from the bankruptcy case, ostensibly on the principle that bankruptcy cannot be permitted to interfere with the smooth running of the financial system.[5]

The exception for criminal proceedings has presented complications with respect to the issue of federal-state relations; *see* §4.28.

§7.8 ~ Police or Regulatory

Courts have faced some challenges in trying to disentangle government actions that are stayed from those that are excepted from the stay under the police or regulatory power. An example is *In re National Cattle*.[6] The debtor, operating in chapter 11, ran a dog track on a license from the state racing commission. The Commission determined that it would revoke the license because of the debtor's failure to demonstrate financial responsibility and long-term viability. The day before the decision was to take effect, the debtor asked the bankruptcy court to prevent it.

The debtor asserted that the revocation violated Section 362(a)(1), as an action against the debtor, and Section 362(a)(3), as an action against property of the estate. The commission argued that it there was no violation of 362(a)(1) because it was acting within its "police or regulatory power."[7] It argued that there was no violation of 362(a)(3) because it did not exercise "control over property of the estate."

---

3. Section 362(b)(1).

4. Section 362(b)(4). Bookkeeping note: effective in 1999, former §362(b)(5) was deleted and its substance combined with a revised §362(b)(4). We don't think the revision makes any substantive difference, and so we believe that pre-amendment case law continue, to be relevant.

5. *See* §§362(b)(6) and (7); *see* also §§555, 556, 559, 560.

6. 179 B.R. 588 (Bankr. N.D. Iowa 1995) Caution: insofar as they involve actions against the state, cases like this need to be read against the background of the Supreme Court's newly-conjured state immunity. *See* §4.24.

7. Cf. §362(b)(3).

The court held that the initiation of proceedings to revoke the license was protected by the police or regulatory power exception and therefore permissible under sections 362(a)(1), read with section 362(b)(4). It held that the actual revocation was an action against property of the estate in violation of Section 362(a)(3), for which the "police and regulatory power" exception does not apply. It's not clear to us that this decision was correct, but it does illustrate the struggle courts face in trying to determine when the government is exercising its police and regulatory power and when it is not.

§7.9 ~ Pecuniary Interest

In *National Cattle*, the court stressed that not all action by a government action is protected by the police and regulatory exception. Courts regularly recognize and distinguish between government action under the police power (which is not stayed) and action by a governmental entity to protect a "pecuniary interest" (which is stayed). *In re Mohawk Greenfield Motel Corp.*[8] explores the limits of the "pecuniary" rule. Mohawk ran a motel. Mayhew, an employee, brought a grievance (alleging sexual harrassment) against Mohawk before the Massachusetts Commission on Discrimination ("MCAD").

While the cases were pending, Mohawk filed for chapter 11 relief. The MCAD case continued and at last, MCAD issued a cease and desist order (which sounds like "police or regulatory"). But MCAD also issued a judgment for damages. MCAD argued that a money judgment was proper because it was exercising police or regulatory power, even though in the form of a money judgment.

The debtor cried foul. It argued that MCAD was merely doing Mayhew's work for her, winning a post-petition judgment for a pre-petition liability, in violation of the stay. The court rejected the argument and allowed the judgment to stand. It relied on a long line of cases, many of them involving things like back-pay awards from the National Labor Relations Board. It found that entry of the money judgment was necessary to "ensure future compliance" and so protected under §362(b)(4).[9]

§7.10 ~ What Kind of Action?

Courts have also been called upon to articulate the limits in the kinds of actions that are prohibited by the stay. Taken at face value, it would seem to prohibit even the filing of a claim against the estate—or for that matter, even the filing of an action for relief from the stay itself. But this is absurd and courts have rightly understood it so.

But there are many difficulties in identifying just what, exactly, is stayed. *Javens v. City of Hazel Park*,[10] is a good example. The court held that the police power exception was sufficient to allow the city to continue to demolish properties on grounds that they violated health and safety laws. The case is interesting because it permits the debtor even to be stripped of property where there is a supervening public purpose.

---

8. 239 B.R. 1 (Bankr. D. Mass. 1999).

9. *Id.* at 22.

10. *In re* Javens, 107 F.3d 359 (6th Cir. 1997).

On the other hand, in *S.E.C v. Towers Financial Corp.*,[11] the court said that a proceeding to prevent future violations of the securities laws was not stayed—which is no surprise – even if the government is also seeking a remedy of disgorgement—which is stayed. *Towers Financial* seems different from *Javens*, in that you couldn't cure the health and safety violations in *Javens* without tearing down the building. But it would seem you could perfectly well make and enforce an injunction without an order of disgorgement.

As to the extent of stay protection, Section 362(b) says that stay continues until the case is closed or dismissed or the time of discharge, whichever is earlier. The discharge carries its own stay-like protection so the effect of the discharge is to continue the stay in perpetuity.[12]

Note that the "police or regulatory" exceptions operate only with respect to sections (a)(1) and (a)(2). The creditor is still bound by (say) section 362(a)(3) which bars any act to obtain property of or from the estate. So when the city gave notice of termination of its solid waste hauling contract, the court held the notice was not a violation of (a)(1) but that it did violate (a)(3).[13]

§7.11 ~ Grounds for Relief

To understand the substantive grounds for relief from the automatic stay, we turn to section 362(d). For purposes of analysis, it will be useful to start with section 362(d)(2). It governs relief with respect to an act against property. So this is the section most often invoked when the mortgagee is trying to foreclose. It provides for relief if

- The debtor does not have an equity in such property; and
- such property is not necessary to an effective reorganization.

Consider the case of DealCo, a manufacturing company with a large warehouse where it maintains a fleet of forklift trucks. SellerCo holds a purchase-money security interest in a forklift truck. The balance due on the contract is $50,000. SellerCo has an appraiser who will testify that the truck is worth $30,000. DebtorCo has an appraiser who will say it is worth $70,000.

If the court accepts the testimony of the DebtorCo's appraiser, then the DebtorCo has equity in the property ($70,000 > $50,000) and wins (at least under (d)(2)(B)—but see the discussion of (d)(2)(A), below). But the opposite is not necessarily true. That is, if the court accepts the testimony of the SellerCo's appraiser,

11. 966 F.Supp. 203 (S.D.N.Y. 1997).

12. *See, e.g.*, §§524(a), 1141.

13. *In re* National Envtl. Waste Corp., 191 B.R. 832 (Bankr. C.D. Cal.1996); aff'd 129 F.3d 1052 (9th Cir. 1997), and cert. denied National Waste Corp. v. City of Riverside, 524 U.S. 952 (1998). Indeed, the city may not have been excepted at all, because the notice may have been an exercise of ordinary commercial rather than police or regulatory power. Yet after all that, the judge went ahead and held he would annul the stay. It appears the notice period was eight years, and the judge apparently didn't think the city should have to start the clock all over again.

it is in effect finding that there is no equity in the property ($30,0000 < $50,000). There remains the question whether the property is necessary for an effective reorganization.

Strategy: The "necessary for an effective reorganization" standard allows the parties—both debtor and secured creditor—to preview to the court their confirmation arguments, even before a plan is filed. The creditor gets a chance to try to convince the court that the case is hopeless and that a successful reorganization is unlikely—the debtor is not a financially viable business, has tried without success to obtain financing, has incompetent management, is incurring administrative debt that it will not be able to pay, or cannot obtain an impaired accepting class of creditors, for example. The debtor gets to preview to the court how it intends to make use of chapter 11 to reorganize. The importance of these arguments may go well beyond the disposition of the lift-stay motion, and a lawyer making these arguments must have one eye on the lift stay hearing and the other eye on the upcoming plan confirmation hearing.

The emerging catchphrase seems to be that statute requires no more than "a reasonable possibility of a successful reorganization within a reasonable time." The phrase apparently owes its popularity to Justice Scalia who used it in dicta in a footnote in his majority opinion in *United Savings v. Timbers of Inwood Forest.*[14]

Generalizing, there are many cases where the court has allowed the debtor simply to buy more time, in the hope of coming up with a better deal, or in the hope of getting the creditor to come to terms.

Strategy: A debtor seeking to defeat a §362(d)(2) motion should consider coming to Court with a substantial-looking plan outline, which shows the Court how the debtor might seek to reorganize and signals to the court that the debtor is focused on obtaining confirmation of a plan without undue delay.

§7.12 ~ SAREs Again

A 1994 amendment added the present Section 362(d)(3), applying to (some) single-asset real estate cases (SAREs).[15] That section imposes a 90-day cap on the stay in a single asset case. The stay may be extended if the debtor has filed a plan or commenced paying interest on the secured claim.[16] Whatever the nuances, the provision is dramatic evidence of the proposition that SAREs are in large measure conflicts over time.

---

14. 484 U.S. 365, 376 (1988). He was quoting the en banc opinion of the Circuit Court below. United Savings v. Timbers of Inwood Forest, 808 F.2d, at 370-71, & nn. 12-13.

15. As defined in Section 101(51)(b) (secured debt no greater than $4 million). Congress has proposed to eliminate the $4 million ceiling, so that this provision would apply to all single asset real estate cases, but as of now the $4 million ceiling remains.

16. The plan must have "a reasonable possibility of being confirmed in a reasonable time." Interest must be at the market rate—yet another opportunity for litigation.

§7.13 ~ Technique: The Two-Edged Sword

There is a lurking trap for the unwary in this litigation over "equity." Again, consider DebtorCo's forklift truck. SellerCo, with a claim of $50,000, may be motivated to lead the court to a low valuation, so as to enhance the chances of relief under Section 362(d)(2). But its very success comes back to haunt it later.

Suppose SellerCo argues for relief based on a valuation of $30,000. The Court finds as a fact that $30,000 is the correct value, but then denies relief on a finding that the property is necessary for an effective reorganization. Later DebtorCo proposes a plan, valuing SellerCo's secured claim at $30,000 and allowing an unsecured claim for the $20,000 deficiency. SellerCo's impulse is to resist again, this time arguing that the $30,000 value is too low—that its secured claim should be set at its whole $50,000. Of course the problem is that SellerCo finds that it must climb over its own prior testimony to get to the result.

Creditors who find themselves embarrassed by this inconsistency like to seek refuge in Section 506(a) which provides that valuation "shall be determined in light of the purpose of the valuation and of the proposed disposition or use of the collateral"—as if to suggest that it is perfectly proper to argue for one value early in the case and another value later on. But there may be less protection here than meets the eye. The judge, at least, is likely to remember her own prior decision, and any effort to achieve a different result is likely to be met with skepticism.

From the standpoint of litigation, perhaps the best advice is to remember the old adage that your words should be sweet because you may have to eat them later. In litigation terms, this would counsel the creditor at the beginning of a case to choose a valuation number he can live with, recognizing that he may well have to live with it throughout the case.

For whatever it may be worth, of course the debtor has the same problem in mirror image. If he sets the value too high at the first hearing, he will find himself eating his words at the time of confirmation.

Strategy: A secured creditor who wants to move for relief from the stay under 362(d)(2) but is concerned about the possibility of wanting to argue for higher valuation at confirmation time might try to get the debtor to agree to the following stipulation:

> The parties agree, solely for purposes of the hearing on Creditor's motion for relief from the automatic stay, that the Debtor has no equity in Blackacre. The parties agree that this stipulation will be binding only in connection with the hearing on Creditor's motion for relief from the automatic stay, and will not preclude or prejudice any party's arguments with respect to valuation at any future time.

The Debtor—also concerned about possibly wanting to take an inconsistent valuation position later in the case—may agree, and the Court, which will be saved a day or two of valuation testimony, may appreciate the stipulation. Remember: the determination under Section 362(d)(2) does not require the court to make a finding with respect to the *extent* to which the creditor is undersecured.

§7.14 ~ The Clay Pigeon Rule

One judge has likened the whole matter of getting relief to the job of the marksman in trapshooting. "Immediately after the bird is thrown," he said, "it is far easier to hit the target—the accuracy required is less. As time passes, in milliseconds, the bird is farther away and the target is more difficult to hit."[17] He continued: "In a §362(d)(2) relief from stay setting, the debtor's burden is similar . . . as time passes, the burden becomes more difficult to satisfy."[18]

This "clay pigeon rule" suggests a litigation strategy: Don't fear that you are asking for relief too early. If you ask for it at the beginning of the case, you probably won't get it. But it sets you up to come back months later and, without actually rubbing his nose in it, to remind that judge that you were there before, and that things really haven't gone as well as he hoped.

§7.15 ~ Another Reason To Ask Early—Running the Meter on Adequate Protection

There is another factor that argues in favor of an early request for relief. At least one judge has held that the right to adequate protection for future loss of collateral value doesn't begin until the creditor seeks relief from the stay.[19]

Comment: The decision in Continental Airlines may not enjoy a wide following, but there is a certain logic in it. If the secured creditor takes back its collateral, and the market value thereafter increases, the creditor benefits; if the collateral declines in value, the secured creditor absorbs the loss. Either way, the creditor takes the risk. But if the creditor seeks adequate protection but does not seek to take back its collateral, it may win either way—if the collateral increases in value, the creditor gets a larger allowed secured claim, and a better recovery in the case. If the collateral declines in value, the creditor gets a superpriority administrative expense claim, for failure of adequate protection, under section 507(b). Forcing a creditor to move for relief from the automatic stay in order to trigger the right to adequate protection for any future diminution in collateral value helps stop the creditor from taking a "heads I win, tails you lose" approach to the risk of collateral value. Of course, it may also lead to clogging the courts' dockets with a lot of lift-stay litigation.

§7.16 ~ Counterrule: A Reason Not To Seek Early Relief

We have provided two good reasons to seek early relief. Now here is a reason not to. Plenty of judges want lawyers for creditors to be "reasonable" and not over-aggressive in interfering with the debtor as it seeks to reorganize. You may argue that it is the lawyer's job to be unreasonable and over-aggressive, but the practical fact is it might get you into trouble. In such a case, the lawyer who is too quick out of the box may be seen as "unconstructive" and be penalized accordingly.

---

17. Matter of Holly's, Inc., 140 B.R. 643, 700 n.90 (Bankr. W.D. Mich. 1992).

18. *Id.*

19. In the Matter of Continental Airlines Inc., 154 B.R. 176, 180-81 (Bankr. D. Del. 1993) (collateral trustees were entitled to adequate protection only for any decline in market value from the time of the filing of the motion).

§7.17 ~ Cause, Including . . .

There is another subdivision to Section 362(d). This is Section 362(d)(1) which allows relief with respect to any stayed action (i.e., not just actions against property). Section 362(d)(1) allows relief "for cause," and adds "including lack of adequate protection." Taken together, these phrases offer about as loosely-textured a mandate as one might imagine. "Cause" is nowhere defined in the Code. "Including" is presumably not exclusive, so one may seek relief for cause other than lack of adequate protection.

"Adequate protection" is defined (in Section 361), but that definition, too, is loosely textured. It provides that adequate protection "may be provided by"—and then identifies three possible means of awarding the prescribed relief. Thus, the broad-gauged mandate to grant relief "for cause" appears calculated to let the bankruptcy court to give relief any time it thinks that relief is dictated by the principles of bankruptcy law or is necessary to protect the interests of non-debtors. For more on adequate protection, *see* §7.19.

Comment: Depending on the facts, "cause" for relief from the stay may include undue delay by a debtor, refusal to negotiate in good faith with creditors, misconduct by a debtor or its management, permitting waste, non-payment of taxes, or hopelessness of a reorganization. But these are only a few examples.

§7.18 ~ Sue on the Policy

A bankruptcy case that involves neither "adequate protection" nor "equity" is *Elliott v. Hardison.*[20] Elliott sued Hardison for personal injury damages arising from an auto accident. Hardison filed for bankruptcy and scheduled Elliott as an unsecured creditor. Eventually the court granted him his discharge. Hardison had no liability insurance, but Elliott had rights under a so-called "uninsured motorist" policy that allowed for compensation in any case where a driver such as Hardison was not insured.

The uninsured motorist policy made it a condition of liability that Elliott obtain a judgment against Hardison. The policy also purported to give the insurer a right against Hardison by subrogation from Elliott's claim. The district court, affirming the bankruptcy court, allowed Elliott to continue with his lawsuit for the purpose of establishing liability, but barred him from collecting from Hardison. Holding that the insurance company had no better rights than Elliott, the court barred the enforcement of the subrogation claim as well.

It is not unusual for a debtor or trustee to stipulate with a creditor that the creditor shall have relief from the stay, with the creditor agreeing in exchange to look only to an insurance policy for its recovery.

§7.19 ~ Adequate Protection

In a number of contexts, the Code provides that the trustee may not do such-and-such unless the non-debtor party gets"adequate protection" of his interest in property of the estate. For example:

- Relief from the automatic stay Section 362(d)(1) (relief from automatic stay "for cause including the lack of adequate protection . . . ");

---

20. 25 B.R. 305 (E.D. Va. 1982).

- Use, sale or lease of property, Section 363(d) (court "shall prohibit or condition . . . use, sale, or lease as is necessary to provide adequate protection . . .); and

- "Priming liens," Section 364(d) (priming lien only if "there is adequate protection of the interest of the holder" of the lien that is primed).

But what is "adequate protection?" The term gets a (nonexclusive) definition in Section 361. It provides that "adequate protection may be provided by" any one of following three items:

- cash payments; or

- an additional or replacement lien; or

- "such other relief . . . as will result in the realization by such entity of the indubitable equivalent of" the non-debtor's interest in the property.

The first two apply to the extent that the action "results in a decrease in the value of such entity's interest in such property." Notably, the Code excludes one possible form of "adequate protection" from the catch-all language of Section 361(3). That is the Code specifies that it is not sufficient simply to allow an administrative expense claim.

The scope of the exclusion is best illustrated by an example. Suppose the secured creditor says: "Your honor I have a claim for $100 secured by collateral worth just $100 which I fear will decline in value. I want protection against the risk of decrease in value." The court responds: "I find you are entitled to adequate protection, and to give you adequate protection, I grant you the right to a first-priority administrative expense claim under section 503(b)(1) to cover any deficiency on your claim."

Per Section 361(3), the administrative expense claim does not satisfy the demand for adequate protection. The reason is clear enough: The estate may be insolvent and unable to pay administrative expense claims, in which case the so-called "adequate protection" will be no protection at all.

If the "adequate protection" doesn't prove adequate, then the aggrieved creditor may have the right to compensation through a "super priority" administrative expense claim under section 507(b), with priority over other administrative expenses. But this is a back-up claim only, available only to the extent that the "real" adequate protection has failed. And the fact remains: 100 percent of nothing is still nothing; and a super priority against an empty estate may be worth just as much.

§7.20 ~ Stay Relief—Procedure

As we have seen, the Code leaves almost all procedural rules to the non-statutory rule-making process, under the mantra of "notice and a hearing." *See* §2.17. The automatic stay is one of the few cases where procedure achieves the dignity of statute. The rules are set forth in Sections 362(e) through (g). The primary purpose appears to be to assure that stay cases will be disposed of quickly, so the creditor's other injuries will not be aggravated by inaction.

With respect to an act against property, Section 362(e) provides that the stay will terminate 30 days after a request for relief unless the court orders it left in effect. Such an order may be the result of a final order from the court. But if the order takes the form of preliminary relief, then the court must conclude its final hearing not later than 30 days after the conclusion of the preliminary hearing.[21]

Further, the statute provides that the stay may continue past the preliminary hearing only if the court finds that there is a reasonable likelihood that the party opposing relief will prevail at the final hearing. The 30-day final deadline may be extended by consent or by the court for Rule 4001 fleshes out the statute. It provides that the motion shall be served on the committee of creditors or (if none) on the 20 largest creditors.

Comment: We are aware of some busy courts that routinely ask creditors to stipulate to leave the stay in place beyond the statutory deadlines so the court doesn't have to fit in a timely hearing. This seems to us to be inconsistent with the aims of Congress in specifying the time limits, but we don't know of any obvious solution to the problem.

The time limits and rules on findings seem calculated to assure, *inter alia*, that the aggrieved party will be able to get quick review. There was some question earlier whether an order denying relief from the stay was even appealable early in the case—or whether the appeal was at best interlocutory, conditioned on the sound discretion of the court. The law appears fairly settled now that the decision denying relief is indeed appealable as a matter of right.[22]

Section 362(f) authorizes relief without notice and a hearing "as necessary to prevent irreparable harm." So, if the debtor is about to leave with the collateral on a flight to a jurisdiction with no extradition treaty, the creditor may be permitted to try to stop him. Rule 4001(a) fleshes out the statute. It provides that relief will be allowed only if it clearly appears from specific facts shown by affidavit or by a verified motion that immediate and irreparable injury, loss, or damage will result to the moving party before the adverse party or the attorney for the adverse party can be heard in opposition, and the moving party's attorney certifies to the court in writing the efforts, if any, which have been made to give notice and the reasons why notice should not be required.

The most notable sanction for relief from the stay is that the action taken is a nullity. Congress in 1984 added Section 362(h) which provides a damage remedy. The statutory remedy is available only for a violation that is willful. On the face of things it is available only to an individual. Some circuits have read it more broadly to apply to partnerships or corporations. At this writing, there is a split in the circuits and the Supreme Court has chosen not to intervene.[23]

---

21. Note that the Code speaks of finishing the "hearing." Suppose the court finishes the hearing on day 29—but then takes the matter under submission, where it continues to languish after a year. Is there a violation of the statute here? Of the spirit, surely, but perhaps not of the letter.

22. Sonnax Industries, Inc., v. Tri Component Products Corp., (*In re* Sonnax Industries, Inc.), 907 F.2d 1280 (2d Cir. 1990).

23. Compare Sosne v. Reinert & Duree, P.C. (*In re* Just Brakes Corporate Sys.), 108 F.3d 881, (8th Cir. 1997), cert. denied, Sosne v. Reinert & Duree, 522 U.S. 947 (1997). (Holding that §362(h) does not extend to corporate debtors) with *In re* Atl. Bus. & Community Corp., 901 F.2d 325, 329 (3d Cir.1990)(holding §362(h) does apply to corporate debtors); Budget Serv. Co. v. Better Homes of Va., Inc., 804 F.2d 289, 292 (4th Cir.1986)(same).

Some courts have also treated violation of the stay as a contempt. This approach would be predicated on the notion that section 362 is a kind of injunction, and contempt is the ordinary remedy for the violation of an injunction. But the analogy may not be as strong as it looks. An injunction is a court order and a contempt is a direct affront to the court. It is not so obvious how a statute can play that role.

§7.21 ~ Practice Point: Don't Violate the Stay

You'll do everybody a favor if you go out of your way to warn your creditor clients against violating the stay, noting the penalties for violation. This includes cautioning not merely against the more obvious abuses,[24] but also warnings against some more insidious hazards—e.g., make sure the creditors reprogram their computers so as not to spit out routine "deadbeat" letters.

§7.22 ~ Setoff Mechanics

We explain elsewhere that the right of setoff is preserved in bankruptcy, but the exercise of setoff is stayed. *See* §12.16-.17. Years back, the mechanics of setoff presented a practical problem, but the Supreme Court seems to have resolved it.

Consider the case of DebtorCo, holder of a deposit account at FirstBank in the amount of $100,000. As it happens, FirstBank also holds a claim against DebtorCo for (as luck would have it $100,000), supported by a contractual right of setoff against the deposit account. DebtorCo files for relief under chapter 11 and attempts to draw on the account. FirstBank points to its right of setoff. DebtorCo counters that setoff is stayed. FirstBank rejoins that it isn't actually "setting off;" rather, it is just imposing an "administrative hold" until the rights are sorted out.

FirstBank's assertion may ring of hairsplitting. But the practical fact is that if the bank lets go of the money, the chances are pretty good that it will never see it again. And FirstBank has another strong card to play. That is: the account appears to qualify as "cash collateral," as that term is defined in section 363(a).[25] And Section 363(c)(2) provides that the trustee may not use cash collateral unless—

- each entity that has an interest in such cash collateral consents; or

- the court, after notice and a hearing, authorizes such use, sale, or lease in accordance with the provisions of this section.

Since it is a given that FirstBank does not consent, the only remaining route is court authorization. And DebtorCo isn't likely to get authorization unless it is able to provide "adequate protection"—perhaps a substitute lien. The problem thus reaches a kind of an impasse.

---

24. *In re* Reed, 11 B.R. 258 (Bankr. D. Utah 1981) (held a stay violation to dump garbage on the debtor's front lawn).

25. I.e., as a "deposit account" … in which the estate and an entity other than the estate have an interest." Section 363(c).

Given this kind of context, in *Citizens Bank of Maryland v. Strumpf*, the Supreme Court held that bank was within its rights to impose the hold pending a determination of its rights. The Bank can't expect to get away with leaving the "administrative hold" in place forever, of course. A sensible course for the bank is to impose the hold and then bring a motion for relief from the automatic stay so as to make the setoff. This may trigger a counter-motion on the part of the debtor to use the cash collateral, and all the issues will be joined at once.

§7.23 ~ Practice Point: Setoff

One of us remembers, as a young lawyer, walking into the bank with the client, standing by while the client drew his funds out of the account, and then walked into the bank manager's office to advise him that the client would be filing for chapter 11. The manager's next line was: "And I suppose you've emptied the account?"

Translated. As a condition of the making a loan, the bank had required the client to maintain a "compensating balance" with the bank. One reason for the compensating balance was that it gave the bank the basis for a right of setoff in the event of the client's default. The client was in default. In the event of a bankruptcy, the right of setoff would have been preserved, although stayed. If there was nothing in the account, there was nothing to set off.

Moral: Before your debtor client files its petition, consider moving deposit accounts to non-creditor institutions.

§7.24 ~ Insulation from the Stay

Elsewhere we have discussed the "bankruptcy remote entity," and the efforts of the Wall Street bar to get special protection for certain securities and financial transactions. *See* §5.11. Some of this impulse is reflected in a couple of Code sections that can be regarded as special exceptions to the automatic stay.

Specifically, Section 559 provides that the bankruptcy of a transferor will not bar the transferee from liquidating his repo contract[26], although he may have to pay over any surplus to the bankruptcy estate. Section 555 creates a liquidation right with respect to "securities contracts" if its elements are met. *See* also Section 556 for commodities or forward contracts, and Section 560 for "swap" contracts.

§7.25 ~ Waiver

It is classic doctrine that you can't waive your right to go bankrupt.[27] For a long time it was thought that you couldn't waive the protection of the automatic stay either, but in recent years there has been some softening in this once firm principle. Recent cases have yielded to a principle that the waiver, while not

---

26. Note the limited definition of "repurchase agreement" under the Bankruptcy Code, but other repurchase agreements may still enjoy protection as "securities contracts" under §555.

27. *In re* Adana Mortgage Bankers, Inc., 12 B.R. 989, 1009 (Bankr. N.D. Ga. 1980) citing Merritt v. Mt Forest Fur Farms of Am., Inc. (*In re* Mt. Forest Fur Farms of Am., Inc.) 103 F.2d 69, 71 (6th Cir. 1939).

self-enforcing, will at least serve as a factor to weigh in the balance when considering whether to give relief.[28]

The trend is perhaps most evident in single asset real estate cases (SARE's). This may be another of those arenas where the special exigencies of the single asset real estate case are creating doctrine you wouldn't expect to find in traditional cases. Thus, the typical single-asset case is really a two-party case in disguise, and the stay waiver is most likely to run into trouble where there are other creditors who weren't privy to the original waiver.[29]

§7.26 ~ Waiving the Stay

Creditor can't bear the thought of debtor going into bankruptcy, thereby tangling creditor in the automatic stay, and messy litigation over relief from the stay. Creditor has a bright idea: do business only with debtors who won't assert the automatic stay. Make it a condition of the loan that the debtor waive, in advance, the right to assert the automatic stay in any later bankruptcy.

Does it sound too good to be true? It should because it is. The court simply isn't going to recognize a wholly prospective pre-petition waiver of the automatic stay—"void against public policy," the judge will say, and he may even mutter something about how it was abusive or overreaching for the creditor even to try.

But this is not quite the end of the story. Even though the wholly prospective waiver is a non-starter, still the creditor may be able to use a stay waiver as part of a workout of a loan already in trouble. If you are giving the debtor more time to work out his problems, or negotiating the dismissal of an existing bankruptcy, you may be able to use a prospective stay waiver to put teeth in your workout deal.

Even here, the judge may be unwilling to enforce the waiver according to his terms. But she may at least take the wavier into account as one factor in making a determination as to whether to grant the lender relief from the stay. In doing so, the judge is likely to consider the entire factors like this:

- What was the context? Was it truly a "restructuring," where the debtor was in trouble and the creditor gave him another chance? Does the "restructuring" look anything like the kind of protection the debtor would have had in chapter 11?

- Did the debtor get sufficient new consideration for the waiver?

---

28. *In re* Shady Grove Tech Ctr. Assocs. Ltd. Partnership, 216 B.R. 386 (Bankr. D. Md.1998), opinion supplemented by *In re* Shady Grove Tech Ctr. Assocs. Ltd. Partnership, 227.R. 442 (Bankr. D. Md.1998) A good general discussion is in Michael St. Patrick Baxter, Pre-petition Waivers of the Automatic Stay, 52 Bus. Law. 577 (1997).

29. *See, e.g.*, *In re* Atrium High Point Ltd.. Partnership, 189 B.R. 599 (Bankr. M.D.N.C. 1995). Here, the waiver was part of a previous confirmed chapter 11 plan. The court held that the waiver was binding on the debtor, but not on nine competing creditors. But *see In re* Cheeks, 167 B.R. 817 (Bankr. D. S.C. 1994) (waiver enforced in a non-SARE).

How do you educate the judge on these issues? One way is to tell the story in the restructuring agreement. For example, do not say:

> Borrower agrees that it will not invoke the automatic stay against the lender in any bankruptcy case.

Better is a full-scale recital of the facts, like the sample in the next section, which demonstrates the *basis* for the stipulation and serves as a contemporaneous statement of the parties intent.

§7.27 ~ Form: Stay Waiver

Here is the kind of full-scale recital we have in mind:

> "Borrower agrees and acknowledges that it is in default under the Loan Agreement because, among other things, it has failed timely to pay principal and interest due to Lender thereunder and because [add other defaults]. Borrower acknowledges that each of these defaults is material that it has no present ability to cure any of its defaults under the Loan Agreement, and that is has no defense to any of its obligations under the Loan Agreement, and Borrower further acknowledges that, because of its uncured defaults under the Loan Agreement, Lender has the absolute and immediate right to foreclose on its collateral and to exercise each and every one of its other rights and remedies under the Loan Agreement, without further notice or opportunity to cure. Borrower acknowledges that by entering into this Workout Agreement and forbearing from the exercise of certain remedies, Lender is allowing Borrower an opportunity to restructure its financial affairs and pay its indebtedness, and is affording Borrower's equity holders a valuable opportunity to retain and increase the value of their equity interests. Lender is also providing a benefit to Borrower's other creditors, because if Lender would foreclose now on its collateral, Borrower's business would cease and Borrower would have no way to pay those other creditors. Although entering into this Workout Agreement delays Lender's exercise of its remedies under the Loan Agreement and imposes risk upon Lender, Lender is willing to give Borrower this one last chance, in lieu of Borrower's filing a bankruptcy petition, to reorganize its affairs and pay its debt. Borrower acknowledges that this Workout Agreement is in lieu of a chapter 11 filing by Borrower and that Lender would not have given Borrower this opportunity unless Borrower agreed that it would not further delay Lender's exercise of its rights and remedies by filing a bankruptcy petition at any time in the future. Accordingly, Borrower hereby agrees that if it files a petition under any chapter of the United States Bankruptcy Code, or any successor or similar provision of federal or state law or if any such petition is filed against Borrower, Lender shall immediately be entitled to relief from the automatic stay (or any similar stay or injunction) in order to foreclose on its collateral and exercise its other remedies under the Loan Agreement or at law, and Borrower hereby (a) consents irrevocably to such relief, (b) agrees not to file any pleading objecting or in any way opposing such relief, and (c) permanently waives any rights to seek any injunction, stay, or other court order which would in any way delay or impair any exercise by Lender of any of Lender's remedies. Borrower acknowledges that, without the foregoing agreements by it, Lender would not have entered into this Workout Agreement."

§7.28 ~ Other Waiver Techniques

Another place to consider stay waivers is in a consensual plan of reorganization, if the lender wants to protect against a subsequent bankruptcy. Here, you may be able to get the bankruptcy court to approve the stay waiver in a plan and confirmation order, which should make it enforceable.

Consider inserting other waivers, including waiver of the right to seek to extend the period to assume or to reject a lease or other executory contract, waiver of the right to seek approval of secured post-petition financing, waiver of the right to seek to use cash collateral, or waiver of the right to seek to confirm a plan that does not pay the creditor in full in cash on the effective date. These may be unenforceable, but it probably does not hurt to try.

Another possible device, on which there appears to be no authority, is an agreement to file only under chapter 7, not in chapter 11. We doubt it would be enforced.

§7.29 ~ Stay Protection for Non-debtors

Chapter 13 includes a "third-party" stay offering protection to non-debtor guarantors or of chapter 13 debtors.[30] Aside from this rule, nothing in the Code expressly authorizes stay protection for non-debtors. Nonetheless, courts have fashioned a variety of principles to give non-debtors protection in a limited but still important class of chapter 11 cases. *See* §17.43.

---

30. Section 1301.

8 Property of the Estate

8 PROPERTY OF THE ESTATE

§8.1 ~ INTRODUCTION: THE HEART OF THE MATTER

The primary role of the bankruptcy trustee is to collect and distribute the property of the estate. It is therefore of the highest importance to know what constitutes as property of the estate.[1] The basic rule is set forth in Section 541(a). It provides that the commencement of the case "creates an estate." It says this estate comprises "all legal or equitable interests of the debtor in property as of the commencement of the case."[2] So as elsewhere, we are thrust back on non-bankruptcy law: what is property for purposes of bankruptcy distribution is whatever would have been property had bankruptcy not intervened.

§8.2 ~ PRE-BANKRUPTCY

The definition says "as of the commencement of the case." This means that the debtor may lose anything that was his at the time of the filing, but he gets to keep whatever he acquires later. You can see the tension in *Wheeler v. Magdovitz*, where the debtor sued his lawyer for malpractice.[3] Magdovitz, the lawyer, prepared a petition and schedules declaring that Wheeler, the debtor, had no assets.[4]

Wheeler signed them; Magdovitz filed them and Wheeler got his discharge. But five years later he was indicted and convicted for concealing assets. He thereupon sued Magdovitz for malpractice. But the question arose—who owned the cause of action? If it was the property of Wheeler "as of the commencement of the case," then it belonged not to Wheeler himself but to his trustee. If it arose later, then it belonged to Wheeler.

Wheeler argued the action was his because it did not "accrue" under state law until injury occurs—and the injury, per Wheeler, was his indictment five years after bankruptcy. The court accepted the assumption that the question was—when did the claim accrue? But it held that there was a "relationship" between Wheeler and Magdovitz dating back before bankruptcy sufficient to date the claim from that time. The court also said that Wheeler knew (or should have known) about the misconduct all along, because it was his own property that was at issue. Wheeler asserted that he was an uneducated person, who simply relied on the advice of his attorney, but the court wasn't impressed.

1. Section 701(1).

2. Section 541(a)(1). So in chapter 7 and 11; some earnings do become property of the estate in chapter 13.

3. *In re* Wheeler, 137 F.3d 299 (5th Cir. 1998).

4. Further proof that the fates have a sense of humor, the debtor's full name was Lawyer Wheeler.

§8.3 ~ Earnings and Human Capital

The general rule is that the debtor's property passes to the trustee. Inevitably, there are exceptions. Perhaps most important, the Code provides that earnings from personal services performed by an individual debtor after the commencement of the case are not property of the estate.[5] This exception helps to explain a standard bankruptcy strategy: the best time to file bankruptcy is the day before you start work on the good new job—that way, you would discharge all your past debts while insulating your future earnings. As a generalization, this probably isn't as true as it used to be, but it's still good as a start.[6]

The exception for personal services may create some anomalous results. The difficulty is that "earning power" may be a capital asset. Normally if I own a capital asset, it becomes an asset of the estate—for example, 100 shares of General Motors stock. My wit, my energy, my learning may count as "human capital." But they do not pass to the trustee because the Code says so.

A dramatic instance is *Ryan v. Lynn*.[7] Ryan and Lynn married while Lynn was in medical school. Later when they divorced, the New Jersey divorce court found his medical degree to be "property" with a value of some $300,000 subject to division under New Jersey's equitable distribution law. Lynn later filed for bankruptcy in Connecticut. Ryan and her attorney sought to block his discharge on the grounds that he concealed an asset by failing to list the medical degree to be "property" subject to administration by the bankruptcy court.

On the face of things, there is a lot to be said for this argument. If we believe that property for purposes of bankruptcy is whatever counts as property under non-bankruptcy law, then the medical degree clearly qualifies. Moreover if we believe that the creditors should have the first crack at the proceeds of the debtor's investments, then the medical education would seem to qualify quite well.

However, the bankruptcy judge, held that Ryan's earning capacity was more akin to wages and thus excluded under Section 541(a)(6). This is surely acceptable under the statute as it stands. But to get a sense of just how close the case might be, consider the case of Harold and Wilma, proud parents of Jed and Jeffrey. Jed is a clever child with good test scores so Harold and Wilma spend $100,000 to buy him two years' worth of education towards board certification as an ophthalmologist. Jeffrey is not so good at the books but he is a hard worker so they buy him a bulldozer. Both Jed and Jeffrey come upon hard times and file for bankruptcy. Nothing can take away Jed's new learning, but Jeffrey will very likely lose the bulldozer.[8]

---

5. Section 541(a)(6).

6. *See* §707(b) (providing that the court may dismiss a case filed by an individual debtor whose debts are primarily consumer debts if the court determines that the granting of chapter 7 relief would constitute a substantial abuse of that chapter). Some courts more or less ignore §707(b), but others use it as a device to leverage high-income debtors into filing a "voluntary" chapter 13.

7. *In re* Lynn, 18 B.R. 501 (Bankr. D. Conn. 1982).

8. The example is overly simple. Jed will not be able to discharge his student loans (absent "undue hardship") and Jeffrey might be able to protect at least part of the dozer value via a "tools of the trade" exception. But these qualifications don't contradict the main point.

Perhaps more surprisingly, the exclusion of earnings applies in chapter 11, just as it does in chapter 7. This at least is the reading of the 9th Circuit in a case involving one FitzSimmons, a lawyer who sought relief in his personal chapter 11.[9] The trustee sought to reach his earnings from his law practice. FitzSimmons resisted, holding that they were "earnings from personal services" and thus not part of the chapter 11 estate. The Circuit acknowledged that some earnings were excluded. But the court held that the interpretation protected only earnings from "personal services," and not "practice earnings." The court remanded to let the lower court sort things out.

It is interesting to speculate on just what the lower court should have done on remand. Suppose these facts: FitzSimmons has 10 employees, aside from himself: five lawyers who earn $40,000 a year each, and five support staffers who earn $25,000 a year each (that makes an annual wage bill of $325,000). The annual "surplus"—i.e., earnings beyond expenses—has run from as high as a million to a low of *negative* $200,000. That is, in at least one year, FitzSimmons has had to dig into his own pocket to pay the help. The average surplus over the past decade has been $200,000.

FitzSimmons comes to the office every day, but he doesn't seem to spend a lot of time writing briefs or going to court. Instead, he spends some of his time popping in and out of other people's offices, asking them how things are going, and some of his time in coffee shops and saloons around the courthouse, chatting with old friends and acquaintances, some of them current or former clients.

One's first thought is to say that schmoozing, etc., isn't work, and that all of the earnings of the firm come from a "business" that is really separate from FitzSimmons himself. But FitzSimmons will say that he is the glue that holds it all together and that nothing would happen without his efforts—thereby, personal services.

The practical result of exclusion is that it lets the debtor continue to earn and spend without answering to the trustee. On the other hand, the typical goal of chapter 11 is confirmation of a plan. Nothing should bar the debtor from voluntarily surrendering earnings to creditors as part of a plan, and if he ever wants win creditor assent for his chapter 11 plan, he may have to.

§8.4 ~ Intangibles

As trustee or DIP, don't overlook the fact that "property" includes intangible property such as accounts receivable, rights of action, patents, copyrights, goodwill, tax attributes, etc. Receivables are familiar stuff: many trustees sue and collect on the debtor's receivables all the time. Rights of action may be less common, but are likewise an estate asset, at least if they accrued pre-petition. For example, the estate might include the "unfair competition" lawsuit against the villain who put the debtor out of business.

Patents, trademarks and copyrights are property of the estate to the extent they were property of the debtor as of the date of the bankruptcy filing. This category of property, seems to be expanding. For example, the Federal Circuit has held that it is possible to patent "business methods."[10]

---

9. *In re* FitzSimmons, 725 F.2d 1208 (9th Cir. 1984).

10. State Street Bank & Trust Co. v. Signature Financial Group, Inc., 149 F.3d 1368. 1375 (Fed. Cir.), *cert denied,* 525 U.S.1093 (1998).

Our best advice is to think as expansively as possible when looking for intangible property of the estate, lest you miss something that may have value.

§8.5 ~ Cyberproperty, Technoproperty, etc.

It is almost a cliche that we live in an era dominated by new species of wealth, generated from cyberspace, from biotechnology, from court-created rights of privacy, etc. Inevitably, we can anticipate litigation over the nature of these rights. Some of this litigation may directly implicate the question of what constitutes "property." Our own guess, however, is that most of it will raise the property interest issue indirectly.

For example, there is already a small body of case law on issues of priority and perfection of security interests in technology-related intangibles; *see* §14, 5-6. We suspect also that courts will get entangled in trying to figure out the distinction between the "property" right in some of these new items and the rules governing executory contracts. And, of course, there are complex multi-jurisdiction issues, since it can be difficult to determine exactly where some of these "techno assets" are located. Perhaps surprisingly, not a lot of this sort of litigation has come to our attention. But the future is young.[11]

§8.6 ~ Bankruptcy Clause (A.K.A. Ipso Facto Clause)

Although Section 541(a) purports to preserve non-bankruptcy rights, Section 541 arms the trustee with a bankruptcy trump-card to play against one kind of interest that would otherwise exist under non-bankruptcy law. This section invalidates a bankruptcy clause. A bankruptcy clause (sometimes known as an "ipso facto" clause) is a contract clause that purports to trigger rights in the non-debtor or obligations on the part of the debtor in the event of the debtor's bankruptcy.

From one perspective, the Code has to include a clause trumping contractual ipso facto provisions. Otherwise, the nondebtor could use the bankruptcy clause in the private contract to negate the general statutory priority scheme. Nevertheless, it has to be recognized as a restriction on non-bankruptcy rights.

The practicing lawyer will see ipso facto clauses in many contexts, broadly drafted to terminate all kinds of rights in the event of a bankruptcy filing. Most of these are unenforceable. One assumes they were tucked into the form file a thousand years ago and persist through a kind of inertia. They probably carry some *in terrorem* effect with unadvised or ill-advised debtors. It falls to debtor's counsel to see to it that no one is misled.

Lawyers have expended a remarkable amount of effort seeking to draft around the ipso facto rule. Most of this effort has come to naught, but one device may have some promise. That is, the ipso facto rule appears not to bar a contract that imposes adverse consequences on a third party in the event of a debtor's bankruptcy.

---

11. For a more detailed discussion of the issues in this section, *see* Mechele Dickerson, *From Jeans to Genes: The Evolving Nature of Property of the Estate*, 15 Bankr. Dev. J. 285 (1999).

Example: NewBank agrees to loan $1 million to DebtorCo, a corporation. The first $100,000 is guaranteed by Gerald, the president and majority shareholder. The contract contains a clause providing that Gerald's guarantee will "spring" from $100,000 to $1 million in the event of DebtorCo's bankruptcy. Since the clause imposes a liability on the third party, not the debtor, we see no reason why it should be held to violate the ipso facto rule.[12]

§8.7 ~ Cleaning Up the Loose Ends

Various subsections of Section 541 help to nail down the loose ends of rules that the courts might (or might not) have guessed on their own account.

Section 541(a)(7) provides that property of the estate includes "any interest in property the estate acquires after the commencement of the case." Note that the operative word here is estate, not debtor. The provision makes clear that the debtor has no direct interest in property acquired by the trustee—but, by negative implication, that the trustee has no direct interest in post-petition property acquired directly by the debtor.

Sections 541(a)(3) and (4) clean up the bookkeeping on trustee avoiding powers. They make clear that property acquired by the trustee in various avoidance actions will become property of the estate.

Section 541(a)(2) provides that property of the estate includes community property. The application of this rule will vary under different marital property regimes, but here is an important example. In California, most property acquired by either spouse during marriage is community property and, as such, is subject to the separate management and control of either spouse. This means that when either spouse goes into bankruptcy, she takes the entire community property with her. The careful planner will want to think through the implications of this rule in relation to the rules on the discharge of community debts[13] and the rules on "community exemptions."[14]

§8.8 ~ Property and Possession

In an earlier time, the question of what property passed to the bankruptcy estate turned at least in part on the question of possession. If the debtor had possession at the time of the filing of the petition, then it might pass to the estate; otherwise, no. But time has softened this view.[15] More modern thinking has long since broken the nexus between "property" and "possession."

The Code, correspondingly, arms the trustee with a number of important powers to force turnover of the debtor's property not in his possession at the time of filing. Thus, Section 542 endows the trustee with a general power to compel turnover, while Section 543 empowers the trustee to force turnover from a custodian (such as an assignee for the benefit of creditors).

---

12. We sidestep the question whether the springing guarantee creates a right of subrogation in favor of the guarantor and against the debtor. We assume that the right can be waived in the loan documents.

13. Section 524(b).

14. Section 522.

15. The Court long ago held that the secured creditors' property right was not in the collateral but the value of his claim, *see* Wright v. Union Central Bank 311 U.S. 273 (1940).

In an a leading case under the Code, the Supreme Court had to consider the rights of the bankruptcy trustee *vis a vis* the Internal Revenue Service as creditor who had repossessed but not yet completed the prescribed liquidation sale.[16] The court held that the trustee could indeed compel turnover.

But Justice Blackmun in his opinion made it clear that the creditor retained any particular rights which would include, for example, its underlying claim, the benefit of any security interest, the right of setoff, and such. Somewhat more interesting is a footnote in which the court says:

> Our analysis in this case depends in part on the reorganization context in which the turnover order is sought. We express no view on the issue whether § 542(a) has the same broad effect in liquidation or adjustment of debt proceedings.[17]

Just why it should be so restricted is not at all clear from reading the statute. In any event, the courts have not generally been as restrictive as the footnote might suggest. Courts have proven willing to grant turnover in substantially any case where the trustee (or DIP) could make a reasonable showing of need for the property, leaving the secured creditor to his monetary remedies as appropriate.

§8.9 ~ Proceeds, Product

Earlier we discussed the "human capital" problem inherent in Section 541(a)(6). Perhaps more troublesome is the other part of Section 541(a)(6). It provides that property of the estate includes "proceeds, product, offspring, rents, or profits of or from property of the estate." This is all well enough—but it makes one wonder what the drafters could have thought of as property in the absence of the section. At least in the commercial context, property can be defined comprehensively as the discounted present value of the expected future cash flows—which is to say, the proceeds, product, rents or profits and, yes, even the offspring. So one might argue that all of these items are already subsumed under the definition of property even without spelling them out.[18]

Section 541(a)(6) cuts off a potential non-bankruptcy right with respect to wages. In a closely related case, the Code is not so generous—the Code permits the trustee to reach forward 180 days after the filing of the petition to reach property acquired by bequest or devise.[19] Together, the two rules suggest hypotheticals that only a law professor can love where the debtor has (a) the prospect of a good new job; and (b) an ailing wealthy relative. He wants to stall filing as late as he can in anticipation of the former, but to file as quickly as he can to preserve his inheritance from the latter.

---

16. United States v. Whiting Pools, 462 U.S. 198 (1983).

17. *Id.*, at 208 n. 17.

18. This issue often arises in the context of the valuation of real estate collateral. The secured creditor will argue that the value of the rents must be added to the value of the underlying property to reach the total value of its secured claim, since it has both a mortgage on the property and a collateral assignment of rents. The debtor, however, will contend that the value of the property is nothing but the present value of the anticipated future stream of rents, so that counting the rents as additional collateral is unfair "double counting."

19. Section 541(a)(5).

We expand on this problem in our discussion of the assignment of "promises," infra. But the problem overlaps with the problem of security interests in post-petition property, on which *see* §13.33.

§8.10 ~ Assignment of "Promises"

Conceptually, perhaps one of the most difficult matters for the bankruptcy court to sort out is the characterization of "promises to pay money."

Example: DebtorCo, the debtor, holds an unsecured claim against Blanche, on her promise to pay $1,000 as the price of a widget which DebtorCo sold and delivered to Blanche last month. The claim is unsecured and there is no negotiable instrument. Implausibly, but to help the example, we will assume that Blanche does not have to pay until a year from today. DebtorCo wants its money now, so it undertakes to transfer the claim to FinCo for $800. Before FinCo collects on the claim, DebtorCo files for bankruptcy. What are the rights of FinCo?

There are a myriad of possible issues here, but for the present we concentrate on one: does FinCo own the claim outright? Or does he hold the claim merely as security for a debt? If he holds it merely as security, then the claim remains property of the estate, subject to FinCo's claim. In that case, almost anything FinCo wants to do with the claim will be subject to the control of the Bankruptcy Court. For example, FinCo will not be able to collect from Blanche unless he gets relief from the automatic stay. His claim will be bifurcated into two claims—one secured, for the value of the collateral, and one unsecured, for the shortfall. In a chapter 11 plan, he may be subject to cramdown.

If FinCo owns the claim outright, then he is free of all these headaches. He can go ahead and take whatever steps necessary to collect the full value of the claim from Blanche just as if the bankruptcy had never taken place.

And so the question arises—how do we tell whether she has a property interest? The answer is not obvious. For some purposes, the Uniform Commercial Code appears to govern the transaction. But the Commercial Code doesn't purport to distinguish between security and outright sale of accounts receivable; it governs both alike.

One beguiling line of inquiry concerns what we may call "risk of loss." Sometimes we say that the person who "owns" something is the person who stands to bear the loss if it declines in value, either through casualty, or through change in the market, or for whatever reason. If it is true that property entails the risk of loss, then the person who has the risk of loss must have the property. Some courts have reasoned exactly this way in just the situation we have before us.[20] The corollary is that if the transferee has the right of recourse back against the transferor-debtor, the transferee does not bear the ultimate risk of loss. This would imply that the transferee is not the owner and the ownership remains with the transferor debtor.

---

20. A prominent example is Bear v. CoBen (*In re* Golden Plan), 829 F.2d 705, 709-10 (9th Cir. 1987) (transferees bore risk of loss so notes not property of the estate); *cf.* Fireman's Fund Insurance Cos. v. Grover, 813 F.2d 266, 270-71 (9th Cir. 1987) (no property where no risk of loss). The Uniform Commercial Code seems to be struggling for the same point, although it puts it backwards. It says that if the transaction is a sale of accounts, then the transferee has no right to deficiency. It would have been better to say that if there is no right to a deficiency, then the transaction is a sale. *See* UCC §9-505. In trying to make sense out of an issue like this, lawyers and judges frequently look to accounting definitions. But new FASB 125, purporting to define when a transaction is a sale for accounting purposes, talks in terms of when the asset is "beyond the reach" of the transferor. Since this is ultimately a question of law, the accountants seem to have bounced the ball back to the lawyers.

A difficulty is that there are plenty of cases where the courts have held that the transferee is the owner even though he has full recourse the transferor-debtor,[21] and others where the courts say that limited recourse is consistent with sale.[22]

This issue may be too arcane to be worth notice in ordinary bankruptcy cases, but it has taken on new life and vigor in the developing law of "bankruptcy remote entities," *see* §5.11. Developers of these bankruptcy remote entities have been testing the limits of the sale-security distinction in an effort to assure that their financing vehicles stay insulated from the bankruptcy process, *see* §8.14.

§8.11 ~ Assignment of Rents

One place where this issue comes into focus is with regard to the assignment of rents under a real estate mortgage. Consider BancCo, holding mortgage on Blackacre to secure a claim of $1 million. Blackacre is an apartment house; virtually all its value is bound up in its capacity to generate income. In the event of default, BancCo would expect to sell the property at a foreclosure sale. As a second-best, BancCo would like to claim the cash flow—in the jargon, the "rents, issues and profits" of Blackacre. But BancCo wants to avoid the toils of Section 541(a)(6) and Section 552(b).

BancCo reasons that if the rents come under an "absolute" assignment, then the rents are not property of the estate and BancCo gets to use them untrammeled by the bankruptcy court. So BancCo drafts the assignment of rents as an "assignment, absolute and not for security purposes."

This is a wonderful way to stop any case, and particularly a SARE case, dead in its tracks—which is, after all, exactly what BancCo wants to do. The trouble is, that everyone knows that BancCo doesn't mean it. Documentation and protestations notwithstanding, BancCo doesn't propose to own the income stream; it just wants to get paid on its debt. Usually, you can tell this from the creditor's own behavior, and sometimes from the so-called absolute assignment itself. For example, many of these provide that the debtor makes an "absolute" assignment of rents to the creditor, but that the creditor grants a license back to the debtor, allowing him to use the rents until default.[23] The very language seems to us to undercut the meaning of the assignment. Moreover, even the purported "absolute" assignment will allow the borrower to keep the rents after the debt is fully repaid, which undercuts the argument that the assignment was intended to be an absolute conveyance of the rents.

We can't resolve all the ambiguities on this one, but we can offer some practical pointers. Here are a few:

---

21. A provocative example is Hatoff v. Lemons & Assocs., (*In re* Lemons & Assocs.) 67 B.R. 198, 209-10 (Bankr. D. Nev. 1986). (Broker's advertisement that the deal is a "sale" outweighs the fact that risk of loss remains with transferor). Note that Hatoff was decided by a lower court in the Ninth Circuit a year before Bear and Fireman's Fund, *supra*. Neither appellate case mentioned Hatoff, although it seems to contradict both of them.

22. *See, e.g.*, Major's Furniture Mart, Inc., v. Castle Credit Corp. 602 F.2d 538, 544 (3d Cir. 1979).

23. The device sounds like a sale-leaseback and is subject to the same conceptual confusion.

- If BancCo asks you to sign an opinion letter assuring that its absolute assignment is bankruptcy-proof, don't do it. None of these are bulletproof. Similarly, be careful if you are asked to give a general enforceability opinion with respect to loan documents which include a purported absolute assignment —you should take a specific exception for this document, or failing that at least make sure your bankruptcy exception is broad enough to cover it.

- If BancCo asks you to draft an absolute assignment, do your best to purge it of anything that smacks of security. We've seen documents that grant an "absolute assignment . . . to secure repayment." This language pretty much shoots itself in the foot.

- If BancCo asks your debtor client to sign an absolute assignment, you will be tempted to let him go ahead, trusting that the court won't enforce it. Don't be too sure. At least it will require some costly explaining, and you might lose.

- BancCo will be willing to grant that license to let the debtor use the rents prior to a default (after all, BancCo wants you to make money from the property so you can pay the debt). But BancCo will typically want to provide that the license can be terminated upon default without notice. Don't hold still for it. At least bargain for some kind of notice and grace period, which (in addition to providing an opportunity to cure) will enable your client to file a chapter 11 petition before its interest in the rents has been terminated.

§8.12 ~ The Fringe of Property—Trust

Some of the most slippery problems in bankruptcy property law involve the matter of property "held for another," most often property "held in trust." Start with a primitive case. An hour before bankruptcy Norman parks his car behind Daniel's chain-link fence. Two hours later he returns and discovers to his consternation that the gate is locked and that the fence bears a large black-on-yellow placard that reads: KEEP OFF; PROPERTY OF TESS, TRUSTEE IN BANKRUPTCY, SUCCESSOR TO DANIEL, DEBTOR.

Tess is the successor to the property of Daniel, of course, but not to the property of Norman. On the facts set forth here, it would seem that nothing more than an unhappy accident put the car within the reach of Tess, and one would hope that Norman could extricate it from her clutches.[24]

Next, consider Doris who owns property and owes debts in her own right, but who also serves as trustee for her nephew, Nestor, under the will of his late uncle Uriah. Doris holds real estate, a bank account, and a strong box, all in the name of "Doris, as trustee for Nestor." Deep-rooted general principles of trust law would recognize that Doris operates under constraint here, empowered only to act in behalf of others.[25] The question arises—if Doris files for bankruptcy, then what becomes of the property held in trust?

---

24. Older cases would say that Norman had no "colorable claim." See James A. MacLachlan, The Law of Bankruptcy §194 at 207 (1956).

25. Restatement (Third) of Trusts, §2, Comment f (1996).

As it turns out, the answer to this question is possibly harder than it needs to be, but in any event certainly harder than it appears at first look. There are several problems. One is that the Code itself deals with the question in a manner that is backhanded, almost inadvertent. You can see this in trying to understand the "property" language in Section 541, and also in trying to grasp its relation with the "trustee avoiding powers" under Section 544. Another is that the doctrines governing express trusts tend to morph into a wholly separate body of doctrine governing so-called constructive trusts. We deal with each of these problems in turn.

§8.13 ~ Who Gets Trust Property?—Section 541(d)

What happens when the debtor files for bankruptcy holding property in trust? The most relevant language seems to come from Section 541(d). In relevant part, it reads as follows:

> Property in which the debtor holds, as of the commencement of the case, only legal title and not an equitable interest . . . becomes property of the estate . . . only to the extent of the debtor's legal title to such property, but not to the extent of any equitable interest in such property that the debtor does not hold.

We can perhaps make sense out of this abstraction if we recall a little black-letter trust law. Traditional doctrine says that the trustee (e.g., Doris) holds only "legal" title, while the beneficiary (e.g., Nestor) holds an "equitable" interest. So the section would seem to say Nestor continues to enjoy his rights as beneficiary of the trust, and in particular that creditors of Doris do not get to share in the trust.[26]

What is the trouble with this reading? One difficulty is that the section apparently was not drafted with the general problem of trusts in mind. Rather, it seems to have been directed at a highly specific (and rather specialized) transaction—the sale of repos.

§8.14 ~ Repos

What is a repo? A repo was originally established as a device to sidestep a restriction on short-term interest rates in the market for commercial bank deposits.[27] In substance, the owner of a pool of mortgages would borrow money, pledging his mortgages as security. But this is illegal; or was illegal under the constraints that brought it into being. So instead of borrowing and giving security, one sold the mortgages with the obligation to repurchase them later.

---

26. There is another provision of Section 541 that would seem to lend itself to the same analysis. That is §541(b)(1), which says that "property of the estate does not include ... any power that the debtor may exercise solely for the benefit of an entity other than the debtor." But this provision seems to have been written with a view towards powers of appointment that the debtor may receive under a will. *See generally* H. Rep. No. 95-595, 1st Sess. at 368-69 (1977); S. Rep. No. 95-989, 2nd Sess. at 83 (1978). *See also* §558, providing that the estate has the defenses of the debtor.

27. There is a good short outline of the repo industry in Linda Allen, Capital Markets and Institutions, 333-61 (1997).

Repos may have started in the mortgage industry, but they have expanded. A wide range of securities are currently financed by means of the repo. In the typical transaction, the "borrower" sells securities to the "lender," subject to the "borrower's" obligation to buy them back at a specified time for a specified amount of money (loan repayment plus interest, in effect). The whole thing is documented using "purchase" and "sale" terminology, so as to make the transaction look like a real sale.

We suspect the use of the repo (rather than secured loan) form is largely, if not exclusively, part of an effort to insulate the transactions from bankruptcy risk, and thereby (the securities firms would argue) reduce the cost of financing.[28] The Wall Street firms that engage in these transactions have become quite sophisticated in their efforts to create "bankruptcy remote" transactions. Through a trade association known as the "Bond Market Association" they have created standard repo documentation which reduces the cost and time of negotiating documentation for each transaction.[29]

From time to time, the documentation has been updated in response to the creation of new types of transactions, and in a continuing effort to stay one step ahead of the bankruptcy laws. The most important problem the repo advocates face is probably the risk that their transactions will be recharacterized as secured loans rather than purchase and sale transactions. The standard form Master Repurchase Agreement itself reflects this strategy—it uses the terms "seller" and "buyer" and expresses an intent that the transactions be treated as purchases and sales, but also contains provisions purporting to create a security interest in favor of the "buyer" (lender) if the transaction is recharacterized as a secured loan.

The repo advocates won a big victory when the Southern District of New York accepted the "sale" characterization in *Granite Partners, L.P. v. Bear Stearns & Co*, although several other courts have recognized that repos are in substance secured loans, rather than purchase and sale transactions.[30] More recently, in the Criimi Mae case, a Maryland bankruptcy court held that the standard bond market association repo form is ambiguous, so that extrinsic evidence is necessary to determine whether a transaction written on that form was intended to be a "true repo" or a secured loan.[31]

The viability of the repo transaction depends upon its being characterized as a purchase/sale, rather than as a secured loan. Those courts that believe it is important for the economy to have bankruptcy remote repo transactions may continue to characterize them as purchase and sale transactions (in what impresses us as result-driven jurisprudence), while those willing to elevate substance over form, regardless of the impact that doing so may have on the financing markets, are likely to recharacterize them as secured loans. This is a battle that will likely be fought out many more times before it is finally resolved.

---

28. Congress has cooperated to some extent by enacting §§555 and 559 of the Bankruptcy Code, which help to insulate certain repos and other securities contracts from the bankruptcy laws.

29. See http://www.bondmarket.com.

30. *In re* Granite Partners L.P.,17 F. Supp. 2d. 275 (S.D.N.Y. 1998). Interestingly, one of those decisions that recognized that repos are, in substance, secured loans, was a case from the Second Circuit — the court of appeals whose decisions are binding upon the court that decided Granite Partners—six years before Granite Partners was decided. *See* U.S. v. Manko, 979 F.2d 900, 902 (2d Cir. 1992) (noting that "[i]n effect, a repurchase agreement is a loan in the amount of the proceeds of the original sale, collateralized by [the security], with interest equal to the difference between the sale and the repurchase prices.").

31. *In re* CRIIMI MAE, 251 B.R. 796 (D. Md. 2000).

§8.15 ~ Beyond Repos

The legislative history gives abundant evidence that the drafters of Section 541(d) were thinking of the repo market and just about nothing else.[32] Defenders argue that it is important to keep this market "bankruptcy remote" to retain the fluidity of the capital market.

Whatever may be the merits of the repo case, the practical fact is that courts can read Section 541(d) to cover "bare legal" title generally, and not just repos. This is at least in part an application of standard principles of statutory interpretation. Reversing a bankruptcy decision, Judge Easterbrook said:

> The bankruptcy court thought that because the legislative history speaks only of secondary mortgage markets, §541(d) is limited to such cases. . . . Legislative history does not carry so much force. Mortgage markets may have been the impetus for §541(d), but statutes often create rules that reach beyond the immediate concerns that spawned them.[33]

For good or ill, the Easterbrook view seems to prevail. Courts regularly read Section 541(d) to apply to transactions that have nothing to do with repos or the secondary mortgage market, often without any comment on the underlying interpretation issue. And it is therefore a good working assumption that where the debtor's only interest in property is that he is trustee of a trust that owns the property, that property will not be within his bankruptcy estate.

§8.16 ~ "Bare Legal Title" and the Trustee's Avoiding Powers

So one problem with 541(d) is the question of scope. A second problem with Section 541(d) is more far-reaching. The problem is that Section 541 deals only with the property of the estate. It says nothing about the powers of the trustee to reach out and recapture assets that are not property of the estate by the use of his avoiding powers.

To understand this problem, consider the case of the debtor who borrows money and gives the bank a traditional mortgage. Using traditional jargon, the creditor is the equitable owner and the debtor retains bare legal title.[34] The debtor would seem to meet the definition of a mere title holder under Section 541(d), suggesting that the mortgagee should enjoy his rights under the mortgage.

But suppose the creditor forgets to record the mortgage. Section 544(a)(3) provides that the trustee may avoid a transfer of real estate that is avoidable by a bona fide purchaser. And the transfer before us is precisely the kind of transfer that the statute seems designed to avoid. *See generally* Chapter 14.

---

32. *See generally* 124 Cong. Rec. S17413 (daily ed. Oct 6, 1978), remarks of Sen. DeConcini; S. Rep. No. 95-989, 2nd Sess. at 83-84 (1978).

33. Belisle v. Plunkett 877 F.2d 512, 516 (7th Cir. 1989).

34. *Cf.* Whiting Pools, 462 U.S. 198, 204, n. 8.

On the same analysis, if the repo seller retains only bare legal title, then the property may be insulated via Section 541(d), but it might still be vulnerable to attack under Section 544. If the repo is characterized as a secured financing, but the seller (borrower) retains possession, then the lender may find not only that he does not "own" the repod property, but that if he has an avoidable security interest in it.

This is perhaps a surprising result. It surely cannot be what the drafters of Section 541(d) had in mind. The explanation must be an oversight—they were so focused on the underlying title issue that they forgot to deal with avoiding powers. But the issue may be mostly a theoretical one. We are not aware of any case in which a repo has been "avoided" under Section 544(a), and if the Bond Market Association and its members succeed in persuading courts that repos are "true sales," then its not likely to happen.

§8.17 ~ Compare: Constructive Trust

You probably remember the scene in Gilbert and Sullivan's operetta, "The Mikado," where Koko has to explain why he said he had executed Nanki-Poo when in fact he had done nothing for the sort. "When your Majesty says, 'Let a thing be done,' it's as good as done practically, it is done because your Majesty's will is law."[35]

Welcome to the world of constructive trust. Any experienced bankruptcy lawyer knows that if the debtor holds the property "in trust," then the nondebtor beneficiary has at least a shot of recapturing it unscathed. And any first year law student knows that constructive means "not"—a "constructive" trust is not a trust at all, but an incantation that the judge uses to sprinkle on over the subject property to protect it from the depredations of the trustee.

Constructive trusts have a way of popping up here and there in bankruptcy law, often unpredictably. The Supreme Court used language of this sort to protect income that the debtor withheld from the debtor's wages, to be paid over to the tax collector.[36] Courts have given the same treatment to assets (and proceeds of assets) received by brokers and dealers from farmers under the Perishable Agricultural Commodities Act (PACA).[37]

The doctrine goes to work perhaps most often in family cases. For example, the Sixth Circuit, deciding In re *McCafferty*[38] had to consider the case of an ex-spouse who wanted to claim a share of the debtor's pension. The court (reversing two lower courts) played the "constructive trust" trump to hold that the portion of benefits awarded to the wife did not become property of the estate.

---

35. W.S. Gilbert, The Mikado, Act II (1875). The Mikado remarks drily that he had furnished "most affecting particulars." Pooh-bah assures him these are "merely corroborative detail intended to give artistic verisimilitude to a bald and unconvincing narrative."

36. Begier v. IRS, 4967 U.S. 53 (1990).

37. 7 U.S.C. §499a *et seq. See* C&E Enters. v. Milton Poulos, Inc. (*In re* Milton Poulos, Inc.) 107 B.R. 715 (B.A.P. 9th Cir. 1989), *aff'd in part and rev'd in part*, 947 F.2d 1351 (9th Cir. 1991).

38. 96 F.2d 192 (6th Cir. 1992).

Other courts have also held that constructive trusts are inconsistent with the general objectives of the bankruptcy system, and are therefore disfavored.[39]

Remember, the point of the constructive trust argument is to upset the pro rata distribution scheme and to push one party to the head of the queue. So, if the estate has $1,000 to distribute and there are five general creditors with claims of $800 each, then each will get 25 cents on the dollar, or $200. But if one of the five persuades the court to hold that $800 of the $1,000 is held in constructive trust for him, then he gets paid in full and the others will get only 6.25 cents on the dollar, or $50.

You have two warring principles at work here. On the one hand, bankruptcy judges like equity of distribution, and resist efforts to upset it. On the other hand, at least some of them tend to favor the occasional non-professional creditor (often an ex-spouse) who will suffer if the commercial creditors walk away with too much.

§8.18 ~ Caution: Equitable Ownership

In the trust cases, we talk of the debtor as the legal owner (sometimes: the *mere* legal owner), leaving the nondebtor with the equitable (superior) claim. In trust law, courts and commentators are pretty consistent in using the language this way. The trouble is, you can find a competing line of cases in which the courts use the language just the other way around.

So, the Ninth Circuit tells us that a person who holds a mere equitable interest will not qualify as a bona fide purchaser.[40] A Federal district court tells us that "it has long been the law that a mere equitable interest in personal property will not support an action for conversion."[41] And a bankruptcy court tells us that "a mere equitable interest in property . . . is not subject to execution."[42]

We suppose we can live with a world where the courts make the same word carry exactly opposite meanings. But it does mean you will have to stay alert when reading cases to make sure exactly what the court is saying and whose side it is on.

---

39. *See, e.g., In re* Stotler & Co., 144 B.R. 385, 388 (N.D. Ill. 1992) ("[A] constructive trust is fundamentally at odds with the general goals of the Bankruptcy Code."); *in re* Behring Int'l, Inc., 61 B.R. 896, 902 (Bankr. N.D. Tex. 1986) ("[t]he reluctance of [b]ankruptcy [c]ourts to impose constructive trusts ... stems from the recognition that each unsecured creditor desires to have his particular claim elevated above the others. Imposition of a constructive trust clearly thwarts the policy of ratable distribution and should not be impressed cavalierly.").

40. Perry v. O'Donnell, 749 F.2d 1346, 1349 (9th Cir. 1984).

41. Tudor Assocs. v. AJ & AJ Servicing, 843 F. Supp. 68, 76 (E.D. N.C. 1993).

42. The court adds: "except an equity of redemption and the perfect[ed?] equity of a purchaser of real estate." *In re* Sandefer, 47 B.R. 133, 136 (Bankr. N.D. Ala. 1985).

§8.19 ~ Pensions

For individual debtors, there is a far more important body of trust law. This is the framework that has come to govern the debtor's pension. Start with some general background. For many individual debtors, perhaps the most important piece of property they will retain at the time of bankruptcy will be their interest in a private pension fund. The stake in the pension fund had become the focus of contention in bankruptcy, partly due to its sheer size, and partly due to a reading that the Supreme Court gave to some pivotal language in the Code. The reading may be correct, but it surely goes far beyond anything the drafters had in mind when they wrote it.

Since the mid-1970s, most pension funds have been governed by the Employee Retirement Income Security Act (ERISA) and related tax statutes. The regime provides important tax advantages for "qualified" pensions. To be "qualified" a pension must contain an anti-alienation provision—a provision that the fund will not be amenable to the claims of creditors.[43] As a matter of tax policy, the common sense of the provision is easy enough to see. After all, without a the anti-alienation rule, the debtor could simply enjoy the tax advantage, then run up debts, then let his creditors collect out of tax-free dollars.

Now, consider what happens when the debtor goes into bankruptcy holding a large chunk of wealth in an ERISA qualified fund—i.e., a fund with an anti-alienation provision. Will the trustee be able to reach the fund?

The short answer is no. The reason is found in Section 541(c)(2). This section provides:

> "A restriction on the transfer of a beneficial interest of the debtor in a trust that is enforceable under applicable nonbankruptcy law is enforceable in a case under this title."

In an important case, the Supreme Court (resolving a split among the circuits) held that this provision served to insulate the ERISA-qualified pension fund.[44] The court reasoned that the ERISA anti-alienation rule qualified as "a restriction .... enforceable under applicable nonbankruptcy law." Note that the result is *not* that the ERISA qualified pension is exempt from bankruptcy administration, but rather that it does not become part of the estate at all.

The decision seems hard to argue with as a matter of statute-reading, although it did make a substantial volume of wealth available to individual debtors—particularly in the upper income brackets—that might otherwise have gone to pay their debt. Equally hard to argue is the proposition that probably neither side had the other in mind when the statutes were written—that is, the bankruptcy scriveners don't seem to have given any specific thought to pension law when they wrote Section 541(c)(2), and the pensions law drafters almost certainly weren't thinking about bankruptcy.

---

43. 29 U.S.C. §1056(d)(1) requires that each qualified pension plan shall provide that benefits provided under the plan may not be assigned or alienated.

44. Patterson v. Shumate, 504 U.S. 753, 759-60 (1992).

Rather, Section 541(c)(2) was drafted with an entirely different situation in mind, and the difference is instructive. What Section 541(c)(2) was created for is the old-fashioned spendthrift trust.[45]

To understand the classic spendthrift trust, consider the case of Uncle who wishes to leave a bequest to Nephew but who fears that Nephew will fritter it away on luxuries rather than using to pay living expenses. Uncle leaves the money in a trust empowered to pay ordinary living expenses but specifically barred from paying claims of creditors, thereby protecting Nephew against his spendthrift tendencies.

Traditionally not all jurisdictions recognized spendthrift trusts: some saw them as encouraging an unwholesome irresponsibility, out of keeping with republican virtue.[46] The Bankruptcy Code takes no explicit position on republican virtue. Rather, Section 541(c)(2) provides that if nonbankruptcy law allows such a restriction, then bankruptcy will respect it as well.

But for present purposes, there is an additional point. That is that even in tolerant regimes, a first principle of spendthrift trust law was that you couldn't "spendthrift yourself."[47] That is, the Uncle might leave money to Nephew subject to a spendthrift bar, but Nephew could not impose such a bar on his own assets.

But ERISA pension funds are very often, in effect, self-settled spendthrift trusts. So the effect of the current reading is that debtors can retain funds in pension trust in volume unanticipated by the drafters and on terms unavailable in traditional spendthrift trust law.

If there is anything that appears unseemly about this relationship, an answer is that this is all a matter of statutory, not Constitutional, law and that Congress could have stopped it any time to limit the available exclusions. Congress, of course, has done nothing of the sort. Rather to the contrary, it has considered a number of proposals to restrict pension exclusions and done nothing about them.[48]

The rules discussed so far do not apply to the debtor's Individual Retirement Account (IRA).[49] The IRA enjoys tax advantages, but it is not protected by the same kind of anti-alienation rule. Rather, the debtor may withdraw, or creditors may levy, at any time. The only relevant consequence is that the debtor may

---

45. A "spendthrift trust" is a "[t]rust in which the interest of a beneficiary cannot be assigned by him or reached by his creditors." Austin W. Scott & William Fratcher, The Law of Trusts, §151 (4th ed. 1987). *See generally* Adam J. Hirsch, *Spendthrift Trusts and Public Policy: Economic and Cognitive Perspectives*, 73 Wash U. L. Q. 1 (1995).

46. A seminal case holds that the spendthrift trust does not violate public policy unless the restraint on alienation amounts to a fraud on creditors. Broadway Nat'l Bank v. Adams, 133 Mass. 170, 173 (1888).

47. *See* Restatement (2d) Trusts §156 (1957); Austin W. Scott & William F. Fratcher, The Law of Trusts §156 (Rev. 4th ed. 1989). Delaware and Alaska recently enacted statutes allowing self-spendthrifting. For a discussion *see* §15.24 ff.

48. Courts have shown themselves correspondingly hospitable to a broad reading of *Patterson*. In Barkley v. Conner, 73 F.3d 258 (9th Cir. 1996), the Ninth Circuit had to consider the status of contributions to an ERISA plan that exceeded the limits eligible for tax protection. The Court held that these were excluded just like the tax-qualified contributions.

49. 26 U.S.C. 408.

have to pay a penalty. But while IRAs are not excluded from the estate, the debtor may be able to exempt part or all them from creditors' claims.[50]

A particularly notorious case is *Solomon v. Cosby*, where Dr. Solomon filed for relief under chapter 13 while facing tort suits for sexual misconduct.[51] Dr. Solomon had some $1.5 million in IRAs, but only some $40,000 in non-exempt assets. He proposed to discharge all claims by paying some $45,000 in installments. The bankruptcy court denied confirmation but the Circuit court reversed, holding that the IRAs were not "disposable income" that must be paid to the creditors.[52]

§8.20 ~ Some Property/Taxation Problems

§8.21 ~ The Tax Year: A Malpractice Trap

The debtor who files for bankruptcy often owes taxes. He may also have potential offsetting deductions. So it makes a difference who owes the taxes and who owns the deductions. Remarkably, he may be able to determine the question by his choice of "tax year." Suppose his normal tax year ends (as most of ours do) on December 30. Suppose he files for bankruptcy July 1. He can elect to terminate his tax year on June 30 (and to start a new tax year on July 1). Or he can do nothing, and the tax year will continue to December 30, as usual.[53]

As we will explain later, we think that usually it makes sense to elect. But election takes thought and action, and non-election happens by itself. Our reading of the cases suggests that a lot of lawyers don't know this, and cost their clients a lot of money by failing to make the election.

We think the whole issue is sufficiently complex that we wouldn't think of wading in without the assistance of specialized tax talent—either a tax lawyer or a CPA. But if you won't consult a specialist—and if you won't even read the rest of this section—at least take our bottom-line advice: when in doubt, elect. This isn't always the right advice, but it's more often right than wrong.

Our explanation follows. We limit our discussion to Federal taxes, for which the rules are set forth in the Internal Revenue Code. Different rules governing state and local taxes are in the Bankruptcy Code itself.[54]

---

50. *See, e.g.*, §522(d)(10)(E) (pension exempt to the extent necessary for support; many state laws have similar provisions). *Cf.* Orr v. Yuhas (*In re* Yuhas), 104 F.3d 612 (3d Cir. 1997) (New Jersey statute that exempted from creditors' claims property held in qualifying trust was restriction on transfer of debtor's IRA, and therefore IRA was excluded from debtor's bankruptcy estate).

51. 67 F.3d 1128 (4th Cir. 1995).

52. As so often happens in these cases, the court then remanded for a finding as to whether the plan was propounded "in good faith" under §1325(a)(3). *Id.* at 1134.

53. 26 U.S.C. §1398(d)(1). *See In re* Haedo, 211 B.R. 149 (Bankr. S.D.N.Y. 1997).

54. *See* §§326, 728, 1146. The applicability of these rules remains open to question in light of the Supreme Court's newfound infatuation with state immunity. *See* §4.24.

§8.22 ~ Loss Carryover Examples

Here are some examples of the tax year problem. In each case, the debtor files for bankruptcy on July 1. Absent bankruptcy, her tax year would end December 30. The question is whether she should make the election to terminate her tax year as of June 30, and start a new tax year on July 1.

Example: In the six months preceding bankruptcy, she had income generating a tax liability of $20,000. If she does not make the election, she will owe the tax as of December 30, and the tax collector will have no right to share in the estate. If she makes the election, she will owe the tax as of June 30, and the tax collector will have a right to share in the estate.

Example: Before last January 1, the debtor accumulated surplus deductions that she could use as "loss carrybacks" to reduce prior year's taxes. If she does not make the election, the loss carrybacks will pass to the trustee to reduce the estate's tax liability. If she makes the election, she will be entitled to use them herself.

Example: In the six months preceding bankruptcy, the debtor accumulated surplus deductions, entitling her to an offset against income. She had no income during the six months preceding bankruptcy, but she anticipates she will have income in the six months after bankruptcy. If she does not make the election, she will be able to use the deductions against her post-petition income. If she makes the election, the trustee gets to use the deductions and her post-petition income is not protected by them.

Note that in the first two examples, the debtor should make the election and in the third, she should not. Since we think the first two cases are far more common than the third, we think the rule should be "when in doubt, elect." Unfortunately, non-election is self-executing, while election takes some planning and thought. The reports are littered with cases where the debtor (or her attorney?) failed to make the election, to her cost.[55]

§8.23 ~ Carryover Law

When an individual files for chapter 11 or chapter 7, the estate is for tax purposes a separate entity.[56] Income of the estate is taxable to the estate and income of the debtor is taxable to the debtor. Per bankruptcy law, property of the debtor passes to the trustee on filing. Per tax law, this kind of transfer usually creates tax consequences. But tax law includes a special exception for bankruptcy, holding that this particular transfer is not a tax-triggering event.[57]

---

55. *See, e.g., In re* Johnson, 190 B.R. 724 (Bankr. D. Mass. 1995) (failure to elect makes entire tax liability a post-discharge obligation).

56. 26 U.S.C. §1398(a).

57. *Id.* §1398(f)(1). And it works the other way around. There is also no tax event when property revests in the debtor after confirmation of a plan. *Id.* §1398(f)(2).

Some tax attributes also pass to the trustee. These include, for example, loss carryovers and similar tax benefits.[58] The Internal Revenue Code provides that the tax attributes that pass to the estate are those that exist on the first day of the tax year in which the case commences.[59] So, suppose the debtor files on August 15. If she makes the election, then the first day of the tax year in which the case commences is August 16. If she fails to make the election, then the first day of the tax year in which the case commences is January 1.

Likewise, the debtor's liability for income tax arises on the last day of the tax year.[60] So if she makes the election, then the estate is liable for taxes on income through the date of filing. If she fails to make the election, then she is liable herself.

§8.24 ~ Income on Default

It seems ironic to think of a debtor on the eve of bankruptcy having income for tax purposes, but it may be easier than it looks.

Example: Consider Delbert, a farmer, who owns Blackacre worth $800,000, subject to a security interest in favor of BancCo for a $1 million note. Delbert's tax basis—the cost of the property, as imputed for tax purposes—is $150,000. Unable to keep up the payments, Delbert surrenders the property to BancCo in exchange for a release on the deficiency claim.

Delbert has two kinds of income. He has income from cancellation of indebtedness (COD income) to the tune of $1 million minus $800,000, or $200,000.[61] He has income on gain in the amount of $800,000 minus $150,000 or $650,000.[62]

---

58. The estate shall succeed to and take into account the following items (determined as of the first day of the debtor's taxable year in which the case commences) of the debtor–

> (1) Net operating loss carryovers; (2) Charitable contributions carryovers; (3) Recovery of tax benefit items; (4) Credit carryovers, etc.; (5) Capital loss carryovers; (6) Basis, holding period, and character of assets; (7) Method of accounting. The method of accounting used by the debtor.; (8) Other attributes to the extent provided in regulations.

Id. §1398(g). *See generally id.* §172(1)(A)(I) & (ii) (operating losses); *id.* §1212(b)(1)(A)-(B) (capital losses); *id.* §170(b) (excess charitable contributions); *id.* §1398(g)(6) (debtor's basis in property). Transfer of federal loss carryovers may be discretionary, *but see* §8.25. Transfer of state and local loss carryovers is mandatory. Section 346(j).

59. 26 U.S.C. §1398(d).

60. *Id.*

61. *Id.* §61(a)(12) (providing for inclusion of reduction of debts in gross income).

62. *Id.* §1001 (providing for recognition of gains or losses on sale or transfer).

The fact of all this income does not mean there will be a huge tax. The debtor (or the estate) may have offsetting losses. Further, gain from sale may sometimes be exempt from tax.[63] And cancellation of indebtedness may not create income if the cancellation is done in a bankruptcy case.[64] For more on foreclosure strategies where there may be COD income and gain, see §8.33.

§8.25 ~ Caution—Fraudulent Transfer

Adding an extra complication to the rules on tax planning for bankruptcy, we need to warn that a couple of courts have held unwound transactions of this sort as fraudulent transfers. A recent example is *Feiler v. Towers*.[65] The court had to consider a loss carryover. The relevant tax law provided that the taxpayer might elect to carry the losses back to offset income from prior years, or forward to protect income in the future. Five months before bankruptcy, the taxpayer elected to carry forward. Election to carry back would have led to a refund of some $266,000 which would have become property of the estate. Election to carry forward left the attribute available to set against post-bankruptcy income unencumbered by the trustee's claim. The appellate panel, upholding a bankruptcy judge, held that the transfer was avoidable on the complaint of the trustee.[66]

§8.26 ~ Exemptions—§522 and Non-bankruptcy Law

In bankruptcy and out, the (individual) debtor will be able to claim some property for himself as exempt from creditor execution. Aside from bankruptcy, every state mandates, by statute, a list of property the debtor may claim as exempt. Traditional exemptions may be understood as providing the debtor with at least minimal means of support (e.g., earnings) or for a chance to start over (e.g., tools of the trade). Some states developed liberal homestead exemptions as a device for luring settlers. More recent exemption laws bear the flavor of institutional lobbying (e.g., life insurance, cemetery lots). As creatures of state law, exemptions necessarily vary from state to state.

The first rule of exemptions is use it or lose it. Translated: normally it is up to the debtor (for which read: his *lawyer*) to claim the exemption. Neither creditor nor court has any duty to claim it for him. This means that if someone is trying to levy against your client, it is up to you to lay your hands on an up-to-date list of exemptions in your jurisdiction, and to claim everything possible.[67] The Norton Treatise maintains a summary of individual state exemption schemes with references to applicable state statutes.[68] Collier also has an "Exemptions" volume that lists the exemptions for each state.[69]

---

63. *Id.* §121 (gain from sale of personal residence). If the taxable event occurs while the debtor is in bankruptcy, it remains an unsettled question whether the exemption protects the trustee.

64. 26 U.S.C. §108(a)(1)(A).

65. *In re* Feiler, 230 B.R. 164 (9th Cir. BAP 1999).

66. The court rested its holding on value/insolvency not intent, so the holding does not present a threat to the debtor's discharge.

67. As we explain below, most exemption claims arise in the context of a bankruptcy filing. Probably most bankruptcy filings today come forth on computerized forms. It appears that the commercial producers of filing forms now include checklists of exemptions as part of their basic package.

68. 2 Norton Bankr. L. & Prac. 2d Ch. 46 App. (1998).

69. Collier on Bankruptcy (15th ed. Rev. 1997).

Claiming the exemption means, first of all, claiming it on the bankruptcy schedules. But for some exemptions, you may have to do more. For example, in Virginia, you can't claim a homestead exemption unless you have recorded a homestead deed.[70] So you'll need to give yourself enough lead time to make sure you've removed any state law obstacles, even before prepare the bankruptcy schedules.

In the run-up to the 1978 Code, bankruptcy reformers focused a lot of scrutiny on the exemption system. They didn't like the inconsistency from state to state. More important, they thought that exemptions in many states weren't generous enough. The obvious solution was to impose a single set of exemptions nationwide.

Creditor lobbyists resisted this federalization of exemptions, and Congress brought forth a compromise, set forth in Section 522. From reading Section 522 alone, you wouldn't guess how it works in practice, so here is a sketch: Section 522 purports to offer the debtor a choice of exemptions. He may take either (a) a scheme of federal exemptions, detailed in Section 522(d); or (b) the exemptions that would have been available under non-bankruptcy law had he never sought bankruptcy relief. [71]

The debtor may also get some protection from state "property" rules, independent of exemptions. For example, some states provide that a husband and wife may hold property in "tenancy by the entireties." Tenancy by the entireties property may not be subject to levy except for joint debts, and this protection may carry over into bankruptcy.[72]

But the section also provided that any individual state might opt out of the Federal exemption scheme. And in fact, as of this writing, some 37 states have opted out, meaning that in these states and federal exemptions are not available, and the debtor's only choice is the state exemptions.

§8.27 ~ Exemption Procedure

You make or exemption claim as part of your initial filing. But here is a procedural curiosity. If the debtor claims an exemption to which he is not entitled, then the trustee must (or a creditor may) file an objection. In a remarkable recent Supreme Court case, the debtor had made a claim of exemption which even the most casual observer might have recognized as invalid. The trustee missed the objection deadline. The Supreme Court let the exemption stand.[73] One wonders if this rule has tempted counsel to make blatantly invalid exemption claims in the hope of trapping the drowsy trustee.

---

70. Va. Code Ann. §34-6 (1999).

71. For example: the Consumer Credit Protection Act, 15 U.S.C. §1673, imposes a 25 percent limit in wage garnishments. There are specific federal exemptions for Social Security payments, 42 U.S.C. §407 and veterans' benefits, 38 U.S.C. §5301.

72. *See, e.g., In re* Ginn, 186 B.R. 898, 902-03 (Bankr. D. Md. 1995).

73. Taylor v. Freeland & Kronz, 503 U.S. 638, 643 (1992). *But cf.* Mercer v. Monzack (*In re* Mercer), 53 F.3d 1, 2-4 (1st Cir. 1995) (explaining and restricting *Taylor*).

§8.28 ~ Partner's Property and the Partnership Debtor

The Code recognizes a distinction between partnership and partner. Correspondingly, the partnership estate does not include the property of individual partners. But a first principle of partnership law is that general partners are liable for partnership debts. May the trustee reach the assets of the general partners?

Section 723 provides that the trustee may reach the assets of the general partner, to the extent that the partner would be liable under non-bankruptcy law. But Section 723 applies only in chapter 7. This seems to suggest that the general partner is insulated from liability in chapters 11 and 12.

Some courts have indeed so held.[74] But others have found means for reaching the general partners even in chapter 11, deploying some combination of Section 541(a) (property of the estate, 544(a) (trustee's hypothetical lien creditor power) and non-bankruptcy partnership law.[75] And the potential of general partner liability may determine whether a plan qualifies under the "best interest" test, because a creditor is entitled in a chapter 11 Plan to receive at least what he would receive in a chapter 7 liquidation, and in the chapter 7 liquidation the trustee would have recourse to the assets of the general partners to satisfy partnership obligations.[76] *See* §18.12.

§8.29 ~ Abandonment

§8.30 ~ In General

Section 554 of the Code provides that the trustee "may abandon any property of the estate that is burdensome to the estate or that is of inconsequential value to the estate." This is common sense. The risk for the creditor is that a dozing or negligent trustee might abandon something that is not burdensome or inconsequential, to the detriment of a creditor recovery.

But the Code requires notice of abandonment, and a trustee who abandons to the prejudice of creditors without notice may find himself paying off on his bond.[77] If a trustee does not abandon on his own, a party in interest may ask the court to order him to abandon. If the property is properly scheduled and not otherwise administered, then at the close of the case it is automatically deemed abandoned to the debtor.

The typical abandonment case is one in which there is simply nothing worth administering. The most famous abandonment case is surely *Midatlantic Nat'l Bank v. New Jersey Dep't of Environmental Protection*.[78] That is the case where the court held that the trustee was not empowered to abandon a

---

74. *See, e.g.*, MBank Corpus Christ v. Seikel (*In re* I-37 Gulf Limited Partnership), 48 B.R. 647, 650 (Bankr. S.D. Tex. 1985).

75. *See, e.g.*, Commercial Bank v. Price (*In re* Nortchcliff Associates), 139 B.R. 361, 371-72 (Bankr. D. Md. 1992) (containing all three justifications).

76. For §723 and the priority of claims, *see* §13.49.

77. Fed R. Bankr. Proc. 6007. *See*, e.g., *In re* Killebrew, 888 F.2d 1516 (5th Cir. 1989).

78. 474 U.S. 494 (1986).

toxic waste site in contravention of state environmental laws reasonably designed to protect health and safety. The decision came during a decade when the courts were coming up with all sorts of devices to effect priority for environmental claims, whether or not it was spelled out in the statute. Its effect does not seem to have extended much beyond the environmental arena.[79]

§8.31 ~ Abandonment to Lien Creditors

A special abandonment rule provides that the trustee shall "dispose of" any property in which an entity other than the estate has an interest, such as a lien, and that has not been disposed of under another section of this title.[80] The provision applies only in chapter 7. The typical case is one in which a creditor has a claim of $1,000 secured by collateral worth $600. Since the claim exceeds the value of the collateral, the estate has no stake, and so it is proper for the trustee to release it.

§8.32 ~ Procedure

The rules provides that notice of intended abandonment must be given to creditors, committees and the U. S. Trustee.[81] Perhaps surprisingly, it does not specify a time (e.g., 20 days, as in so many other similar cases). A party in interest may file and serve an objection within 15 days of the mailing of the notice. Presumably (although the rule doesn't specify) the objection triggers a contested matter under rule 9014.

§8.33 ~ Keep-Away in Tax Cases

The trustee and the debtor may play a game of keep-away over taxes when the property is transferred back to the lender.

Example: Doris, a debtor who owns Whiteacre valued at $6 million, securing a claim of $8 million held by InsCo. Doris' basis in the property is $2.4 million. She is pretty sure she is going to lose the property, and she is thinking about filing for bankruptcy. Should she allow InsCo to take the property now, or should she wait until after the property passes to a trustee? There is no single answer to this question. Surprisingly, the issue is tied up with the law of abandonment.

First, suppose Doris surrenders the property to InsCo in full satisfaction of her debt. She has $2 million in COD income and $5.6 million as gain on sale.[82] She probably faces a tax liability.[83]

---

79. *Cf. In re* Smith-Douglass, Inc., 856 F.2d 12, 17 (4th Cir. 1998) (abandonment proper where no imminent danger to the public health or safety and where the debtor had no unencumbered assets for environmental cleanup).

80. Section 725.

81. Fed. R. Bankr. Proc. 6007.

82. *See* §8.24.

83. She may, of course, offset her income with loss carryovers and similar tax attributes. And if she files for bankruptcy it will be a claim against her estate. So if she is careful and lucky, she may be able to avoid any out of pocket expense.

But suppose she still holds the property, in deep distress, when she files for bankruptcy. The property passes to the trustee, and so do the tax attributes. Ignoring tax, the trustee has no incentive to keep the property. InsCo's claim exceeds the value of the collateral and so there will be nothing left to administer for the estate. Worse for the trustee—but better for Doris—if the trustee loses the property to InsCo, it is the estate that gets the gain from transfer and correspondingly the liability for tax.

Good news for Doris, so far—but necessarily, the trustee will want to toss this hot potato back into her lap by abandoning the property back to Doris, so any action by InsCo is against her and any liability, hers alone—and a post-bankruptcy liability at that. Indeed, if this is the state of the law, it is probably malpractice of the trustee not to abandon, because failure to abandon will create liability for the estate.

Is there any hope for Doris? There may be. An occasional court has held that the act of abandonment is a "taxable event" which itself triggers liability in the trustee.[84] If this is true, then the trustee is no better off abandoning than he would be in losing the property to the bank.

---

84. *In re* Rubin, 154 B.R. 897 (Bankr. D. Md. 1992), *In re* A. J. Lane & Co., 133 B.R. 264, 270-71 (Bankr. D. Mass. 1991); *but see In re* Olson, 100 B.R. 458 (Bankr. N.D. Iowa 1989) (abandonment was not sale) *aff'd* 121 B.R. 346 (N.D. Iowa 1990), *aff'd* 930 F.2d 6 (8th Cir. 1990).

9 How the Debtor Gets to Keep 'His Own' Property

9 How the Debtor Gets to Keep 'His Own' Property

§9.1 ~ Introduction

The benchmark in bankruptcy is that the debtor turns over his property to the trustee, who liquidates it and distributes the proceeds to creditors. If there is a creditor with a security interest that exceeds the value of his collateral, then the trustee may just abandon the property and let the secured creditor and debtor fight it out.

In the teeth of this sort of opposition, does the debtor ever get to keep his own property? Surprisingly often, he does. For purposes of this book, the most important devices for retaining property are in chapter 11, which we deal with in detail later. The following is a catalog of a variety of devices that will work to leave property in the hands of the debtor, notwithstanding the claims of the trustee and of secured creditors. (Later, we call attention to a couple of devices that *won't* work).

§9.2 ~ Confirm a Plan

Confirm a chapter 11 plan—including a cram-down plan. A classic purpose of chapter 11 is to provide a device whereby the debtor gets to hang onto property while creditors' claims are disposed of. Cram-down, in which the debtor may "rewrite the contract" and impose it on the secured creditor, is only the most dramatic of plan devices. *See generally* Chapter 18, below.

Confirm a chapter 13 plan. Chapter 13 provides a bargain-basement plan process for "debtors with a regular income"—usually (but not always) wage-earners. Compare also chapter 12, for "family farmers." Both chapters include a kind of cram-down.

§9.3 ~ Claim it As Exempt

Claim the property as exempt. Section 522 provides that any (individual) debtor may claim property as exempt, either under the bankruptcy statute or under non-bankruptcy law (but, as noted above, most states have exercised their statutory right to "opt out" of the federal system, leaving only state exemptions available).

§9.4 ~ Redeem It

Redeem the property under chapter 7. Sometimes overlooked, Section 722 gives the debtor the right to "buy back" collateral from the secured creditor. The important part is that the debtor gets to redeem the property at a court-imposed valuation, rather than having to bargain on his own. The right applies only to consumer goods securing a consumer debt. It applies only when the property is exempt, or when the trustee is abandoning the property.

So, consider Daniel Debtor who owes $5,000 on his household goods. Although it might cost as much as $6,000 to replace them, the court finds they are worth only $2,000. Daniel may redeem by paying $2,000. Unfortunately for consumer debtors, they must pay the entire buyback price at the time the right is exercised—no installment deals here.

§9.5 ~ Buy It Back

Buy back from the estate "in the market." The trustee is supposed to maximize the value of the estate which means, for practical purposes, he is supposed to sell to the highest bidder. And who is the highest bidder? In many cases it will be none other than the debtor himself. After all, who better than the debtor knows whether that engine leak is really serious or how much change is hidden under the back seat? His "reserve price," as the economists like to say, is likely to be higher than anyone else's. Of course, perhaps sadly, his attachment to "his" property may lead him to overpay for goods that he could easily replace more cheaply.

Unfortunately for the debtor, the typical trustee is not in the business of extending credit. A purchase from the trustee, like the redemption, will probably require cash on the line—and the cash will have to come from some place other than the bankruptcy estate.

§9.6 ~ Reaffirmation

Enter into a deal with the secured creditor. Consider Delia Debtor, who owes $18,000 to CredCo, secured by her two-year-old sports car, worth only $10,000. She can't really handle the installment payments on $18,000 and she certainly can't pony up the cash to redeem under Section 722 at $10,000. But with a little extra scrimping, she might be able to continue with payments on $12,000.

Can she make it happen? Of course she might do it as a cram-down in chapter13 (or even 11 or 12). Nothing requires the secured creditor to take her deal in chapter 7. But the practical fact is that plenty of creditors will be glad to enter into a new contract in which Delia agrees to pay $12,000. Better the new deal, they will reason, than to stand by helpless while Delia tosses the keys on the table and heads off to ride the bus. And there are a significant number of cases where the debtor will reaffirm the debt without modification of the terms or reduction of the amount due, just because he wants to return his property and may not be able to get new credit.

For the creditor, there is one vital threshold here: per Section 524(c) and (d), the reaffirmation agreement must be approved by the court. The criteria for court approval cover a page or two of text, but here are the vital points:

- The deal must be done before the discharge.
- The debtor gets sixty days to rescind.
- The deal must not impose an undue hardship on the debtor.

Caution: If you represent the creditor in a consumer bankruptcy case, don't even think about skipping the reaffirmation process. Sears—the retailer—found itself in the middle of a costly and embarrassing mess in the late 1990s when it came to light that the company regularly failed to file reaffirmation agreements with the court.

Lawsuits and settlements took a 75 percent bite out of earnings in just one quarter. The $60 million fine that Sears paid was apparently the highest for this sort of thing in history. One plaintiff's attorney reportedly walked off with a $7.5 million settlement fee in a resulting class action. Ironically, some industry insiders believe that Sears may have been sidestepping the court in the case of deals it believed too favorable for public notice—apparently Sears didn't want to tip other debtors that they could be rolled.

§9.7 ~ Soldier On

Soldier on. Consider Delbert Debtor, who owes $26,000 to CredCo secured by the van he uses in his plumbing business—value unknown, but certainly less than $26,000. Delbert doesn't have enough cash to redeem under Section 722, and CredCo has made it clear that it is in no mood to deal. On the other hand, someone told Delbert that even if you are going bankrupt, you need to keep your secured creditors happy—and he has never missed a payment.

What if Delbert just keeps on paying, and keeps on driving? He isn't in default (and the creditor can't enforce a "bankruptcy clause": see Section 541(c)). Of course, CredCo's claim may ride through the bankruptcy—that is, the *secured* claim will ride through, though any unsecured claim will be discharged. So if Delbert quits paying later, he may lose the van, but at least he won't be liable for any deficiency claim.

Creditor lobbyists, frustrated and dismayed to be left hanging this way, prevailed on Congress to add Section 521(2), which seems to require the debtor to put up or shut up—either to surrender the property or to reaffirm the debt. But the section doesn't offer what it seems to offer. In the first place, it covers only "consumer" debt, so it appears not to apply to Delbert's plumbing van at all. But in addition, something like half the circuits have virtually read the teeth out of this section, holding, in effect, that there is simply no sanction for failing to do what the section seems to require.[1] This may help to explain why some bankruptcy judges will implore a debtor, not in default, not to make any agreement to reaffirm secured debt.

So much for devices that may help the debtor. Now, consider a couple that may not.

---

1. *See, e.g., In re* Parker, 139 F.3d 668 (9th Cir. 1998); *In re* Boodrow, 126 F.3d 43 (2d Cir. 1997); *In re* Belanger, 962 F.2d 345 (4th Cir. 1992); Lowry Federal Credit Union v. West, 882 F.2d 1543 (10th Cir. 1989).

§9.8 ~ The "New Value" Exception

Here we explain the *new value* exception to the absolute priority rule—and explain why it is, at least, more difficult to implement than it used to be.

The debtor LimCo, a limited partnership is a single asset real estate partnership ("SARE"). LimCo owes $10 million to NuBank, secured by Whiteacre, a strip shopping center, worth perhaps $7. LimCo proposes a cram-down plan in which it will pay $7 million to NuBank, retaining the equity for the old residual owners. NuBank objects that the plan is unconfirmable as a matter of law. NuBank points to Section 1129(b)(2) which provides, in effect, that you can't impose a cram-down without paying the full $10 million (and all other allowed unsecured claims) unless you wipe out the junior (equity) class.

The limited partners respond: it is true that we propose to retain an interest. But the Code says only that we cannot retain an interest *on account of* our pre-petition equity stake. We don't propose to retain our new interest on account of our old interest. Rather we propose (equity) to retain our interest on account of a contribution of *new value*. So the objection does not apply.

Going back to the early 80s, there was a hot debate over whether the Code allowed this particular tactic.[2] A number of cases flatly disallowed it. But many courts gave it their endorsement.

The device became a particular favorite in the late 80s and early 90s among lawyers trying to confirm plans in SARE cases. Debtors propounded (and creditors often accepted) new value plans as a device for avoiding the disastrous (to the partners) consequences of foreclosure, and retaining equity without paying unsecured claims in full.

Note one thing the plan did not propose to do. It did not propose to put the property (or the equity in the reorganized entity, which is essentially the same thing) up for auction, and let the partners bid. The partners feared (accurately, no doubt), that if they went to auction, then the secured creditor would credit-bid against them, or some competing developer would bid up the price. The whole point of the deal was to sidestep the reality of the market, and to hunker down in the warm embrace of a judicial valuation.

Will it fly today? The short answer is probably not. The Supreme Court seemingly put a stake through the heart of the strategy in the *LaSalle* case in the Spring of 1999.[3] Speaking for the Court, Justice Souter reasoned that there was no bar to the old owners' bidding at a general sale—and if they were the highest bidder, winning the sale. He just didn't like the plan where the Court imposed a valuation and the owners got to buy in at that number, without exposing the property (or the equity) to the market.

---

2. Abstruse and intricate as the analysis has become, the topic is necessarily a favorite among professors. One of us has weighed in. *See* John D. Ayer, *Rethinking Absolute Priority after Ahlers*, 87 MICH. L. REV. 963 (1989).

3. Bank of Am. Nat'l Trust and Sav. Ass'n v. 203 N. LaSalle St. Partnership , 526 U.S. 434 (1999).

Strictly speaking, Justice Souter said he left the issue of whether there is a "new value exception" to the absolute priority rule undecided.[4] But this is somewhat misleading, because the Court decided the issue of greatest practical importance.

You might think that this would put an end to the new value argument. But this conclusion is probably too hasty. The Court did not decide how the new equity should be exposed to the marketplace (i.e., is an auction necessary?), whether a court could require cash bids rather than credit bids, or other "procedural" (but potentially very important) issues.

There is also likely to be a fair amount of resistance in the bankruptcy bench and bar, where "new value" has long had a fair amount of support. One straw in the wind may be the opinion of Judge Mary F. Walrath deciding In *re Zenith Electronics Corp.*[5] The case is a complex corporate case, not a single-asset real estate case. It is perhaps distinctive in that the largest creditor (LGE) was also the largest shareholder. In any event, the debtor filed a pre-packaged plan in which LGE agreed to forgive $200 million in debt in exchange for $60 million in new funding, for which it got 100 percent of the new equity. An Equity Committee objected, arguing that *LaSalle* required an open market auction.

Judge Walrath held that *LaSalle* didn't apply because this was a consensual plan, not a cram-down. But she added:

> It is not appropriate to extend the ruling of the 203 North LaSalle case beyond the facts of that case. To do so would require in all cases that a debtor be placed "on the market" for sale to the highest bidder. Such a requirement would eliminate the concept of exclusivity contained in §1121(b) and the broad powers of the debtor to propose a plan in whatever format it desires.[6]

If this attitude is general, there is plenty of room to explore the "new value" issue, even after *LaSalle.*

§9.9 ~ Goodbye to Lien Stripping

Here is a technique that used to work, but doesn't any longer:

It is 1985. Consider the Case of Homer Householder, who owes $125,000 to BankCo secured by a first mortgage on Blackacre his personal residence, worth perhaps $90,000. He's eligible for chapter 13, and he'd love to do a "chapter 13 cramdown"—but Alice, his alert lawyer, has spotted Section 1322(b)(2) which provides that he *cannot* do the chapter 13 cramdown in a case where the only collateral is the debtor's personal residence.

---

4. "We do not decide whether the statute includes a new value corollary or exception, but hold that on any reading respondent's proposed plan fails to satisfy the statute, and accordingly reverse." 526 U.S. at 443 (1999).

5. 241 B.R. 92 (Bankr. D. Del. 1999).

6. *Id.* at 106.

As a second line of defense, Homer has been talking with his father, Grandpa Householder, who has agreed to come up with the entire sum necessary to pay off the loan—if he can do it at $90,000. Ironically, if this were a simple car loan, Homer (and Grandpa) could make it work under Section 722—but this is real estate, and the Section 722 redemption right does not apply.

Frustrated in her more obvious approaches, Alice the lawyer, being a creative and persistent sort, has been studying Section 506, on the status of the secured creditor. This is the section where we learn that the undersecured creditor has a secured claim to the extent of his collateral value, and an unsecured claim for the remainder. It also provides that any lien is "void" if it does not secure an allowed secured claim.

So Alice asks herself: why not simply file for chapter 7 and ask the court to make a finding that the property is worth just $90,000. Then Grandpa could pay the money into the estate (to discharge the secured claim). And the unsecured deficiency claim would vanish with the discharge.

Alice is a little astonished at her own reasoning. After all, it hardly seems plausible that Congress, having provided so many safeguards for cram-down in chapter 11 and 13—and having written a redemption rule for personal property in Section 722—would let you achieve the same result in a fit of absent-mindedness under Section 506. Surely this analysis must be too good to be true?

It is too good to be true. In the case of *Dewsnup v. Timm*,[7] the Supreme Court in effect barred this door as a point of reentry for Homer. Justice Blackmun's opinion has come in for a good deal of criticism—not least from his dissenting colleague, Justice Scalia. Indeed, it depends on a strategy of statutory analysis which no one but Justice Blackmun has ever seemed able to explain.

But smoke and mirrors notwithstanding, the opinion probably reaches the right result: Surely (as Alice suspected), Congress did not intentionally provide for a low-cost end run around the general plan requirements.

Frustrated in chapters 7 and 13, Alice has yet another card up her sleeve. Noting that there is no specific barrier, she files an *individual* Chapter 11 for Homer, intending to impose a classic cram-down plan. But alas for Homer, the creditor lobby beat her to it.

After suffering a few bruises, the creditors prevailed on Congress for some amendatory language to Section 1123.[8] It provides that the proponent of a plan may modify the rights of a secured creditor—but then adds "other than a claim secured only by a security interest in real property that is the debtor's principal residence." The result, which some will find ironic, is that Rockefeller Center and Donald Trump's Atlantic Casino can fly over the barriers of chapter 11, but the son of Grandpa Householder has no place to lay his head.

---

7. 502 U.S. 410 (1992).

8. Section 1123(a)(1), (5).

On the other hand, *Dewsnup* (like *LaSalle* above?) may qualify as a gift that keeps on giving. Note that 1123(b)(5) and 1322(b)(2) speak of cases where the *only* collateral is the personal residence. You can guess where this is going. What if the security agreement covers the personal residence and also something else—say, the debtor's alarm clock, stipulated to be personal property? There is at least a risk that the creditor who makes the "alarm clock loan" will find that by extending beyond real property, he has lost his protection from cram down.[9]

---

9. There is a good discussion in PNC Mortgage v. Dicks, 199 B.R. 674 (N.D. Ind. 1996).

10

Keeping the Ship Afloat

10 Keeping the Ship Afloat

§10.1 ~ Introduction: Not Your Own Man Any More

The goal of the chapter 11 case is the confirmation of the plan. In the meantime, there is a lot to be done just to keep the ship afloat. But the debtor doesn't get to do it just as it chooses. Rather, the debtor must operate within a framework of rules that limit its power to make and implement decisions. Part of the price the debtor pays for the protection of the bankruptcy laws is this limitation on its previously unfettered discretion to run its business. As a general rule, the debtor may undertake "ordinary course" activities without court approval, but must obtain court orders for activities that are not in the ordinary course of business. Not surprisingly, then, there is a lot of debate about what constitutes an "ordinary course" action.

In this section we review three important topics that arise between filing and confirmation. First, we explain Section 363, which is the section under which the debtor sells and leases property and conducts its day-to-day operations. Then we look at Section 364, which permits the debtor to borrow money. Finally, we look at the matter of "operating orders," particularly "first-day orders," where the debtor needs the assent of the court to continue with its business.

§10.2 ~ Use, Sell or Lease—A Path Through Section 363

Section 363 authorizes the trustee (a term which includes the DIP) to "use, sell or lease" property of the estate. Section 363 is forbidding at first blush, but if you follow the right path, the general meaning is tolerably plain. Start with Section 363(c)(1):

> If the business of the debtor is authorized to be operated … and unless the court orders otherwise, the trustee may enter into transactions, including the sale or lease of property of the estate, in the ordinary course of business, without notice or a hearing, and may use property of the estate in the ordinary course of business without notice or hearing.

Now, consider the classic chapter 11. Recall that trustee includes DIP, and that Section 1108 provides that the trustee may continue to operate the business of the debtor until the court tells him to stop. Taken together, these rules provide the basic framework in which the trustee/DIP will continue to operate.[1] The upshot is that in most cases, the same people will continue to operate the business after filing as before, and so long as they operate "in the ordinary course of business" they may do so without court interference.

1. The rule may apply in chapter 7 also, if the Trustee is authorized to continue to operate the business, as he may be under §721. But as a practical matter, he almost never is so authorized, so chapter 11 remains the principal arena.

Contrast operation "other than in the ordinary course of business." Section 363(b)(1) provides that the trustee (including DIP) may "use, sell or lease" property of the estate in this case as well—but only "after notice and a hearing." On notice and a hearing, recall that it usually means no more than notice plus opportunity to be heard, with the burden of prevention falling on the objector. *See generally* §2.17, on "notice and a hearing."

Section 363(c)(2) governs use, sale, or lease of "cash collateral." The phrase is a term of art, defined in Section 363(a). It includes property "in which the estate and an entity other than the estate have an interest ..." The phrase is broad enough to include property held by the debtor subject to a security interest (including a right of setoff). The property covered includes "cash, negotiable instruments, documents of title, securities, deposit accounts or other cash equivalents."[2]

The language will likely cover just about everything that comes to the debtor under his general "working capital" or "revolver" loan where there is a security interest in receivables or inventory. The practical consequence is that in any case where the debtor has a secured working capital loan, and where he hopes to continue to operate in chapter 11, he will usually have to make a deal with the secured creditor at the beginning of the case—or find a new lender to take out the pre-petition lender.[3]

All of the trustee's powers to use, sell, or lease property are governed by an overriding condition that the court, on request, "shall prohibit or condition such use, sale, or lease as is necessary to provide adequate protection of such interest."[4] On the definition of adequate protection, *see* Section 361, and *see* §7.19.[5]

Finally, sales outside the ordinary course on occasion will be so extensive that they undermine the plan process itself—becoming a so-called "*sub rosa* plan." This is particularly an issue where the debtor seeks to sell most or all of the estate's assets.

§10.3 ~ PROCEDURE

The rules specify some of the procedure for sale of property of the estate outside the ordinary course of business. The rules provide that 20 days' notice to creditors and others.[6] Any objection must be filed and served not less than five days before the date set for the proposed action. The objection turns the proposed sale into a contested matter.[7] Emergency sales may be permitted on shorter notice, but usually only under exigent circumstances, such as with wasting assets (e.g., if you wait 20 days to sell a truck load of bananas, you may lose your buyer). *See generally* Section 10.16 ff.

---

2. It also includes proceeds of such cash collateral.

3. "Cash collateral" also includes rents generated by real estate that is subject to a mortgage, deed of trust, and/or assignment of rents, meaning that a single-asset real estate debtor typically has no cash other than cash collateral.

4. Section 363(e). In the same vein, §363(d) provides that the trustee may use, sell, or lease, "only to the extent not inconsistent with any relief granted under" §362, which governs relief from the automatic stay.

5. The trustee has the burden of proof. §363(o)(1).

6. FED. R. BANKR. PROC. 6004(a); Fed. R. Bankr. Proc. 2002(a)(2), (c)(1), (i) and (k). For the special notice in cases governed by the Clayton Anti-trust Act, *see* §363(b)(2).

7. FED. R. BANKR. PROC. 9014.

The sale may be private or by public auction, although where significant assets are being sold, courts tend to favor public sales in order to assure that the estate is receiving maximum valve for the assets.[8] The rule requires the filing of "an itemized statement of the property sold, the name of each purchaser, and the price received." It does not specify who must file the report, but it is surely in the interest of the buyer to see that it is filed, so as to confirm the validity of the sale. Although the rules do not require a court order in all circumstances, a prudent buyer will ordinarily insist on one.

Comment—Procedure for Asset Sales: There is no universal procedure for bankruptcy asset sales, other than the very broad framework established by the statute and the rules. But a certain procedure has developed as a matter of practice, and in one form or another this procedure is generally adopted in major asset sales, the objective being to maximize the sale price through an auction-like mechanism.

It typically works like this: The DIP reaches an agreement with a bidder to purchase the assets for a certain price, and signs a purchase contract, which is subject to higher and better offers by other bidders. (It may also be subject to due diligence, financing, and other contingencies, although the debtor of course tries to eliminate as many of these contingencies as possible). The DIP will then file a motion asking the court to establish bidding procedures.

This motion has two purposes—first to establish a procedure for other bidders to make competing offers and second to protect the initial bidder (sometimes referred to as the "stalking horse") and to compensate that bidder for the risk that, after having spent a lot of time and effort to make the initial bid, and having thereby created interest in the assets that leads to a robust auction, the stalking horse will be outbid. The theory is that if you don't offer such protection and compensation, nobody will be willing to be the stalking horse. Whether this is true or not is the subject of considerable debate among judges and academic commentators.[9]

The particulars of the bidding procedures order will vary depending upon what the DIP negotiates with its stalking horse bidder and what the creditors committee and the court will tolerate. But some common provisions in the procedures order might include:

- The time for submission of competing bids.
- The form of competing bids (for example, must they be all cash, can they be contingent, must they use the same form of proposed contract as the stalking horse, etc.).
- The amount by which competing bids must exceed the initial bid (the "bidding increment").
- Requirements for a bidder to qualify (deposit, demonstration of net worth, etc.).

---

8. FED. R. BANKR. PROC. 6004(f)(1).

9. *See, e.g.,* Bruce A. Markell, The Case Against Breakup Fees in Bankruptcy, 66 Amer. Bankr. L.J. 349 (1992).

- A breakup fee and expense reimbursement payable to the stalking horse if it is outbid (note that breakup fees significantly greater than three percent of the purchase price may face skepticism from the court and creditors).

- Restrictions on the ability of the debtor to shop the deal to other interested bidders (note that when these restrictions become too onerous, they may cause the court concern, and may raise questions about the debtor's fiduciary duty to maximize value; a common compromise is that the debtor may not affirmatively shop the deal, but may respond fully to any inquiries; the creditors committee typically remains free to shop the deal).

- Data room procedures, to make information available to bidders.

There are many other provisions in sale procedure orders; these are just some of the most common ones. After the bidding deadline, there will typically be an auction, if there are competing bidders. Sometimes, this will take place in open court. Other times, it will take place at the office of debtor's counsel. When the highest bid is received, the DIP will seek court approval for the sale to that bidder.

§10.4 ~ Local Rules and Forms

Sale out of the ordinary course is a topic that seems to excite the interest of individual courts. An increasing number of them are creating virtual property exchanges on their court web pages.[10] Many have promulgated local rules, with or without forms, governing the sale process.

---

10. *See, e.g.*, the District of Massachusetts: http://www.mab.uscourts.gov/ntofsl.htm.

As this is being written, the Massachusetts web site also lists an "online auction" of $3 million worth of apparel, by a private auctioneer in a bankruptcy liquidation sale. Online asset liquidation markets appear to be popping up like mushrooms. Anything we say about them here is likely to be outdated by the time you read it, but two that seem to work are:

http://www.fairmarket.com

http://www.bid4assets.com/

§10.5 ~ Asset Sale Order

IN THE UNITED STATES BANKRUPTCY COURT
FOR THE EASTERN DISTRICT OF UTOPIA

In Re: INSOLVENT SUPPLY CORPORATION Debtor-in-Possession	)))))))	Case No. 99-1416-BBL (Chapter 11)

ORDER AUTHORIZING THE SALE OF CERTAIN ASSETS FREE AND CLEAR OF LIENS PURSUANT TO THE TERMS OF A PURCHASE AND SALE AGREEMENT BETWEEN THE DEBTOR AND HUNGRY VULTURE, INC.

This matter comes before the Court on the Motion for an Entry of an Order Approving the Sale of Certain Assets, Known as the "Widget Assets", Free and Clear of Liens, to Hungry Vulture, Inc. (the "Motion"), filed by the Insolvent Supply Corporation ("Debtor") on or about February 15, 2000; a Bidding Procedures Order having been entered by this Court on December 14, 1999; the Court having reviewed the Motion and having heard the statements of counsel and the evidence introduced in support of the relief requested therein at a hearing before the Court which took place on March 9, 2000 (the "Sale Hearing"); all parties in interest having had the opportunity to be heard at the Sale Hearing regarding approval of the Purchase and Sale Agreement between the Debtor and Hungry Vulture, Inc. (the "Purchaser"); and it appearing that sufficient notice of the Motion and the relief requested by this Order have been provided; and it further appearing that no other or further notice hereof is required; this Court hereby makes the following Findings of Fact and Conclusions of Law:

A. The notice the Motion was adequate and sufficient under the circumstances of this proceeding and compiled with the applicable requirements of the Bankruptcy Code (11 U.S.C. §101 et seq.), the Federal Rules of Bankruptcy Procedure, and the Local Rules of this Court.

B. The Court has jurisdiction to hear and determine the Motion and to grant the relief requested in the Motion pursuant to 28 U.S.C. §157 and 1334, and this proceeding is a "core proceeding" within the meaning of 28 U.S.C. §§157(b).

C. The Purchaser has acted in good faith with regard to all matters relating to the purchase of the Widget Assets. The Purchaser constitutes a bona fide good faith purchaser for value. The Purchaser is entitled to the protection of Section 363(m) of the Bankruptcy Code. The price to be paid by the Purchaser for the Widget Assets under Sale Agreement is fair and constitutes reasonably equivalent value for the Widget Assets.

D. No agreement prohibited by Section 363(n) of the Bankruptcy Code exists with respect to the Sale Agreement.

E. The transfer of the Widget Assets to the Purchaser as authorized hereby shall not be subject to any otherwise applicable state, county or local transfer, stamp or similar taxes pursuant to Section 1146(c) of the Bankruptcy Code.

F. The Sale Agreement constitutes a valid and binding contract between the Debtor and the Purchaser, which contract is and shall be enforceable according to its terms.

G. Certain of the Widget Assets are executory contracts. These executory contracts are listed on Schedule 6 to the Sale Agreement (the "Widget Contracts"). The Sale Agreement provides that the Widget Contracts will be assumed by the Debtor and assigned to Purchaser, along with the other Widget Assets. Assumption of the Widget Contracts does not require any cure payment because there are no defaults under any such contracts. Assignment of such contracts to Purchaser, as part of the Widget Assets, constitutes adequate assurance of future performance pursuant to 11 U.S.C. §365(b)(1)(C), because of the financial capacity of Purchaser. No further assurance of future performance by Purchaser is necessary. No non-debtor party to any of the Widget Contracts has filed an objection to the Motion, or otherwise asserted any objection to assumption and assignment to Purchaser of the Widget Contracts.

NOW, THEREFORE, IT IS HEREBY ORDERED THAT:

1. The Sale Agreement, a copy of which is Attachment A to this Order, and all of the transactions described therein or contemplated thereby, including without limitation conveyance of the Widget Assets (which are described on Schedule 1 attached to the Sale Agreement) to Purchaser, are hereby approved and authorized.

2. The Debtor and Purchaser are authorized to enter into the Sale Agreement pursuant to Section 363 of the Bankruptcy Code and to perform their respective duties and obligations under the Sale Agreement.

3. Upon the Closing (as defined in the Sale Agreement), the Purchaser shall acquire title to and become the owner of the Widget Assets free and clear of all liens, claims, encumbrances, judgments, charges, easements, reservations, assignments, licenses, and interests against the Debtor or the Widget Assets. Any liens, claims or encumbrances against the Widget Assets shall attach to the proceeds of sale with the same priority as with respect to the Widget Assets.

4. Pursuant to Section 1146(c) of the Bankruptcy Code, the transfer of the Widget Assets to the Purchaser as authorized hereby shall be free and clear of, and shall not be subject to, any otherwise applicable state, county or local transfer, stamp or similar taxes.

5. The Purchaser shall not be deemed a successor to the Debtor as a result of its purchase of the Widget Assets or other performance under the Sale Agreement, and shall not be liable for any claim (a) against the Debtor or (b) relating in any way to the Widget Assets and arising prior to the Closing.

6. The Debtor, its officers, employees and agents, are authorized to execute such documents and to take or refrain from taking such acts as are necessary and appropriate to implement and effectuate the sale of the Widget Assets to the Purchaser.

7. Each of the Widget Contracts is hereby deemed to be assumed by the Debtor and assigned to the Purchaser pursuant to the Sale Agreement and 11 U.S.C. §365. Purchaser shall not be liable for any obligation under any Widget Contract arising prior to the date of closing under the Sale Agreement.

8. The Purchaser's rights under the Sale Agreement shall remain in full force and effect notwithstanding the confirmation of any plan of reorganization or discharge of the Debtor, and notwithstanding any conversion or dismissal of Debtor's chapter 11 case. The Sale Agreement shall be binding upon and enforceable against any successor to the Purchaser or the Debtor, including any trustee.

9. This Court retains jurisdiction to interpret, implement and enforce the terms of this Order and the Sale Agreement and to resolve any disputes or controversies arising in, under or related to the Sale Agreement.

Dated: March 12, 2000

____

UNITED STATES BANKRUPTCY JUDGE

§10.6 ~ Sale Free and Clear of Liens

§10.7 ~ What It Does and Why It Makes Sense

There is one provision in Section 363 sometimes sufficient in itself to trigger a bankruptcy filing. That is Section 363(f) which provides for a "sale free and clear of liens." More precisely, Section 363(f) says:

> The trustee may sell property under subsection (b) or (c) of this section free and clear of any interest in such property of an entity other than the estate . . .

Consider the problem of your client, BancCo, which has a mortgage on an elixir mine owned by ElixiCo. ElixiCo is in default and your client wants to foreclose. A few minutes' research confirms your worst fears: the collection and mortgage laws of your state are fragmentary and arcane and, in general, unreliable. Moreover, JunCo asserts that it holds a lien on the property and that it will contest the title of anyone who buys at a foreclosure sale unless you leave money on the table for it. As if that weren't enough, the applicable state statutory lien laws are impenetrable and mostly untested, and various government entities have asserted claims against ElixiCo and the mine.

You quickly grasp that you'll have a tough time inducing prospective buyers to take an interest in this mare's nest.[11]

BancCo, like any sensible bank, has always regarded bankruptcy with about the same hospitality and good nature as the mongoose addresses to the snake. And with good reason. Let the debtor go into chapter 11, the next thing you know the debtor will try to cram you down with a 15-year note at a lousy interest rate.

But after a bit of thought, you come to a surprising conclusion: rather than a trap to be avoided, in this case bankruptcy might be just the ticket. Trigger a bankruptcy filing. Let the sale go forward under Section 363, through the bankruptcy court. The secured creditor's lien (if any) attaches to the proceeds. The competing claimants get to argue over their respective interests and the court approves the distribution. The buyer may well pay a premium (or at least full value) for the assurance that he is purchasing the assets free of liens. In short, bankruptcy may be the ideal forum in which to get maximum value for the assets.

§10.8 ~ Statutory Limitations

It isn't quite as easy as all that. For one, the statute itself imposes some restrictions. That is: the sale free and clear may go forward only if —

- applicable non-bankruptcy law permits sale of such property free and clear of such interest;
- lienholder consents;

---

11. And it's no answer to say that BancCo could buy at its own sale. You'd just be buying the problem for yourself, or deferring the difficulties until your inevitable resale.

- the interest is a lien and the price at which such property is to be sold is greater than the aggregate value of all liens on such property;
- the interest is in bona fide dispute; or
- the lien or interest holder could be compelled, in a legal or equitable proceeding, to accept a money satisfaction of such interest.

These requirements are disjunctive, that is, you need to meet only one. Unfortunately, the requirements are not the soul of clarity and there is a good deal of litigation over the question when they have been met. Oddly enough, perhaps the most common ground for a Section 363(f) sale is consent. The reason is that, whatever their differences, the parties often come to court recognizing that they have a common interest in maximizing the size of the pie.

The "aggregate value of all liens" rule has generated a particular problem of interpretation. Consider the case of Blackacre, worth $100,000, subject to a first lien of $80,000 and a second lien of $40,000—total, $120,000. At auction, a stranger bids $100,000.01. May the court confirm the same under the aggregate value rule?

It depends on what you mean by value. Clearly the value of the first lien is $80,000 because it will yield that much in any event. But what of the second lien? The face value is $40,000, and on this reading the sale seems to flunk the aggregate value test. But if the market value of the property is truly only $100,000, then the market value of the second is only $20,000. On this reading the buyer, by bidding $100,000.01, has offered one cent more than the "aggregate value" of all liens and the sale can be confirmed.

We think this second reading is untenable because it proves too much: if this is the rule we can't imagine a sale (at least one for full market value) that could not be confirmed. If Congress had intended only to require that the sale be for full market value, it could have said that. We have to acknowledge, though, that the cases are split and the conflict in the commentary is heated.[12]

The bona fide dispute rule raises the question of what counts as a bona fide dispute. The only real point is that "bona fide" means you cannot manufacture a dispute solely for the purpose of satisfying the rule, and preventing the sale.

§10.9 ~ SALE VERSUS PLAN

Consider Grandma's Pie Co., Inc., of which John C. Grandma is the president and majority shareholder. LoanCo supplies working capital for the company, and holds a security interest in inventory and receivables, as well as a personal guarantee from John C.

---

12. Two cases that consider both sides of the argument are: *In re* Terrace Gardens Park Partnership, 96 B.R. 707, 712-13 (Bankr. W.D. Tex. 1989) (actual value), and *In re* Terrace Chalet Apts. Ltd., 159 B.R. 821, 825-26 (N.D. Ill. 1993) (face value). We have to acknowledge that the well-respected Collier treatise is against us on this one. *See* LAWRENCE KING, 2 COLLIER ON BANKRUPTCY §363 AT 363-31 TO 363-33 (15TH ED. 1992).

The company is in trouble. In discussions with John C., LoanCo says. We don't think we can ever get enough out of LoanCo to satisfy our claim. We think the best disposition of this business is to sell it as a going concern. We think it will fetch a better price if it is sold through a bankruptcy case. So here is what we propose: cooperate with us in making possible the chapter 11 sale. If things go well, we may give you some relief on your guarantee.

And so it goes. John C. causes Grandma's Pie Co. to file a chapter 11petition in the name of the company. The company, with assistance from LoanCo, finds a likely buyer. Grandma's proposes a sale under Section 363(f). LoanCo consents. No other party objects. On behalf of the company, John C. signs the sale documents. The buyer pays the sale price. John C. then either (a) files a liquidating plan, proposing to distribute the cash to stakeholders as their interests may appear; or (b) converts the case to chapter 7 and delivers the cash to the trustee.

What is odd about this scenario? The oddity is that the parties have just accomplished many of the same things that they might have accomplished under a plan[13]—yet they have done it all via a Section 363(f) sale. The question arises: when (if ever) should the court allow the parties to sell substantially all estate assets via Section 363(f) instead of having to satisfy the plan confirmation requirements under Section 1129?

The answer is somewhat of a muddle. The trouble is that the Code seems to contradict itself. A plan requires a hearing and order of confirmation; usually also voting, and an approved disclosure statement. The sale requires just notice and an opportunity to be heard.[14] If the drafters thought the plan provisions were so important, then why did they allow Section 363(f) sales? If they thought the sale route was sufficient, then why did they authorize liquidation through a plan?

We think the decisive issue here is: Does the sale in fact give the stakeholders the kind of protection they would be entitled to under the plan process? Have they had a chance to investigate and evaluate the sale so they can know whether the assets are in fact fetching the best price? Have the assets been reasonably marketed and exposed to higher and better offers? The more you can persuade the court that it is looking at a bona fide sale to the highest bidder, the more likely you are to persuade the court to approve the sale."

Don't agonize too much over the question whether the sale will be cheaper than the plan—it almost always will be. It will ordinarily be quicker too, which is often the factor motivating a 363 sale rather than a plan. Thus, you may raise the stakes if you persuade the court that there is some compelling reason why the sale needs to be done now, rather than later.[15] But this is a devil's bargain. The more you

---

13. Note that §1123(a)(5)(D) provides that a plan may provide for "sale of all or any part of the property of the estate."

14. Recall that on the face of things, you may not need (and indeed, may not even be entitled) to an order confirming a §363 sale, although as we note elsewhere, sale approval orders are common.

15. The strongest case for allowing a quick sale of substantially all estate assets, under §363, without waiting for the plan process to play out, is the case of perishable goods—the assets would lose their value and there would be nothing left to sell under the plan. But many courts have approved such sales in less obvious situations, based on a representation by the debtor (which the court is often not in a position to dispute) that value will be maximized by a prompt sale, and that waiting for the plan process to play out may cost the estate a valuable opportunity. An influential early example is *In re* WHET, Inc., 12 B.R. 743 (Bankr. D. Mass. 1981).

entreat the judge that it has to be done right now, the greater chance she is may suspect you are pulling a fast one on her. So couple your "special circumstance" argument with the strongest possible record on notice and disclosure, and do what you can to obtain consent of the creditors committee.

Discussions of sale outside the plan are not complete without a discussion of Equity Security Holders v. Lionel Corp.[16] Lionel is read as standing for a "good business reason" standard for Section 363(f) sales, and is often relied upon by parties seeking approval of sale of substantially all estate assets. However, it is worth emphasizing that Lionel was not in the least way typical of standard Section 363(f) cases. Rather Lionel was a case where dissenting residual equity holders were seeking to buy (and succeeded in buying) more time in the hope that the market would turn up. *See* §6.19.

§10.10 ~ Sub Rosa Plan

The law grows by increments, and every frontier is a horizon. If you buy the notion of a Section 363(f) sale, then the next logical question is—what if we use the sale to get court approval for a restructuring or a scheme for the payment of creditors? If the Section 363(f) sale looked a little like a plan in disguise, this new deal looks even more so—it appears designed to accomplish everything a plan might, without the protections of voting and the §1129 requirements. Courts and commentators often call it a "sub rosa" plan.

Will it work? Occasionally it will, but the stakes are dramatically higher in this case than they are in the simple Section 363 sale. You face some formidable authority holding that it can't be done.[17] Unless there is a compelling reason to provide the terms of payment of creditors in a sale order, you will encounter less resistance from the court if you limit the proposed sale order to the terms of the sale and related matters, and save the payment of claims for a subsequent (liquidating) plan.

§10.11 ~ Caution: Successor Liability

All this talk of "cleansing sales" may give the impression that you can use the 363(f) sale to cut off all pre-petition claims. You cannot. There remains, at least, the problem of successor liability, which may haunt even a fully confirmed plan and surely will crimp the style of a Section 363(f) sale. Successor liability is a non-bankruptcy law doctrine, applicable most often in product liability situations, pursuant to which an asset purchaser (whether by plan or 363 sale) may be liable for claims against its predecessor. For an introduction to successor liability, *see* §§17.36 ff.

---

16. *In re* Lionel Corp., 722 F.2d 1063 (2d Cir. 1983).

17. The leading case against the creeping plan is *In re* Braniff Airways, Inc., 700 F.2d 935 (5th Cir. 1983). The Circuit court, reversing a district court, refused to bless a pre-plan sale, coupled with contract provisions designed to dictate the contents of a plan. The court pointedly noted that it was not rejecting §363(f) sales *per se*.

§10.12 ~ DIP Financing—A Path Through Section 364

To the outsider, post-petition financing is perhaps the best evidence of the unreality of the bankruptcy system. Lend to a someone in bankruptcy? Surely, the proposition requires an explanation. But experienced bankruptcy professionals know that lending to the DIP is (at least for the lender) a very good deal. It comes with court protection and a priority you can't achieve any place else. Since the arrival of the Bankruptcy Code of 1978, a whole sub-industry has developed to provide post-petition financing under the protection of the Code.

The point is that the lender may be able to get priority over pre-bankruptcy lenders. It will need court approval, but it also gets court protection. Different kinds of post-petition priorities are set forth in Section 364. The following chart offers a graphic summary of the possibilities, in ascending order of difficulty. The second column from the left sets forth the "background condition." The third specifies the degree of court involvement and the fourth spells out the priority.

Comment: The Debtor will often seek approval for post-petition financing on the first day of the case, on an emergency basis. This is often necessary, as the company cannot survive without post-petition advances from its lender. But it does not permit the required 15 days notice to creditors. Rule 4001 allows for this sort of emergency loan approval, but only to the extent necessary to avoid "immediate and irreparable harm." Any approval beyond that will have to wait for a final hearing, on proper notice to creditors. The point here is that the debtor seeking emergency approval under Section 364 must be prepared to show "immediate and irreparable harm" if the approval, in the amount sought, is not forthcoming.

Ascending order of difficulty	**Background condition**	**Court involvement**	**Priority**
First (§364(a))	Authorized to operate and operating in ordinary course	None	Administrative expense
Second (§364(b))	Not authorized to operate; or not in ordinary course	Notice and a hearing	Administrative expense
Third (§364(c))	Financing not available otherwise	Notice and a hearing	"Super priority" administrative expense; or lien on property not otherwise subject to lien; or Junior lien on property that is subject to an existing lien
Fourth (§364(d))	Financing not available otherwise	Notice and a hearing, adequate protection	Senior lien; or equal lien

The first item above—administrative priority, ordinary course—can be understood as a protection for the unsuspecting vendor who continues to supply the debtor as he did before bankruptcy. As to what constitutes "ordinary course," courts have identified two standards. There is a horizontal test—what is ordinary for this business or industry?[18] And a vertical test—did a hypothetical creditor of this business face the same risk he would have faced before the filing or, stated otherwise, what is ordinary in the past operations of this particular company?

For the Section 364(c)(1) super priority, a big issue has been whether it primes even professional fees.[19] Recall that not even a super priority will help you if there is not enough money to pay all competing super priority expenses. Also, the super priority administrative creditor is vulnerable to being subordinated on conversion to chapter 7 because chapter 11 administrative expenses are junior to chapter 7 administrative expenses in a converted chapter 7 case.

The liens available under Sections 364(c)(2) and (3) have no relationship to the super priority in Section 364(c)(1). So, if the lien is insufficient, then the creditor goes to the back of the queue with the unsecured creditors (unless he has some kind of backup super priority in his original authorization).[20]

Technique: In putting these deals together, someone has to act for the debtor/estate. Usually it will be the DIP's counsel, or counsel for an unsecured creditors' committee (or both). Like everyone else, these counsel want to get paid. Expect DIP and committee counsel to insist upon a "carve-out" from the post-petition lender's administrative priority or lien to protect their fees. Negotiated carve-outs are fairly common—but there is nothing automatic about it, so if it isn't part of the deal, it doesn't happen. Note that many courts will require any carve-out to be available on a pro rata basis to all court-approved professionals, so debtor's counsel cannot negotiate the carve-out for himself only.[21]

As to the terms of the borrowing order, courts have shown a curious kind of ambivalence. One can imagine a world in which the court simply deferred to the business judgment of the DIP and let him negotiate the best deal he could. With Section 364 orders, courts are rarely so restrained. They are at pains to recall that the debtor in chapter 11 has little if any bargaining power—perhaps particularly little if the creditor has the "oxygen lien" on cash collateral.

Yet at the end of the day, perhaps more often than not, the court has gone ahead and blessed whatever terms had been called into question. This is perhaps to be expected: no matter how onerous the court may think the terms, if it is a choice between letting the DIP make the deal and closing the business tonight, most courts will come down on the side of the deal.

---

18. Johnson v. First Street Cos. (*In re* Waterfront Cos., Inc.), 56 B.R. 31, 34-35 (Bankr. D. Minn. 1985). *In re* James A. Phillips, Inc., 29 B.R. 391(Bankr. S.D.N.Y. 1983). A loan by an insider trying to salvage a deal may be ordinary course in some sense of the term, but it won't enjoy the protection of this Section. *In re* C.E.N., Inc. 86 B.R. 303, 305-06 (Bankr. D. Me. 1988).

19. *In re* Flagstaff Foodservice Corp., 739 F.2d 373, 76-77 (2d Cir. 1984).

20. *In re* Sobiech, 125 B.R. 110, 114-15 (Bankr. S.D.N.Y. 1991), *aff'd* Mulligan v. Sobiech, 131 B.R. 917 (S.D.N.Y. 1991).

21. RTC v. Official Unsecured Creditors Comm. (*In re* Defender Drug Stores, Inc.), 145 B.R. 312, 317-18 (B.A.P. 9th Cir.1992).

A "poster case" for lenders would be *In re* Western Pacific Airlines.[22] There, the creditor got a senior lien on all assets including causes of action to avoid transfers. He got the right to compel the debtor to assume and assign designated executory contracts. He got veto power over a later plan, and a conditional right to appoint directors to the business—and there was more. The whole deal was larded with an array of loan fees—for commitment, for termination, for providing a facility, and so forth.

The court said the deal was "onerous, costly, and tough." But it said the terms were not "unconscionable, oppressive or punitive."[23] The court seemed impressed that the deal had the enthusiastic support of the creditors' committee.[24]

On the other hand, in a recent Utah case, the debtor asked the court to approve the lender's terms, saying that otherwise the debtor would have to cease operations. The judge refused to approve the loan terms. Then, based on the debtor's own representation, the judge ordered conversion of the case to chapter 7.[25]

One term that has met with some disfavor is the so-called "cross collateral" clause. Consider the case of FinCo, who holds a security interest in the debtor's inventory and receivables for a revolving loan of $5 million. FinCo isn't sure how much its collateral might be worth in liquidation, but concedes it might be worth more as part of a going concern, and so is willing to discuss DIP financing. After some tense negotiations, FinCo and the DIP come up with the following deal: FinCo will extend a post-petition working capital line to the DIP in exchange for a security interest in post-petition receivables. The agreement provides that post-petition collateral will secure post-petition and pre-petition debts, and that pre-petition collateral will secure pre-petition and post-petition debts.

Will it pass muster? Many early cases blessed this kind of arrangement, but a much-noted Eleventh Circuit opinion holds that it is not authorized, and the tide may have shifted toward the Eleventh Circuit view.[26] A variant that may get a warmer reception is the recycling loan. Here the agreement provides that every dollar received from pledged receivables is deemed to constitute a repayment of pre-petition debt and a new advance under the DIP loan facility. Eventually, all the debt will recycle, from pre-petition to post. Our experience is that some (but not all) judges will buy it.

To get the priming lien under Section 364(d), you have to show, first, that you can't get the loan elsewhere. This means putting on evidence that you've tried and failed.[27] The extent of the required showing seems to vary considerably from one court to another.

---

22. 223 B.R. 567 (Bankr. D. Colo. 1997).

23. *Id.* at 572.

24. Refusing to approve a loan because it thought the deal was a violation of the DIP's fiduciary duty to creditors, *see In re* Tenney Village Co., 104 B.R. 562, 567-570 (Bankr. D. N.H. 1989).

25. A district judge promptly reversed, withdrew the reference, and approved the loan. *See In re* Geneva Steel, Bankr. No. 99C-21130 (D. Utah 1999).

26. *See* Shapiro v. Saybrook Mfg. Co., Inc. (*In re* Saybrook Mfg. Co., Inc.), 963 F.2d 1490 (11th Cir. 1992).

27. *In re* Sky Valley, Inc., 100 B.R. 107, 112-13 (Bankr. N.D. Ga. 1988) (three other lenders is enough).

§10.13 ~ ORDERS THE COURT WON'T APPROVE

The following is a list of provisions that attorneys frequent seek to insert into cash collateral or post-petition financing stipulations and orders, but which courts are often reluctant to approve. This list has been compiled from guidelines published by a number of bankruptcy courts throughout the United States.[28] Several caveats are appropriate here.

First, the rules—both written and unwritten—vary significantly from court to court, and, sometimes, from judge to judge. Therefore, you are well advised to check with the court and with local lawyers (if you are not in your home jurisdiction) to see whether there are any particular guidelines that govern cash collateral or post-petition financing orders in the particular court.

Second, even though a court may ordinarily decline to approve a certain provision, if you believe that in your particular case there are unusual facts or circumstances that justify the provision, you should go ahead and seek the relief that you think you need, explaining to the court why, notwithstanding its usual practice or rule, in this case the provision at issue should be approved. We have seen cash collateral and post-petition financing orders approved by courts containing all of these "prohibited provisions."

Finally, you should note that some courts require a movant's counsel to disclose the existence of certain generally-prohibited provisions in a cash collateral or financing agreement. If your court has such a rule, it is critically important that you be up front with the judge, disclose the existence of the provision at issue, and explain its necessity. Given the emergency nature of cash collateral and financing motions, and the length and detail of many agreements that come before the court for approval, the judge often does not have sufficient opportunity to read carefully the agreements between the parties. But there are few ways to lose your credibility with the court more quickly than, on the first day of the case, to get caught trying to sneak something by the judge. In our experience, most judges will make exceptions to these general prohibitions where a true need can be demonstrated and the interests of other parties can be reasonably protected.

The provisions that many courts generally will not permit include the following:

- Cross collateralization clauses, *i.e.*, clauses that secure pre-petition debt by post-petition assets in which the secured party would not otherwise have a security interest.

- Provisions or findings of fact that bind the estate or all parties in interest with respect to the validity, perfection or amount of a secured party's lien or debt.

- Provisions or findings of fact that bind the estate or all parties in interest with respect to the relative priorities of the secured party's lien and liens held by persons who are not party to the stipulation. This would include, for example, an order approving a stipulation providing that the secured party's lien is a "first priority" lien.

---

28. If you practice in the District of Delaware, you may want to obtain a copy of a letter to Delaware Bankruptcy Counsel dated April 2, 1998 from Judge Peter J. Walsh, setting forth certain guidelines for counsel in connection with first-day debtor-in-possession financing orders.

- Provisions in an interim order that permit the secured party's lien to (1) attach to unsecured property of the estate, or (2) have priority over other existing secured creditors in property of the estate that is already subject to a secured creditor's lien. *See* Section 364(c)(2) and (3).

- Waivers of the estate's rights under Section 506(c) (*see* §13.43).

- Provisions that operate to divest the debtor, or any other party in interest, from any discretion in the formulation or proposal of a plan of reorganization, or that limit access to the court to seek any relief under applicable law.

- Releases of liability by the debtor of any claim or cause of action against the secured creditor, including without limitation (1) for the creditor's alleged pre-petition torts, breaches of contract, or lender liability, (2) releases of pre-petition or post-petition defenses and/or counterclaims, and (3) releases of any avoidance actions arising under the Bankruptcy Code.

- Automatic relief from the stay of Section 362(a) upon the debtor's default under a cash collateral or financing agreement or stipulation, conversion to chapter 7, or the appointment of a trustee.

- Adequate protection provisions that create liens on avoidance actions held by the estate or other claims for relief arising under the Bankruptcy Code.

- Waivers, effective upon default or expiration of the term of a cash collateral or financing agreement or stipulation, of the debtor's right to move for a court order pursuant to Section 363(c)(2)(B) authorizing the use of cash collateral in the absence of the secured party's consent.

- Carve outs for administrative expenses that do not treat all professionals on a pro rata basis (for example, carve outs that provide for the fees of debtor's counsel, but not for committee counsel).

- Provisions that create an artificially short period of limitations for the debtor any other party in interest to bring claims or causes of action against a secured creditor (in our experience, it is ordinarily necessary to permit a debtor or committee at least 60 days to investigate and bring any such actions).

- A finding without testimony to the effect that in consenting to the use of cash collateral or extending post-petition financing, a secured creditor is acting in "good faith."

- Provisions applicable in the event of a dispute under the agreement that confer venue on a court other than the Bankruptcy Court which approved the cash collateral stipulation or financing agreement.

- Provisions applicable in the event of a dispute or default under the agreement pursuant to which the debtor waives service of process, *forum non conveniens* notice and hearing or the right to a jury trial.

§10.14 ~ SECURITIES EXEMPTION

Issues of public debt may have to register under the securities laws, and meet the standards mandated through the Securities Exchange Commission. At first look, there would appear to be no reason why this rule should not apply to the trustee/DIP just as it does to any other person. But conforming to SEC rules can be costly and cumbersome, and is hardly compatible with the kind of emergency lending that the debtor may require, and that Section 364 seems designed to facilitate.

Happily for the debtor, the Bankruptcy Code provides an exemption from the securities laws for Section 364 lending. Section 364(f) provides

> Section 5 of the Securities Act of 1933, the Trust Indenture Act of 1939, and any State or local law requiring registration for offer or sale of a security or registration or licensing of an issuer of, underwriter of, or broker or dealer in, a security does not apply to the offer or sale under this section.

The exemption applies to debt securities only, not equity. And it is not available to one who meets the (fairly narrow bankruptcy) definition of an "underwriter," as set forth in Section 1145. This exemption complements the general exemption for "plan securities."

§10.15 ~ MOOTNESS IN CREDIT EXTENSIONS

Consider the case of FinCo, which agrees to extend credit to DebtorCo relying on a bankruptcy court order granting priority under Section 364. The court approves the financing over the objection of the Unsecured Creditors Committee, which promptly takes an appeal. A year later, after FinCo has advanced $1 million, the appellate court finds that the priority arrangement is not authorized under Section 364. The mere threat of losing priority for a year's lending is enough to make the loan officer's stomach churn. On the other hand, DebtorCo can't afford to wait a year until the appeal is final. Is there a way to protect FinCo, and get the money to DebtorCo?

There may be. Section 364(e) provides that the reversal or modification of such an order does not affect such a debt or lien entered into in good faith, unless there was a stay pending appeal. But the Eleventh Circuit held that the provision is only applicable to orders authorized under Section 364, and since cross-collateralization is not authorized by that section, the §364(e) protection will not apply.[29] So, a cautious post-petition lender will limit its advances to what is absolutely necessary until it has a final order approving its loan.

---

29. *In re* Saybrook Mfg. Co., 963 F.2d 1490, 1495 (11th Cir. 1992). In *In re* Swedeland Dev. Group, 16 F.3d 552 (3d Cir.1994), the creditor argued that an appeal of a financing order was moot because a stay was not granted. The court disagreed; it found the appeal not moot with respect to a financing order on which funds remained undistributed.

§10.16 ~ The Dive

You are the new bankruptcy judge of the new bankruptcy court in Indianucky. One day as you are about to close up and go home, your clerk tells you that she has scheduled an emergency hearing. You take the bench and find a copy of a document with this heading:

> EX PARTE MOTION TO USE CASH COLLATERAL, TO BORROW, AND GRANT SECURITY INTEREST, AND ORDER THEREON

You call the motion and receive an appearance from Leonard, counsel to DebtorCo as DIP in chapter 11. DebtorCo is a maker of widgets—a well known and fairly important employer in your town. In fact, you had read about the filing in last night's newspaper, but this is your first formal encounter with the case. With Leonard is Sam, counsel for MidCo, a commercial finance company. Also in the courtroom is Alice, new on the job this week as an attorney with the office of the U. S. Trustee. Leonard explains:

> Good afternoon, Your Honor. I'm sorry to take your time so late in the day and on such short notice, but this is a major case and we have an emergency. We need working capital in order to continue operating. MidCo holds a security interest in everything we own. After discussions with Sam here (Sam smiles and waves), we have reached the following agreement. MidCo has agreed to extend post-petition operating credit (at three points over prime) in exchange for a new security interest in all post-petition assets, and a waiver of all claims or defenses that DebtorCo might have against MidCo. We are acting *ex parte* because we need the financing immediately, and because MidCo has declared that they won't do the deal unless they get a decision right now.

Perhaps it is possible to see why this is one aspect of chapter 11 practice that has most exercised the sensibilities of judges. It's plausible that DebtorCo needs fast action. And there is no good way to quarrel with MidCo's assertion that they need a quick decision—after all, it is their ball and bat, and they can always go home. On the other hand, the judge doesn't want to preside over a daylight raid on the asset pool. If this deal goes through, will there be anything left for unsecured creditors? What are these "claims or defenses" that DebtorCo wants to waive? Are the managers acting like true fiduciaries, or are they just trying to minimize exposure on their personal guarantees?

The judge would love some independent input on this one. Where are the unsecured creditors? Actually, your honor (Leonard responds), I gave telephone notice of this hearing to the 20 largest creditors this morning. I understand that the U.S. Trustee has named seven of them to a creditor's committee, but so far as I know, they have not met or elected officers, and have not retained counsel. In any event, none of them seems to be here. For the U.S. Trustee, Alice contributes that she had heard the motion was coming but that she hasn't been back to her office all day and didn't see the papers until Leonard handed them to her just before this hearing—and she certainly would like more time.

This is the kind of scenario that passed into the folklore as "the dive"—the debtor, as it were, surrendering in the face of the secured creditor's onslaught. The trouble with it from the standpoint of the judge is that every assertion is plausible—and they can't always be right. On the other hand, the debtor is almost certain to need some sort of authorization from the court on critical matters if the case is to go forward.

In the next section, we offer some a kind of scope note, defining the problem. Then we offer some general rules of strategy. Then we outline Rule 4001, the most important source of law on point. Then we give a list of items that are often dealt with by so-called first day orders, with or without contest at the beginning of the case, and we provide some sample first day orders.

§10.17 ~ Strategy—Don't Back Yourself into a Corner

The problem referred to above as "the dive" leads to a complex three-way game of chicken here, between the lender, the debtor, and the court. Of course nothing compels a lender to make a post-petition loan to a debtor. But any experienced judge knows that lenders bluff, because he has seen them back down when their bluff is called. Moreover the judge isn't greatly impressed by the debtor's consent—after all, hostages cheerfully support the demands of their captors when the gun is in their mouth. There are no magic-bullet answers to any of these challenges, but here are some guidelines:

As lender's counsel, remember you need your credibility if you are going to continue to appear in this court. So don't bluff—or more precisely, don't lie. Don't tell the court this is absolutely your last and final offer unless it really is your last and final offer. A better—more honest—approach may be to say: "Your honor, these terms were agreed on by the loan committee, and if any material changes are made, the deal will have to be resubmitted to the committee, and the result is uncertain."

A lot may depend on the attitude and skill of the counsel for the unsecured creditors' committee. The court may look to her as an honest broker, and she may have leeway or leverage that debtor's counsel doesn't have. This is often an excellent up-front opportunity for committee counsel to stake out a central role in the case.

The puzzle for debtor's counsel is the puzzle of the hostage—how to seem to cooperate with the lender while making it clear that you'd be delighted to get some help. Sometimes you encourage committee counsel to play "let's you and him fight." Sometimes you just lay it out for the court: "your honor, we would have loved to get better terms, but these are the best terms the bank would give us so we are constrained to offer our support."

§10.18 ~ First-day Orders

The beginning of a chapter 11 case is like the beginning of a battle. Often the debtor files under pressure or in haste—under threat, for example, of an imminent foreclosure. Even if he has the luxury of order, he will discover that there is plenty to do just to cover the basics. And in the best of cases, he will learn the truth of Napoleon's maxim that no plan survives contact with the enemy.

Virtually every debtor—and debtor's counsel—will find himself scrambling to get the right kinds of court authorization to let matters proceed. Some of these orders are "administrative" (one is tempted to say "paperwork") orders. The debtor may have filed a bare-bones petition, as to prevent a levy. If so, he will need to get an order extending time to file schedules and so forth.[30] And in any event, counsel will want to get himself properly employed—which means, that the DIP will seek an order from the court authorizing the DIP to employ counsel.[31]

30. Fed. R. Bankr. Proc. 1007(c).

31. *See generally* §327.

Other orders will smooth day-to-day operations. For example, the DIP will want to pay the gap wages of continuing employees whose services are needed to keep the case going. This matter of gap wages is conceptually interesting, because there is no specific authorization in the Code to pay any pre-petition creditor until the end of the case. But courts and even creditors seem to recognize that ordinary employees will have to get their regular paychecks if the business is to continue at all. So a pattern has developed whereby the court will authorize the payment now (under what has come to be called the doctrine of necessity) and trust that the issue of authority will somehow take care of itself.[32]

For survival of the chapter 11 debtor, perhaps the most important orders are those that deal with use of cash collateral and post-petition financing. Many operating business debtors will find that virtually all their cash is subject to a security interest held by a working capital lender. Presumably the debtor will need working capital from somewhere. So the situation will compel him to make some kind of a deal for working capital financing—often with the pre-petition lender, but sometimes with a new lender. On this analysis, the debtor will need an order for the use of cash collateral, and a related order for post-petition borrowing, early in the case.

§10.19 ~ RULE 4001

For dealing with the first-day problem, the most important source of law is in rule 4001. Strictly speaking, rule 4001 is not about first-day orders *per se*. It imposes a variety of limitations on agreements and on ex parte hearings and orders. But it does address the kind of problem that arises at the beginning of the case. Perhaps most important, it tries to redefine the problem by minimizing the urgency. The rule provides that a final hearing on a cash collateral motion, or on a motion obtain credit "no earlier than 15 days after service of the motion."[33] It may also give relief at a preliminary hearing before the end of the 15-day period, but only as "necessary to avoid immediate and irreparable harm to the estate pending a final hearing." All motions are to be served on

- Any official committee;
- In a chapter 9 or 11 where there is no unsecured creditors' committee, then on the list of creditors under Rule 1007(d); and
- Any party to an agreement that is subject of the motion.

---

32. A possible partial justification for the first-day wage order is that most or all of these wage claims will be entitled to a (third) priority in any event. Section 507(a)(3). Another partial justification is that labor regulators may close the debtor down if it operates without paying wages. *See, e.g.*, Donovan v. TMC Industries, Ltd., 20 B.R. 997, 1005-06 (Bankr. N.D. Ga. 1982) (Labor Department action under the hot goods act to enjoin shipment of goods produced at below the minimum wage (*i.e.*, zero) held exempt from the automatic stay as "police or regulatory.") But the Fourth Circuit, on the most appealing facts possible, has held that the Code would not authorize payments to personal injury claimants from an emergency treatment fund—and also, that it was not within the court's equitable power to do so. Off. Comm. of Equity Sec. Holders v. Mabey, 832 F.2d 299, 302 (4th Cir. 1987).

33. FED. R. BANKR. PROC. 4001(b), (c).

A motion for approval of an agreement on any of these topics falls under even tighter constraint.[34] Objections may be filed at any time within 15 days of the mailing. If an objection is filed, the court shall hold a hearing on no less than five days' notice. The rule also provides:

> If no objection is filed, the court may enter an order approving or disapproving the agreement without conducting a hearing.[35]

The rule appears to give the court broad power to disapprove the agreement on its own initiative. Apparently it is local practice in many parts of the country for the courts to lay down policies (by rule or otherwise) regarding what sorts of agreements it will, or will not, approve.[36]

Notwithstanding all the constraints, there are cases where counsel will ask the court to grant relief from the stay, or to permit sale of estate property, on short notice. For such occasions, the rule includes a provision governing "ex parte relief." The term "ex parte" is something of a misnomer. It doesn't mean no notice. Rather, it means limited or short notice.

§10.20 ~ Checklist—First-day Orders

Which "first-day" orders will be sought in a particular case depends upon the facts of the case, the needs of the debtor, and the willingness of the court to enter such orders. It would be unusual to have a case where all of the orders listed here are sought and entered on the first day of the case; but this list should be useful as a starting checklist of orders you may want to consider seeking. Some bankruptcy courts are often willing to consider these orders on the first day of a case. However, despite the term "first day orders," many courts will require at least a day or two notice before considering these orders—at least in the absence of truly exigent circumstances.

What "first day orders" seek will depend upon the needs of the debtor and, to some extent, the practices of the particular court before which the case is pending. But here is a list of some first day orders that are common in chapter 11 cases.

Orders that facilitate administration of the estate:

- Order extending time to file schedules, statements and lists.
- Order directing joint administration of related cases.
- Order authorizing employment of professionals.

---

34. Fed. R. Bankr. Proc. 4001(d).

35. Fed. R. Bankr. Proc. 4001(d)(3) (emphasis added).

36. For example, in the District of Massachusetts, local Rule 4003 specifies particular clauses for which approval must be specifically requested. These include provisions for a security interest that binds a party other than the debtor; any waiver of defenses by the debtor; a post-petition lien securing pre-petition debt; a security interest in avoidance recoveries of the trustee; and any provision that grants the creditor relief from the automatic stay.

- Order authorizing retention of "ordinary course" professionals.
- Order establishing interim professional fee procedures.
- Order authorizing procedure for notice.
- Order approving investment guidelines.
- Order authorizing the filing of confidential or proprietary documents under seal.
- Order applying cash management procedures, and authorizing use of pre-petition bank accounts.

Orders that smooth day-to-day operation:

- Orders authorizing debtor to honor pre-petition obligations—

  For wages, benefits, and related taxes.

  For shippers, freight handlers, warehousers.

  For customer claims (on gift certificates, layaways, etc.).

  For essential trade vendors and suppliers.

- Order establishing reclamation procedures.
- Order authorizing debtor to return goods under Section 546(g).
- Order establishing procedure for paying utilities and utility deposits, and prohibiting utilities from terminating service.

Substantive orders:

- Cash collateral order (Section 363(c)(2)).
- Borrowing order (Section 364).
- Order rejecting leases or executory contracts (or extending time for same).
- Some sample first day orders are set forth below. Others are set forth in the appropriate sections of this book.

Strategy: Because there is rarely a creditors committee at the time the first day orders come before the court, and many of the creditors will not be in court, the judge is likely to rely heavily upon the U.S. Trustee's judgment with respect to the appropriateness of the proposed first day orders. Thus, you should consider providing to the U.S. Trustee drafts of the motions and proposed orders before they are filed, and offering to meet with the U.S. Trustee to discuss them and explain their necessity. You may find that this makes your first day motions hearing go more smoothly. There is probably a good chance you can alleviate the Trustee's concerns by discussing the issues and, possibly, making modifications to the proposed orders. And even if you cannot alleviate the Trustee's concerns, it is in your interest as debtor's counsel to know what the Trustee's objections are likely to be in advance of the hearing, so you can be prepared to address them.

§10.21 ~ Form: Order Authorizing Joint Administration

IN THE UNITED STATES BANKRUPTCY COURT
FOR THE EASTERN DISTRICT OF UTOPIA

In Re: INSOLVENT SUPPLY CORPORATION, Debtor-in-Possession	)	Case No. 99-1415-BBL (Chapter 11)
In Re: INSOLVENT DISTRIBUTION CORPORATION Debtor-in-Possession	)	Case No. 99-1416-BBL (Chapter 11)

**ORDER AUTHORIZING JOINT ADMINISTRATION
OF CHAPTER 11 CASES**

This matter comes before the Court upon the motion of Insolvent Supply Corporation and Insolvent Distribution Corporation, the captioned debtors and debtors-in-possession (collectively, "Debtors") for joint administration of their related bankruptcy cases (the "Joint Administration Motion"). Michael L. Bernstein of Arnold & Porter appeared on behalf of the Debtors. Other appearances were as noted on the record.

The Court has reviewed the Joint Administration Motion and has determined that notice thereof was appropriate under the circumstances and was in compliance with Local Rule 101 of this Court. Based upon a review of the Motion and the representations of counsel for this Debtor, the Court finds that good cause and exigent circumstances exist for considering the Joint Administration Motion immediately. Additionally, the Court has determined that the relief requested in the Joint Administration Motion is in the best interest of the Debtors and their respective estates. Accordingly, it is hereby:

ORDERED, that Debtors' chapter 11 cases shall be jointly administered under the case of Insolvent Supply Corporation, Case No. 99-1415-BBL; and it is further

ORDERED, the Court shall hereafter maintain a single docket for the filing of all pleadings with respect to the Debtors' chapter 11 cases; and it is further

ORDERED, the Joint Administration Order herein shall not effect a substantive consolidation of the Debtors' estates, assets, or liabilities, which shall remain separate pending further order of this Court; and it is further

ORDERED, that all pleadings and orders referring to either or both of the above listed cases shall be captioned as follows:

In Re: INSOLVENT SUPPLY CORPORATION and INSOLVENT DISTRIBUTION CORPORATION, Debtors-in-Possession	)))))))))	Case No. 99-1415-BBL (Jointly Administered with Case No. 99-1416-BBL) Chapter 11

Dated: January 13, 2000

____
UNITED STATES BANKRUPTCY COURT

§10.22 ~ Form: Administrative Order Regarding Professional Compensation

IN THE UNITED STATES BANKRUPTCY COURT
FOR THE EASTERN DISTRICT OF UTOPIA

In Re:	)	
INSOLVENT SUPPLY CORPORATION,	)	Case No. 99-1415-BBL (Chapter 11)
Debtor-in-Possession	)	

ADMINISTRATIVE ORDER, PURSUANT TO 11 U.S.C. §§105 AND 331 ESTABLISHING PROCEDURES FOR INTERIM COMPENSATION AND REIMBURSEMENT OF EXPENSES OF PROFESSIONALS

This matter comes before the Court on the Motion for an Administrative Order, Pursuant to 11 U.S.C. §§105(a) and 331, Establishing Procedures for Interim Compensation and Reimbursement of Expenses of Professionals (the "Motion") filed by the above-captioned debtor and debtor-in-possession (the "Debtor"). The Court, having reviewed the Motion and having heard the statements of counsel in support of the relief requested in the Motion at a hearing before the Court on January 11, 1999 (the "Hearing"), and finding that (a) the Court has jurisdiction over the matter pursuant to 28 U.S.C. §§157 and 1334, (b) this is a core proceeding pursuant to 28 U.S.C. §157(b)(2), and (c) notice of the Motion was sufficient under the circumstances; and the Court having determined that the legal and factual bases set forth in the Motion and at the Hearing establish good cause for the relief granted herein;

IT IS THEREFORE ORDERED THAT:

1. Except as may otherwise be provided in a Court order authorizing the retention of specific professionals, all professionals in this case may seek interim compensation in accordance with the following procedure:

> (a) on or before the 15th day of each month following the month for which compensation is sought, each professional shall submit a monthly statement to (i) the Debtor, Thirty Four East Rome Street, Williamsville, Utopia 57195 (Attn: General Counsel), (ii) counsel for the Debtor, Arnold & Porter, 555 Twelfth Street, N.W., Washington, D.C. 20004 (Attn: Michael L. Bernstein), (iii) the Office of the United States Trustee; and (iv) counsel to the Official Committee of Unsecured Creditors (the "Committee"). Each such entity receiving such a statement will have 15 days after its receipt to review it. At the expiration of the 15 day period, the Debtor shall promptly pay 85 percent of the fees and 100 percent of the disbursements requested in such statement, except such fees or disbursements as to which an objection has been served by the Debtor, the U.S. Trustee, or the Committee as provided in subparagraph (b) below.

(b) If the Debtor, the United States Trustee or the Committee object to the compensation or reimbursement sought in a particular statement, they shall, within 15 days of the receipt of the statement, serve upon (i) the professional who submitted the statement to which objections are made and (ii) except to the extent duplicative of the foregoing clause (i), the other persons designated to receive statements in subparagraph (a) above, a written "Notice of Objection to Fee Statement," together with an affidavit setting forth the precise nature of the objection and amount at issue. Thereafter, the objecting party and the professional whose statement is objected to shall attempt to reach an agreement regarding the correct payment to be made. If the parties are unable to reach an agreement on the objection within 15 days after receipt of such objection, the professional whose fee statement is objected to shall have the option of (i) filing the objection with the Court together with a request for payment of the disputed amount, or (ii) foregoing payment of the disputed amount until the next interim fee application hearing, at which time the Court will consider and dispose of the objection if payment of the disputed amount is requested. The Debtor shall be required to pay promptly that percentage set forth above of any portion of the fees and disbursements requested that are not the subject of a Notice of Objection to Fee Statement.

(c) The first statements shall be filed by each of the professionals on or before February 12, 2000. This statement shall relate to the period from the Petition Date through January 31, 2000.

(d) After the first four months, and at four month intervals thereafter, each of the professionals shall file with the Court and serve on the United States Trustee and the other parties identified in subparagraph (a) above an application for interim Court approval and allowance, pursuant to Section 331 of the Bankruptcy Code, of the compensation and reimbursement of expenses requested for the prior four months. The first such application shall be filed on or before June 1, 2000 and shall relate to the period from the Petition Date through May 1, 2000. Any professional who fails to file an application when due shall be ineligible to receive further interim payments of fees or expenses as provided herein until such time as the application is submitted.

(e) The pendency of an objection to payment of compensation or reimbursement of expenses shall not disqualify a professional from the future payment of compensation or reimbursement of expenses as set forth above.

(f) Neither the payment of, nor the failure to pay, in whole or in part, monthly interim compensation and reimbursement as provided herein shall bind any party-in-interest or the Court with respect to the allowance of applications for compensation and reimbursement of professionals.

2. Each member of the Committee is permitted to submit statements of expenses and supporting vouchers to counsel for the Committee, who will collect and submit such requests for reimbursement in accordance with the foregoing procedure for monthly and interim compensation and reimbursement of professionals, and in accordance with 11 U.S.C. §502(b)(3)(F).

3. Notice of any hearing to consider interim applications under 11 U.S.C. §331 shall be sent to: (a) the Office of the United States Trustee; (b) the Debtors and their counsel; (c) counsel for the Committee and (d) all parties who have filed a notice of appearance with the Clerk of this Court and requested such notice, and such notice shall be good and sufficient notice.

4. The Debtors shall include all payments to professionals on their monthly operating reports, detailed so as to state the amount paid to each of the professionals.

5. All time periods set forth in this Order shall be calculated in accordance with Federal Rule of Bankruptcy Procedure 9006(a).

____

UNITED STATES BANKRUPTCY JUDGE

§10.23 ~ Form: Maintenance of Cash Management System/Pre-petition Bank Accounts

IN THE UNITED STATES BANKRUPTCY COURT
FOR THE EASTERN DISTRICT OF UTOPIA

In Re: INSOLVENT SUPPLY CORPORATION Debtor-in-Possession	)	Case No. 99-1415-BBL (Chapter 11)
In Re: INSOLVENT DISTRIBUTION CORPORATION Debtor-in-Possession	)	Case No. 99-1416-BBL (Chapter 11)

ORDER AUTHORIZING
MAINTENANCE OF PRE-PETITION CASH MANAGEMENT
SYSTEM AND MAINTENANCE OF PRE-PETITION BANK ACCOUNTS

Before the Court is the Emergency Motion for Order Authorizing Maintenance of Pre-petition Cash Management System and Pre-petition Bank Accounts (the "Motion"), filed by Insolvent Supply Corporation and Insolvent Distribution Corporation, the above-captioned debtors and debtors-in-possession (the "Debtors").

The Court has read and considered the Motion, the accompanying memorandum and declaration, and all other documents submitted in connection therewith, and has considered the Affidavit in Support of First Day Motions, dated January 11, 1999, Submitted by Insolvent Supply Corporation's Chief Financial Officer, Mr. William Melater (the "Melater Affidavit"). The Court finds that the notice given of the Motion was appropriate under the particular circumstances presented, and that good cause exists to grant the relief requested. The Court further notes that the United States Trustee has consented to the relief sought in the Motion. Therefore, it is hereby ORDERED THAT:

1. The Motion shall be, and hereby is, GRANTED.

2. The Debtors are authorized to continue the use of their cash management system, as described in detail in the Melater Affidavit.

3. The Debtors are authorized to maintain, in their discretion, their pre-petition bank accounts, including their Depository Accounts, Special Reserve Accounts, Payroll Accounts, and General Operating Accounts, as set forth in the Melater Affidavit.

4. Nothing in this Order shall affect any claim of either Debtor against the other Debtor or permit the use of either Debtor's funds to pay expenses or obligations of the other Debtor.

5. The Debtors shall provide a list of all of its bank accounts to the U.S. Trustee within five (5) days after entry of this Order and shall provide notice of any change in the status of such accounts to the U.S. Trustee within five (5) days after any such change.

____

UNITED STATES BANKRUPTCY JUDGE

§10.24 ~ Form: Approving Investment Guidelines

IN THE UNITED STATES BANKRUPTCY COURT
FOR THE EASTERN DISTRICT OF UTOPIA

In Re: INSOLVENT SUPPLY CORPORATION, Debtor-in-Possession	)	Case No. 99-1415-BBL (Chapter 11)
In Re: INSOLVENT DISTRIBUTION CORPORATION Debtor-in-Possession	)	Case No. 99-1416-BBL (Chapter 11)

ORDER PURSUANT TO 11 U.S.C. §345(b)
APPROVING INVESTMENT GUIDELINES

Upon the Motion dated January 12, 2000 (the "Motion") of Insolvent Supply Corporation and Insolvent Distribution Corporation (the "Debtors"), as debtors-in-possession, for an order pursuant to Section 345(b) of Title 11 of the United States Code (the "Bankruptcy Code"), approving the Debtors' investment of cash and cash equivalents, all as more fully set forth in the Motion; and upon consideration of the Affidavit of William Melater, the Debtors' Chief Financial Officer, in Support of First-day Motions and Applications, sworn to on the 11th day of January 2000; and it appearing that the Court has core jurisdiction over this matter; and it appearing that due notice of the motion has been provided to the Office of the United States Trustee (the "Trustee") for the District of Utopia, and to the Debtors' twenty largest known creditors, and that no other or further notice need be provided; and it further appearing that the relief requested in the Motion is in the best interests of the Debtors and their estates and creditors; and upon consideration of the record before this Court; and after due deliberation and good cause appearing therefore, it is

ORDERED that the Debtors are authorized to invest their cash and cash equivalents in accordance with the investment guidelines attached to this Order as Exhibit "A" to the Motion (the "Investment Guidelines"), in addition to the investments permitted by Section 345 of the Bankruptcy Code, for so long as the Debtors operate as debtors-in-possession; and it is further

ORDERED that the Investment Guidelines may be amended by the Court from time to time upon application by the Debtor or by any other party-in-interest; and it is further

ORDERED that the Debtor's compliance with the Investment Guidelines shall be deemed to constitute compliance with Section 345 of the Bankruptcy Code, and the Debtors shall be and hereby are excused from the obligation under 11 U.S.C. §345(b) to obtain a bond from any entity with which money is deposited or invested in accordance with the Investment Guidelines.

____

UNITED STATES BANKRUPTCY JUDGE

EXHIBIT "A"

INVESTMENT GUIDELINES FOR THE SHORT TERM INVESTMENT OF CASH

Allowed investments, in addition to the investments permitted by Section 345 of the Bankruptcy Code, are as follows:

1. Obligations of the U.S. Government and Agencies
   Securities issued or directly and fully guaranteed or insured by the United States government or any agency thereof with maturity no longer than 180 days from the date of investment. Each security shall have an active secondary market.

2. Bank Paper
   Certificates of Deposit, Bankers' Acceptances, Bank Holding Company Commercial Paper, Time Deposits, and Overnight Bank Deposits, in each case with a domestic commercial bank having, at the time of purchase, a combined capital and surplus in excess of $200 million and a long-term debt rating on securities issued by them of A (or equivalent), as listed by either Standard & Poor's or Moody's. Such investments shall have a maturity date of not later than 270 days from the date of investment and shall be limited to the lower of 4% of each bank's combined capital and surplus or $15 million.

3. Commercial Paper
   Commercial paper with final maturities of six months or less from the date of investment of corporations which, at the time of purchase, shall not have a commercial paper rating of lower than A-2 as listed by Standard & Poor's or of lower than P-2 as listed by Moody's, and which shall have a long-term rating, at the time of purchase, of AAA or better as listed by either Standard & Poor's or Moody's. The Debtors shall limit such investments to $15 million of total principal amount per issuer.

4. Repurchase Agreements
   Any repurchase agreement is acceptable if it meets the criteria for direct investments described in paragraphs 1, 2 or 3 hereinabove and if the Debtors, directly through their agents or custodians, either take physical possession of the certificated securities or take possession through appropriate book entries or non-certificated securities. No repurchase agreement shall have a term exceeding 14 days. The Debtors shall limit such investments to $15 million of total principal amount per issuer.

5. Mutual Funds and Similar Investments
   Any funds (such as a mutual fund) investing in the above described securities or commercial paper to the extent that the fund holds investments in excess of $100 million and to the extent that the Debtors' aggregate investment in such fund is less than five percent (5%) of the total amount invested in that fund.

§10.25 ~ Claims of Essential Trade Vendors

IN THE UNITED STATES BANKRUPTCY COURT
FOR THE EASTERN DISTRICT OF UTOPIA

In Re: INSOLVENT SUPPLY CORPORATION Debtor-in-Possession	Case No. 99-1415-BBL (Chapter 11)
In Re: INSOLVENT DISTRIBUTION CORPORATION Debtor-in-Possession	Case No. 99-1416-BBL (Chapter 11)

ORDER PURSUANT TO SECTION 105(A)
OF THE BANKRUPTCY CODE AUTHORIZING DEBTORS TO PAY
PRE-PETITION CLAIMS OF CERTAIN ESSENTIAL TRADE VENDORS

This matter comes before the Court upon the Emergency Motion dated January 12, 2000 (the "Motion") of Insolvent Supply Corporation and Insolvent Distribution Corporation (collectively, the "Debtors"), as debtors-in-possession, for an order pursuant to 11 U.S.C. §105(a) authorizing the Debtors to pay certain pre-petition claims (the "Essential Vendor Claims") of their essential trade vendors (the "Essential Trade Vendors"). Upon consideration of the Motion; and upon further consideration of the Affidavit of William Melater in Support of First-Day Motions and Applications sworn to on the 11th day of January, 2000; and it appearing that the Court has core jurisdiction over this matter; and it appearing that due notice of this Motion has been provided to the United States Trustee for the District of Utopia and the Debtor's twenty largest known creditors, and that no other or further notice need be provided; and it further appearing that the relief requested in the Motion is in the best interest of the Debtors and their estates and creditors because, absent payment of the pre-petition claims of the Essential Trade Vendors, the Debtors would likely be unable to continue to obtain shipments of parts that are essential for the manufacture of their widgets, and would be forced to cease operations and to liquidate; and if further appearing that payment of the Essential Vendor Claims or the terms set forth in this Order is likely to induce the Essential Trade Vendors to continue to do business with the Debtors and to extend acceptable trade credit to the Debtor, which will enable the Debtor to continue to operate and enhance the prospects for a successful reorganization; it is

ORDERED that the motion is GRANTED; and it is further

ORDERED that the Debtors are authorized to pay Essential Vendor Claims in an aggregate amount not to exceed $5,000,000, as set forth in detail on the "Schedule of Essential Vendor Claims" attached to this Order as Exhibit A, subject to the provision of post-petition credit terms and limits by Essential Trade Vendors receiving such payment that are acceptable to the Debtor; and it is further

ORDERED that any Essential Trade Vendor who accepts payment from the Debtors pursuant to this Order shall be deemed to have waived any and all pre-petition claims, of any type, kind or priority, against the Debtors, their assets and properties; and it is further

ORDERED that the Debtors are authorized to obtain written confirmation of the post-petition credit terms and limits to be provided by an Essential Trade Vendor prior to paying such vendor's Essential Vendor Claim; and it further

ORDERED that nothing herein shall require the Debtor to pay the claims of any Essential Trade Vendor.

Dated: January 14, 2000

____
UNITED STATES BANKRUPTCY JUDGE

IN THE UNITED STATES BANKRUPTCY COURT
FOR THE EASTERN DISTRICT OF UTOPIA

In Re: INSOLVENT SUPPLY CORPORATION Debtor-in-Possession	)	Case No. 99-1415-BBL (Chapter 11)
In Re: INSOLVENT DISTRIBUTION CORPORATION Debtor-in-Possession	)	Case No. 99-1416-BBL (Chapter 11)

ORDER AUTHORIZING THE DEBTORS-IN-POSSESSION TO PAY CERTAIN PRE PETITION WAGES, SALARIES AND RELATED TAXES AND EMPLOYEE BENEFITS AND DIRECTING BANKS TO HONOR CERTAIN CHECKS AND FUND TRANSFER REQUESTS

Upon consideration of the motion ("Motion") of Insolvent Supply Corporation and Insolvent Distribution Corporation, as debtors and debtors-in-possession (the "Debtors"), for an order pursuant to 11 U.S.C. §§105(a), 363(b), 507(a)(3), 507(a)(4), and 507(a)(8), authorizing the Debtors to pay pre-petition salaries, wages and related taxes and employee benefits with respect to their current employees (the "Employees") and directing the banks that maintain the Debtors' payroll and other accounts not to dishonor certain checks issued and fund transfer requests made to such employees (the "Motion"); and notice having been provided to the United States Trustee and the Debtors' 20 largest creditors; and after hearing on the Motion on January 13, 2000, the Court being satisfied that the relief sought by the Debtors is necessary and in the best interests of the Debtors and their respective estates, creditors, and equity interest holders; and the Court having jurisdiction to consider this matter; and sufficient cause appearing therefor; and subject to the conditions set forth herein; it is hereby

ORDERED that the Debtors are authorized and empowered to pay the Pre-petition Employee Obligations listed on Schedule A to this Order and the related costs and expenses incurred in connection with the processing of such payments in the manner consistent with the Debtors' pre-petition practices and policies; and it is further

ORDERED that the Debtors are authorized to reissue checks to those employees whose checks were dishonored or which were drawn on now closed accounts; and it is further

ORDERED that the Debtors are authorized and empowered to pay, in the ordinary course of business, all federal, state, and local payroll tax deductions and withholdings pertaining to payments made pursuant to this Order; and it is further

ORDERED that the banks at which each of the Debtors' payroll and other bank accounts are located shall, after having been provided with a certified copy of this Order, honor all checks issued and fund transfer requests made by the Debtors in respect of their Pre-petition Employee Obligations and other amounts, the payment of which is approved herein, to the extent that sufficient available funds are on deposit with such institutions; and it is further

ORDERED that notwithstanding anything to the contrary in this Order, the Debtor shall not pay any pre-petition wage claim in excess of $4,650 per employee, except pursuant to a confirmed plan of reorganization or further order of this Court.

____

UNITED STATES BANKRUPTCY JUDGE

§10.27 ~ Extending Debtor's Time to File Schedules

IN THE UNITED STATES BANKRUPTCY COURT
FOR THE EASTERN DISTRICT OF UTOPIA

In Re: INSOLVENT SUPPLY CORPORATION Debtor-in-Possession	Case No. 99-1415-BBL (Chapter 11)
In Re: INSOLVENT DISTRIBUTION CORPORATION Debtor-in-Possession	Case No. 99-1416-BBL (Chapter 11)

ORDER EXTENDING DEBTORS' TIME TO FILE SCHEDULES, STATEMENT OF FINANCIAL AFFAIRS, AND LISTS PURSUANT TO FEDERAL RULE OF BANKRUPTCY PROCEDURE 1007(c)

Upon consideration of the motion of Insolvent Supply Corporation and Insolvent Distribution Corporation, as debtors-in-possession ("Debtors"), for an Order Extending Time to File Schedules, Statement of Financial Affairs, and Lists Pursuant to Federal Rule of Bankruptcy Procedure 1007(c), without prejudice to seek further extensions thereof for cause shown (the "Motion"); and notice having been provided to the United States Trustee and the Debtors' 20 largest creditors; and after hearing on the Motion on January 13, 2000, the Court being satisfied that the relief sought by the Debtors is necessary and is in the best interests of the Debtors and their respective estates, creditors, and equity interest holders; and the Court having determined that it has core jurisdiction pursuant to 28 U.S.C. §157(b)(2)([illegible]) to consider this matter; and sufficient cause appearing therefor, it is hereby

ORDERED that the time for the Debtors to file schedules, statement of financial affairs, and lists as required by Federal Rule of Bankruptcy Procedure 1007 is hereby extended through and including February 18, 2000, without prejudice to the Debtors' rights to seek further extensions thereof, if necessary, for cause shown.

____
UNITED STATES BANKRUPTCY JUDGE

§10.28 ~ Retaining Managers and Officers

The Code requires court approval for the retention of professional persons.[37] Strictly speaking, it doesn't say anything about the retention of managers. So on the face of things, it appears to allow the DIP to employ its president without court approval at $500,000 a year, while the requiring court approval for the attorney who may draw $75,000. But some courts may have local rules dealing with executive compensation,[38] and abuses could lead to appointment of a trustee.

§10.29 ~ Utility Deposits—Section 366

It is hard to imagine a chapter 11 debtor will not need some sort of ongoing utility service—and many are already behind on their bills when they file. Congress attempted to deal with the problem of utility service with a "good-news/bad-news" rule, set forth in Section 366.

The "good-news" rule (from the standpoint of the debtor) is in clause (a), which provides:

> A utility may not alter, refuse, or discontinue service to, or discriminate against, the trustee or the debtor solely on the basis of the commencement of a case under this title or that a debt owed by the debtor to such utility for service rendered before the order for relief was not paid when due.

But the statute giveth, and the statute taketh away. Clause (b) provides:

> Such utility may alter, refuse, or discontinue service to if neither the trustee nor the debtor, within 20 days after the date of the order for relief, furnishes adequate assurance of payment, in the form of a deposit or other security, for service after such date.

The Section goes on to specify that the court may order "reasonable modification" of the deposit on notice and opportunity to be heard. Typically, a debtor will include among its first day orders a proposed order establishing utility deposit requirements and enjoining the utility companies from terminating service. Most often, this order permits any utility that feels insecure to file a request for a deposit within a specified time period. The debtor and the utility try to negotiate a deposit, and, absent an agreement, the court decides.

---

37. Section 327(a).

38. *See, e.g.*, Maryland Local Rule 2015-1 (requiring debtor to file statement of pre-petition and post-petition compensation of officers and directors and prohibiting payment of post-petition compensation that exceeds pre-petition compensation without court order).

11

Executory Contracts

11 Executory Contracts

§11.1 ~ Introduction: Not Easy

George Treister, one of the smartest bankruptcy lawyers of his generation, used to say that the more he studied executory contracts the less he understood them. Not many others seem to understand them either. Executory contract law is complex—a thicket of artificial distinctions waiting to trip you up. You can't do much about that. What you can do is to try to get some sense of what you are up against.

On the face of things, the topic of executory contracts seems simple enough. Section 365(a) says that "the trustee, subject to the court's approval, may assume or reject any executory contract or unexpired lease of the debtor." But a quick skim over the next six or seven pages of statutory language is enough to show that the scope and meaning of Section 365(a) is more complex than it appears.

Part of the problem is that Section 365 has become the repository of at least as many "special situation" or, if you will, "special interest" rules as any section in the Code. But the deeper problems are conceptual. No one has ever come up with a fully satisfactory definition of what an executory contract is. Nor is it clear why the Code singles out executory contracts and leases as it does.

We begin with a word on procedure and a form of pleading. Then we plunge into a discussion of what it means to be an executory contract, and what it can do for and to you.

§11.2 ~ Procedure

A proceeding to assume, reject, or assume and assign an executory contract or unexpired lease is a contested matter, governed by rule 9014 (unless it is done in the plan).[1] Notice must be given to the other party to the contract, and "to other parties in interest as the court may direct" (and to the U. S. Trustee).[2] Note that there is no general requirement to send notice to all creditors (although the court may require it in a particular case, or it may be required by local rule). Contrast the procedure for sale of property outside the ordinary course of business, where notice to all creditors is standard.

1. Fed. R. Bankr. Proc. 6006(a).

2. Fed. R. Bankr. Proc. 6006(c).

§11.3 ~ Form: Motion to Reject Executory Contract

IN THE UNITED STATES BANKRUPTCY COURT
FOR THE EASTERN DISTRICT OF UTOPIA

In Re:	)
	)
INSOLVENT SUPPLY DISTRIBUTION,	)
	)
Debtor-in-Possession	)
	)

MOTION TO REJECT UNEXPIRED LEASES
FOR CERTAIN WAREHOUSE FACILITIES

The Debtor and Debtor-in-Possession, Insolvent Supply Corporation ("Debtor"), by its counsel, hereby moves for authority to reject the unexpired leases for the seven warehouse facilities listed on Schedule A to this motion (the "Florida Facilities"). This motion is filed pursuant to 11 U.S.C. Section 365(a) and Federal Rule of Bankruptcy Procedure 6006.

In support of its motion to reject the leases on the Florida Facilities, the Debtor represents as follows:

A. FACTUAL BACKGROUND

1. The Debtor filed its voluntary chapter 11 Petition on February 23, 2000. Since that date, the Debtor has remained in possession of its assets and has operated its business as a debtor-in-possession, pursuant to Sections 1107(a) and 1108 of the Bankruptcy Code.

2. On March 12, 2000, the United States Trustee for the District of Utopia appointed an Official Committee of Unsecured Creditors (the "Committee") in this case. No other committees have been appointed.

B. REASONS FOR REJECTING THE FLORIDA LEASES

1. Over the past several years, the Debtor has purchased wiring almost exclusively from Asian countries and has re-sold over 85% of its wiring in states that are west of the Rocky Mountains. The Debtor's east-coast business has diminished considerably. Under these circumstances, it is not profitable to maintain Florida warehouse space.

2. An integral part of the Debtor's reorganization strategy will be to focus its business exclusively on those western states in which it does the most business. The Debtor intends to file a plan of reorganization implementing this strategy as soon as possible. However, the Debtor is not in a position to file such a plan at this time because it is still negotiating the plan terms with the Committee, its secured lenders, and potential sources of exit financing.

3. The Debtor currently pays a total of approximately $650,000 per year in rent (and related charges) for the Florida Facilities.

4. The Debtor has looked into the possibility of selling its leasehold interests in the Florida Facilities, and has consulted Kone Realty, a real estate advisory firm, concerning this possibility. However, the Debtor has determined that each of the Florida Facilities leases is at an above-market rent and there is substantial vacant warehouse space in the regions of Florida in which the Florida Facilities are located. Accordingly, there is no market for the Debtor's Florida leasehold interests.

5. The Debtor is current on all of its post-petition obligations under all leases, including those related to the Florida Facilities. However, the Debtor is not fully utilizing the warehouse space at the Florida Facilities and they are therefore a substantial cash drain. The Debtor seeks to stop this cash drain by rejecting the Florida Facility Leases immediately.

C. LEGAL BASIS FOR RELIEF SOUGHT

1. Section 365 of the Bankruptcy Code permits a debtor-in-possession to assume or reject leases, with court approval. A debtor's decision to assume or reject a lease is evaluated under the "business judgment test." [CITE]. The court should ordinarily defer to a debtor's decision to reject a lease, so long as the decision is a rational one. [CITE] Rejecting a lease for real estate that is not utilized by the debtor and constitutes a cash drain on the estate is consistent with the debtor's obligations as a fiduciary and should be permitted under the business judgment test. [CITE]

2. For the reasons described above, rejection of the Florida Facility leases is in the best interest of the estate and its creditors, and is consistent with sound business judgment. Failure to reject these leases would result in a continued cash drain, with no corresponding benefit, and would impair the Debtor's prospects for a successful reorganization.

3. The Debtor has discussed the rejection of the Florida Facility leases with the Committee, and the Committee has authorized the Debtor to represent to the Court that the Committee supports the Debtor's decision to reject these leases.

D. CONCLUSION

WHEREFORE, the Debtor requests that the Court grant this motion, authorize rejection of the Florida Facility leases as of April 1, 2000, and grant such other and further relief as the Court deems appropriate.

Respectfully submitted,
LAMB, CURRY & RICE, P. C.
/s/________________________________
By: Liddell Beauxpip, Esq. #192837465
Attorney for Debtor
1234 Dingley Dell, Suite #56
Shepherdstown, UT 10203

§11.4 ~ Why It Can't Mean What You Think It Means

Start with the problem of definition. Broadly speaking, under non-bankruptcy law an "executory contract" is any contract that has not been fully "executed." Thus, if the debtor owes $10 to the creditor and has not yet paid, then the contract is "executory" in the broadest sense. But this cannot be what the phrase means in bankruptcy. Consider a simple case. Daniel owes $10 each to Charlie, Carla and Kermit, pursuant to written contracts. He has $10. He files for bankruptcy and his $10 passes to the trustee.

Give "executory contract" its broad meaning and it would seem that the trustee has power to pick and choose—for example, to "assume" the contract with Carla, pay her $10 and leave Charlie and Kermit high and dry. But this is flatly contrary to a basic principle of bankruptcy law—the principle of pro rata distribution. Pro rata distribution is so fundamental to bankruptcy law that it is inconceivable a drafter would dispense with it so lightly. So "executory contract" in bankruptcy must mean something less than it means at non-bankruptcy law.[3]

Here is a second problem. Suppose Daniel owes $10 to Kermit, secured by Daniel's widget, worth $10. Under a broad reading, this secured contract might also qualify as an executory contract under non-bankruptcy law. But the Bankruptcy Code contains special provisions dealing with secured credit. So again, we are compelled to conclude that the drafters meant the category of executory contract to include less than it would include at state law.

§11.5 ~ Why It Matters

So much for what the term cannot mean. We will return later to the question of what it does mean. The immediate next job is to consider why it matters. To consider this question, observe that so far we have identified three separate classes of transactions that the Code seems to recognize.

First, we have ordinary unsecured claims—call them simple contracts; second, claims secured by interests in property of the debtor—call them security interests; and third, executory contracts. Suppose the Donald accepted the transfer of a widget from Tess under a "contract for transfer" and then filed for bankruptcy. The trustee has taken possession of the widget, the transferor remaining unpaid. Donald still owes Tess $10,000; the widget is worth only $6,000. There are $20,000 worth of other assets and $50,000 worth of other claims (all unsecured).

What are the rights of the Tess (and the obligations of the trustee) if we characterize the transferor's deal as (a) a simple contract; (b) a security interest; (c) an executory contract? Consider each of the three in turn.

---

3. For cases holding that a contract in which the only remaining obligation of one party is the payment of money is not an executory contract, *see, e.g., In re* Indian River Homes, 108 B.R. 46, 50 (Bankr. D. Del. 1989); *In re* Gardinier, 50 B.R. 491, 494 (Bankr. M.D. Fla. 1985).

If the deal is a *simple contract*, then the trustee gets to retain the widget as an asset of the estate and the transferor shares pro rata with all other creditors. Total assets are $20,000 + $6,000 = $26,000. Total liabilities are $50,000 + $10,000 = $60,000. So each creditor gets (ignoring costs of administration) 26/60 (or 43 percent) of her claim. For Tess, that means she gets $10,000 x (26/60) = $4,333 on her $10,000 claim.

If the deal is a *security interest*, then Tess has two claims—first, a secured claim to the extent of the $6,000 value of her collateral, and an unsecured claim for the remainder. *See* Section 506(a). In liquidation, Tess will get $6,000 on her secured claim. Her $4,000 unsecured claim will became part of the general mass of unsecured claims. Total assets available for distribution to unsecureds are $20,000.

Total unsecured liabilities are $50,000 + $4,000 = $54,000. Each unsecured creditor will get 20/54 (or 37 percent) of her unsecured claim. For Tess, that means she gets $4,000 x (20/54) = $1,481 on her unsecured claim. Note that this means Tess's total recovery is $6,000 + $1,481 = $7,481 on her $10,000 obligation—or roughly 75 percent of her claim. So, Tess's recovery has risen from 43 percent (in the "all unsecured" case) to 75 percent, while the claims of other unsecureds have fallen from 43 percent to 37 percent.

In a reorganization case, the possibilities are greater. Most notably, the trustee (DIP) in a chapter 11 might try to impose a cram-down plan on the secured claim of Tess. This is possible even though it means rewriting the contract, as long as Tess gets present value not less than her $6,000 secured claim.

If the arrangement is an *executory contract*, the differences are dramatic. Section 365(a) says that the trustee may "assume or reject." But if he assumes, this means that he must assume in toto—*i.e.*, undertaking to pay the $10,000 obligation under the original contract terms. There is no provision for bifurcation into secured and unsecured claims. There is no way to rewrite the contract (without the creditor's consent) as there would be under a cram-down. And if he rejects, he must surrender the widget to Tess. She also retains an unsecured claim for damages due to breach—on the facts set forth here, apparently $4,000.

What are the consequences? It appears that the consequences of rejection are much like the consequences of having a security interest in a liquidation case. Tess winds up with $6,000 plus an unsecured claim for $4,000, so she gets an aggregate recovery equal to 75 percent of her pre-bankruptcy claim, while other unsecureds get only 37 percent. But if the trustee assumes the contract, he must pay $10,000 to Tess out of an estate whose total value is only $26,000. That leaves just $16,000 to satisfy the other $50,000 in claims. Each unsecured creditor will get only 16/50 (or 32 percent) of his claim—less than in any other case.

§11.6 ~ What Countryman Said

So, executory contract in bankruptcy cannot mean the same as executory contract outside of bankruptcy. But it makes a big difference in bankruptcy whether you do (or do not) have an executory contract. The question naturally arises—what does it take to have an executory contract under bankruptcy law? To answer that question, we turn to what must be one of the most influential law review articles in the history of bankruptcy law. The author is the late Vern Countryman, longtime bankruptcy professor at Harvard. The topic is Countryman's attempt to find a workable definition for the term executory contract in bankruptcy.[4]

Countryman undertook to formulate his definition "by a promise similar to one method of sculpting an elephant." That is, you "[o]btain a large piece of stone [and] take a hammer and chisel and knock off everything that doesn't look like an elephant." On that strategy, he offered this definition of executory contract for purposes of the Bankruptcy Act:

> A contract under which the obligation of both the bankrupt and the other party to the contract are so far unperformed that the failure of either to complete performance would constitute a material breach excusing the performance of the other.[5]

This is the so-called Countryman definition, and we wish we had a nickel for every time it has been cited in an opinion on executory contracts.

§11.7 ~ What Countryman Meant

Countryman never really made clear just why he liked this particular definition, but we think we can discern an answer. The clue is: secured credit. Back in the 70s, when Countryman published, the law of secured credit was not so fully developed as it is today. Ideas like "cram-down" and its kin were just coming into full flower. Countryman was an old western populist (he began his career as a law clerk to another populist, Justice William O. Douglas) who never had much taste for secured creditors. Countryman knew the Code definition of executory contract had to be narrower than the state law definition (otherwise, the Code would make no sense.) But he didn't want to write a definition so broad that it would take in secured credit. And his "material breach" definition does just that.

§11.8 ~ But Why?

Countryman's definition has proven hugely influential so he must have been doing something right. But as we said above, the problem gets more puzzling the more you look at it. To see why it is a puzzle, take another look at the hypothetical described above, in which transferor transfers a widget to transferee. The transfer may be (a) an outright transfer, in which case the transferee becomes the owner of the widget; or (b) a transfer of a limited interest, such that the transferee is the lessee. We know that an "ownership" transfer does not fall within the class of executory contract, but that a "lease" transfer does. Assuming (for the moment) that you know how to draw this distinction, the question presents itself: why would you want to?

---

4. *See* Countryman, *Executory Contracts in Bankruptcy, Part I*, 57 Minn. L. Rev. 439 (1973); *Part II*, 58 Minn. L. Rev. 479, 563 (1974).

5. 57 Minn. L. Rev. at 458-461.

Think of it this way. Broadly speaking, the "value" of any cash flow producing asset is the discounted present value of its expected future cash flows. So, if you own a widget that will yield earnings of $100 a year every year forever, and if the appropriate discount rate is 8 percent, then the present value of your widget is $100/0.08 = $1,250.

Now suppose (for whatever reason) that you want to buy not the whole widget, but you do want to use it under a 10-year lease. Can we value the lease interest? We can. To value it, we recognize that we have snipped the perpetuity into two parts, a 10-year term, and the remainder after the 10-year term. We can value each separately. The value of the term is the discounted present value of the first 10 payments. The value of the remainder is the present value of a perpetual payment stream that begins after the 10-year term. Based on this reasoning, and with a little arithmetic, we can see that the value of the term is $671. This means that the value of the remainder is $1,250 - $671 = $579.

When we speak of "ownership," we may think of a perpetuity. But we could just as well "own" a "lease." And each "ownership" interest—the perpetuity and the lease—is subject to the same kind of risks and opportunities.[6]

To consider an extreme example, take the case of HotelCo that owns an interest in two hotels, "O" (for "owned") and "L" (for "leased"). Each is expected to earn $400,000 a year forever and the appropriate discount rate is 10 percent, so the value of each is $400,000/0.10 = $4 million. HotelCo owns O "outright," subject to a 99-year mortgage for $4 million at 10 percent. The mortgage is payable interest only (that is, 10 percent of $4 million—or $400,000) every year for 99 years, with the principal payable as a $4 million balloon payment at the end. Hotel occupies "L" under a 99-year lease at $400,000 a year.

Restated, the only difference between these two deals is—who owns the $4 million residual? But the present value of the $4 million residual, discounted for 99 years at 10 percent, is only $391.29 (that is, about eight one thousandths of a percent of the $4 million value.) If we treat one of these deals under the "secured claim" rules and one on the "executory contract (lease)" rules, then we are letting an awful lot turn on eight one thousandths of a percent.

§11.9 ~ The Role of Non-bankruptcy Law

There is another definitional problem. This one arises from the relationship between bankruptcy and non-bankruptcy law. Courts frequently say that question "what is an executory contract (or lease)" is a question of bankruptcy law, not "state law."[7] This makes sense; indeed if what has been said above makes sense, then it has to be true. But necessarily also, courts must take state law as their point of departure.

And indeed, there is a great deal of state law on the issue. Most of it revolves around the distinction between "ownership transfer (plus security interest)" on the one hand versus "lease" on the other. This is

6. Indeed, if the term of the lease is for the entire remaining useful life of the asset, then, putting aside tax considerations that might apply, the value of the leasehold interest should be the same as the value of owning the asset.

7. *In re* Alexander, 670 F.2d 885, 888 (9th Cir. 1982).

just the kind of distinction that we try to draw in bankruptcy law. So it is nice to know that we can look to state law for an answer. But we are headed for a disappointment. The trouble is that the problem of definition is at least as messy or obscure under state law as it is under bankruptcy law.

The relevant state law is in the Uniform Commercial Code (UCC). *See generally* §12.5. The UCC leaves no doubt that a "lease" is a different kind of transaction from a "sale."[8] It is equally clear that a lease is not a "security interest" governed by Article 9. Section 9-102(1)(a) specifies that Article 9 of the UCC applies "to any transaction (regardless of its form) which is intended to create a security interest in personal property or fixtures. . . ."[9] But the definition of "lease" under the UCC extends to several pages, offering a variety of decision-points and presenting a correspondingly rich menu of possibilities for judicial error. Courts persist in encountering difficulty in making the distinction.[10]

This kind of uncertainty is bound to carry over to bankruptcy law. For example, consider the earlier example where Tess transferred the widget to Daniel. Suppose Tess neglected to perfect (presumably by filing a UCC-1) her interest as a security interest under Article 9. If her transaction is in fact a sale-plus-security-interest, then she is no more than an unperfected secured creditor, doomed to share in the leavings with the other unsecureds. But if her transaction is in fact not a security interest and is instead a "true" lease, then there is no requirement that she perfect and her failure to do so is not culpable. Rather, the trustee remains restricted to the options set forth above—that is, either to assume *in tote* or to reject *in tote* and return the widget to Tess.

A different source of potential confusion arises in the law of "conditional sales." Suppose Tess transfers the widget to Daniel under a contract whereby she purports to retain title until she is paid in full. If the widget is personal property, then the resolution is fairly straightforward. The UCC sets forth in no uncertain terms that a sale plus retention of title is a security interest, notwithstanding its name.[11] And Section 9-102(1)(b) specifically provides that "this Article applies to security interests created by . . . conditional sale."[12]

---

8. *See* UCC Article 2A; *cf.* UCC §1-201(37) (definition of "security interest," including definition of "lease").

9. The text refers to the "old" (or 1972) version of Article 9. The "new" revised Article 9 combines "old" §§9-102(scope) and 9-104(exclusions) into a basic scope principle in new §9-109. Former §9-102(1) and (2) have been combined and shortened into §9-109(a)(1). The revised text omits the word "intended" and says that the article applies to "a transaction, regardless of its form, that creates a security interest in personal property or fixtures by contract." (New) UCC §9-109(a)(1).

10. *Compare In re* Eagle Enters., 223 B.R. 290 (Bankr. E.D. Pa. 1998) (debtor, a waste management firm, had entered in to a "purchase lease agreement" with a German company for a top loader. Lease provided for 12 quarterly payments, it could not be canceled by the debtor, and at expiration of lease debtor had option to purchase for $1.00. Lessor did not file a financing statement and thus moved to have lease assumed or rejected. Court held the lease, under controlling Pennsylvania law, was a security interest; thus, seller moved to the ranks of the unsecured creditors) *with In re* Copeland, 238 B.R. 801 (Bankr. E.D. Ark. 1999). (Lessor/seller was in the business of selling wooden storage sheds. Chapter 13 debtor sought to treat lessor as a secured creditor, bifurcate claim and pay off secured portion over 36 months. Lessor/seller sought to have debtor assume or reject the lease. Despite negligible purchase option and rental payments in excess of value the court held that under Arkansas law when lessee has right to terminate the lease the agreement is *per se* a lease.)

11. UCC §1-201(37).

12. Again, the quotation is from the "old" Article 9. The "new" text omits specific reference to "conditional sale." But it does say that it applies to "a security interest arising under §§2-401 (reservation of title), 2-505, 2-711(3), or 2A- 508(5), as provided in §9-110." (New) UCC 9-109(a)(5).

If the widget should by chance be real estate, the matter is more complicated. Some states—perhaps many—maintain a distinction between "sale plus retention of security," on the one hand, and "sale on land contract" on the other. One might think that here, too, the courts would see past the form to the substance and treat them all as security interests. No doubt often they do. But it is possible to find bankruptcy cases in which the court treats what pretty clearly seems to be a security interest in land as an executory contract because it bears the form of a land contract.[13] The Bankruptcy Code itself treats a land sale contract as an executory contract for purposes of relief to non-debtor transferees.[14]

The Bankruptcy Code itself aggravates this kind of confusion in its treatment of claims against aircraft and vessels. Section 1110 of the Code gives a transferor of aircraft or vessels the right to take possession of the property transferred, notwithstanding the automatic stay, unless the trustee promptly agrees to perform all obligations. The right extends to "a secured creditor with a purchase-money security interest, or of a lessor or conditional vendor of" the property.

So in summary, it seems that if you have property other than Section 1110 property, then if the deal is a lease, you must assume or reject, but if it is a security interest, then you can deal with the transferor under Sections 506 and 1129. On the other hand, if you have Section 1110 property, then if the deal is a lease or a purchase-money security interest, then you must assume or reject (and quickly), but if it is a security interest other than a purchase-money interest, you are bound by ordinary rules governing secured creditors.[15]

The point of all this is not to criticize the Code for seeking to distinguish as it does. The distinction between sale and lease is deep-rooted in the culture of the law, even if not always easy to define in practice. But the discussion should serve as a warning that case law in the area is likely to be unstable and hard to predict.

---

13. *Compare In re* Streets & Beard Farm Partnership, 882 F.2d 233, 235 (7th Cir. 1989) (treating installment land sale contract as security device rather than as executory contract) *with In re* Terrell, 892 F.2d 469, 471 (6th Cir. 1989) (because failure to perform by either party would amount to material breach under state law both parties had unperformed obligations and sale contract was thus executory as defined by federal law). The much cited case of *In re* Booth, 19 B.R. 53 (Bankr. D. Utah, 1982), deserves notice here. This is the case in which Judge Mabey said that the question whether a particular contract is executory will be decided in terms of what benefits the debtor in a particular case. The decision has received much criticism as the most egregious form of result-driven rulemaking. On second look, however, ignoring the principle, Judge Mabey probably got it right as a matter of fact. The deal, which he held to be not an executory contract under his convenience test, appears in any event to be a security agreement in substance. There are several cases that have followed Judge Mabey's definition of executory contract. *See In re* Arrow Air, Inc., 60 B.R. 117, 122 (Bankr. S.D. Fla. 1986); *In re* Detra Fox, 83 B.R. 290, 299 (Bankr. E.D. Pa. 1988).

14. Section 365(i).

15. *See In re* Continental Airlines, Inc., 932 F.2d 282, 288 (3d Cir. 1991), holding that §1110 governs a sale-leaseback agreement, where the debtor first owned the property, then sold it, then leased it back again.

§11.10 ~ Checklist—How to Tell

Here is a list of factors that are referred to in judicial opinions as supporting the conclusion that a lease is (or is not) really a disguised sale/secured transaction. This list is not exhaustive, and other factors may be relevant, but these seem to be the ones upon which the courts rely most often.

- Is the lessor or financing agent also a manufacturer or dealer?
- Does the deal require a down payment?
- Does the deal transfer the risk of decline in value to the transferee?
- Does the lessee bear the risk of loss?
- Does the lessee have an option to purchase at the end of the lease term and, if so, is the purchase price is for little or no additional consideration?
- Is the transferee required to purchase the property upon the occurrence of specified events (such as, but not limited to, upon casualty or condemnation)?
- Does the transferor have the right to declare all lease payments due and payable on default (*i.e.*, as the transferor might have under a real estate mortgage)?
- Did the transferee insist that the debtor sign a financing statement?
- Do the deal papers establish a "sale price?"
- Did the transferor purchase the property in particular for the use of the transferee?
- Did the transferor obtain credit to purchase the property, and do the lease terms track the loan terms?
- Does it appear that the "rental charge" is designed to compensate the transferor for decline in value over the lease term?
- Is there anything in the lease that suggests that the transferee is acquiring equity in the property?
- Does the deal require that the lessee pay all taxes, maintenance and repairs?
- Is the lessee entitled to receive payment of any condemnation awards?
- Does the deal require that the transferee pay sales taxes and obtain any other requisite licenses, registration, and title fees?
- Does it appear that the transaction was structured as a lease instead of a loan to secure tax or accounting treatment benefits, or other benefits?

§11.11 ~ Drafting

If you are called upon to document a transaction where these issues might arise, you should keep in mind the following:

- A statement of the parties' intent in the contract will not likely be dispositive, but it could help your cause, if you want an agreement to be treated as a lease, to state in the contract that the parties intend the contract to be a lease and not a conditional sales contract and that lessor shall be deemed for all purposes to be the owner of the property.

- Leases and conditional/secured sales often have different tax consequences. Do not elect one form over another, or argue that a transaction should be characterized one way or the other, without looking into the tax consequences of each result.

- If your client enters into a lease of property that may be subject to recharacterization, it is often prudent for the "lessor" to file a "protective" UCC-1 financing statement, in case the transaction is recharacterized as a secured sale.

§11.12 ~ Assume and Assign

§11.13 ~ Assume

To explore the scope of Section 365, start with Section 365(a) which provides that "the trustee may assume . . . any executory contract or lease." This means, *inter alia*, that there must be a contract or lease —*i.e.*, otherwise there is nothing to assume. This is not as obvious as it might seem. In a much-cited early case, the bankruptcy judge held that the debtor had no power to assume a lease that had been terminated prior to bankruptcy.[16] Courts have also held that bankruptcy will not intervene to defeat the expiration of a contract under a non-curable notice of default issued before bankruptcy.[17] On the other hand, trustees (or DIPs) have sometimes found ingenious devices to persuade courts that a slender thread of state law right will flower forth into a full-fledged assumption power.[18]

---

16. *See In re* Mimi's of Atlanta, 5 B.R 623. 627 (Bankr. N.D. Ga. 1980), *aff'd*, 11 B. R. 710 (N.D. Ga. 1981).

17. Moody v. Amoco Oil Co., 734 F.2d 1200, 1212 (7th Cir. 1984).

18. *Cf. In re* Stoltz, 233 B.R. 280, 284 (D. Vt. 1998) (district court overturns a bankruptcy court determination that residential lease had expired pre-petition). The court held that until resident of housing authority apartment was disposed of residence by execution of writ of possession the lease was not expired under bankruptcy law. *Id.* Under state law the debtor, despite lease termination, still had a right to cure the default until a writ of possession was executed. *Id. See also In re* Shelco, 107 B.R. 483, 487 (Bankr. D. Del. 1989) (where lease was terminated pre-petition, but tenant had redemption right under state law until time of eviction, lease could still be assumed).

§11.14 ~ TECHNIQUE: TRYING TO DRAFT AROUND IT

When entering into an executory contract with an entity that may become subject to bankruptcy proceedings, it is worthwhile to insert provisions that maximize the chance that you will be able to terminate the contract, if the other party's situation appears to be deteriorating, on short notice-before the other party files bankruptcy. Consider a short term for the contract, renewable an indefinite number of times by mutual consent. Also consider short notice periods for termination or, if you can get away with it, termination effective immediately upon the receipt of notice of default. And consider an "insecurity provision" that allows your client to terminate, on short notice, if it believes in good faith that there has been a material change in the financial position of the other party or that the other party may not be in a position timely to satisfy its contractual obligations.

These are all ways to improve your client's chance of not getting struck as the nondebtor party to an executory contract, although none of them is foolproof.

Perhaps more important, the Bankruptcy Code prohibits the enforcement of so-called *ipso facto* clauses, sometimes called *bankruptcy* clauses, under which the bankruptcy of the debtor terminates the contract. The working of such a clause is perhaps most dramatic in the case of what might be called the "opportunistic default," where the current market rate for the property is higher than the contract rent.

For example, in *In re Sapolin Paints*,[19] in a long-term lease, the rent was 81 cents a square foot while prevailing market rate at the time of the case was $2.88. The question then becomes—who will enjoy the upside? The landlord? Or the other creditors? Not a few chapter 11 cases have been driven by the creditors' attempt to use the bankruptcy process to prevent the landlord from repossessing so they can cause the debtor to assume a lease (and usually also to assign it—*see below*), thereby capturing the premium for themselves.

In deciding whether to assume (or reject), the trustee must, axiomatically, do what is best for the estate. But this rule offers little solace to creditors. The trustee or debtor-in-possession is protected as long his decision is within the scope of his "business judgment," which is the same as saying that the courts will be reluctant to second-guess the debtor/trustee unless they have totally lost confidence in him or there is significant creditor opposition.[20]

If there has been a default, then the trustee cannot assume unless he can (as the jargon goes) *cure and assure*. More precisely, Section 365(b)(1) says he must:

- cure, or provides adequate assurance that the trustee will promptly cure, such default;
- compensate, or provide adequate assurance that the trustee will promptly compensate, for an actual pecuniary loss; and
- provide adequate assurance of future performance.

---

19. 5 B.R. 412 (Bankr. E.D.N.Y. 1980).

20. *See, e.g.*, Orion Pictures Corp. v. Showtime Networks, Inc. (*In re* Orion Pictures Corp.), 4 F.3d 1095, 1099 (2d Cir.1993).

Much executory contract litigation will boil down to a conflict over the scope of the cure-and-assure obligation.

§11.15 ~ Nonmonetary Default

Some ambiguity has developed as to whether a debtor must cure nonmonetary defaults in order to assume an executory contract. The confusion is caused by the language of Section 365(b)(2)(D), which was amended several years ago.[21] We think this confusion is just the result of poor drafting of the amended statute, and that there should be no question that a debtor must cure nonmonetary defaults as well as monetary defaults in order to assume a contract. But, until this is fixed, debtors may still be able to exploit the ambiguity to assume contracts without a full cure.

§11.16 ~ Adequate Assurance

What does it take to give adequate assurance of future performance? In general, the Code does not specify, and this is not the sort of issue on which you are likely to get helpful appellate authority—cases tend to be fact-specific and this kind of issue gets mooted out before it ever gets to court. Congress did enact some specific rules for cases involving shopping centers.[22] They are tough enough that for a lot of landlords, the strategy of choice will be to convince the court that your client is a shopping center. In other situations, the absence of statutory or Appellate Court guidance as to what constitutes "adequate assurance of future performance" is an invitation for counsel to try to spell it out in the agreement.[23]

Remarkably, the Code imposes these obligations only if there has been a default. If the debtor is not in default, then it appears that the trustee can assume without offering anything by way of adequate assurance.

§11.17 ~ Assign (Really Novation)

Far more momentous than the power to assume is the power to assign, under Section 365(f). The force of this rule is that assignment of contracts under the Code is not the same as simple assignment under non-bankruptcy law. Rather, it is better characterized as a "novation." Specifically, Section 365(k) provides that assignment "relieves the trustee and the estate from any liability for any breach ..."

Under state law, an obligor may be able to assign his rights under a contract and he may even delegate performance of his duties. But he cannot relieve himself of liability to the obligee absent the obligee's express consent—which, in the typical case, he is hardly likely to get. Thus an "assignment of the contract" under state law may give the obligee two parties to sue on default, rather than just one.

---

21. For a discussion of this issue, *see In re* Claremont Acquisition Corporation, Inc., 113 F.3d 1029 (9th Cir. 1997).

22. Section 365(b)(3). Since shopping center lessors get special protection, there is a strong incentive to persuade the court that you are a shopping center. But the courts have resisted entreaties to expand the category. *See, e.g., In re* Joshua Slocum, Ltd., 99 B.R. 250, 256-57 (Bankr. E.D. Pa. 1989), *vacated* 922 F.2d 1081 (3d Cir. 1990).

23. For a catalog of possible provisions, *see* David S. Kupetz, *To Assume or Not to Assume: Real Estate Leases in Bankruptcy*, 8 J. Bankr. L. & P. 393, 441 (1999).

But under bankruptcy law, the liability may be transferred without the non-debtor party's consent. Even where a contract specifically provides that it is non-assignable, a debtor-in-possession will generally have the right to assign the contract to a third party, over the nondebtor party's objection.[24]

The Code does require adequate assurance of future performance by the assignee. And in this case (unlike the case of simple assignment), assurance must be forthcoming whether or not there has been a default.[25] Once again, this is a likely focal point for litigation.

§11.18 ~ Non-Assumable, Non-Assignable: Section 365(c), (f) and (e)

The Code does impose some limits on the kinds of contracts that may be assumed or assigned. For example, Section 365(c)(2) provides that the trustee may not assume or assign a contract to make a loan or to issue securities of the debtor.

Thus, if a lender agrees to loan money to a borrower and the borrower files bankruptcy before the loan is funded, the borrower cannot assume the contract and thereby force the lender to make a post-petition loan. The Code also seems to prohibit the assignment of a traditional personal service contract.[26] This is intuitive: if Caruso files for bankruptcy, there is no reason why the Met should have to accept operatic vocal services from an assignee (nor, for that matter, from the trustee).

From thereon, however, the limits on assumption and assignment become somewhat murky. The difficulty arises from the language (seemingly self-contradictory) of Section 365(f), contrasted with Section 365(c).[27] Section 365(f) says:

> [N]otwithstanding a provision in an executory contract or unexpired lease of the debtor, or in applicable law, that prohibits, restricts, or conditions the assignment of such contract of lease, the trustee may assign such contract or lease .

The provision specifies that it applies "[e]xcept as provided in subsection (c) . . . . " And subsection (c)(1)(A) provides:

---

24. The Third Circuit had to cope with this rule in an interesting case involving the transfer of a labor contract. The debtor sold all its assets as a going concern to a third party. The third party assumed the debtor's obligations to a couple of labor unions under two collective bargaining agreements. Later the union tried to look to the debtor for some supplemental payments under the union contract. The debtor argued that he was protected by §365(k). The bankruptcy court agreed but the Circuit reversed. It conceded that §365(k) worked to immunize the debtor after a contract assignment. But it reasoned that §365(k) came into play only if the debtor assigned the entire contract. The court held that the debtor had not assigned the provision in dispute here. American Flint Glass Workers Union v. Anchor Resolution Corp., 197 F. 3d 76 (3d Cir. 1999).

25. Section 365(f)(2)(B).

26. Section 365(c)(1).

27. For the basics on reconciling these two sections, *see* Rieser v. Dayton Country Club Co. (*In re* Magness), 972 F.2d 689 (6th Cir. 1992); *In re* Pioneer Ford Sales, Inc., 729 F.2d 27 (1st Cir. 1984) with.

> The trustee may not assume or assign any executory contract or unexpired lease of the debtor . . . if . . . applicable law excuses a party, other than the debtor, to such contract or lease from accepting performance from or rendering performance to an entity other than the debtor or the debtor in possession.

The clause specifies that it applies "whether not such contract or lease prohibits or restricts assignment of rights or delegation of duties."[28]

The challenge is to read this language in such a way that 365(c) does not cancel 365(f). But in fact Section 365(c)(1)(A) is often read fairly narrowly, especially where the contract is a valuable estate asset. If the nondebtor party cannot point to some specific anti–assignment provision of non-bankruptcy law, or at least convince the bankruptcy court that it entered into the contract with the debtor based on unique characteristics of the debtor, it will likely have an uphill battle in invoking §365(c)(1) to prevent assignment. But where Section 365(c)(1)(A) does apply, it can cause the debtor a real problem that goes beyond the inability to assign the contract to a third party. Note that this section uses the phrase "assume or assign," suggesting that if the debtor cannot assign the contract to a third party under that section, then it also cannot assume the contract—even if it has no intention of assigning it. The problem has probably been most acute in the area of intellectual property—patents, copyrights and the like. The Ninth Circuit has read the language with particular stringency, holding that a debtor who may not assign a patent therefore has no power to assume it—even though he may have the power to cure pre-petition defaults.[29]

§11.19 ~ Anti-Assignment Act

This reading seems to be consistent with the statutory language, which states that a trustee or debtor may not "assume or assign" an executory contract that comes within Section 365(c)(1)(A), but it can have devastating results for the debtor.

Take, for example, a debtor whose major assets consist of government contracts. Under the Anti-assignment Act,[30] a government contract may not be assigned without the government's consent. Because the non-debtor party to the government contract (the government) cannot be compelled to accept performance from an assignee under applicable non-bankruptcy law, it is not surprising that the debtor cannot assign the contracts in bankruptcy.

But under Section 365(c)(1)(A), it appears that the debtor may not even be able to assume the contracts. This would appear to be true even if the debtor were not in default under any of the contracts and if the contracts have nothing to do with the reason for bankruptcy.

---

28. *See also* §365(e)(2) (providing for dealing with *ipso facto* clauses).

29. Perlman v. Catapult Ent., Inc., (*In re* Catapult Entertainment, Inc.) 165 F.3d 747, 750-51 (9th Cir. 1999). Compare *In re* CFLC, Inc. 89 F.3d 673, 679 (9th Cir. 1996) (no power to assign or assume) with Institut Pasteur v. Cambridge Biotech Corp., 104 F.3d 489, 493-94 (1st Cir. 1997) (power to assume).

30. 41 U.S.C. §15.

The result would be to effectively deny such a debtor the ability to avail itself of the protections of the Bankruptcy Code, because it could not take the risk of losing all its contracts. We would be surprised if this was the intent of Congress in drafting this section, but we believe that if this issue were to come before the Supreme Court, the Court would likely interpret the statute as it is written and preclude the assumption.[31]

§11.20 ~ Reject—Consequences of Rejection

You might think that rejection of an executory contract would be less problematic, but the concept of rejection has produced unsuspected difficulties.

In Tote: In the previous section, we saw that if the trustee/DIP wishes to assume an executory contract, he must assume in tote, or *cum onere*—in total and with the burdens. Symmetry would seem to provide that if he rejects, he must reject in tote as well—*i.e.*, surrender all the benefits he enjoys. At first blush, this seems straightforward enough, and it is the general rule. For example, if the trustee/lessee wants to reject a lease for which the debtor is lessee, it seems no more than basic fairness that he surrender the leased property.

But this rule is more complicated than might at first appear. It is one thing to surrender the leasehold for future use: it is quite different to require that the trustee disgorge all benefits acquired prior to rejection. In practice, it turns out that surrender usually means prospective surrender only.

Suppose the trustee does surrender the leasehold property in a declining market. Do we simply leave the lessor without a remedy? We do not. Section 365(g) provides that if the trustee/DIP rejects an executory contract, the non-debtor has a claim effective as of "immediately before the date of the filing of the petition." Normally, you would expect this to be a simple breach-of-contract claim: the non-debtor sues for the unpaid portion of the contract price, less any appropriate "mitigation." (For an important limitation on the damage remedy, *see* discussion of lessor's damages, *see* §11.26 below.) But because the rejection damage claim is a general unsecured claim, it is frequently not worth much. An exception is the contract that is assumed and then subsequently rejected; in that case the rejection damage claim is elevated to administrative priority (which counsels caution before a contract is assumed.)

§11.21 ~ Technique: Multiple Agreements

Non-debtor parties to contracts sometimes face unpleasant results because they have multiple agreements or contracts with the debtor, and the debtor assumes the ones that benefit it and rejects the ones that benefit the nondebtor party—even if, at least in the mind of the nondebtor party, they were all part of one deal.

To avoid this problem, especially in drafting a contract with a financially troubled party, you should consider putting the essential benefits of the contract from the prospective debtor's perspective in the same document that contains the essential benefits from the other party's perspective. If this cannot be

---

31. For a case raising this precise issue, *see* In the matter of West Electronics, 852 F.2d 79 (3d Cir. 1988); *see also* U.S. v. Carolina Parachute Corp., 108 B.R. 100 (M.D.N.C. 1989).

done, at least include a clause in each document stating that, although they are separate documents, they are all part of a single coverall contractual arrangement, and the parties intend that they be treated for all purposes as a single contract. This will increase the chance that the debtor will have to assume or reject the overall deal, rather than "cherry picking."[32]

§11.22 ~ The Limits of Rejection

One important problem emerged in *Burger King v. Rovine*.[33] The debtor ran a restaurant under a franchise from Burger King. In bankruptcy as DIP, the debtor rejected the franchise agreement, and undertook to continue in the restaurant business under another name. Burger King sued to enjoin him. Burger King pointed to the franchise contract, which included a covenant not to compete—that is, a promise by the debtor not to engage in any restaurant business within five miles of the old Burger King and within 18 months of termination.

The franchisor argued that it had a right to the protection of the injunction. It conceded that Rovine had a right to reject, but argued that rejection gave rise to a claim. Claim, as the franchisor happily pointed out, includes not just the right to payment, but also the right to an equitable remedy.[34]

In *Rovine*, the court held for the debtor-franchisee. "An executory contract," the court said, "must be rejected in its entirety or not at all." The purpose of Section 365, the court reasoned, is "to allow the rejection of executory contracts that are burdensome to the estate." Hence, no injunction.

Rovine attracted a lot of attention and a fair amount of criticism. But a good many courts bought its reasoning. An important arena for application was the entertainment industry. Consider the case of Willy the Drummer.

Example: When Willie the Drummer was young and unknown, he signed a contract with Record Co. RecordCo gave Willie a big advance for living expenses, access to a recording studio, and promotional assistance. In exchange, RecordCo is entitled to a percentage of all of the revenues from Willie's first five CDs. If Willie turned out to be a failure (as most of RecordCo's prospects do), RecordCo got nothing. Its big advance to Willie wasn't even repaid. But if Willie turned out to be a hit, RecordCo could look forward to making a lot of money from Willie's first five CDs. Willy's big album shot to the top of the charts. His phone started ringing off the wall, as competing producers beguiled him with prospects of new—and much more favorable—production deals.

Without claiming to be experts in the entertainment industry, we would think it likely that the non-bankruptcy law in Willy's home state gives the RecordCo the right—in the event that Willy threatens to change partners—to some kind of an injunction that would restrict his right to perform while the original contract is in effect.

---

32. For an example of a case where the court recognized that separate documents were part of a single contractual arrangement, which had to be assumed or rejected as a whole, *see In re* Texstone Venture, 54 B.R. 54 (Bankr. S.D. Tex. 1985).

33. 6 B.R. 661 (Bankr. W.D. Tenn. 1980).

34. Section 101(5)(B).

Can bankruptcy help? The evidence is not easy to track, but it appears there are a number of cases where it has helped a lot. We are told that a number of clever bankruptcy lawyers, using *Rovine*-type reasoning, have deployed the threat of bankruptcy to cut new and more favorable deals with their producers— *i.e.*, so as to sidestep the threat of rejection in the bankruptcy court.

Franchises and personal services are not the only realms where this problem seems to arise. Consider the case where the debtor is the lessor or seller of real estate or the licensor of intellectual property. Suppose the DIP/trustee wants to recapture the right and resell (release, relicense) on more attractive terms. In order to make the deal work he will need not only to repudiate the agreement, but also to dispossess the transferee. If the deal is an executory contract, and if rejection implies dispossession of the nondebtor, then it looks like the trustee/DIP can gets what he wants, and that rejection is the way to go.

These problems must have seemed plausible to the drafters of the Bankruptcy Code. We can see that this is so because the Code includes three provisions that seem designed (a) to recognize these arrangements as executory contracts, and (b) to accord statutory protection for the non-debtor. For example, Section 365(h)(1)(A) provides that if the debtor is the lessor of real property and the trustee rejects, then the non-debtor lessee may (if he chooses) "retain its rights under such lease. . . that are in or appurtenant to the real property for the balance of the term . . . ." There is similar language for real estate sales[35] and for intellectual property rights.[36]

A curiosity about this approach is that it may complicate life for other similar transactions that do not have the favor of statutory protection. Consider the case of a lessee of a large moveable crane at a freight harbor, which the court finds to be "personal property" under non-bankruptcy law. The transferee does not come within the protection of the existing lease rules; they are limited to leases of real estate. But by the very act of including special protection for real estate lessees, Congress seems to have conceded that without a special rule, there is no protection.

§11.23 ~ Do the Cases Go Too Far?

Lately, however, there have been signs of a shift in attitude. Critics argue that the old view confuses mere rejection (on the one hand) with wholesale repudiation or termination of the contract (on the other). To read rejection as repudiation (these critics argue) is to turn the executory contract power into an avoiding power. But it is not an avoiding power, and need not be read so broadly.

There is a dispute in the case law on this issue, with some courts viewing rejection of a contract as the equivalent of a breach by the debtor,[37] while others view rejection as a termination of the contract.[38]

35. In §365(i).

36. In §365(n). A version of the real estate rules has been in the Code since 1978. The intellectual property rule is a late addition, largely a response to a single case, Lubrizol Enters. v. Richmond Metal Finishers (*In re* Richmond Metal Finishers Inc.), 756 F.2d 1043 (4th Cir. 1985).

37. *See, e.g., In re* Continental Airlines, 98 F.2d 1450, 1459 (5th Cir. 1993); *In re* Modern Textile, Inc., 900 F.2d 1184 (8th Cir. 1990).

38. *See, e.g., In re* Haw. Dimensions, Inc., 47 B.R. 425 (Bankr. D. Haw. 1985). In an effort to clear up this confusion, the National Bankruptcy Review Commission recommended a change in the assumption/rejection terminology, to use the terms "election to perform" and "election to breach." But the recommendation, like most of the Commission's recommendations, has not been enacted into law.

The distinction can be of practical significance. For example, assume the executory contract contains a liquidated damages provision that is enforceable under applicable state law. The debtor rejects, and one of the parties to the contract seeks to enforce the liquidated damages provision (which party, of course, depends on the amount of the damages).

If rejection is a breach, then the liquidated damages provision may be enforceable. However, if rejection is a termination of the contract, then the liquidated damages provision was presumably terminated along with the rest of the contract, leaving the parties with whatever damages they can prove.

A number of earlier cases embrace the logic of termination. The older view is criticized in a series of law review articles by Michael Andrew of the San Diego bar and Professor Jay Lawrence Westbrook of the University of Texas.[39] The fruit of their work—embracing breach instead of termination—was picked up in the report of the National Bankruptcy Review Commission, and it seems to be making headway in the courts.[40]

An important milestone is *Matter of Austin Development Co.*[41] The debtor's lease was deemed rejected. But a bank, holder of a security interest in the leasehold, stepped in and tried to cure the debtor's default. The landlord argued that the rejection terminated the lease for all purpose, including the right of cure. Judge Edith Hollan Jones,[42] for the panel (specifically citing Andrew), wouldn't buy it. She held that rejection meant that the trustee refused to accept the lease obligation as an administrative expense, but no more.

The Second Circuit has taken the same approach, deciding *In re Lavigne*.[43] The debtor rejected a medical malpractice insurance policy. Later a chapter 7 trustee sought the protection of the policy for so-called "tail-end" insurance (to cover a claim first asserted after the original policy had expired). The insurer argued that rejection ended the right to tail-end insurance. The court disagreed; it held that the trustee retained the right to the tail-end insurance even though the contract had been "rejected."

Courts find at least two different routes to this newer view. Some say they are rejecting the Countryman test.[44] But others believe that they can reach the narrower result without rejecting Countryman outright.[45]

The trend clearly seems to be drifting away from the old "total-rejection" view and in favor of the newer, more limited view. But be assured that we haven't seen the last of it.

---

39. Michael T. Andrew, *Executory Contracts in Bankruptcy: Understanding "Rejection,"* 59 U. Colo. L. Rev. 845 (1988); Jay Lawrence Westbrook, *A Functional Analysis of Executory Contracts*, 74 Minn. L. Rev. 227 (1989); Michael T. Andrew, *Executory Contracts Revisited: A Reply to Professor Westbrook*, 62 U. Colo. L. Rev. 1 (1991).

40. National Bankruptcy Review Commission, Bankruptcy: The Next Twenty Years (Final Report, October 20, 1997) §2.4.1.

41. Sowashee Venture v. Austin Dev. (*In re* Austin Dev. Co.), 19 F.3d 1077 (5th Cir. 1994).

42. Herself a member of the National Bankruptcy Review Commission.

43. Lavigne v. Medical Malpractice Ins. Assn., 114 F.3d 379, 386-87 (2d Cir. 1997).

44. *See, e.g., In re* Drexel Burnham Lambert Group, Inc., 138 B.R. 687, 700-11 (Bankr. S.D.N.Y. 1992).

45. *See, e.g., In re* Bergt, 241 B.R. 17, 29-30 (Bankr. D. Alaska 1999). Bergt contains an exhaustive review of the debate.

§11.24 ~ TIMING

Section 365(a) imposes no limit on the time available for the trustee to assume or reject.[46] Unvarnished, this rule puts the non-debtor in a difficult spot. The trustee will just naturally defer the decision as long as he can—to the plan itself, if possible. But this means that the nondebtor is left hanging, not knowing whether he has a contract or not. This was, in fact, pretty much the rule under the 1978 Code as drafted.

There is a special protective rule for non-residential real property. That rule says that the trustee must assume or reject within 60 days.[47] If the debtor/trustee does neither, then the lease is rejected. Courts routinely agree to extend this period if the Debtor is not in post-petition default and the motion for an extension is timely filed. But the amendment puts the burden of taking the initiative on the debtor-in-possession or trustee, rather than leaving it with the non-debtor.

For leases of personal property (other than consumer goods), another protective rule applies.[48] It provides that "the trustee shall timely perform all of the obligations of the debtor ... first arising from or after 60 days after the order for relief" in a chapter 11 case.[49] This means, in effect, that he will have to keep the lessor current on the lease payments until he decides whether to reject or assume. The same rule applies with respect to leases of non-residential real property.[50]

In a chapter 7 case, the trustee must assume an executory contract or unexpired lease of real or personal property within 60 days, or such longer period as the court permits, or else the contract or lease is deemed rejected.[51]

Independent of these rules, the non-debtor may ask the court to set a deadline by which the trustee must assume or reject,[52] or seek adequate protection of his interest for the interim.[53] He isn't likely to win on the first motion, but he has a chance for some relief if he can show some significant risk or harm he is suffering.

In a chapter 7 case, the executory contract or lease is rejected at the end of 60 days unless assumed.[54]

Strategy: If the debtor assumes a lease and then later rejects the lease, the rejection damage claim will be elevated from a pre-petition unsecured claim to a post-petition administrative claim. So, it often makes sense for the debtor to put off the assumption/rejection decision, and to seek extensions of time to enable it to do so, so that the assumption/rejection decision can be made at a time when the outcome of the reorganization is likely to be more clear. Indeed, the Second Circuit appears to be suggesting this approach in its decision in *In re Klein Sleep Products, Inc.*, 78 F.3d 18 (2d Cir. 1996).

46. *See also* §365(d)(2).

47. Section 365(d)(4).

48. Section 365(d)(10).

49. Except he does not have to honor the *ipso facto* clause.

50. Section 365(d)(3).

51. Section 365(d)(1).

52. Section 365(d)(2).

53. Section 363(e).

54. Section 365(d)(1). Here also, the trustee may seek an extension.

§11.25 ~ The Cap on Damages

One of the more puzzling provisions of the Bankruptcy Code is a set of rules that cap damages for rejection of a lease or executory contract in two specific cases. First, the Code restricts landlords to:

> The rent reserved by [the] lease, without acceleration, for the greater of one year, or 15 percent, not to exceed three years, of the remaining term of such lease[55]

You count the three years from the date of the filing of the petition; or the date on which such lessor repossessed, or the lessee surrendered, the leased property . . . whichever is earlier. The landlord also gets unpaid pre-petition (or pre-repossession) rent.

Example: DebtorCo entered into a ten year lease with monthly rent of $500. Two years later, DebtorCo filed for relief under chapter 11. DebtorCo as DIP rejected the lease and vacated the property. The rent for one year is $6,000. The rent for remaining term of the lease, eight years, is $48,000. So 15 percent = $7,200. The value of three years' rent is $18,000. Landlord has a claim for $7,200.

Note that this is only a cap on damages not a claim for damages. In order to claim the cap amount the lessor must show actual damages up to that amount. The lessor is required to offset security deposits against his claim and is under the normal contractual duty to mitigate his losses.

The legislative history says that the provision is designed to compensate the landlord for his loss while not permitting a claim so large (based on a long-term lease) as to prevent other general unsecured creditors from recovering as dividend from the estate.[56]

But no one has ever given a plausible reason why the landlord's claim, though "large" in any particular case, can be expected to be larger than necessary to compensate the landlord on the same principles used to compensate creditors in general. Surprisingly, the Supreme Court, just two years after it invalidated the Frazier-Lemcke Act as an unconstitutional incursion on property rights, found no constitutional infirmity in the damage cap.[57] The same kind of rule applies to claims by an employee for damages resulting from termination of employment. The cap in employment cases is one year.[58]

---

55. Section 502(b)(6)(A). There is an ambiguity here. Some courts have held that the 15 percent refers to the rent remaining, while others hold that it refers to 15 percent of the term. The more common view appears to be that the landlord gets 15 percent of the rent for the entire balance of the lease term. *See In re* Andover Togs, Inc., 231 B.R. 521, 544 (Bankr. S.D.N.Y. 1999).

56. Bankruptcy Reform Act of 1978, H.R. 595, 95th Cong. §502 (1977). *See also* 124 Cong. Rec. H11110 (daily ed. Sept. 18, 1978) (remarks of Rep. Edwards); S. 17426 (daily ed. Oct. 6, 1978) (remarks of Sen. DeConcini). An account of the history of the provision can be found in Oldden v. Tonto Realty Co., 143 F.2d 916, 920-21 (2d Cir. 1944).

57. Kuehner v. Irving Trust Co, 299 U.S. 445 (1937). Holding the Frazier-Lemcke Act unconstitutional, *see* Louisville Joint Stock Land Bank v. Radford, 295 U.S. 555 (1935).

58. Section 502(a)(7)(A).

§11.26 ~ LABOR CONTRACTS

We call a labor-management collective bargaining agreement a "contract," but it is very far from clear that it is the kind of contract the drafters had in mind when they drafted Section 365. After all, the Supreme Court in 1960 held that a labor contract

> Is more than a contract. . . it is a generalized code. . . [it] covers the whole employment relationship ... it calls into being a new common law—the common law of a particular industry or of a particular plant ... an effort to erect a system of industrial self-government."[59]

Nonetheless, starting in the 1970s, in a number of high-profile cases, debtors in chapter 11 undertook to use the executory contract power to reject their collective bargaining agreements The Supreme Court blessed the strategy in 1984, in the well-known case of *National Labor Relations Board v. Bildisco & Bildisco.*[60]

Congress responded by adopting Section 1113 of the Code affirming the right to reject but adding restrictions to require limited bargaining over rejection in the bankruptcy case. One court found *nine* steps that stood between the DIP and rejection under the new section.[61] The pivot point is that the DIP may not "unilaterally terminate or alter any provisions of a collective bargaining agreement prior to compliance with provisions of [Section 1113]."[62] The ultimate standard seems to be that the union should share in the common suffering.

For example, the court deciding *In re Maxwell Newspapers, Inc.*[63] had to decide whether to let the debtor reject a labor agreement so as to facilitate sale of the business. The court found that unsecured creditors would receive perhaps 13 to 18 cents on the dollar and that equity was virtually worthless. It held that the union's rejection of the company's proposals was not in good faith. The lower court had said:

> Where, as here, a debtor is losing money consistently and does not have the ability to infuse more capital into the business, its best chance for preserving jobs and realizing a return for its creditors is to sell the business. But unless it can escape those collective bargaining agreements which straitjacket it, it may never be able to accomplish a sale.[64]

Well, maybe. But anything is a bargain at the right price, so the true question may not be whether the business can be sold, but at what price. If no sale is possible under the present labor agreement, then a conceivable option would be just to throw the keys on the table and give the business to the union. But in any event, this is not what the law requires, or even allows.

---

59. United Steelworkers of America v. Warrior & Gulf Navigation Co., 363 U.S. 574, 579-80 (1960).

60. 465 U.S. 513 (1984).

61. *In re* Blue Diamond Coal Co., 131 B.R. 633, 643 (Bankr. E.D. Tenn. 1991).

62. Section 1113(f).

63. 981 F.2d 85 (2d Cir. 1992), *affirming in part* 146 B.R. 920 (Bankr. S.D.N.Y. 1992).

64. *In re* Maxwell Newspapers, Inc., 146 B.R. at 929.

§11.27 ~ Employee Buyout

While the Code does not allow a debtor or trustee to "put" the company to its labor unions because of uneconomic collective bargaining in existing contracts, there is an option that is worth considering in such situations - an employee buyout. The company's employees might be persuaded to make the wage and benefit concessions necessary to facilitate a reorganization in exchange for a percentage of ownership of the reorganized business, seats on the board, etc. This approach has been utilized successfully in some cases, but probably should be considered more often than it is.

The number of bankruptcies attributable to collective bargaining arrangements seems to have receded since the 1980s. This fact may a testament to the general health of the economy, or declining power in the labor movement, or to a growing sophistication among unions over when and how to challenge a financially troubled company.

Curiously, the rules on labor contract rejection do not apply in chapter 7—not even, say, in a going concern chapter 7 where the business is to be sold as a whole to a third party. But principles of successor liability under labor law may continue to apply. *See* §17.40. Of greater practical relevance, they appear to apply to—but appear not to contemplate—a "liquidating chapter 11," where the debtor will not survive as an operating business.[65] But a court has solved a comparable problem in a closely analogous provision by subjecting the statutory language to gentle massage.[66]

A related provision, Section 1114 of the Code, governs (and restricts) the power of the DIP to avoid liability for retiree benefits in a chapter 11.

---

65. *See, e.g., In re* Chateaugay Corp., 891 F.2d 1034, 1039 (2d Cir. 1989) (overruling the union's objections to the sale of assets where a mine had been permanently closed). The Court found that the closing was "in good faith." *Id.* at 1038.

66. *In re* Ionosphere Clubs, Inc., 134 B.R. 515, 525 (Bankr. S.D.N.Y. 1991) This was the "liquidating chapter 11" of Eastern Airlines. The court had to consider the applicability of §1114 protecting pension rights. Rights under §1114 depend on what is "necessary to permit the reorganization of the debtor." The Court acknowledged that if read literally, the rule "does not supply a meaningful standard for this Court to apply" in a liquidating chapter 11. *Id.* at 522. The Court therefore (re)read the rule as "necessary to accommodate confirmation of a chapter 11 plan." Since the §1113 rests on the same predicate, we would expect the same (re)reading to apply.

12 Liens

12 LIENS

§12.1 ~ INTRODUCTION: YOUR MOTHER DIDN'T RAISE YOU TO BE AN UNSECURED CREDITOR

Bankruptcy distributes property when there isn't enough to go around. The residual class shares pro rata according to some principle of equity. But nobody wants to be in the residual class. They want to go to the front of the queue where they will get paid first before questions of insufficiency arise.

Broadly speaking, there are two ways to get to the head of the queue. One is to have as priority recognized by the bankruptcy statute. The other is to enjoy some sort of prior right under non-bankruptcy law that will be respected in bankruptcy *See* §13.35 ff. Here, we deal with prior rights created independent of bankruptcy law (but respected in bankruptcy). For convenience, and at the risk of oversimplification, we call these non-bankruptcy rights liens.

Lien is not easy to define. Outside bankruptcy, there is nothing like unanimity on what it means to have a lien—saying nothing of how you get one, or keep one. The Bankruptcy Code offers some help here. It defines a lien as a "charge against or interest in property to secure payment of a debt or performance of an obligation."[1] For our purposes, we might put the point a little differently: we can say that a lien is a relationship to the property of another, such as to give the lienholder a priority right on the property as against competing third parties.

As noted, because the lien is a property right, it puts the creditor at the head of the queue. But there is a corollary advantage. That is: if the creditor truly has a lien, and if the bankruptcy process does not purport to "deal with" the lien, then the lien "rides through"—remains as an encumbrance on the property after the bankruptcy is completed.

Taking that point of departure, it is useful to recognize three kinds of liens. Thus we can identify "consensual" liens that arise by agreement between debtor and creditor—for example, mortgages and personal property security interests. The Code uses the term "security interest," which it defines as a "lien created by agreement."[2]

---

1. Section 101(37).
2. Section 101(51).

Second, we can distinguish "judicial" liens that arise out of the judicial process. The Code defines a judicial lien as a "lien obtained by judgment, levy, sequestration, or other legal or equitable process or proceeding."[3]

And finally, we can point to what we might call "status" liens that arise in favor of creditors in a certain class as a result of their status in the world—as for example, mechanic's liens, attorney's liens on papers, and so forth. The Code doesn't use the term "status lien." It does include the term "statutory lien," which it defines as a "lien arising solely by force of a statute on specified circumstances or conditions, *or* lien of distress for rent, whether or not statutory . . . "[4] So a statutory lien may be a lien not created by statute. This is clumsy, but the point is probably clear enough.

We address each class of lien separately below. But first, a couple of general comments.[5]

§12.2 ~ Property and Contract

The first point to remember about lien law is that it subsists on the borderland between property and contract. So-called consensual liens arise (definitionally) by agreement between debtor and creditor. Status-based liens usually have a contractual basis as well—a mechanic won't get a mechanic's lien unless he makes some kind of deal with the customer. Even judicial liens are frequently contractual in provenance, in the sense that the judiciary intervenes when a deal goes bad.

But all these relationships are noncontractual—call them property-based or perhaps proprietary—in the sense that they purport to bind people who had nothing to do with any underlying contract, and indeed, may never have known about it. We respect these lien rights in bankruptcy (insofar as we do respect them) because we respect non-bankruptcy property rights and we recognize the lien right as a species of property.

This perspective helps to explain one of the oddities of draftsmanship in the Bankruptcy Code. The point of all this theoretical background is to establish that the lien right by definition (often) comes first in bankruptcy—ahead of unsecured claims, but even ahead of the so-called bankruptcy priorities. That is axiomatic. The oddity is that nowhere in the Bankruptcy Code is there any hint of a declaration of this axiomatic rule. Lien rights are not just at the head of the list: they are so far at the head of the list that they are not on the list at all.

Taken in context, this point is perhaps not as bizarre as it may sound. The law is always assuming first principles. Nowhere in the law of divorce, for example, does it specify that you have to be married in

---

3. Section 101(36).

4. Section 101(53) (emphasis added). The definition continues: "but does not include security interest or judicial lien, whether or not such interest or lien is provided by or is dependent on a statute and whether or not such interest or lien is made fully effective by statute."

5. Your authors disagree as to whether these general comments (in §§12.2 and 12.3) have any business in this book. One of us (guess which) thinks they are too theoretical for a practical book. The other thinks they are not theoretical at all, but provide a warning against the kind of snares and traps you may fall into in practice unless you keep your eyes peeled for trouble. We compromise by leaving them in place, with the invitation to ignore them if you see fit.

order to get a divorce: it's just taken for granted. One of us once undertook to research the discussion of secured creditors' (lien) rights in the legislative history of the Bankruptcy Act of 1898, the predecessor of our modern law. He found nothing.

Can we therefore infer that the law did not respect lien rights? We can infer nothing of the sort. Indeed, if you had asked an 1898 drafter why he didn't mention lien rights, he probably would have explained that lien rights, by their proprietary nature, were not part of the bankruptcy process at all. This isn't even remotely true today, of course: secured creditors in bankruptcy get beaten around the head and shoulders all the time. But the basic principle persists.

§12.3 ~ Property and Remedy

One more point of first principle. To assert a "lien right" at non-bankruptcy law is to make not just one, but either or both of two, different claims. It is first of all a claim of *priority* in the sense set forth above. But to say "I have a lien" under non-bankruptcy law is often also to say that "I have a right to special collection remedies, cheaper and more convenient than remedies available to those who do not hold liens."

As a practical matter, these claims are often both true together: lien law does in fact award to the favored both priority rights and special remedies. But it is worth noting for a moment that there is no necessity that this be so. Rather, linking priority and remedy probably arises through a venerable error about the nature of "property." In an earlier day, we supposed that property was unitary and if you were proprietary in one respect (priority), then it followed that you were proprietary in another (remedy).

If we were writing on a clean slate, it is unlikely that we would take the same view today. We live in an age where we recognize that "property" is not an indivisible primary unit, but rather the center of a force field of positive and negative signs, that you can slice and dice into a thousand separate pieces. But the law is a great respecter of tradition and we stick to the old ways. For our purposes, it may be useful only to note that most often it is the priority issues, and not the remedy problems, that exercise the analytical powers of the court.

§12.4 ~ Consensual Lien

The most common lien problem in bankruptcy probably is the conflict over the priority of a creditor whose lien is consensual. The typical "family business" debtor is likely to owe money to the bank on a term loan secured by real estate, and a "working capital loan" secured by inventory and receivables, and any number of "purchase money" loans secured by individual items of personal property. All of these fall under the rubric of consensual liens, and in all cases, the creditor will be seeking to assert his lien rights to get paid first out of the finite pool of assets, at least to the extent of the value of his collateral.

§12.5 ~ Personal Property

Almost all consensual liens in personal property will be governed by Article 9 of the Uniform Commercial Code ("UCC") which is the law (though with many nonuniform variations) in every state in the United

States.[6] This fact yields the happy consequence that personal property security law is widely known and understood. There are textbooks and commentaries, not to mention a visible body of case law. In practice this means that lien issues involving consensual security interests in personal property are most likely to be got right in court—and that the bankruptcy court is the court most likely to get them right, since bankruptcy judges deal routinely with these rules.

The linchpin of Article 9 is Section 9-317(c) of the Commercial Code.[7] It provides that an unperfected security interest is subordinate to the rights of a lien creditor. This lien creditor rule at state law dovetails nicely with the trustee's lien creditor power under Bankruptcy Code Section 544(a)(1); *see* discussion of lien creditor power.

Article 9 also sets forth traffic rules for a number of other priority disputes—for example, priority among competing secured creditors. These rules are important enough in themselves, but it is worth noting that they really don't have a lot to do with bankruptcy. As long as the fight is solely between two secured creditors, there is no issue over the shape of the residual claim and the matter is not properly before the bankruptcy court to do.[8]

§12.6 ~ Real Property

The law of real estate security has a history that is longer and much more fully developed than its parallel in personal property. Moreover, land does not move, so mortgage law has always remained more "local." For both these reasons, mortgage law persists more encumbered by archaic baggage.[9] At least of a matter of history, students of mortgage law had to puzzle over possible distinction between "title theory" and "lien theory" mortgage doctrines. They had to compare and contrast "true mortgage" and "land contract," and other devices such as the "deed of trust."

For personal property, distinctions of this sort were pretty much wiped out by Article 9 of the Uniform Commercial Code, which brought everything together into a single body of law governing any transaction intended to give a security interest. Moreover uniformity meant that there was only one body of personal property security law for the entire nation. The fact of uniformity alone gave it a kind of visibility that meant it was more likely to be understood.

---

6. For the text of the UCC, *see* http://www.law.cornell.edu/ucc/ucc.table.html. A Revised Article 9 has recently been adopted in all 50 states. We cite the revised revision here.

There is an online forum for the discussion of UCC issues. Send a message to listproc@assocdir.wuacc.edu, with the following message in the body: subscribe UCCLAW-L Firstname Lastname.

For individual state versions of the UCC, go to http://www.law.cornell.edu/uniform/ucc.html.

7. Former 9-301(1)(b).

8. The reported cases seem to involve tax liens, not Article 9 interests, but the principle is the same. *See, e.g., In re* Gardner, 913 F.2d 1515, 1519 (10th Cir. 1990) ("the bankruptcy court lacked jurisdiction to resolve the dispute between [the former spouse of the debtor] and the government regarding a lien on nonestate property"). Of course, you will sometimes see such battles fought out in the bankruptcy court, for example, where lien priorities affect plan confirmation, or DIP financing, or adequate protection, and so forth.

9. To track state mortgage statutes, start at http://wwwsecure.law.cornell.edu/topics/mortgages.html.

For real property, matters are not so simple. There is nothing like a "uniform" law of mortgages.[10] A lawyer (or a judge) who runs into a problem of mortgage law will need to master a body of specialized local law where general precedents are frequently of little help.

§12.7 ~ Practice Pointer: Keep State Law In Mind

Our experience is that lawyers in general pay surprisingly little attention to the particulars of state property laws that underlie their bankruptcy cases. One of us has seen an option agreement invalidated because it was held to clog the equity of redemption; a right of first refusal invalidated as a violation of the rule against perpetuities; a potential real estate lien lost because a prevailing plaintiff failed to record his judgment in the appropriate land records; a security interest in personal property avoided because it was recorded in state (but not county) records; and a claim of exemption invalidated because the homestead deed was not recorded in time. Remember that while bankruptcy law administers estate assets, most of the law governing interests in property are state law.

§12.8 ~ Judicial Liens

If mortgage law is a thicket, the law of judicial liens is a swamp. Individual state schemes are almost infinitely various in detail and it would take courage beyond good sense to try to venture far into particulars without a local guide. Still, it is possible to identify the kinds of problems that may arise, and even to say a few (cautious) words about jargon.

The point of departure, as always, is: how to leverage yourself into a position that will put you ahead of other creditors when there isn't enough to go around. One way, of course, is to have a consensual lien or a statutory priority. But what about the ordinary unsecured creditor who sues to collect his claim? Whatever priority he gets will have to arise from the rules governing judicial liquidation of claims— hence, a judicial lien. And with the usual caveats about how local rules vary, here is a generalization: in most cases, he won't be able to get his judicial lien—priority—until after his lawsuit and after judgment.

For example, California law provides that after judgment, the creditor may get a writ of execution, and that levy of the writ of execution creates an execution lien.[11] For personal property capable of manual delivery, you get the lien only when the sheriff actually gets the property into his possession. Surely a lot can happen between the time the creditor realizes that there is a default and the time he finally gets his execution lien.[12]

---

10. Strictly speaking this is wrong. The National Conference of Commissioners of Uniform State Laws in 1985 promulgated a "Uniform Land Security Interest Act." But no one ever adopted it, and it seems to be pretty much a dead letter. On the other hand, there is a restatement; *see* Restatement (Third) of Property: Mortgages (1997). There is also a fine Restatement of Suretyship and Guaranty (1996).

11. Cal. Civ. Proc. Code §697.710.

12. Distinguish the method of getting a "lien"—for purposes of establishing from priority—from the rules that tell you what you have to do to liquidate your claim. Typically, after taking possession of the property, you have to put it up for sale. If there is any surplus available after sale, the surplus goes back to the creditor; but if there is any shortfall the debtor remains liable and the creditor can levy on something else.

Short of the execution lien, California also allows the creditor with a judgment to get a *judgment lien* by recording an abstract of his judgment.[13] The judgment lien is, at least, a cheaper and more convenient method of gaining priority (even if not much faster). It doesn't actually transfer any assets to the hands of the creditor, but it does impose a cloud on the record title, so the creditor knows that if ever the debtor tries to sell the real estate, his phone will ring. Somewhat unusually, California even allows a limited judgment lien against *personal property*, although its coverage is not as extensive.

Seeing how much delay there is between default and lien, the question naturally arises—isn't there some way to get the lien *earlier*, so as to establish priority before others get in line? The answer is a highly circumscribed "yes." The creditor *may* be able to get some sort of lien *prior to judgment* (state law may call it a "prejudgment attachment," or simply "attachment lien"). But there are so many conditions and limitations that the remedy isn't of any practical use in most cases.[14]

Why so many limits on the pre-judgment attachment? The short answer is that they are constitutionally required. There was a time when pre-judgment attachment was the order of the day, perhaps particularly in consumer cases. But in a series of cases in the 1960s and 1970s, the Supreme Court "constitutionalized" the attachment process, holding it governed by an overriding principle of due process. The consequence was that pre-judgment attachment went from being the norm to being, as it is today, the exception.

§12.9 ~ "STATUTORY" LIENS

§12.10 ~ IN GENERAL

Finally, there is a class of cases where a creditor may be able to achieve some sort of lien right that arises peculiarly from his status. For example, traditional common law liens may offer limited protection to innkeepers, or improvers. Many states afford "lien" protection by statute—sometimes even by constitutional mandate—to mechanics and materialmen. Specialized lien law often protects producers of agricultural products.

Bankruptcy treatment of these status liens is a bit tricky unless you keep your eyes open. The Code does not give general recognition to "common law" liens. It does recognize and protect statutory liens. But here comes the confusion. It defines statutory liens to include (a) those created by statute; and also a

---

13. *See, e.g.*, Cal. Civ. Proc. Code §697.340 (real property); *id.* §697.510 (personal property).

14. The experience of California is perhaps typical, if better documented than most. A "pre-constitutional" writ of attachment statute was held invalid in *Randone v. Appellate Department*, 488 P.2d 13, 15 (Cal. 1971). A revised attachment law took effect in 1977. *Id.* §481.010. Use of Attachment is limited to the following conditions: (1) The claim is based upon a contract, *id.* §483.010(a); (2) the claim is for a fixed or readily ascertainable amount of not less than $500, *id.* §483.010(a); (3) that is either unsecured, or undersecured due to a decrease in value of the collateral, *id.* §483.010(b); and (4) it must arise out a commercial transaction, *id.* §483.010(c). The writ of attachment creates a three year lien on the attached property which may be renewed for up to eight years. The statute includes procedures for notice and hearing, apparently calculated to meet the demands of due process. It does allow ex parte attachment upon a showing "that great or irreparable injury would result to the plaintiff if issuance of the order were delayed until the matter could be heard on notice." *Id.* §485.010.

"lien for distress of rent, whether or not statutory."[15] So a statutory lien may or may not be a lien created by statute. For limits on statutory liens, *see* Section 545.

§12.11 ~ Tax Liens (Federal Tax Lien Act)

One class of statutory lien looms so large in bankruptcy practice that it deserves special attention. That is the lien of the Internal Revenue Service under the Federal Tax Lien Act.[16] The act provides that if any person fails to pay any tax, "the amount … shall be a lien in favor of the United States upon all property and rights to property, whether real or personal, belonging to such person."[17] The lien extends from the time the assessment is made until the time the tax is paid or becomes unenforceable by lapse of time.[18] But then the statute goes on to provide that the lien "shall not be valid as against" a long list of competing claimants until a notice of tax lien has been filed.[19]

The Bankruptcy Code recognizes tax liens. But puts one important crimp in the lien claim. That is: in chapter 7, the tax lien is subordinated to senior liens, and also to various bankruptcy priority claims, including claims for administrative expenses, wage claims, consumer lay-away claims and the like.[20]

On its face, this subordination rule applies only in chapter 7. But it makes a difference in chapter 11 as well, when it comes to proving "best interest." *See* §18.2. Recall that to prove best interest, under Bankruptcy Code Section 1129(a)(7), you must prove what the creditor would get in chapter 7. A creditor who is behind the tax lien in chapter 11 may be ahead of it (via subordination) in chapter 7.

Section 6323(f) of the Internal Revenue Code sets the ground rules for tax lien filing. It says that filing shall be "in one office within the State (or the county, or other governmental subdivision), as designated by the laws of such State, in which the property subject to the lien is situated"—or, failing that, with the U. S. district court where the property is situated.[21] So the exact place of filing is left to state law, under the federal criterion. To implement the mandate, most states have adopted the Uniform Federal Tax Lien Registration Act.[22] It prescribes filings with the secretary of state for personal property where the debtor is a corporation of a partnership, and with the county recorder for everything else. Note that this will often be different from the place of filing for ordinary security interests.

---

15. *See supra* note (4) and accompanying text.

16. 26 U.S.C. §§6321-3 (1989).

17. *Id.* §6321.

18. *Id.* §6322.

19. *Id.* §6323(a).

20. Section 724(b).

21. 26 U.S.C. §6323(f)(1)(A), (B). For the District of Columbia, the statute prescribes filing with the Recorder of Deeds, *id.* §6323(f)(1)(C).

22. Cite to the ULA web site for the tax lien act.

The Federal Tax Lien statute and its kin have developed an elaborate encrustation of case-law jurisprudence all their own.[23] The niceties are perhaps most likely to trip up the lawyer who knows a little of the law governing personal property security interests under Article 9 of the Uniform Commercial Code—trip her up because the Tax Lien Statute often talks about the same sorts of issues in language that is similar, but not identical.

To get a flavor of the problem, consider the case where the tax lien applies to a "security."[24] The Tax Lien act says that the tax lien on a security, even though filed, shall not be valid "as against a purchaser of such security who at the time of purchase did not have actual notice or knowledge of the existence of such lien."[25] Recall that Bankruptcy Code Section 545(2) invalidates any statutory lien that is not enforceable against a bona fide purchaser. In a number of cases, DIPs have sought to use the BFP power to avoid the tax lien on a security. Courts have generally rejected the claim, holding that the bona fide purchaser of Section 545 is not the same as the purchaser of Section 6323.[26]

§12.12 ~ Pension Liens

The sponsor of an ERISA-qualified pension plan is liable to make payments quarterly to maintain his plan.[27] Failure to pay triggers a 10 percent excise tax liability. Both liabilities will fall not only on the primary debtor but also on members of its "control group."[28] If the shortfall exceeds $1 million, the liability triggers a statutory lien. Rules governing notice and priority under the pension lien are the same as those for the tax lien.[29]

§12.13 ~ Compare: Insolvency Liens

Perhaps the most noteworthy limitation is a flat prohibition on what you might call "insolvency liens"—liens that are triggered by the debtor's bankruptcy, or insolvency or suchlike. Section 545(1) imposes a flat prohibition on these "insolvency liens." On reflection, it is easy to see that this almost has to be the rule, if the bankruptcy system is to function at all. If the state could write a lien law triggered by bankruptcy, then it could for all practical purposes trump the Bankruptcy Code's own scheme of priority.

---

23. An ALI-ABA publication by William H. Plumb used to hold quasi-canonical status as an interpretation of the Federal Tax Lien Act. *See* William T. Plumb, Jr., Federal Tax Liens (3d ed. 1972), with 1981 Supplement by Harry Shapiro and Joseph Kover, appended. It is, unfortunately, somewhat out of date, but the law changes slowly in this area, and it may still prove useful as a point of departure for the uninitiated. For an outline of what the tax collector believes is the law regarding tax collection (including tax liens), *see* the government's collection manual at its web site:

http://www.usdoj.gov/tax/readingroom/jcmanpdf/manual.htm.

24. "Security" is defined in 26 U.S.C. §6323(h)(4). The term includes stocks and bonds and their close kin.

25. 26 U.S.C. §6323(b)(1)(A).

26. *See, e.g.*, *In re* Janssen, 213 B.R. 558, 564 (B.A.P. 8th Cir. 1997).

27. 26 U.S.C. §412.

28. *Id.* §412(d)(5)(B).; *cf. id.* 4971(e) ("controlled group" defined as "any group treated as a single employer under subsection (b), (c), (m), or (o) of §414.").

29. 26 U.S.C. §§412(n)(5). 4068, 6323(f).

Second, Section 545(2) invalidates any statutory lien that "is not perfected or enforceable at the time of the commencement of the case against a *bona fide purchaser*." This rule appears to parallel the trustee's "bona fide purchaser power" to avoid consensual security interests in real estate, pursuant to Section 544(a)(3). *See* §14.7.

Finally, the Code flatly invalidates all liens for rent, or distress of rent.[30] The legislative history offers no good reason why the landlord is so ill-favored. Perhaps the rule can be read as a parallel to the (equally inexplicable) rule capping landlord's damages for breach of lease.[31]

§12.14 ~ Compare: Setoff

§12.15 ~ The Bankruptcy Code v. the UCC

Section 9-109(d)(1) of the Uniform Commercial Code provides that Article 9 does not apply "to a right of...set-off." The great Grant Gilmore, in his magisterial treatise, sputtered that the provision is "an apt example of the absurdities which result when draftsmen attempt to appease critics by putting into a statute something that is not in any sense wicked but is hopelessly irrelevant."[32]

"Of course," Gilmore continued, "a right of set-off is not a security interest and has never been confused with one: the statute might as appropriately exclude fan-dancing."[33] Gilmore's point is that in the case of setoff, the creditor retains "his own" property against a claim of the debtor, while a security interest is an interest that the creditor holds in property of "another," *i.e.*, the debtor.

Gilmore is right—as long as we think that the UCC is about "property rights" and not just about "priority." But in the years since 1965, we have been drifting away from a purely proprietary theory. A newer attitude is reflected in the Bankruptcy Code, adopted in 1978—which provides that:

> [a]n allowed claim of a creditor secured by a lien on property in which the estate has an interest, *or that is subject to setoff* under Section 553 of this title, *is a secured claim* to the extent of the value of such creditor's interest in the estate's interest in such property, or to the extent of the amount subject to setoff.[34]

[And, the section continues, is an unsecured claim for the remainder.] And the practical fact is that it works pretty well. As we shall see, there are problems with the right of setoff, but defining the boundary with secured credit is not among them.

---

30. Subsections 545(3), (4).

31. Subsection 502(b)(6).

32. Grant Gilmore, Security Interests in Personal Property Vol. 1 §10.7 at 315 (1965). Strictly speaking, he was referring to the predecessor, old §9-104(I).

33. *Id.*

34. Subsection 506(a).

Tactic: If you represent an unsecured creditor and are asked to file a claim on its behalf, remember to find out whether the creditor has any mutual debts with the debtor that would qualify for setoff, and if so, to assert a *secured* claim to the extent of the setoff.

§12.16 ~ Setoff Preserved

Having defined the right of setoff, the Code goes on preserve it. Specifically, Section 553(a) provides (with exceptions):

> This title does not affect any right of a creditor to offset a mutual debt owing by such creditor to the debtor that arose before the commencement of the case under this title against a claim of such creditor against the debtor that arose before the commencement of the case.

For starters, note that this section does not create any right of setoff, but only purports to preserve what existed under non-bankruptcy law. Both claims must arise before the commencement of the case. So there is no right to offset a pre-petition claim against a post-petition claim (although courts have held that it is permissable to set off a post-petition claim against a post-petition debt).

§12.17 ~ But Stayed

While the right of setoff is preserved under Section 553, the exercise of the right is stayed under Section 362(a)(7). This is hardly surprising: it is consistent with the general policy that bars unilateral action to liquidate claims in the pendency of the case. The consequence is that the setoff creditor, just like any other secured creditor, will enjoy his priority, but must wait for general distribution or get relief from the stay.[35]

§12.18 ~ Compare: Recoupment

Having the right of setoff is better than having no right at all, but as we have seen, it is imperfect. We have seen that the creditor is stayed. And he can't set off a pre-petition claim against post-petition debt.

An alternative doctrine that may be of use where setoff is not available is "recoupment"—a traditional "equity" doctrine that allows the court to fashion justice from the entirety of the transaction when otherwise the debtor would be unjustly enriched.[36] To the careless or untrained eye, "recoupment" walks and talks like setoff. But growing body of case law holds that it not setoff, and so the constraints of setoff do not apply.[37] For example, courts have held that the exercise of recoupment is not precluded by the automatic stay and that one may exercise recoupment without regard to the pre-petition/post-petition distinction.

---

35. Where a court finds that a creditor has a valid setoff right, it will usually grant relief from the stay to permit that right to be exercised, but that is not always the case, particularly where the setoff would adversely affect the prospects for a successful reorganization.

36. *See* United States v. Dalm, 494 U.S. 596, 611 (1989) (citing Bull v. United States, 295 U.S. 247 (1935)).

37. "The common law doctrine of recoupment, while frequently merged with the doctrine of setoff in other contexts, is a distinct doctrine in bankruptcy cases." *In re* Davidovich, 901 F. 2d 1533,1537 (10th Cir. 1990). This case provides a good, concise description of the recoupment doctrine.

The argument is not quite as tricky as may at first appear. If the trustee sues the nondebtor for the purchase price of a load of widgets, then the transferee ought to be able to raise a defense of breach of warranty in the trustee's lawsuit without getting all snarled up in the law of setoff.[38] Indeed, at least one court has said that recoupment is the ancestor of the doctrine of "compulsory counterclaim" set forth in Rule 13(a) of the Federal Rules of Civil Procedure.[39]

Although recoupment has the advantage of enabling a creditor to offset pre-petition claims against post-petition debts, and to accomplish the offset without regard to the automatic stay, it is also more limited than setoff in one important respect. The conflicting rights must be part of the "same transaction."[40] There is plenty of litigation over what "same transaction" means. How do you handle, for example, multiple deliveries under the same master supply agreement? You can guess from the question that courts are split.[41]

But the real growth industry has been in the area of government claims. There are any number of cases where the government, as provider of benefits, wants to cancel its obligation for benefits, against some sort of right against the debtor —for an accidental overpayment, perhaps, or maybe for outright fraud. Perhaps the most litigated issue is medicare payments to health care providers—may the government reduce ongoing post-petition payments to a provider to cancel unsatisfied pre-petition obligations from prior cost years? The Third Circuit has held that the activity is not a permissable recoupment because each "cost year" is a separate transaction, so the government must keep paying even while it holds the claim.[42] But there is plenty of authority contra and our guess is that in the long run, the government wins.[43]

---

38. Setoff rules do not apply where the non-debtor's assertion is "essentially a defense to the debtor's claim against the creditor rather than a mutual obligation, and application of the limitations on setoff in bankruptcy would be inequitable." Lee v. Schweiker, 739 F.2d 870, 875 (3rd Cir. 1984).

39. Frederick v. United States, 386 F.2d 481, 487 (5th Cir. 1967).

40. *In re* Davidovich, 901 F.2d at 1537.

41. *Compare In re* California Canners and Growers, 62 B.R. 18 (B.A.P. 9th Cir. 1986) (different transactions) *with In re* B&L Oil Co., 782 F.2d 155, 158-59 (10th Cir. 1986) (same transaction).

42. University Medical Ctr. v. Sullivan (*In re* University Medical Center), 973 F.2d 1065 (3d Cir. 1992).

43. U.S. v. Consumer Health Services of America, Inc., 108 F.3d 390, 395-96 (D.C. Cir. 1997).

13

Priority, Claims and Distribution

13 PRIORITY, CLAIMS AND DISTRIBUTION

§13.1 ~ INTRODUCTION: WHAT ARE WE DOING HERE?

We have seen earlier (in Chapter 7, above) that the job of the trustee is to "[c]ollect and reduce the money the property of the estate . . . and close such estate as expeditiously as is compatible with the best interests of the parties in interest.[1]

In chapter 11, it doesn't work quite that way, but still the bedrock rules for collection and distribution provide a substrate to the chapter 11 plan. So it is important to know who gets paid, and in what order. We take up these topics here.

§13.2 ~ PRO RATA

The basic rule of bankruptcy distribution is pro rata. If there is enough to pay 10 percent of all claims, then each creditor gets 10 percent of his claim.[2]

Example: Ted, the trustee of the estate of Della Debtor is holding $1,440 for distribution. There are three claims. Della owes $1,200 to Alpha, $800 to Betty and $400 to Marshall—a total of $2,400. This means that the trustee has enough to pay 60 percent of all claims (1,440/2,400 = 0.6). So Ted should pay Alpha $720 (1,200 x 0.6). He should pay Betty $480 (800 x 0.6). He should pay Marshall $240 (400 x 0.6). Note that 720 + 480 + 240 = 1,440, so everything checks. Several points are worth noting about pro rata distribution.

First, it only applies to the residual class—usually, although not necessarily, the unsecured class. Other classes get paid in order of "lien" priority or bankruptcy statutory priority (*see* discussion of liens etc.). If a class is paid in full, there is no point in computing pro rata.

Example: Same as above, except the $1,440 property held by the trustee includes $400 as proceeds of the sale of a widget in which Marshall held a perfected security interest. Marshall gets $400, discharging his secured claim. Della still owes $1,200 to Alpha and $800 to Betty—a total of $2,000. After distribution to Marshall, she has $1,040, or enough to pay 52 percent of remaining claims (1,040/2,000 = 0.52). She pays $634 to Alpha (1,200 x 0.52) and $416 to Betty (800 x 0.52).

---

1. Section 704 (1). The duty to collect and close is notably excluded from the duties imposed on a trustee in chapter 11. *See* §1106(a). This makes sense: Chapter 11 contemplates not liquidation and distribution, but the implementation of a "plan." Still, what stakeholders get under a plan is ultimately, at least in part, a function of what they would get in chapter 7. *See, e.g.*, §1129(a)(7) (individual dissenting creditor may defeat a plan if it will give him less than he would get in chapter 7).

2. Section 726(b). Note that this rule applies in chapter 7 only. Interestingly, the rule of *pro rata* distribution doesn't seem to be spelled out. in any other chapter, but no one doubts it is the law.

The secured creditor gets priority only to the extent of his claim. So in the previous case, if the widget had been worth $600, Marshall still would have taken only $400, no more. On the other hand, the secured creditor gets priority only to the extent of his lien. So in the previous case, if Marshall's (total) claim had been worth more than his collateral, he would have been paid as a secured creditor to the extent of the collateral value, and as an unsecured creditor for the remainder.

Example: Same as above, except that the portion of the $1,440 that derives from the widget sale is only $100. Ted pays $100 to Marshall, discharging his secured claim, but leaving Marshall with an unsecured (deficiency) claim of $300. The total of (unsecured) claims is now $2,300 (1,200 + 800 + 300). The total of assets available for distribution is $1,140. Ted has enough to pay 58.26 percent of unsecured claims (1,340/2,300—rounded). So Ted pays $699.13 to Alpha, $466.09 to Betty and $174.78 to Marshall. Note that since Marshall got $100 on his secured claim as well as $174.78 on his unsecured claim, he winds up with some 68.7 percent of his total claim, while the others get less.

Next, note the effect of pro-rata distribution on non-bankruptcy law. We often say that bankruptcy is merely a procedural framework of state law rights. This assertion may be useful as an oversimplification, but it is no more than that. The discharge certainly doesn't just reflect a state law right, and neither does pro rata distribution.

Finally, note that while we have done pro rata distribution for a thousand years, no one has ever (at least not until very recently) offered a compelling explanation for it. We speak vaguely of equity and fairness, without specifying just what is unfair about letting the race go to the swift, as it would without bankruptcy intervention. But here are two possible explanations.

One has passed into bankruptcy folklore as what you might call the "Mad, Mad, Mad, Mad World" explanation, after the comic chase movie where Sid Caesar and a whole bunch of other guys run themselves silly in search of the hidden money. How much cheaper it would have been if they had simply pooled their resources and run a single search instead of half a dozen. Insofar as it implements pro rata distribution, the Bankruptcy Code makes a sharp departure from state law.

The other is perhaps more subtle and elegant. It comes from (then) Professor Thomas Jackson, now the President of the University of Rochester.[3] Jackson makes the case for bankruptcy as a kind of kind of insurance. Suppose an "equal" race in which every creditor knows they would win once out of every 10 times. On standard principles of risk reduction (Jackson argues) each creditor would gladly give up the chance for 100 percent of the pot 10 percent of the time, in favor of 10 percent of the pot every time. Jackson's example has been hugely influential among professors who write about bankruptcy, although it has had no visible impact on the practice of law.

§13.3 ~ Compare: Class Actions

---

3. *See* Thomas H. Jackson, Bankruptcy, Non-Bankruptcy Entitlements, and the Creditors' Bargain, 91 YALE L. J. 857 (1982).

§13.4 ~ Bankruptcy As a Class Action

For the experienced litigator, one way to approach bankruptcy is to think of it as a kind of class action. Class action law aggregates similar claims to save waste, duplication and expense to the parties and to the court. Modern class action law is largely a child of the 1960s; but special pleaders for bankruptcy could rightly say that we've been doing it here for 500 years.

No place is this more evident than in the troubled history of the mass tort claims that arose out of asbestos exposure, and in particular the case of the Manville Corp. Manville went through a huge and much-publicized chapter 11 before the bankruptcy court in Manhattan in the 1980s, where the participants attempted to reach closure on the tort claims. The deal unraveled almost from the start. District Judge Weinstein in Brooklyn asserted jurisdiction over the wreckage and virtually imposed a no-opt-out class action on all parties.[4] But the Second Circuit struck down the Weinstein settlement.[5]

The Second Circuit's decision rests in part on the inferiority of the Weinstein Rule 23 process, as distinct from the bankruptcy process. For example, a chapter 11 reorganization may be approved only after approval by a favorable vote of impaired classes. The Weinstein Rule 23 process contained no such protection. As another example, any creditor may defeat a chapter 11 plan if he can show that he would get less under the plan than he would in liquidation. There was no such protection in the Weinstein Rule 23 class. The court was also troubled by the abrogation of first-in-first-out—which is more intriguing, because one consequence of the typical asset bankruptcy is to supplant the traditional state law, first-in-first-out scheme in favor of a pro rata bankruptcy distribution.

In two important cases lately, the Supreme Court has struck down large non-bankruptcy class action settlements, holding that the settlement mechanism didn't do enough to protect the rights of victims. In Ortiz vs. Fibreboard Corp., the court held that settlement provided too much for lawyers at the expense of litigants, and that it didn't extract enough wealth from the defendants.[6] The court also faulted the settlement for the way it treated "present" claimants against "future" claimants. It is conceivable that the next chapter in this conflict will be written back again in bankruptcy court.

§13.5 ~ Class Actions in Bankruptcy

A separate question is whether you can file a class claim *in* a bankruptcy case. Bankruptcy Rule 7023 adopts the federal class action rule. But the rule is invalid without statutory support and the Code itself is at least inexplicit on the subject. Section 501 specifies a number of "representatives" who may file claims, but the class representative is not on the list. Making a negative inference from silence, a number of courts have held that the claim is not authorized.[7] Others have taken the negative inference in the

---

4. Judge Weinstein's opinion, which occupies upwards of 200 pages of text (plus 70 pages of appendix), is at 129 B.R. 710 (E. & S.D.N.Y. 1991).

5. *In re* Johns-Manville Corp., 982 F.2d 721 (2d. Cir. 1992).

6. 527 U.S. 815 (1999).

7. *In re* Standard Metals Corp., 817 F.2d 625, 632 (10th Cir. 1987), *vacated and rev'd in part on other grounds sub nom.*, Sheftelman v. Standard Metals Corp., 839 F.2d 1383 (10th Cir. 1987).

other direction, holding that class actions should not be barred without clear expression of Congressional intent.[8]

§13.6 ~ Claim

§13.7 ~ The Definition

Section 726 directs the trustee to pay claims. Section 101(5)(A) says that claim means

> right to payment, whether or not such right is reduced to judgment, liquidated, unliquidated, fixed, contingent, matured, unmeasured, disputed, undisputed, legal, equitable, secured, or unsecured.[9]

The first thing to notice about the definition is that it is broad. Consider these three cases:

Daniel, Donald and Della were driving vehicles that injured (respectively) Peter, Paula and Pam. Daniel, Donald and Della each filed for relief in bankruptcy. At the time of filing—

- Peter held a final, non-appealable judgment against Daniel for $100,000.
- Paula had filed suit against Donald for an unspecified amount of damages. Donald has filed an answer in which he denies liability, but the case has not yet come to trial.
- Pam had just realized that she was injured. It had not yet occurred to her that Della might be liable, or that she might have a cause of action against her.

Which of these, if any, holds a claim against the respective bankruptcy estates? The answer is that each has a claim. There may be problems valuing the claims held by Paula and Pam (and indeed, they may be worth nothing), but there is no doubt that the drafters meant to sweep them all in with the expansive language quoted above.

Similarly, consider the case of Harold, the holder of a zero-coupon bond issued by DebtorCo in the amount of $1,000, payable ten years from today. DebtorCo files for bankruptcy today. Does Harold hold a claim? The answer is yes. His claim may be unmeasured and there may be a corresponding problem of valuation, but the fundamental status is beyond doubt.

§13.8 ~ Claim v. Interest

If you are a stockholder rather than a creditor, you do not have a claim but you do have an "interest." The term isn't formally defined in the Code, but you can tease out the meaning pretty clearly. For example,

---

8. *In re* American Reserve Corp., 840 F.2d 487, 492-94 (7th Cir. 1988).

9. Section 101((5)(A). Section 101(5)(B) specifies that "claim" also includes the right to an equitable remedy, "but we can leave the consideration of equitable remedy until later."

Section 1126 provides that a plan must be accepted by a majority in number and two thirds in amount of voting claims. It goes on to say that it must be accepted by two thirds in amount[10] of interests. The legislative history reads this as meaning "equity securities," and so does everyone else.[11]

§13.9 ~ Administrative Expense

If you have a right to payment for administrative expenses, you can expect to get paid better and more quickly than almost anyone else in the case, assuming there are unencumbered assets in the estate. But if you are fastidious, don't call it a claim. The drafters, apparently intentionally, did not write of administrative claims. They reserved the word "claim" for those rights to payment that are not administrative expenses. The difficulty is that they didn't come up with any other word and so people end up talking about administrative claims anyway. For more on administrative expenses, *see* §13.41.

§13.10 ~ Secured Creditors and the Claims Process

Elsewhere we explain that the secured creditor goes to the head of the queue in bankruptcy. You can see this principle at work in the rules governing claims.

Start with Section 506, entitled "determination of secured status." There are two benchmark rules in Section 506. The first is in subsection(a). Heavily edited, it provides:

> An allowed claim . . . is a secured claim to the extent of the value of [the] creditor's interest in [the collateral] and is an unsecured claim [for the balance].

So, consider BancCo, with a claim for $1,000 secured by Blackacre, worth $1,200. BancCo has a secured claim of $1,000. The remaining $200 is available to satisfy other claims against the estate. But then consider LittleCo, with a claim for $1,000, secured by Debtor's inventory, worth $700. Per Section 506(a), LittleCo has two claims—a secured claim for $700 and an unsecured claim for the $300 deficiency. Now, consider the second benchmark rule (in subsection (d)). It reads:

> To the extent that a lien secures a claim against the debtor that is not an allowed secured claim, such lien is void unless . . . such claim is not an allowed secured claim due only to the failure of any entity to file a proof of such claim.

Translated, this rule gives the secured creditor two choices: one, file a claim, participate in the bankruptcy case and thereupon lose his lien; or two, ignore the bankruptcy and let his lien ride through, trusting that he will be able to recover from his collateral later on.

---

10. Note the statute says "majority in amount" rather than "majority in number." So, one equity stakeholder with two-thirds of the equity could outvote 100 other stakeholders who together hold only one third.

11. H.R. Rep. No. 595-95, 1st Sess., at 410-11 (1977). In the same vein, the legislative history to §1129(b)(2)(C) says: "[I]nterests may include the interests of general or limited partners in a partnership, the interests of a sole proprietor in proprietorship, or the interest of common or preferred stockholders in a corporation." *Id.* 412-18.

Taken together, these rules make up a large part of what gives bankruptcy law its personality. They are keystones in the strategy of debtors trying to reorganize under chapter 11 (or chapter 13). And they provide the framework for some of bankruptcy's most bitter and contentious litigation.[12]

§13.11 ~ The Mechanics of Claim

§13.12 ~ To File or Not to File?

If the creditor wants to share in the estate, she will want to make sure that her claim gets on file, either by means of her filling or by virtue of being accepted as prima facie valid through the schedules. She may not need to file if her claim is accepted prima facie—and she may not want to file if filing surrenders to jurisdiction that she'd rather avoid.

In the simple chapter 7 bankruptcy (and in chapters 12 and 13), if the creditor wants to share in any assets, she must file a proof of claim.[13] So in chapter 7 (or 12 or 13), the creditor had better file the claim (and file it on time) if she wants to participate in the case. In the ordinary case, filing the claim isn't hard: you may want to tell your client just to get a form at the stationery store and file it himself.[14]

In chapter 11, the procedure is not so simple. Bankruptcy Rule 3003(a)(1) says that in chapter 11, the schedule of liabilities "shall constitute prima facie evidence of the validity and amount of the claims of creditors." So, many creditors will simply forego the inconvenience and rely on the schedules. This certainly cuts down on the paperwork and it may make sense where most claims are vendor book accounts where the debtor already has the necessary records and there is no dispute.

But it may be dangerous to rely on the schedules. In the first place, the rule doesn't apply if the claim is scheduled as "disputed, contingent or unliquidated." In such case, the creditor must file a proof of claim to have its claim allowed. Perhaps more important, it may be possible for the debtor to amend schedules after filing, so as to remove or "dispute " a previously scheduled creditor. The rules will typically provide that the creditor be notified of such an amendment. But Murphy's law applies in bankruptcy court, and many lawyers would rather file a proof of claim out of caution than trust to the schedules.

Similarly in chapter 7, if the case appears to be a no-asset case, the clerk will mail out a notice asking creditors not to clutter up the file with claims.[15] The obvious purpose of the rule is to keep from clogging the court with claims when there will be nothing to distribute. Here also, however, some cautious lawyers simply aren't willing to let well enough alone. They will file a claim anyway, reflecting that the costs of any failure in the claims process will fall on them while the inconvenience of the extra paperwork will fall on someone else.

---

12. *See, e.g.*, §§9.8-.9.

13. *See* FED. R. BANKR. PROC. 3001-2.

14. Or download it from the web: http://www.uscourts.gov/bankform/index.html or to many individual court web sites.

15. FED. R. BANKR. PROC. 2002(e).

Normally, it is the creditor who files the claim. But the Code does permit the trustee or the debtor to file a claim if the creditor fails to do so. The debtor may wish to file if, for example, he wants to cap a liability, or to assure that a particular creditor receives its pro rata share of estate funds so as to limit its claim against jointly liable nondebtor persons or entities.[16]

Technique: It is up to the bankruptcy judge to adjudicate the validity of the claim. It does not follow that she will necessarily try the lawsuit that arises from the underlying dispute. The question of who hears the lawsuit raises issues of jurisdiction, which we deal with at length elsewhere. *See* Chapter 3 above. But for an illustrative example, suppose the claim alleges "patent infringement," and the trustee's defense is "no patent." The bankruptcy judge might hold (a) that she has formal jurisdiction to hear the patent case; but that (b) she will abstain from exercising the jurisdiction and (c) grant relief from the stay to permit the alleged creditor to bring suit in the appropriate non-bankruptcy forum—and, finally (d) order that the case remain open pending disposition of the patent dispute so that she can deal with the claim.

§13.13 ~ Withdrawing a Claim

Ambrose Bierce said that a lawsuit is a device where you go in a pig and come out a sausage. He may have been thinking of the creditor who files a claim against a bankruptcy estate, only to get hit with a monster counterclaim for which there would have been no bankruptcy jurisdiction unless he filed the claim.

Pummeled by the counterclaim, the creditor's first thought will be to withdraw the claim, hoping thereby to terminate the bankruptcy court's jurisdiction. He may be able to do so—or maybe not. Rule 3006 says that a proof of claim may be withdrawn. It says that withdrawal is a matter of right—unless an adversary proceeding has been filed against the creditor. If the adversary proceeding has been filed, then he may withdraw the claim only with permission of the court, after notice and a hearing.

The problem is a lot like the problem under Federal Rule 41(a) on standards for dismissing a complaint after an answer has been filed.[17] The general principle seems to be that withdrawal should be allowed unless there is prejudice to another party in interest. Of course the real difficulty will be in figuring out what counts as prejudice. But apparently the fact that the estate will lose a tactical advantage does not count as sufficient to deny withdrawal.[18]

---

16. *See generally* §501(c). Cf. *In re* Horner, 1991 Bankr. LEXIS 2188 (Bankr. N.D. Cal. 1992), where the debtor, worried about a nondischargeable tax liability, did not file a claim on behalf of the IRS—but rather pestered the IRS to file the claim in its own behalf. When the IRS finally got around to filing—late—the debtor found itself faced with the task of persuading the court to accept a late claim.

17. *See In re* Fairchild, 969 F.2d 866, 867-68 (10th Cir. 1992).

18. *In re* Armstrong, 215 B.R. 730, 732 (Bankr. E.D. Ark. 1997).

§13.14 ~ Timing

In chapter 7, 12, and 13 cases, the claim "is timely filed if it is filed not later than 90 days after the first date set for the meeting of creditors called under Section 341(a) of the Code."[19] The date will show on the face of the notice of the bankruptcy which the court sends to the creditor. For chapter 11, Bankruptcy Rule 3003(c) says that the court shall fix the time for filing, known as the "claims bar date." Some courts do this sua sponte, while others wait for a motion by the debtor to set a bar date.

This is another one of those cases where it is easy to miss the deadline, and where the aggrieved creditor is likely to try to blame the attorney. In itself this is a factual issue: either the creditor was justified in relying on the attorney, or he was not. But the question naturally arises—can the creditor (or the attorney) save himself by a late filing? The answer is: only sometimes. Rule 9006 provides that he can get an enlargement of time for cause if he asks before the expiration of the original time period; but only for "excusable neglect" if later.[20]

While there will be bar dates for filing claims in any chapter, there is no deadline in the Code or Rules for objecting to a claim.[21] For example, a plan may reserve the power to litigate validity of claims and to assert counterclaims after confirmation. Courts have been reluctant to bless a general reservation of rights in a plan because a creditor might be convinced to support a plan without realizing that the debtor intends to object to its claim (or sue it) promptly after confirmation, but if the reservation of rights is specifically sufficient to give notice, courts are likely to allow it.[22]

§13.15 ~ Amendment

Having filed the proof of claim, the creditor[23] may wish to amend—for example, to raise the dollar amount, or to add a claim of security, among other things. Rules governing amendment of claims roughly follow rules governing amendment of complaints in ordinary civil actions.

An unusual but instructive case is *In Re Kolstad*,[24] where the debtor filed a proof of claim on behalf of the IRS, within the time allowed, but after the time in which the IRS was entitled to file in its own

---

19. FED. R. BANKR. PROC. 3002(c). *Re* the effect of timely mailing, there is a split. *Compare In re* Nimz Transp. Inc. 505 F.2d 177, 179 (7th Cir. 1974) (timely mailing of a properly filed claim raises a presumption of timely receipt) with Chrysler Motors Corp. v. Schneiderman, 940 F.2d 911, 914 (3d Cir. 1991) (no such presumption).

20. The Supreme Court has declared that "excusable neglect . . ." is not limited to situations where the failure to timely file is due to circumstances beyond the control of the filer . . . but may under certain circumstances encompass also "inadvertence, mistake, or carelessness." Pioneer Inv. Serv. Co. v. Brunswick Ass'n Ltd. Partnership, 507 U.S. 380, 388, 390 (1993). But a bankruptcy judge refused to allow a late claim on the plea of an attorney who said he misunderstood the bar date and whose attention may have been distracted by his uncle's funeral. The district court refused to overturn the ruling, holding that the judge did not abuse his discretion. *In re* Au Coton, Inc., 171 B.R. 16, 18 (S.D.N.Y. 1994).

21. *See, e.g., In re* Kolstad, 928 F.2d 171 (5th Cir. 1991).

22. *See, e.g., In re* Hooker Inv., Inc., 162 B.R. 426, 431 (Bankr. S.D.N.Y. 1993). *But cf. In re* Mickey's Enterprises, Inc., 165 B.R. 188, 194 Bankr. W.D. Tex. 1994 (plaintiff's contemplated preference action barred by *res judicata*).

23. Or rarely, the debtor.

24. *In re* Kolstad 928 F.2d 171 (5th Cir. 1991), *reh'g denied* 936 F.2d 571, *cert. denied*, 502 U.S. 958 (1991).

behalf.[25] Thereafter the IRS sought to amend the claim to increase the amount. The debtor objected, arguing that the amendment was offered after the relevant bar date.

The court analyzed cases in which the creditor had initiated the claims process. It concluded that the courts had creditors had been "liberally permitted to cure a defect in the claim as originally filed, to describe the claim with greater particularity, or to plead a new theory of recovery on the facts set forth in the original claim."[26] But they had not been allowed to set forth wholly new grounds of liability.

In this case, the bankruptcy court had allowed the amendment and the circuit court of appeals concluded that there was no abuse of discretion. Contrast *Highland Insurance Co. v. Alliance Operating Corp.,*[27] where the creditor sought to amend an unsecured claim to make it an administrative claim. The court refused to allow the amendment.

§13.16 ~ PRIMA FACIE VALIDITY

The proof of claim constitutes "prima facie evidence of the validity and amount of the claim."[28] This means that if there is no objection, filing alone is sufficient to allow the creditor to share in the estate. If there is an objection, then the burden shifts to the objector to put on evidence sufficient to overcome the prima facie presumption. But once the objector has overcome the presumption, then the ordinary evidentiary burden applies—which is to say, the burden lies on the claimant to convince the court that he should prevail.

In tax cases, the general (non-bankruptcy) rule is that the taxpayer has the burden of proof, no matter who is the plaintiff. A number of taxpayer/debtors hit on the proposition that the burden might be reversed by a bankruptcy filing. Several circuits initially bought this view, but in Raleigh v. Illinois Department of Revenue, the Supreme Court rejected it, and the taxpayer must bear the burden in bankruptcy just as he might otherwise.[29]

The Fifth Circuit offers an instructive exercise for understanding how these burdens work. In *Matter of O'Connor,*[30] the issue was whether the claimant was an insider. The trustee argued that the burden of proving insider status lay on the claimant. The court accepted the proposition in principle, but held that the trustee missed the point. It held that the burden on the claimant came into being only after the trustee presented enough evidence to overcome the rule of prima facie validity.[31]

---

25. *See* F.R. BANKR. PROC. 3004.

26. *In re* Kolstad, 928 F.2d at 175 (quoting *In re* Int'l Horizons, Inc., 751 F.2d 1214, 1216 (11th Cir. 1985).

27. *In re* Alliance Operating Corp., 60 F. 3d 1174 (5th Cir. 1995).

28. Bankruptcy Rule 3001(f).

29. 120 S. Ct. 1951 (2000). The decision is interesting beyond its narrow confines because it is a new affirmation of the view that the rule in bankruptcy will be the rule that might have applied had bankruptcy never occurred. *See generally* Butner v. United States, 440 U.S. 48 (1979).

30. 153 F.3d 258 (5th Cir. 1998).

31. *Id.* at 260-261.

If there are assets, then in due course the trustee will examine the claims and object to any she thinks improper. Most objections are fairly mundane: for example, in a case with unpaid wages, the employee often files his own claim while a state labor officer may file a claim on the employees' behalf. The trustee simply objects to the duplication and then agrees to pay one or the other, as appropriate.

After objection, there will be some sort of hearing on the contest, and there may be a trial. Eventually there will be an adjudication. In large cases, where a debtor or trustee has many similar claim objections to file, you may see "omnibus objections," where the debtor will object in a single pleading to a large number of claims that it believes should be reduced or disallowed for a similar reason.

§13.17 ~ Reconsideration

The Code says that the court may reconsider the allowance or disallowance of a claim for cause and that relief may be readjusted "according to the equities of the case."[32] An Advisory Committee Note says that jurisdiction over reconsideration is "virtually plenary," but there may be less here than meets the eye. Deciding *In re* Colley,[33] the Fifth Circuit held that requests for reconsideration were subject to "the usual Rule 60 standards"—referring to Rule 60(b) of the Federal Rules of Civil Procedure, which authorizes relief for "mistake; inadvertence; excusable neglect; newly discovered evidence; [or] fraud."[34]

§13.18 ~ "Unknown" Claims

§13.19 ~ The Problem

The definition of "claim" in the Code is broad, and it is clear that the drafters meant it so. They wanted to make bankruptcy a "once and for all" measure that would do away with the need for piecemeal litigation later on. But there are some difficulties with this approach. Consider these possibilities:

Example: Paula used to work in the Grenville shipyard where she breathed asbestos fibers. At that time, she did not know that there was any risk involved, but by now many people have died from the exposure. Public health officials have identified that there is a class of people that is "at risk," in the sense that five percent of them will suffer harm from asbestosis in the future. Paula is a member of the class, although she doesn't know it.

Example: Patty uses a hobbyists' carving tool that she bought from ToolCo. In fact, six other people have suffered serious injuries from the use of the an identical product from the same manufacturer. These cases have been widely publicized in the press, but Patty hasn't seen the stories.

---

32. Section 502(j); *see also* Fed. R. Bankr. Proc. 3008.

33. 814 F.2d 1008 (5th Cir. 1987).

34. *See In re* Aguilar, 861 F.2d 873, 874-75 (5th Cir. 1988) (explaining *Colley*). The court sought to clarify the relationship between motions to reconsider under Rule 3008 (governed by Rule 9024, analogous to motions under Federal Rule 60), and appeals under Rule 8002 (analogous to Rule 9023, governed by Federal Rule 59). *Id.* at 874.

Example: Stella is chief of enforcement for the environmental quality agency in the state of Magenta. Edgar runs a small manufacturing plant where he uses toxic chemicals. Edgar buries his used chemicals in barrels. Stella knows about the tanks. She does not know that they have begun to leak, and that the leakage has hit the watershed.

There may be many important distinctions between these cases, but they share a common trait. That is, each of these three—Paula, Patty and Stella—may have a "claim" under an expansive definition of the Bankruptcy Code. Yet if Grenville, or ToolCo, or Edgar, filed for bankruptcy relief today, it is entirely possible that neither Paula nor Patty or Stella would think of herself as a claimant. Even if she did, it might be months or years before she knew in fact whether she was injured, or how much damage the injury caused. We can aggregate these problems together as the problem of "unknown" claims, sometimes "future" claims.[35]

§13.20 ~ Why It Matters

Why does it matter, this problem of the "unknown claim?" Why not simply pay the "known" claims as part of the bankruptcy and leave the "unknown" claims until later? To answer this question, consider this example.

Example: DebtorCo has assets that will be worth $10 as a going concern, $8 in liquidation. It owes $12 to "known" creditors B creditors whose claims had "ripened" before bankruptcy or at least shortly thereafter, based on pre-bankruptcy events. It has "unknown" claims as defined above which everyone agrees will total $7. What are the possibilities?

"Known" creditors will be motivated to try to exclude the "unknown" claimants and sell the assets at the going concern value of $10, allowing for a distribution (ignoring expenses) of 10/12 of all claims.

But a moment's reflection suggests that this will not work. Consider the situation of a prospective bidder. If he knows that he will take the assets encumbered by the $7 in "unknown" claims, then he will not pay $10 for the assets but only $10 - $7 = $3. This would mean: "unknown" claimants get paid in full, known claimants get only 3/12 of their claims.

Known creditors then go back to the drawing board. They now see that their preferred strategy is to promote a quick liquidation, dissipating the assets beyond the reach of unknown creditors. This will allow a distribution of 8/12 of all known claims, with nothing for unknowns.

There is no easy answer here. Therefore it is not surprising that the courts have had trouble coming up with rules to govern the unknown claim.

---

35. Neither name is adequate. In each case, something is known that may lead us to characterize the event as a "claim." And in each case, the argument is that we ought to characterize them as claims at the time of bankruptcy, even though we may not know the details until later.

§13.21 ~ *In re* Frenville

A notorious early unknown claim case is *In re M. Frenville Co.*[36] After Frenville went into bankruptcy, some creditors sued the accountants. The accounts brought an action for indemnity against Frenville. The immediate question was the applicability of the automatic stay. If the accountants had a "claim" effective from the day of bankruptcy, then the indemnity suit was a violation of the automatic stay. But if the claim did not arise until later, then the accountants were not stayed.

The Third Circuit held the indemnity suit was not stayed, holding that the claim did not arise until the accountants could have brought their indemnity suit under non-bankruptcy law. The court reasoned that the accountants could not, as a matter of law, have brought their indemnity suit until after they were sued by the creditors. Therefore, the court concluded, the accountants' claim did not arise until after bankruptcy, and so post-petition, and so not stayed.

The practical effect of *Frenville* was to give the indemnity creditor a clean shot at post-bankruptcy assets, unimpeded by competing pre-bankruptcy creditors' claims. But it is worth noting that it will not always be that way. If the debtor is liquidating, and if (therefore) there will be no post-bankruptcy assets, then the creditor may very well find himself trying to persuade the court that he does have a claim, so he can share in the (finite and terminable) asset pool.

Frenville has been widely criticized and not much followed. Critics say that all the operative facts had taken place before bankruptcy; therefore the court should have held that the claim existed at the time of the petition. This has the appeal of bringing everyone (or at least, most people) at the table at one time in one place, to sort out assets on a principle of equity. But the issue may be tougher than its critics concede.

In *Frenville*, the future claim, although it may have been in some sense unknown at the time of bankruptcy, did at least surface soon enough so it could be dealt with in the ordinary bankruptcy settlement process.

§13.22 ~ Tort Claims

Frenville is a problem, but it is a solvable problem: at least a controversy like this will arise in the "ordinary course" of a bankruptcy case, so it can be sorted out before the assets have been distributed. For a far tougher problem, take a harder look at the personal injury tort cases.

Example: DebtorCo manufactured elixir. Elixir was cheap, useful and popular with consumers, so DebtorCo (and its shareholders) grew rich on the proceeds. Unknown to everyone, elixir threw off imperceptible vapors which lodged themselves in the bodies of anyone exposed to it—those who made elixir, as well as those who used it. After scientist at last exposed the problem, DebtorCo foresaw that it would be held liable in tort as the manufacturer of a defective product. It asked an epidemiologist to estimate the scope of its liability.

In response, the epidemiologist estimated that one million people had been exposed to elixir. It estimated that of this million, five percent (or 50,000) would eventually suffer harm from their prior exposure, and that the damages would be $75,000 each (on average).

36. 744 F. 2d 332 (3d Cir. 1984).

At the time of the disclosure, DebtorCo was an all equity company—aside form the tort claims, it carried no debt. But its aggregate market capitalization (share price times number of shares outstanding) was $1.5 billion. The board of directors, after a brief meeting, agreed that DebtorCo basically belonged to the creditors—the tort claimants, whose aggregate claims exceeded the value of the company. They quickly filed a petition for relief under chapter 11, resigned their office, and turned the company over to a trustee.

The trustee, after consulting with his lawyer, determined that the claims already on file against DebtorCo will result in liability of about $2 billion. This is (a) a little more than half of all the claims that are realistically likely in the case; but (b) about double the net worth.

What is a poor trustee to do? The answer depends on how much he really knows about the case. *If* the report of the epidemiologist is correct, then the trustee simply accepts $4 billion as his total liability number, which means that every creditor gets just ($2 billion)/($4 billion) = 50 cents on the dollar. The trustee pays 50 cents on the dollar to present claims and retains the balance for "future" claims as they arise.

The trouble is that life is never as simple as a classroom hypothetical. Probably no place in the real world would we find an epidemiologist who would make a flat-out estimate of the sort we set forth here—and if we did, the chances are it would turn out to be wrong. None of the present claimants has an incentive to respect the integrity of estimate, and liabilities of this sort just naturally tend to spiral.

If the trustee cannot rely on the estimate (and he can't), he has two bad choices. One is to distribute everything to the present claimants (leaving the future claimants out in the cold). The other is to refuse any distribution until after all the future claims are in (deferring compensation to present claimants on their preestablished claims).

Faced with hard questions like this, courts have not come up with easy answers. One notorious attempt is the device of appointing a representative of the unknown future claims, to try to speak for their interest in the pendency of the case. The future claims representative then negotiates a plan with the debtor, the representative of current creditors, and other constituencies. This device has been restricted almost entirely to a few high-visibility mass tort cases, the most prominent example of which was Johns Manville.[37] For asbestos cases after *Manville*, Congress has enacted §524(g), which contemplates the use of a future claims representative to protect the interests with future claimants.

---

37. This section allows a debtor to propose a plan that creates a trust for the benefit of present and future asbestos claimants. Typically, substantially all of the equity in the reorganized debtor is contributed to the trust, often along with other assets. If 75 percent of the (present) asbestos claimants vote to accept the plan, the court finds the plan "fair and equitable," and the plan satisfies the other statutory requirements, then the court may channel all claims to the trust, enjoining the tort claimants from pursuing the reorganized debtor. The section also contemplates certain third parties (such as prior owners or insurers) making contributions to the trust, in exchange for which they may receive the benefit of the channeling injunction.

Another device is simply to define away the claim. Here, perhaps the most influential discussion is the case *Piper Aircraft* case.[38] The facts in *Piper* are perhaps distinguishable from the elixir example above, but they are close. Piper manufactured light planes. Some of them crashed. Victims (or their representatives) sued the manufacturer, alleging various defects in design and manufacture. Piper filed for bankruptcy and undertook to sell the business to Pilatus. As part of the deal, the court appointed David Epstein to represent the unknown claimants.

Epstein argued for the broadest possible definition of unknown claimant. But the Eleventh Circuit refused to cast the net so broadly. It limited the class to cases where "events occurring before confirmation create a relationship, such as a contract, exposure, impact, or privity."[39] The practical effect was to shift the risk of contingent liability from the present creditor body to the buyer, Pilatus.

§13.23 ~ Environmental Claims

The problem of Stella, above, makes it clear that the same kind of issue arises with respect to "environmental" claims.[40] A principal issue here is timing. Suppose that Edgar generates the toxic waste on Monday, and buries it on Tuesday, and that the container begins to leak on Wednesday, and it hits the watershed on Thursday, and the state discovers and confirms the damage on Friday.

It is not obvious on which day the claim may be said to arise. The issue is complicated by the fact that environmental laws tend to include provisions that purport to reach back and impose liability on prior owners, or users, and that the regulators are busy and have a tough time getting around to all their cases.

An influential approach was propounded by the Seventh Circuit under the old Bankruptcy Act, although it has recently been reaffirmed under the Code.[41] This approach says we have a claim when the claimant can "tie the bankruptcy debtor to a known release of a hazardous substance which a potential claimant knows will lead to . . . response costs."[42] This is similar to the "fair contemplation text" which holds that a "claim" exists where the environmental damage and liability could be fairly contemplated by the parties at the time of the bankruptcy filing.[43] This test is probably the currently accepted standard for determining when an environmental claim arose.

---

38. Epstein v. Official Comm. Of Unsecured Creditors of Estate of Piper Aircraft Corp. (*In re* Piper Aircraft Corp.), 58 F.3d 1573 (11th Cir. 1995).

39. *Id.* at 1577.

40. The principal source of law here is the Comprehensive Environmental Response Compensation and Liability Act ("CERCLA"), 42 U.S.C. §§9601-9675. Many cases also involve state environmental laws.

41. *In re* Chicago, Milwaukee, St Paul & Pacific Railroad, 974 F.2d 775 (7th Cir. 1992); *In re* AM Int'l Inc., 106 F.3d 1342 (7th Cir. 1997).

42. *In re* Chicago, 974 F.2d at 786.

43. *See In re* Jensen, 995 F.2d 925 (9th Cir. 1993); *In re* National Gypsum, 139 B.R. 397 (Bankr. N.D. Tex. 1992).

§13.24 ~ The Problem of Notice

If you accept the idea that unknown (or future) claims are in fact claims for purposes of the bankruptcy case, then the question arises—how do you give "notice" to an unknown claim? Indeed, you could almost stand the point on its head and say—if you can figure out some adequate means for giving notice, then maybe the claims aren't unknown at all.

This problem has a constitutional dimension. Start with the Supreme Court's leading case on notice to the unknown claimant—*Mullane v. Central Hanover Bank & Trust Co.*[44] Some lawyers may remember *Mullane* from their first-year civil procedure course. A trustee in New York was closing out a trust, and met the requirements for constructive notice to beneficiaries by newspaper notice required in a New York banking statute.

Though this statutory requirement for constructive notice was met, the Court held that as to present beneficiaries whose names and addresses were known or readily ascertainable, such notice was insufficient on Fourteenth Amendment due process grounds. "The statutory notice to known beneficiaries is inadequate, not because in fact it fails to reach everyone, but because under the circumstances it is not reasonably calculated to reach those who could easily be informed by other means at hand."[45]

Taking *Mullane* as a benchmark, a good bankruptcy example is the opinion of the Third Circuit in *Chemetron Corp. v. Jones*.[46] Chemetron operated a landfill that received radioactive rubble—a prime candidate for "future claims" if ever you saw one. The bankruptcy court fixed a claims bar date. The court directed (1) that actual notice be provided to all persons known to have claims; and (2) that constructive notice be given to all others by publication. Nineteen months after confirmation, some former "neighbors" and some occasional visitors to the landfill sued Chemetron in state court.

Chemetron moved to dismiss, pleading its chapter 11 discharge. The claimants then asked the bankruptcy court to permit them to file late claims. The bankruptcy court granted the motion, reasoning that they were "known" creditors who should have gotten (but did not get) actual notice of the bankruptcy case. The district reversed, and the circuit upheld the district court.

The Third Circuit pointed out that, at the time of the bankruptcy, none of the (potential) plaintiffs was actually living next to the landfill site. The court of appeals therefore found itself "hard-pressed to conceive of any way the debtor could identify, locate and provide actual notice to these claimants."[47] Therefore, "constructive" (= "published") notice was enough.

---

44. 339 U.S. 306 (1950).

45. 339 U.S. 306, 319.

46. 72 F.3d 341 (3rd Cir.1995), *cert. denied*, 517 U.S. 1137 (1996).

47. 72 F.3d at 347.

A provocative antidote to *Chemetron* is the opinion of Bankruptcy Judge Schmetterer, deciding *Kewanee Boiler Corp. v. Smith*.[48] In Kewanee, 20 months after confirmation the plaintiff was injured by a boiler that had been manufactured some 40 years before. Plaintiff sued the reorganized debtor in state court.

The debtor sought an injunction from the bankruptcy court but the bankruptcy judge refused. He held that the plaintiff was not barred because he held no "claim" at the time of bankruptcy. Or, the judge reasoned, if the plaintiff did have some sort of contingent claim, due process would bar its discharge. For present purposes, perhaps most interesting is the judge's attitude to the matter of notice. He said that "no meaningful notice can be given to individuals who do not yet know they suffer from injury."[49]

The court also noted that nothing in the plan purported to provide for possible future claims. No funds were earmarked for them. No one ever filed a claim in their behalf. No one had suggested that the court appoint a legal representative to act in their behalf.

Another judge who appears to take a dim view of casual use of the notice process is the one who decided *In re Grand Union Co.*,[50] where three personal injury creditors actually got notice of the plan, but the court held it insufficient anyway. The case was a "fast-track" prepackaged plan case, and the "notice" was four pages of single-spaced legalese. The court justified its decision by finding that the notice should have been mailed not just to the litigants but also to their attorney. The governing rule[51] seems at best equivocal on the point, and one suspects the court might not have been so eager to read it as it did had the court not felt that there was a palpable abuse.[52]

§13.25 ~ Tactic—Publication Notice

There are many situations in which it may be in a party's interest to give more notice than the court or the local or federal rules would otherwise require. An example of this is a sale free and clear of liens and claims—where the buyer is hoping that the court order will "cleanse" the purchased assets.

We discussed earlier the question about whether this "cleansing" works in bankruptcy, but it surely does not work with respect to creditors who did not receive constitutionally adequate notice of the sale motion. Another example is a bar date notice, which the debtor will ordinarily want distributed as broadly as possible.

---

48. *In re* Kewanee Boiler Corp, 198 B.R. 519 (Bankr. N.D. Ill. 1996). Schwinn Cycling & Fitness, Inc., v. Benonis (*In re* Schwinn Bicycle Co.) 210 B.R. 747 (Bankr. N.D. Ill. 1997).

49. *Id.* At 530.

50. 204 B.R. 864 (Bankr. D. Del. 1997).

51. Fed. R. Bankr. Proc. 2002(g).

52. The court went on to find that the notice violated the spirit, if not the letter, of Rule 4.2 of the Model Rules of Professional Conduct, which holds that "in representing a client, a lawyer shall not communicate about the subject of the representation with a person the lawyer knows to be represented by another lawyer in the matter, unless the lawyer has the consent of the other lawyer or is authorized by law to do so."

There are many other examples. Parties should consider in every situation not only what notice is required under the rules, but what additional notice, if any, might serve their interests in future litigation. Courts tend to favor more notice rather than less, and will often be receptive to a suggestion for publication notice where there might be "unknown" interested parties, or even to additional notice in trade publications or on the internet. Additional notice in the bankruptcy case may protect your client in the future, but its often incumbent on the lawyer to suggest it to the debtor or the court.

§13.26 ~ Situating "Future Claims"

One reason it's hard to get a handle on the problem of the future claim is that it overlaps with a number of other questions that come freighted with a jurisprudence of their own. For example, the question of liability on a "future claim" often reaches the court entangled with the problem of successor liability—when is the successor liable for the debts of his predecessor, notwithstanding a bankruptcy discharge? We discuss successor liability in the chapter on discharge, this discussion and that are perhaps best read together. *See* §§17.36 ff.

Another closely related issue is the distinction between paying a claim and performing an obligation. This is an issue we turn to here.

§13.27 ~ Payment v. Performance

§13.28 ~ Claim and "Rule"—Environmental Claims Again

Tess, the Trustee, files a MOTION FOR PERMISSION TO ROB BANKS, AND ORDER THEREON. At the hearing on her motion, Tess explains to the judge that she is trustee of DebtorCo, a deeply insolvent estate. She says she could make more money to pay claims if the court would authorize her to rob a few banks.

Motion denied, of course. Yes, of course, it's ridiculous, but the point is non-trivial. The point is that the trustee is bound to follow general laws, just like any other person.[53] The mere fact that he could make more money otherwise is no excuse for ignoring the law. This principle underlies, for example, the exceptions from the automatic stay for police or regulatory action, or for prosecutions under the criminal law. *See* §7.8.

Yet following a rule costs money. So if the nondebtor can succeed in persuading the court that the debtor's "obligation" to him is not a "claim" but a "rule," then the non-debtor has effectively moved himself to the head of the queue.

---

53. *Cf.* 28 U.S.C. §959(b) (trustee's duty to obey applicable state law in operating property under his control). Oddly, the statute doesn't mention local or (non-bankruptcy) federal law. But this section is perhaps best read not as articulating the obligation to obey the law, but as specifying where and how she can be sued.

This point arises at a number of places in bankruptcy law, nowhere more clearly than in the matter of environmental liability. The sovereign enforces a number of environmental laws. The sovereign may have the right to get reimbursement for work done, or to be done. It may have the power to compel performance of a cleanup order, with or without a backup reimbursement right (interestingly, it does not have the support of any general "bankruptcy priority" in seeking to enforce these rights).[54]

It may have the right to enforce ongoing compliance with environmental laws. Or it may have the power to impose penalties. The different categories may require different analysis, but the courts are not always fastidious in maintaining the boundaries.[55]

Starting with the well-known Supreme Court decision in *Ohio v. Kovacs*,[56] there are many cases holding that environmental cleanup orders are, in the last analysis, fights over money and therefore "claims." This means they are dischargeable in bankruptcy (although for whatever it may be worth, it also qualifies them to participate in the assets of the bankruptcy estate).[57]

By contrast, the debtor is responsible, just as any other entity, to obey general laws as part of its ongoing operation—and so also the DIP or trustee. And so if the order is one to "end or ameliorate current pollution," then the DIP/trustee will have to comply.[58] On the same basis, if there is a general rule that says a person cannot use or occupy contaminated property unless he cleans up the contamination, then the DIP/trustee ought to be bound by it just like any other party.[59]

The troubling cases are those that seem to confuse simple obligations to pay money with ongoing duties to obey the law. A notorious early instance is *Penn Terra, Ltd. v. Department of Environmental Resources*.[60] The debtor had operated coal surface mines, although by the time of bankruptcy it had ceased all operations. The Department had served 36 citations against the debtor alleging violation of state environmental laws. After the debtor filed for bankruptcy, the Department sought and got relief from stay to enforce its police power. This seems to us to be a mistake. By the time of bankruptcy, there was nothing left to police; only a question of how to distribute the (trifling) residual assets. The effect of the decision was to give the Department a kind of "first priority" where none was authorized by the Code.

---

54. There is no reason in principle why the government does not acquire a security interest to support its claim for compensation. It is remarkable how rarely it does so.

55. For an admirable summary, *see* Kathryn R. Heidt, *Products Liability, Mass Torts and Environmental Obligations in Bankruptcy: Suggestions for Reform*, 3 AM. BANKR. INST. L. REV. 117 (1995).

56. 469 U.S. 274 (1985).

57. The point is worth remembering in respect of *Kovacs, supra*. In *Kovacs* the government apparently forgot to try to vindicate its right in the bankruptcy case, but then wanted to assert it later. Accepting that a "claim" would have been discharged, the only strategy open to the government was to argue that the right was not a "claim." One can only speculate how many other government agencies (and perhaps even this same one), were at the same time asserting that their rights in other bankruptcies were in fact claims, for the purposes of sharing in distribution.

58. *See In re* Chateauguay Corp., 944 F.2d 997, 1008 (2d Cir. 1991).

59. *In re* CMC Heartland Partners, 966 F.2d 1143, 1146-47 (7th Cir. 1992).

60. 783 F.2d 267 (3d Cir. 1984).

We have the same kind of doubts about *In re* Torwico Electronics, Inc.[61] where the court upheld a cleanup order against the debtor for property that it no longer occupied. The court was impressed by the fact that the debtor still "had[d] access to the site." For the life of us, we cannot imagine why access matters. Just about anyone will give a debtor "access" to anything for the purpose of discharging a liability. The teaching seems to be that "the liability runs with the waste," which might be good environmental policy, but we know of nothing in principle that requires or even justifies a court to so hold.

And (perhaps not surprisingly) we aren't much impressed by the decision of the Supreme Court in *Midatlantic National Bank v. New Jersey Department of Environmental Protection*,[62] where the trustee sought to abandon property as burdensome to the estate. A divided Supreme Court held that the trustee was not empowered to abandon because he was bound by state environmental law that would have prohibited it.

The court cited (among others) precedents from cases where it was held that an owner could not abandon property where there was an imminent danger of harm. But there was no imminent danger of harm here; only risk that the claim would not be paid in full. Once again, the result is to give environmental claims a priority status unrecognized anywhere in the Bankruptcy Code.

It's probably no accident that most of the questionable cases seem to arise somewhere within 50 miles of Camden, New Jersey, where there surely is pressure to find somebody, anybody to pay the environmental claim. But the premise that someone should pay does not support the conclusion that the creditors should pay, by being subordinated to the environmental claim.

§13.29 ~ Injunction as Claim

Section 101(5) says that claim means right to payment, but it doesn't stop there. Rather, Section 101(5)(B) adds that claim means

> Right to an equitable remedy for breach of performance if such breach gives rise to a right to payment ....

This is a startling and in some ways unexpected result. Suppose creditor is buying the valuable Snopes diamond from debtor who files for bankruptcy before having delivered the diamond to creditor. The deal is carried out under the law of Magenta, which provides that for "unique personal property," the creditor has the right of specific performance.

It is perhaps one thing to allow this kind of right between debtor and creditor, but quite another to allow it when it is adverse to creditors. If we let the creditor enforce this right by way of specific performance, then we let him take a valuable asset from the estate while others are going unpaid. Nothing in Code

---

61. 8 F.3d 146 (1993).

62. 74 U.S. 494 (1993).

history suggests that the drafters were really considering this possibility, and in practice we doubt any bankruptcy judge would permit the creditor to divest the debtor of the diamond. On the other hand, there must be some sorts of injunction rights that are clearly enforceable, bankruptcy notwithstanding.

To help sort out this puzzle, a particularly interesting recent case is *In re Udell*.[63] Barry Udell worked for Carpetland in its retail store in Fort Wayne. He signed a contract avowing that if he left Carpetland, he would not engage in any similar business within 50 miles for three years. The contract provided that in the event of breach, Carpetland could get an injunction and "stipulated damages." Udell subsequently quit Carpetland and purchased his own carpet store. He also sued Carpetland for damages, and Carpetland counterclaimed for damages and for an injunction to enforce the restrictive covenant. He also filed relief under chapter 13.

Carpetland, responding, sought relief from the automatic stay, asserting that its right to an injunction was not a claim because it is not dischargeable in bankruptcy. The debtor responded that it was a claim. He called attention to the particular language of the Code definition. It says that claim includes the

> Right to an equitable remedy for breach of performance if such breach gives rise to a right to payment … (emphasis added).[64]

Since Carpetland had a right to damages as well as the right to an injunction (Udell reasoned), it had a claim. And since it had a claim, it was stayed, and the claim would be discharged. The Court of Appeals, reversing, found a deeper meaning in the statute. The Court said that the question was: whether the right to payment was cumulative with the injunction or an alternative to it. It held that the statute intended to turn an injunction into a claim only if the damage remedy was an alternative to the injunction remedy. In Udell's case, the court reasoned, the injunction was not alternative but cumulative, and so not a claim, and so not discharged.

Judge Flaum, in a provocative concurrence, cautioned that the analysis "dodges the plain meaning of the statute." Rather, he said, "let us grant that the statute needs fixing, and … mend an otherwise implausible statute."

Congress has not accepted Judge Flaum's invitation—perhaps because the court did in fact engage in some mending. But he is surely right that there is a problem here.[65]

§13.30 ~ Interest on Claims

Bankruptcy takes time, and time is money. Not surprisingly, the creditor wants not just compensation on his claim, but compensation for lost use of money over time—in a word, "interest." The issue of interest on claims has generated a jurisprudence all its own, with separate rules for claims that are unsecured and for those that are secured. We deal with each by turn.

---

63. 18 F.3d 403 (7th Cir. 1994).

64. Section 101(5)(B).

65. Unpersuaded, and therefore willing to find the injunction right to be a "claim" that is dischargeable. *See In re* Ward, 194 B.R. 703 (Bankr. D. Mass. 1996).

§13.31 ~ UNSECURED CLAIMS

The general rule is that interest on unsecured claims (including undersecured claims) stops accruing at the time of the bankruptcy filing.[66] In the simple unsecured-creditor liquidation case this rule doesn't amount to much: assets will be liquidated and distributed in a matter of a few months, and interest claims would pretty much cancel each other out. It matters more in a reorganization where the creditor's claim may not be paid simply from a pot of cash, but instead over time after plan confirmation.

And, as discussed below, where there is a large secured claim, the rule is important: the secured creditor is allowed to "accrue" post-petition interest to the extent that the value of its collateral exceeds the amount of its claim.[67] If the secured claim is big and the case goes on for a long time, then this interest to the oversecured creditor can eat up all the assets that might otherwise be available to the unsecureds. Thus, the advantage enjoyed by the oversecured creditor over unsecured creditors increases over time.

The issue of allowance of interest as part of a claim can sometimes be more complex than it first seems. Take, for example, a zero-coupon bond due to pay $1,000 ten years from today. Suppose the market rate for such debt is six percent. Then the present trading value of the zero is $1,000/(1.1)10 = $386. The difference between the present value of $386 and the face value of $1,000 can be regarded as compensation for lost use of money, or interest, sometimes original issue discount or just OID. OID has a long history in tax law. Partly on the authority of tax precedents, bankruptcy doctrine seems to accept that OID will be recognized as interest in bankruptcy and dealt with accordingly.[68]

But OID may be tougher to spot and isolate than may at first appear. Suppose a bond with a face value of $1,000 payable tomorrow by DebtorCo, a debtor in chapter 11 who will likely pay no more than 40 cents on the dollar. Just as a rule of thumb, we can expect the bond to trade at $400. But here, the difference between the face amount and the value is not attributable to a present value (or interest) discount, but instead to a "market value" discount. In *In re* Chateaugay Corp.,[69] the Second Circuit purported to recognize that OID should be identified and disallowed as unmatured interest, but that this sort of "market value" discount, in the context of a pre-petition debt for debt exchange, should not. So, you have to look carefully to determine what is OID and what is not.

§13.32 ~ SECURED CLAIMS

The rules governing interest provide another good reason for being a secured creditor. Section 506(b) provides:

---

66. Section 502(b)(2). But creditors do get interest before any money goes back to the debtor, so unsecured creditors will receive post-petition interest in a solvent estate. Section 726(a)(5).

67. Section 506(b).

68. H.R. REP. NO. 595-95, 1ST SESS., AT 352-53 (1977).

69. 961 F.2d 378 (2d Cir. 1992).

> To the extent that an allowed secured claim is secured by property, the value of which . . . is greater than the amount of such claim, there shall be allowed to the holder of such claim, interest on such claim . . . .

Translated, consider BancCo with a claim of $1000 secured by collateral worth $1200, and an interest rate of 10 percent. Unsecured creditors do not get interest. But for BancCo, the meter will continue to run, at least until we exhaust the value of collateral.[70]

You can think of this as "creditor versus debtor" rule if you like, but it is probably better understood as "creditor versus creditor." The money that goes to pay interest on the secured claim generally comes out of the pockets of the unsecured.

§13.33 ~ Interest to Oversecured Creditors

There is a considerable amount of confusing case law dealing with the issue of when a secured creditor's collateral is valued for purposes of determining the extent to which it is oversecured and therefore entitled to post-petition interest. What of the creditor who is oversecured for the first nine months of a year-long chapter 11 case, but undersecured for the last three months and at the time of confirmation. There is also considerable controversy on the related topic of whether an oversecured creditor may receive interest currently during the case, or must accrue it until the end of the case. Often, this is negotiated as part of a cash collateral order.

§13.34 ~ Undersecured Claims—Timbers

If the collateral is worth $1,200 and the claim is only $1,000, then the secured creditor gets interest; so says Section 506(b). But reverse the numbers: what if the claim is $1,200 but the collateral is worth only $1,000—but that there are other "loose assets" in the estate, available *either* to pay interest *or* to apply against unsecured claims?

That issue came before the United States Supreme Court in *United Savings v. Timbers of Inwood Forest Associates, Ltd.*[71] Timbers was a classic single-asset real estate ("SARE") debtor. The property was generating enough to cover operating expenses, with some cash left over. The (undersecured) mortgagee wanted relief from the stay and leave to foreclose under Section 362(d) or, failing that, adequate protection in the form of compensation for lost use of money.

Good practical arguments can be made in favor of the mortgagee here. We have already noted that time is money and that the secured creditor who suffers delay pays a price, even if the nominal value of the collateral remains unchanged. Second, making the debtor compensate for delay is an attention-getter. If the debtor can suspend payments indefinitely, he'll never want to leave chapter 11.

---

70. That would be nearly two years: $\$1,000\,(1.1)^2 = \$1,210$.

71. 484 U.S. 365 (1988).

But whatever the merits of these arguments, the court decided against the mortgagee. The decision took many observers by surprise, perhaps because of its apparent pro-debtor bent, but also because of its indifference to the kinds of policy points raised above. Rather, Justice Scalia turned the case into an exercise of pure statutory interpretation. He found that the statute made no provision for interest on the undersecured claim and as far he was concerned, that was the end of it.

Seen in retrospect, this is perhaps the first of a serious cases in which Justice Scalia has insisted on a strategy of (alleged) plain-meaning interpretation of the Bankruptcy Code—sometimes in sharp conflict with colleagues on the bench, most notably Justice Blackmun.

§13.35 ~ Timbers Circumvented—Section 552(b)

What the statute giveth, the statute can take away. For SARE cases like *Timbers*, the statute has indeed taken away: Congress, partially responding to *Timbers*, added a new Section 362(d)(3), which requires the payment of interest to the secured lender in SARE cases with less than $4 million in secured debt to keep the automatic stay in place past 90 days, if a confirmable plan has not been filed.

But even in real estate cases that are not governed by §362(d)(3)—those wish more than $4 million secured debt—creditors have found some ways to limit the impact of *Timbers*. After *Timbers*, chastened by their loss, creditors went back and took a more careful look at their security agreement. They found that usually, in addition to their interest in real estate, they claim a security interest in rents and profits.

Section 552 of the Bankruptcy Code has always provided that the a security interest in rents or profits will survive the filing of the petition.[72] By aggressive invocation of the rents and profits clause (and the addition of a new Section 552(b)(2)), secured creditors have partially circumvented Timbers. They either negotiate the payment of post-petition interest as the price for consent to an early cash collateral stipulation, or they add the accumulated rents to the real property value and thereby (if the numbers work) become oversecured creditors, who are entitled to post-petition interest.[73]

§13.36 ~ Section 552 On Its Own

Section 552 has played a marquee role in the SARE cases, but its reach is broader and it deserves careful study on its own. Like a lot of sections in the Code, it gives with one hand, then takes away with another. That is: Section 552(a) provides that property acquired after the commencement of the case is not subject to the secured creditor's lien. But then subsection (b)(1) provides that the lien does extend to "proceeds, product, offspring or profits acquired by the estate after commencement of the case."

---

72. *See* §552(b). But note the "equities of the case" exception.

73. There is some conflict regarding whether post-petition rents add to the secured creditors "secured claim." *Compare In re* Kalian, 169 B.R. 503, 506-07 (Bankr. D. R.I. 1994) (secured claim capped by value he would receive on petition day) with *In re* Addison Properties Ltd. Partnership, 185 B.R. 766, 784 (Bankr. N.D. Ill. 1995) (secured claim may include original valuation and also rents and profits under §552).

The lien applies only if the original security interest applied to proceeds, etc.,—but just about any well-drafted inventory or receivables loan will so provide, so this is almost never a problem. As a result, the proceeds of pre-petition accounts receivable are the pre-petition lender's cash collateral, but new accounts receivable generated post-petition are not (absent a post-petition financing arrangement).

Note, there is an "equities of the case" exception in §552(b) that allows the court discretion to cut off or limit a post-petition proceeds lien, although it is not often used.

The practical result of Section 552 is that even a mildly contentious working-capital lender can exercise considerable leverage in a chapter 11 case, since a debtor will often need the cash proceeds of its pre-petition receivables (or other property) to operate post-petition.

§13.37 ~ Bankruptcy Priorities

§13.38 ~ Introduction

Section 507, entitled priorities, purports to tell you who gets paid, and in what order. But this is misleading. We have already seen that there is at least one claimant—the secured creditor—who goes to the head of the queue, even though this right is not specified in the priorities section of the Bankruptcy Code.

We have also seen that claimants can get themselves to the head of the queue in other ways. If you persuade the judge that yours is a claim for an injunction, or not a claim but a rule that the debtor must follow, or a claim that arises out of one of the securities industry exceptions, or a claim based on a trust, then for all practical purposes you get paid ahead of other creditors.

And it is more complicated than that. We will see that there are there are various super priorities ahead of the Section 507 list (including priorities among priorities). Moreover there is a scheme of priorities below Section 507 priorities that apply in chapter 7 before any money goes back to the debtor. And there is a rule of "equitable subordination" which permits courts to change the priority ranking of claims from what is prescribed in the statute. In this section, we consider all of these matters.

§13.39 ~ The Basic Priority Scheme: Section 507

Start with the basic priority scheme in Section 507. In summary, the schedule gives priority in order as follows:

- First: Administrative expenses
- Second: "Gap" creditors in involuntaries—those whose claims were incurred between the petition date and the entry of an order for relief.
- Third: Wages
- Fourth: Employee benefits

- Fifth: Grain and fish claims
- Sixth: "Layaways"
- Seventh: Spousal and child support
- Eighth: Certain taxes
- Ninth: Federal depositories

§13.40 ~ Why?

As with dischargeability, it is natural to ask—why do some creditors get priority when others do not? As with dischargeability, the answer is—it's a muddle. Some creditors, we presume, get priority because of a well-developed public policy that they should be favored: this would surely explain tax and domestic relations obligations as well as the various employment-related claims.[74] We assume there is a good public policy reason to give priority to claims for fish storage (when there is none for, say, okra storage—nor, for that matter, for victims of products that cause birth defects) although we cannot at the moment remember what it is.

We can't think of any particularly good reason for several of these priorities, which seem to us haphazard to the point of fortuity. But we do suspect that lobbying for priority in bankruptcy is good easy politics: we remember a comic strip we saw as kids where Goofy learns that most train wrecks involve the last car of the train—his solution is to take the last cars off all trains. On the same principle, we suspect you could solve a lot of problems by giving everybody a first priority for everything.

Meanwhile, before we get carried away, we should note one important characteristic of the priorities. That is, several of these seem to favor the debtor at least as much as they favor creditors. Wage claims (to take an example) are fully dischargeable in bankruptcy. But as we explain elsewhere, not to pay one's wages is often a crime, and may result in personal officer and director liability.

We suspect that a debtor facing criminal liability is jolly well delighted to see the money go to wage claims as a priority rather than letting the wage claimants take pot luck along with the unsecureds. Most tax claims and claims for domestic obligations will never go away, so once again it is in the interest of the debtor that they get first dibs on the bankruptcy estate.

---

74. The priority for layaways is, we suspect, almost accidental. It seems to have become an issue because one legal aid lawyer got ensnared in a layaway case at just the time the Code was being drafted. *See generally* Philip Schrag and Bruce Ratner, *Caveat Emptor - Empty Coffer: The Bankruptcy Law Has Nothing to Offer*, 72 Colum. L. Rev. 1147 (1972).

§13.41 ~ ADMINISTRATIVE PRIORITY

Usually, an administrative expense must confer a benefit upon the estate. However, courts have recognized that post-petition operation of a debtor's business itself confers a benefit to the estate, such that the incident costs should be entitled to administrative priority, even if the costs themselves are not beneficial to the estate.

Consider the case of the debtor that operates a trucking company. One of its trucks, while making a company delivery, hits a child and causes a $1 million damage claim. We expect the claim would be entitled to administrative priority. Hitting the child and paying a million dollars in damages does not benefit the estate, but the court is likely to recognize that continued operation of the debtor's trucks does benefit the estate, and one of the costs of operating is the occasional liability claim. The most visible possible precedent is *Reading Co. v. Brown*,[75] where the Supreme Court mandated administrative expense treatment for damage claims from property owners for a negligently caused post-petition fire.

The relevant Code language is Section 507(a)(1) which gives a first priority to "administrative expenses allowed under Section 503(b)." Section 503(b)(1)(A) in its turn defines "administrative expenses" as "the actual *necessary* costs and expenses of preserving the estate." We italicize "necessary" to call attention to the fact that some courts have found some wiggle room here.

For example, they have found that the holdover landlord is entitled not to the "contract" rent but only to a "reasonable" rental when the trustee occupies the former business premises of the debtor in the pendency of a liquidation.[76] But many courts have held that insurance (and the costs resulting from a failure to insure) are necessary incidents of doing business and thereby entitled to first priority.

Note that this is also where you get paid: expenses of professionals who represent the trustee/DIP and official committees are administrative expenses, subject to all the rules about appointment, fee applications, etc. *See generally* Chapter 16 below.

Note also that this is where creditors get paid for post-petition financing under Section 364(a) and (b). Indeed, there may be sub-priorities here. One court has held that where the estate was administratively insolvent the professionals might be made to disgorge post-petition payments, but the ordinary course creditors would not.[77] And a claim for failure of adequate protection has a super priority. *See* Section 507(b).

One menacing qualifier to the rule on administrative priorities concerns the instance where the chapter 11 fails and the case converts to chapter 7. Hidden away over in Section 726(b), we find a rule that tells us that there is an internal priority among administrative claimants. Specifically, the Code says that

---

75. 391 U.S. 471 (1968). Reading is a pre-code case, but it has been cited with approval under the Code. *See, e.g.*, Alabama Surface Mining Comm'n v. N.P. Mining Co. (*In re* N.P. Mining Co.), 963 F.2d 1449, 1454 (11th Cir. 1992).

76. *In re* Fisher & Fisher, Inc., 51 B.R. 680 (Bankr. S.D. Ohio 1985) (although lease rate was $3,360 per month, the court found fair market value of occupancy was $1,000 per month for period not covered by 11 U.S.C. §365(d)(3)).

77. *In re* Lochmiler Indus., Inc. 178 B.R. 241, 251-54 (Bankr. S.D. Cal. 1995). For no very obvious reason, this is another issue on which landlords seem to fare less well than others (e.g., vendors).

administrative costs of the chapter 7 hold priority over the administrative expenses of the failed chapter 11.[78]

§13.42 ~ Employee Claims

The third and fourth priority both involve claims by employees unpaid at the time of bankruptcy. This is presumably a worthy purpose and it certainly is not a dead letter by any means, but the priority is not as important as you might think, for several reasons.

The first is that non-bankruptcy law makes it difficult not to pay your wages in the first place. State statutes typically provide that wages must be paid regularly—say, weekly or biweekly. Failure to pay may be a crime. It is often one of those crimes, like the 100 percent penalty for trust fund taxes, where the prosecutor will file charges against everybody who might have been in a position to pay. This is a great motivator, and it tends to get a lot of wages paid independent of the priority.[79] Second, the priority is limited to $4,650 per employee.

As to employee benefits, the 9,000-pound gorilla is the liability to the pension fund under ERISA, enforceable (in part) under Section 1113.

Factor in these two items and the most important realm for the wage claim priority is the gap claim of the employee who was due to get a paycheck on Friday for wages earned by Wednesday—and the debtor files on Thursday. As we suggest elsewhere, even these are likely to get paid in an operating chapter 11, often pursuant to a first day order (for which there is no apparent authority in the Code, but which is nevertheless routinely approved, sometimes under a judicially-created "doctrine of necessity").

§13.43 ~ Taxes

Probably the biggest gobbler, aside from administrative priority, is the eighth priority for tax claims. The priority is Byzantine in its complexity, but the benchmark rule is: priority for taxes less than three years old. For property taxes, the benchmark rule is only one year (although the property tax is nearly always protected by a tax lien). For "trust fund" taxes there is no time limit. Finally the priority applies to any tax assessed within 240 days before bankruptcy.[80] *See* §17.26 (outlining priority and other nondischarged taxes).

The tax priority should not be confused with any tax lien that the tax collector may hold, notably liens under the Federal Tax Lien Act, discussed in §12.11. But Section 724(b) says that in a chapter 7 case, the tax lien is treated as an eighth priority claim, rather than a lien. Section 724 of course does not apply in chapter 11, so there the tax lien remains as a secured claim.

---

78. It works for §§12 and 13 also. Chapter 7 expenses also get priority over expenses of a supplanted custodian.

79. 26 U.S.C. §6672.

80. Assessment occurs when the assessment officer signs the summary record of assessment (Form 23-C, "Assessment Certificate"). Don't take their word for it; ask for a copy of the certificate.

A further aggravation is that tax priority is not the same as tax dischargeability. All priority taxes are nondischargeable, but not all nondischargeable taxes are entitled to priority. For example, taxes filed late (and within two years of bankruptcy) and taxes for which no return was filed are nondischargeable even though not entitled to priority.[81]

Tax penalties wade through some soggy metaphysics. They are "taxes," all right, and on the face of things entitled to the priority.[82] But in chapter 7, insofar as the tax claim is for a penalty, it is subordinated below ordinary Section 507 claims. It is paid, if at all, in the scheme of sub-priorities under Section 726.

The subordination rule does not apply in chapter 11, suggesting that tax penalties stand on a par with other taxes in a reorganization case. Until 1996, some courts were routinely subordinating tax penalties in chapter 11 via Section 510, the provision that allows for "equitable" subordination. But in *U.S. v. Noland*,[83] the Supreme Court said it was improper categorically to subordinate all tax penalties in this way.

§13.44 ~ Superpriorities

We have said that Section 507 sets the priority schedule, and that the secured creditor trumps Section 507. In this section, we identify some statutory priorities that trump Section 507. Some of these even trump the creditor with a pre-bankruptcy secured claim.

§13.45 ~ Benefit to the Collateral

Perhaps the highest priority is the priority that trumps the claim of the perfected security interest. That power is set forth in Section 506(c). The section permits the trustee to recover from property securing an allowed secured claim the reasonable, necessary costs and expenses of preserving, or disposing of, such property to the extent of any benefit to the holder of such claim.[84] No surprise, of course, that the tough cases involving this provision are the ones in which the secured claimant is howling that he didn't enjoy any "benefit" at all.[85]

§13.46 ~ Section 364 Claims

In our discussion of post-petition financing, we have pointed out that the court may gave priority equal to or even superior to existing claims, including existing administrative claims. *See* §10.12. In the case of a loan under Section 364(d), the court may even authorize a priming lien superior to an existing pre-bankruptcy secured claim.

---

81. *See, e.g.*, §523(a)(1)(B).

82. On what is a penalty, *compare In re* Juvenile Shoe Corp. of America, 99 F.3d 898, 903 (8th Cir. 1996) (15 percent pension termination liability a "tax.") with U.S. v. Reorganized CF &I Fabricators of Utah, Inc., 518 U.S. 213, 224-25 (1996) (ERISA funding deficiency a "penalty").

83. 517 U.S. 535 (1996).

84. Only the trustee; no creditor may assert it in his behalf. *See* Hartford Underwriters Insurance Co. v. Union Planters Bank, N.A. (*In re* Hen House Interstate, Inc.), 120 S.Ct. 1942 (2000).

85. *In re* Afco Enters., Inc., 35 B.R. 512, 515 (Bankr. D. Utah 1983) (undersecured creditor must pay administrative expenses incurred to run hotel despite the fact that fair market value decreased and secured indebtedness increase because continuing resort as a going concern was a benefit to the creditor).

§13.47 ~ "Inadequate" Protection

The secured creditor who fails to get relief from the automatic stay (and some other creditors) may have a right to get adequate protection. For example, the court might give the secured creditor an additional or replacement lien.[86] But what if the court miscalculates and the additional or replacement lien turns out to be "inadequate."

Section 507(b) purports to rectify this wrong by providing for a superpriority administrative claim (ahead of other administrative claims) for failed adequate protection. Of course 100 percent of nothing is still nothing, and if the estate has no money for administrative expenses, then the superpriority means nothing.

§13.48 ~ Subpriorities—Section 726

Section 726(a) mandates a of priorities that applies when and if the list in Section 507 is exhausted—which is rarely, so Section 726 doesn't count for a lot in practical terms. But the list includes:

- Late filed claims;
- Penalty claims; and
- Claims for interest.

Note that the list applies only in chapter 7. The main relevance to chapter 11 is that you can't confirm a chapter 11 plan unless you can show that it is in the "best interest of creditors," which means that they will get not less than they will get in chapter 7.[87] So you will have to think through the effect of both Sections 507 and 736 in deciding whether your plan is confirmable.[88]

§13.49 ~ Subordination—Equitable and Otherwise

Section 510(a) mandates that a subordination agreement is enforceable in bankruptcy to the same extent as it is outside. Section 510(c) is much more ambitious. It provides that the court may subordinate all or part of a claim "on principles of equitable subordination." The legislative history says that the rule is designed to codify some venerable case law from the corporate reorganizations of the 1930s.[89] The doctrine is intentionally somewhat free-floating, but a Fifth Circuit opinion points out that equitable subordination generally arise in only three situations:

---

86. Section 361(2).

87. Section 1129(a)(7).

88. At least one court, by reading §726 together with (former) Section 1124(3), held that you didn't need to pay post-petition interest on unsecured claims in a "solvent" chapter 11. *In re* New Valley Corp., 168 B.R. 73, 79 (Bankr. D. N.J. 1004). Acting on the "shoot-the-messenger" principle, Congress effectively overruled this reading by doing away with §1124(3).

89. *See* H.R. Rep. No. 95-595, 1st Sess., at 359 (1977) (Section codifies in part Pepper v. Litton, 308 U.S. 295 (1939), and Taylor v. Standard Gas and Electric Co., 306 U.S. 307 (1938)).

- when a fiduciary of the debtor misuses his position to the disadvantage of other creditors;
- where a third party controls the debtor to the disadvantage of other creditors; or
- when a third party actually defrauds other creditors.[90]

The section provides for subordination of a (creditor's) claim to another claim, or an (equity owner's) interest to another interest. It is unclear why the Code does not permit the subordination of a claim to an interest.

§13.50 ~ Substantive Consolidation

One of the most remarkable bankruptcy doctrines is the one that permits the judge to consolidate "substantively" one bankruptcy case with another. The point of it all is to permit the creditors of the estate that is relatively poorer to share with creditors of the richer estate. The doctrine bears a family resemblance to non-bankruptcy doctrines like "veil-piercing," or "alter ego," but bankruptcy purists are quick to say they are different things.[91] The Second Circuit has said that in order to get substantive consolidation, you need a positive answer to one of these questions:

- Whether creditors dealt with the entities as a single economic unit and "did not rely on their separate identity in extending credit;" or
- Whether the affairs of the debtors are so entangled that consolidation will benefit all creditors.[92]

Courts have limited or conditioned substantive consolidation in countless ways. Interestingly, a number of cases have said that it should be limited so as not to advance the position of a senior secured creditor, as against the unsecureds, or even a junior secured.[93]

There may be a couple of cases in which a debtor's estate has been consolidated with a nondebtor entity, but there is a serious question on whether the bankruptcy court has jurisdiction to do this, and in any event it is exceedingly rare.

---

90. United States Abatement Corp. v. Mobil Exploration & Producing U.S., Inc. (Matter of United States Abatement Corp.), 39 F.3d 556, 561 (5th Cir. 1994).

91. Helena Chemical Company v. Circle Land and Cattle Corp. (*In re* Circle Land and Cattle Corp.), 213 B.R. 870, 876-77 (Bankr. D. Kan. 1997) (holding no jurisdiction to combine a bankruptcy with a non-bankruptcy estate; or, in the alternative, that the proponent had confused substantive consolidation with alter ego).

92. Union Savings Bank v. Augie/Restivo Baking Co. (*In re* Augie/Restivo Co.), 860 F.2d 515, 518 (2d Cir. 1988).

93. *See, e.g.*, Rouse v. United States (*In re* Pronto Enters. Inc.), 141 B.R. 179, 184 (Bankr. W.D. Mo. 1992).

Note the distinction between substantive consolidation, where the assets and liabilities of more than one debtor are combined into a single estate, and joint administration which is much more common, where two or more estates are handled for administrative purposes under one case number, but the assets and liabilities of the estates remain separate.

Substantive consolidation can be effectuated either by a motion or as part of a plan. It is often done in the plan although there is a risk in doing so—if the court holds the required showing has not been made, your plan will be rendered unconfirmable.

§13.51 ~ Partnership and Partner—The "Jingle Rule"

GenCo, a general partnership, is in bankruptcy. It has liabilities of $800 and assets of $560—enough to pay 70 cents on the dollar. Martha is a general partner of GenCo. Aside from her partnership interest, she has assets of $1,000 and liabilities of $1,080—barely solvent.

Definitionally, the fact that we have a general partnership means that Martha is personally liable for partnership debts. But the Bankruptcy Code explicitly recognizes the partnership as an entity, and allows for the filing of a partnership case, to administer partnership property independent of partner property. The question arises—as between partnership and partner, who is liable for which debts? At least two possible solutions come to mind:

First alternative: provide that partner property goes first to satisfy partner debts, with only the surplus (if any) available to satisfy partnership debts. So in this case, $1,000 of Martha's property would go to satisfy her individual debts, with $80 left over for the debts of the partnership. Traditional jargon calls this the jingle rule. Apparently it was the law under the 1898 Act.

Second alternative: put creditors of each on an equal footing with respect to the property of either. On this analysis, we would have total assets of $1,640 (= $1,080 plus $560) and total liabilities of $1,800 (= $1,000 + $800) for the combined entities.

Does it make any practical difference? Under the first rule, creditors of the partner Martha get paid in full, while creditors of the partnership have to settle for 80 percent (that is, 70 percent from the partnership estate and an additional 10 percent from the assets of the partner). Under the second rule, all creditors get 91 percent—an improvement for partnership creditors at the expense of the creditors of Martha.

The Code addresses the problem by giving the trustee of the partnership authority to sue the partners as individuals.[94] He has a claim against each individual estate for the full amount of any deficiency in the partnership estate. The legislative history says that this provision is intended to overrule "the jingle rule."[95]

---

94. Section 723(a).

95. H.R. Rep. No. 595, 95th Cong., 1st Sess. 381 (1977), reprinted in 1978 U.S. Code Cong. of Ad. News 5963, 6337; S. Rep. No. 989, 95th Cong., 2d Sess. 95, reprinted in 1978 U.S. Code of Ad. News 5787, 5881.

§13.52 ~ The Interrelationship with Non-Bankruptcy Priorities

One of the axioms of bankruptcy is that within its own sphere, bankruptcy law is supreme. But bankruptcy also purports to be no more than a procedural framework for the adjudication of previously existing rights. Among other rights, for example, bankruptcy respects valid "liens" that subsist independent of bankruptcy law. These two general principles seem to trump each other.

The question arises—how do you apply a non-bankruptcy priority scheme that seems to trump the bankruptcy law priorities? The classic response comes from *Board of Trade v. Johnson*.[96] The debtor owned a stock exchange seat. In creating the seat, the exchange reserved unto itself the right to be paid first out of any proceeds from sale. The right seemed to pit a contractual priority against the bankruptcy property scheme. But the court held that the since the exchange had created the seat, it could retain the right to determine the conditions of transfer.[97]

In *Artus v. Alaska Dept. of Labor*,[98] the Ninth Circuit affirmed and extended the Board of Trade rule. The court had to consider a state statute which provided that trade creditors be paid first from the sale of a liquor license. The court allowed the state to insist on its priority. The court said that "no statutory bankruptcy policy forbids [Alaska] from giving one creditor a greater right to payment of his claim from a given asset than that conferred on another."[99]

On the other hand, in *U.S. v. Battley*,[100] the court had to consider whether the state tax priority trumped a federal tax lien. This time, the court held for the feds. And in *U.S. v. Stone*,[101] the court had to consider a three-way conflict, between the state as tax collector, some private priority claimants, and the federal government as tax collector. It held that the state tax lien claim trumped the federal tax claim, but that the private wage claim was subordinate to the federal tax claim.

§13.53 ~ Claims Trading[102]

---

96. 264 U.S. 1 (1924).

97. *Id.* at 15.

98. *In re* Anchorage Int'l Inn, Inc., 718 F.2d 1446 (9th Cir. 1983).

99. *Id.* at 1451.

100. 969 F.2d 806 (9th Cir. 1992).

101. 6 F.3d 581 (9th Cir. 1993).

102. Some of the spadework on claims trading comes from an excellent student paper by Geoff Edwards, UC Davis Law '99. For more on claims trading, *see generally* Chaim J. Fortgang & Thomas M. Mayer, *Trading Claims and Taking Control of Corporations in Chapter 11*, 12 Cardozo L. Rev. 1 (1990); Chaim J. Fortgang & Thomas M. Mayer, *Developments in Trading Claims and Taking Control of Corporations in Chapter 11*, 13 Cardozo L. Rev. 1 (1991); Chaim J. Fortgang & Thomas M. Mayer, *Developments in Trading Claims: Participations and Disputed Claims*, 15 Cardozo L. Rev. 733 (1993).

§13.54 ~ THE PROBLEM

Consider the plight of Prez, the president of LittleCo, who just took his company into chapter 11. He prepares for his first serious conference with unsecured creditors. He is uncertain just how much cooperation he can expect to get out of them. But he is consoled by the notion that most of them are longtime suppliers who understand the business and its market—and who, as it happens, pretty much need LittleCo as a customer if they are to stay in business themselves.

Or so he supposed. Imagine his dismay, then when he arrives at the meeting to encounter a roomful of strangers. On inquiry, he is mortified to learn that most of his familiar vendors have decided to cut their losses, and have sold their claims to professional investors with agendas of their own that Prez can barely comprehend. For Prez, this is a welcome to the world of bankruptcy claims trading.

§13.55 ~ THE EXPLOSION IN CLAIMS TRADING

In a sense, claims trading is as American as apple pie. In another sense, claims trading is almost brand new. Twenty years ago, there was scarcely any of it, and the judge tended to look on the exceptional claims trader with skepticism or outright hostility.

Lately, all that has changed. Starting from about 1985, claims trading has exploded into a multi-billion dollar enterprise. Indeed, claims trading continued to flourish even when the number and size of chapter 11 cases declined. In a world where most securities markets are heavily regulated, one senses that at least part of the appeal may be that here is one field where a certain amount of anarchy still reigns.

Claims trading brings with it the virtues and vices that you would expect from an expanded market. For the original claim holder, a vigorous claims market brings the boon of liquidity: it means that any time he wants to get out, there will be a buyer willing to pay a realistic price for his claim. For the claim buyer, it is an investment opportunity. For the system as a whole, it means that assets in general will be more accurately priced.

For the old residuary owners of the debtor, the benefits may not be so obvious. Insofar as claims are priced more "accurately,"—for which read "higher"—it means that the arbs won't be motivated to settle as cheaply as the original claim owners. Moreover the arbs won't have the motive to swallow past losses in exchange for keeping a future customer.

More generally, claims trading in bankruptcy raises the kinds of questions that follow securities trading more generally. For example, how can the obligor assure himself that he is paying the right person? Second, to what extent may a buyer (or seller) take advantage of "private information," about the debtor and the market?

Finally, there is an array of questions about what you might call "strategic" claims trading. How far, for example, should a trader be permitted to buy up claims from one class to protect his stake in another class? Or to what extent (if any) should the law permit a creditor to buy claims for the purpose of becoming a holdout—i.e., to induce other creditors to buy him off for his nuisance value? These are the kinds of questions that have arisen with regard to claims trading on which the existing law is suggestive, but by no means conclusive.[103]

We discuss these issues in more detail below. For the moment, a summary opinion: our reading is that the courts are becoming more hospitable (if sometimes reluctantly) to the process of claims trading. Proponents of trading will continue to have to cope with old and restrictive precedents, along with a certain measure of judicial skepticism. But on this issue at least, the future seems to favor the market transaction.

§13.56 ~ Who Holds the Claim? Rule 3001(e)

One threshold question that arises whenever you allow the assignment of contracts is: how does the obligor know whom to pay? Suppose Otto owes $100 to Betty. One day Ted shows up at Otto's door saying that he just bought the claim from Betty and that Otto should pay him. How is Otto to know whether Ted is correct? The question is important, because if Otto pays Ted and it turns out that Betty still owned the claim (or, worse, that she had transferred it to somebody else), then Otto may end up paying twice.

The law has developed elaborate sets of rules to govern the policing of claim ownership. For example, a principal function of the law of negotiable instruments is to simplify claims transfer by providing that (in general) "the obligation follows the instrument," and that the obligor may and must pay the person who holds the instrument.

Bankruptcy Rule 3001(e) provides a modest system of regulation for the transfer of bankruptcy claims. Rule 3001(e)(2) provides that the transferee shall provide "evidence of the transfer." Then the bankruptcy clerk shall notify the alleged transferor, who has an opportunity to object if he believes he did not transfer his claim. The transferee shall be substituted as owner of the claim only after he wins a challenge (if any) or after the time for challenge has passed.

The rule applies in the case of any transfer that takes place after the original proof of claim is filed, and that is an outright transfer rather than a transfer for security purposes. There is an exception for a note, bond or debenture—but only if "publicly traded." So in bankruptcy, the notice-and-challenge rule will apply even to some negotiable instruments which, outside bankruptcy, would carry their own proof with them.

A group of mostly New York based claims traders and financial institutions have developed standard documentation for the purchase and sale of bankruptcy claims (and other so-called "distressed debt"). This documentation tends not to be used in small or single asset cases, but is routinely used in large chapter 11s, where the most claim trading goes on.

The standard documentation has the advantage of saving a lot of time and money on negotiating claim sale agreements, but it was drafted by claim buyers and is very pro-buyer. A word of advice to those

---

103. It is said also that in a few major cases, the kaleidoscopic nature of the claims trading market was sufficient to make the whole case less manageable—to make it harder to organize creditors or to focus their attention on reorganization.

representing claim sellers: don't accept the line that these documents are unchargeable forms. There is no such thing, and there is some (if not a lot) room to negotiate these agreements.

§13.57 ~ Sources of Law

Aside from Rule 3001(e), there is a rule on fiduciary duties in claims trading, which we discuss below. Beyond that, there is little or nothing in the Bankruptcy Code that directly regulates claims trading. But on occasion, judges have found ways to interfere with deals they felt improper. Among other devices, they have used an earlier version of Rule 3001(e) (now repealed) and Section 1125 mandating disclosure statements for plans. They also deploy Section 1126(e) which provides that the court may "designate any entity whose acceptance or rejection of [a] plan was not in good faith."

§13.58 ~ Claims Trading in the Information Market

We have a long—although contested—tradition in this legal system that holds that information is the cure for the ills of the market.[104] As most law students learn, Justice Brandeis said that "sunlight is said to be the best of disinfectants: electric light the most efficient policeman."[105]

This attitude animates, among other things, the securities laws of the 1930s, which purport to regulate securities markets not by policing the substance of deals but by regulating the flow of information. The same attitude perhaps underlies Section 1125 of the Bankruptcy Code which provides that a proponent may not solicit votes for a plan unless she has provided "adequate information," sufficient to make an "informed judgment about the plan."

A contrary line of thought opposes not disclosure per se, but the regulatory mandate.[106] The argument is that disclosure is costly in any event, and that investors are probably better judges than regulators of how much disclosure they need and how they ought to pay for it.

In a handful of cases, courts have intervened to impose disclosure on the claims trading process. Perhaps the most famous is *Revere Copper and Brass, Inc.*,[107] where the court refused to approve the purchase of trade claims at 20 cents on the dollar. The court conceded that the buyer was not an "insider" and bore no specific fiduciary obligation. But the court found it enough to say that "solicited creditors may be unaware of their rights and options and fall prey to the belief that bankruptcy inevitably will result in their receiving the proverbial ten cents on the dollar or worse."[108]

---

104. Joel Seligman, The Transformation: The History of the Securities and Exchange Commission and Corporate Finance (1981).
105. Louis D. Brandeis, Other People's Money 62 (1914).
106. *The locus classicus* is Frank H. Easterbrook & Daniel R. Fischel, *Mandatory Disclosure and the Protection of Investors*, 70 Va. L. Rev. 669 (1984).
107. 58 B.R. 1 (Bankr. S.D.N.Y. 1985).
108. *Id.* at 2.

The judge in *Revere Copper* relied at least in part on a version of Section 3001(e) that has since been repealed. The evolution of the rule offers interesting insight into the evolving attitude towards claims trading. The earlier version required the assignee to file "a statement of the transferor acknowledging the transfer and the consideration for the transfer."

The advisory committee note explains: "Such a disclosure will assist the court in dealing with evils that may arise out of post-bankruptcy traffic in claims against an estate."[109] An advisory committee note to the current version specifies that the section was "amended to limit the court's role in the adjudication of disputes regarding transfer of claims."[110] The report continues that the new rule "is not intended either to encourage or discourage post-petition transfers of claims . . ." But the new rule is clearly more hospitable than its predecessor.

Revere Copper also relied in part on Section 1125(b), the section requiring disclosure statements. In effect, the court treated the solicitation to purchase claims as a solicitation to support a particular plan and imposed a disclosure obligation accordingly.

We would be surprised to see a decision like *Revere Cooper* these days. So long as the claim purchaser is not buying the claim for an unlawful or blatantly anticompetitive purpose, or affirmatively misleading the claim seller, the court is unlikely to get involved in the sale.

§13.59 ~ "Strategic" Claims Trading

Every beginning student of chapter 11 knows the off-the-rack rule for plan confirmation. You have to get the vote of a majority in number and two thirds in amount of those voting in order to get confirmation. *See generally* §18.4. So a creditor who wants to block a plan doesn't need to own all the claims—or even half of the claims—in order to block a plan. All he needs is "one third plus one."

Then he can, if he wishes, sit back and wait for his phone to ring. If anybody else wants to confirm a plan, they'll have to come to him. Is it lawful to engage in "strategic" claims trading to build this kind of blocking position? There are cases that cast doubt on the tactic, but our experience is that, more often than not, it is permitted.

At least part of the difficulty may be the matter of motive. If you purchase claims to achieve standing so you can propose a plan, then you have at least one decision that says your purpose is not improper.[111]

You may stand on a different footing if you purchase simply to be a holdout, and to extract a premium for your consent.[112] Suppose there are 10 creditors with claims of $40 each (total = $400) who will share in a pot of $100. On the face of things, it appears that each will get 25 percent of her claim.

---

109. Fed. R. Bankr. Proc. 3001(e) (Comm. Note).
110. Fed. R. Bankr. Proc. 3001(e) (Comm. Note 1991 Amend.).
111. *In re* First Humanics Corp., 124 B.R. 87 (Bankr. W.D. Mo. 1991). *See also* Figter Ltd. v. Teachers Insurance & Annuity Ass'n of America (*In re* Figter Ltd.), 118 F.3d 635 (9th Cir. 1997). In allowing a secured creditor to vote purchased unsecured claims, the court noted, *inter alia*, that the creditor was not proposing an alternate plan.
112. *In re* Chateaugay, 78 B.R. 713, 725-26 (Bankr. S.D.N.Y. 1987).

But suppose you need the consent of all 10, and suppose that in fact, each would settle for as little as $7. Any *one* creditor who threatens to withhold his consent may be able to extract up to $3 from each of the other nine, giving him a total recovery of $37, while the others' falls from $10 to $7.

It seems likely that a Court might look with disfavor on as bald a scheme as the one we have set forth here, though heaven knows there are plenty of cases where holdouts seem to have accomplished their purpose.[113] One problem may be that it is difficult to sort out the motives here: a sophisticated "blocking creditor" can cover his strategy under the banner of something more statesmanlike.

A more intricate issue is the question whether you can trade claims into one class so you can protect your position in *another*. Typically, that would mean: can equity buy up debt, so as to compel debt to take a haircut, so as to leave money on the table for equity? The legislative history of the Code seems to suggest that you cannot do so.[114] Although, again, we have seen it happen on any number of occasions.

Tactic: One way for the creditor to block confirmation in the single asset real estate case is simply to buy up all (or enough of) the unsecured claims. They are typically pocket change compared to the mortgage debt and they are claims that will probably be paid anyway because they relate to building management and maintenance which the creditor will typically want to continue. By doing this, the mortgagee can assure that there will be no "consenting class" as necessary to confirm a cram down plan.[115] *See* §18.6.

If the investor buys up 21 claims, does he get to vote once? Or 21 times? *Figler Ltd. v. Teachers Insurance & Annuity Ass'n of America.*[116] holds he gets to vote each of the 21. Recall that this may be important because acceptance of a plan is based on the vote of more than half of the number of claims voted as well as two-thirds of the debt voted. See §1126(c).

§13.60 ~ Fiduciary Trading

A principle that cuts across the developing law of claims trading is the notion of fiduciary duty. A person who is a fiduciary is held to a higher standard than a person in a simple contract relationship.

There is plenty of authority for the proposition that corporate directors, officers and control persons are fiduciaries. So also members of official creditors' committees.[117] On the other hand, it is not always clear which way the train runs on this track. It may be that a person is held to a higher duty because he is a fiduciary. Or it may be that the court finds him to be a fiduciary because it wants to hold him to a higher duty.

---

113. A glaring example is the famous case of Case v. Los Angeles Lumber Products, 308 U.S. 106 (1939), the fountainhead of the famous old "absolute priority rule." In Case, Justice Douglas (for the Court) laid down what became the old chapter X rule—that no junior class could receive anything until all senior classes were paid in full. By refusing confirmation, Justice Douglas seems to have endorsed the strategy of a creditor who bought in for the purpose of becoming a holdout.

114. H.R. Rep. No. 95-595, 225 at 441 (1977), reprinted in 1978 U.S. Code Cong. & Admin. News 5963, 6185.

115. Texas Hotel Sec. Corp v. Waco Dev. Co, 87 F. 2d 395 (5th Cir. 1936) (5th Circuit overruled denial of voting rights to creditor who acquired blocking interest because evidence insufficient to show creditor intent was wholly obstructive).

116. *In re* Figler Ltd., 118 F.3d 635 (9th Cir. 1997).

117. Central Transp. Inc. v. Roberto (*In re* Tucker Freight Lines, Inc.), 62 B.R. 213, 216 (Bankr. W.D. Mich. 1986).

But whichever is the case, the fact is that the courts have sometimes deployed the "fiduciary" label as a means of regulating claims trading classify the claims purchased by the fiduciary below all other creditors' claims.[118]

Courts have not held claims trading by fiduciaries to be invalid per se. But a number of courts have said that it raises a rebuttable presumption that there has been breach of fiduciary duty.[119] In an old chapter X case the court held that the fiduciary's trading was inherently unfair. The court thereupon limited the recovery of the fiduciary claim holder to the amount that it had paid for the claim, not the higher face value.[120]

Strategy: When a member of a creditors committee may want to trade its claim or trade in securities of the debtor, it should establish (and document internally) a strict "ethical wall" so that the people on the trading side of the institution will not have access to any of the information obtained by the institution in its capacity as a committee member. Even then, it is not without risk. One approach is to ask the court to approve a procedure for committee members to trade in debt or equity of the debtor.[121]

---

118. *See* Citibank Venture Capital, Ltd. v. Comm. of Creditors Holding Unsecured Claims, 160 F.3d 982, 988 (3d Cir. 1998).

119. Pepper v. Litton, 308 U.S. 295, 306 (1939); Moulded Products, Inc. v. Barry, 474 F.2d 220, 224 (8th Cir. 1973); *In re* Wingspread Corp., 92 B.R. 87, 93-94 (Bankr. S.D.N.Y. 1988).

120. *See In re* Philadelphia & Western Railway, 64 F. Supp. 738, 740-41 (E.D. Pa. 1946).

121. *See, e.g.*, In the Matter of Federated Dep't Stores, 1991 WL 79143 (Bankr. S.D. Ohio March 7, 1991).

14 Trustee's Avoiding Powers

14 Trustee's Avoiding Powers

§14.1 ~ Introduction: What Makes Bankruptcy Bankruptcy

We turn now to one of the topics that gives bankruptcy its distinctive character: the power of the trustee to "avoid" (invalidate, set aside) certain transactions between the debtor and a third party. We divide our treatment into two parts. In this chapter, we provide a general view of the avoiding powers. In the next, we consider some issues that arise from the most basic of the avoiding powers, the power to set aside fraudulent transfers.

§14.2 ~ Two Hats

Trustee avoiding powers are a mass of often baffling detail and technicality. To get a grip on avoiding powers, it may help to begin by backing off from the detail and taking a look at the big picture.

The trustee wears two hats. Under one, he is successor to the debtor. For example, in a chapter 7 case he must collect and reduce to money the property of the estate.[1] The estate includes all legal or equitable interests of the debtor in property as of the commencement of the case.[2] So, for example, if the debtor had a file of accounts receivable claims against third parties, the trustee could sue on those claims to collect money for the estate.

But the trustee is also the representative of the creditors. In that role, he may exercise rights that would have belonged to creditors before the beginning of the case. Equally important (but perhaps less obvious), he may preempt action by other creditors, who may no longer be able to act on their own.

The trustee's powers are in large part derivative of the powers of creditors at state law. So in order to understand a trustee's powers, we need to start with a review of the powers of creditors at state law.

1. Section 704(1).

2. Section 541(a)(1).

§14.3 ~ The "Strong-Arm Power"—Hypothetical Lien Creditor

In *York Manufacturing Co. v. Cassell*,[3] the Supreme Court considered the claim of a creditor/seller with an unfiled conditional sales contract. State law provided that the contract was invalid against creditors except those holding liens. No creditor held a lien. The Court found that the trustee was not himself a lien creditor. It therefore concluded that he took the property encumbered by the conditional sales contract.

Congress responded swiftly, adding a sentence to the Bankruptcy Act, specifically reposing in the trustee the powers of a lien creditor or a judgment creditor.[4] The legislative history made it clear that the purpose of the amendment was to overrule *York*.[5] Judicial gloss quickly established that the trustee enjoyed these creditors' rights whether or not there was an actual creditor who could have exercised them. The 1910 amendment, carried forward through various permutations and came into the Bankruptcy Act of 1978 as Section 544(a), the trustee's strong-arm power. It is the linchpin of trustee powers under the Code.

Example: Daniel borrows $10,000 from Selma and signs a note and an agreement granting Selma an interest in debtor's valuable banjo pick, worth $10,000, as security for her claim. The agreement is governed by the Uniform Commercial Code. Daniel signs a security agreement, but Selma does not file a financing statement and does not take possession of the banjo pick.

In bankruptcy, Selma demands turnover of her banjo pick to satisfy her claim. Will she prevail? The answer is no. The conclusion follows from the strong-arm power, specifically Section 544(a)(1). That section says:

> The trustee . . .may avoid . . . any obligation incurred by the debtor that is voidable by—a creditor that extends credit to the debtor at the time of the commencement of the case, and that obtains, at such time and with respect to such credit, a judicial lien on all property on which the creditor on a simple contract could have obtained such a judicial lien . . . .

A judicial lien is a "lien obtained by judgment, levy, sequestration, or other legal or equitable process or proceedings."[6]

But who qualifies as such a creditor? To answer this question, we turn to the governing state law, in this case the UCC. We find there in Section 9-301(1)(b), "an unperfected security interest is subordinate to the rights of . . . a person who becomes a lien creditor before the security interest is perfected."

The UCC specifies that a lien creditor is a creditor who gets a lien by attachment, levy or the like.[7] The trustee reasons: I have the rights of a (judicial) lien creditor. A judicial lien creditor trumps an unperfected security interest. Therefore, I trump Selma.

---

3. 201 U.S. 344 (1906).
4. Section 47a(2), Act of June 25, 1910, 36 Stat. 838.
5. *See* 45 Cong. Rec. 2277 (1910).
6. Section 101(36).
7. UCC §9-301.

Contrast this with the situation where Selma files her financing statement a day or an hour before the debtor's bankruptcy petition. Selma's priority position may be avoidable under some other power (cf., the discussion of preferences, infra). But it won't be avoidable under the hypothetical lien creditor power, because she was perfected (however belatedly) before the commencement of the case.

§14.4 ~ Beware of Stipulations

Early in the chapter 11 case, the debtor may be particularly vulnerable to the secured creditor—especially if the debtor needs DIP financing. Plenty of secured creditors will press the advantage and try to get the debtor (as DIP) to stipulate away any potential conflicts over the validity and perfection of the security interest. In fact, defects in security documentation are not uncommon, and the harried debtor will do well to resist or sidestep the pressure as best he can. Failing that, he had better take time to review the existing documentation with care lest he give away a valuable right too cheaply.

The same goes for counsel representing the unsecured creditors' committee. On this issue at least, he is more the ally than adversary to the debtor, and shares the debtor's interest in preserving what he can against the entreaties of the secured creditor.

One common device for resolving the issue is to allow the debtor to waive the challenge (as part of a cash collateral or DIP financing order, for example), but to give the committee a specified period—say, 90 days—to evaluate whether to challenge the lien. This kind of a deal has the virtue of assuring the court that someone is looking into the problem, but giving the secured creditor a kind of closure.

§14.5 ~ Don't Overlook Intangibles

Earlier, we pointed out that "intangibles" may be property of the estate, and that they create problems in part because they are so easy to overlook. They are also property for the purposes of the avoiding powers. But they can be tricky, because the rules are a little different.

For tangible personal property—goods, equipment, inventory—the rules are fairly well developed and familiar: you perfect by taking possession or (more often) by filing a UCC-1. For accounts receivable the rules are a little trickier: you can't possess an account, and so filing is the only route. On the other hand, the rules governing perfection, typically reserved for "secured credit" under Article 9, in the case of accounts also extend to absolute transfers.

Even the judge who has coped with an issue involving intangibles or accounts is less likely to have experience with a patent or a copyright, to say nothing, for example, of a domain name in cyberspace. In sorting out governing law, she is also likely to find herself ensnared in complicating issues. For example, there may be a question of what law applies to a particular transfer:

By our reading, Federal statutes governing patent,[8] trademark[9] and copyright[10] govern "assignment" of rights, without specifying whether this means absolute transfers only, or absolute transfers plus transfers

8. 35 U.S.C. §261.

9. 15 U.S.C. §1060.

10. 17 U.S.C. §201(d)(1).

for security. If these statutes apply to security transfers as well as absolute transfers, then you might conclude that the appropriate place to record your security interest would be with the Patent and Trademark Office or the Copyright Office. For example, a much-noted recent case held that the appropriate way to perfect a security interest in a copyright is in the national registration system.[11] And, there are similar cases for patents and trademarks.

But, perhaps surprisingly, a number of cases under trademark and patent law seem to go the other way: this would mean that the law governing perfection of security transfers is state law under the Uniform Commercial Code.[12] For more on intangibles, *see* §8.3-.4.

§14.6 ~ File Everyplace

Until this ambiguity is resolved, the only safe thing to do is to file in every possible place—that is to say, for patents, with the Patent and Trademark Office, and for copyrights, with the Copyright Office, and for both, with the state "general intangibles" office in order to assure perfection.

§14.7 ~ Hypothetical Bona Fide Purchase

Daniel borrows $10,000 and gives Selma a security interest (lien, mortgage, deed of trust) in Blackacre. State law provides that a mortgage is "void against a bona fide purchaser" unless recorded. Selma neglects to record. Daniel files for bankruptcy relief: the trustee seeks to avoid the mortgage. Under Section 544(a)(1), will the trustee prevail?

The answer depends on the meaning of the phrase bona fide purchaser. If a bona fide purchaser is a species of "creditor with a judicial lien," then the trustee will prevail. But under the law of many states, a bona fide purchaser is not a species of judicial lien-holder.[13] Rather, many states hold that a mortgage trumps a judicial lien even if unrecorded. So if a trustee is no better than a lien creditor, the unperfected mortgage trumps the trustee.

If it is the job of bankruptcy merely to reflect non-bankruptcy rights, then you might think that bankruptcy law would just let the matter rest there. But the drafters of the 1978 Code added Section 544(a)(3) to assure that, with respect to real estate, the trustee enjoyed also the rights of a bona fide purchaser. So in our case, a BFP would trump Selma's unrecorded mortgage, The trustee is a BFP, so he trumps also.

Note that both the lien creditor power and the BFP power exist whether or not such claimant exists. This means that the trustee doesn't have to prove the existence of any particular creditor or BFP. A better way to capture the notion might simply be to say that the filing of the petition makes the trustee a lien creditor (and also a BFP), without more.

---

11. *In re* Peregrine Entertainment, Ltd., 116 B.R. 194, 199 (Bankr. C.D. Cal. 1990).

12. *See, e.g.*, *In re* Cybernetic Services, Inc., 239 B.R. 917, 923 (B.A.P. 9th Cir. 1999).

13. For a classic statement, *see* McGee v. Allen, 115 P.2d 450 (Cal. 1941). You need to read these state cases with care. Often when they talk about a mere lien creditor, they are thinking of someone who got his lien in satisfaction of a pre-mortgage antecedent debt. So they are perhaps better understood as preference cases. But the fact remains, the UCC tells us not to pay attention to the issue of when value was given; rather we pay attention to the lien only.

§14.8 ~ 'Actual Creditor' Power

Now consider a different example. The debtor Harold transfers his valuable refrigerator magnet to his wife Wilma, as a gift, and while insolvent. The transaction probably counts as a fraudulent transfer, voidable outside bankruptcy by an aggrieved creditor under non-bankruptcy law (we will explain in detail later). But in fact Harold didn't know it was a fraudulent transfer: it passes the "golden retriever" test—pure heart and empty head.

A month later, Harold files for bankruptcy. Will the trustee be able to avoid the transfer in the bankruptcy of Harold? In the end, we think the answer is probably "yes," but take it by degrees. First, consider Section 544(a)(1), which gives the trustee the rights of a hypothetical creditor who extends credit and gets a lien on the property of Harold at the moment of bankruptcy. Using this power, will the trustee trump Wilma? Using this power, the answer is no. The reason is that the prior transfer to Wilma, even though constructively fraudulent, is not avoidable by the creditor who extended credit *after* the transfer.[14] By the same reasoning, the trustee gets no rights under 544(a)(3).

Now, consider Section 544(b)(1). This section provides that the trustee may avoid an obligation "that is voidable under applicable law by a creditor holding an unsecured claim." Note that this class of (unsecured) creditor is broader than the class of creditor identified in 544(a). It includes unsecured creditors, not lien creditors. Also, it appears to include a creditor who extends credit at any time, not just at the commencement of the case.

But there is a limit. That is: under Section 544(b)(1), we must prove the existence of an actual creditor —not just a hypothetical creditor, as in 544(a)(1). So we take the trustee's records and search for an actual unsecured creditor against whom this claim was "voidable under applicable law." What sort of creditor will this be? Typically under non-bankruptcy law a (constructive) fraudulent transfer is voidable by one who was a creditor at the time of the transfer. If there is such a creditor and if he remains unpaid at the time of bankruptcy, then we have a creditor who meets the 544(b). The trustee can step into his shoes and avoid the transfer.

Comment: Virtually all Section 544(a) cases involve unperfected security interests. Section 544(b) cases are perhaps more varied. You can conjure such a case any time you can find a statute that protects a general unsecured creditor. Fraudulent transfer law is perhaps the most promising source. Another possible source is the law of bulk transfers under Article 6 of the Uniform Commercial Code (but Article 6 may be on its way out).

So much for the basics of Section 544(b). There is another spin to Section 544(b) that makes it far more dangerous than might appear so far. We discuss it as "the doctrine of *Moore v. Bay*," below §14.11.

---

14. At least, we think this is the law. But the answer depends on state law, and there are a lot of states. Maybe someone will come up with a state law that gives the subsequent creditor a right against the prior "constructively fraudulent" transfer. If that is the case, then the trustee can step into his shoes and we would be wrong. But we don't know of any.

§14.9 ~ A Substantive Law of Fraudulent Transfer

It may be unexceptionable to give the trustee powers to avoid transfers deemed fraudulent under non-bankruptcy law (as he does under Section 544, described above). But then the Bankruptcy Code does something perhaps a bit more contentious. In Section 548, Congress provided the trustee with a separate, federal substantive law of fraudulent transfers: the section largely mirrors the Uniform Fraudulent Transfer Law (UFTA), now on the books in a number of states. *See* Chapter 15 below. In bankruptcy, Section 548 empowers the trustee to avoid certain defined transfers. The transfers defined in Section 548 are largely identical to the transfers rendered avoidable under non-bankruptcy law by the UFTA.

One can be excused if one perceives this as a kind of "piling on." If bankruptcy is merely transparent to state law—and if, when it comes to that, many states have the UFTA anyway—then what is the point of adding substantive fraudulent transfer law to the Bankruptcy Code?

There is no good response to that question, other than to fight the premise. After all, it is not written in the stars that the Bankruptcy Code merely mirrors state law. Apparently Congress has made a decision that avoidance of fraudulent transfers is so integral to the bankruptcy system that we have to have it under federal law, whatever may be the current law of the states. At least Section 548 gives the trustee substantive law to use in states where fraudulent transfer law is fragmentary or undeveloped. It also stabilizes the bankruptcy system in the face of changing state law.

There are cases where seemingly similar state law may award broader powers to the trustee than Section 548 accords. The Section 548 statute of limitations, for example, is only one year; under the laws of Texas (for example) a four-year statute applies.[15] This is often the most important difference between the two. The bottom line is that the prudent trustee who thinks she has a fraudulent transfer claim and under will ordinarily allege causes of action under both state law (via Section 544(b)) and under Section 548.

§14.10 ~ Debtor Avoiding Powers

We need to discuss yet one more class of avoiding power. Section 522(f) provides that the individual debtor, not the trustee, may avoid certain pre-bankruptcy transactions. For example, Section 522(f)(1) provides that the debtor may avoid a judicial lien. But he may avoid the lien only to the extent that such lien impairs an exemption to which the debtor would have been entitled. For example, suppose the debtor has $4,000 in a bank account. Two weeks before bankruptcy, a creditor slaps a lien on the bank account. Now the debtor wants to claim it as exempt under Section 522(d)(5). Section 522(f) empowers him to do so.

Note the important novelty here. This is the first avoiding power that we have seen which works on the initiative (and to the benefit) of the debtor, not the trustee or the DIP. This power came into the law as part of the Bankruptcy Code of 1978. There is no prior analog. For other debtor avoiding powers, *see* Sections 522(f)(2)(g) and (h).

---

15. Tex. Bus. & Com. Code Ann. §24.010(a), (b) (Vernon Supp. 1990).

§14.11 ~ "In the Overshoes of the Creditor"—Moore v. Bay

A trap that awaits the transaction planner, found in Section 544(b)(1), gives the trustee the power to avoid any interest or obligation that is "voidable under applicable law by a creditor holding an unsecured claim." The provision sounds innocuous enough on its face. But start with an example.

Example: Suppose Daniel, being insolvent, makes a (constructive) fraudulent transfer of property worth $1 million to Theresa. Under the state law governing fraudulent transfers, the transaction might be avoidable by any creditor with a claim against Daniel at the time of the transfer, but not by a future creditor. Against all expectations, Daniel pays off all of his extant creditors (or so he believes) and continues life unencumbered. Unfortunately, he falls into debt a second time, accumulating $1 million in new claims. This time, with debts but no assets, he files for bankruptcy.

Examining Daniel's books and records, the trustee finds one $10 claim that remains unpaid from before the fraudulent transfer. On the authority of Section 544(b)(1) (and invoking the $10 claim), trustee sues Theresa to avoid the $1 million transfer. Theresa, admitting the facts as pleaded, offers $10 in full settlement of all claims.

Enter the doctrine of *Moore v. Bay*.[16] The trustee says: no, if I find one creditor with a claim that remains unpaid, then I get to set aside the entire transfer. So I want, not $10, but $1 million. Such is the (reputed) holding of the Supreme Court. Or in standard jargon: the trustee gets to avoid the transaction in toto and not just pro tanto. Thus we meet one of the oddest doctrines in the history of bankruptcy law: the idea that a Section 544(b)(1) trustee "stands in the overshoes of the creditor" and to set aside the entire transaction for a trifling claim.

So far as we know, no one has ever come up with a convincing justification for the doctrine of *Moore v. Bay*. Rather, commentators like to make their points by attacking it. "Ill-considered," growled the great Professor Maclachlan.[17] "Cryptic and unsatisfactory" said the great Professor Gilmore.[18] Modern commentators have not been much kinder.

The commentators take the same kind of perverse glee in pointing to the legislative history of Section 544(b)(1). It says that this section "follows *Moore v. Bay*" (though you might never have guessed it from reading the statute itself).[19] So Justice Holmes' doctrine remains part of the law.

Comment: We suspect that *Moore v. Bay* cases are like Elvis sightings—more often reported than confirmed. You have to have some fairly unusual conditions—a statute that protects unsecured creditors and an "overlooked" claim. The result is so counterintuitive that courts are probably happy to find a way around it, or simply not to recognize it in the first place. The real importance is twofold. One, it's a nightmare to transaction planners, threatening a major penalty for a minor slipup. And two, it's wonderful negotiating leverage for the trustee/DIP who is lucky enough to have the argument available in his toolkit.

---

16. 284 U.S. 4 (1931).

17. James Angell Maclachlan, Bankruptcy 330 (1956).

18. Grant Gilmore, Security Interests in Personal Property 466 (1965).

19. *See* H.R. No. 595-95, 1st Sess. at 370-1 (1977); S. Rep. 989-95, 2d Sess. at 85 (1978).

§14.12 ~ Counter-rule: Caplin v. Marine Midland

Cynics and revolutionaries like to say that for every situation the law has two rules—rather a rule, and a counter-rule, allowing the judge to chose either at she sees fit to govern the situation. We won't speak about the law in general, but the insight may be a pretty good description of *Moore v. Bay* when measured against *Caplin v. Marine Midland Grace Trust Co.*[20] Caplin stands for the proposition that a trustee does not have standing to bring causes of action that belong to creditors individually.

A typical modern example is *Schertz-Cibolo-Universal City v. Wright.*[21] EGHT was a bankrupt provider of health care and Wright was the trustee. Some of the health care beneficiaries sued some of the principals of EGHT on charges of fraud and mismanagement. The trustee intervened, alleging that the lawsuit belonged to him. The Court of Appeals gave a split decision. It held that the trustee owned those causes of action that derive from a direct injury to the bankruptcy estate. But it said that the beneficiaries owned those causes that involved direct injury to them. The difference is important: if the beneficiaries own the claim, then they get all the money. If the trustee owns it, then he must divide it pro rata among all creditors—a class which would include beneficiaries and others.

§14.13 ~ Preferences—Section 547

Consider the case of Dawson who owes $100 each to the Alpha, Betty and Carol. His assets are worth just $100. The claim to Carol takes the form of a note payable on demand. Carol, not knowing anything about Dawson's financial situation, decides that she needs the money to take a vacation. She asks him to pay $100 and he pays. At the time he paid Carol, Dawson thought that his fortunes would improve and he would be able to pay all his debts. But they did not improve, and 89 days after the transfer, Dawson files for bankruptcy.

The trustee sues Carol to recover $100, alleging that the transfer is a voidable preference on the authority of Section 547. The judge rules for the trustee. Carol turns over the money and the trustee distributes it (net of expenses) pro rata among all creditors including Carol (whose claim was reinstated when she got paid the $100).

Welcome to the world of the voidable preference.

§14.14 ~ Why Preferences?

A core purpose of bankruptcy law is to provide for the "equitable" distribution of debtor property under some scheme of distribution (*e.g.*, pro rata) that will supervene over the race to the courthouse of non-bankruptcy law. Consistent with this principle, you wouldn't want to let creditors go ahead and make piecemeal levies after bankruptcy begins. This is *one* reason for Section 362 of the Bankruptcy Code, which stays any action to take property from the estate: leave the property with the estate so the trustee can carry out the statutory scheme.

---

20. 406 U.S. 416 (1972).

21. 25 F.3d 1281 (5th Cir. 1994).

Section 362 sets a bright line for invoking the stay—the filing of the petition. Bankruptcy may indeed be amenable to a bright-line definition. Maybe you can't be more or less bankrupt, but people are more or less insolvent all the time. You can probably anticipate the problem here. If creditors see bankruptcy coming (and they often do) they will pick and choose among the debtor's assets on the eve of bankruptcy. When the trustee finally shows up, she will find that the grab is over, and there's nothing much left for her to distribute.

It is for this reason that the bankruptcy statute contains a mechanism permitting the trustee to reach back before bankruptcy to undo certain transactions for the purpose of bringing property back into the estate. This is the power to avoid preferences, set forth in Section 547. Note that the preference power is one that exists entirely independent of state law. As a general matter, state law does not outlaw preferences—after all, a debtor who prefers one creditor over another is at least paying a debt. But note that there are some state preference laws, and occasionally a creative trustee will rely upon one.[22]

§14.15 ~ Prima Facie Case

The trustee's prima facie case for a preference is set forth in Section 547(b). It provides that the trustee may avoid any transfer of an interest of the debtor in property to (or for the benefit of) a creditor; for or an antecedent debt; made while the debtor was insolvent;[23] on or within 90 days before the filing of the petition; and that enables the creditor to receive more than the creditor would have received in chapter 7.

The first thing to note about this transaction is that Dawson did owe the money. It cannot be wrong to pay a debt. So surely Dawson stands on a different moral footing from debtors who spirit assets into concealed bolt-holes where creditors won't find them—or from debtors who spend all their cash on riotous living. On the other hand, if you let the transaction stand, you cannot possibly run a system of bankruptcy. A primary purpose of bankruptcy is orchestration: dividing up the assets according to some principle of equity. If you let the debtor pick and choose, or give free reign to the creditor with the greatest leverage, then orchestration will not work.

But the second thing to note is that this was not a scheme to orchestrate claims. Neither Dawson nor Carol had any intent to defeat the bankruptcy distribution scheme—indeed, on the evidence, neither gave bankruptcy any thought at all. Transferee knowledge used to be an element of the prima facie case; no longer.

---

22. *See* David A. Skeel, Jr., *Rethinking the Line Between Corporate Law and Corporate Bankruptcy,* 72 TEX. L. REV. 471 (1994) (national survey of state preference statutes). They do not seem to be used very often. But *see, e.g., In re* Rexplore Drilling, 971 F.2d 1219 (6th Cir. 1992) (affirming the avoidance of a judgment as a preference under the Kentucky preference statute).

23. "Insolvency" means the balance-sheet test—assets minus liabilities. But assets, for this purpose, will not include exempt property, or property transferred with the intent to defraud. *See generally* §101(32).

§14.16 ~ Examples

Here are some examples that will clarify the nature and extent of preference law. Assume that the debtor is insolvent at the time of all transfers from debtor to creditor.

- Debtor borrows $100 from butcher five years before bankruptcy. He repays butcher 91 days before bankruptcy (t - 91) Not a preference. Outside the 90 days (*but see* below on insider transfers).[24]

- Twenty minutes before bankruptcy, Debtor buys a widget (worth $100) from WidgetCo, paying cash. Not a preference, because not a transfer for an antecedent debt. This seems reasonable when you reflect that no creditor is made any worse off by the transfer, since Debtor got value for value.[25]

- Debtor buys a widget from WidgetCo for $100 at t-91, giving WidgetCo a security interest which WidgetCo promptly perfects, At bankruptcy, Debtor's only asset is the widget, still worth $100. Not a preference. WidgetCo has first claim on the widget via its security interest, which gives it no more than it would get in chapter 7.

- Same as the previous case, except Debtor pays WidgetCo $100 cash on t - 2. Still not a voidable preference. WidgetCo has gained $100 but it has lost his secured position, so it is no better off than it would be in chapter 7.

- Two years before bankruptcy, Debtor borrows $100 from NewBank and grants NewBank a security interest in a widget. At the time of the making of the loan, NewBank neglects to perfect its security interest. Three days before bankruptcy, NewBank finally perfects. The transfer will be treated as a voidable preference. The transfer is the granting of the security interest. The transfer was made when it was perfected.[26] Since it was made three days before bankruptcy to secure a debt incurred two years before bankruptcy, it is a transfer for an antecedent debt. Academics sometimes argue that the "delayed perfection" problem is conceptually different from the "preference" problem and ought to be dealt with separately. But there is no doubt that under the Bankruptcy Code, preference analysis applies.[27]

§14.17 ~ Exceptions

Aside from Section 547(b), note that Section 547(c) sets forth certain exceptions—transactions which, presumably, meet the definition of preference under 547(b), but which will not be avoidable because the Code says so. The exceptions, roughly in order of importance, are:

---

24. If the debtor pays by check, then the transfer is made when the check clears the bank. Barnhill v. Johnson, 503 U.S. 383 (1992).

25. *See also* the discussion of §547(c)(1) below.

26. Section 547(e)(2)(B).

27. The Bankruptcy Code has its own ten-day reach-back period for delayed perfection; *see* §14.21.

- Transfers in the ordinary course of business.[28]
- "Substantially contemporaneous exchange."[29]
- There is a 20-day safe harbor for delayed filing of purchase money security interests.[30] This provision overlaps with Section 547(c)(1) (on contemporaneous exchange) and 547(e)(2) giving a general safe harbor for delayed perfection.
- Cases where the transferee receives a preference and later advances offsetting *new value*.[31]
- There is a provision designed to prevent the inventory or receivables creditor from ginning up the inventory or receivables accounts.[32]
- In a consumer case, transfers aggregating $600.[33]
- Domestic obligations.[34]
- Certain statutory liens.[35]

§14.18 ~ Burden of Proof

The trustee has the burden of proof in a preference case. With reference to the matter of insolvency, Section 547(f) gives him the benefit of a presumption of insolvency for the 90-day period prior to the bankruptcy filing. By conventional wisdom, this is an evidentiary presumption only. That is, if the trustee alleges insolvency and no one introduces any contrary evidence, he wins. If there is some contrary evidence, then the burden of proof remains on the trustee as it would with other elements.

§14.19 ~ Insider

Special rules apply when the transferee is an insider. Consider the case where Debtor paid $100 to Brother 364 days prior to Debtor's bankruptcy filing, in satisfaction of an antecedent unsecured debt

---

28. Section 547(c)(2). The statute sets three criteria: (1) debt incurred in ordinary course; (2) payment in ordinary course; and (3) according to ordinary business terms. "Ordinary business terms" might mean (a) ordinary in the trade; or (b) ordinary between this debtor and this creditor. The cases (and the commentary) are divided. *See generally In re* Tolona Pizza Products Corp., 3 F.3d 1029 (7th Cir. 1993).

29. The Code requires that the transaction be both (a) intended as and (b) in fact a substantially contemporaneous exchange. From our point of view, such a transaction isn't a preference at all because it is not a payment on account of an antecedent debt, and so doesn't even need to be in the list of exceptions. But Congress put it there, in §547(c)(1).

30. Section 547(c)(3).

31. Section 547(a)(4).

32. Section 547(c)(5).

33. Section 547(c)(8).

34. Section 547(c)(7).

35. Section 548(c)(6).

while insolvent. If the other elements are met, the transaction may be avoidable even though outside the 90-day period. This is so because Brother qualifies as an insider, for whom the reach-back period is not 90 days, but one year.[36]

§14.20 ~ DePrizio

Here is a preference case that rocked the bankruptcy bar a few years back, and may have the power to haunt us again.

Bank loans $1 million to DebtorCo. Gary, who is the president and controlling shareholder of DebtorCo, gives his personal guarantee. DebtorCo slides into financial trouble. Gary, worried about exposure on his guarantee, sees to it that DebtorCo pays $500,000 to Bank. One hundred days later, DebtorCo files for chapter 11.

Is this a preference? At first look, you would say no. The repayment was outside the 90 period. Bank is not an insider, so the one-year insider rule cannot apply.

But on a second look, the answer is not so clear. A preference is a payment "to or for the benefit of a creditor." Obviously, Bank is a creditor—but perhaps less obviously, so also is Gary, who has a contingent subrogation claim against DebtorCo for anything he pays on his guarantee.

Bank is not an insider of DebtorCo, but clearly Gary is. The payment went to the Bank, but it was for the benefit of Gary. So the one-year period applies. Not so surprising, perhaps, to find that the trustee can recover from Gary, the insider. The surprise is that the trustee can recover the (insider) transfer also from the (non-insider) Bank.

Such was the reasoning of Judge Easterbrook for the Seventh Circuit, in the case that became famous as *DePrizio*.[37] On the face of the statute, Judge Easterbrook was probably right. The bizarre part is that it puts the Bank in a worse position with the guarantee than it was without. It seems unlikely (to put it mildly) that this was what Congress had in mind.

Many courts followed the Seventh Circuit (although some declined to do so), and as a result *DePrizio* became a very important issue for bankruptcy lawyers, transactional lawyers, and bankers. All sorts of solutions were invented to the *DePrizio* reasoning. Probably the most common device was to include a waiver of subrogation provision in the guarantee. The reasoning was that if the guarantor waived the right of subrogation, then he wasn't creditor of the estate, and so the transaction could not be "for the benefit of an insider who is a creditor." Some courts held that it worked.

---

36. Who is an insider? *See* §101(31). The definition uses the word "includes" and therefore is not exhaustive. To test its limits, compare two circuit opinions considering whether an ex-wife, though not specifically within §101(31), nonetheless qualified as an "insider" under the statute's general reach. The cases reach opposite results, and are very likely distinguishable on their facts. *Cf.* Browning Interests v. Allison (*In re* Holloway), 955 F.2d 1008 (5th Cir. 1992) *with* Miller v. Schuman (*In re* Schuman), 81 Bankr. 583 (9th Cir. BAP 1987).

37. Levit v. Ingersoll Rand Financial Corp. (*In re* V.N. DePrizio Construction Corp.), 874 F.2d. 1186 (7th Cir. 1989).

Under pressure from financial institutions and the finance bar, Congress stepped in with a remedy. Congress acted not by amending Section 547 itself, but by amending the remedy provision in Section 550. The amended Section 550 specifies that the trustee may not recover a preference from a party that is not an insider if the preference payment was outside of the 90-day period. So, under our example, the trustee could still seek to recover the payment from Guarantor (although that is often hopeless), but could not recover the payment from Bank, because Bank was not an insider.

Why are we bothering with all this if *DePrizio* has been, in effect, repealed? First, you will still get a lot of questions about it from transactional lawyers and lender clients, and you need to be able to respond. Second, if you understand *DePrizio* and how it was repealed, you probably understand preference law pretty well. Third, there may be areas where *DePrizio* still creates problems. An example is *In re Williams*.[38] The Bank did not get an outright transfer of property, but it did perfect a security interest in the one-year period. The court held that the legislative *DePrizio* fix did not reach the perfection of a security interest, and invalidated the transfer.

§14.21 ~ Timing—Made when Perfected, etc.

Perhaps the most difficult interpretative problems under Section 547 involve the late-filed security interest. In an earlier example, we saw that a transfer was deemed made when perfected, and so a late-perfected security interest became a transfer on account of an antecedent debt. We also noted that there was a "safe harbor" rule for late perfection. The rules are intricate and deserve careful attention. Consider a security interest in personal property, governed by Article 9 of the Uniform Commercial Code ("UCC"). We start with Section 547(e)(2). This section defines when the transfer is made. It sets two rules, as follows:

- The transfer is made when it takes effect between the parties, if it is perfected *at* or within 10 days *after* the time it takes effect. This is the grace period rule. Section 547(e)(2)(A).

- Otherwise, the transfer is made when perfected. Section 547(e)(2)(B).

So, these rules define when the transfer is made. But when is it perfected? The answer is in Section 547(e)(1)(B). It provides that the transfer "is *perfected* when a creditor on a simple contract cannot acquire a judicial lien that is superior to the interest of the transferee." This bankruptcy perfection rule dovetails pretty well with the state law set forth in the Uniform Commercial Code Section 9-301(1)(b). So we can infer that perfection under the Uniform Commercial Code counts as perfection under the Bankruptcy Code. Now, consider some examples (assume the debtor is insolvent at all relevant times):

- On January 5, Della signs a UCC financing statement in favor of Carla covering a security interest in equipment. On January 14, Della borrows $500 from Carla, granting Carla a security interest in a widget which Della holds as equipment. The transfer is made when it takes effect between the parties because it is perfected when made. No preference.

38. 234 B.R. 801 (Bankr. D. Ore. 1999).

- On January 5, Della borrows $500 from Carla, granting Carla a security interest in a widget which Della holds as equipment. On January 14 Della signs, and Carla files, a UCC financing statement granting a security interest in equipment. The transfer is made when it takes effect between the parties because it is perfected within 10 days after it takes effect between the parties. No preference.

- Same as in the previous example, except that Carla does not file the financing statement until January 16. The transfer is not perfected within 10 days after the time when it is made. Therefore, made when perfected, on January 16. Hence a transfer for an antecedent debt, and apparently a preference.[39]

These cases are fairly straightforward. Now, consider a trickier case:

- On January 5, Della signs a UCC financing statement in favor of Carla covering a security interest in equipment, and borrows $500 from Carla. Carla files the financing statement the same day. On January 14, Della grants Carla a security interest in a widget which Della holds as equipment. The transfer is made when it takes effect between the parties.

But note the difference. In this case, the transfer of *security* is made on January 14, while the loan was made on January 5, so the transfer is for an antecedent debt. It appears to be a preference, although once again, the "contemporaneous exchange" exception might apply. Summarizing:

- Loan and security agreement January 5, filing January 14. The grace period applies, and the transfer is made January 5.

- Loan and filing January 5, security agreement January 14. The grace period does not apply, and the the transfer is made January 14.

Courts also have to cope with timing problems under Section 547(c)(3), the protection for purchase money interests. The Supreme Court in 1998 held that the 20-day grace period in that section trumps a longer grace period available under state law.[40]

Caution: For the creditor, there is one easy way to avoid all these nightmares. That is: do it right the first time. Make sure you understand what you have to do to perfect your security interest (Real estate? Personal property? What kind of personal property? Which jurisdiction?). This is even more important with the new amendments to Article 9, which will (in some respects) change the way things have been done for many years. Malpractice carriers report that failure to perfect a security interest is a major source of malpractice claims.

§14.22 ~ Statutory Liens

The Bankruptcy Code takes a somewhat unsympathetic view of state-law "statutory liens"—liens created by statute, independent of agreement or judicial process.[41] The Code provides that the trustee may avoid

39. Although the transferee may have a long-shot exception argument under the contemporaneous exchange rule of §547(c)(1).

40. Fidelity Financial Services, Inc. v. Fink, 522 U.S. 211 (1998).

41. Section 101(53) (definition) and §545.

a statutory lien that is an insolvency lien—*i.e.*, a lien triggered by the debtor's insolvency. More specifically, Section 545 provides that the trustee may avoid any lien to the extent that it first becomes effective:

- on the filing of bankruptcy;
- on the filing of a non-bankruptcy insolvency case;
- when a custodian is appointed or authorized to take possession;
- when the debtor becomes insolvent;
- when the debtor's financial condition fails to meet a certain standard; or
- at the time of a levy other than the creditor holding the statutory lien.

You can think of these rules as preserving the integrity of the bankruptcy system—if the state could write insolvency liens, it could effectively trump the priority scheme of the Bankruptcy Code.

A statutory lien is also avoidable if it is not perfected at the commencement of the case against a BFP.[42] This rule brings statutory liens in line with consensual liens under Section 544(a)(3).

Perhaps more surprisingly, the Bankruptcy Code invalidates a lien for rent or distress of rent.[43] This rule parallels the rule that caps the damages for the lessor creditor.[44] Just why lessors should be so disfavored remains unclear.

§14.23 ~ Post-petition Transfers

Consider the case of Dahlia, the debtor in a bankruptcy case, who remains in possession of property of the estate. She undertakes to transfer the property to a third party. She may (or may not) incur liability for making the transfer, but we leave that issue for another time and place; *see, e.g.*, §17.6. The question for the moment is: what becomes of the property "transferred?"

The answer probably lies in §549, which gives the trustee broad power to avoid post-petition transfers. We note two limitations. One, he may not be able to avoid good-faith "gap" transfers in involuntary cases after filing but before the entry of an order for relief. And two, he may not recover from a good faith purchaser for value of real estate, unless the fact of the bankruptcy appeared in the real estate records. The practical teaching of this last rule is: trustee, record any place you think you may own real estate, or risk personal liability on your bond when the real estate is transferred out from under you.

---

42. Section 545(2).

43. Section 545(3), (4).

44. *See, e.g.*, §502(a)(6). Of course, the landlord gets some special protections, too. *See, e.g.*, §365(b)(3).

§14.24 ~ Compare: Premature Setoff Under Section 553

The potential for creditor setoff creates a risk similar to the risk of preferential transfer, but the Code provides a separate rule (in Section 553) and the differences are noteworthy. As discussed in chapter 12 above, Section 553 (together with Section 362(a)(7)) provides that the right of setoff is preserved but stayed. But the Code also provides an avoidance rule designed to prevent the creditor from improving its setoff position within 90 days prior to the filing of bankruptcy.[45]

A creditor needs to think through the effect of this rule before exercising a setoff on the eve of an anticipated bankruptcy. In some cases, the effect of the rule is to make it more worthwhile for the creditor to wait until after the bankruptcy is filed to seek to exercise its setoff, even though it will then have to seek relief from the automatic stay to do so.

§14.25 ~ Reclamation (Section 546)

Consider the case of RetCo, a full-service retailer, hammered by new competition on the internet. For weeks, RetCo has been preparing to file for relief under chapter 11. Meanwhile every day, trucks roll up to the loading dock and unload inventory from vendors who sell on unsecured credit. Up to the moment of filing, they have been getting paid regularly every 30 days (okay, maybe 45, as RetCo careens into a cash crunch). From the moment of filing, the vendors have nothing but an unsecured claim.

Is there any relief for the vendors? There is. They have a limited right to reclamation of the goods (or an equivalent) via the Uniform Commercial Code. They have a somewhat more expansive right to get the goods back if the judge find it is appropriate, on motion of a trustee. We consider each of these in turn.

§14.26 ~ Via the UCC

Start with the seller's reclamation right as defined in UCC. Section 2-702(b) provides, in part:

> When the seller discovers that the buyer has received goods on credit while insolvent, he may reclaim the goods upon demand made within ten days after receipt. . . .

Outside of bankruptcy, this is straightforward enough: if the seller finds the debtor is insolvent, and makes a timely reclamation notice, he gets the goods back. And when or where is the seller most likely to find that the buyer is insolvent? Why when he goes into bankruptcy, of course. The trouble is, the rule seems to run smack into the avoiding powers of the Bankruptcy Code, such as Section 544(a) and 547, discussed above.

The Bankruptcy Code offers some relief for the repossessing transferor. The critical provision is Section 546(c). It provides that the rights of the trustee are subject to:

---

45. *See* §553(a).

> Any statutory or common-law right of the seller of goods that has sold goods to the debtor, in the ordinary course of business, to reclaim such goods if the debtor has received such goods while insolvent.

It is tolerably clear that UCC 2-702 qualifies as such a statute, but note that the rights and requirements under the Bankruptcy Code differ from the UCC. Section 546(c) goes on to say that the seller asserts his claim by making a reclamation "demand in writing." Contrast the UCC, which says "reclaim . . . on demand." The Bankruptcy code specifies "in writing," while the UCC contains no such requirement, and seems to permit an oral reclamation demand (although even outside bankruptcy a prudent vendor would make the demand in writing).

And then there is the matter of timing. Section 546 says the seller may not reclaim unless the demand was made "before 10 days after receipt of the goods by the debtor; or if the 10 days expires after the commencement date, then before 20 days after receipt of the goods by the debtor." So the Bankruptcy Code gives the seller an extra 10-day grace period when bankruptcy intervenes.

But even if the seller jumps through the right hoops, he often does not get the goods back from the debtor. Rather, the Bankruptcy Code says that the court may deny reclamation if the court "grants an administrative priority; or secures the claim by a lien."

Note one further limit. UCC Section 2-702 (b) says that "if misrepresentation of solvency has been made to the particular seller in writing within three months before delivery the ten day limitation does not apply." This would seem to give the seller more leeway in reclamation. The trouble is that nothing protects this "late" reclamation under the Bankruptcy Code. That is: it would seem that unless the reclamation is done within the Section 546(c) period, it is vulnerable to attack under Sections 544(a) or 547.

These rules are stringent on their face, and courts have read them with full stringency. For example, the right doesn't apply unless the debtor still has the goods in its possession at the time of the demand, and it is up to the seller to prove that he did.[46] Another limitation is the prior "dragnet lien," discussed below.

What does the seller get from Section 2-702(b)? In many cases, not very much. The fuse is short enough that many creditors miss it. But a vigilant creditor can obtain a considerable benefit. The right of reclamation can enable the trade creditor to convert an unsecured claim into a secured or administrative priority claim.

§14.27 ~ Court-ordered Reclamation

Aside from UCC Section 2-702, there is another route to reclamation via Bankruptcy Code Section 546(g). That provides that the court may order return of the goods if it finds "that a return is in the best interests of the estate." The court may act only on motion of the trustee or DIP, but return is permitted only "with consent of the creditor." The motion must come within 120 days of the order for relief.

---

46. *In re* Rawson Food Service, Inc., 846 F.2d 1343, 1348-49 (11th Cir. 1988).

§14.28 ~ Reclamation Action

Neither the Code nor the UCC specifically requires that you file a lawsuit to assert the reclamation claim. You need only serve a written notice. But if you make a demand and then do nothing for a long time, a court may hold that you have waived your right. So a vigilant creditor may want to file a complaint (see a sample complaint below), if it does not receive a satisfactory response to its reclamation demand.

In large cases, debtors will often ask the court to implement a universal reclamation procedure, to economize on proceedings governing reclamation claims.

§14.29 ~ Form: Complaint for Reclamation

[Here is a basic form for a reclamation complaint. Note this is an adversary proceeding, so you will need to pay the filing fee and follow the adversary proceeding rules.]

IN THE UNITED STATES BANKRUPTCY COURT
FOR THE EASTERN DISTRICT OF UTOPIA

In Re: INSOLVENT SUPPLY CORPORATION, Debtor	)	Case No. 99-1415-BBL (Chapter 11)
ACE BANJO PICK Plaintiff, v. INSOLVENT SUPPLY CORPORATION Defendant	)	Adversary Proceeding No.____

COMPLAINT FOR RECLAMATION

Ace Banjo Pick hereby files its Complaint for Reclamation against the debtor-in-possession, Insolvent Supply Corporation, and states as follows:

A. Plaintiff is Ace Banjo Pick ("ABP"), a creditor and party in interest in the above-captioned case. ABP conducts its business at 900 Roxbury Road, Paradise City, Utopia 94944.

B. Defendant Insolvent Supply Corporation is a Delaware corporation with offices located at 1497 Erewhon Blvd., Carson City, Utopia 94949. The Defendant filed a chapter 11 petition in the United States Bankruptcy Court for the District of Utopia on November 19, 1999, and has continued to operate its business as a debtor-in-possession since that date. The Defendant's business is the wholesale distribution of banjo picks.

C. This Court has jurisdiction over this adversary proceeding pursuant to 28 U.S.C. §§157 and 1334 and 11 U.S.C. §546(c). This is a core proceeding under 28 U.S.C. §157(b)(2)(A), (E) and (O).

D. During the period from November 12, 1999 through November 17, 1999, ABP, in the ordinary course of its business, sold on credit and delivered to the Defendant certain banjo picks, with an invoice price totaling $510,000.00

E. On the date of delivery of the goods to Defendants, Defendants were insolvent.

F. By letter dated November 20, 1999, ABP made written demand (the "Demand") upon Defendants for the return and reclamation of the said goods. A copy of the Demand, with enclosures, is attached hereto as Exhibit "A" and is incorporated by reference as if set forth fully herein.

G. The Demand was sent by certified mail to Mr. William Melater, Chief Financial Officer for the Defendant, 1497 Erewhon Blvd., Carson City, Utopia 94949.

H. Upon information and belief, Defendants received the Demand.

I. Upon information and belief, the goods were in Defendant's possession when the Demand was received.

J. Defendants have failed and refused to comply with ABP's request for turnover of the goods.

WHEREFORE, ABP requests that this Court grant the following relief:

1. Enter an order directing Defendants to turn over and physically deliver to ABP the goods described in Exhibit "A" hereto;

2. Enter an order providing that, in the event said goods have been disposed of, Defendants be required to turn over to ABP the proceeds from the sale of said goods;

3. In the alternative, grant ABP a superiority administrative claim in the Debtors' bankruptcy cases in the amount of $510,000.00 or a lien in that amount on assets of the Debtor's bankruptcy estate; and

4. Award ABP such other and further relief as the Court deems just and appropriate.

Respectfully submitted,
LAMB, CURRY & RICE, P. C.
/s/______________________________
By: Liddell Beauxpip, Esq. #192837465
Attorney for Plaintiff
1234 Dingley Dell
Suite #56
Shepherdstown UT 10203

§14.30 ~ Form Demand Letter

[See the reclamation complaint in the previous section.]

ACE BANJO PICK, INC.
900 Roxbury Road
Paradise City, Utopia 94944

November 20, 1999

BY FAX AND CERTIFIED MAIL

Mr. William Melater
Chief Financial Officer
Insolvent Supply Corporation
1497 Erewhon Blvd.
Carson City, Utopia 94949

Re: Reclamation Demand

Dear Mr. Melater:

Reference is made to the annexed invoices. Insolvent Supply Corporation received from Ace Banjo Pick, Inc. the goods listed on such invoices. No part of the purchase price for such goods has been paid.

We have been advised that Insolvent Supply Corporation has filed a voluntary petition for relief under chapter 11 of Title 11 of the United States Code on November 19, 1999. Insolvent Supply Corporation was insolvent on the date the shipment of the goods listed on the annexed invoices was received.

In the exercise of our reclamation rights under Section 2-702 of the Uniform Commercial Code and Section 546(c) of the United States Bankruptcy Code, we hereby demand the immediate return of the goods listed on the annexed invoices. Kindly advise us promptly that you will honor this demand and we will arrange to pick up the goods.

We understand that the bankruptcy laws may not allow us to receive the goods immediately, and this letter is not intended to violate any stay imposed by the bankruptcy laws, but merely to assert our rights under the referenced sections of the Uniform Commercial Code and the United States Bankruptcy Code.

Sincerely,
David Ross
Credit Manager

§14.31 ~ Dragnet Lien

We have tried to give an account of how to exercise the right of reclamation against the bankruptcy trustee. But oftentimes, the real enemy of the reclaiming creditor is not the bankruptcy trustee. Rather, it is the prior inventory secured creditor with a "dragnet lien" that applies to any after-acquired property.

A recent illustration is *In re Arlco*.[47] Galey shipped textiles to the debtor on open account. The debtor did not pay on time and Galey demanded reclamation. CIT asserted its rights under prior security interest with an after-acquired property clause. The judge held that CIT's prior security interest trumped Galey's reclamation right. In *Arlco*, it appeared that CIT's claim was large enough to exhaust all the assets. *In re Diversified Food Service Distributors, Inc.*[48] is a case where the prior lien threatened to exhaust part of the value of the property in question. The court held that the prior lender was indeed prior, but it held that the reclaiming seller had the right to the remainder.

---

47. 239 B.R. 261 (Bankr. S.D.N.Y. 1999).

48. 130 B.R. 427 (Bankr. S.D.N.Y. 1991).

§14.32 ~ Form Avoidance Complaint

IN THE UNITED STATES BANKRUPTCY COURT
FOR THE EASTERN DISTRICT OF UTOPIA

In Re: INSOLVENT SUPPLY CORPORATION Debtor	)	Case No. 99-1415-BBL Chapter 7
DONALD L. KOLLEKTBAK, Chapter 7 Trustee, Plaintiff, v. VICTIM, LLP Defendant	)	Adversary Proceeding No.____

COMPLAINT TO RECOVER PREFERENTIAL TRANSFER AND FRAUDULENT CONVEYANCE

COMES NOW Donald L. Kollektbak, chapter 7 Trustee for the estate of Insolvent Supply Corporation, by his counsel, Smith & Jones, and brings this action against Victim, LLP to recover preferential transfers and fraudulent conveyances, alleging as follows:

1. The jurisdiction of this Court is founded upon 28 U.S.C. Section 1334.

2. This adversary proceeding is brought pursuant, *inter alia*, to Rule 7001 of the Federal Rules of Bankruptcy Procedure and Sections 547, 548 and 550 of Title 11 of the U.S. Code.

3. This is a core proceeding within the meaning of 28 U.S.C. Section 157(b)(2)(F).

4. On or about October 22, 1999, Insolvent Supply Corporation (hereinafter the "Debtor") filed a petition in this Court for relief under chapter 11 of Title 11 of the U.S. Code.

5. By an Order entered on or about November 25, 1999, the Debtor's chapter 11 case was converted to a case under chapter 7 of the Bankruptcy Code.

6. Donald L. Kollektbak ("Trustee") is the duly appointed and qualified Trustee for the Debtor's estate.

7. Victim, LLP ("Defendant"), a Utopia limited liability partnership, was a pre-petition lender to the Debtor and, on information and belief, had other pre-petition business dealings with the Debtor.

COUNT I: PREFERENTIAL TRANSFERS

8. The Trustee incorporates each of the foregoing paragraphs of this Complaint and makes the same a part hereof.

9. On or about January 5, 1999, Defendant made an unsecured loan to Debtor in the original principal amount of $40,000 (the "Loan").

10. On or about October 4, 1999, which was within ninety (90) days before the date of the filing of its bankruptcy petition, the Debtor transferred cash in the amount of $15,000, by wire transfer, to the Defendant, as a partial repayment of the Loan (the "Payment").

11. The above referenced Payment was on account of an antecedent debt.

12. The Debtor was insolvent at the time of the Payment.

13. The Payment enabled the Defendant to recover more than the Defendant would receive as a creditor if (a) the bankruptcy case were a case under chapter 7 of Title 11 of the United States Code; (b) the Payment had not been made; and (c) Defendant received payment of its debt to the extent provided for by the provisions of Title 11 of the United States Code.

WHEREFORE, on the foregoing Count I, the Plaintiff, Donald L. Kollektbak, chapter 7 Trustee, respectfully requests that this Court enter judgment against the Defendant for $15,000.00, or in such other amount as may be proven at trial, plus interest thereon, the costs of this action, and for such further relief as this Court may deem just.

COUNT II: FRAUDULENT CONVEYANCES

14. The Trustee incorporates each of the foregoing paragraphs of this Complaint and makes the same a part hereof.

15. On or about March 8, 1999, which was less than one year prior to the date of the Debtor's bankruptcy filing, the Debtor transferred funds in the amount of $10,000 to Defendant by a check numbered 141, drawn on the Debtor's account at Eighth National Bank.

16. The foregoing $10,000 payment was not a payment on the Loan.

17. Upon information and belief, Debtor received no consideration in exchange for the $10,000 payment.

18. Upon information and belief, the Debtor transferred said funds with the intent to hinder, delay or defraud the entities to which it was or became, on or after the date of the transfers, indebted.

19. The Debtor transferred said funds to the Defendant in exchange for less than a reasonably equivalent value and (a) was insolvent on the date of transfer, or said transfer caused it to be insolvent; (b) was engaged in business or a transaction, or was about to engage in business or a transaction, for which any property remaining with the Debtor was an unreasonably small capital; or (c) intended to incur debts that would be beyond the Debtor's ability to pay as such debts matured.

WHEREFORE, on the foregoing Count II, the Plaintiff, Donald L. Kollektbak, chapter 7 Trustee, by counsel, respectfully requests that this Court enter judgment against the Defendant for $10,000, or in such other amount as may be proven at trial, plus interest thereon, the costs of this action, and for such further relief as this Court may deem just.

Respectfully submitted,

SMITH & JONES

By: ________________________________

Nathan Lee Kesef, Esq.
Utopia Bar No. 141711
8381 Recovery Road
Utopia City, Utopia 98899
(646) 814-8114

Attorneys for Donald L. Kollektbak
Chapter 7 Trustee

§14.33 ~ Chart Avoiding Powers

SECTION	WHAT IT COVERS	REACH-BACK
544(a)(1)	(Hypothetical) lien creditor	(None; as of the filing)
544(a)(3)	(Hypothetical) bona fide purchaser (real estate only)	(None; as of the filing)
544(b)	State law fraudulent conveyance and other state law avoidance	State law, but often longer than §548
546(c)	Reclamation	10 days (usually)
545	Statutory liens	(None; as of the filing)
548	Fraudulent transfer • Intent • Insolvency plus less than reasonably equivalent value	One year (*but see* 544(b))
547	Preferences	90 days (insider—one year)
549	Post-petition transfers	After petition date

15

Fraudulent Transfers

15 Fraudulent Transfers

§15.1 ~ Introduction: This Stuff Has a History

This is the second of two chapters on trustees avoiding powers. Here we deal with a number of issues that surround the most ancient avoiding power—the power to avoid fraudulent transfers.

§15.2 ~ What Your Wife's Brother-In-Law said at Thanksgiving

"So you're a bankruptcy lawyer?" your wife's brother-in-law tells you over drinks before Thanksgiving dinner. "I don't worry about bankruptcy. I transferred all my property to my wife's name."

Even the neophyte in the world of bankruptcy law will recognize the folly and potential for disaster in this bald statement. The brother-in-law appears to have carried out the crudest form of fraudulent transfer.[1] It probably won't work: in bankruptcy, we can expect the transfer to be avoided and the property recovered for the bankruptcy estate. But that may be only the beginning. The fraudulent transfer may cause the debtor-transferor to lose his bankruptcy discharge. In extreme cases, the conduct may be a crime. And the problem doesn't end with the debtor-transferor. The lawyer who led him into this mess may face civil or even criminal liability of his own.

Fraudulent transfer law thus lies at the core of our understanding, and misunderstanding, of the bankruptcy process—so pervasive that we find it at many places throughout this manuscript.[2] Here we limit ourselves to outlining the substance of fraudulent transfer law. We try to put it in the context of its history. We also point to some places where the substance of fraudulent transfer law occurs under other names.

§15.3 ~ Background

For fraudulent transfer issues in bankruptcy, we have a full complement—indeed, perhaps a surplus—of fraudulent transfer law. The Bankruptcy Code offers its own substantive law of fraudulent transfer in Section 548.[3] But in many cases, the trustee will deploy Section 544(b) to avail himself of state law. *See generally* §14.14. Necessarily state law will vary from state to state. But some 40 states have adopted

---

1. Salomon v. Kaiser (*In re* Kaiser), 722 F.2d 1574, 1582-83 (2d Cir. 1983); Travelers Indemnity Co. v. Cormaney, 138 N.W.2d 50, 56-57 (Iowa 1965).

2. *See, e.g.*, §2.13, §16.19, §17.6.

3. The text of the UFTA is at http://www.law.upenn.edu/bll/ulc/fnact99/1980s/84.htm. For lists of states adopting particular uniform acts, go to http://www.law.cornell.edu/uniform/vol7.html#frtra.

the Uniform Fraudulent Transfer Act (UFTA) which bears many similarities to (and a few important differences from) Section 548. Some four states retain the old Uniform Fraudulent Conveyance Act (the "UFCA"), a predecessor. The most important of the UFCA holdouts is New York.

Nevertheless, to begin with the current statute law is perhaps misleading. The reason is that fraudulent transfer law has a long and well-documented "pre-statute" history. Indeed no field of statute law (with the possible exception of the Statute of Frauds) is so immured in its caselaw history. Inevitably judges will read the current statutes through the prism of this history. And the history explains why, even in jurisdictions with no more than rudimentary fraudulent transfer law, we may nonetheless find a developed law of fraudulent transfer.

§15.4 ~ Two Kinds of Fraudulent Transfer

Against this background, we turn to the prima facie case.[4] The first thing to note is that the statute provides for the avoidance of *two* kinds of fraudulent transfer. Call them "intentional" transfers and "equivalent value" transfer. We summarize.

§15.5 ~ The Classification

- First, "intentional" transfers, as defined in Section 548(a)(A): "Made . . . with actual intent to hinder, delay or defraud. . . ."

- Second, "equivalent value" transfers, as defined in Section 548(a)(B):

> Received less than a reasonably equivalent value in exchange for such transfer or obligation; and
>
> > was insolvent at the time, or became insolvent as a result, of the transfer;
> >
> > or was engaged (or was about to engage) in a business or transaction, for which any property remaining was an unreasonably small capital;
> >
> > or intended to incur, or believed she would incur, debts beyond her ability to pay as they matured.

§15.6 ~ Why it Matters

Just the briefest glance will suggest that there must be ways in which these categories blur into each other. For example, making a transfer by gift surely qualifies as making a transfer for "less than a reasonably equivalent value." Yet the fact that the transfer was by gift may also serve to give evidence of intent to hinder, delay or defraud. Indeed, we would speculate that most intentional fraudulent transfers are also transfers for less than a reasonably equivalent value.

---

4. For convenience, we give primary attention to §548.

But difficult as it may be to distinguish in some cases, we think it is important to get it right. One, it affects the *prima facie* case. We can easily imagine a case where the trustee could prove less than a reasonably equivalent value, but might not be able to prove intent.[5] We can also imagine, if a bit less easily, where the trustee could not meet the standard of proof on value but could prove intent.[6]

The solution is perhaps obvious: if you can do so within the bounds of good faith, plead both, and hope that the evidence will support judgment on at least one count. Of course, only one recovery is permitted.

Of even greater practical importance, the difference between "intent" transfers and "equivalent value" transfers is critical to other aspects of fraudulent transfer law. Denying a discharge requires a showing of intent to hinder, delay or defraud, for example.[7] Intent is also critical to the bankruptcy crime.[8] In short, about the worst that can happen to an equivalent-value transfer is that it will be avoided. But the intent transfers bring a lot more grief in tow.

Finally, the issue may be important as affecting a limitation on the trustee's recovery. *See* limitation on remedy, below.

§15.7 ~ Transfer

We speak of transfers in fraud of creditors. But the definition of transfer in Section 101(54) is not intuitively obvious. For example, the definition includes "removal or concealment" of property—which may be enough to justify those cases where the debtor transfers money from one pocket to the other, in the hope of taking advantage of an exemption. *See* §15.25. It may also explain a case like *In re Bernard*,[9] where the court held that withdrawal of funds from a bank account for purposes of preventing attachment counts as a fraudulent transfer.

§15.8 ~ Actual Fraud

Section 548(a)(1) denounces transactions done with "actual intent" to hinder, delay or defraud. But there is a difficulty here: How do you define "actual" intent? As a practical matter seldom—and as a matter of strict metaphysics, perhaps never—do we know the mind of another sufficient to know his "actual" intent, as distinct from (we assume) his intent presumed at law.

So the fact is that (virtually) always and in (virtually) every case, we are working with external indicia from which we infer state of mind. It is for this reason that the law has developed what have come to be called "badges of fraud"—indicia that may be used of evidence of the internal state. The drafters of the UFTA went so far as to include a non-exclusive catalog of badges in Section 4(b) of its text. They are:

---

5. This is probably the posture of most of the LBO cases, discussed below at §15.18ff.

6. Many jurisdictions set a higher standard of proof (for example, clear and convincing rather than mere preponderance of the evidence) for intent cases. *See, e.g.*, United States v. Gleneagles Inv. Co., 565 F.Supp. 556, 580 (M.D. Pa. 1983).

7. *In re* Goldschein, 241 B.R. 370 (Bankr. D. Md. 1999).

8. *Id.*

9. 96 F.3d 1279 (9th Cir. 1996).

- the transfer or obligation was to an insider;
- the debtor retained possession or control of the property transferred after the transfer;
- the transfer or obligation was disclosed or concealed;
- before the transfer was made or obligation was incurred, the debtor had been sued or threatened with suit;
- the transfer was of substantially all the debtors' assets;
- the debtor absconded;
- the debtor removed or concealed assets;
- the value of the consideration received by the debtor was reasonably equivalent to the value of the asset transferred or the amount of the obligation incurred;
- the debtor was insolvent or became insolvent shortly after the transfer was made or the obligation was incurred;
- transfer occurred shortly before or shortly after a substantial debt was incurred; and
- the debtor transferred the essential assets of the business to a lienor who transferred the assets to an insider of the debtor.

The statute says that consideration "may be given" to these "among other factors." The official commentary elaborates that the list

> is a nonexclusive catalogue of factors appropriate for consideration by the court in determining whether the debtor had an actual intent to hinder, delay, or defraud one or more creditors. Proof of the existence of any one or more of the factors enumerated in subsection (b) may be relevant evidence as to the debtor's actual intent but does not create a presumption that the debtor has made a fraudulent transfer or incurred a fraudulent obligation.

The commentary also sets forth a representative sampling of the supporting case law. There is no comparable list in the Bankruptcy Code or the UFCA. But insofar as the list is a crystallization of the case-law tradition, and insofar as the Bankruptcy Code crystallizes the same tradition, this kind of case law would seem as relevant in bankruptcy as otherwise.[10]

---

10. *See* Dionne v. Keating (*In re* XYZ Options, Inc.), 154 F.3d 1262 (11th Cir. 1998) (badges of fraud the same under Alabama, Arizona or bankruptcy law); Max Sugarman Funeral Home Inc. v. A.D.B. Investors, 926 F.2d 1248, 1254 (1st Cir. 1991).

§15.9 ~ Two Classic Frauds

This isn't a treatise on fraud in general, but there are two frauds so common in bankruptcy practice that they deserve special mention.

One is the Ponzi Scheme named after its master practitioner, Charles Ponzi, who fleeced a whole community of small savers around Boston just after World War I. Here is a Ponzi Scheme: I promise to double your money in a week. Two people "invest" one dollar and then, a day later, two more. I pay $2 each to the first two, using their own money, plus the money invested by the next two. I am broke again, of course. But then the word gets around and the next thing you know, there is a line of eager investors waiting for the chance to throw their money at me. I pay each new wave from funds contributed by the next wave.

A moment's math will suggest that it can't last very long: an amazing number of Ponzi schemes emerge, only to collapse in ruins. But if you are sufficiently deft about siphoning off some of the inflow (and sufficiently willing to commit grand theft), we suppose you can funnel some of the proceeds into your secret bank account.

Ponzi schemes probably existed long before Ponzi, and surely have survived him. After the collapse of the Soviet Union, Russia and the former Soviet republics found themselves afflicted with investor frauds that were no more than Ponzi schemes. Under one name or another, Ponzi schemes continue to flourish in bankruptcy law.[11]

The other classic fraud is the "bust-out." You know how the bust-out works if you watched Episode #23 of the second season of "The Sopranos" on HBO. That's the one where Davey Scateno, sporting goods merchandiser and compulsive gambler, finds himself caught in the clutches of the mob goons who force him to use his carefully honed vendor credit to charge up everything you can imagine and then collapse into bankruptcy after the bad guys skim off all of the swag.

This is the kind of misconduct that may lose the individual debtor his discharge, or at least make him vulnerable to an exception for discharge. But the deal was a scam from the start, so presumably the perpetrators intend to put themselves beyond the reach of the law.

§15.10 ~ Reasonable Value

The trustee who seeks to avoid a fraudulent transfer on "reasonably equivalent value" grounds is relieved of the need of proving actual intent. But he must prove "less than a reasonably equivalent value" and one of the three other predicates set forth in §15.5 above.

§15.11 ~ Solvency

Of the three predicates, perhaps the toughest recurrent issue is the matter of proving insolvency. As elsewhere in the Code, insolvency means "balance sheet" insolvency—liabilities exceeding assets.[12] Note that in counting assets we exclude exempt property and also include property that has been the

---

11. *See, e.g.*, *In re* The Bennett Funding Group, 220 B.R. 742 (Bankr. N.D.N.Y. 1997).

12. Section 101(32). The statute says debts . . . greater than . . . property, but it amounts to the same thing.

subject of intentional fraudulent transfer. So, suppose the debtor has assets of $100 and liabilities of $80, but that of the $100, the debtor transferred $45 worth, with the intent to hinder, delay or defraud. For purposes of testing solvency, the assets are $100 minus $45 or $55. So we have: assets, $55, liabilities, $80, for a net worth of negative $25 and the debtor is insolvent.

Proving insolvency can be a formidable hurdle, particularly in the case of transferor who is trying to hinder, delay or defraud. The UFTA specifies that the plaintiff/creditor has the benefit of an evidentiary presumption of insolvency if he can show that the debtor is generally not paying his debts as they come due.[13] There is a similar presumption in the Bankruptcy Code for preference cases, but not for cases of fraudulent transfer.[14] We would predict that the judge will generally be willing to accord the same sort of presumption anyway.

§15.12 ~ Contingent Claims

Proving insolvency becomes even more complicated when, as is common, some of the debtor's liabilities (or even his assets) are contingent. Contingent liabilities might include, for example, liability on a guarantee, an indemnification obligation, or a prospective product liability claim. Properly, the value of the liability (or asset, as the case may be) is not the face value, but the face value multiplied by the probability that the contingency will occur. So if the debtor is the guarantor on a $100 note, and there is a 20 percent chance that he will have to pay on his guarantee, then the value is $100 x. 0.2 = $20.[15]

§15.13 ~ Unreasonably Small Capital, Intent to Incur Debts

Somewhat more puzzling are the remaining two classes of cases under 548(b)(2)(B). These are the ones in which the debtor is not "balance sheet" insolvent but where the debtor either was engaged (or about to engage) in a business or a transaction, for which any property remaining with the debtor was an unreasonably small capital,[16] or intended to incur, or believed that it would incur, debts that would be beyond its ability to pay as they matured.[17]

There are few reported cases decided under either of these criteria where the other criteria are not also present.[18] But one case that does appear to rely on the "unreasonably small capital" rule is *O'Donnell v. Royal Business Group, Inc.*[19] The court said that the debtor " may not have been insolvent in the balance sheet sense." But it found that the debtor's "cash flow was strained to the breaking point" by the transaction. It found that the debtor "was plainly unable to pay its obligations as they came due." This established,

---

13. *See* UFTA §2(b). The language parallels language in the involuntary provision of the Bankruptcy Code, §303(h)(1); and in the Uniform Commercial Code, UCC §1-201(23).

14. *See* §547(f).

15. For a good discussion, *see* Covey v. Commercial National Bank of Peoria, 960 F.2d 657 (7th Cir. 1992).

16. Section 548(a)(B)(ii)(II).

17. Section 548(a)(B)(ii)(III).

18. *See, e.g.*, In the Matter of Christian and Porter Aluminum Co. 316 F. Supp. 1340, 1342 (N.D. Ca. 1970) (finding both unreasonably small capital and intent to incur debts beyond capacity to repay).

19. *In re* Oxford Homes, Inc., 160 B.R. 1 (Bankr. D. Maine 1995).

the court concluded "a reasonable likelihood of demonstrating that [the debtor] had unreasonably small capital and was equitably insolvent at the time of the [transaction]."[20]

The matter of "unreasonably small capital" presents the extra complication that it seems to fold into the non-bankruptcy law of "thin capitalization," which may become relevant to bankruptcy via Section 510.[21] *See* §13.47.

§15.14 ~ Charitable Contributions

A remarkable recent addition to Section 548 insulates an important class of religious and charitable contributions from attack as fraudulent transfers. The language is in Section 548(a)(2), added in 1994. It provides that a transfer to a religious or charitable contribution is insulated from "value" attack if

- the contribution is less than 15 percent of the debtor's gross annual income; or (if higher)
- the transfer was consistent with the practice of the debtor in making charitable contributions"[22]

The provision is part of a package of amendments designed to insulate religious and charitable contributions from bankruptcy attack.[23] Debtors may get further protection (with limits still undefined) from the Religious Freedom Restoration Act of 1993.[24] Charitable contributions that exceed these limitations may be vulnerable to attack as fraudulent transfers. And if "intentional fraud" can be proven, any charitable contribution is subject to avoidance.

§15.15 ~ Value

Section 548 bears its own definition of value. It says that "'value' means property, or satisfaction or securing of a present or antecedent debt of the debtor."[25] So paying a debt, counts as value, insulating the payment at least from the "reasonable value" prong of Section 548. Of course, the payment of a debt may, on appropriate facts, qualify as a voidable preference. *See* §14.13 ff. An interesting case on which your authors know of no controlling (modern) authority, goes like this:

---

20. *Id.* at 16. Oxford Homes was a leveraged buyout ("LBO") case. *See generally* §15.18. *Cf.* Lackawanna Pants Mfg. Co. v. Wiseman, 33 F.2d 482, 485 (6th Cir. 1943) (transferor not left with unreasonably small capital because he had no capital to begin with).

21. *See, e.g., In re* Vadnais Lumber Supply, Inc., 100 B.R. 127, 137-38 (Bankr. D. Mass. 1989).

22. Definitions of charitable contribution and qualified religious or charitable entity or organization are taken from the Internal Revenue Code; *see* §548(d)(3).

23. *Cf.* §§707(b), 544(b) and 1325(b)(2)(A) as amended by the Religious Liberty and Charitable Donations Protection Act of 1998, Pub. L. No. 105-183, 112 Stat. 517 (1998).

24. 42 U.S.C. §2000bb (1993). In City of Boerne v. Flores, 521 U.S. 507 (1997), the Supreme Court held the act unconstitutional as applied to state conduct. But bankruptcy is federal, not state law, and so the act may remain constitutional as a limitation on bankruptcy law. *Cf.* Christians v. Crystal Evangelical Free Church (*In re* Young), 141 F.3d 854 (8th Cir. 1998).

25. Section 548(d)(2)(A).

Debtor owes $10 each to Alfa, Betty and Marshall. He has $10. He pays the $10 to Betty saying: "I hereby discharge my debt to you. And I must say it gives me great pleasure not only to pay you, but also to hinder and delay those other two."

Fairly clearly, the transaction qualifies as a voidable preference. The question arises whether facts that make out a prima facie case of preference may also qualify as an (intentional) fraudulent transfer. The issue is important, because there is nothing intrinsically evil about giving or taking a preference; it may simply be avoided. But as we have seen, from an intentional fraudulent transfer, all sorts of nightmarish consequences can ensue. On the one hand, we see no reason in principle why a preference may not, in the right case, also count as an intentional fraudulent transfer. On the other hand, we know of no modern case that says so.

The definition also says that 'value' … does not include of unperformed promise to furnish support to the debtor or to a relative of the debtor. We can imagine the cases where the sheriff is on his way to auction the transferor's farm. Transferor deeds it to his daughter in exchange for a promise of lifetime support. Presumably this promise would count as consideration for a simple contract; evidently otherwise for fraudulent transfer law.

It may help to compare the Code's fraudulent transfer definition of value with the more familiar definition from first-year contract law. A little reflection will show that the Code definition is *broader* in that it includes payment of an antecedent debt. But it is narrower insofar as it excludes a promise to render services in the future.

§15.16 ~ Limitation on Remedy—Value

Based on what we have said so far, Section 548 would seem a threat to the interests of innocent transferees. But it is not so extensive. Section 548(c) provides that "a transferee . . . that takes for value and in good faith has a lien or may retain any interest transferred . . . to the extent that such transferee … gave value to the debtor in exchange for such transfer."[26]

Section 551 adds its own language protecting transferees and also protects transferees of transferees. It provides that the trustee may not recover from

> "a transferee that takes for value, including satisfaction or securing of a present or antecedent debt, in good faith, and without knowledge of the voidability of the transfer avoided."

The same section provides a safe harbor for any "good faith transferee" of a transferee who passes the test set forth above.

---

26. Torcise v. Community Bank of Homestead (*In re* Torcise), 116 F.3d 860, 867-68 (11th Cir. 1997) (jury instructions in §548(c) case).

§15.17 ~ Timing (and Dating)

The power to avoid under Section 548 applies only to transfers made within one year before the filing of the petition.[27] State statutes are significantly longer, which may give the trustee the appropriate incentive to bypass Section 548 and try to bring his action via Section 544(b).

There may be an issue in some cases as to when the transfer is "made." Section 548(d) provides that the transfer is not made as long as it can be trumped by a bona fide purchaser. The scope of the provision is unclear. On the one hand, BFP rules typically arise only in real estate cases. On the other hand, consider the case where the transferor and transferee deliberately agree to strive to conceal the transfer. It seems likely that a court, even without the assistance of a specific mandate, might find that the transfer is not "made" until someone had a reasonable chance to find out about it.

§15.18 ~ LBOs

Back in the late 80s, we went through a gale of corporate restructuring that changed the face of American capitalism. One tool was the leveraged buyout (LBO), where an acquirer purchases a corporation by borrowing money (leverage) and pledging the assets of the target corporation as security. The understanding is that buyer will pay off the loan with earnings from the acquired corporation. Sometimes the deals worked as planned; sometimes they did not. When they did not, it was time to call in the bankruptcy lawyers.

We want to consider the position of the old creditors—those who loaned money to the pre-buyout target. When the curtain rises, they hold claims against OldCo, the pre-buyout debtor. At the end of the second act, they find themselves confronting the wreckage of a failed deal—their obligor is unable to pay their claims and all of its assets are pledged to secure the acquisition financing. The question arises—do they have any claim against anyone who thrust them into this misfortune? More precisely, is there way to characterize the whole transaction as a voidable fraudulent transfer?

The answer is: Maybe, but it's a tough case to prove. Taken as a whole, creditors probably lose these cases more often than they win, unless there is strong evidence of outright corporate looting. But the fraudulent transfer argument is not frivolous. As a minimum, we suspect it has some settlement value.[28]

What sort of theory supports these cases? Usually, it is a version of "constructive fraud." The target granted a lien on its assets, in exchange for no value; all of the "value" went to the target's shareholders. As a result, the corporation was rendered insolvent or left with unreasonably small capital. When it falls apart, the old creditors of the target end up empty-handed. The bank that provided the acquisition financing forecloses on the assets, after the old shareholders have walked off with their pockets full of money.[29] Sometimes there is also an allegation of actual fraud, but it is harder to prove.

---

27. Contrast: the statute of limitations governing the time after filing during which the trustee may bring a cause of action belonging to the debtor at the time of filing—normally two years. *See* §546(a)(1)(A); *cf.* §108(a).

28. For a good summary of the case law, *see* Sally S. Neely, *Leveraged Buyouts: Fraudulent Conveyances or What*, 804 PLI/CO 321 (PLI 1993).

29. *Cf.* O'Donnell v. Royal Business Group, Inc. (*In re* Oxford Homes, Inc.), 180 B.R. 1, 16 (Bankr. D. Maine 1995) ("a fundamental feature of leveraged buyouts is that equity is exchanged for debt").

Of course, there are defenses to the theory. Among them, it is often possible to put together a case showing significant value to the target as a result of the transaction. The defendants may also be able to make a credible solvency case. An example may help.

§15.19 ~ LBOs: An Example

Harold and Wilma spent 30 years building up AceCo, a manufacturer and seller of defenestrators. Using tried-and-true business methods, AceCo was able to generate earnings of some $9 million per year—fairly low by industry standards, but enough to satisfy the demands of Harold and Wilma and the other stockholders—all family members and most on the company payroll. Here is a balance sheet:

AceCo
Balance Sheet (Original)
(In Millions)

Assets		Liabilities & NW	
Cash	$5	Banks	$35
Acc'ts Rev	$10	Suppliers	$30
Inventory	$12	Total	$65
Plant	$30		
Equipment	$33	Net Worth	$25
Trans Fees	$5	Net Worth	$10
Total Assets	$90	Total L & NW	$90

One day Harold was in his office pouring over the accounts when he heard a loud varooming outside the front door. It was the sound of a perfectly restored 1969 Porsche. Out of it stepped a man in a $2,000 suit wearing a Rolex the size of a grapefruit. He introduced himself to Harold as Lance, an entrepreneur. Lance told Harold that he felt the assets of AceCo were substantially underperforming, and that he and his "group" wanted to take over the company so they could put their ideas to work. He said he was willing to pay AceCo shareholders $70 million for their stock—nearly three times what Harold believed to be its realistic value.

Harold couldn't believe his ears. Faced with the chance for unheard-of cash, Harold quickly persuaded other stockholders to join in tendering their shares to Lance. Lance promptly produced the money and the deal was closed. Harold and the other shareholders all moved to a new gated community outside Palm Desert.

Harold was only vaguely aware of how Lance intended to pay for AceCo, to say nothing of his plans for operation. Had Harold inquired, he would have learned the following particulars. Lance was backed by VentureCo, a large lender. Lance and VentureCo agreed that AceCo's assets were substantially undervalued. On that basis, VentureCo agreed to lend AceCo the sum of $125 million.

The funds were distributed as follows: $70 million went to pay off existing shareholders. $20 million went to pay off existing bank debt. Another $5 million of VentureCo loan proceeds went to cover transaction fees—legal fees, investment banking fees and the like. The remainder went into the operation of the business. The existing $30 million in supplier loans were left in place (but could be expected to turn over fairly quickly in the ordinary course of business). Also left in place was $15 million in the old bank debt, representing unsecured long-term notes not due for another five years.

In exchange for its loan, VentureCo got a security interest in all company assets. None of the other creditors had any security. The balance sheet of the reorganized company looked like this:

AceCo
Balance Sheet (After Buyout)
(In Millions)

Assets		Liabilities & NW	
Cash	$5	VentureCo	$125
Acc'ts Rev	$10	Old Unsec Bank	$15
Inventory	$30	Suppliers	$30
Plant	$70	Total	$170
Equipment	$60		
Trans Fees	$5	Net Worth	$10
Total Assets	$180	Total L & NW	$180

The reorganized company did, in fact, pay off its old debts to suppliers in a matter of months, replacing them with new obligations, mostly to the same suppliers. Meanwhile, it did institute some important economies. Most notably, it persuaded its employees to accept a 20 percent, across-the-board wage cut, convincing them that without it, the company would fold and they would lose their jobs altogether.

But it quickly became apparent that Lance's hopes for the company were extravagant, and that it could not make anything like the money he had hoped it to make. Last month Lance informed creditors that an independent appraisal showed the assets to be worth no more than $150 million as a going concern, $125 million in liquidation. VentureCo remains unpaid, as does the old bank debt. Meanwhile suppliers' claims have burgeoned to $60 million.

Lance has proposed an out-of-court plan of reorganization with the following terms: VentureCo's loan will be reaffirmed in full. Unsecured claims (including the $60 million in suppliers' claims and the $15 million in old bank debt) will be given new claims totaling $15 million, or 25 cents on the dollar, for their old claims. Lance and his associates will remain the owners of the re-reorganized company.

VentureCo has agreed to this plan. Lance has been soliciting the consent of unsecured claimants, and it appears that more than half have consented. Others, including the holders of the old bank debt, object. Lance has indicated that if he gets sufficient consents, he will take the company into a "prepackaged" Chapter 11. The balance sheet of the re-reorganized company would look like this:

AceCo
Balance Sheet (Reorganized)
(In Millions)

Assets		Liabilities & NW	
Cash	$5	VentureCo	$125
Acc'ts Rev	$10	"Old" Debt	$15
Inventory	$20	Total	$140
Plant	$60		
Equipment	$50	Net Worth	$10
Trans Fees	$5		
Total Assets	$150	Total L & NW	$150

§15.20 ~ LBOs: What Can We Make of It?

Think of this as a law school exam. The last paragraph says you represent a dissenting, unpaid, pre-LBO creditor. Do you have a cause of action against anyone to avoid a fraudulent transfer? The analysis should include whether there was actual intent to hinder, delay, or defraud creditors; whether the target was insolvent, rendered insolvent or left with unreasonably small capital; whether the target received reasonably equivalent value in exchange for pledging its assets to the LBO lender; whether the defendants (often, the old shareholders or the lenders) have defenses under 548(c) or 551; and what is the (practical) remedy if the plaintiff prevails.

The two best-known cases on the topic go in opposite directions, but a comparison helps you to see what is at stake in the issue. In *United States v. Tabor Court Realty*,[30] the Third Circuit upheld a trustee's fraudulent transfer action against an LBO. Three years later in *Kupetz v. Wolf & Vine*,[31] the Ninth Circuit went the other way.

But in *Tabor*, the court found intentional fraud—an elaborate device to spirit the assets out of the reach of creditors. The shareholders themselves appear to have been active participants, if not initiators. Wolf and his wife were much more appealing defendants. There is not the slightest evidence that they gave any thought to looting the corporation; Mr. Wolf just wanted to retire.[32] Clearly, the court was not eager to upset the expectations of a seller who was just trying to get on with his life.

Remarkably, both the Third and Ninth Circuits have both since backed away from their earlier positions. In *Lippi v. City Bank*,[33] faced with a defendant who perhaps not as sympathetic as the Wolfs, the Ninth Circuit allowed the fraudulent transfer action to continue. More recently in *Lowenschuss v. Resort International, Inc.*,[34] the Third Circuit rejected an action against a shareholder.

The circumstances of *Lowenschuss* are important. The court's decision was based upon its conclusion that the payment received by the shareholder was a "settlement payment" which, under Section 546(e), is exempt from the application of the constructive fraud provisions of Section 548 (as well as certain other avoidance provisions). The court determined that the securities "settlement payment" exception applied because the cash that was paid to the shareholder was funnelled through two financial institutions; if the cash had been paid directly to the shareholder, the literal terms of Section 546(e) would not have applied. Whatever one thinks about the Third Circuit's decision, it will have the effect of limiting substantially the ability to recover LBO payments under a fraudulent conveyance theory, at least in that circuit, since it is common for payments to shareholders as part of an LBO transaction to run through a "financial institution."

§15.21 ~ Present and Future

One important difference between the Bankruptcy Code and the UFTA concerns the class of creditors protected. Specifically, the UFTA distinguishes two classes of cases:

---

30. 803 F.2d 1288 (1986).

31. 845 F.2d 842 (1988).

32. We are told that Wolf and his wife sat in the front row of the public area during the argument in the Ninth Circuit, and that Wolf wore a cardigan sweater.

33. 955 F.2d 599 (1992).

34. *In re* Resorts International, Inc., 181 F.3d 505 (1999).

- Present and future—cases that can be brought by a creditor whose "claim arose before or after the transfer;" and

- Present only—those that can be brought only by one who was a creditor at the time of the transfer.

Present only cases are those where the prima facie case involves less than a reasonably equivalent value and insolvency. All other cases are present and future cases. There is no such distinction in the Section 548.

§15.22 ~ Comparison: Bulk Sales Law

Earlier, we explained the rudiments of the bulk sales provision of the Uniform Commercial Code. *See* §6.30. We outlined the classic bulk sales case: the merchant who turns his inventory into cash, with the intention of skipping town. We remarked that the bulk sales problem could turn into a real nightmare in bankruptcy. Now is the time to explain this problem.

For starters, note that the classic bulk transfer bears at least a family resemblance to a fraudulent transfer. At least as we have set forth the facts, it rather smells of a transfer with the intent to hinder, delay or defraud. On the other hand, although we may suspect the intent of the transferor in a bulk transfer, there is no requirement that the objecting creditor show actual intent to hinder, delay or defraud.

Another curiosity about bulk sale is the matter of the location of the property. In the typical bulk sale, the difficulty is that the debtor/transferor no longer has possession of the inventory—rather, the traded it for far more pocketable money.

A novelty of the bulk sale statute is that it protects creditors without adjective—including vendors and other unsecured creditors who do not have the protection of security agreements. A statute of this sort might have made good sense in an era when the law of security interests was incomplete or impenetrable or just the exception. It is perhaps harder to justify in an era when just about anyone can effect a security interest, for the price of a little boilerplate, so long as the debtor agrees.

Aside from its historical curiosity, perhaps the most important fact about the bulk sale is its relationship to *Moore v. Bay* and the specter of Section 544(b). We saw above how *Moore v. Bay* empowers the trustee to step into the "overshoes" of a $10 creditor and set aside a million-dollar transaction. *See* §14.11. We made the point that there aren't many *Moore v. Bay* cases around any more, in part because the trustee cannot invoke it unless he finds a real unsecured creditor with a non-bankruptcy avoidance powers. Unsecured creditors don't usually have avoidance powers—but one place where they get them is in the bulk sale law.

The problem is aggravated by the fact that one of the most notorious of all *Moore v. Bay* cases arose in the context of the bulk sale law. The case is *Verco Industries v. Spartan Plastics*.[35] Verco sold some personal property to Spartan and received, inter alia, a promissory note for part of the purchase price.

---

35. Actually, under a California variant, even more arcane and slippery than the original.

Before delivering the property to Spartan, Verco filed for relief under chapter 11. By way of avoiding a bulk sale, DIP Verco sued Spartan on its promissory note. The bankruptcy judge rejected the suit, holding that Spartan was relieved of its obligation since Verco still had the property. The appellate panel reversed, and the Circuit upheld the appellate panel, giving DIP Verco the right to sue on a promissory note for goods it had not yet delivered and still possessed.

With respect to the learned court, we think *Verco* gets just about everything backwards. Typically it is the transferee who has the goods, after the transferor gets (and vanishes with?) the money. Here, Verco still the goods in possession. Indeed, the court seemed to regard this as a kind of transfer plus retention of possession which, as we have seen, is often voidable as a fraudulent transfer. But in the typical fraudulent transfer case, the hitherto unsuspected transferee is appearing out of nowhere to lay claim to goods that the creditors thought would be theirs. Here, the creditors in effect have the goods, and are trying to get the money as well.

Under the circumstances, we have some sympathy with transactional lawyers who want to defang bulk transfer. If Verco is the law, then *Moore v Bay* is as strange as they say it is.[36] So we are not surprised that the "drafters" of U.C.C. Article 6, unable to win outright repeal, have sought at least to limit its effect. Specifically, the "remedies" provisions do all that they can to avoid the language of "fraud" or "avoidance," and to make it clear that aggrieved creditors are restricted to "actual" damages.[37] We are not aware of any case where a creditor has run into a Moore v. Bay problem under the revised Article 6, but the threat seems sufficiently large to cause concern.

§15.23 ~ Dividend Statutes

Consider the case of LittleCo, a struggling small public company that owes $1 million to creditors and has assets worth perhaps $800,000. The directors of LittleCo, reconciled to the notion that things are going from bad to worse, resolve that they will get as much money to shareholders as possible. They therefore vote a "special dividend" of $100,000. The effect of the dividend will, of course, be to reduce the size of the asset pool to $700,000, while keeping the liabilities unchanged.

Has LittleCo made a fraudulent transfer? Almost certainly. From the recital, it appears that the directors intended to hinder, delay or defraud creditors. LittleCo also made a payment for which it received less than a reasonably equivalent value while it was insolvent. But they have also very likely violated yet another set of rules as well. Just about every state has a dividend control statute that restricts the payment of dividends by a corporation that is insolvent or on the edge of insolvency.

Perhaps the commonest form of dividend control statute is the version in the Revised Model Business Corporation Act, which is the law of about half the states. Under the Act, a board of directors may authorize distributions to its shareholders unless either:

---

36. Your authors are informed that the bulk transfer defect in Verco was as follows: the statute required the buyer to publish a notice of bulk transfer in a legal newspaper for the Municipal Court for the *Central* district of Orange County. Instead, it filed in a paper for the *Western* district. It is hard to imagine any angel dancing on a smaller pinhead.

37. UCC §6-107.

(i) the corporation would not be able to pay its debts as they become due in the usual course of business; or

(ii) the corporation's total assets would be less than the sum of its total liabilities in a dissolution.[38]

The statute clearly echos traditional fraudulent transfer statutes. It is perhaps an interesting question why these dividend statutes exist more or less side by side with the fraudulent transfer statutes, yet independent of them and in another part of the Code. The reasons are perhaps cultural: traditional corporate lawyers don't think of themselves as doing bankruptcy law and tend to look for their own rules in their own Codes. So some overlap is perhaps inevitable.

There are some noteworthy differences, however. Perhaps most important, the typical dividend statute provides a remedy not just against the corporation but also against the directors. This probably helps in two ways. One, the remedy against the directors may be easier to pursue than any remedy against the disparate and scattered shareholders. And two, the threat of personal liability may help to keep the directors on their toes in the first place.

§15.24 ~ Fraudulent Transfer and "Asset Protection"

We turn now to a number of tactics on the fringe between asset protection (or perhaps debtor protection) and outright fraud. This material could as well go in any of several other chapters. They could have been dealt with as matters of property of the estate or exemptions, or discharge. Insofar as most of these involve the active participation of the attorney, they could well have gone in a chapter on professional conduct. We include them here because the most frequent challenge on these devices is under the law of fraudulent transfer.

§15.25 ~ Exemption Planning

A particular headache in the run-up to bankruptcy is the matter of "exemption planning." Start with a simple example. In California, it used to be the law that the debtor could have an exemption of $1,000 for an account in a savings and loan association, but not in a bank. No one doubted that it was good lawyering to tell the client to get his last dollars out of the bank and to redeposit them in a savings and loan, so as to make sure he got full protection from the exemption. Indeed arguably (although we know of no case on point), failure to do so would have been malpractice.

No one, in short, found the simple account-switch to be "abusive." But what of the lawyer who makes a specialty of (say) turning all the debtor's liquid assets into cash and shipping them to Texas or Florida, with instructions to invest everything in a jurisdiction famous for its liberal exemption laws protecting real estate?

---

38. RMBCA §6.40(c).

One's first thought might be that this bit of exemption planning is a fraudulent transfer. It isn't really. No one is trying to get the money back from the third party seller of real estate (who, in any event, appears to have given fair consideration). Indeed, in the strict sense there wasn't any transfer at all—just the transmutation from the (nonexempt) lefthand pocket of the overalls to the (exempt) right-hand pocket.

Fans of the device like to invoke the explicit endorsement in the legislative history of the Bankruptcy Code. Both the House and Senate Reports on the 1978 Code say:

> As under current law, the debtor will be permitted to convert nonexempt property into exempt property before filing a bankruptcy petition. The practice is not fraudulent as to creditors, and permits the debtor to make full use of the exemptions to which he is entitled under the law.[39]

But this is one piece of legislative history the courts have not embraced unthinkingly. Rather, they have plowed into a muddle of seeming inconsistency, perhaps illustrated by the Minnesota twins, a notorious pair of exemption cases, decided the same day by the Eighth Circuit.

In *Norwest Bank Nebraska v. Tveten*,[40] the first of these cases, the debtor Tveten, a 59-year-old Minnesota physician with no dependents, owed creditors almost $19,000,000, mostly in the form of personal guaranties on a number of investments. Several creditors sued him. One got a judgment for $140,000. Tveten had property worth $700,000. Minnesota law provided an exemption for funds in life or annuity contracts issued by fraternal benefit societies.

After talking to a lawyer, Tveten undertook to turn a number of hard assets into cash. For example, he sold land to his brother and his parents (at its market value). He sold his home. He liquidated his life insurance and his retirement accounts. He put all the money into fraternal benefit policies, and filed for bankruptcy. For this behavior, a creditor objected to his discharge. The bankruptcy court denied the discharge. The district and the circuit court (2-1) affirmed.

In *Hanson v. First National Bank*[41] (the other "twin") decided the same day, the Circuit had to consider the case of the Hansons, South Dakota farmers. Facing financial trouble, the Hansons liquidated some of their property (but, unlike Tveten, not all). They put the proceeds into state qualified-exemptions. Then they filed for bankruptcy.

The bank objected to the exemption claim (*sic*—not the discharge). The bank asserted that none of the property was ever transferred to the buyers. The Hansons acknowledged that the vehicles were stored at their home; they said that the son was living with them while finishing school. They admitted they occasionally used the vehicles, they did so only with the express permission of the son. He later sold the motor home. They admitted that the household goods stayed with them, but they explained that the brother could not retrieve them because he was in Alaska.

---

39. H.R. REP. NO. 95-595 1ST SESS., at 361 (1977), S. REP. 95-989, 2D SESS., at 76 (1978).

40. 848 F.2d 871 (8th Cir. 1988).

41. 848 F.2d 866 (8th Cir. 1988).

The bank argued that a transfer to family members while at the same time retaining possession amounted to a classic badge of fraud. The bankruptcy court upheld the exemption. The district and circuit courts affirmed.

Judge Arnold, dissenting in *Tveten* and concurring in *Hanson*, avowed that he was able to discern no principled difference between the two. The fact that Tveten is a doctor and Hanson a farmer may be a difference, but cannot be a difference of principle. In fact, most commentators sympathize with Judge Arnold.

The state of the law seems to remain: what may be malpractice not to do in some cases (or circuits)—may also be grounds for denial of discharge in others. Perhaps this is a pretty good case for the application of the old restatement principle: pigs get fat and hogs get slaughtered. Translated, the more aggressive or exotic or enterprising your exemption plan, the more likely you are to run into trouble.

We don't think this is a cure-all. The practical question remains: what's a poor lawyer to do? We don't have an easy answer to that one. We suspect the best you can do is to explain the situation to the client —warts and all—and to get the client to make some informed choices about what sorts of risks he will be willing to run.

§15.26 ~ The Bowie Kuhn Maneuver

Suppose you live in the state of Borealis, up near the Arctic Circle, where the homestead exemption is capped at $8,000 and the mean February temperature is 12 below zero. Your icebox factory has been struggling for years but lately it has become clear that you won't be able to keep going much longer—and that you are likely to come up woefully short on your business debts, all of which you have personally guaranteed. After careful thought, in a few swift moves you turn all your assets into cash and move to Florida—a state known, among other distinctions, for some fairly liberal exemption laws, including a homestead exemption that is unlimited as to amount.[42] You pack all your wealth into some exempt annuities and a nice little mansion near the beach, sure in the knowledge that your assets will be beyond the reach of your creditors.

Some would criticize this kind of forum-shopping as a blatant evasion of the spirit of the law, the worst sort of fraudulent transfer. Others are more benign. Borealis, after all, has never been a Garden of Eden in the winter. Lots of people move to Florida for all sorts of reasons—and anyway, South Dakota has an unlimited homestead exemption, and you don't see people clamoring to escape their creditors by moving out there!

So who's right? The answer is, of course—a little of both. But in any event, Florida has gained itself a reputation, justified or otherwise, as the exemption capital of the United States. Former Baseball Commissioner Bowie Kuhn, laboring under liabilities he incurred in the collapse of his law firm, is only the most famous of a flight of sun birds who took wing from a low-homestead jurisdiction with the hope of basking secure in the Florida sun. Not all of them brought it off.[43] But at least one Florida court has

42. Fla. Const. Art. X, §4(a)(1). Florida does, however, impose limitations on the size of the homestead property.

43. *In re* Coplan, 156 B.R. 88 (Bankr. M.D. Fla. 1993), the bankruptcy judge invalidated a homestead claim as a fraudulent transfer—then allowed the debtors to claim the kind of exemption they would have enjoyed had they never left Wisconsin!

held that it would be a violation of the Florida constitution to deny the debtor an exemption, even if his purpose was to hinder, delay or defraud.[44]

As we write, Congress is considering amendments to the Bankruptcy Code that might limit the availability of these "unlimited" homesteads in bankruptcy. But there has been no action yet, and there seems to be considerable resistance from legislators in the generous-homestead states.

§15.27 ~ Offshore Asset Protection

No discussion of fraudulent transfers would be complete without a discussion of the nascent and explosive "offshore asset protection industry," designed to put debtors' assets beyond the reach of creditors and in particular, beyond the reach of traditional fraudulent transfer laws.[45]

In crude outline, the deal works like this. The debtor transfers all his assets to a trust (which, one way or another, he controls). The trust is located in some postcard sovereignty on the other side of the planet—a favorite is the Cook Islands.[46] As a result of no accident at all, it happens that the fraudulent transfer (if you can call them that) laws of the Cook Islands are distinctively suited to preserving the integrity of the transfer and defeating the efforts of any foreign creditor to reach them.

For example, a familiar standard of proof for the plaintiff in fraudulent transfer cases is "preponderance of the evidence."[47] In the Cook Islands, in order to establish a fraudulent transfer, the plaintiff must submit proof "beyond a reasonable doubt."[48] The burden applies both on the question of whether the transfer was fraudulent, *and* to the question whether it rendered the transferee insolvent.

Cook Island law also offers a short statute of limitations. The limitation period is: (a) two years after the creditor's claim for payment accrues; or (b) one year after the transfer, whichever is earlier.[49] Cook Island law also makes itself hospitable to so-called duress clauses, where the self-settlor is automatically removed as a trustee if he is under duress—*i.e.*, subject to a lawsuit in the U.S.[50]

Finally, the statute provides that no foreign judgment shall be effective against a Cook Island trustee "notwithstanding (a) the provisions of any treaty; (b) the provisions of any statute; [or] (c) any rule of law or equity.[51] Presumably, creditors must start over again in the courts of the Cook Islands (where there appear to be no bankruptcy laws in any event).

---

44. Bank Leumi Trust Co. v. Lang, 898 F. Supp. 883, 887 (S.D. Fla. 1995).

45. For a thorough discussion of offshore investments and trusts (including a country by country review), *see* Barry Spitz, International Tax Havens Guide (1999).

46. A former New Zealand colony in the South Pacific. Other favorites are Mauritius, Nevis, St. Kitts and St. Vincent.

47. Gabaig v. Gabaig, 717 P.2d 835, 838 (Alaska 1986).

48. Section 13B(1) (Cook Islands) International Trusts Act 1984, as amended.

49. Section 13B3(a) & (b) (Cook Islands) International Trusts Act 1984, as amended.

50. *See* the discussion in FTC v. Affordable Media LLC, 179 F.3d 1228, 1240 n. 9 (9th Cir. 1999).

51. Section 13C (Cook Islands) International Trusts Act 1984, as amended.

A recent variant on the Cook Islands scheme is to try to achieve the same result under domestic U.S. law. In particular, both Alaska and Delaware have passed revisions to their trust law, seemingly with the purpose of trying to achieve Cook-like results in a less exotic venue.[52]

To put matters in perspective, one needs to recognize the Cook Island fandango, judged on traditional principles, is a fraudulent transfer, and a pretty crude one at that.[53] The enterprise has under a fair amount of criticism in the business and professional press. Some of this criticism seeks to distinguish protection against "good" creditors (typically, ex-spouses) and presumptively "bad" creditors (e.g., malpractice claimants), though why a paraplegic should be less morally worthy than a suburban spouse is not immediately obvious.

Other criticism focuses on the creative manipulation of notions of sovereignty. But on this point, it may be useful to take the long view. That is: criticisms of "island sovereignties" today are in principle no different from criticisms of the "abuse" of out–of-state incorporation when that first practice first appeared in the 19th Century.

For good or ill, there can be little doubt that the offshore trusts have succeeded in shielding uncountable assets from creditor claims, largely through frustration and delay. On the other hand, lately there have been some dramatic signs of judicial hostility. In two recent cases, bankruptcy judges have "repatriated" offshore assets into the bankruptcy estate—in one of those two, the judge also denied the discharge.[54] The doctrinal weak point in each case was the choice of law clause: the judges weren't willing to accept a "unilateral expatriation" at creditors' expense. In another case, the court denied a discharge of a debtor for what it called his "disingenuous and untruthful testimony" under questioning about an offshore trust.[55]

It is not clear from the record that any of these cases ever put a dime back in the pockets of creditors. Perhaps a more ambitious attack on the device is a recent Ninth Circuit decision, upholding the decision of a district judge who jailed two defendants for contempt after they sought to protect themselves behind

---

52. *See* The Alaska Trust Act, effective April 2, 1997, Alaska Laws, SLA 1997, Ch. 6 (H.B. 101); and the Delaware "Qualified Dispositions in Trust Act," as amended in part by §§36 and 37 of the Banking and Financial Services Amendments Act of 1998, enacted March 30, 1998, effective for trusts becoming irrevocable after July 9, 1997, 12 DCA §§3570-3576 (1997); *see also*, 6DCA §§1304, 1305, 1309. Missouri appears to have similar legislation dating back to 1989, although it has received less attention. 3 Missouri: V.A.M.S. §§428.005_428.059, 456.020, 456.080 (1989). There has been a good deal of controversy over the potential merits of Alaska and Delaware trusts, not least among proponents of competing models. One obvious problem would seem to be that Alaska and Delaware are bound to respect the judgments of other states as a matter of constitutional law under the full faith and credit clause. The Cook Islands have no such constraint.

53. *See, e.g.*, Cioli v. Kenourgios,, 211 P. 838, 841-42 (Cal.App.1922) (debtor's sale of all assets and shipment of proceeds out of the country held to e fraudulent conveyance notwithstanding adequacy of consideration).

54. Marine Midland Bank v. Portnoy (*In re* Portnoy), 201 B.R. 685, 701-03 (Bankr. S.D.N.Y. 1996) (transfer held invalid; discharge denied for concealing assets from the estate); *In re* Brooks, 217 B.R. 98 (Bankr D. Conn. 1998).

55. *In re* Lawrence, 227 B.R. 907, 916-17 (Bankr. S.D. Fla. 1998). The court also referred the matter to a U.S. attorney for possible perjury prosecution, and entered its order without prejudice to the trustee's right to seek sanctions against the debtor's counsel under Rule 9011. *Id.* at 918.

a "duress clause."[56] The couple claimed they were "unable" to persuade the trustee to return the assets. The Circuit upheld the district judge, holding that the avowals of incapacity were a charade. The court said that United States courts do not have to recognize structures which are designed to "frustrate and impede the United States courts. . . ."[57]

§15.28 ~ Third-party Rights—Section 550

Section 550 governs the trustee's recovery. Section 550(a) provides that the successful trustee may recover from the initial transferee, or from "any immediate or mediate transferee"—that is, from transferees of transferees.

But Section 550 also imposes important limits on the property of the trustee. Specifically, Section 550(b) protects a transferee who herself is a bona fide purchaser. To get the protection, the transferee must take for value,[58] in good faith; and without knowledge of the voidability of the transfer avoided. The burden of proof on these BFP elements is on the transferee.[59]

Section 550(e) provides that a good faith transferee also gets a lien to give her recompense for improvements she may have made while in possession. The lien will secure the lesser of the cost of the improvement; or any increase of value of the property as a result of the improvement.

Finally recall the case of the transferee who receives a preference between 90 days and one year of the bankruptcy filing. That transferee is vulnerable under special insider rule of Section 547(b). But what about the transferee of that transferee? Section 550(c) specifies that this "second generation" transferee is not liable unless she herself is an insider.

§15.29 ~ Preservation for the Estate—Section 551

Section 551 provides that if the trustee may avoid a transfer, then she may also preserve it for the benefit of the estate. The rule applies in a fairly narrow class of cases, more often observed in the classroom than in practice. But here is an example:

Example: Debtor owns Blackacre, worth $100,000. Debtor grants a security interest in Blackacre to FirstBank. Later, debtor grants a "junior" security interest to SecondBank. Later still, Debtor files for bankruptcy. On inquiry, Trustee determines that SecondBank perfected its security interest, but that FirstBank failed. Trustee may avoid the unperfected transfer (under Section 544(a), and perhaps also under Section 547). But if he does so, SecondBank will advance to first place, ahead of Trustee. So instead, Trustee preserves the transfer under Section 551, and slips in ahead of SecondBank.[60] As a result, the unsecured creditors, rather than SecondBank, benefit from the avoidance.

---

56. Affordable Media LLC, 179 F.3d at 1239.

57. The trial judge in Affordable Media is a former bankruptcy judge.

58. Here again, the Code says that "value" includes "satisfaction or securing of a present or antecedent debt." §550(b)(1).

59. *In re* Nordic Village, Inc., 915 F.2d 1049, 1055-56 (6th Cir. 1990), *rev'd on other grounds*, 503 U.S. 30 (1992).

60. *See, e.g., In re* Kors, Inc., 819 F.2d 19, 24-25 (2d Cir. 1987). Kors adds an important fillip. Apparently "FirstBank" had entered into a subordination agreement, putting itself behind "SecondBank" as a matter of contract law. The court held that the Trustee could preserve FirstBank's transfer, but that he was bound by the subordination agreement.

16 The Role of the Lawyer

16 The Role of the Lawyer

§16.1 ~ On Looking Yourself in the Mirror, Etc.

The sensible lawyer will concern herself with issues of professional responsibility (PR) in any case, if not as a matter of self-respect, then at least as a matter of common prudence. Surely she wants to look herself in the face in the mirror in the morning. But in any event, she wants to avoid having her fees disallowed, or be sued for malpractice, or disbarred, or prosecuted for a crime. All of these concerns conspire to keep PR issues on the front burner.

In some sense, issues of professional responsibility are no different in bankruptcy than they are anyplace else. The lawyer is an advocate and also an officer of the court in this case just as in any other. But the substance and structure of the bankruptcy case both serve to give these issues a special twist for bankruptcy lawyers.

§16.2 ~ Structure

First, as to structure. All lawyers are bound by the rules governing lawyer PR in any case, but issues of bankruptcy PR are most likely to arise when the lawyer is acting on authorization of the court—as counsel to the DIP, or to the trustee or to a committee.[1] For these cases, the Code sets specific standards for employment and retention, and the court maintains close control of fees, providing a framework bound to generate PR issues.[2]

Second, as to substance. Oversimplified, most conventional litigation is a two-party affair while bankruptcy, almost by definition, involves multiple parties.[3] And not only multiple parties, but parties with shifting alliances, so that today's enemy is tomorrow's friend. To take a simple example: the creditor is adverse to the debtor on the basic question of the collection of the debt.

---

1. The "general law" of lawyer PR can be found in the ABA Model Rules of Professional Conduct (the "Model Rules") and the American Law Institute's Restatement (Third) of the Law Governing Lawyers.

2. Specific bankruptcy provisions are discussed below. One curiosity about bankruptcy PR is that it is not always completely clear just which PR law the court is applying. This is perhaps due to the fact that a lot of PR law arises out of the same primordial soup and is presented at a level sufficiently abstract that you can shape it to fit a variety of special situations. But there are some flat-out contradictions. For example, §504 of the Bankruptcy Code imposes a flat bar on fee-splitting. More recent PR rules permit and sometimes even encourage fee-splitting insofar as it encourages specialization.

3. Good general background on multiparty relationships is in Geoffrey C. Hazard, Jr., *Triangular Lawyer Relationships: An Exploratory Analysis*, 1 Geo. J. Legal Ethics 15 (1987).

But any single creditor may be the ally of the debtor in seeking to protect the debtor's bankruptcy discharge —provided the claim of the individual creditor will survive, free of competition from other adverse claims. In the same vein, creditors may work happily together—and with the debtor—to gang up on another creditor in (for example) an action to avoid a preference. Parties who are at loggerheads over underlying liability may find themselves nonetheless constrained to work together in the formulation of a plan. All of these concerns tend to blur the distinctions that govern ordinary rules of client loyalty.

Another problem of substance concerns the public attitude to bankruptcy itself—a topic discussed at greater length elsewhere , *see* §6.14.To repeat, the problem is that we don't have a consensus as to just how far the DIP in chapter 11 can "tilt to equity." Is the DIP solely the agent of creditors, or may he seek to salvage something for the old residuary owners, even if at creditors' expense? This is a problem in any event. It becomes a PR problem, because the question of what the lawyer can do is governed in large part by the question of what the client can do. If the client is permitted to tilt to equity, then there can be no problem in the lawyer's helping him to do so, but if the client is constrained, then the lawyer may be constrained as well.

In this framework, it is possible to sketch the layout of the playing field. In most of our discussion below, we will focus on the role of the attorney who represents a DIP, because that is where many of the problems come up and the cases get written. But most of what we say here would apply to any "professional person" —accountant, etc.—working for a trustee—including DIP. And a good bit of it also applies to an attorney representing a committee.

§16.3 ~ Employment (Adverse Interest and Disinterested)

Section 327(a) provides that "the trustee, with the court's approval, may employ one or more attorneys [etc.] that do not hold or represent an interest adverse to the estate and that are disinterested persons . . ."[4] Therefore, the point of departure is you don't get paid unless your employment is authorized, and that your meet specific threshold criteria.[5] We discuss the criteria briefly and then say a word about the employment process.

4. Contrast the more relaxed standard for committee counsel in §1103. It provides that the counsel may not hold an adverse interest, but specifies that representing one or more individual creditors at the same time that you represent the class is not *per se* an adverse interred.

5. For an exception, *see* §503(b)(4), discussed at §16.13.

§16.4 ~ Form Application for Employment

IN THE UNITED STATES BANKRUPTCY COURT
FOR THE EASTERN DISTRICT OF UTOPIA

In Re:	)	Bankruptcy Case
	)	99-1415-BBL
INSOLVENT SUPPLY CORPORATION,	)	Chapter 11
	)	
Debtor-in-Possession	)	
	)	

APPLICATION OF DEBTOR FOR APPROVAL
OF THE EMPLOYMENT OF SMITH & JONES
AS ATTORNEYS FOR THE DEBTOR

Insolvent Supply Corporation (the "Debtor") respectfully requests this Court's approval of the employment of Smith & Jones as attorneys for the Debtor and Debtor-in-Possession, pursuant to 11 U.S.C. §§327, 328 and 1107 and Rule 2014 of the Federal Rules of Bankruptcy Procedure, on the following grounds:

Jurisdiction and Venue

A. This Court has jurisdiction over this matter pursuant to 28 U.S.C. §1334.

B. This is a core proceeding pursuant to 28 U.S.C. §157(b)(2)(A).

C. Venue is proper in this Court pursuant to 28 U.S.C. §§1408 and 1409.

Background

A. On December 22, 2000, the Debtor filed a voluntary petition for relief under chapter 11 of the Bankruptcy Code. No trustee, examiner or committee of creditors has been appointed in this case. The Debtor continues to own and manage its property and to conduct its business affairs as a debtor-in-possession.

B. The Debtor desires to retain counsel to assist it in the performance of its duties in this case. The professional services for which the Debtor desires to employ counsel include, but are not limited to, legal services as may be required or deemed by the Debtor to be desirable in connection with the administration of this case in accordance with the powers and duties of a debtor-in-possession as set forth in the Bankruptcy Code and applicable bankruptcy law, representing the Debtor in connection with all motions, other contested matters and adversary proceedings that may arise in connection with the case, and advising and representing the Debtor in connection with the formulation and confirmation of a chapter 11 plan.

C. The Debtor has selected Smith & Jones because Smith & Jones has considerable experience and knowledge in bankruptcy and related matters. The Debtor believes that the applicant is well-qualified and able to represent the Debtor in this case in an efficient and timely manner.

D. Smith & Jones has stated its desire and willingness to act in this case and to render the necessary professional services as counsel to the Debtor.

E. To the best of the Debtor's knowledge, Smith & Jones represents no other entity in connection with this case, is a disinterested person, as that term is defined in Section 101(14) of the Bankruptcy Code, and represents or holds no interest adverse to the Debtor, creditors, any party in interest, their respective attorneys or accountants, the United States Trustee, or any person employed in the office of the United States Trustee, except to the extent disclosed in the Verified Statement of Albert E. Smith Pursuant to Bankruptcy Rule 2014 (the "Verified Statement"), as that Verified Statement may be amended from time to time. A copy of the Verified Statement is attached to this Application as Exhibit A.

F. Smith & Jones shall make appropriate applications to this Court for compensation of attorneys' fees and reimbursement of expenses as required by the Bankruptcy Code and the Federal Rules of Bankruptcy Procedure. Subject to the Court's approval, Smith & Jones will perform all services at its customary hourly rates as those rates are in effect during the applicable time period for the principals, associates and paralegals who render services on the Debtor's behalf. A copy of Smith & Jones' engagement letter, which includes the firm's current customary hourly rates, is attached hereto as Exhibit B and incorporated herein by reference.

G. Smith & Jones reserves the right, subject to applicable law, to request additional fees based on the results obtained in this case, the degree of urgency required of counsel, and other factors relevant to the determination of fair and reasonable compensation.

H. No previous application for the relief sought herein has been made to this or any other court.

WHEREFORE, Insolvent Supply Corporation respectfully requests that an Order be entered authorizing and approving the employment of Smith & Jones as counsel to the Debtor and for such other and further relief as is just and proper.

Respectfully submitted,

INSOLVENT SUPPLY CORPORATION
By:________________________________
Irving Insolvent, President
88 Fluid Drive
New Vision, Utopia, 99989
(111) 234-5678

Presented by:

SMITH & JONES, PC
By:________________________________
Nathan Lee Kesef, Esq.
Utopia Bar No. 141711
8381 Recovery Road
Utopia City, Utopia 98899
(646) 814-8114

§16.5 ~ Adverse Interest

There are two constraints: "adverse interest" and "disinterestedness." Take them in order.

§16.6 ~ What Is It?

First, the rule on adverse interest bears a strong family resemblance to the rule governing simple conflicts in any other field of law. Typically you can't represent both creditor and debtor in the same bankruptcy case any more than you would represent both victim and insurer in a personal injury lawsuit.[6]

The difficulty is that questions of adverse interest aren't so easily cubby holed. Suppose your firm represents BankCo a major bank in your town with claims against a thousand debtors including DebtorCo. It happens that all BankCo work concerning DebtorCo has been handled by another firm. Can you represent DebtorCo as DIP in its chapter 11?[7]

The objection is obvious. The Model Rule says that the lawyer shall not represent the client if the representation will be directly adverse to or materially limited by the lawyer's responsibilities to another client unless, *inter alia*, the lawyer reasonably believes there will be no adverse effect.[8] This is a promising start,

6. *Cf.* Model Rule of Professional Conduct Model rule 1.7 (1982) [hereafter Model Rules] (conflict of interest in general); *id.* 1.9 (duty to former client).

7. For starters, note that this isn't a matter that can be settled simply by consent. Of course, the bank consents, or you wouldn't be here. The people who speak for the DIP appear to consent, but there are two difficulties. One, it may not be clear whether the spokesman for the DIP, in his fiduciary role, really understands what he is consenting to. And two, there may be a question whether he should be permitted to consent away the interests of all the creditors even if he does understand.

8. Model Rules Model Rule 1.7.

but it is too abstract to be conclusive. Is the bank "directly adverse" to the debtor? What will count as an adverse effect? All this would seem to be open to case law articulation which, surprisingly or not, remains thin.[9]

Even if we did know the answer, the question would remain—how far does the rule extend? Suppose BankCo is not a big creditor of DebtorCo but only a middle-sized creditor—or, by contrast, suppose BankCo is not a big client of the firm, but only a middle-sized client. Or, not a present client, but a former client, or a potential future client! Or, not a creditor of DebtorCo and not a client of the firm, but a creditor of the firm. The possibilities are virtually endless, and it is unlikely that you will find any short generalization that will accompany them all.

§16.7 ~ Disclosure

Under the circumstances, the best advice we can give is: when in any kind of doubt, disclose the relationship, and let the court decide. The reports are littered with horror stories of counsel who have found themselves disencumbered of fairly large fees that counsel had already pocketed (and spent?) after perceived violation of the conflicts rules. Our reading is that the sting in these cases is the non-disclosure: the judge feels she was misled and is cutting the fee as a sanction, and perhaps as a warning to others.[10]

Indeed, the courts favor disclosure so much that they have begun to fashion an independent requirement of disclosure, broader than the underlying rule of adverse interest itself.[11] We confess we don't quite understand how it can be wrong not to disclose something that is not wrong in itself. On the other hand, we think the new infatuation with disclosure can be used as a sword as well as a shield. Thus, we suggest that counsel can sometimes can seize the moral high ground by seeming to reach out to flag potential PR issues before they become a problem ("We do not thing that x is a conflict, but the court should know . . . " etc.).

In this same vein, it can hardly be surprising that courts have found the obligation of disclosure to be *ongoing—i.e.*, if the situation changes after the case starts, you have to amend or update your disclosure.[12]

Much of what we have said so far about adverse interest also applies to the matter of "disinterestedness."[13] But disinterestedness has some quirks of its own that need separate attention.

---

9. We don't know of a "big bank" case, but many cases involve attorneys who do, or did, represent shareholders. *See, e.g., In re* Hot Tin Roof, Inc., 205 B. R. 1000, 1004 (B.A.P. 1st Cir.1997).

10. *See, e.g., In re* Crivello, 134 F.3d 831,839 (7th Cir. 1998) (Court has discretion over fee awards, but "if any evidence exists to support an inference of [intentional nondisclosure], then the Court should not fall prey to the professional's story of confusion, miscommunication, or negligence. We believe a Bankruptcy Court should punish a willful failure to disclose the connections required by [Rule] 2014 as severely as an attempt to put forth a fraud upon the court." *In re* Maui 14K, Ltd., 133 B.R. 657, 660 (Bankr. D. Hawaii 1991) ("denial of all compensation is justified regardless of actual harm to the estate").

11. *See In re* Park-Helena Corp., 63 F. 3d 877, 881-82 (9th Cir. 1995) (holding that failure to comply with the disclosure rules is sanctionable even if proper disclosure would have shown that the attorney had not actually violated any provision of the Bankruptcy Code or rules).

12. *In re* Begun, 162 B.R. 168, 177 (Bankr. N.D. Ill. 1993).

13. Section 101(14).

§16.8 ~ Check the Conflicts

Because the disclosure requirement is ongoing, we think the process of checking conflicts should be ongoing as well. As the case goes on, your firm will get new clients and new lawyers. Meanwhile the cast of characters in the case will change (claims will be traded, old investors will bail out, etc.). Make a new conflicts check every few months and file supplementary disclosures as necessary.

§16.9 ~ Disinterestedness

Courts sometimes use adverse interest and disinterestedness interchangeably, but in fact they are very different things. While adverse interest is in large measure a creature of general law, disinterestedness is a bankruptcy term of art. In order to qualify as a disinterested person, the applicant must not be "a creditor, an equity security holder, or an insider" of the debtor, or an investment banker of the debtor; or an officer, director, or employee of the debtor, or of an investment banker of the debtor."[14]

This provision leads to some severe results. Consider the case of Oliver the lawyer and Chad, the CEO of DebtorCo. Oliver and Chad were fraternity brothers together. Oliver incorporated DebtorCo and has served as its corporate secretary and a director. Last year when DebtorCo first ran into difficulties, Oliver let the bill slide and DebtorCo now owes Oliver's firm some $30,000—about half of one percent of the firms annual gross revenues.

Should Oliver be permitted to represent DebtorCo as DIP in its chapter 11? For a thoughtful lawyer, the case is not an easy one. A lawyer should not represent anyone where his personal involvement is so great that he cannot give detached advice (we have always assumed that this is the point of the old canard about the lawyer representing himself and having a fool for a client).[15]

As we say, we think this is an issue that requires some thought—but the Code will have none of this. It imposes a flat prohibition that bars, *e.g.*, any creditor (no matter how slight the claim) or any officer (no matter how technical and formal the office) from serving as counsel for the DIP.

The disinterestedness rule may be in the Code as a result of a drafting error. The history is as follows: back in the runup to the 1978 Code, the Securities and Exchange Commission proposed a new chapter 11 that would have looked a lot like old chapter X. Recall that under old chapter X, there was a general presumption that the existing officers and directors were the villains and that they must exit in a clean sweep. Ignoring the propriety of this assumption, certainly it makes sense to say that if management must leave, then their kept professionals should leave also.

But the chapter 11 model as adopted rejects that premise almost completely. Rather, retaining the debtor in possession (as DIP) is the norm. It appears that during some drafting session in the runup to the 1978 act, the drafters decided to snip out all the disinterestedness provisions governing management and the trustee—but then forgot to excise the comparable provisions governing professionals.

---

14. There is a residual catch-all category in §101(14)(E). But it is sufficiently abstract that it hasn't generated a lot of independent litigation.

15. *Cf.* Model Rule 1.7 cmt. 6: ("the lawyer's own interests should not be permitted to have an adverse effect on representation of a client").

Your authors also believe that the disinterestedness rule is too stringent as it stands, and they would be happy to see Congress change it. But we disagree among ourselves as to just what should happen in the meantime. In particular, some courts have cooked up *de minimis* exceptions of one sort or another to try to restrict the impact of the disinterestedness rule.[16] One of us believes these are disingenuous and ought to be discouraged. The other believes that the original rule is bad law, and that the courts ought to be encouraged to find creative approaches to bad law.

A lawyer who is also a creditor may be tempted to consider whether he can solve his disinterestedness problem by simply arranging to be paid before the case begins. Perhaps he can but, in getting paid, he probably has taken a preferential transfer which would seem to create a problem all its own.

A different sort of suggestion is to simply waive the claim. Recognizing that most unsecured creditors' claims in chapter 11 are worth significantly less than face value anyway, he might well decide that he is better off waiving the claim in exchange for the valuable opportunity to represent the DIP. Once the lawyer has relinquished his claim, then he is no longer a creditor, and the bar should not apply.

Yet another solution might be to sell the claim. We are not aware of any case where the court has rejected this approach. Finally, if all else fails and you still want to be in the case, consider employment as special counsel, as authorized in Section 327(e). *See* §16.12.

§16.10 ~ SELF-DEALING

Aside from the specific bars in Section 327, the attorney needs to keep in mind general limitations on self-dealing. We have noted elsewhere that the trustee is barred under pain of criminal penalty from buying property from the estate.[17] On the same general principle an attorney, by virtue of fiduciary role, may be restricted in his dealings with the estate. Thus, there is a general duty on the lawyer to safeguard confidential client information.

Beyond the general duty, the new Restatement of the Law Governing Lawyers provides that "a lawyer who uses confidential information of a client for the lawyer's pecuniary gain other than in the practice of law must account to the client for any profit made."[18] The lawyer is released from these duties if the client consents after being adequately informed.[19]

The commentary to Section 112 explains:

> "The strict confidentiality duty of the Subsection is warranted for prophylactic purposes. A lawyer who acquires confidential client information as the result of a representation should not be tempted by expectation of profit to risk a possibly incorrect assessment of future harm to a

---

16. *In re* Rusty Jones, Inc., 134 B.R. 321, 346 (Bankr. N.D. Ill. 1991).

17. *See generally* Chapter 18.

18. RESTATEMENT (THIRD) OF THE LAW GOVERNING LAWYERS §112(2)(1998).

19. RESTATEMENT (THIRD) OF THE LAW GOVERNING LAWYERS §114(1998).

client. There is no important social interest in permitting lawyers to make unconsented use or revelation of confidential client information for self-enrichment in personal transactions."

The commentary provides that "the sole remedy of the client for breach of the duty is restitutionary relief in the form of disgorgement of profit" (with a cross-cite to the comparable rule in the Restatement, Second, of Agency). But then, somewhat obscurely, it adds that state lawyer disciplinary rules "differ over whether such self-enriching use or disclosure constitutes a disciplinary violation in the absence of prejudice to the client."

Indeed, some states do impose more severe limitations under their lawyer codes. For example, California imposes an absolute bar against buying property at any foreclosure or trustee's sale.[20] The drafters many not have been thinking of a bankruptcy trustee when they wrote the rule, but it may well be sufficient to apply to a bankruptcy sale.

§16.11 ~ Saving Rules

§16.12 ~ Special Counsel

There are a couple of limited escape hatches for lawyers seeking employment in the estate, but who do not meet the standards of Section 327(a). First, Section 327(e) allows the trustee (with court approval) to employ "for a specified special purpose" a lawyer who has represented the debtor. The representation must be in the best interest of the estate. The attorney must not hold an adverse interest with respect to the matter on which she is to be employed—*i.e.*, a lower barrier than the general adverse interest bar of Section 327(a). There is no requirement of "disinterestedness."

The rule appears to be designed to cover the case of a lawyer who was doing a particular project for the debtor at the time of filing, and where there would be costs and no benefits to bringing on new counsel. An example might be the case of lawyer employed to handle a personal injury claim. Courts have been alert not to let counsel use the Section 327(e) exception as a sidestep to the general rule of Section 327(a).

Comment: Note that the saving rule of Section 327(e) is not available to any professional other than the attorney. But we have seen judges who stretch the point to allow employment of other professionals, most notably accountants, under this section.

§16.13 ~ Substantial Contribution

In a limited class of cases unappointed counsel may recover for his role in making a "substantial contribution" to the case. Sometimes this enables counsel for a creditor who takes an action that benefits all creditors to get paid from the estate, although in practice the standard is a fairly high one. Section 503(b)(3) authorizes the payment of actual, necessary expenses to creditors in a number of situations, including

---

20. Cal St. Rule of Prof. Conduct 4-300 (1996).

those who make such a contribution. Section 503(b)(4) authorizes "reasonable compensation for professional services" in support of those creditors. We wouldn't expect this to work as an end run around the requirements of Section 327(a), so debtor's counsel who wants to get paid will have to get his employment approved first.

§16.14 ~ Creditor Representation

There are a couple of saving rules that may solve some of the more frustrating problems of counsel facing the brick wall of disinterestedness and adverse interest. Perhaps the most noteworthy is Section 327(c). It provides that

> a person is not disqualified for employment under this Section *solely because of* such person's employment by or representation of a creditor, unless there is objection by another creditor or the United States trustee, in which case the court shall disapprove such employment if there is an actual conflict of interest (emphasis added).

Counsel sometimes look to this rule as the solution to all their problems, but we wouldn't get carried away. Note that it removes a bar for one who *represented* a creditor, but it says nothing about the lawyer who is a creditor—which is the kind of problem that causes so much head-banging under the disinterestedness rule.

A different sort of protection is available to counsel who wants to represent a committee, which is governed not by Section 327, but by Section 1103. Section 1103(b) provides that the attorney may not represent an adverse interest while representing the committee. But it specifies:

> Representation of one or more creditors of the same class as represented by the committee shall not per se constitute the representation of an adverse interest.[21]

§16.15 ~ Who Is Your Client?

So much for the fundamentals of adverse interest and disinterestedness as prescribed by Section 327. But there is a deeper PR problem here: call it the problem of client loyalty. Obviously, a lawyer should be loyal to his client. But as we saw earlier, when it comes to representing the DIP, there is great controversy over just what the client can so, *see* §6.14. So the lawyer's duty of loyalty has to be understood in terms of the client's duty of loyalty. For starters, we suspect that the lawyer can't do anything that the client can't do. On the other hand, as we suggest below, probably the lawyer can, and perhaps he must, do some things that the DIP is not likely to do on his own.

One way to approach the problem is to consider the DIP as a fiduciary.[22] He is a fiduciary if and insofar as he owes a fiduciary duty to creditors. On this reading, the creditors are the beneficiaries of this fiduciary relationship. You could hold the lawyer liable to the creditors, then, either by saying that the lawyer is a

---

21. The protection also explicitly extends to accountants.

22. On the background of fiduciary liability for DIP counsel, *see generally* Bruce A. Markell, *The Folly of Representing Insolvent Corporations*, 6 J. Bankr. L. & P. 403, 413-24 (1997).

direct representative of the beneficiaries,[23] or that the beneficiary, though a third party non-client, has some sort of right against the lawyer based on the fiduciary duty of the original client.[24] In most cases, either analysis would get you to the same place.

Translated into chapter 11 terms, as we said earlier, the question is—how much can the DIP tilt towards equity? We have already said that we think this an open question. We suspect the best answer is that he can do so "some, but not too much."[25] Earlier we pointed to the famous *Kendavis* case, which seems to say that any tilt to equity is too much. It remains to note that *Kendavis* is a fee case—just the kind designed to give nightmares to the lawyer who is trying to serve his client while not getting crosswise with the court.

For the lawyer with a sour stomach after reading *Kendavis*, an antidote is *In re DN Associates*[26] out of the First Circuit, which, we think, states a rule often applied though less often articulated. Counsel for the DIP filed a plan that purported to save the old residual owners. The plan failed, and the court confirmed a creditor plan. Thereupon DIP counsel sought fees for his work in the case. Over creditor objection, the court authorized the fee request in full. The decision was upheld by the district court and the court of appeals. Unanimously, these three opinions support the proposition that "tilt to equity" is no bar to fees.[27]

§16.16 ~ The Application for Employment

We have seen that you can't get fees unless your employment was authorized. That means that at the beginning of the case, your client, the DIP files, an "application to employ counsel." Per rule 2014, the application

> shall state the specific facts showing the necessity for the employment, the name of the person to be employed, the reasons for the selection, the professional services to be rendered, any proposed arrangement for compensation and, to the best of the applicant's knowledge, all of the person's connections with the debtor, creditors, any other party in interest, their respective attorneys and accountants, the United States trustee, or any person employed in the office of the United States trustee.

---

23. *See, e.g., In re* Clarke's Estate, 188 N.E.2d 128, 130 (N.Y. 1962) ("an attorney for a fiduciary has the same duty of undivided loyalty to the *cestui* as the fiduciary himself").

24. *See, e.g.*, Willner's Fuel Distributors, Inc., v. Noreen, 882 P.2d 399, 405 (Alaska 1994).

25. 91 B.R. 742 (Bankr. N.D. Texas 1988). We also said we think the Kendavis language goes far beyond the facts.

26. 144 B.R. 195 (Bankr. D. Maine 1992), *aff'd sub nom.* Casco Northern Bank v. DN Associates, 3 F.3d 512 (1st Cir. 1993).

27. The fact remains, however, that whatever the definition, it is the DIP and not the debtor that is the client. For example, a noteworthy Fifth Circuit decision denotes that counsel cannot be compensated from assets of the estate for services rendered after the appointment of a trustee. Andrews & Kurth v. Family Snacks, Inc. (*In re* Pro-Snax Distributors, Inc.), 157 F.2d 414 (5th Cir.1998).

The professional shall attach a verified statement setting forth any such connections. *See also* Rule 2016 on applications for compensation. This means, among other things, that the lawyer will need a good system for checking the firm's records to identify conflicts. In an age of the mega firm, this in itself is no easy trick.[28]

§16.17 ~ U.S. Trustee Approval

Many judges look to the U. S. Trustee for help on employment applications. Some require that the U.S. Trustee sign off before the application is approved. It's probably a good idea to ask for U.S. Trustee approval on any application for employment, and to get the approval into the record.

§16.18 ~ Checklist: Conflicts Check

Your firm should have a detailed written conflicts-check policy, and follow it in every case. Consider, for example:

- Maintain a computerized list of every client and each adverse or potentially adverse party, and update it as new adverse parties are identified.

- When a new matter comes in, run the name of the debtor, all known affiliates of the debtor, officers and directors of the debtor, all known creditors, any major equity holders, and any other known interested parties through the database.

- For each connection you identify, speak to the lawyer who handles the other party and determine whether there is a potential conflict.

- As a supplement to the computer check, send a memo to everyone in the firm inquiring whether there is a conflict. This is a good backup protection against computer error. It also allows you to surface business conflicts that might give you reason to pass up a case, even in the absence of formal conflicts.

- Assign one lawyer (or in a big firm, a committee) to serve as PR specialists. When in doubt, consult the PR specialist.

- Make it clear that nobody will be permitted to open as new matter without going through these steps.

§16.19 ~ Client Misbehavior (and Whistle-Blowing)

A different kind of problem emerges when the client misbehaves, or makes it clear he intends to misbehave. It is a problem because it poses a conflict between two sets of duties that fall on the lawyer, each plausible and important. One is the duty of loyalty to the client, including the duty to maintain client confidences. Typically the lawyer has no duty to disclose information received in confidence about the client—and

---

28. *Cf.* Model Rule 1.10.

indeed may be liable to the client if he does disclose. The counterpoise is the lawyer's duty to redress or prevent wrongdoing, perhaps coupled with his duty as an officer of the court. A conflict over the appropriate boundary between these duties rocked the bar in the 1980s, and remains among the most contentious issues in PR today.[29]

One version of the problem is the case where the lawyer believes the client intends to commit a crime that is likely to result in economic loss. On this issue, the law (for the moment ignoring bankruptcy law) is in hopeless disarray. Of the 50 states, only two say that the lawyer must disclose information in this case. Another 29 states say that he *may* disclose it—but another 20 prohibit disclosure! Another version involves the client's prior or contemporaneous perjury (or other fraudulent conduct before a tribunal). Here, no state allows discretion—but 38 states say that he must disclose to rectify the wrong, while 13 say that he must not![30]

Aside from PR law, there is another source of doctrine that runs at least parallel to the PR framework and at least in some cases may flatly contradict it. This is the so-called "crime-fraud exception." The exception arises in the rules of evidence. Evidentiary rules typically provide that the lawyer may not be compelled (absent the consent of the client) to reveal client confidences. The exception, as articulated in the Uniform Rules of Evidence, provides:

There is no privilege under this rule . . . if the services of the lawyer were sought or obtained to enable or aid anyone to commit or plan to commit what the client knew or reasonably should have known to be a crime or fraud.[31]

The problem takes on special urgency where the lawyer is representing a DIP (or trustee) for at least two reasons. First, what the lawyer does for the DIP takes place in the context of a court proceeding, where both his client and he are directly answerable to the court for virtually everything they do—making the lawyer (and the client?) in some sense an officer of the court. Second, the lawyer and the client work together in an ongoing relationship, where the lawyer's silence is not mere preservation of a confidence but is arguably active participation in present wrongdoing. These problems are at least aggravated by the general uncertainty over DIP duty, outlined elsewhere.

---

29. The most notorious allegation against a lawyer in an ongoing negotiation is not a bankruptcy case, but bankruptcy-like: it was the episode that pitted the Office of Thrift Supervision versus the firm of Kaye, Scholer, Fierman, Hays & Handler over its representation of Charles Keating, the Savings and Loan entrepreneur. The conflict was settled short of judicial decision so there is not the kind of authoritative record that lawyers like to depend on, *but cf.* Willam H. Simon, *The Kaye Scholer Affair: The Lawyer's Duty of Candor and the Bar's Temptations of Evasion and Apology*, 23 L. & Soc. Inquiry 243 (Spring 1998).

30. The Restatement says the lawyer may "use or disclose confidential client information when and to the extent necessary to prevent . . . substantial financial loss as the result of a crime or fraud that the client has committed or intends to commit." An optional extra clause adds: "and in the commission of which the lawyer's services were or are being employed." Restatement (Third) of Law Governing Lawyers, §117A (1998).

31. Unif. R. Evid. 502(d)(1).

Example: Consider the problem of Lori, a lawyer who represents DebtorCo as DIP in its chapter 11. DebtorCo speaks through Chad, the CEO and majority shareholder. Lori thinks she has a good working relationship and that the client understands his responsibilities as DIP—until one night when she receives an anonymous phone call telling her that Chad has been funneling money out of DebtorCo into his personal offshore trust account.

We take it for granted that the allegations, if true, constitute a crime. So apparently as a minimum, under the crime-fraud exception, Lori might be compelled to testify in a criminal case.[32] But this doesn't solve Lori's immediate problem in the middle of the night, while she still represents the client. What should she do?

For starters, we believe that Lori owes it to herself to make at least some inquiry on her own to see whether the charges have any basis. If she believes they are true, then the conventional wisdom dictates that she should confront Chad with the charges and to explain that what he has done is wrong (but of course he knew that—otherwise why all the elaborate deception). Traditional lore says that she is supposed to counsel him to correct his misdeed, but this will not be as easy as it sounds—after all, an amended cash flow statement reporting that money was in truth stolen is bound to get someone's attention.

The conventional wisdom says that Lori's next step is to withdraw from the case—but only after court authorization (we would assume), because that is how she got into the case in the first place.[33] But the problem does not end there. The question is whether she merely picks up her slippers and tiptoes away or whether she is obliged to make a noisy withdrawal, with full disclosure and a panoply or accusations.

Lori is perhaps more likely to be tempted by the possibility of a nudge-and-wink withdrawal, where she announces her intention to withdraw for "differences with the client," trusting that the court will understand from her silence that this file glows in the dark and needs to be handled with special care.

A variation on the client wrongdoing problem occurs in the pre-petition phase, where the lawyer and the client are doing bankruptcy planning. Suppose the client owns the valuable Snopes diamond which he "neglects to mention" during his pre-petition interview with the paralegal doing the schedules. The oversight is later discovered: the client loses the diamond and probably also his discharge—and he may find himself on the fast track to the penitentiary.

We think that in any event, the lawyer must make clear to the client that the consequences of concealment may be swift and severe, and that his freedom is worth more than the odd bauble. This is common decency; but also, as a matter of elementary self-preservation, the lawyer wants to make sure that if there is any wrong-doing, it will not stick to him.

---

32. *See, e.g.*, U.S. v. Ballard, 779 F.2d 287 (5th Cir. 1986) (testimony of lawyer admissible in criminal proceeding against former client).

33. *See* Model Rule 1.16 (allowing withdrawal if "the client persists in a course of action involving the lawyer's services that the lawyer reasonably believes may be criminal or fraudulent").

The lawyer must document that he explained to the client that he must disclose everything, along with the consequences of misbehavior. And heaven help him if it appears that he knew about the diamond (and said nothing) at the time the schedules were filed—or, worst of all, that it was somehow his idea.[34]

We think perhaps you can get some help on this issue from a well-drafted initial interview form. It will help to make sure that you don't forget the important warnings. For our initial interview lists, *see* §§5.21-.22.

§16.20 ~ Independent Investigation

And there is one more level of complexity. That is—how far most the lawyer go in making an independent investigation of the client's (mis)behavior? The point of departure might be that she has no duty. But we think this rule needs qualification, for at least two reasons. One is the notion that the lawyer is an "officer of the court." Particularly in DIP cases, where the court often feels short of guidance, there is a tendency on the part of the judges to look to the lawyer to do at least some of what you might think of as trustee duties. Properly handled, this can be an advantage: a lawyer's reputation with the court can be a marketable commodity that can help her to build her practice.

A second reason is that there is a fine line between failure to investigate and willful ignorance. A court may well take the attitude that if counsel is around the DIP all the time, then one way or another he ought to have found out what DIP was up to.

A conspicuous case is *In re Wilde Horse Enters., Inc.*,[35] where the court denied all fees to counsel for, among other things, failure to investigate the good faith of the debtor in a prospective sale. Some lawyers tend to think of Wilde Horse and a very few cases like it as exceptional, limited to lower courts and special facts. But you get the same sort of attitude from the Ninth Circuit itself, deciding *In re Perez*.[36]

§16.21 ~ More on Getting Employed and Getting Paid

Elsewhere we made the basic point about employment as a professional person to represent the trustee or the DIP.[37] The point is: your employment must be authorized by the court. Otherwise, no fees from the estate. And within the principle, judges retain the power to disallow fees or to cut or change from what is allowed.[38] The statute allows "any . . . party in interest" to take part in a fee dispute, but foresees a special role for the U.S. Trustee.

---

34. There is a useful discussion of the problem in *In re* Matthews, 154 B.R. 673 (Bankr. W.D. Tex. 1993). This was a fee application case. The court questioned what it saw as an inordinate amount of time spent gathering information and preparing schedules and statements. The attorney argued that he had a duty to investigate so as not to mislead the court. The court conceded that counsel had a duty to investigate, but said that if she felt was being misled, she should have withdrawn.

35. 136 B.R. 830 (Bankr. C.D. Calif. 1991).

36. 30 F.3d 1209, 1219 (9th Cir. 1994).

37. Section 330(a). Most of what is said here applies also to counsel for a committee of creditors or for any other official committee authorized to retain counsel as an expense of the estate, §1103(a).

38. Section 330(a)(2).

And indeed, in virtually every District, the U. S. Trustee reviews and comments on fee applications. Unless he is prepared for a big fight, counsel might as well master the relevant U. S. Trustee fee guidelines and abide by them.[39] In crude summary, counsel will get fees based on an hourly rate appropriate to the community or the case, with the remote possibility of a "lodestar" kicker for unusual services and the less remote possibility that the court will cut some of the fees requested.[40]

Inevitably, counsel complain about the fee application process as a bureaucratic complication. But these complaints need to be put in perspective. There was a time when the general rule (at least in the 9th Circuit) was that you couldn't earn more than the annual earnings of a U. S. District Judge.[41] Meanwhile unpaid creditors tend to view any money that flows to professionals as a form of ill-gotten gain.

Our suspicion is that judges actually cut fee applications less than they think they should—driven by the conviction that the requests are probably excessive, but that they can't guess exactly where, or by how much, or whose. Under the circumstances, the judge is bound to welcome an application that tells a convincing story, at a sufficiently low level of abstraction, of what counsel did, and why it helped, and why it took so much time.

Note: This would be the appropriate place for a sample fee application, were we to offer one. After some thought, we have decided not to offer a sample fee application here. The reason is that here, perhaps more than anywhere else, anything that smacks of boilerplate puts you at the risk of trouble. Rather, what you need to do in your fee application is to specify exactly what you did in this case (rather than simply to tote up time in general categories). You need also to describe how your work contributed to progress in this case. And of course you need to support it all with detailed time entries—perhaps amplified by summary charts to make it all easy to follow.

This sounds like work. It is work. But many courts will allow you to get paid for it—*i.e.*, will allow reasonable fees for expenses incurred in preparing the fee application.

For law governing fee applications, a conventional point of departure is Johnson v. Georgia Highway Exp., Inc.—not a bankruptcy case, but it has achieved quasi-canonical status in bankruptcy fee cases.[42] The appeal of Johnson is that it lists 12 factors of sufficient generality that they can support any result.[43]

---

39. For detail, GUIDELINES FOR REVIEWING APPLICATIONS FOR COMPENSATION AND REIMBURSEMENT OF EXPENSES FILED UNDER 11 U.S.C. §330 (Appendix A to 28 C.F.R. §58), can be found at http://www.usdoj.gov/ust/rules_reg.htm.

40. For a recent case awarding a lodestar kicker to counsel as compensation for bringing down a recalcitrant debtor, *see In re* Vista Foods USA, Inc., 234 B.R. 121 (Bankr. W.D. Okla. 1991).

41. *In re* Beverly Crest Convalescent Hospital, Inc., 548 F.2d 817 (9th Cir. 1976, as amended 1977).

42. 488 F.2d 714 (5th Cir.1974).

43. We know a trial judge who states a general rule: when the court of appeals names more than three factors, you can ignore all of them.

The 12 factors are:

- time and labor required
- novelty and difficulty of the issue
- skill required
- preclusion of other employment
- customary fee, whether the fee is fixed or contingent
- time limitations
- amount involved and results obtained
- experience, reputation, and ability of counsel
- undesirability of the case
- nature and length of professional relationship with the client
- awards in similar cases.

Just about everything said so far applies to fees for representing the DIP (or trustee) in the chapter 11 case. Contrast the rules governing counsel for the debtor. Counsel does not need authorization to represent the debtor (indeed in advance of filing, how could he get it?). But the court retains explicit authority to examine the fees of counsel for the debtor, and to make adjustments as appropriate. In practice this translates into a system where the court sets a typical fee for debtor representation, which counsel will be able to get without second-guessing. If he wants more, he had better be prepared to persuade the court that the case justifies it.

The corollary is that normally counsel will not be able to take fees from the estate for representing the debtor individually, as distinct from the estate.[44]

One persistent source of lamentation: some courts outside the high-rent districts persist in the notion that high-priced big city counsel should settle for lower local fees when they practice in their courts. *See*, for example, *Hassett v. Goetzmann*,[45] holding that a Washington, D.C., lawyer who charged $400 an hour at home would have to settle for $175 for the privilege of working in Syracuse, as that was the rate charged for similar services by lawyers of reasonably comparable skill, experience and reputation.

---

44. There is an interesting exception for chapter 12 and 13 cases. *See* §330(4)(B).

45. 1998 U.S. Dist. LEXIS 12703, *10 (Bankr. N.D.N.Y.). There is a sharp split in authority on the question whether the Code allows compensation to the debtor's attorney for services performed after the appointment of a trustee. Compare *In re* Top Grade Sausage, Inc., 227 F.3d 123, 130 (3rd Cir. 2000) (allowed) with *In re* American Steel Prod., Inc., 197 F.3d 1354, 1357 (11th Cir. 1999) (not allowed).

It is interesting to wonder whether the big city lawyers thought there was anyone up there truly offering similar skill, experience and reputation. Remarkably, the fee issue is not one for the out-of-towners alone. Often, the locals are glad to see the big city guys come in with their higher rates because it softens up the court for their own fee increases, and because large cases tend to create lots of "local counsel" work.

In light of all this, we think there are good arguments for the out-of-town lawyers to employ local counsel when they come to the outlander district. The local counsel can save you from falling into all the traps of local practice, particularly prevalent on the issue of fees. And there are plenty of judges who think it is good form to provide work for the home folks in any event.

Comment: We think there is a trend toward allowing big-city rates even in outlying jurisdictions where lower rates usually prevail, at least in complex cases. On the other hand, if you are the out-of-towner who regularly charges rates higher than local rates, it's a point you probably want to surface clearly in your initial application for employment. If the judge is really going to allow you only $175 an hour, you are better off knowing that early.

§16.22 ~ Interim Fees

We know a trustee who says: I am in the only business in the world where a four-year-old receivable is good news. Translated: bankruptcy professionals often have to wait for their fees. But time is money, the grocer doesn't take credit, and in a big case you will want to do what you can to get paid as you go along.

The evolving standard seems to be to allow interim fee applications roughly every 120 days, which is consistent with Section 331, governing interim compensation. In a big case, some courts allow fees monthly, subject to a holdback. This is common in large Delaware cases and is becoming more common in other districts. Lawyers routinely seek, and courts enter, orders like the one below early in chapter 11 cases.

§16.23 ~ Form Interim Fee Order

IN THE UNITED STATES BANKRUPTCY COURT
FOR THE EASTERN DISTRICT OF UTOPIA

In Re:	)	
INSOLVENT DISTRIBUTION	)	
CORPORATION,	)	
Debtor-in-Possession	)	Case No. 99-1416-BBL (Chapter 11)
	)	

ADMINISTRATIVE ORDER, PURSUANT TO 11 U.S.C. §§105 AND 331, ESTABLISHING PROCEDURES FOR INTERIM COMPENSATION AND REIMBURSEMENT OF EXPENSES OF PROFESSIONALS

This matter comes before the Court on the Motion for an Administrative Order, Pursuant to 11 U.S.C. §§105(a) and 331, Establishing Procedures for Interim Compensation and Reimbursement of Expenses of Professionals (the "Motion") filed by the above-captioned debtor and debtor-in-possession (the "Debtor"). The Court, having reviewed the Motion and having heard the statements of counsel in support of the relief requested in the Motion at a hearing before the Court on January 11, 1999 (the "Hearing"), and finding that (a) the Court has jurisdiction over the matter pursuant to 28 U.S.C. §§157 and 1334, (b) this is a core proceeding pursuant to 28 U.S.C. §157(b)(2), and (c) notice of the Motion was sufficient under the circumstances; and the Court having determined that the legal and factual bases set forth in the Motion and at the Hearing establish good cause for the relief granted herein;

IT IS THEREFORE ORDERED THAT:

1. Except as may otherwise be provided in a Court order authorizing the retention of specific professionals, all professionals in this case may seek interim compensation in accordance with the following procedure:

   (a) on or before the 15th day of each month following the month for which compensation is sought, each professional shall submit a monthly statement to (i) the Debtor, Thirty Four East Rome Street, Williamsville, Utopia 57195 (Attn: General Counsel), (ii) counsel for the Debtor, Arnold & Porter, 555 Twelfth Street, N.W., Washington, D.C. 20004 (Attn: Michael L. Bernstein), (iii) the Office of the United States Trustee; and (iv) counsel to the Official Committee of Unsecured Creditors (the "Committee"). Each such entity receiving such a statement will have 15 days after its receipt to review it. At the expiration of the 15-day period, the Debtor shall promptly pay 85 percent of the fees and 100 percent of the disbursements requested in such statement, except such fees or disbursements as to which an objection has been served by the Debtor, the U.S. Trustee, or the Committee as provided in subparagraph (b) below.

(b) If the Debtor, the United States Trustee or the Committee object to the compensation or reimbursement sought in a particular statement, they shall, within 15 days of the receipt of the statement, serve upon (i) the professional who submitted the statement to which objections are made and (ii) except to the extent duplicative of the foregoing clause (i), the other persons designated to receive statements in subparagraph (a) above, a written "Notice of Objection to Fee Statement," together with an affidavit setting forth the precise nature of the objection and amount at issue. Thereafter, the objecting party and the professional whose statement is objected to shall attempt to reach an agreement regarding the correct payment to be made. If the parties are unable to reach an agreement on the objection within 15 days after receipt of such objection, the professional whose fee statement is objected to shall have the option of (i) filing the objection with the Court together with a request for payment of the disputed amount, or (ii) foregoing payment of the disputed amount until the next interim fee application hearing, at which time the Court will consider and dispose of the objection if payment of the disputed amount is requested. The Debtor shall be required to pay promptly that percentage set forth above of any portion of the fees and disbursements requested that are not the subject of a Notice of Objection to Fee Statement.

(c) The first statements shall be filed by each of the professionals on or before February 12, 2000. This statement shall relate to the period from the Petition Date through January 31, 2000.

(d) After the first four months, and at four month intervals thereafter, each of the professionals shall file with the Court and serve on the United States Trustee and the other parties identified in subparagraph (a) above an application for interim Court approval and allowance, pursuant to Section 331 of the Bankruptcy Code, of the compensation and reimbursement of expenses requested for the prior four months. The first such application shall be filed on or before June 1, 2000 and shall relate to the period from the Petition Date through May 1, 2000. Any professional who fails to file an application when due shall be ineligible to receive further interim payments of fees or expenses as provided herein until such time as the application is submitted.

(e) The pendency of an objection to payment of compensation or reimbursement of expenses shall not disqualify a professional from the future payment of compensation or reimbursement of expenses as set forth above.

(f) Neither the payment of, nor the failure to pay, in whole or in part, monthly interim compensation and reimbursement as provided herein shall bind any party-in-interest or the Court with respect to the allowance of applications for compensation and reimbursement of professionals.

2. Each member of the Committee is permitted to submit statements of expenses and supporting vouchers to counsel for the Committee, who will collect and submit such requests for reimbursement in accordance with the foregoing procedure for monthly and interim compensation and reimbursement of professionals, and in accordance with 11 U.S.C. §502(b)(3)(F).

3. Notice of any hearing to consider interim applications under 11 U.S.C. §331 shall be sent to: (a) the Office of the United States Trustee; (b) the Debtors and their counsel; (c) counsel for the Committee and (d) all parties who have filed a notice of appearance with the Clerk of this Court and requested such notice, and such notice shall be good and sufficient notice.

4. The Debtors shall include all payments to professionals on their monthly operating reports, detailed so as to state the amount paid to each of the professionals.

5. All time periods set forth in this Order shall be calculated in accordance with Federal Rule of Bankruptcy Procedure 9006(a).

____
UNITED STATES BANKRUPTCY JUDGE

Dated: _______________

§16.24 ~ Attorney Duties in Litigation

Anyone who litigates in Federal court will be familiar with "Rule 11," the civil procedure rule that imposes duties on counsel who sign pleadings in civil cases. Bankruptcy has its own "Rule 11" in "Rule 9011" of the Bankruptcy Rules. The placement is important: because it appears in the "9000" series, we know that it applies to "adversary proceedings" (under the 7000 series) and also to the more general categories of motions, contested matters, etc., in the main case.

Rule 9011 requires that every pleading or motion must be signed by an attorney or a party (with an address and telephone number).

It provides that anyone who presents the document thereby certifies that it:

- Is not interposed for any improper purpose, such as to harass or to cause unnecessary delay or needless increase in the cost of litigation;

- The claims, et cetera, are warranted by existing law or a non-frivolous argument for the extension, modification, or reversal of existing law or for the establishment of new law;

- The allegations have evidentiary support, or (if specifically so identified) are likely to have evidentiary support after a reasonable opportunity for further investigation or discovery; and

- The denials of factual contentions are warranted on the evidence; or (if specifically so identified) are reasonably based on a lack of information or belief.

[All these avowals are based on the attorney's "knowledge, information and belief formed after an inquiry reasonable under the circumstances."]

Anyone who violates the rule may be liable for an "appropriate sanction ... sufficient to deter repetition of such conduct or comparable conduct by others similarly situated." Sanction proceedings may be initiated by a party on motion or by the court on its own initiative. The rule specifically does *not* apply to abuse under the adversary discovery rules.

One place where sanctions have been used in the bankruptcy forum is in testing the limits of "good faith filing,"[46] *See* §5.7.

§16.25 ~ Other Professionals

In discussing the role of the "professional," so far we have focused mainly on the attorney. But the attorney is hardly the only "professional" in the bankruptcy case. Surely the category includes also the outside auditor/accountants for the DIP/trustee or the committee—surely also the investment bankers. It may (though there is a slippery slope here) apply to brokers, auctioneers, appraisers, expert witnesses, "consulting liquidators," and so forth. We won't pretend to canvass all the problems that may arise with these other professionals, but we think we can offer some guidance on important issues.

First: We think it is the job of the lawyer for the DIP/trustee to be alert to the problem—to identify who is a "professional" for purposes of Section 327(a), to make sure they get proper authorization, to work out the terms of payment and such. When in doubt, apply.

Second: Bankruptcy lawyers are used to working by the hour (mostly). Other professionals have different conventions. Real estate brokers work on commission, personal injury lawyers expect contingency fees, investment bankers want flat fees paid monthly (plus "success" fees), and so forth. You may have to educate the judge on why these different fee devices are appropriate in a particular case.

§16.26 ~ Checklist—Time Limits

The easiest way to get sued for malpractice is to blow a deadline. Making the record is a no-brainer: either you missed it or you didn't. And the excuses always sound lame. These facts help to explain all those "excusable neglect" cases, where the litigant is trying to persuade the court that it should grant forgiveness in the teeth of the plain facts. The nominal supplicant is the client, but behind most of these you see the grinning teeth of the insurance carrier.

---

46. Grunewaldt v. Mutual Life Ins. Co. (*In re* Coones Ranch), 7 F.3d 740 (8th Cir. 1998).

Bankruptcy is loaded with deadlines. We don't pretend to catalog all of them here. But we do offer a list of some of the most important, including those we think most likely to get you into trouble.

- Time for objecting to discharge and dischargeability in chapter 7—Rules 4004 and 4007. The rule says not later than 60 days after the first date set for the Section 341 meeting. You'll find the date on the front of the "notice of commencement of case;" *see* Official Form 9. The deadline applies to discharge actions and to those dischargeability actions that must be filed in the bankruptcy case, per Section 523(c). For others, you can file any time. *See generally* §17.29.

- Time for filing a claim in chapter 7—bankruptcy rule 3001. The limit here is ninety days after the date set for the 341 meeting. This date also appears on the face of the notice of commencement, Official Form 9—but note that in apparent no-asset cases, the form will direct that *no* claims be filed. For more on claims filing, *see generally* §13.14.

- Time limit for serving the summons—within 10 days following issuance, rule 7004(e). The answer is due within 30 days of the issuance of the summons, rule 7012(a). Contrast: 120 days for service of the summons in an ordinary civil action, with 20 days after service for the answer.[47] *See generally* §3.20.

- Time to file a notice of appeal—bankruptcy rule 8001. The limit is 10 days after entry of judgment —*i.e., not* 30 days, as is the case with ordinary federal civil actions. *See generally* §§4.13 ff.

- Time during which only the debtor may file a plan—Section 1121. The statute gives you 120 days, except as otherwise ordered. You get an extra 60 days to get confirmation. In small cases creditors rarely file plans and so debtors' lawyers may drift into the habit of letting exclusivity expire. Big mistake: you don't want to explain to your client how you got ambushed by a creditor plan when you might at least have asked the court to extend the exclusive period. Note that the limit in "small business" cases is only 100 days—which is a principal reason why debtors don't feel motivated to accept treatment as a "small business case." *See* §6.14.

- Time to assume or reject a lease of nonresidential real property—Section 365(d)(4). You get 60 days from the time of the petition unless the court orders otherwise. An extension order must come within the original 60 days, so the trustee/DIP will have to move quickly. In chapter 7, executory contracts not assumed within 60 days are deemed rejected.[48] This rule can be embarrassing to a trustee who doesn't even find out what is in the estate until after the 60-day deadline. See generally §11.25.

- Time you can reach back to undo a preference—per Section 547(b), 90 days from the time of filing (or one year for insiders). This is important when you are negotiating with a debtor who has made an avoidable preference. You may need to insist on filing, or to bring an involuntary, in order to capture the 90-day time cap.[49] *See generally* §§14.11 ff.

---

47. Fed. R. Civ. Proc. 4(j), 12(a).

48. Section 365(d)(1).

49. Compare also the time limit for bringing an avoidance action after the bankruptcy has begun (two years or longer; *see* §546).

- Time to reach back to avoid a fraudulent transfer. Under Section 548, only one year before the filing of the petition. Under non-bankruptcy law, incorporated via Section 544(b), the time is set by state statute of limitation and may be much longer. Note that the debtor is required to disclose pre-bankruptcy transfers only within a year before the petition.[50] A crafty debtor may seek to delay filing until after the one-year cutoff in the hope to keep it secret. *See* Chapter 15.

- Time for advance notice of the confirmation hearing—Rule 2002(b) says 25 days. It is one of a number of rules in Section 2002 setting minimum notice standards (mostly 20 days). We suspect that these rules are often violated because no one is alert enough to pick up on them. But it could be awfully embarrassing to show up for the confirmation hearing with your client, your witnesses, your ballots and so forth—only to have the judge send you packing because you didn't provide enough notice. *See* Chapter 18.

50. *See* Official Form 7, Question 10.

17 Discharge and Dischargeability

17 Discharge and Dischargeability

§17.1 ~ Introduction: Not What You Might Hope

If the individual debtor plays by the rules—files his schedules, discloses all his property, appears at the meeting of creditors and so forth, then at the end of the case, the debtor gets a discharge. His remaining liability on his unpaid debts is canceled. Indeed, far and away the majority of all bankruptcy cases are filed by individuals who seek the discharge, and most of them get it.[1] But the discharge may not provide all the comfort it seems to offer at first glance.

For the debtor, part of the problem is practical. If the creditor holds a security interest in, say, the auto the debtor needs to drive to work, then debtor may have to keep paying the secured creditor to retain the automobile (for more on reaffirmations, *see* §9.5). If the creditor is the credit union of which the debtor's father-in-law is a director, then he may have to repay the debt just to keep peace in the family. If the debtor wants the creditor to continue to extend credit to it after bankruptcy, then he may have to pay the debt off even if it is legally dischargeable. And some people still can't bear the thought of not paying their debts; discharge or no discharge, they will insist on following through.

The Code also provides its own catalog of debts that will remain nondischargeable even though the debtor gets the discharge overall.[2] On a day-to-day basis, this matter of nondischargeability is probably a lot more important than the matter of the discharge overall. There are plenty of cases where the debtor will have an undisputed right to the general discharge, but where some exception or other will threaten to carve so large a hole in the protection as to make the bankruptcy scarcely worth the bother.

One reason why this is so is the matter of creditor incentive. Consider the problem of your client, CreditCo, holder of a claim against Dawson Debtor for $100,000, secured by the "Barbarelli Messenger," an exquisite little gold statue last seen in Debtor's possession. Debtor says it was stolen. You don't believe him. You believe he melted it down and hid the gold inside a souvenir model of the Eiffel Tower. Debtor has other liabilities totaling $1 million and no other assets. He does, however, have the capacity to earn money in the future.

---

1. *See generally* §§727, 1141, 1228, 1328.

2. *See generally* §523. Note that the Code has a separate discharge provision for every chapter but only one section (in general chapter 5) purporting to govern all cases of dischargeability. But the matter is a little more complicated than it may appear. Not all of §523 is applicable in chapter 13 (*see* §1328(a)), nor, indeed, in chapter 11 (*see* §1141).

A review of law persuades you that you might have a cause of action to deny Debtor's discharge, perhaps under Section 727(a)(2) ("removed, destroyed, mutilated, or concealed" property), (a)(4) (false oath), or (a)(5) (failure to explain loss of assets). But you also have a respectable shot at an exception to discharge under Section 523(a)(2) (obtaining property by actual fraud) or perhaps (a)(6) (willful and malicious injury).

As a matter of litigation strategy—between your Section 727 action and your Section 523 action, which do you prefer? A moment's reflection and the question almost answers itself. Assuming your goal is to get paid, then you'd usually rather have the 523 action—because if the debtor gets his (general) discharge while your claim alone survives, you are in the best of all possible worlds. You are in the ironic position of being the debtor's ally with regard to his Section 727 case, just as you want to win under Section 523.

There are limits to this reasoning. Sometimes you may have grounds for a Section 727 case, but not for a Section 523. And, of course, sometimes, the debtor's future prospects are so slim that neither case is worth the time and effort.

§17.2 ~ Discharge v. Priority

It is useful also to distinguish the denial of (or exception to) discharge from the matter of priority. The short point is that there is no relation between the two. Consider the matter of "debtor wrongdoing," such as gives grounds for an exception to discharge under Section 523(a)(2), (4) or (6). There is no corresponding priority for any of these claims. By contrast, wages and employee benefits are entitled to priority under Section 507(a)(3) and (4), but there is no corresponding exception to discharge.[3]

Indeed, the relationship can be trickier than it appears. Under Section 523(a)(7), there is an exception to discharge "a fine, penalty, or forfeiture payable to and for the benefit of a governmental unit." But under Section 726(a)(4), claims for fines or penalties (and also claims for punitive damages) are subordinated to general unsecured claims. This presents an interesting strategic choice. Counsel who undertakes to persuade the Court that his client's claim is a fine or penalty (for purposes of enjoying the exception to discharge) may find that he has talked himself out of a distribution under Section 726(a).

§17.3 ~ Discharge

For dischargeability, as defined above, the Code sets a single rule that applies in all chapters. For "discharge," there is a separate rule for each chapter. We begin by considering the discharge in chapter 7.

---

3. There may be leverage elsewhere that will effectively except wage claims from discharge. For example, non-payment of wages is a crime in many jurisdictions, and the potential defendant may work very hard to see to it that the wages are paid so as to remove the threat of criminal liability. And the debtor can scarcely expect to continue to run his business unless he pays his employees. But the general point remains.

§17.4 ~ Discharge for "Individuals" Only

Section 727(a)(1) bars the discharge if "the debtor is not an individual." This means, among other things, that there is no discharge for partnerships or corporations (note that this is chapter 7 only—the chapter 11 rule is different).

The case of the partnership is nonproblematic. At least with respect to general partners, the point of partnership is unlimited liability, so you can't really give a discharge to the partnership independent of the (general) partners. On the other hand, nothing bars the individual partners from getting their own individual discharges in their own bankruptcy proceedings. *See* §17.43.

The case of the corporate discharge is more puzzling. The legislative history says the bar "will avoid trafficking in corporate shells,"[4] although it is far from clear that there ever was a market for corporate shells, or if so, that it needed to be discouraged, or if so, that the Bankruptcy Code was the proper place to do it. But on the other side of the coin, there is probably no point to a discharge in a corporate chapter 7 liquidation. The corporation's assets will be sold, so all that will remain, in the usual case, will be the corporate shell. A limited liability entity, with no assets and no ongoing business, has no need for a discharge. The usual course will be either to dissolve the corporation under state law or, perhaps more commonly, just let it languish.

§17.5 ~ Only Once Every Six Years

Section 727(a)(8) bars the debtor from getting the chapter 7 discharge more than once every six years. A few debtors will find themselves struggling to fend off creditor action long enough to reach beyond the six year period (count time from date of filing to date of filing).

Section 727(a)(9) provides that a debtor who receives a discharge in chapter 13 may get a discharge in chapter 7 within six years thereafter, but only in two classes of cases. First, he may get the new discharge if he paid 100 percent of all claims. But secondly, he may also get it if he paid only 70 percent of claims and "the plan was proposed by the debtor in good faith, and was the debtor's best effort." Don't confuse this rule with the similar (but not identical) rule governing the issue of when you get the super discharge in chapter 13. *See* §6.26.

§17.6 ~ Wrongdoing, Fraudulent Transfer

Section 727(a)(2) bars the discharge when

> the debtor, with *intent* to hinder, delay, or defraud a creditor or an officer of the estate charged with custody of property under this title, has transferred, removed, destroyed, mutilated, or concealed, or has permitted to be transferred, removed, destroyed, mutilated, or concealed –
>
> - property of the debtor, within one year before the date of the filing of the petition; or
> - property of the estate, after the date of the filing of the petition.

---

4. H.R. Rep. No. 95-595, 1st Sess. at 384 (1977).

This is a kind of a fraudulent transfer rule, but note that it is limited to intentional fraud and does not bar the discharge in the case of mere technical (constructive) fraudulent transfers. Intentional concealment of this sort may also be a crime. So on appropriate facts, the debtor may (a) see the transfer avoided and the property recaptured for the estate, (b) lose his discharge, and (c) suffer a criminal penalty.

Note that 727(a)(2) doesn't say anything about harm to the estate. Consider this case:

Dawson owns Mona Lisa, a famous painting. Fearing that his creditors may get it, he transfers it to his cousin Ted. Later, as his troubles get worse, he seeks advice from Lisa, a lawyer. Lisa asks him if he has made any transfers by gift. Dawson freely tells Lisa about the transfer of the Mona Lisa.

What is Lisa's next move? If Dawson files for bankruptcy leaving the transfer undisturbed he almost certainly will lose his discharge under 727(a)(2). On the other hand, if he gets the painting back from Ted, it is not clear that he has improved his lot. After all the statute speaks about transfer not repentance, and the transfer remains a fact even after the return. Plausible as this may sound, the Ninth Circuit was able to read a no-harm-no-foul rule into the subtext to save the transferor's discharge.[5]

The statutory reach-back period is one year before the petition, just as in avoidance actions under Section 548. But the Ninth Circuit recently held that the one year runs from the time the transfer is effective between the parties.[6]

§17.7 ~ NONCOOPERATION

Sections 727(a)(3), (a)(5), and (a)(6) bar a broad the discharge for a broad range of conduct which might be lumped together generally under the head of noncooperation. All of these may be read, at least in part, as preventive rather than penal. They provide leverage to compel debtor cooperation—and in particular, a lever for counsel to make sure that his client does what he is supposed to do. Also, they all need to be understood in the context of the debtor's privilege against self-incrimination, guaranteed by the Fifth Amendment.

Among specifics, Section 727(a)(3) bars the discharge where

> the debtor has concealed, destroyed, mutilated, falsified, or failed to keep or preserve any recorded information, including books, documents, records, and papers, from which the debtor's financial condition or business transactions might be ascertained, unless such act or failure to act was justified under all of the circumstances of the case.

---

5. *See In re* Adeeb, 787 F.2d 1339, 1343 (9th Cir. 1986). *But see In re* Davis, 911 F.2d 560, 562 (11th Cir. 1990).

6. *In re* Roosevelt, 87 F.3d 311 (9th Cir. 1996).

It parallels subsection 727(a)(5) which bars the discharge where:

> the debtor has failed to explain satisfactorily, before determination of denial of discharge under this paragraph, any loss of assets or deficiency of assets to meet the debtor's liabilities.

But with these, compare Section 727(a)(6) which provides that the debtor will lose his discharge where he has refused in the case:

- to obey any lawful order of the court, other than an order to respond to a material question or to testify;
- on the ground of privilege self-incrimination, to respond to a material question approved by the court or to testify, after the debtor has been granted immunity with respect to the matter concerning which such privilege was invoked; or
- on a ground other than the properly invoked privilege against self-incrimination, to respond to a material question approved by the court or to testify.

The protective language about the Fifth Amendment is perhaps superfluous: after all, the Constitution trumps, and the Fifth Amendment protection would subsist even if the statute tried to deny it. But the statute makes clear that the debtor will not, in the ordinary case, lose his discharge for a properly pleaded Fifth Amendment defense.

The statute does recognize one (apparently constitutional) exception. Section 344 provides:

> Immunity for persons required to submit to examination, to testify, or to provide information in a case under this title may be granted under [the Federal immunity statute].

Section 344 should be read together with Section 727(a)(6), quoted above. Together, they mean that the debtor may invoke the privilege without jeopardizing his discharge unless the prosecutor goes before a district judge and gets an affirmative grant of use immunity in a particular case. Since this almost never happens in practice, the practical effect is that the debtor's privilege is virtually complete.

§17.8 ~ Interfering with the Process

Section 727(a)(4) bars the discharge for a mixed bag of misconduct that may be categorized as interference with the bankruptcy process. The section says the court shall not grant the discharge if the debtor knowingly and fraudulently, in or in connection with the case

- made a false oath or account;
- presented or used a false claim;
- gave, offered, received, or attempted to obtain money, property, or advantage, or a promise of money, property, or advantage, for acting or forbearing to act; or

- withheld from an officer of the estate entitled to possession under this title, any recorded information, including books, documents, records, and papers, relating to the debtor's property or financial affairs.

Once again, there is a good deal of overlap between this provision and the "bankruptcy crimes" statutes in Title 18; *see* §2.13.

§17.9 ~ Insider Misconduct

Subsections (a)(2) through (a)(6) bar the discharge for a range of misconduct in a particular bankruptcy case. Subsection (a)(7) extends the bar to misconduct "in connection with another case . . . concerning an insider." There is a (non-exclusive) definition of "insider" in Section 101(31). It links, *e.g.*, the debtor and the corporation of which he is a director, officer or person in control. So the principal who meddles improperly with his corporate case may find that he has spoiled chances for his individual discharge.

§17.10 ~ Waiver of Discharge

Section 727(a)(10) provides that the discharge is barred when "the court approves a written waiver of discharge executed by the debtor after the order for relief under this chapter." Hardly any debtor will ever want to waive the discharge, although the matter of waiver may arise in collateral litigation—*e.g.*, settling a criminal case. Perhaps the most important point of Section (a)(10) is that it limits the terms on which waiver will be available—making clear, for example, that there will be no anticipatory waivers in the boilerplate of form contracts.

§17.11 ~ Dismissal

A little noticed possible side door around the discharge is in Section 349, which provides for dismissal of the bankruptcy case. The section provides that dismissal does not bar discharge in a later case. But it bears the qualification "unless the court, for cause, orders otherwise."

This seems to raise the prospect of a "dismissal with prejudice" having the same effect as denying the discharge. So far as we can tell, no court has used the dismissal rule of Section 349 as a quick-and-dirty substitute for denying discharge under Section 727. But they have done something very close. That is, several courts have used dismissal with prejudice in an attempt to control serial or abusive filings, barring the debtor either temporarily[7] or permanently[8] from ever seeking bankruptcy relief.

We don't think these cases are quite the same because they typically involve debtors who have no apparent interest in the discharge, but instead are trying to use the bankruptcy proceeding to hold onto property. But counsel for the debtor will want to read potential stipulated dismissal papers with special care.

---

7. Walker v. Stanley, 231 B.R. 343, 351 (N.D. Cal. 1999); *In re* Frieouf, 938 F.2d 1099, 1104-05 (10th Cir. 1991).

8. *In re* Casse, 198 F.3d 327, 334-42 (2d Cir.1999) (thorough discussion of dismissal with prejudice).

§17.12 ~ Dischargeability

There are currently 17 numbered exceptions to discharge in Section 523. Congress keeps adding new ones, and never seems to remove any, so the list can be expected to grow. Some of the 17 are too specialized to admit extensive discussion here.[9] But it is possible to draw some tentative generalizations. For example, an important class of cases involves some sort of debtor wrongdoing—fraud, or willful and malicious injury and the like. Some turn not on the conduct of the debtor, but on the nature of the obligation.

Thus, for example, most tax claims are excepted from discharge, as are most domestic obligations. Further, it is useful to identify those cases (in fact, very few) where the Code applies what you might call a "best efforts" rule, testing the scope of the discharge by the debtor's capacity to repay. Finally, we can identify a couple of classes of nondischargeability that emerge from the Code itself. We start with this last category first.

§17.13 ~ Not Scheduled, Not Discharged

Practically speaking, perhaps the most important rule of dischargeability practice is: if a claim is not scheduled, it is not discharged. This is an oversimplification, but it is good enough for starters.

§17.14 ~ Strategy: List All Debts

Insist that the client list every debt, no matter how trifling, or no matter or how determined he is to repay it. This is easier said than done: the client will often come up with (apparently) good reasons why somebody or other should be left off the schedules. Your job is to talk him out of it. Or, failing that, at the very least make sure that you can document that the choice to exclude was his choice and not yours, and that in omitting the claim, he acted against your advice. You don't want him changing his mind later about the decision to omit—and then pointing the finger at you as the one who let him let the debt survive.

This is a good point of departure but, in fact, the situation is a little more complicated. What the Code says is that there is no discharge for an unscheduled debt "unless (the) creditor had notice or actual knowledge of the case in time" to file his claim.[10] This offers a kind of desperation defense where a creditor tries to sue post-discharge on an unscheduled claim: the debtor has the option of trying to persuade the court that the creditor had notice or actual knowledge, notwithstanding the omission. Compare also Section 726(a)(2) and (3) (awarding a junior priority to some late-filed claims).

As with claims in general, there is a no-schedule exception where the creditor might have had a case of debtor wrongdoing under Section 523(a)(2), (4) or (6). In this case, the debt survives under Section 523(a)(3), unless the claim was scheduled in time for the creditor to have an opportunity to pursue a non-dischargeability action under Section 523(a)(2), (a)(4), or (a)(6).

---

9. Section (a)(16) (excepting co-op and condo dues); §(a)(17) (excepting debts for fees in prisoner appeals); §§(a)(11) and (12) (excepting obligations to federal depository institutions).

10. Section 523(a)(3) (emphasis added).

The rules require a bit of extra thought in the (typical) no-asset case. Suppose that two years after discharge (and after the case is closed), Clarence Creditor sues Deborah Debtor on a pre-petition claim. To her chagrin, Deborah discovers that Clarence was not scheduled. If the case was a no-asset case, Deborah will be tempted to try to (a) reopen the case; (b) amend the schedules; and (c) seek a declaration that the debt is discharged in any event. She will argue: Your Honor, I know I am late, but look at the record. There were no assets to distribute anyway, so Clarence was not harmed. It is a case of no harm, no foul.

There is hope for Deborah here, but it is not a slam dunk. Courts are not eager to let Deborah think up easy, cost-free excuses for missing deadlines.[11] The case law is extensive and inconsistent, but a lot of it seems to go against the debtor, so prepare the schedules with care.

§17.15 ~ Denial is Forever

We made the point elsewhere that the denial of the discharge lasts forever. With limited exceptions, if the discharge is denied, then it stays denied and the debts in question cannot be discharged in any subsequent case. Section 523(a)(10) confirms this principle, granting an exception to discharge for any debt that was or could have been listed in a prior case where the discharge was denied.

§17.16 ~ False Statement

A frequently litigated question relates to the scope of the "false statement" exception to discharge in Section 523(a)(2). Just at first glance, it is clear that the language is forbiddingly technical: a minefield of litigation technicalities to thread one's way over.

The difficulties are probably best understood in terms of history. The scope of the false-statement exception has always been a contentious issue in Congress, with creditors unwilling to excuse wrongdoing, while the debtor lobby seeks to resist any appearance of creditor overreaching. The language we see before us can be regarded as Congress' declaration that you may be able to get your exception here, but that it won't be easy.[12]

Perhaps a good way to get a handle on the section is to pose a case of the kind that attracted Congress' attention back a generation ago, before many of the statutory refinements.

Example: It is 1968. Deborah and Donald Debtor are husband and wife. Donald is in the South Pacific with the United States Navy while Deborah is living alone in San Diego. She runs short of money for basic expenses. She goes to LoanCo, a specialist in consumer loans. Lannie, the manager, presents her with an application form. On the back, it says, other debts, and leaves three blank lines. Deborah tells

---

11. *See, e.g.*, Matter of Faden, 96 F.3d 792, 796-97 (5th Cir. 1996). The court held that the debtor has the burden of proving that the creditor had timely notice or knowledge so as to overcome §523(a)(3). More interestingly, the court held that amendment is not permissible in any event where the original failure to schedule was intentional.

12. The courts, for their part haven't done much to simplify matters. There are a number of important Supreme Court cases construing §523 (and its predecessors), along with a virtual torrent of lower court opinions—most of the latter very fact-specific.

Lannie that she's not sure what all her debts are, but she's pretty sure there are more than three. Lannie says—it's okay, this is for purposes of information only. So she lists three small department store charge cards—neglecting three others and the $800 that she owes to the hospital for emergency medical care. She further fails to tell Lannie about some debts run up by Donald last time he was home on leave—necessarily, because Donald never told her, and she will be as disappointed as anyone when she finds out about them.

In any event, LoanCo makes the loan and Deborah defaults and files for bankruptcy. On a complaint seeking an exception to discharge, LoanCo will allege that Deborah got the loan on the strength of a false financial statement.[13] This is true enough as far as it goes, but as many will think that it misses the point. By conventional standards, Deborah hardly set out to mislead. Given what Lannie said, LoanCo can hardly be said to have been misled (but in any event, he has since changed jobs and cannot be found). Moreover there is a good chance that even if Deborah had told them everything, LoanCo would have made the loan anyway.

§17.17 ~ "Financial Condition"—Section 523(a)(2)(B)

This helps to explain the fairly intricate path that LoanCo must follow to win its case. We direct our attention to Section 523(a)(2)(B). On facts like these, LoanCo can get an exception to discharge only if it shows a statement in writing—

- that is materially false;
- respecting the debtor's or an insider's financial condition;
- on which the creditor to whom the debtor is liable for such money, property, services, or credit *reasonably relied*; and
- that the debtor caused to be made or published with intent to deceive.

Clearly LoanCo can show that there was a "writing . . . respecting the debtor's . . . financial condition," and that it was false. But every other contention is in dispute: materiality, intention to deceive, reasonable reliance. So LoanCo's chances of prevailing are sharply circumscribed. And generalizing, the hurdles seem sufficiently high so as to put sharp limits on the amount of successful 523(a)(2)(B) litigation.[14]

---

13. In the 60s, the case would have been tried in state court. These days, it would be in the bankruptcy court. *See* §17.30.

14. Among recent cases, *see, e.g*, Bellco First Fed. Credit Union v. Kaspar (*In re* Kaspar), 125 F.3d 1358, 1362 (10th Cir. 1997) (computer generated credit application not a written statement for purposes of §523(a)(2)(B)); First Nat'l Bank v. Pontow, 111 F.3d 604, 609-10 (8th Cir. 1997) (bank's practice of discarding "borrowing base certificates" is a strong suggestion that the Bank didn't rely on them); Tallant v. Kaufman (*In re* Tallant), 218 B.R. 58, 70-71 (B.A.P. 9th Cir.1998) (failure by debtor/attorney to include personal liability in written profit and loss for law practice was not materially false because the statement accurately reflected finances of law practice).

§17.18 ~ Other Than Financial Condition—Section 523(a)(2)(A)

Scanning reported cases, one draws the inference that there are far more dischargeability proceedings these days under subsection (a)(2)(A) than under (a)(2)(B). There are two possible reasons why. One is the difficulty of making an (a)(2)(B) case, as set forth above. The other is the explosion of credit card debt and related ATM debt, which seems to invoke (a)(2)(A) more directly than (a)(2)(B).

Section 523(a)(2)(A) provides another kind of false statement exception. It provides an exception for credit obtained by "false pretenses, a false representation, or actual fraud, other than a statement respecting the debtor's or an insider's financial condition." To understand how it works, consider this case:

Example: Della, the single mother of three, who has always prudently managed her limited resources. She has a credit card at BankCo with an overdraft privilege, but until lately, she was careful never to use the overdraft line. Everything on the original credit card application with truthful and until early this year, she always made at least the minimum payment on time. On the February 1, disaster overtakes her: she loses her job. The same week, her eldest child leads her on a frantic chase to the emergency room, leaving her with an $800 uninsured bill.

From then on, she never seemed to catch up. Over the next three months, she used the card for a variety of household expenses including, for the first time, some overdraft draws. Her outstanding balance trebled from its previous high to $9,000. During the last week in April, she took the maximum draw every day. On May 1, she filed for bankruptcy. On her schedules, she listed her cash holdings at $50, and claimed an exemption for miscellaneous household goods and supplies. BankCo filed a complaint for an exception from discharge under Section 523(a)(2)(A) for the credit card debt. At trial, Della does not take the stand and there are no witnesses. Without objection, the bank introduces the credit card statements, and both sides rest.

What can we make of this case? First, note that the bank, stuck with a truthful application, seems to have abandoned any hope of success under (a)(2)(B). What the bank must be alleging is that her use of the card while in desperate straits is a representation of an intent to repay—and that no reasonable person would have been able to entertain such an intent, given her straits.

Some readers will find this sort of argument credible. Many courts, however, seem not to have found it persuasive. Recognizing that the cases are fact-specific, still a growing body of case law suggests we look at the debtor's subjective intent, and if it appears that this debtor actually intended to pay, then the debt is dischargeable, no matter how unrealistic the intention might appear to a third person.[15] But other courts have sided with the creditor, holding that use of a credit card constitutes a representation of intent and ability to repay.[16]

---

15. *See, e.g.*, Rembert v. AT&T Universal Card Servs. Inc. (*In re* Rembert), 141 F.3d 277, 282-83 (6th Cir.) (gambler's subjective statement of belief that she could win enough to repay cash advances—coupled with payments to card issuer—evidence lack of fraudulent intent), *cert. denied*, 525 U.S. 978 (1998); *cf.* Providian Banncorp v. Shartz *(In re* Shartz) 221 B.R. 397 (B.A.P. 6th Cir.1998) (reading *Rembert* as saying that use of the card alone is no longer enough for a Section 523(a)(2)(A) case).

16. *See, e.g.*, American Express v. Hashemi (*In re* Hashemi), 104 F.3d 1122 (9th Cir. 1996) (use of card is representation of intent/ability to repay); *In re* Borror, 132 B.R.194, 196. (Bankr. M.D. Fla. 1991) (same).

If creditors have had trouble with the lower courts under this section, they have received a couple of recent gifts from the Supreme Court. *Cohen v. De La Cruz* holds that the 523(a)(2) exception extends beyond the compensatory award and includes treble damages, attorney's fees, and costs.[17] In *Field v. Mans*,[18] the Supreme Court held that the creditor's reliance need be only justifiable, not reasonable. The latter point may appear to be one of surpassing technicality. But there is more litigation than you might think over the issue of creditor reliance. *Field v. Mans* seems to have offered important new cover for creditors in fraud cases.

§17.19 ~ MORE ATM LAW: SECTION 523(A)(2)(C)

Recall Della, the debtor in the previous section. Unfortunately, Section 523(a)(2)(A) may not be the end of her problems. The bank will likely also seek relief under Section 523(a)(2)(C). It provides:

> For purposes of subparagraph (A) of this paragraph, consumer debts owed to a single creditor and aggregating more than $1,075 for luxury goods or services incurred by an individual debtor on or within 60 days before the order for relief under this title, or cash advances aggregating more than $1,075 that are extensions of consumer credit under an open end credit plan obtained by an individual debtor on or within 60 days before the order for relief under this title, are presumed to be nondischargeable.

The pivot point here is: "presumed to be nondischargeable." The presumption is rebuttable, but it is up to the debtor to offer an explanation.[19] Note that the consumer debts must be for luxury goods or services, but the cash withdrawals may not be so limited: evidently any kind of cash withdrawal will do. Della may have used the cash advance to buy baby food, but on a literal reading of the statute, this fact doesn't seem to be relevant.

Note that nothing precludes the use of Section 523(a)(2)(A), as appropriate, for ATM cases that do not fit the narrow confines of (a)(2)(C).

§17.20 ~ DAMAGES—523(D)

One more warning for the creditor thinking about bringing a Section 523(a) case—watch out for Section 523(d). This section provides that if the debtor wins, and if the creditor's position was not substantially justified, then the debtor can get judgment for costs and attorney's fees. The Second Circuit BAP had to consider the case of a debtor who had lost her job, was separated from her husband, was hospitalized for a suicide attempt, was unable to work and used cash advances for food, gas, clothing, diapers and baby formula. The bankruptcy court refused to grant an exception to discharge, and awarded attorney's fees. The appellate court upheld the decision and left open the opportunity to file a motion for extra costs for the appeal.[20]

---

17. Cohen v. De La Cruz, 523 U.S. 213, 218 (1998).

18. 516 U.S. 59 (1995).

19. AT&T Universal Card Servs. Corp. v. Ellingsworth (*In re* Ellingsworth), 212 B.R. 326, 339-40 (Bankr. W.D. Mo. 1997).

20. AT&T Universal Card Servs. Corp. v. Williams (*In re* Williams), 224 B.R. 523, 532 (2d Cir. BAP 1998). The court held that the costs are not authorized under §523(d) itself, but may be under appellate rule 38. Fed R. App Proc. 38.

§17.21 ~ Fraud or Defalcation

Conceptually, some of the most interesting dischargeability litigation involves Section 523(a)(4), which grants an exception "for fraud or defalcation while acting in a fiduciary capacity, embezzlement, or larceny."

A particularly troublesome issue has been the question of what counts as "fiduciary capacity." Courts interpreting bankruptcy law generally agree that just because the state *calls* it "fiduciary" doesn't mean that it is "fiduciary for purposes of Section 523(a)(4)"—else a state could make anything it wanted nondischargeable just by stamping the scarlet "F" on its forehead.[21]

A recent Fifth Circuit opinion offers a useful sketch of how to recognize a fiduciary relationship.[22] The Texas Lottery Act provided that the proceeds of ticket sales "be held in trust for the benefit of the estate." The court conceded that a statute may create an "(a)(4)" trust, but only if (a) it includes a definable trust *res*, and (b) imposes 'trust-like' duties. Here, the court noted, the debtor was required only to remit money—there was no requirement of a separate bank account. Also, the debtor was not in a "position of ascendancy" over the state: there was no "difference of knowledge or power" in the debtor's favor. Therefore, no trust.[23]

In the same vein but on a slightly different issue, the same court held that a jury finding of wrongful misappropriation of trade secrets was not necessarily a finding of embezzlement. For example, one could misappropriate wrongfully but with an honest belief of entitlement—in which case, no embezzlement.[24]

§17.22 ~ Willful and Malicious

Section 523(a)(6) provides an exception to discharge for "willful and malicious injury by the debtor to another entity or to the property of another entity." The Supreme Court pretty much rewrote the agenda for this section in 1998 in *Kawaauhau v. Geirger*, when it held that a medical malpractice judgment grounded in reckless or negligent conduct does not fall within the definition of willful and malicious.[25] Interpreting *Kawaauhau*, the Fifth Circuit has said that *three* remaining readings of willful and malicious are possible:

- any tort classified as intentional;
- any tort substantially certain to result in injury; or
- any tort motivated by a desire to inflict injury.

---

21. *See, e.g.*, Fowler Bros. v. Young (*In re* Young), 91 F.3d 1367, 1371-72 (10th Cir. 1996).

22. Texas Lottery Comm'n v. Tran (Matter of Tran), 151 F.3d 339 (5th Cir. 1998).

23. Remarkably, some (but not all) courts have held that an attorney who takes money from a client is not a fiduciary for purposes of §523(a)(4). *See, e.g.*, R.E. America, Inc. v. Garver (*In re* Garver), 116 F.3d 176, 179-80 (6th Cir. 1997).

24. Miller v. J.D. Abrams Inc. (Matter of Miller) 156 F.3d 598, 602-04 (5th Cir. 1998).

25. 523 U.S. 57, 61 (1998).

The Fifth Circuit held that mere intent was not enough; but that either of the remaining two standards would be sufficient to support the exception.[26]

One tantalizing question that will perhaps continue to perplex the courts is the relationship between willful wrongdoing and the kind of risk-taking that debtors do with other people's money. In *Chrysler Credit Corp. v. Perry Chrysler Plymouth, Inc.*,[27] the debtor took $100,000 of funds held in trust for Chrysler and took them to Las Vegas, where he lost it in about three days. The Fifth Circuit held the debt nondischargeable under Section 523(a)(6).

It is provocative to compare that case with *Heinhold Commodities & Securities, Inc. v. Hunt*,[28] where the plaintiffs alleged that certain debts were nondischargeable because they were fraudulently procured when the debtor issued bad checks and made a false financial statement. In Heinhold, the creditors were brokerage houses and the debtor was a high-volume "day trader" in bond futures. His account often fell below formal margin requirements, but he regularly covered shortfalls. An unusual string of unsuccessful trades left him in bankruptcy.

But the court found no intent to injure. In a long discussion of the problem of intent, the court said, "where the objective unreasonableness of the debtor's proposed technique for repayment of the plaintiff is revealed, the debtor's professed subjective good intent is impugned and the debtor must demonstrate that he subjectively intended to succeed at an unreasonable scheme. This burden is not insurmountable."[29] In a footnote, the court added: "No other facts appearing, a debtor who intends to cover a check tomorrow by winning the Irish Sweepstakes is acting beyond the standards of a reasonably prudent man."[30] And in another footnote on how the debtor might meet his burden of showing intent, the court said:

> One example might be the debtor who at the time of incurring a debt plans a trip to Las Vegas to gamble and expects to win enough money to pay the debt. Such would be an objectively unreasonable scheme and the burden would be on the debtor to come forward with further proof. Conceivably, were the debtor to prove his ability at "card counting" and a long history of success at the card tables, a court might find that the debtor carried his burden . . . . In the example above of a debtor intending to cover a bad check by winning the Irish Sweepstakes, what if the debtor proves he holds all of the tickets? What if the debtor's psychiatrist testifies that a television set "told" the debtor he would win the sweepstakes?[31]

The court didn't attempt to answer its own question. The footnote leaves one wondering what should have been done with *Perry* had Perry been able "to prove his ability at 'card counting.'" Perhaps Chrysler got off too easy.

---

26. J.D. Abrams Inc. 156 F.3d at 603-04.

27. 783 F.2d 480 (5th Cir. 1986).

28. 30 B.R. 425 (M.D. Tenn. 1983).

29. *Id.* at 442.

30. *Id.* at n. 31.

31. *Id.* at n. 31.

§17.23 ~ Drunk Driving

Here is a kind of case that attracted a good deal of adverse commentary. Daniel gets behind the wheel of his car late one night, having had far too much to drink. He weaves out of the parking lot and plows into a car driven by Carla, who is injured, and whose car is demolished. Carla sues Daniel to get compensation for her injuries. When Daniel files for bankruptcy Carla files a complaint seeking an exception from under Section 523(a)(6), alleging willful and malicious injury.

Daniel's response: it couldn't have been willful because I was too drunk to form a purpose. Ungracious as this may sound, it appears to have worked—at least long enough for the drunk driving lobby to prevail on Congress for a special exception. Current Section 523(a)(9) provides an exception for death or personal injury caused by the debtor's operation of a motor vehicle if such operation was unlawful because the debtor was intoxicated from using alcohol, a drug, or another substance.

This provision may be enough to dispose of Daniel's argument, but note the limitations. Carla will have to show that the operation was unlawful because of intoxication. Our criminal law colleagues say there is an offense known in the trade as a "wet reckless," where Daniel, though impaired by alcohol, is not drunk enough to be charged with driving while intoxicated. Carla may find to her chagrin that the "lesser" charge isn't sufficiently precise to win her the protection of subsection (a)(9). She remains free, of course, to try to sustain the "willful and malicious" case under subsection (a)(6).

§17.24 ~ Fines and Restitution Orders

Section 523(a)(7) provides an exception "to the extent that [the] debt is for a fine, penalty, or forfeiture payable to and for the benefit of a governmental unit." There is an exception for tax penalties.

Criminal sentences these days often include an order that the defendant make restitution for his wrongdoing. In the early years of the current Code, courts had some difficulty figuring out what to do with restitution orders. The perplexity led to the addition of current Section 523(a)(13), providing an exception "for any payment of an order of restitution under Title 18, United States Code." Note that this restitution rule applies only to the federal criminal code, suggesting that state restitution orders remain dischargeable. Contrast the rule on fines and penalties, discussed above, which appears not to be so limited.

For a case where a state with a consumer protection order succeeded in missing out on this and three other possible exceptions, *see* Matter of Towers,[32] where the court held that a civil restitution order payable to the state was not exempted by subsection (a)(7). The court held that the sum was not for the benefit of the state because the state paid all such recoveries over to the actual injured parties (although it did not have to).

The court said the state also missed its opportunity to take advantage of subsections (a)(2), (a)(4) and (a)(6) because it "snoozed through" two prior bankruptcies. The state argued that there were good policy reasons for skipping the prior bankruptcies because it was waiting until it finished underlying litigation. But the court said the policy arrow pointed just the other direction: the purpose of Section 523(c) (the court said) is to try to get dischargeability issues disposed of promptly.

---

32. 162 F.3d 952 (7th Cir. 1998), *cert. denied*, Illinois *ex rel.* Ryan v. Towers, 119 S. Ct. 2340.

As an added confusion, observe that there is no discharge under chapter 13 of any debt incurred "for restitution, or a criminal fine, included in a sentence on the debtor's conviction of a crime."

§17.25 ~ TAXES

Section 523(a)(1) provides an exception to discharge for tax debts. It is broad-gauged and will cover most tax debts, but there are a few limits that the debtor might slip through.

The exception covers all taxes entitled to priority under Section 507(a)(8), and then some.[33] For a checklist, see the next section.

Timing: There are "time caps" that cut off the rights of the government against the taxpayer. They are best seen in terms of some examples.

Example: Debtor files for bankruptcy on April 1, 2001. He owes income taxes for 1996 and 1997. The debtor filed returns for each year, and the tax was due in each case on April 15 of the following year. A three-year time cap applies.[34] The 1997 tax is nondischargeable because it is due on April 15, 1998, which is within three years of the filing of the petition. The 1996 tax is dischargeable because it is it is due on April 15, 1997, more than three years before the filing of the petition.

Example: Debtor files a tax return on September 1, 2000, for the tax year ending December 31, 1995. The IRS issues its assessment for that taxable year in January, 2001. The 240-day rule applies. The tax is nondischargeable because the assessment was made within 240 days of the filing, even though the taxes go back more than three years.

Suppose the debtor foresees that his tax debt will be nondischargeable in bankruptcy. To sidestep the constraint, he borrows money from BankCo and pays the tax debt. After a respectful pause (to obviate the imputation of outright fraud), he files for bankruptcy relief, seeking to discharge the debt to BankCo which, after all, is not a tax debt. Will he get the protection of the discharge? The answer is no.[35]

§17.26 ~ CHECKLIST: NONDISCHARGEABLE TAXES

Priority Taxes (Section 507(a)(8))

- Withholding taxes.
- Any income or gross receipt tax for which return was due (including extensions) within three years before the bankruptcy filing.

---

33. For example, late filed taxes and taxes and taxes for which no return is filed are nondischargeable even though not entitled to priority. Section 523 also picks up "gap taxes" in involuntary cases under §502(f), included via §507(a)(2).

34. Section 507(a)(8)(A)(i).

35. *See* §523(a)(14).

- Taxes assessed within 240 days before filing of bankruptcy petition. The 240-day period is tolled while offer in compromise is pending and for 30 days thereafter.

- Unassessed taxes that are assessable after the bankruptcy filing. For example, if a debtor is under audit for prebankruptcy years at time of filing, those taxes, once assessed, are priority, and therefore nondischargeable.

- Certain employment taxes.

- Certain excise taxes.

- Certain customs duties.

- A property tax assessed prior to the petition date which was due within one year prior to petition date.

Nonpriority, but also Nondischargeable

- If fraudulent return or willful attempt to avoid tax, the taxes, interest, and penalties are nondischargeable.

- Return, if required, is not filed or is filed after the date on which last due and within two years prior to bankruptcy filing.

Penalties and Interest

- Penalties that compensate the government for actual pecuniary loss are priority. Others are nonpriority in chapter 7, but treatment is less clear in chapter 11.

- Pre-petition interest is priority (and therefore nondischargeable) if the tax on which it accrued is priority.

Finally, debts incurred to pay nondischargeable federal taxes are nondischargeable.

§17.27 ~ Domestic Obligations

Section 523(a) includes two provisions excepting domestic obligations from discharge. The older and more pervasive is Section 523(a)(5), which excepts obligations "for alimony to, maintenance for, or support of (a) spouse or child." Then it adds (somewhat cryptically) that it will apply only if "such liability is actually in the nature of alimony, maintenance, or support." Whatever one can say for the draftsmanship, the effect of the provision is clear enough. Consider a state like California, where local law draws a sharp distinction between obligations for support (on the one hand) and division of marital property on the other. Section 523(a)(5) excepts the support obligation but leaves the obligation under the property division fully dischargeable.

This inconsistency of treatment led Congress in 1994 to adopt current Section 523(a)(15). It excepts property settlement obligations, but it imposes a "best efforts" and "balancing of equities" test which, taken together, offer to provide a variety of issues in litigation. Specifically, the provision says that the obligation is excepted

- unless the debtor does not have the ability to pay such debt from income or property of the debtor not reasonably necessary to be expended for the maintenance or support of the debtor or a dependent of the debtor and, if the debtor is engaged in a business, for the payment of expenditures necessary for the continuation, preservation, and operation of such business;

- or discharging such debt would result in a benefit to the debtor that outweighs the detrimental consequences to a spouse, former spouse, or child of the debtor.

§17.28 ~ Student Loans

Student loans are conceptually interesting because they are one place where the Code imposes a general best efforts test. Thus, Section 523(a)(8) provides an exception for a government-funded student loan unless "excepting such debt from discharge . . . will impose an undue hardship on the debtor and the debtor's dependents." This provision and its predecessors have created a body of Dickensian case law in which the judge tries to determine the limits of the debtor's capacity to repay. The nearest thing to a "general rule" would be the "three part test" propounded by the Second Circuit deciding *Brunner v. New York State Higher Educ. Services Corp.*[36] The court summarized the three parts:

- that the debtor cannot maintain, based on current income and expenses, a 'minimal' standard of living for herself and her dependents if forced to repay the loans;

- that additional circumstances exist indicating that this state of affairs is likely to persist for a significant portion of the repayment period of the student loans; and

- that the debtor has made good faith efforts to repay the loans.

The court added that "the first part of this test has been applied frequently as the minimum necessary to establish 'undue hardship.'"[37]

Caution. There used to be a time cap in the student loan exception, such that the debtor could discharge the loan altogether, without meeting the undue hardship test, after seven years. Congress struck out the time limit in 1998.

---

36. 831 F.2d 395 (2d Cir. 1987).

37. *Id.* at 396.

§17.29 ~ Limit on Dischargeability

There are several other limits on dischargeability in statutes other than the Bankruptcy Code. We note the ones that we have located in the margin, but for all we know there are still others tucked away somewhere.[38]

§17.30 ~ Litigating Discharge

Consider Ben the beneficiary a trust of which Frank is the trustee. Frank takes money out of the trust and spends it on himself. Thereupon he files for bankruptcy. Ben sues in bankruptcy court for a determination that the debt is nondischargeable under Section 523(a)(4). Ben also asks the bankruptcy court to give him judgment on the underlying claim. Clearly, the bankruptcy court is the proper (indeed it is the only) place to adjudicate the issue of dischargeability. May it also give judgment on the underlying claim? The answer appears to be yes, although we have seen courts hold otherwise.[39]

---

38. Loans for the education of health professionals are often part of the Health Education Assistance Loan (HEAL) program. The statute authorizing the HEAL program, 42 U.S.C. §292f(g), provides that such loans are not dischargeable unless payment would be "unconscionable." 42 U.S.C. §292f(g)(2). For a case in which the bankruptcy judge refused dischargeability of some $200,000 worth of student loans, mostly HEAL loans, held by a dentist afflicted with spina bifida and living with her husband on an income of some $20,000 a year, *see* Barrows v. Illinois Student Assistance Commission 182 B.R. 640, 650 (Bankr. D. N.H. 1994). Discharge is denied for debts incurred under the Antiterrorism and Effective Death Penalty Act of 1996, 18 U.S.C. § 3612(e) & (f); and for certain medical specialists under 37 U.S.C. §302g(e).

39. *In re* Sieger, 200 B.R. 636, 639 (Bankr. N.D. Ind. 1996).

§17.31 ~ Form Complaint to Determine Discharge and Dischargeability

IN THE UNITED STATES BANKRUPTCY COURT
FOR THE EASTERN DISTRICT OF UTOPIA

In Re: DOROTHEA DEBTOR Debtor	Case No. 99-10490-BBL Chapter 7
FASTFOOD FRANCHISE, INC. Plaintiff, v. DOROTHEA DEBTOR Defendant.	Adversary Proceeding No. ___

COMPLAINT TO DETERMINE NONDISCHARGEABILITY OF DEBT
PURSUANT TO 11 U.S.C. §523(a)
AND FOR DENIAL OF DISCHARGE
PURSUANT TO 11 U.S.C. §727(a).

Plaintiff, Fastfood Franchise, Inc. ("Plaintiff"), by its attorneys, Freshstart & Denile, brings this action against the Debtor and Defendant, Dorothea Debtor ("Debtor"), seeking a determination that certain debts owed by the Debtor to Plaintiff are nondischargeable pursuant to 11 U.S.C. §523, and that the Debtor is not entitled to a discharge under 11 U.S.C. §727, and for other relief. In support of its complaint, Plaintiff states, alleges, and complains as follows:

INTRODUCTION

1. The Debtor filed a voluntary chapter 7 petition on December 18, 1999.

2. Plaintiff files this complaint seeking to except from discharge certain debts pursuant to 11 U.S.C. §§523(a)(2) and 523(a)(4). In addition, Plaintiff seeks a determination that the Debtor is not entitled to a discharge pursuant to 11 U.S.C. §§727(a)(2) and (a)(4).

JURISDICTION AND VENUE

3. This adversary proceeding arises in the case of *In re Dorothea Debtor*, No. 99-10490-BBL, now pending in this Court under chapter 7 of Title 11 of the United States Code. This Court has jurisdiction of this adversary proceeding pursuant to 28 U.S.C. §1334 and 11 U.S.C. §523. This is a core proceeding under 28 U.S.C. §157(b)(2)(I).

4. Venue is proper in this Court pursuant to 28 U.S.C. §1409, as this is a proceeding arising under Title 11 in a case pending in this Court.

DESCRIPTION OF THE PARTIES

5. Plaintiff, Fastfood Franchise, Inc., is a Kentucky corporation with its principal place of business in Lexington, Kentucky.

6. On information and belief, the Defendant, Dorothea Debtor, is a citizen and resident of Utopia, residing at 144 Elm Road, Harrison, Utopia.

STATEMENT OF THE FACTS

I. The Fastfood Franchise System

7. Plaintiff operates and franchises the nationwide chain of Fastfood restaurants known as "Choke Quick and Cheap." All Choke Quick and Cheap restaurants are operated by franchisees, pursuant to franchises granted by Plaintiff.

8. Prospective franchisees are required to complete written applications to become a franchisee, in order to assure that they have the requisite financial stability, business experience, character, and other qualifications to be a Choke Quick and Cheap franchisee.

9. The Choke Quick and Cheap franchise application process requires detailed disclosures by the applicant of, among other things, assets, liabilities, work history, and sources of income, as well as personal and business references.

10. Plaintiff typically provides inventory and other financing to its franchisees, and the franchise application therefore also serves as an application for financing from Plaintiff.

11. Fastfood Franchise relies upon the financial and other representations made by a prospective franchisee in his or her franchise application in deciding whether to grant a franchise and in deciding whether to extend financing to an applicant.

II. The Debtors' Franchise

12. On or about October 10, 1995, Debtor completed an application to become a Choke Quick and Cheap Franchisee (the "Application"). A copy of the Application is attached hereto as Exhibit A.

13. The Application contained material, false information concerning the Debtor and her financial experience, income, assets, and liabilities.

14. For example, the Debtor made the following false and fraudulent statements in the Application: (a) Debtor stated that she owned a Ferrari automobile with a value of $150,000, when in reality she owned no car at all; (b) Debtor stated that she had $160,000 in her brokerage account at Jonestown Investments, when in reality she had only $1,000 in that account; (c) Debtor stated that she had no liabilities at all, when in reality she had (and still has) a judgment against her in the amount of $375,000 in favor of Joe's Burger System, for nonpayment of franchise fees to that entity; (d) Debtor stated that she had no criminal record, when in reality she was convicted in 1991 of grand larceny, for stealing over $500,000 from Joe's Burger System, while she was a franchisee of that system, (e) Debtor did not list her experience with Joe's Burger System in the "past employment" section on the Application, although she was employed full time in that capacity for six years; (f) Debtor stated that her current income at the time she completed the Application was $80,000 per year, when in reality, upon information and belief, her income was in the range of $20,000 to $25,000 per year; and (g) Debtor stated on the Application that she had run a business in Lapland, Norway for 7 years, with revenues of at least $4.5 million per year, when in reality Debtor did not run any such business and indeed has never even been to Norway.

15. Based upon the Application, Plaintiff entered into a Franchise Agreement with the Debtor for a Choke Quick and Cheap restaurant located in Utopia, referred to herein as the "Utopia Restaurant." A copy of the Franchise Agreement for the Utopia Restaurant is attached hereto as Exhibit B.

16. Based upon the Application, and in connection with the operation of the Utopia Restaurant, Plaintiff also provided inventory financing to Debtor. As of the petition date, Debtor owed Plaintiff $175,000 under this inventory financing arrangement.

COUNT I
THE DEBTORS OBTAINED MONEY, PROPERTY AND SERVICES BY FALSE PRETENSES, FALSE REPRESENTATIONS, OR ACTUAL FRAUD

17. Plaintiff incorporates herein by reference each and every allegation set forth in the paragraphs above and realleges the same as though set out here in full.

18. Pursuant to 11 U.S.C. §523(a)(2)(A), an individual debtor may not be discharged from any debt obtained by false pretenses, a false representation, or actual fraud, other than a statement respecting the debtor's or an insider's financial condition. Pursuant to 11 U.S.C. §523(a)(2)(B), an individual debtor may not be discharged from any debt obtained by the use of a statement in writing, that is materially false, respecting the debtor's financial condition, on which the creditor relied, that the debtor made with an intent to deceive.

19. Debtor's misrepresentations in the Application, as described above, concerning her financial condition, including her assets, liabilities, and income (collectively, the "Financial Misrepresentations"), were materially false.

20. The Financial Misrepresentations were made with an intent to deceive Plaintiff.

21. The Financial Misrepresentations did actually deceive Plaintiff and induced Plaintiff to grant a franchise to Debtor and to extend inventory financing to Debtor.

22. Plaintiff actually and justifiably relied upon the Financial Misrepresentations.

23. But for the Financial Misrepresentations, Plaintiff would not have granted Debtor a franchise for the Utopia Restaurant and would not have extended the related financing to Debtor.

24. The Financial Misrepresentations constitute "the use of a statement in writing, that is materially false, respecting the Debtor's financial condition, on which the creditor relied, that the debtor made with an intent to deceive."

25. Debtor also made material misstatements on the Application other than those relating to her financial condition, including those misstatements referred to in Paragraph 14(d), (e), and (g) above (the "Non-Financial Misstatements").

26. The Non-Financial Misstatements were made with the intent to deceive Plaintiff by inducing Plaintiff to grant a franchise to Debtor and to extend financing to Debtor, and did actually deceive Plaintiff by inducing Plaintiff to grant a franchise to Debtor and to extend financing to Debtor.

27. The Non-Financial Misstatements were material.

28. Plaintiff actually and justifiably relied upon the Non-Financial Misstatements.

29. The Non-Financial Misstatements constitute false pretenses, false representations, and actual fraud.

30. Accordingly, the debt owed by Debtor to Plaintiff, is nondischargeable under 11 U.S.C. §§523(a)(2)(A) and 523(a)(2)(B).

COUNT II

THE DEBTORS COMMITTED FRAUD OR DEFALCATION WHILE ACTING IN A FIDUCIARY CAPACITY, EMBEZZLEMENT OR LARCENY

31. Plaintiff incorporates herein by reference each and every allegation set forth in the paragraphs above and realleges the same as though set out here in full.

32. Pursuant to 11 U.S.C. §523(a)(4), an individual debtor may not be discharged from any debt "for fraud or defalcation while acting in a fiduciary capacity, embezzlement or larceny."

33. While the Debtor was a franchisee, she stole $20,000 from the cash register at the Utopia Restaurant, which funds were, under the terms of the franchise agreement, the property of Plaintiff.

34. As a result of these actions, Debtor was convicted in the Circuit Court of Utopia County, Utopia of grand larceny, a felony under Utopia Code Section 2-34(a), and was sentenced to two years in the Utopia Prison.

35. The theft referenced above, which formed the basis for Debtor's criminal conviction, constitutes larceny.

36. Accordingly, the debt of $20,000, owed by Debtor to Plaintiff, for repayment of the amounts stolen by Debtor from the cash register, is nondischargeable under 11 U.S.C. §524(a)(4).

COUNT III

THE DEBTORS' DISCHARGE SHOULD BE DENIED UNDER §727(a)(4) DUE TO THE DEBTORS' KNOWING AND FRAUDULENT FALSE OATH OR ACCOUNT

37. Plaintiff incorporates herein by reference each and every allegation set forth in the paragraphs above and realleges the same as though set out here in full.

38. Pursuant to 11 U.S.C. §727(a)(4), an individual debtor shall be denied discharge if it can be shown that the individual debtor knowingly or fraudulently made a false oath or account.

39. On the Debtors' bankruptcy schedules, the Debtors represent that she made no transfers or gifts of any of the Debtor's property within one year immediately proceeding the commencement of this case. *See* Debtors' Statement of Financial Affairs, answers to questions 7 and 10. The Debtors certified under penalty of perjury that these representations were true and correct.

40. The Debtor was asked by counsel for Plaintiff, at the Section 341 meeting in this case, on February 2, 2000, whether she had "conveyed any personal property to any family members within the past one year." Her response was as follows: "Absolutely not; I have never given anything to anyone in my family."

41. However, the Debtors testified at a recent Rule 2004 examination taken by Able Bank Corporation's counsel, in contradiction to the representations that she made on her bankruptcy schedules and at the Section 341 meeting, that, in fact, the Debtor did transfer her Rolls Royce automobile, with a market value of approximately $125,000, to the Debtor's mother, for no consideration, only eight days prior to filing her bankruptcy petition. See Transcript of Able Bank Corporation's Rule 2004 examination of Dorothea Debtor, at page 31-32.

42. The Debtor's omission of the transfer of her Rolls Royce on her bankruptcy schedules, and her false answer at the Section 341 meeting in response to a question concerning transfer of assets, constitute knowing and fraudulent false oaths and accounts.

43. Accordingly, the Debtor should be denied a discharge.

COUNT IV
THE DEBTORS' DISCHARGE SHOULD BE DENIED UNDER §727(a)(2) DUE TO THE DEBTORS' FRAUDULENT TRANSFER OF ASSETS WITHIN ONE YEAR BEFORE HER BANKRUPTCY FILING

44. Plaintiff incorporates herein by reference each and every allegation set forth in the paragraphs above and realleges the same as though set out here in full.

45. Pursuant to 11 U.S.C. §727(a)(2), an individual debtor shall be denied discharge if it can be shown that the individual debtor "with intent to hinder, defraud, or delay a creditor . . . has transferred . . . property of the debtor, within one year before the date of the filing of the petition."

46. The transfer of the Debtor's Rolls Royce automobile to the Debtor's mother, eight days prior to her bankruptcy filing, for no consideration, as described in Count III above, was intended to hinder, defraud, or delay creditors of the Debtor, including, without limitation, Plaintiff.

47. Accordingly, the Debtors should be denied a discharge.

PRAYER FOR RELIEF

WHEREFORE, Plaintiff prays for

48. A determination that the indebtedness of the Debtors to Plaintiff, in the amount of at least $195,000 is nondischargeable;

49. An order determining that the Debtor is not entitled to a discharge under 11 U.S.C. §727 and denying said discharge;

50. Attorneys' fees and costs; and

51. Such other relief as the Court may deem just and appropriate.

Respectfully submitted,

FRESHSTART & DENILE, PC
By:________________________
Cleopatra Q. Denile #6767676
Attorneys for Plaintiff
1111 Temple Boulevard
Breezeway, Utopia, 99979
(530) 752-4704

§17.32 ~ Overlap: Section 523 and Section 727

Consider the case of Debtor who owed $2 million to Creditor, secured by Debtor's $2 million widget. In a fit of pique, but intending to do harm to the creditor, Debtor destroys the widget. He then files for bankruptcy. Creditor wants his $2 million claim to survive the bankruptcy so he researches the law of discharge. He concludes that he might have a pretty good case for exception to discharge under Section 523(a)(6) (willful and malicious injury). But the facts appear also to support an exception to discharge under Section 727(a)(2) ("with the intent to hinder, delay, or defraud a creditor . . . injured . . . property.")

Creditor has standing to sue on either ground. What should he do? The obvious answer: sue on both, and take judgment on either one, as the facts justify.

This may be a good strategy, but there are two reasons for caution.

- If you win the Section 523 action, your claim survives the bankruptcy while other claims are discharged. If you win the Section 727 action, then all claims survive. So if you are really interested in getting paid, then you want the Section 523 action to succeed and the Section 727 action to fail.

- If your action is under Section 523, then you can settle with the debtor pretty much at your discretion. If your action is under Section 727, then some courts will not allow you to settle unless you give notice to all creditors. If the Court believes you are using the leverage of a Section 727 action to coerce a settlement of the Section 523 case, the Court may not approve any settlement of the Section 727 action, even with broader notice.[40] Thus, the Section 727 action may limit the creditor's power to maneuver.

§17.33 ~ Relationship to Non-bankruptcy Law

Courts have had a lot of trouble disentangling the bankruptcy dischargeability rules from the underlying liability rules under non-bankruptcy law. The leading case is *Brown v. Felsen*.[41] The creditor sued the debtor for breach of contract and fraud. The parties entered into a stipulated judgment on the contract action and dismissed (with prejudice) the fraud counts. The debtor promptly filed for bankruptcy. On the creditor's complaint for an exception to discharge, the debtor argued that the state judgment was res judicata.

But the Supreme Court wouldn't go along. The Court noted that the creditor didn't need the fraud evidence in order to get his judgment at state law. So, the Court reasoned, the creditor should not be barred from introducing evidence on the point now that it was in issue. The Court held that the bankruptcy court is not limited to the record in the prior state proceeding, and that the creditor might offer evidence on the fraud issue.

---

40. *See, e.g., In re* deArmond, 240 B.R. 51 (Bankr. C.D. Cal. 1999).

41. 442 U.S. 127, 131-39 (1979).

There remains the question how the non-bankruptcy trial was conducted. *Grogan v. Garner* is the classic case here.[42] The creditor got judgment against the debtor for securities fraud. The debtor filed for bankruptcy and the creditor sought an exception under Section 523(a)(4). The debtor acknowledged the fraud judgment, but said it was acquired only on "preponderance of the evidence." The bankruptcy standard, he argued, was the higher clear and convincing barrier. But the Supreme Court held that preponderance of the evidence was enough.

§17.34 ~ A Good State Record Works Wonders

The practical result is that collateral estoppel applies in dischargeability cases, and a good state court record will save you trouble when you try to prove up your nondischargeability claim in the bankruptcy case. Thus, suppose the debtor has been convicted of criminal fraud, before bankruptcy, in a case involving your claim. File your nondischargeability action in bankruptcy and file a motion for summary judgment on collateral estoppel grounds, documenting the criminal fraud judgment as part of your case. It may save you the cost of a trial.

§17.35 ~ Chapter 11 Discharge

Chapter 11 has its own discharge provision—in Section 1141(d). It provides that confirmation of the plan discharges the debtor from any debt that arose before confirmation, whether or not the claim was allowed or a proof of claim filed.[43] Clearly, this is more than the debtor gets in chapter 7.

Note there is no general schedule of exceptions to discharge, such as you find in Section 523 (*but see* below on the chapter 11 discharge for individuals). This seems to suggest, for example, that confirmation will discharge a claim involving fraud, defalcation, willful misconduct, etc. It also appears to provide for discharge even if the claimholder never knew anything about the bankruptcy, although this may raise constitutional questions; and in any event has driven some of the litigation on "unknown claims;" *see* §13.24.

There are two important exceptions. First, confirmation does not discharge an *individual* chapter 11 debtor from any debt that would have been excepted from discharge under Section 523.[44] Contrast this rule with the comprehensive discharge for individuals in chapter 13 under Section 1328(a),and consider the debtor who owes a debt for, *e.g.*, willful and malicious injury, nondischargeable in chapter 7 via Section 523(a)(6). The debtor may be able to escape the debt in chapter 13.[45] But he is stuck with it in chapter 11.

Second, confirmation does not discharge the debtor if:

---

42. 498 U.S. 279 (1991).

43. The section also discharges debts under §§502(g), (h) and (i).

44. Section 1141(d)(2).

45. *See, e.g.* Soloman v. Cosby, 67 F.3d 1128 (4th Cir. 1995).

- The plan provides for liquidation of all or substantially all of the property of the estate,
- The debtor does not engage in business after consummation of the plan, and
- The debtor would be denied a discharge under Section 727(a) of this title if this case were a case under chapter 7 of this title.[46]

§17.36 ~ Successor Liability—The Problem

Consider the case of DebtorCo, a small manufacturing company in chapter 11. The owners of DebtorCo sell all the assets of DebtorCo to NewCo.[47] They thereupon pay all (known) creditors in full. They distribute the surplus among themselves and depart for parts unknown.

Months later, NewCo receives a summons and complaint in a state court lawsuit captioned "Charlie v. NewCo." In the complaint, Charlie alleges that he is a creditor of DebtorCo who was somehow overlooked in the liquidation and distribution. He alleges that under non-bankruptcy law, his claim against the "predecessor" DebtorCo continues against the successor NewCo. After the appropriate briefing and argument, the court finds in favor of Charlie and against NewCo. NewCo thereupon finds itself "paying twice" for the assets of DebtorCo.

The question arises: could NewCo have avoided the problem by "cleansing" the assets through the bankruptcy court—getting DebtorCo to file for bankruptcy relief and then buying the assets through the court via some sort of "judicial sale?"

This looks promising. But as we shall see in a moment, it probably will not work. But to get a grip on the problem, first take a look at "successor liability" under non-bankruptcy law.

§17.37 ~ Successor Liability Under Non-bankruptcy Law

What sort of successor will be held liable independent of bankruptcy law? The answer must inevitably remain imprecise, but some useful generalizations are possible.

First, if the new business is a mere technical restructuring of the old, then liability will likely continue. This is almost a no-brainer: no one would suppose that the John D. Jones Co. could free itself of past debts merely by changing its name to J. Donald Jones Inc.[48] Second, if the successor by contract assumes the liability, the successor will be liable on his contract obligation.[49] Third, there are cases

---

46. Section 1141(d)(3).

47. The sale might be a part of a plan under §1129, or a "sale outside the ordinary course" under §363(b). The issues may differ; the debtor gets a discharge under §1141, while the buyer may take free and clear of liens under §363 (*see* §363(f)). Most of the cases arise under chapter 11, but the §363 problem could arise in a chapter 7 case also.

48. The same goes for more elaborate restructurings, combinations, etc., along as underlying ownership remains the same. *See generally* 15 William Meade Fletcher Cyclopedia of the Law of Private Corporations §7122 (perm. Ed. Rev. vol 1990 & 1994).

49. *See, e.g.*, Kessinger v. Grefco, Inc., 875 F.2d 153, 153 (7th Cir. 1989).

where the court finds the transaction to be a fraud on creditors, and holds the successor liable as the transferee on a fraudulent transfer.[50]

None of these is any stretch of pre-existing doctrine, and none presents any special conceptual difficulties for the bankruptcy court. Two other classes of cases may be more contentious. One of these two you might call the "same product line tort" cases. OldCo made widgets, an inherently dangerous product. OldCo sold all its assets to NewCo. OldCo distributed all the sale proceeds and dissolved. NewCo continued in the widget business. Plaintiff, who bought a widget from OldCo, files a personal injury lawsuit against NewCo. Some courts will allow the action to go forward on the proposition that NewCo is doing the same kind of business.[51]

Another class of cases are those where the courts impose some "public" obligation (usually drawn from federal law) on the successor solely because the obligation is seen to be important, and because the successor is the successor. This doctrine won a foothold a generation ago under federal labor law.[52] It has extended into a number of other fields, but its most notable growth has come in environmental and employment law.[53]

§17.38 ~ Successor Liability Under Bankruptcy Law

Now, take another look at DebtorCo and NewCo. This time NewCo, more careful than before, encourages DebtorCo to file for relief under chapter 11. NewCo then buys the assets from the estate, in a sale "outside the ordinary course of business" under Section 363. *See* §10.2. Then DebtorCo files a liquidating plan which provides that the assets will be distributed among creditors as their interests may appear. The court confirms the plan and closes the case. Note that DebtorCo did not get (and was not entitled to) a discharge.

As before, Charlie sues NewCo for a liability first incurred by DebtorCo. Assume for purposes of analysis that Charlie would have a valid "successor" claim under non-bankruptcy law. The question now arises —will the intervening bankruptcy insulate the claim?

Language in the Bankruptcy Code may seem to suggest that it will. For example, Section 363(f) says that "the trustee may sell property . . . free and clear of any interest in such property of an entity other than the estate."

---

50. *See, e.g.*, Schmoll v. ACandS , Inc., 703 F. Supp. 868 (D. Or. 1988), aff'd 977 F.2d 499 (9th Cir. 1992); Lumbard v. Maglia, Inc., 621 F. Supp. 1529 (S.D.N.Y. 1985).

51. A leading case is Ray v. Alad Corp. 560 P.3d 3 (Cal. 1977). Ray has been read as imposing liability on the basis of the same product line, pure and simple. A somewhat narrower view is to impose liability if there is a "continuity of enterprise." Cyr v. B. Offen & Co., Inc., 501 F.2d 1145 (1st Cir. 1974).

52. For the labor law background, see NLRB Twenty-first Ann. Rep. 14 (1956), accepted in Radio & Television Broadcast Technicians Local Union v. Broadcast Serv. of Mobile, Inc., 380 U.S. 255 (1965) (per curiam); *see also* Golden State Bottling Co. v. NLRB, 414 U.S. 168 (1973).

53. On the growth of the labor law doctrine, *see, e.g.*, Steinbach v. Hubbard, 51 F.3d 843, 845 (9th Cir. 1995) ("federal common law successorship doctrine . . . now extends to almost every employment law statute"). On environmental law, *see, e.g.*, U.S. v. Mexico Feed and Seed Co., 980 F.2d 478, 486 (8th Cir. 1982); United States v. Carolina Transformer Co., 739 F. Supp. (E.D.N.C. 1989), *aff'd*, 978 F.2d 832, 838 (4th Cir. 1992). Excellent background and history is available in Phillip I. Blumberg *The Continuity of Enterprise Doctrine: Corporate Successorship in United States Law*, 10 FLLA. J. INT'L L. 365 (1996).

If this isn't sufficient, we can imagine DebtorCo selling to NewCo not under Section 363 but under a plan. Section 1123(a)(5)(D) clearly authorizes sale as part of a chapter 11 plan. And Section 1141(c) (the chapter 11 discharge) says that "the property dealt with in the plan is free and clear of all claims and interests of creditors, equity security holders, and of general partners in the debtor."

These sections offer a possible background for *American Living Systems v. Bonapfel*,[54] perhaps the first important Code case to hit these issues head on. The debtor manufactured mobile homes. He sold its assets in bankruptcy under Section 363(f). Prior to the sale, the plaintiff sued the debtor in state court. The plaintiff knew about the bankruptcy, but never filed a claim.

After the sale, the plaintiff joined the buyer as a defendant in the state court suit. The buyer thereupon went back to bankruptcy court and asked for an injunction against the lawsuit, and a declaration that Section 363(f) precluded successor liability. The court agreed. The judge offered two reasons:

- [I]f a plaintiff asserts a claim grounded on successor liability after a bankruptcy sale, he, in effect, receives a priority over those claims which were paid in accordance with the Bankruptcy Code.[55]

- The court emphasized the "negative impact that potential successor liability claims would have on the trustee's ability to sell assets of the estate at a fair price."[56]

American Living Systems is a good point of departure because it poses the issue so sharply, and makes the case in favor of "cleansing" so well. We can imagine the prospective buyer kicking the tires on the assets and then telling the court:

> Your honor, anything is a bargain at the right price, but what I want is closure. I am willing to pay full market value for the assets unencumbered by the claims, but I don't think it should be my business to worry about what comes later. Let me pay the money into the court and let the court decide how it should be distributed, and to whom.

Appealing this may be. But it is not the way the law has gone. Rather, more recent courts have engaged in an agonizing reappraisal of the doctrine of cleansing, and have often held that bankruptcy sales do not provide a shield against successor liability claims that would survive under applicable non-bankruptcy law.

Some of this rethinking begins with a close reading of the statute. For example, a number of cases have noted that Section 363(f) allows sale free and clear of interests—but says nothing directly about claims. A secured creditor may have an "interest" in property sold. We may well want to cut off the "interest" to facilitate the sale. But no one asserts that we thereby terminate his "claim." Indeed in the ordinary case it is conceded that his claim survives and is transferred to the proceeds.

---

54. *In re* All American of Ashburn, Inc. 56 B.R. 186 (Bankr. N.D. Ga.), *aff'd* 805 F.2d 1515 (11th Cir. 1986).

55. *Id.* At 190.

56. *Id.*

Many courts have held that unsecured claim is not an "interest" and therefore not barred under Section 363(f).[57] On similar reasoning, other courts have held that the buyer gets no more protection from Section 1141(c).[58]

Perhaps the most influential of all no-cleansing cases is the decision of the Seventh Circuit in *Zerand-Bernal Group, Inc. v. Cox*.[59] The purchaser got a court order authorizing the sale of assets "free and clear of any liens, claims or encumbrances of any sort." It further reserved jurisdiction in the bankruptcy court to adjudicate products liability claims.

Four and a half years later, the plaintiff joined the purchaser in a products liability case. The purchaser thereupon went back to bankruptcy court to get an injunction against the state court action.

The Seventh Circuit rejected the plea, holding that there was no *jurisdiction* for an adversary action. The court held that it could be justified only if the matter was either "related to" or arising under the bankruptcy jurisdiction statute (*see* chapter 3). But the court held that this case was neither.[60]

§17.39 ~ Successor Liability and "Unknown Claims"

The cases, in short, appear to conflict with each other. Is there a way to resolve this conflict? We think there may be. The clue is in the timing of the claim.

Start with *American Living Systems*, above. In *American Living Systems*, the products liability lawsuit was already pending at the time of the sale, and the plaintiff knew about the bankruptcy. These facts present the most attractive case for drawing the plaintiff into the bankruptcy process.

Contrast a case like *Fairchild Aircraft Inc. v. Campbell*.[61] The debtor manufactured airplanes. The plane in question was manufactured pre-petition. The accident didn't happen until after the assets were sold out of the bankruptcy estate. The pre-petition manufacture may have been enough to qualify the right as a "claim" within the meaning of the Bankruptcy Code. But that fact was not enough to persuade the judge that the plaintiff had the protection he deserved.

---

57. A leading case is Volvo White Truck Corp. v. Chambersburg Beverage, Inc. (*In re* White Motor Credit Corp.), 75 B.R. 944 (N.D. Ohio 1987). *But cf. See, e.g., In re* Savage Industries, Inc., 1993 WL 763407, (D. Mass. Oct 19, 1993).

58. Wilkerson v. C.O. Porter Machinery Co., 237 N.J. Super. 282, 567 A.2d 598 (N.J. Super. Ct. Law Div. 1989). The analysis is a bit intricate, but worth repeating. The *Wilkerson* court begins by noting that the debtor will not get a discharge in this case, because the case involves a sale of substantially all the assets, and the Code bars a discharge for the corporate debtor who is selling substantially all his assets. *See* §1141(d)(3). So the buyer cannot hide behind the discharge of the debtor. Since he cannot hide behind the discharge of the debtor, the court argued, the only substantive basis is Section 363(f). But the court held §363(f) inapplicable, on grounds set forth above.

59. 23 F.3d 159 (7th Cir. 1994).

60. For a state court opinion discussing and deciding the bankruptcy issue, *see* Lefever v. K.P. Hovnanian Enterprises Inc., 734 A.2d 290 (N.J. 1999) (state successor liability survives "free and clear"sale; 4-3 decision).

61. *In re* Fairchild Aircraft Corp., 184 B.R. 910 (Bankr. W.D. Texas 1995).

The problem, then, can be understood as a problem of "unknown" or "future" claims. We deal with that issue in chapter 13. We won't go so far as to say that every successor liability case is an unknown claim case (we're sure this is not the case). But we think the two concepts get entangled, and need to be understood together.

§17.40 ~ Labor Claims

Issues of successor liability arise sometimes, although less often, in labor law cases, where the question is whether a sale of assets will terminate a labor contract. The important point to keep in mind here is that there are really two separate issues in the labor cases. One is the liability for pre-petition (or pre-rejection) damages. The other is the question of the ongoing relationship. Under non-bankruptcy law, a successor may be bound to recognize and bargain with the predecessor's union, even if not bound by the precise terms of the predecessor's contract.[62]

The underlying non-bankruptcy law of successor liability in labor cases is similar, though not identical, to what we find in products liability. The general rule is that the successor is not bound by the collective bargaining contract negotiated by his predecessor.[63] But the successor may be liable if it is the mere alter ego of the predecessor."[64] Even without an alter ego finding, the purchaser may be a successor if there is a substantial continuity of operations.[65]

§17.41 ~ What Is At Stake?

Why does the bankruptcy system care about the successor liability cases? A Seventh Circuit judge said that shield cases

> stand for the proposition that it is desirable, perhaps even necessary, to shield purchasers of failing businesses from liability incurred by their predecessors. Such protection is viewed as a means of encouraging market growth . . . . Fear of successor liability . . . would "chill" sales in bankruptcy . . . .[66]

What can this mean? We think it can mean at least two things, each rather different from the other.

---

62. *E.g.*, Fall River Dyeing & Finishing Corp. v. NLRB, 482 U.S. 27 (1987).

63. NLRB v. Burns Int'l Sec. Servs., Inc., 406 U.S. 272 (1972), affirmed in Fall River Dyeing, *supra*.

64. That is, if there is "a mere technical change in the structure or identity of the employing entity . . . to avoid the effect of labor laws, without any substantial change in its ownership or management."

65. Factors to be considered include:

> Whether the business of both employers is essentially the same; whether the employees of the new company are doing the same jobs in the same working conditions under the same supervisors; and whether the new entity has the same production process, produces the same products and basically has the same body of customers.

Fall River Dyeing, Id., 482 U.S. at 43.

66. Chicago Truck Drivers v. Tasemkin, 59 F.3d 48 (7th Cir. 1995).

First, it can mean that the debtor will pay more for a "clean deal" than he will for a deal encumbered by unsatisfied claims—or, what may be the same thing, a deal where there is doubt over prior claims. This seems to us as perfectly legitimate interest and we would want to try to find a way to serve it in the bankruptcy forum.

But it can also mean something rather different, namely that the deal may be more valuable to the purchaser (and therefore to the estate) if you can simply terminate prior valid (though not yet disclosed) claims. This may be true enough as a matter of fact, but we think it is terrible as a rule of law. Generating value to the estate by extinguishing otherwise valid (future) claims is effectively not much more than transferring value from future claimants to current creditors or shareholders. We can't think of any good reason why this should be the law.

We labor the point now because we think this kind of reasoning has a way of creeping into bankruptcy cases, at many points. It comes up when we find parties asking the court to excuse the debtor from the obligation to abide by, say, environmental laws, or other general principles which ought to apply to all alike. If the debtor can't afford to abide by general rules, then we think the answer is that it shouldn't be in business, and the "bankruptcy excuse" should not be a defense. And it seems to us that this is the trend in the law, so that bankruptcy "cleansing sales" will be harder to come by.

§17.42 ~ Drafting a Cleansing Provision

As counsel for the buyer, how do you cleanse the assets of pre-sale claims? The short answer is: You probably can't, and you'd better not sign any opinion letters without some carefully qualified exceptions. What you can do however is to increase the likelihood that your client will not be subjected to successor liability claims. You do this by doing your best to give notice to everyone who might be a claimant (which may include published notice) and by drafting an order that has the support of the major constituencies and that purports to offer the "cleansing" protection.

Some judges will sign orders that say something like:

> "Purchaser is not and shall not be deemed to be a successor to Debtor under any state or federal law, and shall not be liable for any claims (a) against Debtor and/or (b) relating to the Purchased Asset and arising before the Closing Date, under any theory of successor liability or otherwise."

If your client is the asset purchaser, it is probably worth your while to seek inclusion of such a provision. If no one objects, it just might stick. But you should warn your client that some later court may hold it invalid anyway.

§17.43 ~ Third-party Releases

Consider these three cases.

- InsCo is a liability insurer. InsCo wrote policies of insurance for ToxCo, the maker of a product that has proven to be toxic, and has generated hundreds of millions of dollars worth of liability claims. ToxCo is in chapter 11. All parties agree that ToxCo will never confirm a plan unless everybody knows how much money will have to come from InsCo.

- Pebble was a partner in Stone & Hardrock, a large national law firm. Chester Flint, the managing partner, made all the important partnership decisions and kept all the books and records in his personal safe. Pebble thought he was doing well with a personal net worth of about $2 million and so was chagrined to find, when the partnership went into chapter 11, that its true net worth was negative $50 million.

- Prez is president and majority shareholder of LittleCo, a debtor in chapter 11. Prez has so far avoided filing, but he faces large personal exposure on debts that he guaranteed for LittleCo, and also as a person responsible for LittleCo's unpaid trust fund taxes.[67]

Prez, Pebble and InsCo share a common goal. Each would like to dispose of its individual liability as part of an existing chapter 11 case without filing itself. Will they be able to do so? The short answer is that InsCo and Pebble may have a chance, at least if they make a substantial contribution to a global settlement, but that Prez may have to seek relief on his own.

The general question is: When may a third party, not itself a chapter 11 debtor, get relief in a debtor's chapter 11 case? On the face of things, you might think the answer was "never." No specific provision of chapter 11 offers any relief to a non-debtor. Meanwhile, Section 524(e) provides that "discharge of a debt of the debtor does not affect the liability of any other entity on, or the property of any other entity for, such debt." Also, Section 1301 does offer limited relief for a co-debtor, suggesting that the drafters knew perfectly well how to write third-party protection if they wanted to. On reasoning such as this, some courts have refused outright to validate any third-party release as part of a plan.[68]

But a second thought will suggest several ways in which the first guess may be too quick. First, there may be some cases in which it is in the interest of the creditors to get at least interim protection for a non-debtor. For example, consider the non-debtor who is an officer of the debtor, where the non-debtor's full attention is required to make the debtor's case go forward. Second, there may be good reasons to enforce relief with respect to a creditor who consents to non-debtor relief as part of a chapter 11 plan, even if you don't enforce it against a dissenter (or a non-voter). Perhaps it is no surprise, then, that courts have developed a rather narrow body of doctrine allowing "third party release" as part of a chapter 11 plan.

Perhaps the most visible cases are the "mass tort" cases, where the court imposes a general release as part of a global settlement of a complex multiparty litigation.[69]

---

67. 26 U.S.C. §6672.

68. *See, e.g.*, Underhill v. Royal, 769 F.2d 1426 (9th Cir. 1985); Field v. Zale Corp. (*In re* Zale Corp.), 62 F.3d 746 (5th Cir. 1995).

69. *See, e.g.*, MacArthur Co. v. Johns-Manville Corp., 837 F.2d 89, 93 (2d Cir. 1988), *cert. denied*, 488 U.S. 868 (1988).

A bit closer to home are the arising from professional (usually law firm) partnership breakups, where the reasoning is either that the non-debtor partners won't be motivated to settle unless they get releases[70] and usually because the non-debtors are kicking in assets to help fund the plan.[71]

A forced release, binding on dissenters, is one thing; release by consent is quite another. Some courts have refused to bless even consensual releases that arise through the plan. Others, while recognizing that coercion may be an issue, have held that the releases in the particular plan at issue where not coerced and were therefore binding on those who gave consent.[72]

A bankruptcy judge has come up with a list of factors that are likely to prove influential in deciding whether or not to impose a third-party release.[73] They include:

- *Indemnity*. A release may be proper where the non-debtor would have a "right over" against the debtor—as in the case of a guarantor, who might have a claim for indemnity if he paid the debtor's debt.
- *Substantial contribution*. The non-debtor has come up with assets to help fund the plan.
- *Necessary*. The reorganization deal will fall through without it.
- *Support*. The affected creditors have voted overwhelmingly to accept it.
- *Payment*. The plan provides a mechanism for the payment of all, or substantially all, of the claims of the class or classes affected by the injunction.

A Delaware bankruptcy judge had occasion to apply this list of factors, deciding *In re* Zenith Electronics Corp.[74] The plan purported to release certain derivative claims against certain third parties who had contributed to the reorganization. As to direct claims, however, the court refused to go so far. It agreed to recognize the release as effective against creditors who had voted for the plan, but refused to impose it on those who had not.

Technique: In sum, courts are hesitant to impose third-party releases on dissenters, or they think the release was coerced, but they are more willing to uphold the release where it was given by consent. This means you should do what you can to persuade the court that the release was consensual. One approach is to include on your plan ballot a separate box where creditors can accept (or reject) the third-party release, often in exchange for the right to share in a pool of funds provided by the third party, which

---

70. *See, e.g.*, Monarch Life Ins. Co. v. Ropes & Gray, 65 F.3d 973 (1st Cir. 1995).

71. *See, e.g., In re* Heron, Burchette, Ruckert & Rothwell, 148 B.R. 660 (Bankr. D.D.C. 1992); Myerson & Kuhn v. Brunswick Associates Ltd. (*In re* Myerson & Kuhn), 121 B.R. 145 154 (Bankr. S.D.N.Y. 1990).

72. *See, e.g., In re* West Coast Video Centers., 174 B.R. 906 (Bankr. E.D. Pa. 1994).

73. *In re* Master Mortgage Investment Fund Inc., 168 B.R. 930, 935 (Bankr. W.D. Mo. 1994).

74. 241 B.R. 92 (Bankr. D. Del. 1999).

would supplement the distribution being made by the estate. In this way, you may be able to persuade the court to validate the release as a contract (at least as to those who vote for it) even though the Code allows discharge for "debtors" only.[75]

§17.44 ~ Compare: Individual Relief on Trust Fund Taxes

It's not quite the same as a third party release, but the Supreme Court has laid down one rule that has proven helpful for those who want to protect individual debtors through the corporate chapter 11. The case is *United States v. Energy Resources Co.*[76] The corporate debtor failed to pay some taxes, including some trust fund taxes. Liability for the trust fund taxes extended also to individuals. The corporate debtor's chapter 11 undertook to deal with the trust fund taxes at the expense of other taxes that did not enjoy trust fund status. The bankruptcy court permitted this, and the Supreme Court affirmed.

§17.45 ~ Temporary Relief

Aside from permanent non-debtor releases (discharge), there is the more limited question of whether the court will grant temporary relief to a non-debtor. A few courts have been willing to grant temporary protection to a non-debtor in the pendency of a third-party reorganization, sometimes on analogy to a preliminary injunction in the non-bankruptcy context.[77] These injunctions (under Section 105) are still unusual, but may be granted where the court is persuaded that the full attention of a debtor's principal is needed in order to facilitate a reorganization, and that he is likely be distracted if he must spend his time defending the personal action.

§17.46 ~ Channeling Injunctions

As we suggested above, these issues of multiparty relief take on full flower in the complex multi-party cases like the "mass tort" cases of the 1980s. Here of all places is where the court may feel itself impelled to impose an injunction to channel all the litigation into the bankruptcy forum—hence channeling injunctions. One attempt to deal with the problem of successor liability and the problem of the future claim is the channeling injunction, where the court tries to structure a procedure to put all the claims litigation through the bankruptcy estate.

The procedure was developed in part in the notorious mass tort asbestos cases in the 1980s, although it has spread somewhat beyond the asbestos cases.[78] It typically works like this: the court appoints a representative to speak for the unknown or future claims. The stakeholders negotiate a plan. The plan anticipates the continuation of the debtor as a going concern. Typically, the plan creates a trust for the

---

75. The leading case is *In re* AOV Industries, 792 F.2d 1140 (D.C. Cir. 1986).

76. 495 U.S. 545 (1990).

77. *See, e.g., In re* United Health Care Org., 210 B.R. 228 (S.D.N.Y. 1997), *vacated on other grounds sub nom.*, Olson v. Amersco New England II. L.P. (*In re* United Health Care Org.), 147 F.3d 179 (2d Cir. 1998). The analogy seems inexact. In the typical temporary injunction case, the expectation is that a permanent injunction will follow. In the temporary-relief bankruptcy cases, the proponent is conceding or indeed stressing that he won't be seeking final relief.

78. *See, e.g.*, Kane v. Johns-Manville Corp., 843 F.2d 636 (2d Cir. 1988).

benefit of claimants, and their claims are "channeled" into the trust; an injunction is issued to preclude claimants from asserting their claims against the reorganizing debtor. The trust is funded, in the typical case, with cash and equity in the reorganized debtor. Allowed tort claims are paid from the trust. rather than afflicting the reorganized debtor or any successor to the debtor. Of course, the precise terms differ from case to case.

The most famous of these is perhaps *MacArthur Co. v. Johns-Manville Corp.*,[79] involving Manville's multibillion dollar liability for harm due to asbestos. The debtor reached an agreement compromise with some insurers who thereafter sought to invoke the protection of the injunction. Another creditor complained. The Second Circuit held that there was inherent equitable power to fashion a kind of channeling order, even if only granted by implication.

The statutory basis of these channeling injunctions was open to question. In 1994 Congress adopted Section 524(g) which purported to authorize channeling injunctions in asbestos cases and (what may be more important) to bless those already in place. At least one bankruptcy court has suggested (in dicta) that the policy of Section 524(g) might empower a bankruptcy judge to use the residual injunction power in Section 105 to reach a similar result in a non-asbestos case.[80]

There are relatively few successful cases involving channeling injunctions. The process is sufficiently cumbersome and expensive that it is usually worthwhile considering only in the largest and most complex mass tort cases. Also, the result is unattractive to current equity holders, and to managers who view themselves as beholden to equity owners, since it necessarily reduces the fund available to pay old equity.

§17.47 ~ Challenging "Invalid" Releases

Finally, there is the question whether a third-party release invalid in itself may nonetheless be binding if not properly challenged. In the famous old case of *Stoll v. Gottlieb*,[81] the district court affirmed a plan including a non-debtor release. A bondholder (who had not appeared earlier) asked the court to vacate or modify its order as without jurisdiction. The court refused. The bondholder did not appeal, but he did challenge the release in a later state court action. On review, the Supreme Court assumed, but did not decide that the district court was without jurisdiction to grant the third-party release. Nevertheless, the Court held that the district court order denying the motion to vacate was *res judicata* for any later state proceeding.

In Corbett v. MacDonald Moving Services, Inc.,[82] the plan discharged a parent company for withdrawal liability under a pension plan. The pension trustees woke up to what had happened and launched a collateral attack. The court held that the discharge was res judicata. The trustees argued that res judicata can never

---

79. *In re* Johns-Manville Corp., 837 F.2d 89 (2d Cir. 1988).

80. *In re* Fairchild Aircraft Corp., 84 B.R. 910, 933 n.28 (Bankr. W.D. Tex. 1995). The legislative history to §524(g) avows that it does not intend to speak one way or another on channeling in cases other than asbestos cases.

81. 305 U.S. 165 (1938).

82. 124 F. 3d 82 (2d Cir. 1997). *See also* Republic Supply Co. v. Shoaf, 815 F.2d 1046 (5th Cir. 1987).

foreclose the question of subject matter jurisdiction, but the court rejected the argument. The court held that the creditors had had the opportunity to raise subject matter jurisdiction before the plan was confirmed, but didn't do so.

§17.48 ~ Attacking an "Invalid" Order

A couple of years ago, Paula Plaintiff sued Daniel Defendant on a personal injury claim and won $280,000. Defendant posted a bond to stay execution while he appealed. Just recently the appeals court upheld the judgment and it became final. Hours later Defendant filed for relief under chapter 11 at its "principal place of business," 800 miles away. The same day, the bankruptcy court issued an injunction forbidding enforcement of the appeal bond.

Paula is in a quandary. If she wants to challenge the bankruptcy injunction, she'll have to go 800 miles away and get involved in the bankruptcy case. If she goes back to the trial court, she'll be closer to home. She believes she also stands a better chance of getting relief from the home-town court (with whom the bond was posted) than with the bankruptcy court (in charge of "reorganizing the debtor"). She has just about made up her mind to go after the bond in the local court.

She had better think again. *In Celotex Corp. v. Edwards*,[83] the Supreme Court had to consider just such a case as Paula's. It held that the appropriate place to challenge the injunction was in the bankruptcy court (or on appeal), and not by a collateral attack in state court.

Like Paula, Mr. and Mrs. Edwards sought relief in the trial court, which granted their request. The Court of Appeals noted the existence of the Section 105 injunction. But it held that the injunction didn't apply, reasoning that Celotex had ceased to have any interest in the bond once the Edwards' judgment had been affirmed.

The Fifth Circuit also questioned the merits of the bankruptcy injunction. It remarked that a supersedeas bond was designed to protect creditors in exactly this sort of the case—that is, when the debtor is unable to pay after a decision on appeal.

But a sharply divided Supreme Court reversed. The majority held that the bankruptcy court had jurisdiction to issue the temporary injunction, and that the appropriate way to challenge it was by appeal, not by collateral attack.

The court never directly ruled on the merits of the injunction. But the majority remarked on the fact that there were some 200 creditors claiming the right to execute on bonds in the case. Allowing exercise on these bonds (as the court observed) might remove the linchpin of any reorganization plan.

The court also noted that the there were possible claims of preference or fraudulent transfer against the bond, and that the injunction had the effect of preserving the status quo pending resolution of these claims.

---

83. 514 U.S. 300 (1995).

18 Confirmation

18 CONFIRMATION

§18.1 ~ INTRODUCTION: THE ANVIL

There are two reasons to understand the confirmation procedure in chapter 11 of the Bankruptcy Code. One is obvious: to know what you have to do to win confirmation, or to block it, as the case may be. The other is less obvious, but perhaps equally important. Chapter 11 is the anvil upon which settlements are hammered out. In order to know what to settle for, you need to know what can be achieved under a chapter 11 plan. In this section, we outline the basics of confirmation. Then we work through an example, to show the basics at work. Then we elaborate on some of the general principles with which we began.

§18.2 ~ A BROAD OVERVIEW OF THE PLAN PROCESS

Here is a strategy of what you need to do to confirm a plan. The permissible components of a plan are set forth in Section 1123.[1] The requirements for confirmation are set forth in Section 1129 ("The court shall confirm only if . . . ."). First, identify the classes of claims or interests that are set forth in your plan. Then with respect to each class, ask whether you can satisfy the requirements of confirmation with respect to that class. If the answer is no with respect to any class, then start over. If the answer is "yes" with respect to each class, then ask whether you can meet the general requirements of plan confirmation.

As to each particular class, ask the following questions:

- Is the class unimpaired? See the definition in Section 1124 (defining "impairment"). If the class is "unimpaired," then the class is, for most practical purposes, "out of the case," and you don't need to worry about them any more (an oversimplification, but it will do for now). *See* Section 1129(a)(8)(B). *See also* Section 1126(f).

- If not unimpaired, then the class must be impaired. If the class is impaired, do you have the votes to confirm? For a class of claims, this requires more than half in number of claims voting and two thirds in amount of debt voted. For interests, it requires two thirds in amount.

1. *See, e.g.*, §1123(a) (A plan shall . . .") and 1123(b) ("a plan may . . .").

If you have the votes of an impaired class, you confirm with respect to that class—but with one important qualification. That is, even if you have the votes, still a dissenter in a class may be able to block confirmation of the plan if he can show that he is getting less than he would get in liquidation under chapter 7. This is the meaning of Section 1129(a)(7). It implements the so-called best interests test. If your plan satisfies the best interest test, then you may impose the plan on the dissenting minority in a class.

But even if you don't have the votes, you may be able to impose your plan on a class under Section 1129(b) if it is fair and equitable. This is the so-called "cram-down" rule. The cram-down is a device whereby the proponent imposes a plan without the consent of the creditor, or even of a class of creditors.

How do you do a cram-down? Consider the question separately for secured creditors and for unsecured creditors.

First, as to secured creditors, there are two important possibilities:[2]

- one, you sell the creditor's collateral free and clear of liens, with the lien attaching to the proceeds of sale and the creditor receiving a stream of payments equal to the value of its collateral (or other "indubitable equivalent" treatment). This is the meaning of Section 1129(b)(2)(A)(ii); or

- two, you rewrite the contract, allow the secured creditor to retain its lien, and give the creditor a stream of payments with a present value equal to the value of his collateral. This is the gist of Section 1129(b)(2)(A)(i).

But do not confuse

- *reinstating* the original contract and leaving the creditor unimpaired under Section 1124; with

- *rewriting* the original contract under Section 1129(b)(2)(A)(i).

Second, as to unsecured creditors—you can cram-down the plan only if unsecured claims are paid in full under the plan or no junior class receives anything on account of its junior claim or interest.[3]

To review, the ways to obtain confirmation with respect to an individual class are:

- leave the class unimpaired;

- obtain the requisite votes plus satisfy the best interests test; or

- cram-down the class.

2. There is a third possibility, the so-called indubitable equivalent rule of §1129(b)(2)(A)(iii), which isn't as important as the other two rules set forth above. Its most frequent use is in so-called "dirt for debt" cases, where the debtor satisfies the secured claim by conveying the collateral to the creditor. *In re* Sandy Ridge Dev. Corp., 881 F.2d 1346 (5th Cir. 1989), *reh'g, en banc, denied,* 889 F.2d 663 (5th Cir. 1989).

3. The unsecureds may be paid either in full on confirmation day or (following the analogy of the secured claim) in installments over time, with interest. Section 1129(b)(2)(B)(ii).

Next, consider the other, more general requirements of Section 1129(a). Of these, perhaps the most important is Section 1129(a)(10). This section says that if any class is impaired, then at least one class must vote for the plan.

Translated, this means that you cannot confirm a plan that crams down all classes. If you propose a cram-down plan, it must be that at least one class is impaired (or else why the cram-down?). And if so, you must get the accepting votes of at least one impaired class. This sometimes leads to a desperate scramble in which the proponent tries to leave a class impaired (even though it would be easy to pay the class off) so that the proponent can then solicit and obtain the consent of that class, so as to fulfill the requirements of Section 1129(a)(10)! Hardly surprising that some courts have termed this tactic "artificial impairment."[4]

Focus also on Section 1129(a)(11) which provides that "confirmation is not likely to be followed by the need for further financial reorganization of the debtor." This is the so-called feasibility rule, carried over with a long encrustation of case law from the pre-1978 Code. Note that the "feasibility" rule has the effect of imposing on the judge the job to make findings as to the prospective viability of the debtor's business.

§18.3 ~ The Non-Impaired Claim

Section 1129(a)(8) provides that a class of claims or interests is bound by a plan if it "is not impaired under the plan." How do you determine whether a class is impaired? The answer is in Section 1124. That section provides that a class is impaired unless the plan meets one of two criteria.

First, the claim is unimpaired if the plan "leaves unaltered the legal, equitable, and contractual rights to which such claim or interest entitles the holder of such claim or interest." Imagine an installment loan on which the debtor undertakes to "pay in full" on different terms, with compensation for lost use of money. The proponent may be able to confirm such a plan over the creditors' objections, but he will do so, if at all, under Section 1129(b), the cram-down rule.

What if the debtor chooses not to reinstate the contract, but to simply pay off the creditor in cash? Our view is that if the debtor pays face value plus interest until the time of payment, then the claim is unimpaired under Section 1124(1) and the debtor is home free. We think you can count on this, but you have to leap over a little convoluted case law and legislative history to get there.[5]

---

4. *Compare* Windsor on the River Assocs., Ltd. v. Balcor Real Estate Fin., Inc. (*In re* Windsor on the River Assocs., Ltd.), 7 F.2d 127 (8th Cir. 1993) (artificial impairment disapproved because it renders Section 1129(a)(10) a nullity, and because it is absurd) *with* L & J. Anaheim Assocs. v. Kawasaki Leasing Intel, Inc., (*In re* L & J. Anaheim Assocs.) (artificial impairment by a creditor of its own claim – increasing the value of the claim – approved over debtor's objection).

5. Prior to 1994, the Code expressly provided that if you cashed out the creditor, then the creditor was unimpaired. One court read this provision as relieving a solvent debtor of the obligation to pay post-petition interest. *In re* New Valley Corp., 168 B.R. 73 (Bankr. D. N.J. 1994). Congress responded by repealing the cash-out provision. We think you can read §1124(1) as we propose—but if the debtor is solvent, he will have to pay post-petition interest. *See, e.g., In re* Cross Creek Apts., 213 B.R. 532, 536-7 (Bankr. E.D. Tenn. 1997); *In re* Atlanta Stewart Partners, 193 B.R. 79, 82 (Bankr. N.D. Gal. 1996).

§18.4 ~ Consenting Class

Even if a class of claims is impaired under the plan, it may nonetheless be bound if the class has accepted the plan.[6] For claims, the basic rule is that a class has accepted if the plan has been accepted by a majority in number and two-thirds in amount of those accepting or rejecting.[7] Consider the following three cases. In each case, there are 10 creditors with claims aggregating $100,000:

- Nine creditors holding claims totaling $65,000 vote in favor of the plan. The remaining creditor, holding a claim of $35,000, votes against. The class has not accepted, even though the vote is nine to one in favor, because less than two-thirds in amount accepted the plan.

- Six creditors holding claims of $99,000 vote in favor of the plan. Four creditors holding claims totaling $1,000 vote against. The class has accepted the plan even though the numerical vote is less favorable, because the amount vote exceeds two thirds.

- Two creditors holding claims totaling $2 vote in favor of the plan. One creditor holding a claim of $0.95 votes against. The remaining seven creditors holding claims totaling $99,997.05 do not vote. The class has accepted even though most do not vote.

The most important consequence of acceptance is, of course, that a dissenting minority of the class will nonetheless be bound by the plan.[8] An important practical consequence is that a junior class may participate in the distribution even though the senior ("accepting") class has not been paid in full. For example, suppose the debtor has assets of $100 and liabilities of $150, all owed to a single class of creditors. A majority in number and two thirds in amount of all creditors vote to accept a plan which undertakes to pay 50 percent of all claims. The debtor thereby may discharge $150 in claims by paying $75, leaving $25 for the residual equity class. This is a departure from the regime that prevailed under chapter X of the old Bankruptcy Act, where it was necessary that each class be paid in full before any junior received anything.[9]

There is one important exception to this rule of majority control. It is set forth in Section 1129(a)(7)(A). It provides that a holder of a claim is bound if she has accepted the plan *or* if she receives at least what she would "if the debtor were liquidated under chapter 7." Consider this example. There are 100 creditors with claims totaling $100,000. The plan proposes to pay 10 percent of all claims. Of these, 99 creditors, holding claims totaling $99,000, vote to accept. The remaining creditor, with a claim of $1,000, votes to reject. Under Section 1129(a)(8), the plan would appear to be binding on the dissenter.

The plan proposes to pay 10 percent of all claims. The dissenter proves that in chapter 7 liquidation, she would get 11 percent of her claim. She has shown that the plan does not offer at least what she would get in liquidation under chapter 7, and the plan may not be confirmed. By corollary, if the plan had provided for payment of 12 percent of all claims, then the dissenter would have been bound by the plan.

---

6. *See* §1129(a)(8)(A). On the definition of "acceptance," *see generally* §1126.

7. *See* §1126(c).

8. *See* §1129(a)(7).

9. Case v. Los Angeles Lumber Products, Inc., 308 U.S. 106 (1939).

This is the so-called "best interests" test. To understand the role of the best interest test, consider this case. The debtor files for relief under chapter 11. By resourceful obstruction and delay, he so frustrates the creditor that the creditor is willing to accept even less than he would get in a chapter 7 liquidation rather than stay in the case. The best interests test prevents this result.

The best interests test seems to envision a debtor with two values—one a (higher) value as a going concern and the other a lower value in liquidation. This sometimes the case, but surely not always. It is easy to imagine cases where the debtor is worth more in liquidation than is as a going concern. Perhaps the most obvious are the cases of "bad business, good dirt," where the debtor is occupying real estate that could be more profitably deployed in another business.[10]

In other cases, going concern and liquidation value may be the same. This is usually the posture of single-asset real estate cases, where the debtor is one real estate venture—say a medical office building or a strip shopping center that will either continue in the hands of the original owners or be sold as is.

§18.5 ~ Practice Point—Liquidation Analysis

If you need to prove best interests, you will want to include in your disclosure statement a "liquidation analysis" which will show what the creditor will get in liquidation. Doing a good liquidation analysis will require a careful analysis of what would really happen if the debtor were liquidated under chapter 7. You must, therefore, deduct (hypothetical) commissions and professional fees. You need to consider the timing of any possible sale, and the tax consequences. You will have to think your way down the priority ladder, to make sure you can show what must be paid to whom—not forgetting "chapter 7 only" rules such as the tax claim subordination (under Section 724(b)) or the rights of a partnership trustee (under Section 723). Not surprisingly, there is plenty of room for litigation over the meaning and application of the best interest rule.[11]

§18.6 ~ Cram-down

If a class is impaired but does not vote for the plan, the plan may not be confirmed under the standards of Section 1129(a). But it may nonetheless be confirmed pursuant to Section 1129(b). This is the famous (or infamous) cram-down provision.[12] It provides that the court shall confirm a plan, even without a favorable vote "if the plan does not discriminate unfairly, and is fair and equitable with respect to each class of claims or interests that is impaired under, and has not accepted, the plan."

---

10. One of the largest of modern bankruptcy cases was the case of the Penn Central railroad system, which reorganized itself from an unprofitable railroad into a valuable real estate holding company.

11. *See generally* David Gray Carlson, *Secured Creditors And The Eely Character Of Bankruptcy Valuations*, 41 AM. U.L. REV. 63 (1991).

12. *See generally* Kenneth W. Klee, *All You Wanted to Know About Cram Down Under the New Bankruptcy Code*, 53 AM. BANKR. L. J. 133 (1979).

"Fair and equitable," is a term with a history, but it does not mean what it used to mean. Under old chapter X (prior to 1978), it meant that *all* senior classes had to be paid in full before any junior class was paid anything. This is the absolute priority rule of *Case v. Los Angeles Lumber Products*.[13] Such "absolute priority" treatment was mandatory anytime *any* creditor insisted on it, even if the overwhelming majority of creditors agreed to waive the protection. That isn't the rule today. But some of the flavor of Los Angeles Lumber has worked its way into the statutory definition of fair and equitable, set forth in Section 1129(b)

First, consider the rule as it applies to a secured claim—Section 1129(b)(2)(A). What does it require? Here is an example: There is one secured creditor with a claim of $1 million, secured by collateral worth $1 million. Under terms of the original agreement the debtor was to have discharged the obligation in equal annual installments over five years (with interest as prescribed by the contract). The debtor now proposes to pay the loan in annual installments over ten years with interest at a rate to be determined by the court. Is this sufficient for a cram-down? The answer turns largely on the choice of interest rate. If the rate is sufficient to compensate the creditor for delay (and extra risk), then it is sufficient for purposes of the plan.[14]

But now, suppose the debtor owes $1 million to the secured creditor, and the collateral is worth only $600,000. The debtor proposes to pay that $600,000 sum in installments over ten years (with appropriate interest). Does the plan meet the standard for cram-down of the secured claim? It does. Note that the creditor here has two claims—a secured claim to the extent of the $600,000 collateral value and an unsecured claim for the ($400,000) deficiency.[15] The cram-down is effective for the secured claim. The unsecured claim will be dealt with elsewhere.

13. 308 U.S. 106 (1939).

14. Section 1129(b)(2)(A)(II).

15. *See* §506(a).

Now, consider the rule of Section 1129(b)(2)(B), defining fair and equitable for the unsecured claim.[16] In this subsection, the Code in effect requires either that the class be paid in full **or** that no junior class take anything under the plan. Under Section 1129(b)(2)(A) (the secured claim provision) there is no such provision regarding the rights of junior classes. Consider this example. DebtorCo owes $1 million to NewBank, secured by Blackacre, which is worth $600,000. Debtor has other assets of $300,000 and owes 20 other claims with an aggregate liability of $850,000, all unsecured. The balance sheet looks like this:

DebtorCo
Balance Sheet

Assets		Liabilities & NW	
Blackacre	$600,000	NewBank	$1,000,000
Other	$300,000	Other	$850,000
		Total L	$1,850,000
		Net Worth	<$950,000>
Total	$900,000	Total L&NW	$900,000

For simplicity, ignore the requirement of a consenting class under Section 1129(a)(10). DebtorCo proposes a plan that will cram down the mortgage at $600,000. He proposes to lump the bank's deficiency claim and the other unsecured claims into a single unsecured class with claims totaling $1,250,000.

16. The Code also provides for cram-down of an equity interest. The issue would ordinarily arise only if there were more than one equity class—for example, if the debtor had issued preferred stock, in addition to common stock. The rules are conceptually similar to the cram-down rules discussed here, but the issue arises so rarely in practice that we won't deal with it further here. *See generally* 1129(b)(2)(C).

DebtorCo proposes to pay this class $200,000 and to leave the residual $100,000 with the old equity owners. The proposed balance sheet looks like this:

DebtorCo
Balance Sheet

Assets		Liabilities & NW	
Blackacre	$600,000	NewBank	$600,000
Other	$300,000	Other	$200,000
		Total L	$800,000
		Net Worth	$100,000
Total	$900,000	Total L&NW	$900,000

May the court confirm the plan? The court may not confirm the plan as a cram-down plan, because the unsecured class is not being paid in full while a junior class (the old equity) is retaining something. Note by contrast that if a majority in number and two thirds in amount of the unsecured class had voted in favor of the plan, then it might have been confirmed even though the equity class retained an interest.

A final note on valuation. Suppose that Blackacre in the previous example is an operating business with a going concern value of $600,000, while the liquidation value is only $450,000. For purposes of cram-down, may the proponent use the (lower) liquidation value rather than the higher value of the going concern? He may not. The settled view is that for purposes of cram-down, if the business is to continue then the creditor has a right to participate in the business as a going concern. Contrast the best interests rule under Section 1129(a)(7), discussed above.[17]

§18.7 ~ EXAMPLE: DEFENESTRATORS, INC.

Here is an example that will show you the confirmation provisions at work. Defenestrators, Inc., is a firm devoted to the manufacture of novelty items out of recycled waste products. Its most important asset is some half-completed research on possibilities for the development of silk purses. Defenestrators is convinced that its research effort will come to fruition soon, but the fact is that it has not produced anything yet, and if abandoned it would probably be worthless.

17. *See generally* Isaac Pachulski, *The Cram Down and Valuation under Chapter 11 of the Bankruptcy Code,* 58 N.C.L. Rev. 926 (1980).

Defenestrators owes $1,755,000, as follows:

- $100,000 in chapter 11 priority administrative expenses (including attorneys' fees);[18]
- $50,000 in priority taxes;[19]
- $1 million to SP, holder of a claim secured by Blackacre, Defenestrators's plant and warehouse, which is itself worth $1 million;[20] and
- $605,000 to unsecured creditors.

The court has determined that in liquidation, SP and priority creditors would be paid in full, and that unsecured creditors would divide about $121,000 (*i.e.*, 20 cents on the dollar).

Defenestrators has attracted the attention of AngelCo, Inc., a lender who funds high-risk ventures, at correspondingly high interest rates. AngelCo, Inc., has no prior relationship with Defenestrators or any of its principals. AngelCo, Inc., has agreed to provide the funds necessary to support a plan of reorganization for Defenestrators under chapter 11.

Defenestrators therefore now proposes a plan the outlines of which are as follows: Defenestrators will assume the SP claim on the terms set forth below, intending to meet the payments out of post-discharge earnings. It proposes to discharge other claims by paying $325,000 in cash at confirmation. Of this sum, $150,000 will go to administrative and priority claims; the balance will be distributed as set forth below. AngelCo, Inc., will provide the $325,000, to be repaid out of post-confirmation earnings, and secured by a security interest in all unencumbered property.

Having won court approval for its disclosure statement,[21] Defenestrators has submitted its plan (together with the disclosure statement) to all relevant parties, and has solicited their votes as necessary under the Code. The following is an outline of treatment accorded each class, together with comments on confirmability.

- **Class I** consisting of 75 Creditors with claims under $100 will be paid in full, a total of $5,000. The court has determined they would get $1,000 on liquidation.[22]

Comment: This appears to be a class of administrative convenience, or (less politely) of "nuisance" claims—small claims, where the cost of soliciting votes, etc., might exceed the cost of simply paying

18. Section 507(a)(1).

19. Section 507(a)(8).

20. Section 506(a).

21. Section 1125.

22. Sections 1124(1), 1129(a)(7).

them off. The Code expressly allows the proponent to carve out an administrative convenience class and to dispose of it by paying the class in full.[23] Note that there is no substantive basis for distinguishing these administrative convenience claims from other unsecured claims, but plans rarely flounder on the issue of the administrative convenience class.

We can think of only two ways in which you are likely to get in trouble here. One is where you try to define certain very large claims as part of the class, so as to give them favorable treatment. The other is where you try to manipulate the "convenience" class by means of "artificial impairment" to obtain an impaired accepting class. Otherwise, the plan is confirmable with respect to this class.

- **Class II** consists of 75 trade creditors with claims totaling $500,000. The court has determined they would get $100,000 on liquidation. The debtor proposes to pay this class a total of $150,000 in cash on confirmation. Sixteen creditors representing $300,000 worth of claims have returned ballots. Nine creditors representing $201,000 worth of claims voted in favor. The rest voted against.[24]

Comment: This is the class at the core of the chapter 11 process. The creditors are unsecured. They are clearly impaired. But they have voted by majority in number and two thirds in amount in favor of the plan, and they are getting more than they would get in liquidation. So, the plan is confirmable with respect to this class (*but see* the note on classification below).

- **Class III** consists of 25 persons who have products liability claims against the debtor, deemed to be worth $100,000.[25] The court has determined that they would get $20,000 in liquidation. The debtor proposes to pay these creditors a total of $20,000 in two annual installments of $10,000 each, the first payable one year after confirmation and the second payable two years after confirmation. Five creditors holding claims totaling $16,000 returned ballots. Of these, four creditors holding claims totaling $14,000 voted in favor; one creditor holding a claim of $2,000 voted against.[26]

Comment: Once again, we have unsecured creditors whose claims will be impaired. They have voted in favor of the plan. Also, the creditors will get a sum equal to what they would get in liquidation. But the plan may not pass the best interests test. The reason is the payment will come in installments, and there is no provision for compensation for lost use of money. Thus, if the market interest rate is anything greater than zero, the creditors are getting a sum with a present value less than the liquidation value, and a dissenting creditor should be able to block the plan under Section 1129(a)(7) (*see also* the note on "classification" below).

---

23. Section 1122(b).

24. Sections 1124, 1129(a)(8), 1126(c), 1129(a)(7)(A), cf. §1325(a)(4).

25. The court has the power to estimate the claims for purposes of the plan even if the litigation is not completed yet and the claims are therefore not liquidated. Section 502(c).

26. Sections 1124, 1129(a)(8), 1126(c), 1129(a)(7)(A), cf. §1325(a)(4).

- **Class IV** consists of one creditor, SP, who has a claim for $1 million, secured by the debtor's factory, Blackacre, which has been appraised at $1 million. Under the contract, Debtor is supposed to pay the claim with interest a rate of 10 percent, which is specified to mean 10 annual payments beginning one year from today at $162,745. Debtor proposes to extend the payment term to twenty years, retaining the same interest rate and reducing the payment to $117,460.[27]

Comment: This is a classic cram-down plan: the proponent undertakes to rewrite the contract, giving the creditor a payment stream with a present value equal to his claim. Will the proposal pass muster? It will if the proponent has chosen the correct interest rate. On the face of things, it would appear that the proponent may not have chosen the right rate. He has selected 10 percent for the (20-year) cram-down, which is the same as the rate in the current (10-year) contract. But, other things being equal, a longer contract is ordinarily more risky than a shorter contract because it is more vulnerable to the fluctuation in interest rates. This would seem to argue for a higher interest rate.

Final note on classification: note that Classes I, II and III above all comprise unsecured creditors. On the face of things, there would seem to be no basis for distinguishing among them. Courts have shown a willingness to accept (and indeed, the statute seems to authorize) separate treatment for Class I. As to Classes II and III, it may be tougher to think of a good justification for separate classification. But courts have often allowed separate classification in cases of this sort, particularly when they do not believe the separate classification was done for the purpose of manipulating the voting to obtain an accepting creditor class. *See* §18.13.

§18.8 ~ A Tax Reason for Chapter 11: COD Income

Tax issues in chapter 11 are a subspecialty of their own, for the most part beyond the scope of this book. But there is one basic tax rule important enough that it motivates some chapter 11 cases, and so we mention it here. The rule is: cancellation of debt (COD) does not create income.[28] This rule is more compassionate than the rule that applies outside bankruptcy. Outside bankruptcy, COD creates income to the extent the COD renders the debtor solvent.[29] Inside, there is no income effect at all. The rule is important enough to drive plenty of deals into bankruptcy that could otherwise perfectly well be done elsewhere.

But the COD does not come completely free. Although the debtor doesn't get *income* from COD, he must figure the COD as an offset against tax attributes. These attributes include:

- Net operating losses (NOLs);
- Investment tax credits and such;
- Capital losses;

27. Sections 1124, 1129(a)(8), 1129(b)(2)(A).

28. 26 U.S.C. §108(a)(1)(A).

29. *Id.*, §108(a)(1)(B).

- Tax basis in other assets;
- Passive activity losses; and
- Foreign tax credits.

The debtor doesn't have to make the offset until after he has figured his tax for the year of the COD, so he will be able to use some of the attributes even though a COD is pending.[30] And to the extent the COD exceeds the value of the attributes, the surplus escapes tax altogether.

Under an old rule, a stock for debt plan (in which the creditors surrender debt claims in exchange for stock) did not trigger COD consequences at all. This rule was far more attractive to the debtor, and probably drove the plan (or even the decision to file bankruptcy in the first place) in a lot of cases. Unfortunately for plan proponents, it was repealed effective in 1995.

The COD triggers tax consequences. But what sort of conduct triggers a COD? The question is urgent in a situation where the debtor seeks a modification from his creditors. The IRS has issued an extensive regulation seeking to specify when a modification is significant enough to trigger tax consequences.[31] For example, the regulation provides that a change of interest rate is a modification if it changes the rate by (a) more than 1/4 of one percent; or (b) five percent of the annual yield—whichever is greater.[32]

The rule provides some important safe harbors. For example, the rule specifies that a forbearance to collect a debt will *not* count as a modification during a chapter 11.[33]

Even with the COD rules, many debtors will approach the end of chapter 11 with "surplus" losses—carryovers and such that it cannot offset against its own income. These surplus losses are naturally attractive to an entity with lots of income and few deductions.

§18.9 ~ PROCEDURE

The typical sequence is as follows:

- Debtor files the petition, initiating the case.
- Debtor negotiates with creditors (sometimes with the participation of committees).

---

30. This is something to keep in mind when planning emergence from chapter 11—when do you want the discharge to occur from a tax perspective?

31. Treas. Reg. §1.1001-3.

32. *Id.*, §1001-3(e)(2).

33. *Id.*, §1001-3(c)(f).

- After reaching a tentative agreement, debtor drafts a disclosure statement. If the court approves of the disclosure statement, the debtor distributes it to creditors and equity security holders along with the plan and a ballot.

- If it gets the requisite votes, the debtor then asks the court for confirmation.

- After a hearing, the court enters an order of confirmation.

- The debtor pays creditors as provided for in the plan.

There is an almost infinite range of variations possible on this bare-bones scenario. For example, in some cases, the plan may accompany the petition (a "prepackaged plan;" *see* §18.15). In some cases, the creditors will get paid at confirmation, and in others, over time after confirmation. Sometimes it is a creditor (or creditors, or a committee) who proposes the plan; there may even be competing plans. If the plan proposes merely to reinstate all claims and interests, there will be no voting (and probably no disclosure statement).

§18.10 ~ Some Important Time Rules

Within this basic framework, you will need to master a few basic rules governing the time for major plan events. Here are some of the most important time limits:[34]

- For filing a plan: The Code does not specify a particular deadline for filing a plan. But it does provide that only the debtor may file a plan within the first 120 days of the case (the "exclusive period").[35]

- To get confirmation: If the debtor files his plan within 120 days, then it gets an extra 60 days (a total of 180 days of exclusivity) to solicit votes.[36]

- Notice of hearing on adequacy of disclosure statement: 25 days.[37]

- For voting on the plan: the court shall fix the date "on or before approval of the disclosure statement."[38] Typically, this means that the proponent includes with its proposed disclosure statement a proposed order which includes deadlines (usually left blank for the court to fill in) for voting, as well as for objections to confirmation. In some districts the court may issue a form order instead.

---

34. Many of these time limits can be changed by court order. Check the particular sections.

35. Section 1121(b); and *cf.* the special 100-day limit for small business cases in §1121(c).

36. Section 1121(c)(3); *cf.* §1121(e)(2) (in small business cases, 160 days).

37. Bankr. R. 2002(b), 3017.

38. Bankr. R. 3017(a).

- For the hearing on confirmation: set by the court, typically in the same order that approves the disclosure statement.
- For filing objections to confirmation: set by the court, but at least 25 days.[39]
- To make the Section 1111(b) election: any time prior to the disclosure statement approval.[40]

§18.11 ~ More About Major Plan Concepts

§18.12 ~ Best Interests and the Partnership Debtor

One of the more puzzling limitations in bankruptcy law concerns the right of the trustee against the general partner of an insolvent partnership. Section 723 provides that the trustee of an insolvent partnership has a right to collect from the general partner, to the extent the general partners is liable under non-bankruptcy law. This is fine as far as it goes. The trouble is that Section 723 applies in chapter 7 only and there is no comparable rule in chapter 11.

There is no obvious reason for this inconsistency. It comes into focus when the court has to consider the applicability of the "best interest" test for a partnership plan. Under the best interest test, the court must find that the creditors are getting not less than they would get in chapter 7. The rule would seem to require that the court consider what a chapter 7 trustee would recover under Section 723, even if it is not included in the chapter 11 estate.

§18.13 ~ Classification

Consider the chapter 11 case of Daniel, who has $10 and owes $1 to Moe, $10 to Larry and $100 to Shemp. Under his plan he undertakes to pay Moe is in full because his claim is too small to worry about. He proposes to pay $4 to Larry because he is a trade creditor with whom he wants reasonably good relations in the future. He proposes to pay the $6 to Shemp because Shemp is a personal injury creditor whom Daniel never saw before and hopes never to see again.

Ignoring other constraints, is it proper to classify these claims in so different a manner? On the surface of things, you might think not. On the face of things, all are simple unsecured claims with no statutory priority, and no basis for equitable subordination. It is said that the job of bankruptcy is to implement non-bankruptcy rules, and it appears they would all stand on the same footing under non-bankruptcy law. Moreover, Section 1122 says that "a plan may place a claim or an interest in a particular class only if such claim or interest is substantially similar to the other claims or interests of such class."[41] And Section 1129(b) provides that a cram-down plan may be confirmed only if it does not "discriminate unfairly."

---

39. Bankr. R. 2002(b), 3020(b).

40. Rule 3014. *See* §9.7.

41. *See also* Bankr. R. 3013.

But things are never that simple. In fact the courts have carved out some notable (though limited) modifications to these classification rules that permit certain creditors to be placed in different classes—and treated differently—even though they would be treated the same under non-bankruptcy law.

Start with Moe. Section 1122(b) itself provides (by way of exception) that the plan may designate an "administrative convenience" class and give them separate treatment—usually by paying them in full. There usually isn't much dispute about this kind of administrative convenience classification, though there may be an issue as to whether (as here) an administrative convenience class should get 10 percent of the estate.

But on a much more ambitious plane, with or without good justification, a couple of early Courts of Appeals decisions blessed schemes that distinguished different kinds of unsecured creditors. For example, the Third Circuit upheld separate classification for physicians, malpractice victims, employee benefit plan participants and trade creditors, all within the same case.[42] And the Sixth Circuit upheld separate classification for a claim resulting from rejection of a collective bargaining agreement.[43]

In both these cases, the claimants at least look different, whether or not there is a principled basis for the court's decisions. But some of the more ambitious classification law seems to come from a rather different source—the "single asset real estate cases" (SARE's) that drove the docket through so much of the 1980s, *see* §5.7.

In the typical SARE, the debtor had a kind of "yaks and sparrows" balance sheet—one monster secured liability held by the bank, and a handful of unsecured claims that are almost infinitesimal by comparison. The proponent had two problems: One, the deficiency claim of the bank, if allowed to vote, would swamp all other claims. Two, the bank needed to find at least one consenting class to win confirmation under 1129(b). A typical strategy was: classify trade and deficiency separately. "Impair" the trade in some minor way and get their consent. Then, cram down the deficiency claim.

Some courts gagged at this kind of manipulation as a kind of sophistry.[44] But others went so far as to hold not only that the court *may* classify nonrecourse deficiency claims separately—but that it *must* do so because of the different nature of their claims.[45]

§18.14 ~ Controlling the Confirmation Progress

The campaign to create or destroy the impaired accepting class has generated a jurisprudence all its own. We have seen cases where debtors incur new secured debt from a friendly, unaffiliated, lender on the eve of bankruptcy, evidently for no purpose other than to create a separate class (consider: buy a new truck

---

42. *In re* New Jersey Medical Center, 817 F.2d 1055 (3d Cir. 1987).

43. *In re* U.S. Truck Co., Inc., 800 F.2d 581 (6th Cir. 1986). For more on why labor claims are different, *see* (section on rejecting executory contracts).

44. A leading noncooperator is *In re* Greystone III, 995 F.2d 1274 (5th Cir. 1991).

45. *In re* Woodbrook Associates, 19 F.3d 312 (7th Cir. 1994). *See generally* Linda Rusch, *Single Asset Cases and Chapter 11: The Classification Quandary* (Published in Single Asset Real Estate Bankruptcies: Current Developments and Legislative Issues (ABA and ABI 1987)).

with a purchase money security interest). Perhaps more often, we have seen a secured creditor simply buy up the trade claims, so it will control the confirmation process.

§18.15 ~ Prepackaged Plans

A properly constructed chapter 11 plan, once accepted by the appropriate majority vote, is binding on dissenters. There is usually no way to bind dissenters under non-bankruptcy law. So binding the minority is perhaps the most noteworthy distinction between a chapter 11 plan and an informal workout.

Of course, chapter 11 has its costs and so a proponent will want to resist invoking the protection unless he absolutely needs it. This tradeoff suggests a strategy: draft a workout plan and disclosure statement and solicit consent outside bankruptcy. If you get 100 percent support, fine; implement the plan and get on with your life. If you fall short, take your petition, plan and disclosure statement down to the bankruptcy court along with the consents already gathered and file a pre-packaged chapter 11 plan.

So-called "prepacks" have received a great deal of notoriety in recent years and their proponents talk as if the strategy were invented just day before yesterday. This approach betrays a lack of perspective. Years ago, there were judges who wouldn't even accept a chapter 11 filing unless the plan was stapled to the back of the petition.[46]

Chapter 11 itself contemplates the use of prepackaged plans. Thus, Section 1126(b) specifically provides that the proponent may use pre-petition acceptances if the voting creditor received the equivalent of a disclosure statement.

The Southland case, confirmed in 1991, is a good example of the nature and risks of a prepack.[47] Southland was the entity that owned most of the 7-Eleven convenience stores. The firm went through a management buyout in 1987. The deal appears to have been ill-considered. Almost immediately, the company began selling off assets to pay debt. Within a matter of months, vulture investors started buying up Southland bonds and pushing the company towards chapter 11.

Southland indeed filed for chapter 11 in 1991, plan in hand. But a group of dissident investors persuaded the bankruptcy judge that the pre-bankruptcy solicitation materials were not sufficient to validate the pre-bankruptcy votes and that the time to vote was inadequate. He ordered a new vote.[48] The decision derailed the original prepack, but in the end, the adversaries were able to logroll a settlement that got the company out of bankruptcy quickly and cheaply.[49]

---

46. Another and more disreputable ancestor of the modern prepack is the "protective committee" that was used to organized many of the federal court receiverships that reorganized so many corporations – including virtually every railroad – in the 19th Century. The procedure was so riven with insider favoritism as to give rise to a conviction that it was the receivership and not the debtor that was the real railroad in the case. *See generally* Jacob Trieber, *The Abuses of Receiverships*, 19 YALE L. J. 275 (1910).

47. There is a good summary of the Southland case in Hilary Rosenberg, THE VULTURE INVESTORS 231-67 (1992).

48. *In re* the Southland Corp., 124 B.R. 211 (Bankr. N.D. Tex. 1991).

49. For one court's idea of how to do a prepack, see http://www.nysb.uscourts.gov/pdf/prepackguidelines.pdf.

§18.16 ~ Timing

Prepacks are perhaps most common in cases where the debtor is unlikely to survive a prolonged stay in bankruptcy (turning off customers, drying up trade credit).

But if you want to be quick with the bankruptcy, go slow with the paperwork and the voting. Put together good disclosure materials and make sure you give creditors plenty of time to review them. Otherwise you can expect a challenge in the case from the dissenters who will argue that you are trying to pull the wool over everyone's eyes. And because in a prepack you do not obtain court approval of the disclosure statement prior to solicitation of votes, if the disclosure statement is subsequently determined to have been inadequate, the debtor will be forced to resolicit, often at great cost.

§18.17 ~ Pre-Negotiated Plan

Short of a prepack, another strategy is to do a pre-negotiated plan. This is the case where you negotiate your deal with major creditors (or a committee) before the filing, but defer solicitation of acceptances until after. The virtue of the pre-negotiated plan is that it doesn't seem to usurp as much of the court's jurisdiction: you leave the court in charge of the disclosure and solicitation process and thereby raise the comfort level of the judge. And you eliminate the risk that you will solicit votes using a disclosure statement that the court later finds to have been inadequate. The trade off, of course, is that the prenegotiated plan doesn't get you out of bankruptcy as fast as the prepack.

§18.18 ~ Disclosure Statement

Section 1125(b) provides that you may not solicit acceptance or rejection of a plan without a court-approved disclosure statement, containing adequate information. This adequate information is defined as:

> Information of a kind, and in sufficient detail, as far as is reasonably practicable in light of the nature and history of the debtor and the condition of the debtor's books and records, that would enable a hypothetical reasonable investor typical of holders of claims or interests of the relevant class to make an informed judgment about the plan.

The section goes on to specify that it "need not include such information about any other possible or proposed plans." The legislative history calls the disclosure process "the heart of" the current chapter 11.[50] Other passages make it clear that the intent that the disclosure rule is not intended to be as inflexible as the rules governing, for example, prospectuses or annual reports under the securities laws.

There are two major ways you can go wrong with disclosure: too little disclosure and unauthorized disclosure or solicitation. For all the centrality of the provision, there is almost no reported case law on too little disclosure. The reason probably is that these issues get thrashed out at the disclosure statement hearing: if the judge makes it clear that she isn't satisfied with the amount of disclosure, then either the proponent coughs up some more or the plan is withdrawn.

---

50. H.R. Rep No. 95-595, 95th Cong. 1st Sess 408 (1977).

On the matter of unauthorized disclosure, perhaps the leading case is the opinion of the Third Circuit deciding *Century Glove v. First Am. Bank of New York.*[51] A plan proponent circulated a draft plan, unsupported by a disclosure statement. An adversary argued that this was an impermissible solicitation. But the circuit refused to go so far. It held that proponent was within his rights because he didn't actually solicit a vote. More recently, a bankruptcy judge held that a plan proponent who was not the debtor violated both Sections 1125 and 1121 (on exclusivity) when it circulated a plan during the debtor's exclusivity period.[52] The bankruptcy judge criticized the *Century Glove* decision, but the cases might well be distinguishable on their facts. The bottom line: any solicitation materials, whether in support of a plan or in opposition to one, must be approved by the court. If you oppose a plan, the bankruptcy judge may be willing to approve a letter to be sent to creditors and shareholders opposing the plan, but do not send the letter without the court's permission.

§18.19 ~ Raise Confirmation of Objections Early

Plan opponents may be able to use the hearing on the disclosure statement as their first shot across the bow of confirmation, hoping to show that the plan is unconfirmable on its face. Some judges will resist the effort, and tell you to save it for the hearing on confirmation. Others will take the view that it is a waste of time and money to go all the way to the confirmation hearing on a plan that is defective from the start.[53] Our advice is if you think you have a real basis for objecting to confirmation, then go ahead and raise it at the disclosure statement hearing. At best, you might win; short of that, you might at least get a chance to educate the judge on your argument, and to plant seeds of doubt in his mind. But don't be too surprised if he tells you to save it for confirmation.

§18.20 ~ Settling a Disclosure Statement Dispute

Plan proponents often find that the best way to settle a disclosure statement objection often is simply to yield. For example, consider the plan of DebtorCo, where the payout is based on a future income stream. BigBank, the largest creditor, thinks the projections are overstated by a factor of 25 percent. On this basis BigBank asks the court to withhold approval from the disclosure statement. What is DebtorCo to do? It is nowhere unless it can get approval on the disclosure statement, and it can't expect to go to the court of appeals on this issue alone. So DebtorCo's next line is: "Judge, we think the disclosure statement is adequate as it stands, but if the court sees fit, we will add a line saying that BigBank thinks we have overstated our projections by 25 percent." It won't always work, but it is often the best solution available.

§18.21 ~ Disclosure and the Securities Laws

This section covers disclosure requirements and exemptions that are part of the plan and confirmation process. On securities exemptions under Section 364, *see* §10.14.

---

51. 860 F.2d 94 (3d Cir. 1988).

52. *In re* Clam-All Corp., 34 BCD 380 (Bankr. D. Mass. 1999). *See also In re* California Fidelity, Inc., 198 B.R. 567 (9th Cir. BAP 1996). Before a disclosure statement was approved, the debtor's principal told creditors he opposed a plan proposed jointly by the chapter 11 trustee and the creditors' committee. The court held that this was a "solicitation" and thus violated §1125.

53. *See, e.g., In re* Copy Crafters Quickprint, Inc., 92 B.R. 973 (Bankr. N.D.N.Y. 1988).

§18.22 ~ The Exemption For Plan Securities

The debtor under a plan typically incurs new obligations to holders of claims and interests. Many of these obligations will trade in interstate commerce. Ordinarily, claims and interests of this sort are securities that must conform to the Federal securities laws.[54] For example, under the securities laws it is usually unlawful for a person to sell a security unless a registration statement is in effect. The question necessarily arises: to what extent must the proponent of a chapter 11 plan comply with the securities laws?

A short answer is that chapter 11 exempts the plan process from some, but by no means all, of securities law. A good chapter 11 lawyer will need to know at least the limits of his exemption, and when to bring securities lawyers on board.

Begin with Section 5 of the Securities Act.[55] Section 5 provides that if an entity wants to issue securities, it must first prepare and file a registration statement with the Securities and Exchange Commission ("SEC"). The registration statement provides information about the issuer and the offering. The SEC staff reads and comments on the registration statement. The issuer may respond with changes. The issuer then distributes a prospectus, which is a portion of the registration statement. The issuer is barred from selling or drumming up sales before filing with the SEC. After filing, but before the registration statement becomes effective, he may offer to sell, but not sell. After the registration statement is approved, he may sell the securities.

Compare the Bankruptcy Code. The proponent drafts its plan; then (per Section 1125) it seeks approval of the disclosure statement. If the court approves, then the disclosure statement may be distributed to holders of claims or interests. Only after getting approval of the disclosure statement may anyone solicit acceptance or rejection of the plan.

Suppose the consideration offered to creditors under the plan constitutes a security under securities law. Must the debtor get approval both of the prospectus and also the disclosure statement and plan? The answer is no. Bankruptcy Code Section 1145(a) provides that Section 5 of the Securities Act does not apply to the offer or sale under the plan of a debtor:

- in exchange for a claim or interest; or
- principally in exchange and partly for cash or property.

---

54. "The securities laws" means, chiefly: (1) the Securities Act of 1933; and, to a lesser extent (2) the Securities Exchange Act of 1934, together with a half dozen other laws governing corporate finance, almost all dating from the Great Depression of the 1930s. Note that "old chapter X" of the (defunct) Bankruptcy Act, repealed in 1978, arose out of the same intellectual stew and represented the same general attitude both towards regulation and towards finance. As the text suggests, the new Bankruptcy Code represents a somewhat more relaxed and flexible attitude to the problem of disclosure than the Depression statutes.

55. 15 U.S.C. §77e.

The protection extends not just to notes and shares, but also to warrants, options, rights to subscribe and so forth. It extends not only to securities of a debtor, but to those of an affiliate issued under a joint plan, and to those of a merger partner.[56]

But there are some noteworthy limitations. For one, the exemption insulates only securities issued under a plan. It does not cover securities issued independently to finance a plan. More over, the protection extends only to the Federal securities laws. The debtor may also have to cope with state securities laws. Here, sometimes he will find an exemption and sometimes not.

Finally, the exemption extends only to equity securities. But the plan proponent may well wish to offer debt. There is no general exemption under Section 1145 for debt. Issuance of public debt may bear its own disclosure and compliance obligations, including those of the Trust Indenture Act of 1939.[57]

One reading of this exemption is that Congress intended to treat the disclosure statement as the functional equivalent of the prospectus. But there may be more to it than that. Recall that Section 1125 specifies that "adequate information" for a disclosure statement means (only) what "is reasonably practicable in light of the nature and history of the debtor and the condition of the debtor's books and records." The legislative history adds that "Reporting and audit standards devised for solvent and continuing businesses do not necessarily fit a debtor in reorganization."[58] It seems clear that it was the purpose of Congress to allow a more relaxed standard, at least for small, uncomplicated cases, than the standard that would apply under Federal securities laws.

§18.23 ~ No Exemption for Fraud

The securities laws do more than merely require documentation. They also police against fraud. And while the issuer will usually be protected by exemption from the registration requirements, he is not exempt from the rules against fraud.[59]

The fraud exception arose in connection with Public Service of New Hampshire, one of the largest bankruptcies in modern history.[60] Shareholders of the reorganized debtor brought a fraud action based on alleged false representations in the plan solicitation. The shareholders had raised the same objections in the plan confirmation process but lost the point and failed to appeal. Reasoning that they had had their chance, the court enjoined filing of the post confirmation action. The court in dicta added that fraud not addressed in the confirmation process might be an appropriate ground for postconfirmation relief.

---

56. Section 1145(c) specifies that the exempted offer *is* a "public offering," for purposes of securities law. This might appear to be a restriction, but in fact it is just the reverse. The point is that since it is a "public offering" it cannot be a "private placement" governed by Rule 144. Therefore, restrictions on private placements will not apply to the plan.

57. 15 U.S.C. §77aaa. Section 1145 does provide that the Trust Indenture Act does not apply to a note issued under the plan that matures not later than one day after the effective date of the plan.

58. Senate Report No. 95-989.

59. *See generally* 1933 Act §17, 15 U.S.C. §77q.

60. Public Service Co. v. Richards, 148 B.R. 702 (Bankr. D. N.H. 1992).

§18.24 ~ RESELLERS

So far we have considered the problem of the plan proponent. But there is a another problem facing the person who receives the securities typically, the creditor who takes them in exchange for his claim. Often the creditor wants to sell the securities as soon as possible. This impulse puts him at risk of becoming an underwriter who is liable under the securities laws in his own right.[61] Happily for this creditor, the Bankruptcy Code offers some relief.

The Code proceeds by setting forth its own definition of underwriter, more narrow than the general definition under the Securities Act.[62] It then provides that an entity that meets the bankruptcy definition of underwriter is not an underwriter for purposes of the Securities Act. This has the effect of insulating him from the underwriter liability of the Securities Act as he acts to resell his securities.[63]

More specifically, the Securities Act says that an entity is an underwriter any time it acquires the security with a view to distribution.[64] The Bankruptcy Code restricts the class to include only one who purchases a claim with a view to distribution. So the traditional vendor-creditor who works with the debtor to compromise his own claim will not count as an underwriter but the new class of secondary-market arbitrageurs probably will.

§18.25 ~ REPORTING

In addition to the prospectus, the debtor may be obliged to file periodic reports with the SEC. These would include, for example, the 10-K annual report and the 10-Q quarterly report. On the face of things, there is nothing to exempt the debtor from these reporting requirements. But the SEC has proven flexible in issuing "no-action letters," to permit late filing, or even under some circumstances to waive the filing requirement altogether. For example, in Carnegie International Corp., the SEC issued a no-action letter agreeing to accept monthly financial statements filed with the bankruptcy court in lieu of the regular 10-Ks or 10-Qs.[65]

But absent a no-action letter, it would be prudent for a debtor to assume that it must satisfy the SEC reporting requirements while in chapter 11, particularly where its stock continues to trade.

---

61. 15 U.S.C. §77b(11).

62. Section 1145(b)(1).

63. Section 1145(b)(3).

64. Securities Act of 1933, 1933 §2(11), 15 U.S.C. §77b(a)(11).

65. Available July 1, 1983. For a good succinct description of the reporting requirements of a debtor and the relief available through the no-action letter mechanism, *see* 4 Norton Bankr. Law & Practice 2d §96:23 (West 2001).

§18.26 ~ INTEREST

Before the court can confirm a cram-down plan over the objection of a secured creditor, it must find that the present value of the payment stream equals the value of the collateral. This means it is essential to choose the correct interest rate. For example, suppose the plan proposes to pay $1 million at the end of 10 years. If the discount rate is five percent, then the present value is $614,000. If the rate is nine percent, then the present value is $422,000.[66] So if the collateral is worth $500,000, then he is underpaid at nine percent but overpaid at five.[67]

There is a dizzying variety of interest-rate cases out there. Analysis is not simplified by the fact that the cases come from at least three different chapters (12 and 13, as well as 11). On the principle that the dollar doesn't know who owns it, a case from any chapter should be good authority for the others. But one has to wonder whether the courts will really apply rules made for a four-year-old Pontiac or a 10-acre truck garden to a multinational oil company.

The interest rate issue is, perhaps more than any other issue that arises in chapter 11, a battle of the experts. Investment bankers, commercial lenders, economists, real estate brokers, professors of corporate finance, industry-specific experts, and others present a wide variety of complex theories, in an effort to convince the court that a higher or lower rate of interest is appropriate. There are those who suspect that many judges understand only a small fraction of the evidence presented on these issues and tend to come out someplace in the middle most of the time. If that is true, it is probably more often the fault of the experts and the lawyers who prepare them than it is of the judges (who, after all, in many cases are not experts in finance).

It is critically important to chose the right expert. This means someone who can qualify as an expert in the particular field and has impressive qualifications, but also someone who can present the concepts in a way that the judge is likely to understand them. The most impressive MIT professor or the head of high yield trading at New York's most prestigious investment bank will not do your case much good if the judge cannot understand him.

Subject to these cautions, the interest rate case law seems to be coalescing into several views:

- *Cost of Funds.* A variety of lower court cases and at least one circuit (the Second), purport to compensate the creditor for his "cost of funds," specifically excluding any compensation for profit.[68]

---

66. This assumes annual compounding, and rounds to the nearest thousand. The formula is C[1/(1+r)n], where C = $ 1 million and r = the interest rate.

67. To turn the point around, if the value of the collateral is $500,000, then at five percent compounded annually, the payment at the end of 10 years should be $814,000 and at nine percent, $1,184,000. The present value of $1 million would be $500,000 only if the rate happened to be 7.18 percent. Note that the higher the rate, the lower the present value of the future payment. So normally it will be the debtor pushing the court to accept a low rate and the creditor, a high.

68. The circuit case is GMAC v. Valenti (*In re* Valenti), 105 F.3d 55 (2d Cir., 1997) (chapter 13).

- *Forced Loan.* This approach seeks to compensate the creditor for what it would have cost him to make the loan at the time the plan is confirmed. But these forced loan cases themselves subdivide into at least two parts. Some simply focus on the contract rate.[69] Another approach is crystallized in Koopmans v. Farm Credit Services, where Judge Easterbrook, for the Seventh Circuit, held that the creditor is entitled to the rate of interest it could have obtained had it foreclosed and reinvested the proceeds in loans of equivalent duration and risk.[70]

- *Band of Investment.* A third body of cases follows what you might call the band of investment approach. This approach is not so much a substantive rule as a device for determining a rate when you can't compare it with any loan in the marketplace, which is common in the case of cram-down notes. An exhaustive review of this technique is set forth *In re Crosscreek Apartments, Ltd.*,[71] where the court accepted the debtor's proposal for a blended rate of 8.68 percent. The court noted that the blended rate was just about two percent higher than the extant rate for (risk-free) T-bills of a comparable term, as if to recognize that the creditor needs some compensation for the risk in the deal.

  Here is an example of how the technique might work. DebtorCo is liable on a $7 million loan secured by a factory worth $7.2 million. A commercial lender might make a take a first mortgage for 65 percent of that amount, or $4.68 million, at eight percent. A venture capital firm might be willing to take a second for 20 percent, or $1.44 million, at a rate of 13 percent. That leaves $880,000 on which no lender would lend, so the debtor would have to go to the equity market where the going rate is 24 percent. Blend these together and you get a combined rate of about 9.4 percent.[72]

- *The Riskless Rate Plus Risk Premium.* Start with the riskless rate. That is likely to be the interest rate for Treasury instruments with a maturity equal to the maturity of the proposed cram-down note. Then, determine the ways in which the proposed cram-down note is more risky than a Treasury instrument, and assign a "premium," typically expressed in basis points, for each identified risk. Add the total of the risk premiums to the riskless (Treasury) rate to calculate the appropriate interest rate.

- *Corporate Bond Equivalent.* This approach requires the expert to assess the risks of the proposed loan and find a corporate bond with a comparable level of risk, preferably in the same or a very similar industry. The yield on that bond will provide guidance as to the appropriate interest rate for the cram-down loan. An alternative to finding a comparable bond is for the expert to determine how the cram-down loan would be rated by a rating agency if it were a corporate bond, and then determining the expected interest rate for a bond with that rating in the relevant industry.

---

69. *See, e.g.*, GMAC v. Jones, 999 F.2d 63 (3d Cir. 1993).

70. 102 F.3d 874 (7th Cir. 1996) (chapter 12).

71. 213 B.R. 521 (Bankr. E.D. Tenn. 1997).

72. More precisely: the weighted sum of the interest payments is $658,400, which is about 9.4 percent of $7 million. To amortize a loan like this over 20 years would require a payment of about $1.11 million per year.

There are certainly other means of calculation interest rates, and not all of these theories will apply will to every loan. And if you look carefully at the theories, you will see that there is considerable overlap. Sometimes, it works best to combine the theories, showing the court that you can reach nearly the same conclusion with several different approaches (and sometimes more than one expert).[73]

§18.27 ~ THE 1111(B) ELECTION

The strangest rule in chapter 11 is probably not all that common in practice, but no discussion of plan confirmation can ignore it. This is the mysterious "1111(b) election" that purports to give a secured creditor a second line of defense if he thinks the cram-down is too harsh. The rule is so counterintuitive that you'll need to read it with care because you would never guess what it says on your own. Start with an example:

Example: LimPart, a limited partnership, owns Blackacre, a medical office building, subject to a non-recourse secured mortgage note in favor of BankCo in the amount of $5 million. Blackacre is worth $3 million. LimPart proposes a cram-down plan in which it will replace BankCo's note with a single payment note payable at the end of 10 years and with a present value of $3 million. Since BankCo is a nonrecourse creditor, LimPart proposes to pay nothing on the $2 million deficiency claim.

Note that if Blackacre is in fact worth $3 million, and if the present value of the proposed single-payment note is $3 million, then LimPart has met the basic requirements for cram-down under Section1129(b). But what are the rights of BankCo under Section 1111(b)? Take it in two steps.

First step: LimPart won't have its way with respect to the deficiency claim. Section1111(b)(1)(A)(i) provides that the claim "shall be allowed or disallowed . . . the same as if the holder of such claim had recourse . . . whether or not the holder has such recourse . . . ." So LimPart needs to make some provision for the $2 million deficiency. But—

Second step: instead, BankCo can elect to have its entire claim treated as secured. If BankCo elects, then its entire $5 million claim is a secured claim.[74]

At this point, the thoughtful reader will ask—why doesn't *everybody* make the election and require that the entire claim be treated as a secured claim? The answer is in Section 1129(b)(2)(A)(i)(II), which defines what the creditor gets on account of its secured claim. That section says the creditor gets payments:

- totaling *at least the allowed amount* of such claim; but
- of a (discounted present) *value* equaling the value of the collateral.

---

73. For some idea of the complexity of the interest rate arguments, and how the courts approach them, have a look at *In re* Bloomingdale Partners, 155 B.R. 961 (Bankr. E.D. Ill. 1993); *In re* SM104 Limited, 160 B.R. 202 (Bankr. S.D. Fla. 1993); *In re* Sherwood Square, 107 B.R. 872 (Bankr. D. Md. 1989).

74. Section 1111(b)(2).

Apply it to LimPart. The plan said that LimPart would make a single payment at the end of 10 years. It did not specify the amount. But if LimPart promises to pay $5 million at the end of 10 years, then it has met part one of the test set forth above. To know the discounted present value of this $5 million claim, we have to have a (discount) interest rate. But suppose the rate is 5.24 percent. If the rate is 5.24 percent, then the discounted present value of the 10-year payment turns out to be $3 million—and we have met part two of the test.

Which is to say—even though the creditor has a $5 million secured claim, we have discharged it by paying no more than we would pay on the secured claim under the original plan. Or to turn the point around, by making the election, the secured creditor loses whatever he stood to get on the unsecured deficiency claim!

Two questions present themselves. One, why would anyone make the election? And two, why did Congress do anything so (apparently) strange?

To the first question, the short answer is—usually he wouldn't. But we can identify two (rather specialized) occasions on which it might be useful:

- *Capture Upside.* The claim is $5 million and the judicial valuation is $3 million, as above. The creditor is sure the valuation is wrong (or that it is right, but that the market will recover) and that the debtor may be back facing foreclosure at some point, or may decide to sell the property. If he makes the election, then in the subsequent sale or foreclosure (or bankruptcy) he has a secured claim for his full $5 million. If he does not make the election, then he will have a secured claim for only $3 million.

- *Defeat Plan.* There are some times that making the §1111(b) election can kill a plan on feasibility grounds. For example, assume the claim is $5 million and the present value is $3 million as before, but the useful life of the asset is only three years. From the projections, the court finds that the debtor will be able to pay $3 million at the end of three years, but not $5 million. The annual amortization payments necessary to keep the $3 million loan in place over $3 years, and to pay a total of $5 million, are: $557,000, $660,000 and $783,000. The debtor concedes he can't meet these cash flow obligations and the plan therefore cannot be confirmed.

Why did Congress do it? There appears to be no documentary evidence. But bankruptcy folklore offers this account: apparently it had something to do with rules applied by bank regulators. The bank's main objective is to avoid having to "write down" the value of the loan from $5 million to $3 million. Evidently regulators (who must have been deeply deficient in first principles of present value) would allow the loan to stay on the books at $5 million as long as the *face value* was $5 million, even if the discounted present value were much less.

§18.28 ~ Tradeoff: Losing Control of the Class

We've seen that the 1111(b) election requires that the creditor surrender his unsecured claim. In dollar terms, this may not be a great loss: unsecured creditors in chapter 11 often get just pennies on the dollar. But there is another tradeoff here. That is, by surrendering its unsecured deficiency claim, the creditor no longer has the power to vote in the unsecured class. The deficiency claim alone is often enough to control the unsecured class and thereby defeat the plan. So the giving up class control may be too high a price to pay, even if the dollar loss is trifling.

§18.29 ~ How Much Can You Do in the Plan?

One recurrently troublesome issue is the limit of the plan process. There are two kinds of problems:

- What sorts of provisions are flatly prohibited under the plan process? The principal issue here is the scope of third-party releases—plan provisions that purport to "discharge" others, not themselves debtors in the chapter 11 case.

- What sorts of plan provisions, though not flatly impermissible, undertake to deal with issues that should be dealt with elsewhere in the chapter 11 case? The principal issue here is the matter of claims adjudication—cases in which the proponent seeks to limit or eliminate claims via the plan process, instead of via a claims adjudication proceeding.

Casting a shadow on both these questions is the nature and scope of "finality" —the question whether a plan provision, invalid in itself, is enforceable if no one thinks to challenge it in the right place at the right time.

§18.30 ~ Finality

Under what circumstances should a plan provision, invalid in itself, subsist because it was not challenged in the right place, at the right time? To get a handle on the issue, we can compare two Fifth Circuit cases.

The first case is *Republic Supply v. Shoaf*,[75] a guarantor case. Shoaf was the individual guarantor of a corporate debt. The corporation defaulted. Republic, the creditor, sued Shoaf as guarantor. The corporation went into chapter 11. The debtor proposed a plan that, *inter alia*, purported to release Shoaf. Republic voiced an objection in open court, but never formally objected in writing. The plan was confirmed, and the order of confirmation was not appealed. Later Republic pressed its suit against Shoaf. He amended his answer to plead the plan as *res judicata*.

Reversing the district court, the Fifth Circuit held for Shoaf. It reasoned that the creditor was just trying to achieve a back-door appeal of the plan. The court noted that both Shoaf and Republic had participated in the plan process, and that the confirmed plan amounted to a final judgment on the merits. So, the court concluded, notwithstanding any illegality, the doctrine of *res judicata* barred Republic's claim.

In 1998 the Fifth Circuit came back to the issue, deciding *IRS v. Taylor*. *Taylor*,[76] the chapter 11 debtor, scheduled a liability for a nondischargeable "trust fund tax" claim, *see* Section 17.43 The schedules pegged the claim at $80,000, but listed it as unliquidated, disputed and contingent. The plan mentioned

---

75. 815 F.2d 1046 (5th Cir. 1987).

76. 132 F.2d 256 (5th Cir. 1998).

no such debt, but also declared that any such debts were discharged. The IRS received a copy of the plan. The IRS also filed, but then withdrew, a claim against Taylor for a personal income tax.

One month after confirmation, the IRS assessed a claim on the trust fund tax for some $96,000. Taylor asked the court to declare that he was not indebted. Taylor argued that the bankruptcy court had the power to adjudicate the tax liability.[77] He pointed out that the claim was scheduled, that the plan mentioned trust fund liability in general, and that the IRS had participated in the case (on the personal tax issue). And he relied on *Shoaf* for the proposition that the issue was *res judicata*.

But the Fifth Circuit, again reversing, wasn't buying. The court said that *Shoaf* was a general rule, subject to competing concerns expressed in the Bankruptcy Code. It cited a string of pre-*Shoaf* cases in which the proponent had sought to adjudicate a lien issue via the plan rather than through the claims process. The ironic result is that an "invalid" provision—third-party discharge—survives, while an issue that could have been dealt with in bankruptcy—claims adjudication—does not.

§18.31 ~ Checklist: What You Must Prove to Confirm a Chapter 11 Plan

Here is a summary of what you have to prove to confirm a plan, organized more or less in order of importance. In organizing for your confirmation hearing, you should sift through your evidence with some such checklist in mind and make sure that you have something to offer on every point. Then prepare a "trial brief," or something of the sort, itemizing what you have to offer, and why, and have a competent witness available to testify. If there is no opposition, some judges will accept an offer of proof rather than requiring an actual witness, but at least you have offered the judge a basis to make her findings. And of course if there is opposition, then you are ready to join the issue.

A. The core provision: unimpaired/accepted/cram-down (Sections 1129(a)(8), 1129(b)). With respect to each class, you must show either:

   1. That the class is *unimpaired* (Section 1124 plan); or

   2. That it has *accepted* the plan (Section1126).

If you can't show either of these, you get a second bite at the apple—a chance to impose a cram-down ("fair and equitable") plan under Section 1129(b), of which more later.

B. With respect to each impaired claim, you must show also that the creditor holding such claim has:

   1. Accepted the plan; or

77. Under §505.

2. Will receive not less than it would receive in chapter 7 (Section 1129(a)(7)).

The combined effect of 1129(a)(8) and (a)(7) is that you can bind dissenters by a vote as long as they are getting not less than they would get in chapter 7. One consequence is that just about every plan or disclosure statement will have to have a liquidation analysis—a showing of what the creditors would get in chapter 7.

C. Feasibility. Per Section 1129(a)(11), the court must find that "confirmation of the plan is not likely to be followed by the liquidation, or the need for further financial reorganization, of the debtor or any successor to the debtor under the plan, unless such liquidation or reorganization is proposed in the plan." You'll probably need a witness (perhaps the same one who does your liquidation analysis) to assure the court that this plan makes financial sense.[78]

Some "protection against insiders" rules. There are several provisions that can best be understood as trying to prevent insiders from spiriting away the assets of the estate. These include:

1. Insiders (Section 1129(a)(6)). The plan proponent must disclose the identity of any insider that will be employed or retained by the reorganized debtor, and the nature of any compensation to be paid to such insider.

2. Court Approval for Payments. Any payments to be made in connection with the plan and incident to the bankruptcy case must be approved by or are subject to approval by the court as reasonable (Section 1129(a)(4)).

3. Officers and Directors (Section 1129(a)(5)).

   a. The plan proponent must have disclosed the identity and affiliations of any individual proposed to serve as a director, officer, or voting trustee of the debtor.[79]

   b. The court must find that their continuation in office is in the *best interests* of creditors and equity security holders and with public policy.

---

78. *Cf. In re* Clarkson, 767 F.2d 417 (8th Cir. 1985) (debtor's failure to prepare income tax returns over five years makes it virtually impossible to formulate an informed expectation as to the prospects for reorganization).

79. The rule also applies to affiliates under joint plans, and to successors.

D. Some rules on payment of claims and fees:

1. Bankruptcy fees filing fees and quarterly fees must be paid no later than the effective date of the plan (Section 1129(a)(12)).

2. Administrative expenses (and allowed "involuntary gap" claims) must receive cash equal to the allowed amount of such claim, unless they agree otherwise (Section 1129(a)(9)(A)).

3. Priority claims must be paid in full in cash on the effective date unless they have agreed otherwise by class vote (Section 1129(a)(9)(B)). For a special rule on tax priorities, *see infra.*

4. Special rule on priority tax claims (Section 1129(a)(9)(C)). The plan may stretch out priority tax claims over six years from the time of assessment, so long as the collector gets a present value equal to the allowed amount of the claim. This is an important substantive provision, and probably drives some chapter 11 cases.

E. Special rule for retiree benefits. The plan must provide for their continuation in conformity with Section 1114 (Section 1129(a)(13)).

F. Some general allegations. These are usually boilerplate, although there has been some litigation over the meaning of "good faith" in the context of the plan.

1. Plan Complies with the Code. The plan must comply with applicable provisions of the Bankruptcy Code.

2. Proponent Complies with the Code. The proponent of the plan must comply with applicable provisions of the Bankruptcy Code.

3. Good Faith. The plan must have been proposed in good faith and not by any means forbidden by law.

G. Acceptance By At Least One Impaired Class. If any class is impaired, then at least one impaired class must have accepted the plan (Section 1129(a)(10)). This rule has two implications:

1. If you are not impairing anyone, then you don't need solicit or get acceptances. This is not quite trivial: once in a while your plan will simply reinstate every one, and in those cases it is no small virtue to be free of the expense of disclosure and solicitation.

2. If you are trying to do a cram-down plan, you need to find at least one impaired class. *See infra.*

H. A couple of special rules for special cases:

1. Regulated industries (Section 1129(a)(6)). Any governmental regulatory commission with jurisdiction over the rates of the debtor upon confirmation of the plan

   a. must have approved any rate change provided for in the plan, or

   b. such rate change is expressly conditioned on such approval.

I. Cram-Down (Section 1129(b)). Section 1129(b) provides that the court may "rewrite the contract" and impose the plan on a dissenting class. This is the so-called "cram-down" rule. There are three general requirements—

1. The court may impose the cram-down under Section 1129(b), only if all requirements of Section 1129(a) are met, except the requirement of accept or unimpaired under Section 1129(a)(8). This means, among other things, that the proponent must show that there is at least one impaired consenting class, per Section 1129(a)(10).

2. The plan must not discriminate unfairly.

3. The plan must be fair and equitable. This enables the judge to deny confirmation when he believes the plan is unfair in any respect. But most judges do not interpret the provision as a roving commission for the judge to do anything he wants.[80] Rather, a plan will usually be held to satisfy the "fair and equitable" requirement if it meets the following standards:

   a. Cram-down of Secured Claims. The creditor must:

      (1) Retain his lien on his collateral (or on the proceeds of the sales of his collateral) and receive either:

         (a) Deferred cash payments that equal the present value of his claim; or

         (b) The "indubitable equivalent." Nobody really knows what the "indubitable equivalent" is, but it may include surrendering the property—"dirt for debt."[81]

---

80. Or maybe it is. *See, e.g., In re* D & F Constr., Inc., 865 F.2d 673 (5th Cir. 1989).

81. *See generally* U.S. *ex rel.* United States Farmers Home Administration (*In re* Arnold and Baker Farms, 85 F.3d 1415 (9th Cir. 1996), *cert. denied*, 117 S.Ct. 681 (1997).

b. Unsecured Claims. Either:

(1) Each holder must receive payments with a present value equal to his claim; or

(2) No junior claim or interest may receive anything under the plan.

c. Equity Interests. Either:

(1) Holder of interest receives the greatest of any fixed liquidation preference, fixed redemption price, or the value of the equity interest; or

(2) No more junior interest receives anything under the plan.

There are a couple of other provisions in this section. But since they are not in Sections 1129(a) or (b), we think they are not issues on which the court must make findings, and so not part of your *prima facie* case. You will, of course, want to be ready for them if they arise.

A. The court, may confirm only one plan (Section 1129(c)). It amuses us to speculate on whatever may have caused Congress to spell out so obvious a rule. Of greater practical relevance, the Code goes on to say that if more than one plan is proposed and is held to satisfy all of the confirmation requirements, then "the court will select one of the plans to confirm, after considering the preferences of creditors *and* equity security holders." So equity remains a voice, even when there are competing plans.

B. The court will not confirm a plan if it finds that principal purpose of the plan is:

1. The avoidance of taxes,[82] or

2. The avoidance of the application of Section 5 of the Securities Act of 1933.

---

82. The Code specifies in this case that the Court may act only "upon the request of a governmental unit" and that the governmental unit has the burden of proof. Occasionally, you may see a governmental entity raise this objection when a single asset real estate case is resolved, as many are, by conveying the property to the secured lender, with the goal of saving transfer and recordation taxes under §1146(c).